Implemei
GAAS
2010–11

Implementing GAAS 2010–11

A Practical Guide
to Auditing and Reporting

Peter Chidgey
Sarah Nendick
BDO LLP

a Wolters Kluwer business

Wolters Kluwer (UK) Limited
145 London Road
Kingston upon Thames
Surrey
KT2 6SR
Telephone: 144(0) 844 561 8166
Facsimile: 144(0) 870 247 1184
email: customerservices@cch.co.uk
website: www.cch.co.uk

Disclaimer

This publication is sold with the understanding that neither the publisher nor the authors, with regard to this publication, are engaged in rendering legal or professional services. The material contained in this publication neither purports, nor is intended to be, advice on any particular matter.

Although this publication incorporates a considerable degree of standardisation, subjective judgment by the user, based on individual circumstances, is indispensable. This publication is an 'aid' and cannot be expected to replace such judgment.

Neither the publisher nor the authors can accept any responsibility or liability to any person, whether a purchaser of this publication or not, in respect of anything done or omitted to be done by any such person in reliance, whether sole or partial, upon the whole or any part of the contents of this publication.

Telephone Helpline Disclaimer Notice

Where purchasers of this publication also have access to any Telephone Helpline Service operated by Wolters Kluwer (UK), then Wolters Kluwer's total liability to contract, tort (including negligence, or breach of statutory duty) misrepresentation, restitution or otherwise with respect to any claim arising out of its acts or alleged omissions in the provision of the Helpline Service shall be limited to the yearly subscription fee paid by the Claimant.

British Library Cataloguing-in-Publication Data

A catalogue record for this book is available from the British Library.

Typeset in-house at Wolters Kluwer (UK) Ltd
Printed and bound in the UK by Hobbs the Printers Ltd

CONTENTS

PART 2 REPORTING

PART 3   ACCOUNTING SYSTEMS AND INTERNAL CONTROLS

PART 4   EVIDENCE

PREFACE

From a UK GAAS perspective the major event of the year was clearly the publication in October 2009 of the revised ISAs for UK and Ireland which comprised:

- 33 new International Standards on Auditing (UK and Ireland) (ISAs (UK and Ireland));

- A new International Standard on Quality Control (UK and Ireland) 1 (ISQC (UK and Ireland) 1); and

- A revised Statement of the Scope and Authority of APB Pronouncements.

This represents the culmination of the UK part of the IAASB's Clarity Project which reformatted the 33 standards in a 'clarified' form and also revised a number to update them for changes in the business environment and for current thinking. These were issued as exposure drafts in April 2009 and were referred to in last year's edition, and incorporated as UK standards with very little change.

Because, for all intents and purposes the first audits required under the new standards are those for 31 December 2010 year ends, this is a year of transition in the UK as firms adjust their procedures and methodologies ready for this deadline. Therefore, we have taken the approach in this book of setting out the existing pre-clarification requirements and showing what the changes will be as we consider this is of most help to those coping with the new standards.

The expansion of the Statement of the Scope and Authority of APB Pronouncements reflects the fact that standards are now in one of two kinds – the old-fashioned black-lined versions – requirements indicated by 'should' – which includes the Engagement Standards for Reporting Accountants and the Ethical Standards for Auditors and Reporting Accountants as opposed to the clarified standards which use the international conventions of no black-lining and requirements indicated by 'shall'. Whilst for the moment this should not present too many practical problems in the longer term it will prove unwieldy.

The question of whether the EU will adopt the standards is still an open one. Recent changes in both the European Parliament and in the European Commission have meant that the anticipated progress has not taken place and indeed there is now some doubt as to whether IAS will be eventually incorporated in European law. Whilst in the short term this will have no real effect for the UK, for the longer term it raises the spectre of the EU developing its own rules as the PCOAB has done in the US. This would only lead to increased complexity for multi-national audits.

As far as the future is concerned, the aftermath of the financial crisis has produced a number of voices calling for a fresh look at the audit function. It is likely attention will be focused particularly on the scope of audit reporting and whether this can be developed to give additional assurance on such matters as valuations and risk disclosures, both of which have become of increasing importance in companies' annual reports. These have traditionally been areas which auditors have been reluctant to go into because of potential liability issues, so it will be interesting to see whether any progress can be made here.

The other main developments in the UK for which we have updated the book include:

- PN 26 – *Audit documentation for a smaller entity*
- Draft PN 10 (revised) – *Money laundering – Guidance for Auditors*
- Draft PN 10 – *Audits in the Public Sector*
- Bulletin 2009/3 – *Audits of Charities in the UK – updated reports*
- Bulletin 2009/4 – *Guidance on Going Concern*
- ES3 (revised) – *Long association with the audit engagement.*

As with earlier editions, we have kept to our conventions of:

- where there is an existing guideline in an area and a proposed Standard or Practice Note, we have, unless indicated in the text, examined the subject from the point of view of the proposal on the basis that it is a more authoritative and up-to-date indication of GAAS;

- international standards and other overseas guidance are discussed in detail when they have been exposed by the APB in a national context although we indicate the main effects of significant proposals, and

- where new Standards have been issued but in a number of cases the old guidelines have not been withdrawn, we have ignored the old guidelines except where they have provided helpful insights.

Finally, we would like to acknowledge the contributions of Chris Kirton, Don Bawtree, Peter Lewis, Philip Rego, Nick Carter-Pegg and Fiona Raistrick who have helped in the drafting of various chapters. Their help has been invaluable.

Peter Chidgey
Sarah Nendick
BDO LLP

May 2010

PART 1
INTRODUCTION

1 THE NATURE OF AUDITING STANDARDS

1.1 INTRODUCTION

For the purpose of this book Generally Accepted Auditing Standards (GAAS) are the rules which are acknowledged as those by which auditors can measure their performance and by which others can measure them. These may be formal or informal, written or unwritten. In the widest sense these standards are set by a variety of groups:

- government in the form of legislation;
- professional or standard setting bodies in the form of pronouncements of varying authority;
- courts in judgments on cases involving auditors;
- practitioners whose 'internal' standards may become a generally accepted 'norm' especially in areas where there are no public pronouncements.

In practice it is the professional or standard setting bodies who are the greatest source of authority in this area. Traditionally, government has not become involved in the detail of auditing; UK legislation specifies the matters on which auditors must report but it has been left to the professional bodies to issue detailed standards and guidance covering how auditors collect the evidence to support their opinion and the form that opinion takes in different circumstances. A similar approach has developed in recent years in the area of 'general' standards, for example, independence or maintaining competence, where detailed regulation has again been left to the professional bodies.

For these reasons, this book concentrates mainly on the standards and guidance issued by professional and standard setting bodies as the main source of GAAS, referring where necessary to the decisions of courts or to the practices of firms where these are relevant.

1.2 LIMITATIONS OF STANDARDS

Because of the nature of auditing the development of a framework of Auditing Standards which will provide answers to all the questions and problems faced by auditors is not feasible. There will always be judgements over questions – such as how much evidence is enough in a given case? – to which Auditing Standards will not provide a solution. This is aggravated by the relationship between auditing and accounting. Auditors form opinions on financial statements, the preparation of which involves, amongst other things, appraisals of the likely outcome of uncertain future events. Auditing Standards are also constrained by this uncertainty. Also, methods of producing financial statements adapt to changing circumstances and auditors must be able to adapt their approaches. Because of this GAAS can only be a framework to assist auditors in making judgements and forming opinions, not a rigid system of rules.

1.3   AUTHORITATIVE BODIES

In the main, GAAS emanates from the pronouncements of authoritative bodies which have been established to issue standards and which are accepted by audit practitioners and the bodies which regulate them as having that authority. From the point of view of this book GAAS encompasses not only the standards issued by those bodies but also any guidance on their application.

What constitutes GAAS, in practice, is subject to evolution and change. Auditors in the UK must have regard to a large number of pronouncements issued by various bodies in order to ascertain what actually constitutes GAAS. The main bodies which either issue or have issued standards or related guidance are:

- Auditing Practices Board (APB);
- International Auditing and Assurance Standards Board (IAASB); and
- various other accountancy bodies, for example, The Institute of Chartered Accountants in England and Wales (ICAEW) which issues guidance through its Audit Faculty.

Increasingly auditors have also had to have regard to the pronouncements of the International Auditing and Assurance Standards Board (IAASB). In December 2004 this process took a step forward when the APB issued all of the International Standards of Auditing (ISAs) as ISAs (UK and Ireland) supplemented with additional guidance from a UK and Ireland perspective. Further detail is given below.

1.4   THE AUDITING PRACTICES BOARD

The Auditing Practices Board was established in 1991 by the Consultative Committee of Accountancy Bodies (CCAB). In April 2002, the new APB commenced its activities and adopted the extant guidance previously issued by the old APB. The new APB was at the time a subsidiary of the Accountancy Foundation. Following the publication of the reports of the Consultative Group on Audit and Accounting (CGAA) and the Government 'Review of the Regulatory Regime of the Accountancy Profession' the Auditing Practices Board fell under the remit of the Financial Reporting Council (FRC).

The FRC was established in 1990 to promote good financial reporting through its, then, two subsidiaries, the Accounting Standards Board and the Financial Reporting Review Panel. When the FRC's original remit was enlarged it took a more pro-active role in relation to corporate governance, compliance with company law and accounting standards. It also assumed new responsibilities in relation to overseeing the self-regulation of the professional bodies.

The FRC has five subsidiary boards:

- the Accounting Standards Board;
- the Financial Reporting Review Panel;
- the Auditing Practices Board;
- the Professional Oversight Board for Accountancy; and
- the Accountancy Investigation and Discipline Board.

The FRC and its subsidiaries are funded jointly by the accountancy profession, business and the Government.

In October 2009, and following the publication of the Revised ISAs (UK and Ireland), the APB issued a revised Scope and Authority of Pronouncements which is applicable to engagements relating to financial periods ending on or after 15 December 2010. The Statement sets out:

- an overview of the types of document issued by the APB;
- the level of authority associated with each type of document; and
- the regulatory regime supporting APB pronouncements derived from legislation and the rules of the accountancy bodies.

The Statement includes the *Auditors' Code* which sets out the principles that the APB expects to guide the conduct of auditors, as well as underlying its own guidance and the ethical standards of the professional bodies. The code is set out in **Table 1**.

TABLE 1: *The Auditors' Code*

Accountability

Auditors act in the interests of primary stakeholders, whilst having regard to the wider public interest. The identity of primary stakeholders is determined by reference to the statute or agreement requiring an audit: in the case of companies, the primary stakeholder is the general body of shareholders.

Integrity

Auditors act with integrity, fulfilling their responsibilities with honesty, fairness, candour, courage and confidentiality. Confidential information obtained in the course of the audit is disclosed only when required in the public interest, or by operation of law.

Objectivity and independence

Auditors are objective and provide impartial opinions unaffected by bias, prejudice and compromise and conflicts of interest. Auditors are also independent, this requires them to be free from situations and relationships which would make it

---

probable that a reasonable and informed third party would conclude that the auditors' objectivity either is impaired or could be impaired.

Competence

Auditors act with professional skill, derived from their qualification, training and practical experience. This demands an understanding of financial reporting and business issues, together with expertise in accumulating and assessing the evidence necessary to form an opinion.

Rigour

Auditors approach their work with thoroughness and with an attitude of professional scepticism. They assess critically the information and explanations obtained in the course of their work and such additional evidence as they consider necessary for the purposes of their audit.

Judgement

Auditors apply professional judgement taking account of materiality in the context of the matter on which they are reporting.

Clear complete and effective communication

Auditors' reports contain clear expressions of opinion and set out information necessary for a proper understanding of that opinion. Auditors communicate audit matters of governance interest arising from the audit of financial statements with those charged with governance of an entity.

Association

Auditors allow their reports to be included in documents containing other information only if they consider that the additional information is not in conflict with the matters covered by their report and they have no cause to believe it to be misleading.

Providing value

Auditors add to the reliability and quality of financial reporting; they provide to directors and officers constructive observations arising from the audit process; and thereby contribute to the effective operation of business, capital markets and the public sector.

The APB issues pronouncements covering:

- quality control:
  - International Standards on Quality Control (UK and Ireland);
- the framework of fundamental principles:
  - the Auditor's Code;
- ethical and engagement standards:
  - APB Ethical Standards for Auditors or Reporting Accountants;

- Standards for Investment Reporting (SIRs); and
- International Standards on Auditing (UK and Ireland) (ISAs (UK and Ireland)); and

- guidance:
  - Practice Notes; and
  - Bulletins.

1.4.1 International Standards of Auditing (UK and Ireland)

International Standards of Auditing (ISAs) are issued by the International Auditing and Assurance Standards Board (IAASB). In recent years the IAASB has functioned as the independent standard setting body under the auspices of the International Federation of Accountants (IFAC).

In May 2004, the APB announced their intention to adopt the ISAs issued by the IAASB for use in the UK and Ireland, first reviewing all of the SASs to identify instances where they contain higher standards than those contained in the equivalent ISAs, and supplementing the ISAs accordingly. The resultant International Standards of Auditing (UK and Ireland) ('ISAs (UK and Ireland)') were issued, first for consultation, and then in final form in 2004. They were effective for the audit of financial statements for periods commencing on or after 15 December 2004.

The IAASB undertook a major overview of ISAs from October 2005 to March 2009, revising some and clarifying all of the standards (see **1.5.1**).

Following a consultation process the APB agreed to update UK and Irish auditing standards in line with the IAASB clarified ISAs. These revised ISAs will be effective for the audits of financial statements for periods ending on or after 15 December 2010 (see **1.5.2** below).

The APB believed the change to international-based standards provided the following strategic advantages:

- maintaining the stature of UK and Irish standards internationally, particularly following earlier accounting and auditing failures, and the anticipated requirement from the European Commission for ISAs to be adopted by all Member States; and
- allowing the APB to benefit from future improvements to ISAs.

Because of the publication date and period of reference for this publication we refer to both the existing ISAs (UK and Ireland) which are effective for the audit of financial statements with year ends before 15 December 2010 and the clarified ISAs (UK and Ireland) which are effective from that date. The terms 'existing standards' and 'clarified standards' are used throughout to differentiate between them.

The ISAs (UK and Ireland) comprise both the standards (which are set out in bold type), which are prescriptive, and explanatory and other material designed to assist auditors in interpreting and applying the standards but which is not prescriptive.

The members of the CCAB undertake to adopt all auditing standards (ISAs (UK and Ireland)) promulgated by the APB. Failures by auditors to comply with the relevant standards will therefore be enquired into by the appropriate accountancy body.

Only members of a Recognised Supervisory Body (RSB) are eligible for appointment as auditors of limited companies. The ISAs (UK and Ireland) constitute the technical standards adopted by the RSBs to be applied in company audit work. The RSBs must also monitor and enforce compliance with them.

APB pronouncements, in particular ISAs (UK and Ireland), are likely to be taken into account when the adequacy of the work of auditors is being considered in a court of law or in other contested situations.

Like SAS 100 *Objective and General Principles Governing an Audit of Financial Statements* before it, Clarified ISA (UK and Ireland) 200 *Objective and General Principles Governing an Audit of Financial Statements* is a 'grandfather standard' and sets out a number of basic principles and assumptions on which all other standards are based.

Clarified ISA (UK and Ireland) 200 requires auditors to conduct their audits in accordance with ISAs (UK and Ireland) and with an attitude of professional scepticism. This means that the audit should be approached with a questioning mind, with auditors making critical assessments of the evidence obtained, remaining alert for contradictions or evidence which makes them question the reliability of documents or management representations.

Auditors should also comply with the APB's Ethical Standards (see **Chapter 2**) and other ethical pronouncements issued by their professional body.

Clarified ISA (UK and Ireland) 200 requires auditors to plan and perform their work in order to reduce audit risk to an acceptably low level, having regard to the requirements of the Clarified ISAs (UK and Ireland), their professional body, legislation and the terms of the engagement. Auditors must make an assessment of the audit risk, but are not responsible for the detection of misstatements that are not material to the financial statements taken as a whole.

1.4.2 Practice Notes

The APB also issues Practice Notes to assist auditors in applying audit standards of general application to particular circumstances in specific industries. Practice

Notes are persuasive rather than prescriptive although they are indicative of good practice and have similar status to the explanatory material in SASs. At the date of this publication 16 Practice Notes are in issue and others are at Exposure Draft stage. Some Practice Notes have been updated, or are in the process of being updated following the adoption of Clarified ISAs (UK and Ireland).

1.4.3 Bulletins

Bulletins have the same status as Practice Notes and are issued to provide auditors with timely guidance on new and emerging issues. At the date of writing 29 bulletins are in issue. As with Practice Notes, there is an ongoing process of updating Bulletins following the adoption of Clarified ISAs (UK and Ireland).

1.5 INTERNATIONAL AUDITING AND ASSURANCE STANDARDS BOARD

As well as the ISAs, the IAASB issues other guidance which is of relevance to UK auditors despite not being adopted directly by the APB.

1.5.1 IAASB's Clarity Project

In October 2005, the IAASB announced a project aimed to improve the clarity of its ISAs. This project involved:

- setting an overall objective for each ISA;
- improving overall readability and understandability of ISAs by redrafting; and
- replacing the word 'should' with the word 'shall' to emphasise that requirements are relevant to virtually all circumstances.

The project was completed in March 2009 when 36 newly updated and clarified ISAs were issued. They are effective internationally for the audits of financial statements for periods commencing on or after 15 December 2009.

1.5.2 APB Adoption of clarified ISAs

Throughout the length of the IAASB's Clarity Project the EU has made no announcements on the likely adoption date of the new suite of ISAs in Europe. The APB had commented that they would await adoption of the guidance by the EU before introducing them to the UK and Ireland.

However, in October 2008 the APB commenced a consultation process to determine whether UK and Irish auditing standards should be updated for the new international ISAs. In their consultation paper, the APB stated that as no timetable for endorsement of the ISAs had been announced by the EU, adoption was likely to be later than the effective date established by the IAASB, which is accounting periods commencing on or after 15 December 2009.

In a consultation paper the APB put forward the view that the Clarity Project has improved guidance on important topics such as auditing groups, estimates (including fair values) and related party transactions and that there was merit in introducing these changes to UK and Irish standards as soon as possible.

In March 2009, the APB announced its intention to adopt the clarified ISAs as new UK and Irish auditing standards, effective for all the audits of financial statements for periods ending on or after 15 December 2010. An exposure draft of the complete set of the revised ISAs was published in April 2009 and the finalised ISAs (UK and Ireland) were issued in October 2009. The clarified ISAs (UK and Ireland) contain some additional paragraphs of supplementary material (grey-lined paragraphs) which are necessary to:

- address specific UK and Irish legal and regulatory requirements;
- provide other guidance relating to legal and regulatory matters relevant to an audit; and
- maintain other current APB requirements and guidance which are necessary to prevent changes in audit practice to the detriment of audit quality.

However, changes to the international ISAs mean that these additional grey-lined paragraphs are far fewer in number than in the previous suite of ISAs (UK and Ireland).

The consultation process also supported the view that the same auditing standards should be applied to all audits, regardless of size. This removes the risk of creating a two tier auditing system, which could undermine the credibility of smaller audits.

One exception is ISA 700 *Forming an Opinion and Reporting on Financial Statements* which was not adopted by the APB. The APB instead issued ISA (UK and Ireland) 700 *The Auditor's Report on Financial Statements* which addresses the requirements of company law and also provides for a more concise auditor's report, addressing issues raised in the consultation process (see **Chapter 3**).

1.5.3   Transition

The clarified ISAs (UK and Ireland) published in October 2009 are effective for audits of financial statements for periods ending on or after 15 December 2010. However, earlier adoption is permissible and so audit firms are likely to adopt the new guidance for all audits performed after a certain date, irrespective of their year ends. For example, a firm may introduce changes to their audit practices from 31 December 2010, which will be used for any outstanding audits for year ends prior to this date. This would encompass the 15 December 2010 application date as well as audits for year ends earlier in 2010 which have not yet commenced and ensure that audit teams are not required to swap between different methods depending on the audit year end.

1.6 OTHER GUIDANCE

Guidance on auditing before the development of the APB (and its predecessor, the APC) came mainly from the statements on auditing of the ICAEW which dealt with particular aspects of auditing practice. Most of the original statements have now been superseded by ISAs (UK and Ireland) or Auditing Standards and guidelines but the few remaining are set out in the **Appendix** to this book.

In addition, the auditing committee of the ICAEW, which was part of their Financial Reporting and Auditing Group, from time to time issues statements (FRAGs) on particular topics, for example, *Reports on Internal Controls of Investment Custodians made available to Third Parties*. This role has now been assumed by the Audit and Assurance Faculty of the ICAEW, which was formed in 1995. These are also listed in the **Appendix**.

1.7 OTHER SOURCES OF AUDITING STANDARDS

This book has taken a narrow definition of GAAS, i.e., based on the pronouncements of standard setting bodies except for those areas where decisions of courts indicate a duty. We have not ignored other sources, and in some areas and where necessary we have drawn on:

- auditing textbooks;
- the published manuals of some of the larger firms; and
- model audit files/methods published by the various institutes.

These have, however, only been used to a limited extent as illustrative material because:

- such information is only a partial indication of the standards applied in practice; and
- such standards will often be higher than GAAS although they may be in the process of becoming generally accepted.

2 AUDIT REGULATION

2.1 INTRODUCTION

Only registered auditors may accept appointment as company auditors in the UK. This has been the case since the relevant provisions of the Companies Act 1989 became effective on 1 October 1991 and this requirement is retained in the Companies Act 2006. Audit firms, or in some cases individuals, must be registered with a Recognised Supervisory Body (RSB). In order to qualify as an RSB, an organisation must have rules to ensure that its members, who are therefore qualified to accept appointments as company auditors, are properly regulated and monitored. To date the Institute of Chartered Accountants in England and Wales (ICAEW), the Institute of Chartered Accountants of Scotland (ICAS), the Institute of Chartered Accountants in Ireland (ICAI) and the Association of Chartered Certified Accountants (ACCA) have become RSBs for this purpose.

The RSB's regulations must cover the following areas:

- qualification of auditors;
- control of audit firms by qualified individuals;
- fit and proper persons;
- professional integrity and independence;
- technical standards;
- procedures to maintain competence; and
- meeting claims.

The rules must also provide for monitoring and enforcement, membership eligibility, investigation of complaints and discipline.

The Review of the Regulatory Regime of the Accountancy Profession (the 'DTI Review'), published in January 2003 stated that the APB should take over the professional bodies' responsibilities for setting standards for independence, objectivity and integrity. The APB commenced this process with the publication of five Ethical Standards in October 2004 and an Ethical Standard, *Provisions Available for Smaller Entities* in December 2004 ('ES – PASE'). These are discussed in **2.5** and **2.6** below.

At the time of issuing the five Ethical Standards and the ES – PASE, the APB stated that they would be subject to ongoing review. The first review was commenced in the spring of 2007 and changes were effective for audit periods commencing on or after 6 April 2008. At that time, the need for further review of certain items was identified and the resulting Exposure Draft of further amendments was issued in March 2009. It is discussed in **2.7** below.

In July 2006, the ICAEW issued additional ethical guidance for its members in its Code of Ethics. Further details are given in **2.8** below.

A number of changes were made to the Audit Regulations which were effective from 1 January 2003. These dealt with the need to be registered before accepting an audit appointment, a requirement for registering Institute approval of new Responsible Individuals and a change in the definition of an audit in respect of charities.

The Companies (Audit, Investigations and Community Enterprise) Act 2004 states that RSBs are not able to be directly involved in carrying out standard setting, disciplinary functions and monitoring. They may however, comment on draft auditing standards, provide information for monitoring visits or refer cases to the independent disciplinary body. Typically the APB sets standards and the Professional Oversight Board for Accountancy ('the POBA') has responsibility for disciplinary matters and for monitoring via the Audit Inspections Unit (AIU) (see **2.13** below).

In October 2006, the APB issued the Ethical Standard for Reporting Accountants (ESRA) based on the threats and safeguards approach used in ES 1 to 5 and applicable for all engagements governed by the SIRs, which are covered in **Chapter 50**. The ESRA is discussed in **50.9**.

2.2   QUALIFICATION

The Companies Act states that for a qualification to be recognised it must, among other things, involve:

- a course of theoretical instruction;
- examinations; and
- three years' practical training.

2.3   CONTROL OF AUDIT FIRMS

A firm may not be recognised as a registered auditor unless it is controlled by qualified persons. In simple terms this means that a majority of the members of the firm are qualified persons although certain of the RSBs have in fact imposed more stringent requirements than this.

2.4   FIT AND PROPER PERSON

An RSB must have adequate rules and practices designed to ensure that persons eligible under its rules are fit and proper persons to be so appointed. This will normally involve ensuring that there is a suitable procedure for notification, both to the firm by partners and employees and to the RSB by the firms, of matters relating to partners and employees in respect of:

● financial integrity and reliability;
● convictions or civil liabilities; and
● good reputation or character – including previous disciplinary procedures with professional bodies or other regulatory organisations.

2.5 PROFESSIONAL INTEGRITY AND INDEPENDENCE

In October 2004 the APB issued its *Ethical Standards for Auditors* covering integrity, objectivity and independence.

● Ethical Standard 1, *Integrity, Objectivity and Independence*;
● Ethical Standard 2, *Financial, Business, Employment and Personal Relationships*;
● Ethical Standard 3, *Long Association with the Audit Engagement*;
● Ethical Standard 4, *Fees, Remuneration and Evaluation Policies, Litigation, Gifts and Hospitality*; and
● Ethical Standard 5, *Non-audit Services Provided to Audit Clients*.

These five APB Ethical Standards replace previous guidance issued by the accounting profession. This is in line with the recommendations of the Review of the Regulatory Regime of the Accountancy Profession (the 'DTI Review') which stated that the APB should take over the professional bodies' responsibilities for setting standards for independence, objectivity and integrity.

This move was also suggested by the final report of the Co-ordinating Group on Audit and Accounting Issues, which recommended that the responsibility for setting standards to uphold auditor independence should be transferred to a body that would be independent of the professional accountancy bodies.

In April 2008, the Ethical Standards were revised to incorporate a number of issues which had arisen during the initial application of the standards.

The Ethical Standards (Revised) also incorporate the requirements set out in:

● the EC Recommendation on 'Statutory auditors' independence in the EU: a set of the fundamental principles'; and
● Section 8 of the International Federation of Accountants ('IFAC') 'Code of Ethics for Professional Accountants',

so that when auditors follow the APB standards they will also have complied with the principles set out in the international guidance.

The Ethical Standards (Revised) also consider the recommendations of the Combined Code and the Smith Report to develop the role of audit committees.

The APB's aims were to develop standards that:

- are rigorous, complete and likely to be effective in practice in upholding the integrity, objectivity and independence of auditors;
- enhance public confidence in the quality of the audit; and
- are clear to auditors, audit committees and those monitoring audits.

They have set out the fundamental principles which auditors are expected to follow in ES 1 (Revised) and then applied those principles to address particular areas of concern in other standards. A 'threats and safeguards' approach has been used in drafting the Standards, identifying the threats that can arise and giving examples of the safeguards that may be suitable. The Standards have been drafted to be relevant to the audits of both large and small entities, publicly traded or privately owned.

Ethical Standards 1, 2, 4 and 5 (Revised) are effective for the audits of financial statements for periods beginning on or after 6 April 2008. Ethical Standard 3 (Revised) underwent further amendment and was reissued in October 2009. It is effective for the audits of financial statements for periods commencing on or after 15 December 2009.

Further amendments to the remaining Ethical Standards outlined in **2.7** below have been deferred until responses are received on the APB's consultation on non-audit services which is detailed in **2.8**.

Following the public consultation on the Ethical Standards, the APB issued a further Ethical Standard, *Exemptions Available for Smaller Entities* ('ES – EASE') alongside the five final Standards. This is discussed in section **2.6**.

2.5.1 Ethical Standard 1 (Revised): Integrity, Objectivity and Independence

APB Ethical Standard 1 (Revised) (ES1) states:

> 'Public confidence in the operation of the capital markets and in the conduct of public interest entities depends, in part, upon the credibility of the opinions and reports issued by the auditors in connection with the audit of the financial statements. Such credibility depends on beliefs concerning the integrity, objectivity and independence of the auditors and the quality of audit work they perform.'

It defines each of the terms, integrity, objectivity and independence as follows:

- 'integrity requires not only honesty but a broad range of related qualities such as fairness, candour, courage, intellectual honesty and confidentiality';
- 'objectivity is a state of mind that excludes bias, prejudice and compromise and that gives fair and impartial consideration to all matters that are relevant

to the task in hand, disregarding those that are not. Objectivity requires that the auditors' judgement is not affected by conflicts of interests'; and

- 'independence is freedom from situations and relationships which make it probable that a reasonable and informed third party would conclude that objectivity is either impaired or could be impaired'.

The Standard requires firms to establish formal and written policies and procedures to ensure that those in a position to influence the conduct and outcome of an audit act with integrity, objectivity and independence. This should involve the leadership of the firm engendering an environment where ethics are considered more important than commercial considerations, and designating an 'ethics partner' to have overall responsibility for the firm's policies and procedures.

The policies and procedures in place should include those set out in **Table 1**.

TABLE 1: Ethical policies and procedures

- requirements for partners and staff to report where applicable;
- family and other personal relationships involving an audit client of the firm;
- financial interests in an audit client of the firm;
- decisions to join an audit client;
- monitoring of compliance with the firm's policies and procedures relating to integrity, objectivity and independence. Such monitoring procedures include, on a test basis, periodic review of the audit engagement partners' documentation of their consideration of the auditors' objectivity and independence, addressing, for example:

  - financial interests in audit clients;
  - economic dependency on audit clients;
  - the performance of non-audit services; and
  - audit partner rotation;

- prompt communication of identified breaches of the firm's policies and procedures to the relevant audit engagement partners;
- evaluation by audit engagement partners of the implications of any identified breaches of the firm's policies and procedures that are reported to them;
- reporting by audit engagement partners of particular circumstances or relationships as required by APB Ethical Standards (Revised);
- prohibiting members of the audit team from making, or assuming responsibility for, management decisions for the audit client. The revision to ES1 published in 2008 added the specific guidance that an auditor should not be involved in the decision making of the audited entity;
- operation of a disciplinary mechanism to promote compliance with policies and procedures; and
- empowerment of staff to communicate to senior levels within the firm any issue of objectivity and independence that concerns them; this includes establishing clear communication channels open to staff, encouraging staff to use these channels and ensuring that staff who use these channels are not subject to disciplinary proceedings as a result.

All firms of more than three partners who are responsible individuals should designate a partner in the firm as 'ethics partner'. The ethics partner will have responsibility for:

- the adequacy of the firm's policies and procedures relating to integrity, objectivity and independence, their compliance with APB Ethical Standards, and the effectiveness of their communications to partners and staff within the firm; and
- providing related guidance to individual partners.

The ethics partner should be suitably experienced and hold sufficient authority within a firm.

Firms with three or less partners where it is not practicable to designate an ethics partner should ensure that the relevant issues are regularly discussed by all partners. Sole practitioners should discuss with the ethics helpline of their professional body any matters where a difficult or objective judgement must be made.

Auditors should identify and assess threats to their objectivity and apply safeguards that will either eliminate or reduce the threat to an acceptable level. The principal types of threat are set out in **Table 2**.

TABLE 2: Types of threats to objectivity

- Self-interest threat – the auditor has financial or other interest that would affect their decision making.
- Self-review threat – if auditing their own non-audit work.
- Management threat – the firm has made judgements or taken decisions that are the responsibility of management.
- Advocacy threat – the auditor has acted as an advocate and has supported a position taken by management in an adversarial context.
- Familiarity (or trust) threat – the auditor has a close personal relationship with the client.
- Intimidation threat – the auditor is influenced by fear or threats.

The significance of threats should be considered throughout the audit, but at least when:

- considering whether to accept or retain an audit engagement;
- planning the audit;
- forming an opinion on the financial statements;
- considering whether to accept or retain an engagement to provide non-audit services to an audit client; and
- potential threats are reported to the audit engagement partner.

This assessment of threats should be documented, together with details of actions taken as a result of identified threats. The firm should have procedures in place to ensure that any possible threats are reported to the audit engagement partner or the ethics partner. The audit engagement partner should not accept or continue an audit engagement if it is concluded that a threat to objectivity and independence cannot be reduced to an acceptable level.

At the end of the audit process, but prior to issuing the audit report, the audit engagement partner should reach an overall conclusion on whether any threats to objectivity and independence have been properly addressed. If they are unable to conclude that this is the case, the audit report should not be issued, and the firm should resign.

In the case of listed companies and public interest clients the assessment, and documentation of the assessment, should be reviewed by an independent partner and those charged with governance should be informed of any significant facts and matters that bear on the auditors' objectivity and independence on a timely basis.

For all clients, the key elements of the audit engagement partner's consideration of objectivity and independence should be communicated to those charged with governance. These may include:

- the principal threats, if any, to objectivity and independence identified by the auditors, including consideration of all relationships between the audit client, its affiliates and directors and the audit firm;
- any safeguards adopted and the reasons why they are considered to be effective;
- any independent partner review;
- the overall assessment of threats and safeguards; and
- information about the general policies and processes within the audit firm for maintaining objectivity and independence.

The minimum requirements for listed companies are set out in **Table 3**. These were updated in the revision to ES 1 published in April 2008.

TABLE 3: Minimum contents of communications with those charged with governance for listed clients

- a written disclosure of relationships that bear on the auditor's objectivity and independence, any safeguards that are in place and details of non-audit services provided to the audited entity and the fees charged in relation thereto;
- written confirmation that the auditor is independent;
- details of any inconsistencies between APB Ethical Standards (Revised) and the company's policy for the supply of non-audit services by the audit firm and any apparent breach of that policy; and
- an opportunity to discuss auditor independence issues.

2.5.2 Ethical Standard 2 (Revised): Financial, Business, Employment and Personal Relationships

ES 2 (Revised) sets out a number of requirements and prohibitions relating to auditor and client relationships.

Financial relationships

The Standard states that the audit firm, or a person in a position to influence the conduct and outcome of the audit, should not hold:

- any direct financial interest in an audit client or affiliate of an audit client;
- any indirect financial interest in an audit client or an affiliate of an audit client, where the investment is material to the audit firm or the individual and to the intermediary (e.g., an open-ended investment company or a pension scheme); or
- any indirect financial interest in an audit client or an affiliate of an audit client, where the person holding it has both:

  - the ability to influence the investment decisions of the intermediary; and
  - actual knowledge of the existence of the underlying investment in the audit client.

There are no safeguards that can mitigate such threats and the individual involved should either dispose of the whole financial interest, dispose of part of the interest so that the remaining part is not material or the firm or individual concerned should withdraw from the audit. Ethical Standard 2 (Revised) gives further details of the remedies required.

This requirement also extends to:

- an immediate family member of the person who can influence the conduct and outcome of the audit;
- partners in the same office as the engagement partner; or
- the immediate family of such partners.

Financial interests held by audit firm pension schemes

There are no safeguards that can eliminate or reduce the self-interest threat to an acceptable level where the pension scheme of an audit firm has a financial interest in an audit client and the firm has any influence over the trustees' investment decisions. In such a situation the audit firm would be required to resign from the audit. Where the pension scheme invests in a client through an intermediary such as a collective investment scheme, and the firm cannot influence the investment decisions, the ethics partner must consider whether the position is acceptable, having particular regard to the materiality of the investment to the pension scheme.

Loans and guarantees

There are similar restrictions as those for financial relationships where firms, persons able to influence audits and immediate family members of such persons make loans to, or guarantee the borrowings of, an audit client.

This also extends to accepting a loan from, or having borrowings guaranteed by, an audit client.

The only exemptions for these restrictions are:

- the audit client is a bank or similar institution; and
- the loan or guarantee is made in the ordinary course of business on normal business terms; and
- where the client makes the loan or guarantee to the audit firm, it is neither material to the audit firm or the client, or where the client makes the loan or guarantee to a person able to influence the audit or their immediate family members it is not material to that individual.

Business relationships

Audit firms and persons able to influence audits (and their immediate family members) should not enter into business relationships with audit clients except for the purchase of goods or services in the normal course of business where the transaction is not material to either party.

Examples of business relationships that may create self-interest, advocacy or intimidation threats include:

- joint ventures with the audit client or with a director, officer or other senior management;
- arrangements to combine services or products and market them with reference to both parties;
- acting as a distributor or marketer of any of the audit client's products or services; or
- other commercial transactions such as the audit firm leasing office space from the audit client.

Employment relationships

Audit staff should not:

- be employed by both audit firm and audit client;
- be loaned by the firm to the client, except if the audit client agrees that the member of staff will not hold a management position and will not have responsibility for management decisions or preparing or recording accounting entries; or
- be involved in auditing any work they performed whilst on loan with the client.

If a former partner of the firm joins an audit client, the firm must ensure that all connections with the partner are severed before any further audit work is performed for that client. This includes settling outstanding financial interests and ensuring that the partner does not participate or appear to participate in the firm's business or professional activities.

Firms should have procedures to ensure that partners or senior audit team members are required to notify the firm as soon as there is a potential for them to become employed by an audit client. Other members of the team should notify the firm as soon as their employment by an audit client becomes probable. Any such person must be removed from the audit team immediately and the work they performed on the current and most recent audit should be reviewed.

When a partner becomes a director, including a non-executive director, or enters a key management position with an audit client within two years of acting as an engagement partner, the firm must resign as auditors. Reappointment cannot take place until the two-year period has elapsed. If any other audit team member joins the client within the two-year window, the firm should consider whether the composition of the current audit team remains appropriate.

Similarly, a partner or an employee of an audit firm should not accept a governance role with an audit client. A prohibited governance role would be appointment to the board of directors or any subcommittee of that board or to any position in any entity which holds directly or indirectly, more than 20 per cent of the voting rights of the audit client. Where a governance role is accepted by an immediate or close family member, or another partner or employee in the office, safeguards can usually be put in place to mitigate any threats.

When staff who were involved with the preparation of the financial statements transfer from audit client to audit firm they should not be involved in the audit of that client for a period of two years from leaving the audit client.

Family and other personal relationships

The Standard states that:

> a relationship between a person who is in a position to influence the conduct and outcome of the audit and another party does not generally affect the consideration of the auditors' objectivity.

However, this may not be the case where a family relationship exists and that family member also has a financial, business or employment relationship with the audit client. The significance of any threat will depend on:

- the relevant person's involvement in the audit;
- the nature of the relationship between the relevant person and his or her family member; and
- the family member's relationship with the audit client.

Therefore partners and professional staff should report any immediate family (i.e., spouse and dependents), close family (i.e., parents, non-dependent children and siblings) and other personal relationships involving an audit client, to their firm where they consider it might create a threat to independence or objectivity. Such information should be passed to the engagement partner who will be able to assess the threat to independence and objectivity and apply appropriate safeguards.

The audit engagement partner should also consider whether any external consultant involved in the audit will be objective, and document the rationale for their conclusion.

2.5.3 Ethical Standard 3 (Revised): Long Association with the Audit Engagement

The Standard states that firms should monitor the length of time that audit engagement partners, key audit partners and staff in senior positions serve as members of the engagement team for each audit.

The Standard suggests rotating the audit partners and senior members of the audit team after a period of time. For listed and public interest entities, the maximum period is determined as five years. A suggested maximum of ten years is given for non-listed clients, although this is not mandatory and alternative safeguards could be applied. Where the individual is not rotated from the audit after ten years the reasons for this should be documented and these facts communicated to those charged with governance.

For listed and public interest entities, the Standard states that partner rotation is the only permissible safeguard. **Table 4** sets out the time limits for rotation.

TABLE 4: Time limits for partner rotation for listed and public interest entities

In the case of listed companies and other public interest entities the audit firm should establish policies and procedures to ensure that:

- no one should act as audit engagement partner or as independent partner for a continuous period longer than five years;[1][2]
- where an independent partner becomes the audit engagement partner, the combined period of service in these positions should not exceed five years; and

---

[1] The revision to ES3 published in October 2009 and effective for the audits of financial statements for periods commencing on or after 15 December 2009 allows the five year rule to be extended to seven years where the audit committee (or equivalent) of the entity decide that such an extension is necessary to safeguard the quality of the audit and this is agreed by the audit firm involved. This may be where substantial change has recently been made or will be made to the nature or structure of the entity's business or there are unexpected changes in the senior management of the audited entity. In such circumstances, alternative safeguards should be put in place to reduce any threats to an acceptable level. Disclosure of the extension must be made to the shareholders as soon as possible and again in each of the subsequent years.

[2] Where an audit client becomes listed or public interest the period before the listing etc. will be taken into account when calculating the five years elapsed. However, if on listing the partner has served four years or more, they can serve up to two further years.

> • anyone who has acted as the audit engagement partner or the independent partner, or held a combination of such positions, for a particular audit client for a period of five years should not hold any position of responsibility in relation to the audit engagement until a further period of five years has elapsed.

A seven-year limit is imposed for rotation of key audit partners. A key audit partner is an audit partner, or other person performing the function of an audit partner, of the engagement team (other than the audit engagement partner) who is involved at the group level and is responsible for key decisions or judgements on significant matters, such as on significant subsidiaries or divisions, or on significant risk factors that relate to the audit of that client. Additionally, the seven-year limit applies when the key audit partner becomes the engagement partner. The 'cooling off' period before the key audit partner can assume any responsibility in relation to this client is two years.

The same seven-year limit is relevant to other partners and staff in senior positions after which time a review of the threats and safeguards relevant to objectivity and independence must be made. Where there are threats identified a suitable safeguard may be to remove the member of staff from the audit team.

2.5.4 Ethical Standard 4 (Revised): Fees, Remuneration and Evaluation Policies, Litigation, Gifts and Hospitality

Fees

The Standard sets out the following requirements in relation to fees:

• sufficient partners and staff with appropriate skills must be used on an audit, irrespective of fees charged;
• an audit should not be undertaken on a contingent fee basis;
• audit partners should be informed if other non-audit services are to be provided to the client on a contingent fee basis;
• for listed companies, the audit engagement partner should disclose to the audit committee in writing any contingent fee arrangements for non-audit services;
• fees and payment arrangements should be agreed with the client prior to the audit firm being appointed for the following period; and
• where overdue fees arise, the audit engagement partner, together with the ethics partner, should consider whether it is necessary to resign.

The revision to ES 4 published in 2008 added the requirement that audit fees should not be influenced or determined by the provision of non-audit services to the audit client.

Remuneration and evaluation policies

The Standard states that the audit team should not include in its objectives the selling of non-audit services to the audit client, and team members should not be evaluated or remunerated based on their success in selling non-audit services.

Litigation

Unless insignificant, the audit firm should not continue or accept an audit engagement where litigation is in progress or is probable.

Gifts and hospitality

The Standard states that the audit firm and those in a position to influence the conduct and outcome of the audit (and their immediate family) should not accept gifts from an audit client other than low-value items of a promotional or commemorative nature. Neither should they accept hospitality unless it is reasonable in terms of its frequency, nature and cost.

The audit firm should establish policies on the nature and value of gifts and hospitality that may be accepted from and offered to audit clients, their directors, officers and employees.

2.5.5 Ethical Standard 5 (Revised): Non-Audit Services Provided to Audited Entities

Ethical Standard 5 (Revised) states that a firm must consider whether acceptance of a non-audit service engagement may give rise to threats to objectivity. If this is the case they must either not accept the non-audit service engagement or provide the non-audit service having resigned their positions as auditors. Procedures should be in place to ensure that the possible provision of non-audit services is notified to the audit engagement partner prior to accepting the work.

The audit engagement partner should ensure that those charged with governance of the audit client are informed of all significant facts relating to non-audit services that may have a bearing on the auditors' objectivity and independence. For listed clients they should also be informed where their policy on obtaining non-audit services from their auditor is inconsistent with the requirements of the APB's Ethical Standards (Revised), and if their own policy has been breached.

The Standard then details risks to objectivity that may arise from the provision of the following services:

- internal audit;
- information technology;
- valuation;
- actuarial valuation;
- litigation support;

- taxation;
- legal;
- recruitment and remuneration;
- corporate finance;
- transaction-related services; and
- accounting.

It also suggests safeguards which could be put in place, if any, to allow auditors to continue their work in an independent and objective manner.

2.6 ETHICAL STANDARD, PROVISIONS AVAILABLE FOR SMALL ENTITIES

2.6.1 Background

The consultation process for the five ethical standards raised a number of issues where commentators believed the requirements of the standards to be unworkable for smaller entities. One area where there was particular concern was the restrictions on the provision of non-audit services unless 'knowledgeable management' were able to oversee all non-audit services provided by the entity's auditors. It was considered unlikely that smaller entities would have sufficiently knowledgeable management, thus causing accounting and taxation work to be given to a firm other than the auditors. This would have meant the loss of a single, cost-effective source of business advice for such companies. As a result ES 5 (Revised) requires 'informed' rather than 'knowledgeable' management, maintaining the need for the client to take responsibility for judgements arising from non-audit services, whilst clarifying the required level of competence.

The APB do not want to reduce the requirements for smaller companies as, if they fall below the audit exemption limits, they may be requesting an audit on the instigation of a third party who would probably expect full ethical standards to apply. Therefore they issued *Provisions Available for Small Entities* (PASE) with a view that the ES – PASE should apply for a period of three years. In this period the APB will consider:

- the extent to which companies have taken advantage of the increased level of audit exemption;
- the reasons for, and main users of, audits that continue to be undertaken of companies below the audit exemption threshold;
- the views of owners of small entities and users of small entity audited accounts on the independence and objectivity of auditors; and
- the feasibility of an alternative assurance service to meet the needs of users of small entity audited accounts.

Other areas where concerns were raised were the 10 per cent economic dependence test in ES 4 (Revised) and the two-year 'cooling off' period on a partner accepting a management role. These are also addressed in the ES – PASE.

The ES – PASE is effective for the audits of financial statements for periods commencing on or after 15 December 2004.

2.6.2 Non-audit services

The ES – PASE exempts auditors, when working for a Small Entity client, from adhering to the requirement in paragraph 28 of ES 5. A Small Entity client is defined in **Table 5**.

TABLE 5: Definition of a Small Entity client

For the purposes of the ES – PASE, a 'Small Entity' is:

- not a listed company, or an affiliate thereof;
- any company that meets two or more of the following requirements in both the current financial year and the preceding year (the Companies Act 2006 definition):

  - not more than £5.6 million turnover;
  - not more than £2.8 million balance sheet total;
  - not more than 50 employees.

- any charity with an income of less than £5.6 million;
- any pension fund with less than 1,000 members (including active, deferred and pensioner members);
- any firm, bank and building society, regulated by the FSA (including any mortgage firm or insurance broker that will be regulated from early 2005), which is not required to appoint an auditor under the FSA Handbook on Supervision;
- any credit union which is a mutually owned financial cooperative established under the Credit Unions Act 1979 and the Industrial and Provident Societies Act 1965 (or equivalent legislation);
- any entity registered under the Industrial and Provident Societies Act 1965, incorporated under the Friendly Societies Act 1992 or registered under the Friendly Societies Act 1974 (or equivalent legislation), which meets the Companies Act 1985 definition of a small company, set out above;
- any registered social landlord with less than 250 homes; and
- any other entity, such as a club, which would be a Small Entity if it were a company.

Where an entity falls into more than one of the above categories, it will only be a Small Entity if it meets the criteria of all relevant categories.

Paragraph 28 requires auditors to assess whether management at the audit client are able to make independent judgements and decisions based on the information provided by the non-audit service. It also states that if management are not suitably able, there are likely to be no other safeguards available to reduce management threat to objectivity and independence to an acceptable level as auditors are increasingly likely to take decisions and make judgements which should be made by management.

Small Entity auditors taking advantage of the exemption from paragraph 28 of ES 5 (Revised) are not required to apply safeguards provided:

- the audit client has 'informed management'; and
- the audit firm extends the cyclical inspection of completed engagements that is performed for quality control purposes to include a random selection of audit engagements where non-audit services have been provided to ensure that there is documentary evidence that 'informed management' has made relevant judgements and decisions themselves.

The fact that the exemption has been applied should be disclosed in the auditor's report and further disclosure in line with the example in **Table 8** should be made in the financial statements or auditor's report.

In addition, the auditors of a Small Entity will have exemption from the requirements of paragraph 73 of ES 5 (Revised) which states that:

'the audit firm should not undertake an engagement to provide tax services to an audit client where this would involve acting as an advocate for the audit client, before an appeals tribunal or court in the resolution of an issue:

(a) that is material to the financial statements; or
(b) where the outcome of the tax issue is dependent on a future or contemporary audit judgment.'

Where use is made of the exemption from either paragraph 28 or 73 of ES 5 (Revised), the working papers should document this fact and the audit report should disclose that advantage has been taken of the exemption. Where a paragraph 28 exemption is used details of the non-audit service should be given in the audit report; when a paragraph 73 exemption is used a description of the relevant circumstances should be included.

2.6.3   Economic dependence

The ES – PASE gives an exemption for Small Audit Firms from paragraphs 23 and 26 of ES 4 (Revised), the 10 per cent and 15 per cent fee limits (see **2.5.4** above). Small Audit Firms are those with three or less partners that are responsible individuals.

The exemption is available as long as the firm discloses the breaches of the expectation that fees will amount to between 10 and 15 per cent to the ethics partner and to those charged with governance of the client.

2.6.4   Partners joining an audit client

An audit firm of a Small Entity is exempt from the requirement of paragraph 43 of ES 2 (Revised) as long as the firm takes appropriate steps to ensure that there have been no significant threats to the audit team's integrity, objectivity and independence and discloses the fact that it has taken advantage of the exemption in its audit report. Example steps for a Small Audit Firm to take are set out in **Table 6**.

Paragraph 43 of ES 2 (Revised) requires an audit firm to resign from an engagement for a two-year 'cooling off' period if a former partner of that firm is appointed as a director or in a key management position at the client, if that partner had acted as audit engagement partner, independent partner, key audit partner or partner in the chain of command at any time in the two years prior to this appointment.

Where this exemption is used, the fact must be disclosed in the auditor's report and further disclosures in line with the example in **Table 8** should be made in the financial statements or the auditor's report.

TABLE 6: Possible steps for a Small Audit Firm to take to guard against threats to independence relating to paragraph 43 of ES 2 (Revised)

- assess significance of the self-interest, familiarity or intimidation threats having regard to:

  - the position the individual has taken at the audit client;
  - the nature and amount of any involvement the individual will have with the audit team or the audit process;
  - the length of time that has passed since the individual was a member of the audit team or firm; and
  - the former position of the individual within the audit team or firm, and

- if that threat is anything other than clearly insignificant, apply safeguards such as:

  - considering the appropriateness or necessity of modifying the audit plan for the audit engagement;
  - assigning an audit team to the subsequent audit engagement that is of sufficient experience in relation to the individual who has joined the audit client;
  - involving an audit partner or senior staff member with appropriate expertise, who was not a member of the audit team, to review the work done or otherwise advise as necessary; or
  - perform a quality control review of the audit engagement.

2.6.5 *Audit report wording*

The ES – PASE gives example wording for the disclosure required in the audit report when any exemption given by the ES – PASE is used. The example wording is reproduced in **Table 7**.

TABLE 7: Example audit report wording where an ES – PASE exemption has been used

"Basis of audit opinion

We conducted our audit in accordance with International Standards on Auditing (UK and Ireland) issued by the Auditing Practices Board. An audit includes examination on a test basis, of evidence relevant to the amounts and disclosures in the financial statements. It also includes an assessment of the significant estimates and judgements made by [the directors] in the preparation of the financial statements, and of whether the accounting policies are appropriate to the [company's] circumstances, consistently applied and adequately disclosed.

We planned and performed our audit so as to obtain all the information and explanations which we considered necessary in order to provide us with sufficient evidence to give reasonable assurance that the financial statements are free from material misstatement, whether caused by fraud or other irregularity or error. In forming our opinion we also evaluated the overall adequacy of the presentation of information in the financial statements.

We have undertaken the audit in accordance with the requirements of APB Ethical Standards (Revised) including APB Ethical Standard – Provisions Available for Small Entities, in the circumstances set out in note [x] to the financial statements.

Opinion

In our opinion . . . "

Examples of the disclosures required when certain exemptions are applied are also provided by the ES – PASE, as these are reproduced in **Table 8**.

TABLE 8: Example disclosures where exemptions are used

Management threat in relation to non-audit services (2.6.2 above)

In common with many other businesses of our size and nature we use our auditors to prepare and submit returns to the tax authorities and assist with the preparation of the financial statements.

Advocacy threat – tax services (2.6.2 above)

In common with many other businesses of our size and nature we use our auditors to provide tax advice and to represent us, as necessary, at tax tribunals.

Partners joining an audit client (2.6.4 above)

XYZ, a former partner of [audit firm] joined [audit client] as [a director] on [date].

2.7   REVIEW OF ETHICAL STANDARDS

2.7.1   Background

When the Ethical Standards were first published, the APB announced their intention to update their contents on a regular basis. The first of these updates was published in April 2008. Following this update a further consultation was performed on a number of issues and the resulting Exposure Draft of further amendments was published in March 2009. Comments were requested by 15 June 2009.

Changes outlined in the proposal relating to the extension of rotation periods for audit engagement partners on listed company audits were introduced in the revision to ES3 issued in October 2009 and are effective for the audit of financial statements commencing on or after 15 December 2009.

Other amendments proposed in the March 2009 consultation paper have been deferred pending responses to the October 2009 consultation on audit firms providing non-audit services to listed companies that they audit (see **2.8** below).

The areas where amendments are proposed but have not yet been actioned are:

*   remuneration and evaluation policies for key partners involved in audits;
*   partners and staff in governance roles for an audit client;
*   the provision of non-audit services relating to securitisation and restructuring services;
*   the provision of direct assistance to the audit team by internal auditors;
*   the definition of an audited entity's 'affiliates'; and
*   the financial interests of partners joining the firm.

Further details of the proposed amendments are set out below.

2.7.2   Remuneration of key partners

As part of their work the FRC's Audit Investigation Unit identified that some firms were permitting senior specialist personnel from outside of the audit function, but who were involved in the audit, to be rewarded for selling non-audit services to audited entities, or for their performance to be evaluated on the basis of non-audit services sold in this way.

The Exposure Draft now makes it explicit that all key partners involved in the audit should not be rewarded or evaluated on the basis of non-audit services sold to audit clients. This, however, does not extend to partners (other than key partners involved in the audit) and staff from non-audit disciplines who are assigned to the audit and who undertake a substantial part of some of the audit procedures.

2.7.3 Governance

Ethical Standard 2 (Revised) has a restriction on all partners and employees of the audit firm who undertake audit work from serving as a director or officer of an audit client. In the draft revision to the IFAC Code this restriction is extended to all partners and employees of a firm, not just those involved in audit. The APB therefore, proposes to extend the restriction in ES 2 (Revised) in the same way.

2.7.4 Restructuring and securitisation services

Increasingly audit firms are being requested to provide restructuring advice to their clients and some commentators are of the opinion that this can pose a conflict of interest.

APB Bulletin 2008/10 *Going Concern Issues During the Current Economic Conditions* includes guidance in this area (see **13.10**), and the Exposure Draft proposes that this guidance be brought into ES 5 (Revised) as well. The proposed new section to ES 5 (Revised) will provide examples of the type of services included in the category of restructuring services and sets out the requirements and guidance associated with their provision to an audited entity.

Following the Treasury Committee's inquiry into Northern Rock, the APB proposes to amend the examples of transaction related services in ES 5 (Revised) to clarify that assurance services on transactions, such as those relating to securitisations are covered by this guidance. This means that the performance of securitisation services is prohibited where:

- there is reasonable doubt as to the appropriateness of a related accounting treatment;
- such services are provided on a contingent fee basis and:
  - the fees are material to the firm; or
  - the outcome is dependent on a future or contemporary audit judgment; or
- the engagement would involve the firm undertaking a management role.

2.7.5 Internal auditors

There are instances when personnel from a company's internal audit function directly assist the external auditor in carrying out external audit procedures. This is different to when the external auditor relies on work already performed by the internal audit function or the external auditor agrees that the internal audit function should undertake certain work and then places reliance on that work.

Some commentators believe that this makes the internal audit function part of the audit team, and results in dual employment which is not permitted under paragraph 36 of ES 2 (Revised).

The APB intends to update ISA (UK and Ireland) 610 to include reference to ES 2 (Revised) and to set out the threats relating to using internal audit in this way. The audit procedures to be followed when the internal audit department assists the external auditor with their procedures will be similar to those already outlined in ISA (UK and Ireland) 610 which are currently used when external auditors rely on the work already performed by the internal audit department.

2.7.6   Affiliates

The APB proposes an amendment to its definition of an 'affiliate' to include a 'clearly insignificant' test. Although this does not go as a far as the IFAC Code's 'materiality' test, it does minimise the scope for subjectivity and guides audit firms to a more cautious approach.

2.7.7   Financial interests of new partners

As part of the consultation process after introducing the Ethical Standards in 2004, some commentators noted difficulty in appointing new partners from outside the firm where these individuals have existing financial interests involving entities that the firm audits which they are unable to unwind without significant penalties.

The APB proposes to amend the guidance to relax the prohibition on all partners holding financial interests in audit clients for new partners joining a firm where there is no market for disposal of such financial interests. This is providing that the new partner is not involved in the provision of any services to the entity and that they work in a different part of the firm to the audit engagement partner.

2.8   CONSULTATION ON NON-AUDIT SERVICES

2.8.1   Background

In October 2009, the APB issued a document entitled *Consultation on Audit Firms Providing Non-Audit Services to Listed Companies That They Audit*. This was in response to the Treasury Select Committee's report *Banking Crisis: reforming corporate governance and pay in the City* which was published in May of that year. The Treasury Select Committee's report called for a review of the appropriateness of auditors providing non-audit services to their audit clients, stating:

> We strongly believe that investor confidence, and trust in audit would be enhanced by a prohibition on audit firms conducting non-audit work for the same company, and recommend that the Financial Reporting Council consult on his proposal at the earliest opportunity.

The Treasury Select Committee reports that commentators remain sceptical that audit independence can be maintained when non-audit services are provided, and in particular that auditors may be less critical of accounts when there is a potential risk that fees from non-audit services may be jeopardised. Because the concerns raised by the Select Committee are couched in terms of investor confidence, the APB's consultation paper focuses primarily on the provision of non-audit services to listed companies.

2.8.2 Services provided

The nature of other services provided by audit firms to their clients varies enormously. Some non-audit services derive directly from the audit, such as advice on compliance with accounting standards or on internal control weaknesses identified during the audit. Other services are performed by auditors because they are required by legislation or regulation, such as reporting on regulatory returns or on government grants. For these reasons a total ban on the provision of other services may be problematic.

Other services can only be provided by auditors under certain circumstances and when conditions set out in the Ethical Standards to avoid significant threats to auditor objectivity are met. Examples of such services are internal audit or tax planning advice.

Companies argue that involving auditors who already have a good knowledge of the client's business is cost effective and allows those charged with governance to focus on key business activities. For auditors, becoming more involved in their client's operations is argued to assist with risk identification and efficient auditing. It is also stated that multi-disciplinary firms attract and retain the best partners and staff, thus enabling the retention of specialists often needed for an audit.

Investors, regulators and some commentators argue that providing additional services causes the views of the auditor to become more closely aligned with management and increases the economic reasons why auditors will not challenge management during the audit. Prohibitions on the provision of other services to listed clients may also enhance opportunities for mid-sized accountancy firms.

2.8.3   *Managing the risks*

As a result of reviews following the collapse of Enron in 2001, the audit and accountancy profession in the United Kingdom has been subject to increased regulation and imposition of tougher auditor independence standards. Audit committees have also become increasingly involved in the approval of the supply of non-audit services by listed company auditors, and disclosure requirements regarding non-audit services have increased.

As detailed above, Ethical Standards require an assessment of both threats to independence and potential safeguards against identified threats. In addition, ES 5 sets out a number of situations where the undertaking of services by the auditor is prohibited, covering services in areas such as:

- internal audit;
- information technology;
- valuation;
- actuarial;
- tax;
- litigation support;
- legal;
- recruitment and remuneration;
- corporate finance;
- transaction-related services; and
- accounting.

Research and data reviews indicate that the effect of the guidance, together with other economic factors, is that non-audit fees paid to listed company auditors have declined both in absolute terms and as a percentage of audit fees.

It is against this background that the APB requested comments from all stakeholders – investors, companies and their directors and management and accountants – as well as other interested parties as to whether the provision of non-audit services currently impacts on confidence in the independence of auditors and whether, and in what form, there should be any change to the current arrangements. Comments were requested by the end of January 2010.

2.9   ICAEW CODE OF ETHICS

2.9.1   *Background*

In July 2006, the ICAEW issued its own *Code of Ethics* ('the Code') to assist its members in meeting the highest standards of professional conduct. The Code runs to 174 pages and replaces the previous *Guide to Professional Ethics*. It is effective from 1 September 2006 and applies to all ICAEW members (including students), affiliates, employees of member firms and member firms themselves (together 'professional accountants'). It is applicable to all professional and business activities, whether remunerated or voluntary.

The Code is based on IFAC's *Code of Ethics* and adopts a principles-based approach, with threats to the fundamental principles and related safeguards illustrated by a series of case studies.

The Code is split into four sections dealing with:

- issues of general application to all members; and
- issues of specific interest to:
  - members in practice;
  - members in business; and
  - members undertaking insolvency work.

2.9.2   *The fundamental principles*

The Code sets out five fundamental principles that must be complied with at all times. These are set out in **Table 9** below.

TABLE 9: Five fundamental principles in the ICAEW Code of Ethics

Integrity

A professional accountant should be straightforward and honest in all professional and business relationships.

Objectivity

A professional accountant should not allow bias, conflict of interest or undue influence of others to override professional or business judgements.

Professional Competence and Due Care

A professional accountant has a continuing duty to maintain professional knowledge and skill at the level required to ensure that a client or employer receives competent professional service based on current developments in practice, legislation and techniques. A professional accountant should act diligently and in accordance with applicable technical and professional standards when providing professional services.

Confidentiality

A professional accountant should respect the confidentiality of information acquired as a result of professional and business relationships and should not disclose any such information to third parties without proper and specific authority unless there is a legal or professional right or duty to disclose. Confidential information acquired as a result of professional and business relationships should not be used for the personal advantage of the professional accountant or third parties.

> *Professional Behaviour*
>
> A professional accountant should comply with relevant laws and regulations and should avoid any action that discredits the profession.

The environment in which professional accountants operate may lead to specific threats to these fundamental principles. As it is impossible to envisage every possible threat that may occur, the Code sets out a conceptual framework which requires professional accountants to identify, evaluate and address these threats individually rather than just comply with a predetermined set of rules. Where professional accountants identify significant threats they should apply suitable safeguards to eliminate them or reduce them to an acceptable level.

When considering whether a threat is significant, professional accountants should consider both quantitative and qualitative factors. Where suitable safeguards cannot be applied, the professional accountant should not accept, or should resign from, the engagement.

2.9.3 Threats and safeguards

The Code sets out the following types of threats to the fundamental principles:

- self-interest threats, as a result of the financial or other interests of a professional accountant or of an immediate or close family member;
- self-review threats, when a previous judgement needs to be re-evaluated by the professional accountant responsible for that judgement;
- advocacy threats, when a professional accountant promotes a position or opinion to the point that subsequent objectivity may be compromised;
- familiarity threats, when, because of a close relationship, a professional accountant becomes too sympathetic to the interests of others; and
- intimidation threats, when a professional accountant may be deterred from acting objectively by actual or perceived threats.

Each type of threat may arise in relation to the professional accountant themselves or in relation to a connected person such as a close family member, a fellow partner or other professional associate.

There are two main types of safeguard set out in the Code:

- safeguards created by the profession, legislation or regulation; and
- safeguards in the work environment.

The first category includes, but is not restricted to:

- educational, training and experience requirements for entry into the profession;
- continuing professional development requirements;
- corporate governance regulations;
- professional standards;

- professional or regulatory monitoring and disciplinary procedures; and
- external review by a legally empowered third party of the reports, returns, communications or information produced by a professional accountant.

The actual safeguards used will depend on the circumstances. In assessing whether the safeguards are reasonable, professional accountants should consider what a reasonable and informed third party would consider to be acceptable.

2.9.4 Conflict resolution

When applying the fundamental principles, conflicts may arise. The Code states that it is preferable for such conflicts to be resolved within the organisation before obtaining advice from the Institute or legal advisors. Where necessary professional accountants should consult with other appropriate persons within the organisation.

When conflicts occur, professional accountants should consider:

- relevant facts;
- relevant parties;
- ethical issues involved;
- fundamental principles related to the matter in question;
- established internal procedures; and
- alternative courses of action.

If, having exhausted all possibilities, the conflict remains unresolved, the professional accountant should refuse to remain associated with the matter creating the conflict. This may involve a firm resignation from an engagement or an individual withdrawing from an engagement team or resigning from a firm.

2.10 TECHNICAL STANDARDS

The body must have rules and practices as to the technical standards to be applied in company audit work and the manner in which they are to be applied. In practice, the UK bodies have adopted the Auditing Standards and guidelines and registered auditors must be able to demonstrate compliance with these. For example, the *Audit Regulations and Guidance* issued in December 1995 by the ICAEW, ICAS and ICAI, state that where the Audit Registration Committee (ARC) has to decide whether registered auditors have complied with Auditing Standards they will consider, in addition to the standards themselves, any relevant guidance in ISAs (UK and Ireland), SASs, Practice Notes and Bulletins.

In practice, to comply with audit regulations firms will normally be expected to have procedures covering, in addition to the areas mentioned above:

- acceptance of appointment and reappointments; and

● quality control.

2.10.1 *Acceptance of appointment and reappointment*

A firm will normally be expected to have procedures which ensure that before accepting an appointment, and also in considering whether to accept reappointment as auditor of a company, issues of the firm's independence and those of its competence to act are addressed. In addressing competence to act the firm must assess whether or not the partners and employees have the necessary skill and training for the particular type of appointment.

2.10.2 *Quality control*

There must be an adequate system of quality control (see **Chapter 20**). This will involve not only ensuring adequate review procedures but also some measure of quality assurance procedures, for example, 'hot' review of work by independent partners before the opinion is signed off and also 'cold' review procedures to ensure that work has been properly carried out in accordance with the firm's procedures. Quality control will also ensure that the various procedures necessary to ensure compliance with the regulations of the RSB have been carried out.

2.10.3 *Control of confidentiality and independence*

A firm must have procedures to ensure that staff are aware of confidentiality and independence issues. Confidentiality applies to the information obtained during the course of professional work and the obligation not to disclose or use it. Firms need to be able to demonstrate that they have procedures to ensure that such issues have been brought to the attention of staff. This can be demonstrated by having staff certify their awareness of the procedures. Additionally, as regards independence, the firm should circulate details of listed companies of which it is the auditors to both partners and employees to enable them to identify any potential conflicts.

2.11 MAINTAINING COMPETENCE

There must be adequate arrangements to ensure that persons eligible for appointment as a company auditor continue to maintain an appropriate level of competence in the conduct of company audits. This is done by ensuring that there are satisfactory arrangements for training and continuing professional education (CPE) for members of bodies – the levels of desired CPE are normally set out in the rules of the various RSBs.

Although an audit firm's ability to audit rests with its partners and staff, these may change over time. As a result, to demonstrate its competence a firm must use audit manuals, audit programmes, checklists and standard procedures.

The amount of formal documentation and procedures will depend on the size of the firm and its clients. Even the smallest firm is likely to need some documentation such as audit programmes, but as it grows in size, or as its clients become more complex in their nature, procedures may need to be developed further to assist staff to carry out audit work in accordance with audit regulations.

2.12 MEETING OF CLAIMS

There must be adequate rules to ensure that any registered auditor has adequate professional indemnity insurance (PII) cover to secure them against claims arising out of company audit work. In order to become a registered auditor a firm must demonstrate that there is sufficient PII cover in place.

2.13 OTHER AREAS

In addition to the above, each RSB must have rules relating to eligibility for membership, disciplinary arrangements, investigation of complaints and keeping a published register of members. It must also take into account the costs of any rules it makes in terms of the benefit to be obtained and be involved in the promotion and maintenance of Auditing Standards.

The changes to audit regulations effective from 1 January 2003 made three main changes to the regulations, namely:

- adding a rule explicitly stating that a firm or member of an Institute must be registered by a RSB before accepting an audit appointment;
- requiring firms to formally apply before appointing a new Responsible Individual (RI), rather than just informing the registering Institute of the new RI; and
- a clarification that the Regulations apply to all charities, not just those registered under the Charities Acts 1992 and 1993 in England and Wales.

2.14 THE PROFESSIONAL OVERSIGHT BOARD FOR ACCOUNTANCY

Following the Government's announcement that the new regulatory regime for financial reporting, auditing and the accounting professions would fall within the remit of the Financial Reporting Council (FRC), the Professional Oversight Board for Accountancy ('the POBA') was set up.

The POBA aims to support investor, market and public confidence in the financial stewardship and governance of listed and other entities by providing:

- independent oversight of the regulation of the auditing profession by the recognised supervisory and qualifying bodies;
- monitoring of the quality of the auditing function in relation to 'economically significant entities'; and
- independent oversight of the regulation of the accounting profession by the professional accountancy bodies.

In relation to audit, the POBA intends to achieve its aims by:

- working for the FRC in discharging the Council's responsibility for authorising professional accountancy bodies to act as supervisory bodies and to offer a recognised professional qualification; and
- monitoring audit quality through an independent Audit Inspections Unit (AIU) which will monitor audit quality by reviewing audit processes and agreeing with audit firms amendments to their procedures where appropriate. In severe cases, the AIU will recommend appropriate regulatory action to the recognised supervisory bodies and refer matters to the Financial Reporting Review Panel (FRRP).

The AIU took over responsibility from the Joint Monitoring Unit (JMU) for monitoring the audit of listed companies and major charities and pension funds, i.e., the entities whose activities have the greatest potential to impact on financial and economic stability.

2.15 THE QUALITY ASSURANCE DIRECTORATE

Since the responsibility for regulatory and disciplinary issues fell to the FRC, the ICAEW have set up their own arrangements for monitoring the audits not covered by the AIU (see **2.13**). The Quality Assurance Directorate (QAD) operates on similar grounds to the old JMU and reports their findings to the ICAEW.

2.16 AUDIT REPORTS

The audit regulations apply to audits of companies, building societies, credit unions, registered charities, friendly and provident societies, and persons authorised under the Financial Services and Markets Act. An audit for this purpose is when an opinion is expressed on the financial statements, or an extract from them under companies' legislation or that governing those other regulated entities.

Where auditors of one of these entities reports on its financial statements, the report must be signed in the name of the firm, together with the phrase 'registered auditor(s)'. Other opinions that are required to be given by registered auditors, for example the report on the transfer of non-cash assets to a public company, are also covered by the regulations and auditors must also sign these as 'registered auditor(s)'.

Occasionally reports are given on entities which are not covered by the regulations but which the auditors sign as registered auditors, either by choice or because of a specific requirement. If an RSB receives a complaint about such a report enquiries may be made into the general standard of the firms' audit work, including non-regulated work.

2.17   WORKING PAPERS

Audit regulations now include specific requirements concerning the retention period of audit working papers and situations where audit work is carried out by another firm.

2.17.1   *Retention of working papers*

Registered auditors are now required to keep their audit working papers for a period of six years from the balance sheet date to which they relate. Although this regulation only came into force on 1 January 2000, it applies to any papers created before that date. Where a firm previously destroyed its working papers within a shorter period, any papers already destroyed do not have to be recreated. However, the ICAEW indicated in its publication *Audit News* in October 1999, which announced the new regulation that any firm which continued with a shorter retention period between that date and 1 January 2000 would have to be prepared to justify its actions.

The guidance to the regulation notes that the working papers do not have to be on paper but may be on microfilm or on a computer, in which case there should be adequate methods of retrieving them. Records should be kept of which files have been destroyed.

Firms are advised to exercise caution in deciding whether files should be destroyed as the papers may serve another purpose to which a longer retention period applies.

2.17.2   Work carried out by other auditors

Where auditors subcontract audit work to another firm they should retain a right of access to the working papers if they are not handed over to the auditors at the end of the engagement. Any decision to destroy the papers in question should be made by the registered auditor and not the other firm.

The guidance suggests that where the work is to be performed by another firm which itself is not a registered auditor, it may be appropriate for the engagement letter between the two firms to include the full text of the relevant audit regulations regarding working papers.

PART 2
REPORTING

3   THE AUDIT REPORT

3.1   INTRODUCTION

This Chapter examines the auditor's report on the annual financial statements of a company reporting in accordance with the Companies Act 2006. Modifications to the auditor's report are discussed in **Chapter 4**. Other Companies Act reports on annual financial statements are considered in **Chapter 5**, while other reports under the Companies Act are considered in **Chapter 6** and reports to the FSA on investment businesses in **Chapter 8**. Reports on accounts prepared by accountants are considered in **Chapter 7**.

3.2   THE STANDARDS

The current version of ISA 700 *The Auditor's Report on Financial Statements* was issued in October 2009 and provides standards on reporting covering:

- the aim of the audit report;
- the contents of the audit report; and
- modified reports.

The process of updating ISA 700 was removed from the introduction of revised ISAs (UK and Ireland) based on the IAASB's Clarity Project because of the enactment of the Companies Act 2006. The revision to ISA (UK and Ireland) 700 was published in March 2009, and reissued without further amendment in October 2009 as part of the suite of final clarified standards. Like the clarified standards, ISA (UK and Ireland) 700 is effective for the audit of financial statements for periods ending on or after 15 December 2010.

The main changes in the revision to ISA (UK and Ireland) 700 are set out in **3.3**.

One of the changes made by the Companies Act 2006 is to require that audit reports are signed by the 'Senior Statutory Auditor'. This is effective for financial periods beginning on or after 6 April 2008 and is further explained in **3.12** below. In April 2008, the APB issued Bulletin 2008/6, *The 'Senior Statutory Auditor' under the United Kingdom Companies Act 2006* which sets out the role of the Senior Statutory Auditor and provides relevant sign off wordings for auditor's reports. The example reports in this chapter and throughout this publication that require a revised sign off for accounting periods commencing on or after 6 April 2008 have been updated accordingly. For accounting periods before this date, reference should be made to earlier editions of this publication.

3.2.1 Other guidance

In ISA (UK and Ireland) 700, the APB refers readers to 'the most recent version of the APB Bulletin, *Auditor's Reports on Financial Statements in the United Kingdom*' for example company reports. The most recent version is Bulletin 2009/2 which was released in April 2009 in response to the publication of ISA (UK and Ireland) 700 the previous month. Examples in this chapter have been updated in line with the recommendations of that Bulletin. The examples in the Bulletin are effective for periods beginning on or after 6 April 2008 and ending on or after 5 April 2009.

In January 2001 the APB issued two bulletins in response to the changing focus on auditors' reports as a result of the increasing use of the Internet as a medium for publishing financial material. Bulletins 2001/1 *The Electronic Publication of Auditors' Reports* and 2001/2 *Revisions to the Wording of Auditors' Reports on Financial Statements and the Interim Review Report* are considered in section **3.18** below. The example audit reports in this chapter, and throughout the book, take into account these Bulletins. The issue of FRS 18 *Accounting Policies* prompted the APB to issue Bulletin 2000/3 as guidance to auditors on the application of SAS 600 when reporting on financial statements which fall within the scope of a Statement of Recommended Practice (SORP), but contain a departure from the SORP's requirements. This guidance is still relevant following the publication of the updated ISA (UK and Ireland) 700.

The Director's Remuneration Report Regulations 2002 ('the Regulations') came into force on 1 August 2002. The Regulations require certain public companies to produce a Remuneration Report containing detailed information about directors' remuneration for periods ending on or after 31 December 2002. Some of the information specified for inclusion is to be audited, and auditors must state in their report whether the 'auditable part' of the Directors' Remuneration Report has been properly prepared in accordance with the Companies Act 1985. Reports in this Chapter for relevant listed companies have been updated in accordance with the guidance in the related APB Bulletin, 2002/2, *The United Kingdom Directors' Remuneration Report Regulations 2002*, which was published in October 2002. Details of the Bulletin are given in **3.17** below.

In January 2003 the Audit and Assurance Faculty of the ICAEW issued Technical Release Audit 1/03, *The Audit Report and Auditors' Duty of Care to Third Parties* following an earlier judgement in the Scottish courts, *Royal Bank of Scotland* v *Bannerman Johnstone Maclay and others* ('Bannerman'). The aim of 1/03 is to assist auditors in managing the risk of inadvertently assuming a duty of care to third parties in relation to their audit reports. Further details are discussed in **3.20**.

In April 2006, the Audit and Assurance faculty of the ICAEW issued AAF 02/06, *Identifying and managing certain risks arising from the inclusion of reports from auditors and accountants in prospectuses (and certain other investment circulars)*. This publication develops the principles in 01/03 for reporting accountants. It is detailed in **50.9.**

3.3   ISA (UK AND IRELAND) 700 (REVISED)

3.3.1   Main changes

As a result of the consultation process which followed the APB's *The Audit Report: A time for change?* paper issued in December 2007, the two main areas where change was requested were:

- a shorter auditor's report; and
- making the report more informative.

Reducing the length of the audit report has been achieved in the new 'Statement of the Scope of an Audit' section, discussed in **3.10** below, as well as by reducing the length of the description of the auditor's responsibilities.

The APB is of the opinion that wholesale changes to make the auditor's report more informative is best coordinated on an international basis through the work of the IAASB. However, there is increased guidance in the updated ISA (UK and Ireland) relating to the ability of auditors to highlight matters which they regard as relevant to a proper understanding of their work as additional comments in their report.

3.3.2   Discussions with those charged with governance

The APB recommends that auditors discuss the changes to their reports with those charged with governance. The ISA (UK and Ireland) sets out the following areas as ones of particular interest:

- the advantages and disadvantages of the various alternative approaches to the description of the scope of the audit, permitted by ISA (UK and Ireland) 700; and
- matters that auditors may wish to include in the auditor's report under the heading 'Other Matter'.

3.4   AIM OF THE AUDIT REPORT

The aim of the report is to provide information to the reader on the respective responsibilities of the directors and the auditors and information on what an audit entails.

ISA (UK and Ireland) 700 requires that auditors' reports should contain a clear expression of opinion based on review and assessment of the conclusions drawn from evidence obtained in the course of the audit. The other standards expand this basic principle.

The auditor should evaluate whether:

- the financial statements adequately refer to or describe the relevant financial reporting framework;
- the financial statements adequately disclose the significant accounting policies selected and applied;
- the accounting policies selected and applied are consistent with the applicable financial reporting framework, and are appropriate in the circumstances;
- accounting estimates are reasonable;
- the information presented in the financial statements is relevant, reliable, comparable and understandable;
- the financial statements provide adequate disclosures to enable the intended users to understand the effect of material transactions and events on the information conveyed in the financial statements; and
- the terminology used in the financial statements, including the title of each financial statements, is appropriate.

3.5   CONTENTS OF AN AUDIT REPORT

The ISA (UK and Ireland) requires that an audit report should contain the following information:

- a title which identifies to whom the report is addressed;
- an introduction that identifies the financial statements which have been audited;
- the responsibilities of those charged with governance;
- the responsibilities of the auditors;
- the scope of the audit of the financial statements (see **3.10** below);
- the auditor's opinions on the financial statements (see **3.11**);
- the manuscript signature of the Senior Statutory Auditor signing for and on behalf of the audit firm (see **3.12**);
- the auditors' address; and
- the date of the auditors' report.

The standard recommends that using a standard format with appropriate headings will help the user to understand the report. However, it also points out that the report should reflect the particular assignment.

3.6   TITLE

The term 'Independent Auditor' is usually used in the title in order to distinguish the report from reports that might be issued by others who have not complied with the APB's *Ethical Standards for Auditors* (see **Chapter 2**).

3.7   ADDRESSEE

Where the auditors are reporting on a company, the report should be addressed to the members as the audit is undertaken on their behalf. For other types of reporting entity the addressee will depend on the terms of the engagement, for example, where the auditors are reporting on a pension fund they will address their report to the trustees.

3.8   INTRODUCTORY PARAGRAPH

This section should refer to the pages of the report that contain the financial statements and the date of, and period covered by, the financial statements, and is to ensure that there is no confusion over the subject matter of the auditors' report. Bulletin 2001/1 (see **3.18**) outlines the situation where the Annual Report is to be published electronically and the statements covered by the audit report may not be determined from page numbers alone. Here, auditors are required to refer explicitly to the primary statements and notes covered by the audit report.

Technical Release Audit 1/03 was issued in January 2003 to assist auditors in managing the risk of inadvertently assuming a duty of care to third parties in relation to their audit reports. The Technical Release is discussed in detail in section **3.20** below.

3.9   RESPECTIVE RESPONSIBILITIES OF THOSE CHARGED WITH GOVERNANCE AND AUDITORS

Those charged with governance have a responsibility to prepare the financial statements and auditors are responsible for auditing and expressing an opinion on those financial statements in accordance with applicable legal requirements and International Standards on Auditing (UK and Ireland). A paragraph in the auditor's report should state these responsibilities clearly.

3.10 SCOPE OF THE AUDIT OF THE FINANCIAL STATEMENTS

This new section was introduced by the update to ISA (UK and Ireland) 700 in March 2009. In an attempt to reduce the length of auditor's reports, the report should now either:

- cross refer to a 'Statement of the Scope of an Audit' that is maintained on the APB's website (*www.frc.org.uk/apb/scope/UKP* for publicly traded companies or groups, or *www.frc.org.uk/apb/scope/UKNP* for non-publicly traded companies or groups);
- cross refer to a 'Statement of the Scope of an Audit' that is included elsewhere within the Annual Report; or
- include the description of the scope of an audit from **Table 1** below.

When the Statement of the Scope of an Audit is included elsewhere in the Annual Report, the format in **Table 1** should also be used.

TABLE 1: Statement of the Scope of an Audit to be included in the auditor's report

'An audit involves obtaining evidence about the amounts and disclosures in the financial statements sufficient to give reasonable assurance that the financial statements are free from material misstatement, whether caused by fraud or error. This includes an assessment of:

- whether accounting policies are appropriate to the [*describe nature of entity*] circumstances and have been consistently applied and adequately disclosed;
- the reasonableness of significant accounting estimates made by [*describe those charged with governance*]; and
- the overall presentation of the financial statements.'

3.11 AUDITOR'S OPINIONS

3.11.1 True and fair

ISA (UK and Ireland) 700 requires that the report should contain a clear expression of the auditors' opinion on the financial statements and on any further requirements of statute or the particular assignment.

The opinion may be unqualified or qualified. Qualifications are considered in detail in **Chapter 4**.

Where the opinion is unqualified, this means that, in the auditors' opinion, the financial statements give a true and fair view and have been properly prepared in accordance with the relevant accounting framework.

The auditor's opinion should indicate the financial reporting framework upon which the financial statements are based. In the UK these will normally be:

- International Financial Reporting Standards (IFRSs) as adopted by the European Union and, for consolidated financial statements of fully listed companies, Article 4 of the IAS Regulation (1606/2002/EC); or
- UK Generally Accepted Accounting Practice, which comprises applicable UK Company Law and UK Accounting Standards as issued by the ASB.

Where an auditor is also required to report on compliance with a second financial reporting framework, the second opinion must be clearly separated in the opinion section by the use of a subheading.

3.11.2 Opinion on other matters

Other reporting requirements may be set out in legislation or by the terms of engagement agreed with the entity. Such opinions may be required as:

- a positive statement in the auditor's report (such as the opinion whether the information in the directors' report is consistent with the accounts); or
- by exception (for example if the company has not maintained adequate accounting records).

If the auditor is required to report by exception, the opinion should be given under the heading 'Matters on which we are required to report by exception'. If there is nothing to report by exception, the section must still be included in the report, but would be set out in accordance with the wording stipulated in ISA (UK and Ireland) 700, which is reproduced in **Table 2**.

TABLE 2: Example paragraph where there is nothing to report by exception

Matters on which we are required to report by exception

We have nothing to report in respect of the following:

[*give details of item to be reported on*]

3.12   SIGNATURE

3.12.1   Senior Statutory Auditor

Where the auditor is a firm, the Companies Act 2006 sets out the requirement for the Senior Statutory Auditor to sign the auditor's report in his own name for and on behalf of the audit firm. The Auditing Practices Board was tasked with issuing guidance with respect to the term 'Senior Statutory Auditor' and this was published in April 2008 as Bulletin 2008/6, *The 'Senior Statutory Auditor' under the United Kingdom Companies Act 2006.*

The Senior Statutory Auditor is required to sign in his own name for reports:

- prepared in accordance with ss495, 496 and 497 of the Companies Act 2006, that is audit reports which provide a true and fair opinion;
- on voluntary revisions of annual accounts and reports (see **5.6**); and
- on auditor's reports on abbreviated accounts (see **5.4**).

This requirement is effective for accounting periods commencing on or after 6 April 2008.

There are no legal requirements for eligibility to be appointed as a Senior Statutory Auditor. In practical terms each partner in an audit firm previously authorised to act as an engagement partner and sign the auditor's report in the firm's name is likely to assume the role of Senior Statutory Auditor.

In signing auditor's reports in their own name as the Senior Statutory Auditor, the individual does not take on any additional legal responsibility for the audit or the report than they would previously have had prior to the Companies Act 2006.

If more than one partner is involved in an audit it is important to determine which individual is acting as the engagement partner and therefore assumes the role of Senior Statutory Auditor.

The Bulletin suggests that it would be pragmatic for the audit firm to have a contingency plan as to who would succeed as senior statutory auditor in the event that the audit is at an advanced stage but the senior auditor is unable to sign the auditor's report.

If another audit partner is actively involved in the audit engagement, a suitable contingency plan may be for that other partner to work in parallel with the senior statutory auditor and be able to take over as senior statutory auditor if the need arises.

If no other partner has worked in parallel with the senior statutory auditor, then the APB is of the view that in such exceptional circumstances it is permissible for the engagement quality control reviewer to be appointed as the replacement senior statutory auditor where:

- the engagement quality control reviewer has completed his or her review; and
- the audit is at an 'advanced stage' as defined by Bulletin 2008/2 which deals with the auditor's association with preliminary announcements.

This is subject to the condition that the engagement quality control reviewer is eligible to be appointed as the senior statutory auditor.

Once an engagement quality reviewer has been appointed as a replacement senior statutory auditor he or she can no longer act as the engagement quality control reviewer because his or her objectivity may have been impaired through assuming the role of senior statutory auditor.

3.12.2 Signing

The requirements of the Companies Act 2006 for the Senior Statutory Auditor to physically sign the auditors' report in their own name, extends only to the copy of the auditors' report to be provided to the client upon completion of the audit. In all but this 'signing copy', the name of the Senior Statutory Auditor needs to be stated, but the signature does not need to be reproduced. The copy of the auditor's report sent to the Registrar of Companies only requires the name of the Senior Statutory Auditor to be stated, not their signature, together with a signature in the name of the firm.

Under s503(3) of the 2006 Act, only the Senior Statutory Auditor can sign the 'signing copy' of the auditors' report. If they are absent at the time of signing, the signature can be obtained by electronic means, such as e-mail or fax.

3.12.3 Joint auditors

Where a company has appointed joint auditors, each audit firm will designate their own Senior Statutory Auditor. When the auditors' report is signed, each firm's Senior Statutory Auditor must sign the report in their own name for and on behalf of their firm.

3.13 DATE

ISA (UK and Ireland) 700 requires that:

- before the auditors can give an opinion on the financial statements they must have been approved by the directors and the auditors must have considered all of the available evidence; and
- the auditors' report has to be dated as at the date the opinion is expressed.

The significance of the date of the auditors' report is that they are informing the reader that they are aware of events up to that date and have considered the effect of these on the financial statements.

Before they sign the audit report the following must have occurred:

- receipt of the approved financial statements, together with any accompanying information, from the directors;
- review of all the documents which the auditors are required to consider in addition to the financial statements, for example, the directors' report; and
- completion of all the procedures thought necessary by the auditor to be able to form an opinion, including a post balance sheet event review.

The Senior Statutory Auditor must sign in manuscript and date the report expressing an opinion on the financial statements for distribution with the financial statements. Firms must therefore have procedures to ensure reports are not signed before the above events have occurred.

The report should also state the location of the auditors' offices, typically the city or town in which the office that has responsibility is based.

Although the date of the auditors' report has to be after the directors have approved the financial statements, it does not mean that the auditors cannot commence their work until the directors have approved the financial statements. Rather, they cannot conclude it until this has happened. In many cases the preparation of the financial statements will take place at the same time as the auditors are gathering evidence.

Although they will normally be in a position to give their opinion at the same date as the financial statements are approved, it does not have to be on the same day. Unless the auditors have gathered all their evidence and completed their work at that time (including a post balance sheet event review) they are unable to sign their report despite the directors approving the financial statements.

Where the date the opinion is expressed is before the final printing of the financial statements, the auditors will have to ensure the drafts on which they form their opinion are sufficiently clear for them to assess the overall presentation. One area to be especially aware of is where the directors have approved the profit and loss account and the balance sheet, but the notes have yet to be finally completed. In such cases the auditors will have to delay giving their opinion until they are finished.

Where the date the auditors sign their report is later than the date of approval they may need to obtain additional assurances from the directors that there have been no events in the intervening period that would affect the financial statements. They will also need to have their own procedures for reviewing subsequent events and assessing their impact on the financial statements.

3.14   UNMODIFIED AUDITOR'S REPORTS EXAMPLES

ISA (UK and Ireland) 700 refers to example auditor's report in the most recent version of its Bulletin *Auditor's Reports on Financial Statements in the United Kingdom*. The current version is Bulletin 2009/2 published in April 2009.

A simple auditor's report for a non-listed company not preparing group accounts is provided in **Table 3**.

TABLE 3: Example simple auditor's report

- *Company does not prepare group accounts*
- *UK GAAP used for individual company financial statements*
- *Company does not meet the Companies Act definition of a quoted company*
- *Financial statements contain no surrounding information other than the Directors' Report*

Independent auditors' report to the members of XYZ Limited

We have audited the financial statements of [entity name] for the year ended [date] which comprise [state the primary financial statements such as the Profit and Loss Account, the Balance Sheet, the Cash Flow Statement, the Statement of Total Recognised Gains and Losses] and the related notes. The financial reporting framework that has been applied in their preparation is applicable law and United Kingdom Accounting Standards (United Kingdom Generally Accepted Accounting Practice).[1]

Respective responsibilities of directors and auditors

As explained more fully in the Directors' Responsibilities Statement [set out [on pages ...]], the directors are responsible for the preparation of the financial statements and for being satisfied that they give a true and fair view. Our responsibility is to audit the financial statements in accordance with applicable law and International Standards on Auditing (UK and Ireland). Those standards required us to comply with the Auditing Practices Board's (APB's) Ethical Standards for Auditors.

Scope of the audit of the financial statements

A description of the scope of an audit of financial statements is [provided on the APB's web-site at *www.frc.org.uk/apb/scope/UKNP*]/[set out [on page x] of the Annual Report].

Opinion on financial statements

In our opinion the financial statements:

- give a true and fair view of the state of the company's affairs as at ... and of its profit [loss] for the year then ended;
- have been properly prepared in accordance with United Kingdom Generally Accepted Accounting Practice; and
- have been prepared in accordance with the requirements of the Companies Act 2006.

Opinion on other matters prescribed by the Companies Act 2006

In our opinion the information given in the Directors' Report for the financial year for which the financial statements are prepared is consistent with the financial statements.

Matters on which we are required to report by exception

We have nothing to report in respect of the following matters where the Companies Act 2006 requires us to report to you if, in our opinion:

---

[1] Auditors may include a 'Bannerman Statement' as part of the opening section of their report (see **3.20**).

- adequate accounting records have not been kept or returns adequate for our audit have not been received from branches not visited by us; or
- the company's financial statements are not in agreement with the accounting records and returns; or
- certain disclosures of directors' remuneration specified by law are not made; or
- we have not received all the information and explanations we required for our audit.

[*Signature*]
John Smith (Senior statutory auditor)
For and on behalf of ABC LLP, Statutory Auditor
Address
Date

The following example is for a publicly listed company. Further variations are set out in Bulletin 2009/2.

TABLE 4: Example auditor's report for fully listed company using IFRSs where the scope of the audit is described on the APB website or elsewhere in the annual report

- *Group and parent company financial statements not presented separately*
- *IFRSs as adopted by the European Union used for both group and parent company financial statements*
- *Company does meet the Companies Act definition of a quoted company*
- *Section 408 exemption relating to parent company's own income statement not taken*

Independent auditors' report to the members of XYZ Limited

We have audited the financial statements of [entity name] for the year ended [date] which comprise [specify the financial statements such as the Group and Parent Company Statements of Financial Position, the Group and Parent Company Statements of Comprehensive Income, the Group and Parent Company Statements of Cash Flow Statements, the Group and Parent Company Statements of Changes in Equity,] and the related notes. The financial reporting framework that has been applied in their preparation is applicable law and International Financial Reporting Standards (IFRSs) as adopted by the European Union.[2]

Respective responsibilities of directors and auditors

As explained more fully in the Directors' Responsibilities Statement [set out [on page . . .]], the directors are responsible for the preparation of the financial statements and for being satisfied that they give a true and fair view. Our responsibility is to audit the financial statements in accordance with applicable law and International Standards on Auditing (UK and Ireland). Those standards required us to comply with the Auditing Practices Board's (APB's) Ethical Standards for Auditors.

Scope of the audit of the financial statements

A description of the scope of an audit of financial statements is [provided on the APB's web-site at *www.frc.org.uk/apb/scope/UKP*]/[set out [on page x] of the Annual Report].

---

[2] Auditors may include a 'Bannerman Statement' as part of the opening section of their report (see **3.20**).

Opinion on financial statements

In our opinion the financial statements:

- give a true and fair view of the state of the group's and of the parent company's affairs as at ... and of the group's and the parent company's profit [loss] for the year then ended;
- have been properly prepared in accordance with IFRSs as adopted by the European Union; and
- have been prepared in accordance with the requirements of the Companies Act 2006 and, as regards the group financial statements, Article 4 of the IAS Regulation.

Opinion on other matters prescribed by the Companies Act 2006

In our opinion:

- the part of the Directors' Remuneration Report to be audited has been properly prepared in accordance with the Companies Act 2006; and
- the information given in the Directors' Report for the financial year for which the financial statements are prepared is consistent with the financial statements.

Matters on which we are required to report by exception

We have nothing to report in respect of the following:

Under the Companies Act 2006 we are required to report to you if, in our opinion:

- adequate accounting records have not been kept by the parent company, or returns adequate for our audit have not been received from branches not visited by us; or
- the parent company financial statements and the part of the Directors' Remuneration Report to be audited are not in agreement with the accounting records and returns; or
- certain disclosures of directors' remuneration specified by law are not made; or
- we have not received all the information and explanations we required for our audit.

Under the Listing Rules we are required to review:

- the directors' statement, [set out [on page]], in relation to going concern; and
- the part of the Corporate Governance Statement relating to the company's compliance with the nine provisions of the June 2008 Combined Code specified for our review

[*Signature*]
John Smith (Senior statutory auditor)
For and on behalf of ABC LLP, Statutory Auditor
Address
Date

3.15   DIRECTORS' RESPONSIBILITY STATEMENTS

ISA (UK and Ireland) 700 requires that auditors should distinguish between their responsibilities and those of the directors. This is achieved by making reference in the auditor's report to a statement contained elsewhere in the financial statements or accompanying information.

Example Statement of Directors' Responsibilities are set out in **Tables 5 to 8**. Bulletin 2006/6 suggests that legal advice on the exact wording of the statement may be sought in complex situations and that the wording applicable to publicly traded companies will vary depending on the rules of the market on which its securities are traded.

TABLE 5: *Example wording of a description of the directors' responsibilities for inclusion in a non-publicly traded company's financial statements, reporting under UK GAAP*

The directors are responsible for preparing the Directors' Report and the financial statements in accordance with applicable law and regulations.

Company law requires the directors to prepare financial statements for each financial year. Under that law the directors have elected to prepare the financial statements in accordance with United Kingdom Generally Accepted Accounting Practice (United Kingdom Accounting Standards and applicable law). Under company law the directors must not approve the financial statements unless they are satisfied that they give a true and fair view of the state of affairs of the company and of the profit or loss of the company for that period. In preparing these financial statements, the directors are required to:

- select suitable accounting policies and then apply them consistently;
- make judgements and accounting estimates that are reasonable and prudent;
- state whether applicable UK Accounting Standards have been followed, subject to any material departures disclosed and explained in the financial statements [except for small or medium-sized companies as defined by the Companies Act];
- prepare the financial statements on the going concern basis unless it is inappropriate to presume that the company will continue in business.

The directors are responsible for keeping adequate accounting records that are sufficient to show and explain the company's transactions and disclose with reasonable accuracy at any time the financial position of the company and enable them to ensure that the financial statements comply with the Companies Act 2006. They are also responsible for safeguarding the assets of the company and hence for taking reasonable steps for the prevention and detection of fraud and other irregularities.

TABLE 6: *Example wording of a description of the directors' responsibilities for inclusion in a fully listed company's financial statements*

- *Group accounts prepared under IFRS*
- *Parent company accounts prepared under UK GAAP*

The directors are responsible for preparing the Directors' Report and the financial statements in accordance with applicable law and regulations.

Company law requires the directors to prepare financial statements for each financial year. The directors are also required to prepare financial statements for the group in accordance with International Financial Reporting Standards (IFRSs) as adopted by the European Union and Article 4 of the IAS Regulation. The directors have chosen to prepare financial statements for the company in accordance with United Kingdom Generally Accepted Accounting Practice.

Group financial statements

International Accounting Standard 1 requires that financial statements present fairly for each financial year the company's financial position, financial performance and cash flows. This requires the faithful representation of the effects of transactions, other events and conditions in accordance with the definitions and recognition criteria for assets, liabilities, income and expenses set out in the International Accounting Standards Board's 'Framework for the preparation and presentation of financial statements'. In virtually all circumstances, a fair presentation will be achieved by compliance with all applicable IFRSs. A fair presentation also requires the directors to:

- select suitable accounting policies and then apply them consistently;
- present information, including accounting policies, in a manner that provides relevant, reliable, comparable and understandable information; and
- provide additional disclosures when compliance with the specific requirements in IFRSs is insufficient to enable users to understand the impact of particular transactions, other events and conditions on the entity's financial position and financial performance.

Parent company financial statements

Company law requires the directors to prepare financial statements for each financial year. Under company law the directors must not approve the financial statements unless they are satisfied that they give a true and fair view of the state of affairs of the company and of the profit or loss of the company for that period. In preparing these financial statements, the directors are required to:

- select suitable accounting policies and then apply them consistently;
- make judgements and accounting estimates that are reasonable and prudent;
- state whether applicable UK Accounting Standards have been followed, subject to any material departures disclosed and explained in the financial statements;
- prepare the financial statements on the going concern basis unless it is inappropriate to presume that the company will continue in business.

The directors are responsible for keeping adequate accounting records that are sufficient to show and explain the company's transactions and disclose with reasonable accuracy at any time the financial position of the company and to enable them to ensure that the financial statements comply with the Companies Act 2006. They are also responsible for safeguarding the assets of the company and hence for taking reasonable steps for the prevention and detection of fraud and other irregularities.

*[Where financial statements are published on a website, see **3.18.2**]*

Financial statements are published on the group's website in accordance with legislation in the United Kingdom governing the preparation and dissemination of financial statements, which may vary from legislation in other jurisdictions. The maintenance and integrity of the group's website is the responsibility of the directors. The directors' responsibility also extends to the ongoing integrity of the financial statements contained therein.

TABLE 7: *Example wording of a description of the directors' responsibilities for inclusion in a fully listed company's financial statements*

- *Group accounts prepared under IFRS*
- *Parent company accounts prepared under IFRS*

The directors are responsible for preparing the Directors' Report and the financial statements in accordance with applicable law and regulations.

Company law requires the directors to prepare financial statements for each financial year. The directors are also required to prepare financial statements for the group in accordance with International Financial Reporting Standards (IFRSs) as adopted by the European Union and Article 4 of the IAS Regulation. The directors have chosen to prepare financial statements for the group and the company in accordance with IFRSs.

International Accounting Standard 1 requires that financial statements present fairly for each financial year the company's financial position, financial performance and cash flows. This requires the faithful representation of the effects of transactions, other events and conditions in accordance with the definitions and recognition criteria for assets, liabilities, income and expenses set out in the International Accounting Standards Board's 'Framework for the preparation and presentation of financial statements'. In virtually all circumstances, a fair presentation will be achieved by compliance with all applicable IFRSs. A fair presentation also requires the directors to:

- consistently select and apply appropriate accounting policies;
- present information, including accounting policies, in a manner that provides relevant, reliable, comparable and understandable information; and
- provide additional disclosures when compliance with the specific requirements in IFRSs is insufficient to enable users to understand the impact of particular transactions, other events and conditions on the entity's financial position and financial performance.

The directors are responsible for keeping adequate accounting records that are sufficient to show and explain the company's transactions and disclose with reasonable accuracy at any time the financial position of the company and to enable them to ensure that the financial statements comply with the Companies Act 2006. They are also responsible for safeguarding the assets of the company and hence for taking reasonable steps for the prevention and detection of fraud and other irregularities.

TABLE 8: *Example wording of a description of the directors' responsibilities for inclusion in a non-listed company's financial statements (including AIM listed companies)*

- *Group voluntarily prepares accounts under IFRS*
- *Parent company voluntarily prepares accounts under IFRS*

The directors are responsible for preparing the Directors' Report and the financial statements in accordance with the applicable law and regulations.

Company law requires the directors to prepare financial statements for each financial year. The directors have chosen to prepare financial statements for the group and the company in accordance with International Financial Reporting Standards (IFRSs) as adopted by the European Union.

International Accounting Standard 1 requires that financial statements present fairly for each financial year the company's financial position, financial performance and cash flows. This requires the faithful representation of the effects of transactions, other events and conditions in accordance with the definitions and recognition criteria for assets, liabilities, income and expenses set out in the International Accounting Standards Board's 'Framework for the preparation and presentation of financial statements'. In virtually all circumstances, a fair presentation will be achieved by compliance with all applicable IFRSs. A fair presentation also requires the directors to:

- consistently select and apply appropriate accounting policies;
- present information, including accounting policies, in a manner that provides relevant, reliable, comparable and understandable information; and
- provide additional disclosures when compliance with the specific requirements in IFRSs is insufficient to enable users to understand the impact of particular transactions, other events and conditions on the entity's financial position and financial performance.

The directors are responsible for keeping adequate accounting records that are sufficient to show and explain the company's transactions and disclose with reasonable accuracy at any time the financial position of the company and to enable them to ensure that the financial statements comply with the Companies Act 2006. They are also responsible for safeguarding the assets of the company and hence for taking reasonable steps for the prevention and detection of fraud and other irregularities.

3.16   SMALL COMPANIES

The Financial Reporting Standard for Smaller Entities

The introduction of the Financial Reporting Standard for Smaller Entities (FRSSE) led the APB to issue guidance for auditors of companies adopting this all-embracing accounting standard. Bulletin 1997/3 *The FRSSE: Guidance for Auditors* covers four areas of concern:

- whether auditors consider other accounting pronouncements when assessing the truth and fairness of the financial statements;
- the responsibility of auditors with regard to voluntary disclosures made in such financial statements;
- the effect of the FRSSE on ISAs (UK and Ireland); and
- the effect of the FRSSE on the auditors' report on the financial statements.

The FRSSE notes that, where it does not address a particular matter, reference may be made to other pronouncements to establish best practice and hence the Bulletin advises that in such cases auditors would also need to refer to them.

Voluntary disclosures made in financial statements prepared under the FRSSE are subject to audit. Where such disclosures are outside the financial statements but elsewhere in the annual report the requirements of ISA (UK and Ireland) 720 should be followed (see **Chapter 13**).

Only ISA (UK and Ireland) 550 *Related Parties* is directly affected by the FRSSE. FRS 8 requires materiality to be considered from the point of view of 'individual' related parties as well as the reporting entity. The FRSSE, on the other hand, like IAS 24, only requires materiality to be considered from the point of view of the reporting entity. The guidance in the ISA (UK and Ireland) on this is therefore not relevant (see **30.5**).

Where financial statements apply the FRSSE, the introductory section of the auditors' report has to be amended. Example wording for an unmodified audit report for a company preparing financial statements under the FRSSE is given in **Table 9**.

TABLE 9: Example unmodified auditor's report for a company preparing financial statements under the FRSSE

Independent auditors' report to the shareholders of XYZ Limited

We have audited the financial statements of [entity name] for the year ended [date] which comprise [state the primary financial statements such as the Profit and Loss Account, the Balance Sheet, the Cash Flow Statement, the Statement of Total Recognised Gains and Losses, the Reconciliation of Movements in Shareholders' Funds] and the related notes. The financial reporting framework that has been applied in their preparation is applicable law and the Financial Reporting Standard for Smaller Entities [Effective April 2008] (United Kingdom Generally Accepted Accounting Practice applicable to Smaller Entities).[3]

Respective responsibilities of directors and auditors

As explained more fully in the Directors' Responsibilities Statement [set out [on pages ...]], the directors are responsible for the preparation of the financial statements and for being satisfied that they give a true and fair view. Our responsibility is to audit the financial statements in accordance with applicable law and International Standards on Auditing (UK and Ireland). Those standards required us to comply with the Auditing Practices Board's (APB's) Ethical Standards for Auditors [, including 'APB Ethical Standard – Provisions Available for Small Entities (Revised)', in the circumstances set out in note [x] to the financial statements].

Scope of the audit of the financial statements

A description of the scope of an audit of financial statements is [provided on the APB's website at *www.frc.org.uk/apb/scope/UKNP*]/[set out [on page x] of the Annual Report].

Opinion on financial statements

In our opinion the financial statements:

● give a true and fair view of the state of the company's affairs as at ... and of the company's profit [loss] for the year then ended;
● have been properly prepared in accordance with United Kingdom Generally Accepted Accounting Practice applicable to Smaller Entities; and
● have been prepared in accordance with the requirements of the Companies Act 2006.

---

[3] Auditors may include a 'Bannerman Statement' as part of the opening section of their report (see **3.20**).

Opinion on other matters prescribed by the Companies Act 2006

In our opinion the information given in the Directors' Report for the financial year for which the financial statements are prepared is consistent with the financial statements.

Matters on which we are required to report by exception

We have nothing to report in respect of the following matters where the Companies Act 2006 requires us to report to you if, in our opinion:

- adequate accounting records have not been kept or returns adequate for our audit have not been received from branches not visited by us; or
- the financial statements are not in agreement with the accounting records and returns; or
- certain disclosures of directors' remuneration specified by law are not made; or
- we have not received all the information and explanations we required for our audit; or
- the directors were not entitled to prepare the financial statements and the directors' reporting accordance with the small companies regime.

[*Signature*]
John Smith (Senior statutory auditor)
For and on behalf of ABC LLP, Statutory Auditor
Address
Date

The Small Companies and Groups (Accounts and Directors' Report) Regulations 2008

ISA (UK and Ireland) 700 gives no guidance on cases where a small company takes advantage of the exemptions set out in Sch. 1 to SI 2008/409 *The Small Companies and Groups (Accounts and Directors' Report) Regulations 2008.* These Regulations effectively supersede Sch. 8 of the Companies Act 1985 and set out the reduced requirements for small companies, rather than the exemptions.

Although the disclosure requirements are limited, the financial statements should still show a true and fair view. The auditors of a company which prepares its accounts under Sch. 1 to SI 2008/409 are still therefore required to form an opinion on whether the financial statements give a true and fair view. The normal wording for an unqualified opinion should be used.

3.17   APB BULLETIN 2002/2, THE UNITED KINGDOM DIRECTORS' REMUNERATION REPORT REGULATIONS

3.17.1   Introduction

With effect from 1 August 2002 the UK Government brought into force Regulations that require quoted companies to prepare a Directors' Remuneration Report for each financial year. This report contains specified information, some of which is subject to audit.

Section 497 of the Companies Act 2006 requires auditors of quoted companies to include within their report on the annual accounts their opinion as to whether the 'auditable part' of the Directors' Remuneration Report has been properly prepared in accordance with the Companies Act.

In October 2002, the APB issued Bulletin 2002/2, *The United Kingdom Directors' Remuneration Report Regulations 2002*, to provide auditors with guidance about their responsibilities with respect to the unaudited part of the Directors' Remuneration Report and illustrations of the revised audit report and statement on Summary Financial Statements.

The guidance in **Chapter 5** on Summary Financial Statements reflects this.

3.17.2   Companies affected by the rules

The regulations apply to 'quoted' companies. A quoted company is defined as a company incorporated under the Companies Act 2006:

- whose equity share capital has been included in the official list; or
- is officially listed in an European Economic Area (EEA) state; or
- is admitted to dealing on either the New York Stock Exchange of the exchange known as Nasdaq.

The definition does not include companies traded on the Alternative Investment Market (AIM).

3.17.3   The 'auditable part' of the Directors' Remuneration Report

Auditors are required to report on the disclosures in the 'auditable part' of the Directors' Remuneration Report. The 'auditable part' is the part which contains the information required by Pt. 3 of Sch. 8 to *The Large and Medium-sized*

Companies and Groups (Accounts and Reports) Regulations 2008 (SI 2008/410).

3.17.4   Reporting on the Directors' Remuneration Report

Auditors report on the Directors' Remuneration Report as part of their report on the financial statements. As they are not required to audit all of the information in the Directors' Remuneration Report, they must clearly identify the elements that have been audited. If this cannot be done by cross-reference, auditors should set out the particulars that have been audited within the auditors' report. It is not satisfactory for auditors to describe what they have audited as 'the disclosures required by Pt. 3 of Sch. 8 to *The Large and Medium-sized Companies and Groups (Accounts and Reports) Regulations 2008* (SI 2008/410)'.

An example report for a quoted company is set out in **Table 4**.

3.17.5   The Directors' Remuneration Report as a separate document

If a quoted company issues its Directors' Remuneration Report as a separate document, the scope of the auditors' report in the Annual Report will still be required to include the parts of this separately published report which are to be audited.

When the Directors' Remuneration Report is issued as a separate document, auditors should:

- when their report is unqualified, encourage the directors to indicate in the Directors' Remuneration Report where the report can be found; or
- when their report contains a qualification, adverse opinion or disclaimer which is relevant to the Directors' Remuneration Report, encourage directors to reproduce the relevant parts of the auditors' report as part of the Directors' Remuneration Report. If the directors refuse to comply with this request, the Bulletin suggests that auditors should consider whether to resign.

3.18 CHANGES TO AUDIT REPORTS RESULTING FROM ELECTRONIC PUBLICATION

3.18.1 Background

In January 2001, the APB published two Bulletins covering changes required to audit reports as a result of a number of developments in the Listing Rules and the way financial statements are circulated to members.

Bulletin 2001/1 *The Electronic Publication of Auditors' Reports* was published in response to the enactment of the Companies Act 1985 (Electronic Communications) Order 2000 ('the Order'). The Order enables companies, subject to certain conditions, to meet their statutory reporting obligations to shareholders by distributing financial statements and certain other reports (including summary financial statements) electronically, or to post their financial statements on their website and advise shareholders of this.

Published at the same time, Bulletin 2001/2 *Revisions to the Wording of Auditors' Reports on Financial Statements and the Interim Review Report* includes revisions to standard audit reports as a result of the Order and its implications for the readers of audit reports, as well as changes to responsibility for the Listing Rules in the United Kingdom.

The Companies Act 2006 set out additional requirements to facilitate electronic communication with shareholders. This was one of the first areas of the new Companies Act to be implemented and was effective from 20 January 2007. It is discussed in **3.18.3** below.

3.18.2 Electronic publication of audit reports

As stated above, following the enactment of the Order, companies may either send their members copies of the annual financial statements by electronic means or post the annual financial statements on their website and advise their members of this, rather than post hard copies to them. The purpose of the Bulletin is to provide guidance to auditors in each of these circumstances, and also in the more common current situation where annual financial statements, accompanied by the auditors' report, are published on an entity's website.

Although ISA (UK and Ireland) 700 has now been revised, the guidance in Bulletin 2001/1 is still relevant where an entity publishes their annual financial statements electronically, either by email or by posting them on their website.

The main aim of the guidance is to ensure that auditors' duty of care is not extended solely as a result of their report being published in electronic rather than hard-copy form. In addition, as information published on websites is available in many countries with different legal requirements, it must be clear which legislation governs the preparation and dissemination of financial statements.

Additional work to provide assurance on the integrity of an entity's website is considered a separate engagement and is not covered in the Bulletin.

Directors' responsibilities

The fact that financial statements are reproduced or published electronically does not change the responsibilities of the directors concerning preparation, dissemination and signing of financial statements. The APB's view is in order to comply with their responsibilities, directors will still produce paper-based versions of their financial statements.

At the request of the Department of Trade and Industry, the Institute of Chartered Secretaries and Administrators (ICSA) has issued guidance on information published on corporate websites. If a company wishes to publish its financial statements on its website, auditors should enquire whether the directors have obtained a copy of this guidance and are following its recommendations relating to the presentation of the annual report and accounts.

The main ICSA recommendations are set out in **Table 10**. Auditors should be aware of these, as non-compliance of any of these by an entity may mean auditors are unable to agree to the electronic publication of their audit report.

TABLE 10: *Summary of ICSA recommendations for electronic publication of the annual report and accounts*

- inclusion of a 'watermark' or 'banner' on each page containing statutory or audited information to ensure that the status of that information is clear;
- add a warning message each time a user moves from or to a statutory or audited part of a website;
- not mixing statutory and non-statutory or audited and unaudited information on any one page;
- including a link to the statutory part of the website on the homepage;
- at any early stage ask auditors for clearance for the publication of audited information on the website;
- ask auditors to confirm that they agree with the way information is being presented, including the exact format of their audit report;
- listed companies should have procedures in place to ensure that no price sensitive information is published prior to notification of the relevant authorities; and
- ensure they comply with s434 of the Companies Act 2006, which states that statutory accounts must be published with the relevant auditors' report and that non-statutory accounts must be accompanied by a statement that they are not statutory accounts.

The directors' responsibility statement should include reference to the fact that legislation in the United Kingdom governing the preparation and dissemination of financial statements may differ from legislation in other jurisdictions.

Hard-copy reports cannot be amended unless a revised printed version is issued to shareholders. However, it is easy for all or part of an electronic report to be amended without it being apparent that a revision has occurred. Inaccurate information may be placed on a website by a company employee (either accidentally or maliciously) or by a person outside the organisation who is able to gain access to the website.

Directors should therefore establish a regular procedure for checking that statutory or audited information has not been tampered with. Auditors will have no further responsibility for either the controls in place or the integrity of the information on a website once it is issued in electronic form. The APB recommends that directors state clearly in their statement of responsibilities that the maintenance and integrity of the website is their responsibility alone. If the directors' statement does not make this clear such as in **Table 6** above, or if the auditors otherwise consider it appropriate, they should add a note to the bottom of their audit report. The example wording from the Bulletin is given in **Table 11** below.

Where auditors are aware that the financial statements no longer agree to the set the directors have approved, they should inform the directors and request that they be amended immediately. If the necessary amendments are not made, auditors should obtain legal advice and consider resignation.

Auditors' considerations

When companies publish their annual report on their website or distribute it electronically, auditors should:

- review the process used to derive the electronically published financial statements from the manually signed version;
- check the electronic version is identical to the manual accounts; and
- check that conversion to the electronic version has not distorted the overall presentation (e.g., by use of different fonts or colour to highlight certain information).

In addition, for future reference, auditors should obtain a printed copy of the electronic version that they have reviewed.

Auditors are not expected to perform the above procedures on any prior period information. Prior period information should be clearly identified as such, or the auditors should request management to delete it.

Auditors' report

Three main issues should be considered in relation to the wording of the audit report:

- identification of the nationality of the accounting and auditing standards applied;
- identifying the financial statements that have been audited and the information that has only been reviewed or read by the auditors; and
- limiting the auditors' association with any other information distributed with the annual report.

Bulletin 2001/2 deals with the first issue, by requiring reports to state that the standards used are those relevant in the United Kingdom. This means that the relevant jurisdiction is clear to readers in other countries. In addition, auditors should ensure that their report gives sufficient of their address to enable readers to understand in which country the auditors are located.

Where the directors' responsibility statement does not include the statement relating to different legislation requirements in different jurisdictions referred to above, the auditors should include a statement at the foot of their report. The example wording from the Bulletin is given in **Table 11** below.

TABLE 11: *Possible notes for inclusion at the foot of audit reports presented on a website*

1. The maintenance and integrity of the [name of entity] website is the responsibility of the directors; the work carried out by the auditors does not involve consideration of these matters and, accordingly, the auditors accept no responsibility for the changes that may have occurred to the financial statements since they were initially presented on the website.

2. Legislation in the United Kingdom governing the preparation and dissemination of financial statements may differ from legislation in other jurisdictions.

Hard-copy annual reports will have page numbers by which auditors can identify the financial statements that have been audited in their report. Where Hypertext Mark-up Language (HTML) has been used to publish annual reports on a website, page numbers are often no longer included and thus identification of audited information is difficult. Where a Portable Document Format (PDF) file is used, page numbers generally continue to be effective.

Therefore, where page numbers are no longer an effective way of identifying audited information the APB recommends that the auditors' report describes, by name, the primary statements that comprise the financial statements. The same technique can be used to identify information that has been reviewed, or read, by the auditors.

The problem of identifying other information in the annual report, which the auditor has neither audited, reviewed nor read, is exacerbated by the use of hyperlinks that allow the user to move easily from one area of the website to another. To reduce misunderstandings, auditors should request that readers are warned when they move from an audited to an unaudited part of the website. An additional safeguard is for auditors to request that all audited information, such as disclosures relating to directors' emoluments, are included within the financial statements. If the scope of the audit report is not clear because of the use of hyperlinks, the report itself should list in detail all the areas within its scope.

Where auditors are not satisfied with the proposed presentation of the audited financial statements and their report, they should request that the presentation is amended. If the presentation is not amended, the auditors should refuse to give their consent for the electronic release of their audit report. If the report is used without their consent, the auditors should seek legal advice and consider resigning from the engagement.

The electronic report should have the same date as the manually signed version. Amending the manual report for electronic publication (such as the substitution of the names of primary statements for page numbers) does not constitute a new audit opinion. The auditor is not required to perform any further subsequent events work, as the date of the opinion has not changed.

Engagement letters

The responsibilities of directors and auditors in relation to the electronic publication of financial statements should be clarified in the engagement letter. The engagement letter should also state that directors must seek the consent of their auditors for the electronic publication of their audit report. This will ensure that auditors have a right to request amendments to the wording or presentation of an electronic audit report.

The engagement letter should note that:

- the auditors recognise that the company may wish to publish its financial statements and the auditors' report on its website or distribute them electronically;
- the presentation of the financial information and auditors' report is the responsibility of the directors;
- the directors should advise the auditors in advance of the intended electronic publication;
- the auditors reserve the right to withhold consent to the electronic publication of their report if the audited financial statements or the audit report itself are presented in an inappropriate way;
- the directors are responsible for controls over the maintenance and security of the website;
- examination of the controls over maintenance and integrity are outside the scope of the audit; and
- where applicable, directors are responsible for establishing and controlling

the process for electronically distributing the Annual Report to shareholders and the Registrar of Companies.

3.18.3 The Companies Act 2006

One of the first parts of the Companies Act 2006 to be implemented was that relating to the electronic communication by companies with shareholders, debenture holders and others with an effective date of 20 January 2007.

The 2006 Act considers the use of electronic means for all communications, whereas the 1985 Act only considered it in certain areas. Subject to the individual's right to continue to receive information in paper format, companies should, under the new Act, be able to default to electronic communication.

A key change is to allow publication of documents on a website as a default where:

- the company's articles of association or a shareholder resolution permit those documents which should be supplied to a shareholder to be published on a website; and
- a person has not objected to receiving information via a website within 28 days of being 'individually' asked.

For communication via email rather than a website, an individual is still required to provide positive consent to receiving communications in this way.

However, even if a member or debenture holder has agreed to receive communications electronically, they still retain the right to request a hard copy under the 2006 Act.

3.19 DEPARTURE FROM SORPS

The Auditing Practices Board issued Bulletin 2000/3 to provide guidance to auditors on the application of SAS 600 when reporting on financial statements that fall within the scope of, but contain a departure from, a Statement of Recommended Practice (SORP). Its guidance remains relevant in relation to ISA (UK and Ireland) 700.

The Bulletin *Departure from Statements of Recommended Practice for the Preparation of Financial Statements: Guidance for Auditors* is effective for accounting periods beginning on or after 24 December 2000, or for any financial statements where FRS 18 *Accounting Policies* has been applied before that date.

3.19.1 Requirements of FRS 18

FRS 18 requires an entity to select accounting policies that are most appropriate to its particular circumstances and give a true and fair view. This selection includes consideration of whether accepted industry practices, such as those detailed in a SORP, are suitable.

Paragraph 58 of FRS 18 states that where an entity falls within the scope of a SORP it should state:

- the title of the SORP; and
- whether the financial statements have been prepared in accordance with the current requirements of that SORP.

If there is a departure from the requirements of the SORP, the entity should give a brief description of how the financial statements depart from the recommended practice. However, the effect of the departure need not be quantified unless this is required to give a true and fair view.

3.19.2 Audit considerations

When an entity's financial statements fall within the scope of, but depart from, an SORP, the auditors should assess whether:

- the departure is reasonable and that the treatment adopted is more appropriate to give a true and fair view;
- the requirements of FRS 18 to disclose the departure have been complied with.

In making their assessments, auditors should consider:

- consistency with accounting policies used in prior periods;
- directors' justification for changes to accounting policies;
- if the alternative accounting policies comply with applicable accounting standards, UITF Abstracts, legislation and industry-specific rules and regulations;
- impact on the financial statements; and
- level of compliance with the SORP by other entities in the industry.

3.19.3 Audit opinion

If, as a result of their assessment, the auditors are of the opinion that the financial statements do not give a true and fair view, they should issue a qualified or adverse opinion. Non-compliance with the disclosure requirements outlined above will usually result in a qualified opinion.

Reporting options are detailed in the flowchart in **Table 12.**

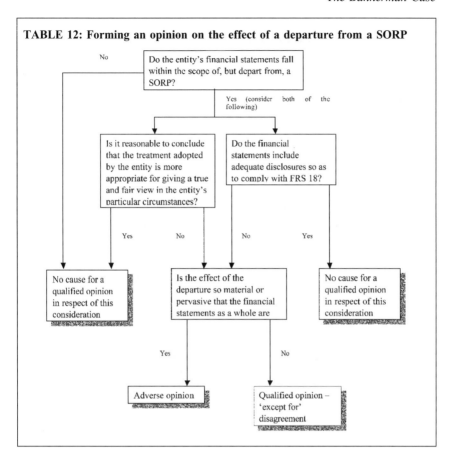

TABLE 12: Forming an opinion on the effect of a departure from a SORP

3.20 THE BANNERMAN CASE

3.20.1 Introduction

As a result of the legal judgement in the Scottish Court of Session in the *Bannerman* case, auditors have considered whether they should include additional wording in their audit reports to protect against exposure to third party claims. The ICAEW issued Technical Release 1/03 in January 2003, and this guidance contains a suitable wording for inclusion in audit reports. They have discussed the format and inclusion of such wording with Leading Counsel.

In the *Bannerman* case the judge held that, although there was no direct contact between Bannerman (the auditors) and the third party, knowledge gained by Bannerman through the course of their normal audit work was sufficient, in the absence of any disclaimer, to create a duty of care towards the third party. The absence of a disclaimer was an important circumstance supporting the finding of a duty of care by the judge.

3.20.2 Auditors' responsibilities

The Technical Release is clear that the responsibilities of auditors are not changed as a result either of the *Bannerman* case or the release of 1/03. It states that 'the best risk management policy is for firms to take the steps that are necessary to carry out quality audits'.

3.20.3 Recommended wording

It is clear that auditors automatically assume responsibility for the audit report to the shareholders as a body. The *Bannerman* case indicates that the absence of a disclaimer may, depending on the facts of the case, make auditors liable to third parties.

The ICAEW therefore suggests the following wording is included in the first or second paragraph of all audit reports.

> 'This report is made solely to the company's members, as a body, in accordance with Chapter 3 of Part 16 of the Companies Act 2006. Our audit work has been undertaken so that we might state to the company's members those matters we are required to state to them in an auditor's report and for no other purpose. To the fullest extent permitted by law, we do not accept or assume responsibility to anyone other than the company and the company's members as a body, for our audit work, for this report, or for the opinions we have formed.'

The wording, or a variation of it, may also be suitable for inclusion in other reports issued by auditors.

It is important to note that the inclusion of this paragraph in audit reports does not means that auditors can never agree to take on responsibilities to third parties, or that they may inadvertently assume a duty of care through subsequent comments or actions inconsistent with the wording of this paragraph. Where auditors are aware of circumstances which may give rise to a duty of care, they should disclaim this responsibility by writing a letter to the third party in line with guidance in Technical Release Audit 4/00 (see **Chapter 42**).

3.20.4 Engagement letters

The Technical Release also contains suggested wording for inclusion in an engagement letter, to inform clients about the clarification paragraph in the audit report. This is not mandatory, and is set out in **Chapter 21**.

3.21 READING AUDIT REPORTS

When SAS 600 was first issued, there was some concern that there would be problems at annual general meetings where auditors were asked to read their report to the members present. In response to this the ICAEW issued FRAG 1/94 *Reading of auditors' reports at annual general meetings*. This suggested that there were two options, either:

- to read out the full report; or
- to read out 'highlights' of the report.

Where highlights were read out it should be made clear that this was not the full report and where there were any modifications to the normal wording of the report these were noted.

In March 2000, the Technical & Practical Auditing Committee of the ICAEW's Audit Faculty reviewed the FRAG in the light of the changes in corporate governance. It decided that the 'short' form of the audit report contained in the FRAG could be misleading, as it did not:

- cover the current 'read' and 'review' responsibilities of the expanded version of the report made on listed companies; nor
- highlight some of the restrictions of the audit report as shown in the full accounts, particularly with regard to not considering risks and controls.

The Committee therefore concluded that the use of the short form of audit report should be discontinued, noting that if auditors were asked to read their report at AGMs, they should consider whether it was appropriate to abbreviate it at all.

4 MODIFIED AUDITOR'S REPORTS

4.1 INTRODUCTION

In **Chapter 3** the content and format of unmodified auditor's reports was considered. Where auditors are unable to issue an unmodified report, their report may follow a number of formats, which are discussed below.

As with unmodified reports, guidance on modified auditor's reports is provided by ISA (UK and Ireland) 700, *The Auditor's Report on Financial Statements* and Bulletin 2009/2, *Auditor's Reports on Financial Statements in the United Kingdom.*

Internationally, ISAs 705 *Modifications to the Opinion in the Independent Auditor's Report* and 706 *Emphasis of Matter Paragraphs and Other Matter Paragraphs in the Independent Auditor's Report* contain guidance in relation to modified reports. Despite their contents being a duplication of the guidance in ISA (UK and Ireland) 700, the APB published UK and Ireland versions of both ISA 705 and 706 in October 2009.

All three clarified ISAs (UK and Ireland) are effective for the audit of financial statements for periods ending on or after 15 December 2010.

4.2 TYPES OF MODIFICATION

An auditor's report is considered to be modified in the following situations:

- matters that do not affect the auditor's opinion:
  - emphasis of matter;
- matters that do affect the auditor's opinion:
  - disclaimer of opinion;
  - adverse opinion;
  - qualified opinion.

Table 1 contains a navigation aid to help auditors select the correct type of report.

TABLE 1

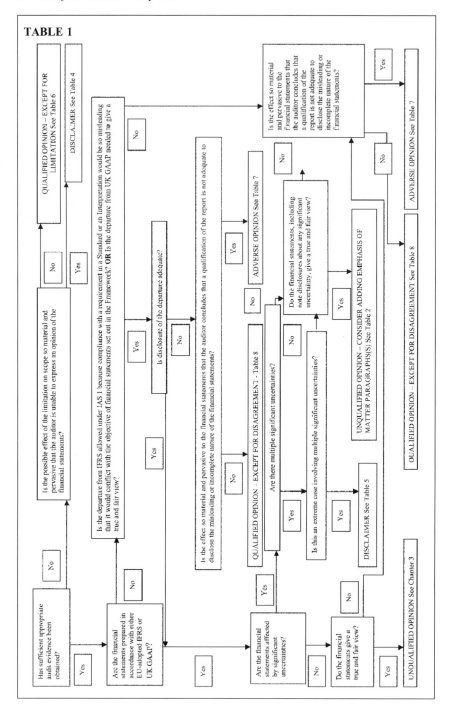

4.2.1   Emphasis of matter

In some circumstances, the audit report may be modified by adding an emphasis of matter paragraph to highlight a matter which is included in a note to the financial statements. Typical examples are where the going concern basis of preparation is appropriate but a material uncertainty exists (see **Chapter 13**) or where a significant uncertainty exists, the resolution of which depends on future events and which may affect the financial statements.

A significant uncertainty is one which, if it is not fully disclosed in the financial statements, would be seriously misleading, for example the outcome of major litigation. The nature of an uncertainty is that it can be expected to be resolved in the future when there will be sufficient evidence available to assess its outcome. In other circumstances where such evidence is available, or could reasonably be expected to be available, but it is not made available to the auditors, there is a limitation of scope which may lead to a qualification or disclaimer of opinion (see **4.2.2** below).

When assessing whether an uncertainty is significant, auditors should consider:

- the risk that the estimate associated with the uncertainty is likely to change;
- the range of possible outcomes of the uncertainty; and
- the consequences of those outcomes on the view given by the financial statements.

Where auditors decide that the uncertainty is significant they must include in their report an explanatory paragraph (**Table 2**) which describes the matter, the effect on the financial statements and, where practicable, quantifies it. Where quantification is not possible, this should be stated. A reference to the notes to the financial statements alone is not sufficient. The explanation in the audit report must be such that a reader can appreciate the principal points at issue and their implications.

TABLE 2: *Unqualified with explanatory paragraph on fundamental uncertainty*

Independent auditor's report to the members of ABC Limited

. . . .

Scope of audit

A description of the scope of an audit of financial statements is [provided on the APB's web-site at *www.frc.org.uk/apb/scope/UKNP*]/[set out [on page x] of the Annual Report].

Opinion on financial statements

In our opinion the financial statements:

- give a true and fair view of the state of the company's affairs as at 31 December 20.. and of its profit for the year then ended;
- have been properly prepared in accordance with United Kingdom Generally Accepted Accounting Practice; and
- have been properly prepared in accordance with the requirements of the Companies Act 2006.

Emphasis of matter – possible outcome of a lawsuit

In forming our opinion, which is not qualified, we have considered the adequacy of the disclosures made in the financial statements concerning the possible outcome of litigation against B Limited, a subsidiary of the company, for an alleged breach of environmental regulations. The future settlement of this litigation could result in additional liabilities and the closure of B Limited's business, whose net assets included in the consolidated balance sheet total £ ... and whose profit before tax for the year is £ .... . Details of the circumstances relating to this significant uncertainty are described in note .... .

Opinion on other matter prescribed by the Companies Act

In our opinion the information given in the Directors' Report for the financial year for which the financial statements are prepared is consistent with the financial statements.

Matters on which we are required to report by exception

We have nothing to report in respect of the following matters where the Companies Act 2006 requires us to report to you if, in our opinion:

- adequate accounting records have not been kept or returns adequate for our audit have not been received from branches not visited by us; or
- the company's financial statements are not in agreement with the accounting records and returns; or
- certain disclosures of directors' remuneration specified by law are not made; or
- we have not received all the information and explanations we required for our audit.

[*Signature*]
John Smith (Senior statutory auditor)
For and on behalf of ABC LLP, Statutory Auditor
Address
Date

As with any inherent uncertainty, where the disclosure of a fundamental uncertainty in the financial statements is insufficient, or its outcome is materially misstated, the auditors should qualify their report on the grounds of disagreement.

Other matters

Where auditors consider that a matter other than those presented or disclosed in the financial statements is relevant to the user's understanding of the audit, ISA (UK and Ireland) 700 encourages the inclusion of a paragraph in the auditor's report setting out details of the matter. The information should be included under the heading 'Other Matter' or another appropriate heading.

Such paragraphs will typically be used:

- to provide further explanation of the auditor's responsibilities for the audit of the financial statements or of the auditor's report thereon;
- where reporting by exception on corporate governance matters (see **Chapter 15**); or
- if an amendment to other information in a document containing audited financial statements is necessary to correct an material inconsistency and the entity refuses to make the amendment.

4.2.2 Qualified opinions

Qualified opinions arise from either a limitation of scope or a disagreement over an accounting treatment or disclosure. There are three possible outcomes, as illustrated in **Table 3**:

- *'disclaimer' of opinion*, where there is a limitation of scope which is so material or pervasive that the auditors are unable to form an opinion;
- *'adverse' opinion*, where the effect of the disagreement is so material or pervasive as to lead the auditors to conclude that the financial statements are seriously misleading; and
- *qualified opinion*, which is given when the limitation of scope or disagreement is not so material or pervasive as to require either an adverse opinion or disclaimer of opinion.

The decision whether an qualified opinion is sufficient has to be made based on the potential impact on the true and fair view given by the financial statements.

Whenever any opinion other than an unqualified one is given, auditors should include a clear description of all the substantive reasons for the report and a quantification of the likely effects on the financial statements, if possible.

TABLE 3: Types of qualification		
Effect	*Limitation of scope*	*Disagreement*
Material but not pervasive		Except for
Material and pervasive	Disclaimer	Adverse

4.2.3 Limitation of audit scope

Where there is a limitation of scope which prevents the auditors from obtaining sufficient evidence they should:

- describe the factors leading to the limitation in the opinion section of their report; and
- issue a disclaimer where the possible effect is so material or pervasive that they are unable to express an opinion; or

- in other cases issue an opinion qualified as to the possible adjustments that might have been necessary had the limitation not existed.

The ISA (UK and Ireland) does not define the term 'limitation of scope' but it is generally understood to be where the auditors are unable to express an unqualified opinion because their work has been restricted, they have not been able to carry out alternative procedures and as a result have had insufficient evidence on which to conclude on either the statements as a whole or a particular area. An example of this is an entity with a significant amount of cash sales over which there is no system of control upon which the auditors can rely and where no alternative procedures are possible.

Examples of disclaimers of opinion ('unable to' form an opinion, **Table 4 and 5**) and a report which is qualified on an 'except for' basis (**Table 6**) are provided below.

In assessing whether there is a limitation of scope, auditors must have regard to the evidence that they would reasonably expect to be available to support a particular figure or disclosure. The expectation of reasonable availability of evidence is critical to the decision on the limitation of scope. In all cases where there is a lack of evidence leading to a limitation of scope the auditors should take all possible steps to obtain alternative evidence to support an unqualified opinion. Inherent uncertainties are not in themselves a limitation of scope as, because of their nature, the auditors would not expect to find a great deal of information.

The details given about the nature of the limitation should distinguish between those which are imposed on the auditors and those which are outside their control or the control of the directors. Examples of these are:

- lack of a system of control over cash sales or refusal of directors to allow the auditors to contact a third party who holds stock on behalf of the entity (limitations imposed on the auditors);
- the auditor was not appointed until after the year end and so could not attend the stock take and there is no alternative evidence of existence (limitations outside the control of the auditors and the directors).

TABLE 4: Extract from an example 'disclaimer' of opinion

Scope of audit

A description of the scope of an audit of financial statements is [provided on the APB's web-site at *www.frc.org.uk/apb/scope/UKNP*]/[set out [on page x] of the Annual Report].

Opinion: disclaimer on the view given by the financial statements

The audit evidence available to us was limited because we were unable to observe the counting of physical stock having a carrying amount of £X and send confirmation

---

letters to trade debtors having a carrying amount of £Y due to limitations placed on the scope of our work by the directors of the company. As a result of this we have been unable to obtain sufficient appropriate audit evidence concerning both stock and trade debtors.

Because of the possible effect of the limitation in evidence available to us, we are unable to form an opinion as to whether the financial statements:

- give a true and fair view of the state of the company's affairs as at [date] and of its profit [loss] for the year then ended;
- have been properly prepared in accordance with United Kingdom Generally Accepted Accounting Practice; and
- have been prepared in accordance with the requirements of the Companies Act 2006.

Opinion on other matter prescribed by the Companies Act 2006

Notwithstanding our disclaimer on the view given by the financial statements, in our opinion the information given in the Directors' Report for the financial year for which the financial statements are prepared is consistent with the financial statements.

Matters on which we are required to report by exception

In respect solely of the limitation of our work referred to above:

- we have not obtained all the information and explanations that we considered necessary for the purpose of our audit; and
- we were unable to determine whether proper accounting records had been kept.

We have nothing to report in respect of the following matters where the Companies Act 2006 requires us to report to you if, in our opinion:

- returns adequate for our audit have not been received from branches not visited by us; or
- the financial statements are not in agreement with the accounting records and returns; or
- certain disclosures of directors' remuneration specified by law are not made.

[*Signature*]
John Smith (Senior statutory auditor)
For and on behalf of ABC LLP, Statutory Auditor
Address
Date

TABLE 5: Extract from an example of multiple disclaimers

Opinion: disclaimer on the view given by the financial statements

In forming our opinion we have considered the adequacy of the disclosures made in the financial statements concerning the following matters:

- [significant uncertainty 1]
- [significant uncertainty 2]
- [significant uncertainty 3]

Because of the potential significance, to the financial statements, of the combined effect of the three matters referred to in the paragraph above, we are unable to form an opinion as to whether the financial statements:

- give a true and fair view of the state of the company's affairs as at [date] and of its profit [loss] for the year then ended;
- have been properly prepared in accordance with United Kingdom Generally Accepted Accounting Practice; and
- have been prepared in accordance with the requirements of the Companies Act 2006.

Opinion on other matter prescribed by the Companies Act 2006

Notwithstanding our disclaimer on the view given by the financial statements, in our opinion the information given in the Directors' Report for the financial year for which the financial statements are prepared is consistent with the financial statements.

Matters on which we are required to report by exception

We have nothing to report in respect of the following matters where the Companies Act 2006 requires us to report to you if, in our opinion:

- adequate accounting records have not been kept or returns adequate for our audit have not been received from branches not visited by us; or
- the financial statements are not in agreement with the accounting records and returns; or
- certain disclosures of directors' remuneration specified by law are not made; or
- we have not received all the information and explanations we required for our audit.

[*Signature*]
John Smith (Senior statutory auditor)
For and on behalf of ABC LLP, Statutory Auditor
Address
Date

TABLE 6: *Extract from an 'except for' report*

Scope of audit

A description of the scope of an audit of financial statements is [provided on the APB's website at www.frc.org.uk/apb/scope/UKNP]/[set out [on page x] of the Annual Report].

Qualified opinion arising from limitation in audit scope

With respect to stock having a carrying amount of 3X the audit evidence available to us was limited because we did not observe the counting of the physical stock as at 31 December 20X1, since that date was prior to our appointment as auditor of the company. Owing to the nature of the company's records, we were unable to obtain sufficient appropriate audit evidence regarding the stock quantities by using other audit procedures.

Except for the financial effects of such adjustments, if any as might have been determined to be necessary had we been able to satisfy ourselves as to physical stock quantities, in our opinion the financial statements:

- give a true and fair view of the state of the company's affairs as at [date] and of its profit [loss] for the year then ended;

- have been properly prepared in accordance with United Kingdom Generally Accepted Accounting Practice; and
- have been prepared in accordance with the requirements of the Companies Act 2006.

Opinion on other matter prescribed by the Companies Act 2006

In our opinion the information given in the Directors' Report for the financial year for which the financial statements are prepared is consistent with the financial statements.

Matters on which we are required to report by exception

In respect solely of the limitation on our work relating to stocks:

- we have not obtained all the information and explanations that we considered necessary for the purpose of our audit; and
- we were unable to determine whether proper accounting records had been maintained.

We have nothing to report in respect of the following matters where the Companies Act 2006 requires us to report to you if, in our opinion:

- returns adequate for our audit have not been received from branches not visited by us; or
- the financial statements are not in agreement with the accounting records and returns; or
- certain disclosures of directors' remuneration specified by law are not made.

[Signature]
John Smith (Senior statutory auditor)
For and on behalf of ABC LLP, Statutory Auditor
Address
Date

In the example in the Bulletin, reference to both the failure to obtain all information and explanations considered necessary and to determine whether proper records have been maintained are included in the opinion paragraph. These follow the main opinion and are restricted to the area in which the lack of scope has occurred.

Imposed limitation of scope

ISA (UK and Ireland) 700 refers to cases where directors or management restrict access to sensitive information such that an effective audit cannot be carried out. This may occur where there is a statutory requirement for an audit but the owners are indifferent to the requirement, for example:

- an owner-managed business; or
- an overseas controlled entity which requires an on-shore report.

In these cases the owners or directors may be prepared to accept a disclaimed opinion for a nominal fee so long as they have a set of accounts that may be filed at Companies House.

The ISA (UK and Ireland) sets out the opinion of the APB that acceptance of such an engagement would not be compatible with auditors' obligations from the point of view of their legislative duties, auditing standards and the ethical guidance issued by their Professional Bodies.

Therefore, if auditors are aware, before accepting an audit engagement that the directors of the entity, or those who appoint its auditors, will impose a limitation on the scope of their work which they consider likely to result in the need to issue a disclaimer of opinion on the financial statements, they should not accept that engagement.

Where auditors become aware after accepting an engagement of such a restriction, the ISA (UK and Ireland) requires that they should consider whether to resign if the limitation is not removed. Alternatively they may decide to continue the engagement and then not seek reappointment. Factors they would take into account in deciding on the most appropriate course of action are the extent to which any work is complete and what is in the best public interest. The guidance suggests that the imposition of such a limitation may be a matter for any statement on the circumstances of ceasing to hold the office of auditor or for professional clearance letters to possible successor auditors.

4.2.4 Disagreement

ISA (UK and Ireland) 700 requires that where the auditors either disagree with the accounting treatment or the disclosure of a matter in the financial statements and the effect is material to the financial statements they should:

- describe the substantive factors giving rise to the disagreement, the implications for, and, where practicable, a quantification of the effect on, the financial statements; and either
- issue an adverse opinion where the possible effect is so material or pervasive that the financial statements are seriously misleading; or
- issue a qualified opinion indicating that it is expressed except for the effects of the matter giving rise to the disagreement.

The examples given in Bulletin 2009/2 include an adverse (**Table 7**) and a qualified 'except for' opinion (**Table 8**). It should be noted that in the example of the qualified opinion the opinion paragraph is clearly titled indicating the reason for the qualification, i.e., disagreement about accounting treatment to distinguish it from a qualification due to a limitation of scope which should also be clearly titled.

TABLE 7: *Extract from an adverse report*

Adverse opinion

As more fully explained in note ... no provision has been made for losses expected to arise on certain long-term contracts currently in progress, as the directors consider

---

that such losses should be off-set against amounts recoverable on other long-term contracts. In our opinion, provision should be made for foreseeable losses on individual contracts as required by [*specify accounting standard*]. If losses had been so recognised the effect would have been to reduce the profit before and after tax for the year and the contract work in progress at 31 December 20.. by £ . . . .

In view of the effect of the failure to provide for the losses referred to above, in our opinion the financial statements:

- do not give a true and fair view of the state of the company's affairs as at 31 December 20.. and of its profit for the year then ended; and
- have not been properly prepared in accordance with United Kingdom Generally Accepted Accounting Practice.

In all other respects, in our opinion the financial statements have been prepared in accordance with the requirements of the Companies Act 2006.

Opinion on other matter prescribed by the Companies Act 2006

Notwithstanding our adverse opinion on the view given by the financial statements, in our opinion the information given in the Directors' Report for the financial year for which the financial statements are prepared is consistent with the financial statements.

Other matters on which we are required to report by exception

We have nothing to report in respect of the following matters where the Companies Act 2006 requires us to report to you if, in our opinion:

- adequate accounting records have not been kept or returns adequate for our audit have not been received from branches not visited by us; or
- the financial statements are not in agreement with the accounting records and returns; or
- certain disclosures of directors' remuneration specified by law are not made; or
- we have not received all the information and explanations we required for our audit.

[*Signature*]
John Smith (Senior statutory auditor)
For and on behalf of ABC LLP, Statutory Auditor
Address
Date

TABLE 8: *Extract from an 'except for' disagreement report*

Qualified opinion arising from disagreement about accounting treatment

Included in the debtors shown on the balance sheet is an amount of £ . . . due from a company which has ceased trading. XYZ plc has no security for this debt. In our opinion the company is unlikely to receive any payment and full provision of £ . . . should have been made, reducing profit before tax and net assets by that amount.

Except for the financial effect of not making the provision referred to in the preceding paragraph, in our opinion the financial statements:

- give a true and fair view of the state of the company's affairs as at 31 December 20.. and of its profit for the year then ended;

- have been properly prepared in accordance with United Kingdom Generally Accepted Accounting Practice; and
- have been prepared in accordance with the requirements of the Companies Act 2006.

Opinion on other matter prescribed by the Companies Act

In our opinion the information given in the Directors' Report for the financial year for which the financial statements are prepared is consistent with the financial statements.

Matters on which we are required to report by exception

We have nothing to report in respect of the following matters where the Companies Act 2006 requires us to report to you if, in our opinion:

- adequate accounting records have not been kept or returns adequate for our audit have not been received from branches not visited by us; or
- the financial statements are not in agreement with the accounting records and returns; or
- certain disclosures of directors' remuneration specified by law are not made; or
- we have not received all the information and explanations we required for our audit.

[*Signature*]
John Smith (Senior statutory auditor)
For and on behalf of ABC LLP, Statutory Auditor
Address
Date

When referring to the disagreement, it is not sufficient for the auditors merely to refer to the relevant note in the financial statements without giving further details. The reader must be able to judge the facts to understand their impact on the financial statements from the audit report alone.

4.2.5   Adverse opinions or disclaimers of opinion

Where auditors have expressed an adverse opinion or disclaimed an opinion on the financial statements as a whole, auditors cannot issue an unmodified opinion on a part of the financial statements under the same financial reporting framework.

4.2.6   Multiple uncertainties

Auditors are permitted to issue a disclaimer of opinion in the case of multiple uncertainties where 'the cumulative nature and possible effect of the multiple uncertainties are such that it is not possible to form an opinion'. This may be despite obtaining sufficient evidence about each individual uncertainty, but where it remains unclear how the interaction of the uncertainties affects the financial statements.

5 OTHER REPORTS ON FINANCIAL STATEMENTS

5.1 INTRODUCTION

This Chapter considers other reports that auditors may be required to make on a company's financial statements. It covers the reports on:

- summary financial statements;
- abbreviated accounts;
- exemptions for small and medium-sized groups;
- revised financial statements; and
- preliminary announcements.

The main source of guidance on reporting on abbreviated accounts, small and medium-sized groups and revised financial statements comes from Practice Note 8 *Reports by Auditors under Company Legislation in the United Kingdom*. The examples in the appendix to Practice Note 8 were updated in Bulletin 2007/1 issued in January 2007. At the same time the APB announced its intention to review the body of Practice Note 8 prior to the Companies Act 2006 coming into force.

Following the publication of Bulletin 2009/2 *Auditor's Reports on Financial Statements in the United Kingdom* in April 2009, the format of standard auditor's reports was changed for accounting periods ending on or after 5 April 2009. Until revised guidance is issued in relation to the reports in this chapter, this publication retains the examples from the most recent specific material.

For periods commencing on or after 6 April 2008 guidance on summary financial statements is from Bulletin 2008/3 *The Auditors' Statement on the Summary Financial Statement in the United Kingdom.*

Abbreviated accounts guidance is found in Bulletin 2008/4 *The Special Auditor's Report on Abbreviated Accounts in the United Kingdom* for periods commencing after 6 April 2008.

For revised accounts guidance is found in Bulletin 2008/5 *Auditor's Reports on Revised Accounts and Reports, in the United Kingdom* for periods after 6 April 2008.

For preliminary announcements guidance comes from Bulletin 2008/2 *The Auditors' Association with Preliminary Announcements Made in Accordance with the Requirements of the UK and Irish Listing Rules.*

For some reports there is additional guidance on the procedures necessary to support such reports and the source of this has been noted below.

Internationally, IFAC released a Consultation Paper in relation to a planned revision to International Standard on Review Engagements (ISRE) 2400 *Engagements to Review Financial Statements in September 2008*. ISRE 2400 applies when a practitioner who is not the auditor of an entity undertakes an engagement to review the financial statements. The proposals for its revision are discussed in **5.8** below.

5.2 SUMMARY FINANCIAL STATEMENTS

5.2.1 Legal background

Under s426(1) of the Companies Act 2006 and the Companies (Summary Financial Statement) Regulations 2008, companies in the United Kingdom may send summary financial statements (SFSs) to their shareholders instead of the full report and accounts. There are strict requirements as to the contents of the summary financial statements.

Previously an option for listed companies only, the possibility of preparing summary financial statements was extended to all companies from 1 January 2005.

These financial statements must be accompanied by a statement from the company's auditors that the summary statement is consistent with the full accounts and that it complies with s426(1) and the Regulations. There is no need to include the auditors' report on the full financial statements unless this is either qualified or contains a statement concerning proper accounting records or inadequate returns under or failure to obtain certain necessary information and explanations.

5.2.2 Auditing Standards and Guidelines

The guidance in relation to summary financial statements comes from Bulletin 2008/3 *The Auditor's Statement on the Summary Financial Statement in the United Kingdom* for periods commencing after 6 April 2008. This Bulletin superseded Bulletin 1999/6 *The Auditors' Statement on the Summary Financial Statement*.

Where quoted companies prepare a Summary Financial Statement they are required to include either the whole, or a summary, of certain information concerning directors' remuneration contained in the notes to the financial statements and in the Directors' Remuneration Report. The relevant information is:

- the aggregate amount of directors' emoluments;
- a statement of the company's policy on directors' remuneration for the next following financial year; and
- the performance graph.

The last two items are not required to be audited, but should be read as required by ISA (UK and Ireland) 720.

5.2.3 Audit procedures

As with any assignment, auditors should ensure that their responsibilities and terms of engagement with reference to the SFS are included in an engagement letter.

Auditors should plan to carry out their work on the SFS at the same time as completing the audit so that their statement under s426(1) of CA 2006 and their audit report can be issued at the same time.

They should plan their work so that they can report:

- on the consistency of the SFSs with the full financial statements; and
- whether the SFSs comply with s426(1) as applicable and the Regulations.

These are not independent of each other as consistency is required by the Regulations. The Regulations require that where additional information is necessary to achieve consistency with the full financial statements this is included in the SFS. The auditors are not required to state whether the SFSs give a true and fair view and it is unlikely that this will be the case.

Consistency

It is the issue of consistency that concerns the auditors the most. There is no guidance on the definition of consistency. The most simplistic interpretation is that the information should be taken directly from the full statements.

The other extreme is that users should be able to reach the same conclusion as they would from studying the full accounts. If the latter view is taken then the amount of information required would be so great that there would be no advantage to providing summary financial statements. Accordingly, the former view is invariably taken. This is supported by the Bulletin, which comments that users of SFS do not have the same expectations of SFS as they do of the full financial statements.

The Bulletin gives four instances when inconsistency may occur:

- where information has been incorrectly extracted from the full financial statements, which should generally be easy to identify and correct;
- where headings that are used in a summary primary statement are incompatible with the statutory headings in the full financial statements;

- where the information given has been summarised too much or too selectively; or
- where, in the opinion of the auditors, the summary needs to give more information than is required by the Regulations to achieve consistency. For example, details of an exceptional item are not specified by the Regulations but may be necessary if the summary is to be consistent with the full financial statements and the user is to gain a reasonable understanding of them.

Where inconsistencies have been identified, the auditors should discuss the matter with the directors so that corrections can be made to whichever set of financial statements is incorrect. If no agreement is reached the auditors should modify their statement under s427(4)(d) or s428(4)(d) of CA 2006 to include a description of the inconsistency. The inconsistency will also mean that the accounts do not comply with the Regulations and should also be qualified in this respect.

Compliance with s427(4)(d) or s428(4)(d) of CA 2006 and the Regulations

The auditors should include all matters required by the Regulations and s427(4)(d) or s428(4)(d) of CA 2006 within the scope of their examination. This includes the summarised directors' report, the aggregate figure required in respect of directors' emoluments and any statements specifically required by the legislation.

Where there are items in the SFS which, although not inconsistent with the full financial statements, are not properly derived from them, then a modification of the report may be necessary.

If the report on the full financial statements has been qualified, then it will be necessary for the auditors to decide whether or not there is sufficient disclosure of the matter in the SFSs for the user to understand the qualification. This will be in addition to the reproduction of the report itself. They may consider that to achieve this, extra notes would have to be included in the SFSs that are not specifically required by the Regulations.

Although not addressed in the legislation, the Bulletin suggests that where there was an explanatory paragraph referring to a fundamental uncertainty in the auditors' report in the full financial statements, this should also be referred to in their report on the SFS. Where the explanatory paragraph in the report on the full financial statements includes a reference to a note accompanying the full financial statements, but does not reproduce the information in that note, that information should be reproduced in the SFS.

Other information

If the SFSs are being sent out with other information the auditors should ensure that it is clear that their report relates to the summary only and not to any other information. The Bulletin suggests that the auditors read the other information before it is sent out to ensure that they are not aware of any apparent misstatements or material inconsistencies. If there is any disagreement this should be discussed and changes made as appropriate. Where changes are not made, the Bulletin suggests that the auditors may need to take legal advice.

5.2.4 *Reporting*

The auditors' statement should include the following elements:

- addressee – normally the shareholders;
- introductory paragraph – identifying the SFS by reference to page numbers;
- respective responsibilities of the auditors and the directors;
- basis of opinion – indicating that the work was carried out in accordance with the relevant Bulletin;
- opinion – regarding the consistency with the full financial statements and the compliance with the legislation; and
- other information – for example, a qualification in the auditors' report on the full financial statements would require the reproduction of that audit report.

The auditor will consider whether to include a paragraph in accordance with the Bannerman judgement and Technical Release 1/03 (see **3.20**).

The report should be dated when the auditors sign the report in manuscript, which must be after the directors have approved the SFS. The Bulletins recommend that this is the same day as the audit report on the full financial statements in order to avoid the impression that the report on the SFS updates that on the full financial statements. If the SFS report is signed at a later date, the report should state that the auditors have not considered the effect of any events between the two dates.

Examples of an unmodified report under CA 2006 is shown in **Table 1** below.

TABLE 1: Report on summary financial statements under CA 2006

Independent auditors' statement to the shareholders of ABC Plc

We have examined the summary financial statements of ABC Plc [which comprises the Summary Consolidated Profit and Loss Account, Summary Consolidated Balance Sheet, Summary Consolidated Statement of Total Recognised Gains and Losses, [Summary Consolidated Cash Flow Statement] [and the Summary Directors' Remuneration Report] [set out on pages ... to ...].[1]

Respective responsibilities of directors and auditors

The directors are responsible for preparing the [*summarised annual report*] in accordance with United Kingdom law.

---

[1] Auditors may include a 'Bannerman Statement' as part of the opening section of their report (see **3.20**).

Our responsibility is to report to you our opinion on the consistency of the summary financial statement within the [*summarised annual report*] with the full annual financial statements [, the Directors' Report] [and the Directors' Remuneration Report], and its compliance with the relevant requirements of section 428 of the Companies Act 2006 and the regulations made thereunder.

We also read the other information contained in the [*summarised annual report*] and consider the implications for our report if we become aware of any apparent misstatements or material inconsistencies with the summary financial statement. The other information comprises only [the Chairman's Statement and the Corporate Governance Statement].

Basis of Opinion

We conducted our work in accordance with Bulletin 2008/3 issued by the Auditing Practices Board. Our report on the company's full financial statements describes the basis of our audit opinion[s] on those financial statements, the Directors' Remuneration Report and the Directors' Report.

Opinion

In our opinion the summary financial statement is consistent with the full annual financial statements, the Directors' Report and the Directors' Remuneration Report of ABC Plc for the year ended 31 December 20.. and complies with the applicable requirements of section 428 of the Companies Act 2006, and the regulations made thereunder.

Registered Auditors
Address
Date

Where the date is after the date of the auditors' report on the full financial statements the following words should be added:

'We have not considered the effects of any events between the date on which we signed our report on the annual financial statements [insert date] and the date of this statement.'

5.3 ABBREVIATED ACCOUNTS

5.3.1 *Legal background*

Companies which meet the criteria set out in the Companies Act 2006 for small and medium-sized companies are entitled to file abbreviated or modified financial statements with the Registrar of Companies. These have to be prepared in accordance with s396(3) of the 2006 Act but are not required to give a true and fair view. There is no provision for group accounts to be prepared on an abbreviated basis.

Those companies who have elected to prepare their individual accounts using IFRSs cannot prepare abbreviated accounts.

5.3.2   Guidance

Guidance for auditors of abbreviated accounts is provided in Bulletin 2008/4 *The Special Auditor's Report on Abbreviated Accounts in the United Kingdom* for periods commencing on or after 6 April 2008. This supersedes Bulletin 2006/3 of the same name.

5.3.3   Audit procedures

Where abbreviated accounts are prepared to be delivered to the Registrar, they must be accompanied by a copy of a special report of the auditor. The Companies Act does not state to whom the report should be addressed, but in absence of guidance, the Bulletin states that the report should be addressed to the company. Despite the fact that abbreviated accounts must be properly prepared in accordance with the relevant provisions, the auditor's opinion cannot be in terms of 'true and fair'. Instead it is limited to whether:

- the directors are entitled to the exemptions claimed; and
- the abbreviated accounts have been properly prepared under the Act.

The report should be dated as close as possible to the date of the report on the full financial statements, and preferably on the same day. If there is a significant delay in reporting on the abbreviated accounts it may give the impression that the report on the full accounts is being 'updated'. In practical terms, this means that auditors may be required by the directors to confirm informally in advance of the preparation of abbreviated accounts that the exemptions are available. Where the report on the abbreviated accounts is dated later than that on the full financial statements, the abbreviated report should state that auditors have not considered the effect of any events between the two dates.

If the auditors cannot confirm that the directors are entitled to the exemptions, they should report this to the directors and full accounts will have to be filed with the Registrar.

If the report on the full financial statements is qualified, abbreviated accounts may be prepared so long as they are an accurate extract. If the qualification relates to one of the criteria for exemption, the auditors should consider the maximum possible misstatement that this would give rise to. Where this means that the company would exceed the limits full accounts will have to be filed with the Registrar. If the auditors have disclaimed on the financial statements then this will normally prevent them from assessing the criteria at all.

A reproduction of the report given on the full financial statements is not required unless the report on the full financial statements has been qualified. Where this is the case, the Act requires that the report given on that full financial statements is reproduced together with sufficient material either in the accounts or following the auditors' report, to ensure that the reader is able to understand the qualification fully.

In addition, if the report on the full financial statements contains a statement under s498(2)(a) or (b) CA 2006 (accounts, records or returns inadequate or accounts not agreeing with records and returns) or s498(3) CA 2006 (failure to obtain necessary information and explanations), the special report should set out that statement in full under the heading 'other information'.

Under CA 2006, where the auditor is a firm, the report must be signed by the Senior Statutory Auditor in his own name for and on behalf of the auditor in line with the requirements of Bulletin 2008/6 *The 'Senior Statutory Auditor' under the United Kingdom Companies Act 2006.*

TABLE 2: Report on abbreviated accounts under CA 2006

Independent auditors' report to XYZ Limited under section 247B of the Companies Act 1985

We have examined the abbreviated accounts of XYZ Limited set out on pages ... to ..., together with the financial statements of the company for the year ended ... prepared under section 396 of the Companies Act 2006.[2]

Respective responsibilities of directors and auditors

The directors are responsible for preparing the abbreviated accounts in accordance with section 444 [section 445 if medium-sized] of the Companies Act 2006. It is our responsibility to form an independent opinion as to whether the company is entitled to deliver abbreviated accounts to the Registrar of Companies and whether the abbreviated accounts have been properly prepared in accordance with those provisions and to report our opinion to you.

Basis of opinion

We conducted our work in accordance with Bulletin 2008/4 issued by the Auditing Practices Board. In accordance with that Bulletin we have carried out the procedures we consider necessary to confirm, by reference to the financial statements, that the company is entitled to deliver abbreviated accounts and that the abbreviated accounts are properly prepared.

Opinion

In our opinion the company is entitled to deliver abbreviated accounts prepared in accordance with sections 444(3) [section 445(3)] of the Companies Act 2006, and the abbreviated accounts have been properly prepared in accordance with those provisions.

Other information

[*This section is only to be included where there is such information*]

---

[2] Auditors may include a 'Bannerman Statement' as part of the opening section of their report (see **3.20**).

[signature] John Smith (senior statutory auditor)
for and on behalf of ABC LLP, Statutory Auditors
Address
Date

There is no legal requirement to reproduce the report on the full financial statements where this contains a reference to a fundamental uncertainty or some other explanatory paragraph. The Bulletin notes that the legislation only sets out minimum requirements and does not preclude other information being provided where the auditors consider it to be important.

Hence, the APB recommends that both the explanatory paragraph, and sufficient information for it to be properly understood, are included in the special report under the heading 'other information'.

It is preferable for the same auditors to report on both full and abbreviated sets of accounts. If there is to be a change of auditors and the new auditors are to report on the abbreviated accounts they only need to perform additional work if they have grounds to doubt the accuracy of their predecessor. Where such a change occurs it should be indicated in the report.

5.4 EXEMPTIONS FOR SMALL AND MEDIUM-SIZED GROUPS

5.4.1 Legal background

Under Companies Act 2006 small groups of companies may choose not to prepare group accounts. Where the directors have taken advantage of the exemptions under s398 and in the auditors' opinion they are not entitled to do so, the 2006 Act requires that this be stated in the auditors' report on the parent company's financial statements. A suitable wording for the additional opinion paragraph is given in **Table 3**.

Prior to 6 April 2008, when the 2006 Act became effective, a similar exemption was available for medium-sized groups.

If the auditors do not believe that the directors are entitled to the exemption they should initially discuss the matter with them. Directors should be made aware that where they file parent company accounts with such a qualification the Registrar of Companies may decide to investigate the matter.

5.4.2 Audit procedures

Although there is no specific guidance on the procedures to be carried out it is reasonable to assume that similar considerations to those described under abbreviated accounts (see above) would apply to the exercise auditors must carry out to assess whether the limits which allow the directors to claim the exemption have been complied with.

TABLE 3: Additional opinion paragraph where not eligible for group accounts exemption

Other matters

As detailed in note .. to the financial statements, the directors have taken advantage of the exemptions in s398 of the Companies Act 2006 from preparing group accounts. In our opinion, they are not entitled to do so because the group does not qualify as a small-sized group.

5.5 REVISED FINANCIAL STATEMENTS

5.5.1 Legal background

The Companies Act 2006 allow directors to withdraw financial statements which have been found to be defective after they had been filed with the Registrar of Companies. In addition, the court has powers to make directors revise defective accounts.

5.5.2 Auditing Guideline

In addition to the reporting guidance in Practice Note 8, an exposure draft of an auditing guideline was published in May 1991 by the APC entitled *Auditors' Reports on Revised Annual Accounts and Directors' Reports*, which covers the procedures necessary to give such a report. There is no indication of when or if the APB intend to revisit this and it does not form part of their current programme.

5.5.3 Types of revision

Revision of accounts may be by:

- issue of replacement financial statements;
- supplementary note, to be appended to the existing financial statements; or
- revision to the directors' report.

In each case the auditors have to report on the revision and the directors' statement of the reason why the original financial statements are now considered incorrect. They must consider if the statement by the directors of the reason for the revision is sufficient for the reader to obtain a clear picture of the relevant facts. It is also necessary to consider if the method of revision is appropriate and whether any further adjustments are necessary.

Where the only revision is to the directors' report, the auditors have to make a positive statement that it is consistent with the information in the financial statements, unlike normal reports where they need only report on any inconsistency.

Bulletin 2008/5 sets out individual example reports under the Companies Act 2006 for:

- revision by replacement; and
- revision by supplementary note

and both are reproduced in **Tables 4** and **5** below.

It is possible to revise abbreviated financial statements where these alone prove to be defective. In these instances, auditors are only required to report on the preparation of the abbreviated financial statements, rather than the revision.

Where either the full revision or supplementary note option is chosen, there should be a statement of directors' responsibilities under the Regulations. As with the annual financial statements this may be either in the auditors' report or elsewhere in the financial statements or accompanying information. The responsibilities that should be noted are shown in **Table 6.**

Where it is necessary to qualify such a report, the considerations are the same as for reports on other financial statements. For example, if the auditors consider that the reasons for the revision given by the directors are inadequate they should qualify and give further details in their report.

TABLE 4: Annual financial statements revised by replacement under CA 2006

Independent auditors' report to the shareholders of XYZ Limited

We have audited the revised financial statements of XYZ Limited for the year ended ... which comprise [state the primary financial statements such as the Profit and Loss Account, the Balance Sheet, the Cash Flow Statement, the Statement of Total Recognised Gains and Losses] and the related notes. These revised financial statements have been prepared under the accounting policies set out therein and replace the original financial statements approved by the directors on ...

The revised financial statements have been prepared under the Companies (Revision of Defective Accounts and Report) Regulations 2008 and accordingly do not take

---

account of events which have taken place after the date on which the original financial statements were approved.[3]

Respective responsibilities of directors and auditors

The directors' responsibilities for preparing revised financial statements in accordance with applicable law and United Kingdom Accounting Standards (United Kingdom Generally Accepted Accounting Practice) and for being satisfied that they give a true and fair view are set out in the Statement of Directors' Responsibilities.

Our responsibility is to audit the revised financial statements in accordance with relevant legal and regulatory requirements and International Standards on Auditing (UK and Ireland).

We report to you our opinion as to whether the revised financial statements give a true and fair view and are properly prepared in accordance with United Kingdom Generally Accepted Accounting Practice and are prepared in accordance with the requirements of the Companies Act 2006 as they have effect under the Companies (Revision of Defective Accounts and Report) Regulations 2008. We also report to you whether in our opinion the information given in the [revised] Directors' Report is not consistent with the revised financial statements.

In addition we report to you if, in our opinion, the company has not kept proper accounting records, if we have not received all the information and explanations we require for our audit or if disclosures of directors' benefits, remuneration, pensions and compensation for loss of office specified by law are not made.

We read the [revised] Directors' Report and consider the implications for our report if we become aware of any apparent misstatements within it.

We are also required to report whether in our opinion the original financial statements failed to comply with the requirements of the Companies Act 2006 in the respects identified by the directors.

Basis of audit opinion

We conducted our audit in accordance with International Standards on Auditing (UK and Ireland) issued by the Auditing Practices Board. An audit includes examination, on a test basis, of evidence relevant to the amounts and disclosures in the revised financial statements. It also includes an assessment of the significant estimates and judgements made by the directors in the preparation of the revised financial statements, and of whether the accounting policies are appropriate to the company's circumstances, consistently applied and adequately disclosed.

The audit of revised financial statements includes the performance of additional procedures to assess whether the revisions made by the directors are appropriate and have been properly made.

We planned and performed our audit so as to obtain all the information and explanations which we considered necessary in order to provide us with sufficient evidence to give us reasonable assurance that the revised financial statements are free from material misstatement, whether caused by fraud or other irregularity or error. In forming our opinion we also evaluated the overall adequacy of the presentation of information in the revised financial statements.

---

[3] Auditors may include a 'Bannerman Statement' as part of the opening section of their report (see **3.20**).

Opinion

In our opinion:

- the revised financial statements give a true and fair view, seen as at the date the original financial statements were approved, of the state of the company's affairs as at ... and of its profit for the year then ended;
- the revised financial statements have been properly prepared in accordance with United Kingdom Generally Accepted Accounting Practice seen as at the date the original financial statements were approved;
- the revised financial statements have been properly prepared in accordance with the provisions of the Companies Act 2006 as they have effect under the Companies (Revision of Defective Accounts and Reports) Regulations 2008;
- the original financial statements for the year ended ... failed to comply with the requirements of the Companies Act 2006 in the respects identified by the directors in the statement contained in note .. to these revised financial statements; and
- the information given in the [revised] Directors' Report is consistent with the revised financial statements.

Emphasis of matter – revision of ...

In forming our opinion on the revised financial statements, which is not qualified, we have considered the adequacy of the disclosures made in note x to these revised financial statements concerning the need to revise the .... The original financial statements were approved on ... and our previous report was signed on that date. We have not performed a subsequent events review of the period from the date of our previous report to the date of this report.

[Signature] John Smith (senior statutory auditor)
For and on behalf of ABC LLP, Statutory auditor
Address
Date

TABLE 5: Annual financial statements revised by supplementary note under CA 2006

Independent auditors' report to the shareholders of XYZ Limited

We have audited the revised financial statements of XYZ Limited for the year ended ... which comprise [state the primary financial statements such as the Profit and Loss Account, the Balance Sheet, the Cash Flow Statement, the Statement of Total Recognised Gains and Losses] and the related notes. These revised financial statements replace the original financial statements approved by the directors on ... and consist of the attached supplementary note together with the original financial statements which were circulated to members on ....

The revised financial statements have been prepared under the Companies (Revision of Defective Accounts and Report) Regulations 2008 and accordingly do not take account of events which have taken place after the date on which the original financial statements were approved.[4]

---

[4] Auditors may include a 'Bannerman Statement' as part of the opening section of their report (see **3.20**).

5. Other Reports on Financial Statements

Respective responsibilities of directors and auditors

The directors' responsibilities for preparing revised financial statements in accordance with applicable law and United Kingdom Accounting Standards (United Kingdom Generally Accepted Accounting Practice) and for being satisfied that they give a true and fair view are set out in the Statement of Directors' Responsibilities.

Our responsibility is to audit the revised financial statements in accordance with relevant legal and regulatory requirements and International Standards on Auditing (UK and Ireland).

We report to you our opinion as to whether the revised financial statements give a true and fair view and are properly prepared in accordance with United Kingdom Generally Accepted Accounting Practice and are prepared in accordance with the requirements of the Companies Act 2006 as they have effect under the Companies (Revision of Defective Accounts and Report) Regulations 2008. We also report to you whether in our opinion the information given in the [revised] Directors' Report is not consistent with the revised financial statements.

In addition we report to you if, in our opinion, the company has not kept proper accounting records, if we have not received all the information and explanations we require for our audit or if disclosures of directors' benefits, remuneration, pensions and compensation for loss of office specified by law are not made.

We read the [revised] Directors' Report and consider the implications for our report if we become aware of any apparent misstatements within it.

We are also required to report whether in our opinion the original financial statements failed to comply with the requirements of the Companies Act 2006 in the respects identified by the directors.

Basis of audit opinion

We conducted our audit in accordance with International Standards on Auditing (UK and Ireland) issued by the Auditing Practices Board. An audit includes examination, on a test basis, of evidence relevant to the amounts and disclosures in the revised financial statements. It also includes an assessment of the significant estimates and judgements made by the directors in the preparation of the revised financial statements, and of whether the accounting policies are appropriate to the company's circumstances, consistently applied and adequately disclosed.

The audit of revised financial statements includes the performance of additional procedures to assess whether the revisions made by the directors are appropriate and have been properly made.

We planned and performed our audit so as to obtain all the information and explanations which we considered necessary in order to provide us with sufficient evidence to give us reasonable assurance that the revised financial statements are free from material misstatement, whether caused by fraud or other irregularity or error. In forming our opinion we also evaluated the overall adequacy of the presentation of information in the revised financial statements.

Opinion

In our opinion:

- the revised financial statements give a true and fair view, seen as at the date the original financial statements were approved, of the state of the company's affairs as at ... and of its profit for the year then ended;
- the revised financial statements have been properly prepared in accordance with

United Kingdom Generally Accepted Accounting Practice seen as at the date the original financial statements were approved;

- the revised financial statements have been properly prepared in accordance with the provisions of the Companies Act 2006 as they have effect under the Companies (Revision of Defective Accounts and Reports) Regulations 2008;
- the original financial statements for the year ended ... failed to comply with the requirements of the Companies Act 2006 in the respects identified by the directors in the statement contained in the supplementary note; and
- the information given in the [revised] Directors' Report is consistent with the revised financial statements.

Emphasis of matter – revision of ...

In forming our opinion on the revised financial statements, which is not qualified, we have considered the adequacy of the disclosures made in the supplementary note concerning the need to revise the .... The original financial statements were approved on ... and our previous report was signed on that date. We have not performed a subsequent events review of the period from the date of our previous report to the date of this report.

[Signature] John Smith (senior statutory auditor)
For and on behalf of ABC LLP, Statutory auditor
Address
Date

TABLE 6: Directors' responsibilities with regard to revised financial statements under CA 2006

Under s454 of the Companies Act 2006 the directors have the authority to revise financial statements or a directors' report if they do not comply with the Act. The revised financial statements must be amended in accordance with the Companies (Revision of Defective Account and Report) Regulations 2008 and in accordance therewith do not take account of events which have taken place after the date on which the original financial statements were approved. The Regulations require that revised financial statements show a true and fair view as if they were prepared and approved by the directors, as at the date of the original financial statements.

There is no specific guidance on what the auditors should do if they do not agree that there are grounds for revision but the directors decide to go ahead with the revision. However, as the auditors must give an opinion on whether the revision is in accordance with the Regulations and these only permit revision in certain circumstances, where they disagree with it, they will have to give an adverse opinion. This is because the revised financial statements have not been prepared in accordance with the Regulations and may also be on the grounds that in their opinion the original financial statements did comply with the requirements of the Companies Act.

The auditors will need to assess whether the discovery that leads to the revision indicates that proper accounting records have not been kept and the effect this has on their report.

There is no duty on auditors to search for further evidence after they have signed their report, but if they do become aware of anything that they should have known at the original date of signing they should inform the directors immediately and consider whether revision is necessary.

When deciding on the best course of action once an error is discovered, various factors should be taken into consideration, including the proximity to the next set of financial statements. It may be better to make a prior year adjustment rather than carry out a revision, if the error is discovered during the course of the next year's audit due to the costs and value of the information that will result from a revision. This is not precluded by the Regulations and will often be the best course of action if a significant amount of time has elapsed since the incorrect financial statements were produced.

5.5.4   Procedures

In determining the extent of audit procedures necessary, auditors should analyse the matter giving rise to the revision and consider:

- whether the nature of the matter suggests that errors in the financial statements may be pervasive, for example the discovery of fraud;
- whether the facts discovered since the approval of the financial statements affect past assumptions in areas of judgement, for example provisions;
- the extent of any consequential changes to the form of financial statements which arise from the matter. For example, group financial statements may be required for the first time; and
- any steps taken by the directors to investigate and correct the defect.

Where the auditors have changed since the date of the original financial statements which have subsequently been found to be defective, the new auditors should make the required reports, unless the previous auditors have been specifically engaged by management and they are still eligible to report as 'registered auditors'.

Where the auditors reporting on the original and revised financial statements are the same, it is unlikely that a re-performance of the original audit will be required. However, in determining the extent of their examination, the auditors should assess the risk of other misstatements in the original accounts. Where different auditors are reviewing the revised accounts the amount of work that is necessary will depend on the reason for the revision and their assessment of risk.

Based on their assessment of this, they should determine appropriate review procedures to identify any significant events in the period since the approval of the original financial statements. Such a review must be sufficient to:

- ensure that the factors which have led the directors to determine that the original financial statements were defective have been properly reflected in the proposed adjustments; and

- identify any further adjustments which should be made to the revised accounts.

Auditors would therefore normally undertake the following specific procedures:

- review of the original audit plans (and programmes) in the light of the analysis of the matter leading to revision and the extent to which additional audit evidence is required should be considered;
- reassessment of the various matters of judgement involved in the preparation of the original financial statements;
- obtaining evidence specific to the adjustments made to the original financial statements;
- review of the period after the date on which the original financial statements were approved;
- review of the revised financial statements to the extent that, in conjunction with the conclusions drawn from the other audit evidence obtained, there is a reasonable basis for the opinion on the financial statements; and
- consideration of any legal and regulatory consequences of the revision.

Each of these steps may in turn indicate a need for further procedures.

Engagements to report on revised directors' reports should be conducted following the principles outlined above.

5.6 PRELIMINARY ANNOUNCEMENTS

5.6.1 Background

Following a change to the Listing Rules of the Financial Services Authority a listed company may choose to publish a preliminary announcement, but is not required to do so. However, when a company does issue a preliminary announcement it is required by the Listing Rules to have agreed the announcement with the company's auditors prior to publication, although the Listing Rules do not set out what form the agreement with the auditor should take. Neither do they set out the extent of work expected by the auditor.

In July 1998 the Accounting Standards Board issued a non-mandatory Statement containing guidance on the content of preliminary announcements.

5.6.2 Guidance

Main guidance on this issue is in APB Bulletin 2008/2 *The Auditors' Association with Preliminary Announcements Made in Accordance with Requirements of the UK and Irish Listing Rules*. This supersedes Bulletin 2004/1 that provided guidance on the 'legitimate and important role [auditors of listed companies] play in the process leading to the orderly release of preliminary announcements'. The updated Bulletin:

- reflects the change in the Listing Rules to move from a mandatory to a permissive regime for the publication of preliminary announcements;
- reflects the change in the Listing Rules to require preliminary announcements to give details of any likely modification (rather than qualification) of the auditor's report required to be included with the annual financial report;
- reflects the introduction of ISAs (UK and Ireland); and
- continues to emphasise the need for the auditor to consider the way in which alternative performance measures and management commentary are presented in preliminary announcements before agreeing to their release.

In February 2003, the APB wrote to all auditors of listed companies to alert them to the possibility that shareholders may sometimes be misinformed by the way in which 'pro forma' financial information is included in unaudited preliminary announcements, and to emphasise the need for auditors to consider the way in which pro forma information is presented before agreeing to the release of preliminary announcements. A further letter was issued in December 2003 reminding auditors of the February 2003 letter.

5.6.3   Terms of engagement

From the auditors' point of view, the objective of the engagement is to report that the preliminary figures are consistent with the financial statements which are being or have been audited.

The scope of any engagement to review a preliminary announcement should be clearly established with the client and any public statements must also make this clear. The terms of the engagement should be set out either in a separate engagement letter or by incorporating them within the standard engagement letter.

In particular, auditors are required to agree the contents of the preliminary statement, whether or not its contents exceed the minimum laid down by the Listing Rules.

The Bulletin contains example paragraphs for inclusion in an engagement letter where a preliminary announcement is being made. These are shown in **Table 7** (audit complete) and **Table 8** (audit not yet complete).

5.6.4   Procedures

A preliminary announcement may be based on financial statements where the audit report has been finalised, or on financial statements whose audit is at an advanced stage. Whilst there is the expectation that the figures in the preliminary announcement will be consistent with those in the final audited financial statements, this cannot be guaranteed where the full financial statements are yet to be approved.

The Bulletin defines an 'advanced stage' as being where the audit has been completed, including appropriate reviews by personnel not otherwise involved in the audit, subject only to the following:

- clearing outstanding audit matters which the auditors are satisfied are unlikely to have a material impact on the financial statements or disclosures in the preliminary announcement;
- completing audit procedures on the detail of note disclosures to the financial statements that will not have a material impact on the primary financial statements and completing their reading of the other information in the annual report in accordance with ISA (UK and Ireland) 720, *Other information in documents containing audited financial statements*;
- updating the subsequent events review to cover the period between the issue of the preliminary announcement and the date of the auditors' report on the financial statements; and
- obtaining final signed written representations, where relevant, from management and establishing that the financial statements have been reviewed and approved by the directors.

TABLE 7: Example paragraphs for engagement letter where audit is complete

Review of preliminary announcement

The Listing Rules state that 'a preliminary statement of annual results ... must be agreed with the company's auditor prior to publication'. As directors of the company, you are responsible for preparing and issuing any preliminary announcement and ensuring that we agree to its release.

We undertake to review the preliminary announcement having regard to Bulletin 2008/2 *The Auditors' Association with Preliminary Announcements Made in Accordance with the Requirements of the UK and Irish Listing Rules*, issued by the Auditing Practices Board. Accordingly, our review will be limited to checking the accuracy of extraction of the financial information in the preliminary announcement from the audited financial statements of the company for that year, considering whether any 'alternative performance measures' and associated narrative explanations may be misleading and reading the management commentary, including any comments on, or separate presentation of, the final interim period figures, and considering whether it is in conflict with the information that we obtained in the course of our audit.

You will provide us with such information and explanations as we consider necessary for the purposes of our work. We shall request sight of the preliminary announcement in sufficient time to enable us to complete our work. The Board/Committee of the Board will formally approve the preliminary announcement before we agree to it.

TABLE 8: Example paragraphs for engagement letter where audit is not yet complete

Review of preliminary announcement

The Listing Rules state that 'a preliminary statement of annual results ... must be agreed with the company's auditor prior to publication'. As directors of the company, you are responsible for preparing and issuing the preliminary announcement and ensuring that we agree to its release.

We undertake to review the preliminary announcement having regard to Bulletin 2008/2 *The Auditors' Association with Preliminary Announcements Made in Accordance with the Requirements of the UK and Irish Listing Rules* issued by the Auditing Practices Board. Accordingly, our review will be limited to checking the accuracy of extraction of the financial information in the preliminary announcement from the audited financial statements of the company for that year, considering whether any 'alternative performance measures' and associated narrative explanations may be misleading and reading the management commentary, including any comments on, or separate presentation of, the final interim period figures, and considering whether it is in conflict with the information that we have obtained in the course of our audit.

You will provide us with such information and explanations as we consider necessary for the purposes of our work. We shall request sight of the preliminary announcement in sufficient time to enable us to complete our work. The Board/Committee of the Board will formally approve the preliminary announcement before we agree to it. You will also make available to us the proposed text of the company's annual report.

We will not agree to the release of the preliminary announcement until the audit is complete subject only to the following:

- clearing outstanding audit matters which we are satisfied are unlikely to have a material impact on the financial statements or disclosures insofar as they affect the preliminary announcement;
- completing audit procedures on the detail of note disclosures to the financial statements that will not have a material impact on the primary financial statements and completing our reading of the other information in the annual report in accordance with ISA (UK and Ireland) 720 *Other information in documents containing audited financial statements*;
- updating the subsequent events review to cover the period between the date of the preliminary announcement and the date of our auditor's report on the financial statements; and
- obtaining final signed written representations from management and establishing that the financial statements have been reviewed and approved by the directors.

The scope of our work will be necessarily limited in that we will only be able to check the consistency of the preliminary announcement with draft financial statements on which our audit is incomplete. Accordingly, we shall not, at that stage, know whether further adjustments may be required to those draft financial statements. Consequently, there is an unavoidable risk that the company may wish to revise its preliminary announcement in the light of audit findings or other developments occurring between the preliminary announcement being notified to a regulatory information service and the completion of the audit.

In the event that we disagree with the release of the preliminary announcement we will send you a letter setting out the reasons why.

The Bulletin provides a list of audit procedures which will normally be carried out by the auditors in relation to the preliminary announcement, regardless of whether that announcement is based on a draft statement or extracted from audited financial statements. These procedures will ensure that there are no material differences expected between the preliminary and final figures:

- checking that the figures in the preliminary announcement covering the full year have been accurately extracted from the audited or draft financial statements and reflect the presentation to be adopted in the audited financial statements. For example, any summarisation should not change the order in which items are presented where this is specified by law or accounting standards;
- considering whether the information (including the management commentary) is consistent with other expected contents of the annual report of which the auditors are aware; and
- considering whether the financial information in the preliminary announcement is misstated. A misstatement exists when the information is stated incorrectly or presented in a misleading manner. A misstatement may arise, for example, as a result of an omission of a significant change of accounting policy disclosed or due to be disclosed in the audited financial statements.

Auditors should also consider whether the preliminary announcement includes:

- the directors' statements required by s435 of the Companies Act 2006; and
- the minimum information required in interim reports under Listing Rule 9.7A.1.

5.6.5 *Pro forma information*

The APB's alert to auditors of listed companies in February 2003 (reiterated in December 2003) regarding misleading pro forma information or 'alternative performance measures' (APMs) included in preliminary announcements states that, whilst much pro forma information is of use to shareholders, it has the greatest potential to be misleading when:

- it is given greater prominence than the statutory numbers;
- there is no description of the APM;
- the APMs resemble defined performance measures but do not actually have the characteristics of the defined measures; or
- adjusted numbers are not reconciled to the statutory numbers.

The essence of this warning has been included in the body of the updated Bulletin.

Pro forma information will typically include adjustments of statutory results to exclude certain items to give alternative earnings figures, such as EBITDA, to exclude certain business segments or to reflect significant non-adjusting post balance sheet events, such as disposals or acquisitions.

Therefore Bulletin 2008/2 recommends that prior to auditors agreeing the release of a preliminary announcement, they should consider whether:

- appropriate prominence has been given to the statutory numbers;
- any APMs are clearly and accurately described, stating the purpose for which it has been prepared;
- any APMs are reconciled to the statutory numbers; and,
- any APMs are not misleading in the form or context in which they are given.

5.6.6   Management commentary

Auditors should read any management commentary in the preliminary statement, together with any other narrative disclosures and any final interim period figures, and consider whether they are in conflict with the information that they have obtained in the course of their work. If it is available, auditors should also read the text of any Chairman's Statement, operating and financial review or similar document to be included in the annual report to ensure no discrepancies with the preliminary statement.

5.6.7   Directors' approval

The preliminary statement should state the date on which it was approved by the directors. Auditors do not agree the preliminary announcement until the Board has formally approved its entire content.

5.6.8   Modification of the auditor's report

The Listing Rules require that where an auditor is likely to issue a modified report (that is a qualification or emphasis of matter), any preliminary announcement should make reference to this. The directors should give adequate prominence to this information in the announcement and auditors should consider whether this is the case.

When giving details of the likely modification, care should be taken to comply with s435 of the Companies Act 2006 which states that an auditor's report on the statutory accounts cannot be published with non-statutory accounts.

5.6.9   Reporting

Auditors are not required to prepare an audit report on the preliminary announcement. However, the Bulletin recommends that, to avoid possible misunderstanding and to make explicit their agreement to the preliminary announcement, they should issue a letter to the company to signify their agreement. An example of this letter is shown in **Table 9**.

TABLE 9: Example report on preliminary announcement

Dear Sirs

In accordance with the terms of our engagement letter dated [ ], we have reviewed the attached proposed preliminary announcement of XYZ plc for the year ended [ ]. Our work was conducted having regard to Bulletin 2008/2 *The Auditor's Association with Preliminary Announcements Made in Accordance with the Requirements of the UK and Irish Listing Rules* issued by the Auditing Practices Board. As directors you are responsible for preparing and issuing the preliminary announcement.

Our responsibility is solely to give our agreement to the preliminary announcement having carried out the procedures specified in the Bulletin as providing a basis for such agreement. In this regard we agree to the preliminary announcement being notified to a Regulatory Information Service.

[*Insert paragraph* below only where the preliminary announcement is made before the audit is complete.*]

Yours faithfully
Registered auditors
Address
Date

* As you are aware we are not in a position to sign our auditor's report on the annual financial statements as they have not yet been approved by the directors and we have not yet [*insert significant procedures that are yet to be completed, for example completing the subsequent events review and obtaining final representations from directors*].Consequently there can be no absolute certainty that we will be in a position to issue an unmodified audit opinion on financial statements consistent with the results and financial position reported in the preliminary announcement. However, at the present time, we are not aware of any matters that may give rise to a modification to our report. In the event that such matters do come to our attention we will inform you immediately.

Fundamental uncertainty

The Bulletin also states that where the final audit report does, or will, contain an explanatory paragraph dealing with a fundamental uncertainty, the auditors must not agree to the preliminary announcement unless the directors have made mention of the fundamental uncertainty. It is the directors' responsibility to make this disclosure and the preliminary announcement need not refer to the auditors in this respect.

Disclosure of the fundamental uncertainty must also be made where such conditions exist at the time of clearance of the preliminary announcement, even if it is likely that this uncertainty will be resolved by the time the final audit report is signed. If the matter is cleared before the final audit opinion is given, the change in circumstances since the preliminary announcement should be disclosed in a note to the financial statements.

Unresolved matters

If the precise details of a matter giving rise to a qualification or explanatory paragraph are critical to the full understanding of the auditors' report, and this matter is still to be resolved, the Bulletin strongly recommends that the auditors should not agree to the release of the preliminary announcement containing information about a qualification until the matter is resolved.

5.6.10   Announcements not agreed

Where the auditors are not in agreement with the content of the preliminary announcement, they should communicate this to the directors in a letter setting out the reasons for this disagreement and advising the directors not to release the announcement to a Regulatory Information Service.

Where they become aware that the company has released the announcement, without first obtaining their consent, they should first ascertain the reasons for this. If the announcement was released inadvertently, the Bulletin advises auditors to remind the directors of their obligations under the Listing Rules to obtain the auditors' agreement. However, where an announcement with which they disagree has been released, the Bulletin advises taking legal advice with a view to notifying the Listing Authority of the fact that the announcement had not been agreed.

5.7   ISRE 2400

5.7.1   Introduction

International Standard on Review Engagements (ISRE) 2400, *Engagements to Review Financial Statements* applies when a practitioner who is not the auditor of an entity undertakes an engagement to review financial statements. The principles contained therein should also be applied to reviews of other historical information.

The IAASB have announced their plans to undertake a review of ISRE 2400 particularly in relation to aligning the ISRE with:

- the *International Framework for Assurance Engagements*;
- other ISREs, including ISRE 2410 on the review of interim financial information (see **Chapter 16**); and
- revised and redrafted ISAs.

In response to this, IFAC commissioned a report setting out areas in need of revision. This Consultation Paper was issued by IFAC in September 2008.

The areas identified were:

- the objective of reviewing historical financial information;
- consideration of a 'moderate level of assurance' and engagement risk;
- conditions for engagement acceptance;

- evidence required to support the review engagement report;
- communication with those charged with governance;
- reporting and communicating with users; and
- removing cross references to ISAs and ensuring that ISREs can stand alone.

The IAASB plan to commence work on the update to ISRE 2400 in 2009.

6 OTHER STATUTORY AUDIT REPORTS

6.1 INTRODUCTION

This Chapter considers the other types of reports that auditors may be required to make under the Companies Act. It covers the reports on:

- distributions;
- purchase and redemption of own shares;
- re-registration of companies;
- allotment of shares otherwise than for cash; and
- transfer of non cash assets.

The guidance on the form of these is contained in Bulletin 2008/9 *Miscellaneous Reports by Auditors required by the United Kingdom Companies Act 2006*. For some reports there is additional guidance on the procedures necessary to support such reports and the source of this has been noted below.

Under The Companies Act 2006 (Commencement No. 5, Transitional Provisions and Savings) Order 2007 (SI 2007/3495 (C. 150)), Sch. 4, para. 51, there is no longer a requirement for auditors of a private company to make a report on the directors' statutory declaration to provide financial assistance for the purchase of its own shares or those of a holding company. This is effective in relation to financial assistance given on or after 1 October 2008.

Following the publication of Bulletin 2009/2 *Auditor's Reports on Financial Statements in the United Kingdom* in April 2009, the format of standard auditor's reports was changed for accounting periods ending on or after 5 April 2009. Until revised guidance is issued in relation to the reports in this chapter, this publication retains the examples from the most recent specific material.

6.2 DISTRIBUTIONS: QUALIFIED REPORTS

6.2.1 Legal background

Section 837(4) of the Companies Act 2006 requires that where the auditors' report on a company's financial statements contains a qualification, before those statements may be used to justify a distribution, it is necessary for the company's auditors to make a further statement. This must be laid before the members in general meeting, and cover the effect of the qualification on the company's ability to make a distribution.

6.2.2 Guidance

The statement may be issued as a separate report to the members and sent to the company secretary, or as an additional paragraph in the normal report to the members. This will depend upon the individual circumstances.

The report is restricted to the consideration of the effect of the last qualification on the company's distributable profits. The auditors are required to state whether the subject matter of the qualification is material for determining whether the proposed distributions, and any which have not yet been proposed, are permitted. Some qualifications will not be material because of their nature, for example, if the qualification related to the misclassification of creditors due within one year, there would be no effect on distributable profits.

Other qualifications will by their nature be potentially material. For example, a qualification for failure to make a provision in respect of the carrying value of properties could have an adverse effect on the distributable reserves of the company. Here the auditors would have to assess the maximum potential write down, if known, before they could say whether the proposed distribution was permitted.

It should be noted that fundamental uncertainties do not give rise to a qualification and as a consequence will not result in the need for a report under s837(4).

If they are unable to quantify the effect of the qualification, its effect would have to be assessed as material for the purposes of determining the distributable reserves, unless auditors can conclude that the qualification either does not impact distributable profits or that its possible impact could only be favourable. In this case the auditors would have to state either that the qualification is material or that they are unable to form an opinion whether it is material. Whatever opinion is given, legally the company could pay a dividend so long as a statement, irrespective of its conclusion, is laid before the members. It is only when the auditors do not provide such a statement that the distribution is illegal.

A disclaimer of opinion on the financial statements as a whole would be material as the auditor would be unable to form an opinion on the amount at which the company's distributable profits are stated.

The following tables provide suitable wordings for these reports. **Table 1** is where a separate report is given and the amount of the proposed distribution is known. If the proposed dividend is as yet unquantified, the wording in **Table 2** should be used or if a statement is to be made about 'any distribution' **Table 3** should be used. If a separate report is not required, the additional paragraph should be based on **Table 4**. All these examples are effective where a distribution is made on or after 6 April 2008.

If a separate statement is made, the date used should be that on which the statement is completed and will need to be by the date of the distribution.

TABLE 1: Report required on company's ability to make a distribution

Statement of the Independent Auditor to the [members/shareholders] of XYZ Limited pursuant to s837(4) of the Companies Act 2006

We have audited the financial statements of XYZ Limited for the year ended ... in accordance with International Standards on Auditing (United Kingdom and Ireland) issued by the Auditing Practices Board and have expressed a qualified opinion thereon in our report dated ....[1]

Respective responsibilities of directors and auditors

[Summarisation of directors' responsibilities with respect to the financial statements referred to in the introductory paragraph]. They are also responsible for considering whether the company, subsequent to the balance sheet date, has sufficient distributable profits to make a distribution at the time the distribution is made.

Our responsibility is to report whether, in our opinion the subject matter of our qualification of our auditors' report on the financial statements for the year ended ... is material for determining, by reference to those financial statements, whether the distribution proposed by the company is permitted under s830 [s831/832[2]] of the Companies Act 2006. We are not required to form an opinion on whether the company has sufficient distributable reserves to make the distribution proposed at the time it is made.

Opinion

In our opinion the subject matter of that qualification is not material for determining, by reference to those financial statements, whether [the distribution of £ ... /the interim/final dividend for the year ended ... of £ ...] proposed by the company is permitted under s830 (*s831/832*) of the Companies Act 2006.

Statutory Auditor
Address
Date

TABLE 2: Alternative opinion paragraph where amount of distribution not known

In our opinion the subject matter of that qualification is not material for determining, by reference to those financial statements, whether a distribution of not more than £ ... by the company is permitted under s830 (*s831/832*) of the Companies Act 2006.

---

[1] Auditors may include a 'Bannerman Statement' as part of the opening section of their report (see **3.20**).
[2] Section 831 should be used for public companies and ss831 and 832 if the company is also an investment company.

> **TABLE 3: Alternative opinion paragraph concerning ability to make 'any distribution'**
>
> In our opinion the subject matter of that qualification is not material for determining, by reference to those financial statements, whether any distribution proposed by the company is permitted under s830 (*s831/832*) of the Companies Act 2006.

> **TABLE 4: Additional paragraph concerning ability to make a distribution for audit report on annual accounts**
>
> *Statement pursuant to [s837(4)/839(6³)] of the Companies Act 2006*
>
> *Respective responsibilities of directors and auditors*
>
> In addition to their responsibilities described above, the directors are also responsible for considering whether the company, subsequent to the balance sheet date, has sufficient distributable profits to make a distribution at the time the distribution is made.
>
> Our responsibility is to report whether, in our opinion the subject matter of our qualification of our auditors' report on the financial statements for the year ended ... is material for determining, by reference to those financial statements, whether the distribution proposed by the company is permitted under s830 [s831/832[4]] of the Companies Act 2006. We are not required to form an opinion on whether the company has sufficient distributable reserves to make the distribution proposed at the time it is made.
>
> *Opinion*
>
> In our opinion the subject matter of the above qualification is not material for determining whether [the distribution of £ ... /the interim/final dividend for the year ended ... of £ ...] proposed by the company is permitted under s830 (*s831/832*) of the Companies Act 2006.
>
> Statutory Auditor
> Address
> Date

6.3 DISTRIBUTIONS: INITIAL DISTRIBUTIONS

6.3.1 Legal background

Where a company wishes to make a distribution during its first accounting period, or after its end but before the accounts have been laid before the members in general meeting, initial accounts have to be prepared. These accounts should be prepared under the accounting provisions of the Companies Act, although in the case of a parent company group accounts are not required.

---

[3] Section 837(4) applies where the last annual accounts are used. Section 839(6) applies where initial accounts are used and are qualified.
[4] Section 831 should be used for public companies and ss831 and 832 if the company is also an investment company.

Where the company concerned is a public company, the auditors are required to issue an audit report on these accounts in accordance with s839(5) of the 2006 Act.

6.3.2 Guidance

This report may be addressed to the directors, as there is no statutory requirement for it to be sent to anyone else, and should identify the period covered by the initial accounts. As with any report, the audit should be carried out in accordance with ISAs (UK and Ireland) and this should be stated in the report.

The auditors are required to comment on whether the accounts have been properly prepared in accordance with ss395 to 397 and the regulations made there under of the Companies Act 2006, that is, the accounts give a true and fair view and are in accordance with the accounting provisions of the Act. This, in effect, means that the procedures necessary to support such an opinion could be almost as extensive as those necessary to support the opinion on annual financial statements. If the report is qualified then a paragraph on whether the matter is material to the distribution must be included (see **Table 4** above).

An example report is shown in **Table 5**. This example is effective where a distribution is made on or after 6 April 2008.

TABLE 5: Report on initial accounts of a public company wishing to make a distribution

Report of the Independent Auditor to the directors of XYZ Plc under s839(5) of the Companies Act 2006

We have examined the initial accounts of XYZ Plc for the period from ... to ... which comprise [state the primary financial statements such as the Profit and Loss Account, the Balance Sheet, the Cash Flow Statement, the Statement of Total Recognised Gains and Losses] and the related notes. The initial accounts have been prepared under the accounting policies set out therein.[5]

Respective responsibilities of directors and auditors

As described ... the directors are responsible for the preparation of the initial accounts in accordance with applicable law and United Kingdom Accounting Standards (United Kingdom Generally Accepted Accounting Practice).

Our responsibility is to report to you our opinion as to whether the initial accounts have been properly prepared within the meaning of s839(4) of the Companies Act 2006.

---

[5] Auditors may include a 'Bannerman Statement' as part of the opening section of their report (see **3.20**).

Opinion

In our opinion the initial accounts for the period from ... to ... have been properly prepared within the meaning of s839(4) of the Companies Act 2006.

[Signature]
John Smith (Senior Statutory Auditor)
for and on behalf of ABC LLP, Statutory Auditor
Address
Date

6.4   PURCHASE AND REDEMPTION OF OWN SHARES

6.4.1   *Legal background*

Where a private company decides to redeem or purchase its own shares wholly or partly out of capital, this has to be approved by a special resolution of the company. A directors' declaration is required concerning the amount by which the purchase price exceeds any available profits (the permissible capital payment) and the solvency of the company. This statement has to be accompanied by an auditor's report.

The auditor's report should be addressed to the directors and states that the amount specified as the permissible capital payment has been properly determined and that the solvency statement is reasonable. The report should be made and dated in the week prior to the meeting which passes the special resolution.

6.4.2   *Guidance*

The auditor's report:

● should not be dated earlier than the declaration;
● cannot be qualified and should not be issued unless unqualified.

An example of the report is shown in **Table 6**. It is effective for reports dated on or after 1 October 2009.

There is no published guidance on the procedures that are necessary to support such a report. In general, before giving the report the auditors must:

● be satisfied that the directors' assumptions are realistic and consistently applied;
● review the cash flow forecasts;
● review asset and liability values, including provisions and future commitments;

- confirm that any support being received from lenders or group companies will be continued; and
- ensure that the permissible capital payment calculation is correct, taking into account any movements since the relevant accounts were prepared. These relevant accounts need not be audited but must be sufficient to enable a reasonable judgement to be made as to the financial position of the company.

TABLE 6: Report for private company redeeming or purchasing shares out of capital

Report of the Independent Auditor to the Directors of XYZ Limited pursuant to s714(6) of the Companies Act 2006

We report on the attached statement of the directors dated . . . , prepared pursuant to the Companies Act 2006, in connection with the company's proposed [purchase]/ [redemption] of . . . (*number*) [ordinary]/[preferred] shares by a payment out of capital.[6]

Basis of opinion

We have inquired into the state of the company's state of affairs in order to review the bases for the directors' statement.

Opinion

In our opinion, the amount of £ . . . specified in the directors' statement as the permissible capital payment for the shares to be [purchased]/[redeemed] is properly determined in accordance with ss710 to 712 of the Companies Act 2006.

We are not aware of anything to indicate that the opinion expressed by the directors in their statement as to any of the matters mentioned in s714(3) of the Companies Act 2006 is unreasonable in all the circumstances.

Statutory Auditor
Address
Date

6.5   RE-REGISTRATION OF COMPANIES

6.5.1   *Legal background*

When a private company wishes to re-register as a public company, it has to deliver certain documents to the Registrar of Companies before it will be issued with a new certificate of incorporation. These include a copy of the company's balance sheet, at a date not more than seven months before the application, together with an auditor's report on that balance sheet which is either:

- unqualified; or

---

[6] Auditors may include a 'Bannerman Statement' as part of the opening section of their report (see **3.20**).

- qualified and the auditor expresses an opinion that the qualification is not material for determining the net assets of the company,

and a further written statement from the auditor. If the last financial statements are at a date more than seven months before, an up-to-date balance sheet will need to be prepared and audited.

The auditor's statement should confirm that the company's net assets are not less than the total of its share capital and non-distributable reserves.

6.5.2 Guidance

The procedures to support such a report may be restricted to a simple examination of the amounts in the relevant financial statements. The report should indicate that the work is limited to such an examination.

If the balance sheet is qualified, the auditor will have to state that this is not material for the purposes of determining whether at the balance sheet date the net assets of the company were not less than the aggregate of its called-up share capital and non-distributable reserves. The considerations required for this are similar to those for the effect of qualifications on distributions. Where this is the case an extra paragraph will need to be inserted in the auditor's statement as illustrated in **Table 7**.

The auditor's report should not be dated earlier than the date of the audit report on the relevant balance sheet.

If there has been a change of auditor, the new auditor can accept the balance sheet audited by their predecessors unless the audit report contains a material qualification. The new auditor should refer in their report to the firm that has carried out the audit of the relevant balance sheet.

The following examples should be used:

- a balance sheet from the previous annual financial statements is reported on without qualification (**Table 7**);
- a balance sheet from the previous annual financial statements is reported on with a qualification in respect of proper preparation in accordance with the Companies Act 2006, but the qualification is not material (**Table 8**);
- a specially prepared balance sheet is reported on without qualification (**Table 9**); and
- a specially prepared balance sheet is reported on with a qualification in respect of proper preparation in accordance with the Companies Act 2006, but the qualification is not material (**Table 10**).

The examples are effective for reports made on or after 1 October 2009.

TABLE 7: Statement required when a private company wishes to re-register as a public company – previous balance sheet with no qualification

Statement of the Independent Auditor to the directors of XYZ Limited for the purpose of s92(1)(b) and (c) of the Companies Act 2006

We have examined the balance sheet and related notes of XYZ Limited as at ... which formed part of the financial statements for the year then ended which were audited by [us]/[name of firm].[7]

Respective responsibilities of directors and auditors

The company's directors are responsible for the preparation of the balance sheet and related notes.

It is our responsibility to:

- report on whether the balance sheet has been properly prepared in accordance with the requirements of the Companies Act 2006; and
- form an independent opinion, based on our examination, concerning the relationship between the company's net assets and its called up share capital and undistributable reserves at the balance sheet date.

Opinion concerning proper preparation of balance sheet

In our opinion the audited balance sheet as at ... has been properly prepared in accordance with the requirements of the Companies Act 2006.

Statement on net assets

In our opinion, at ... the amount of the company's net assets (within the meaning given to that expression by s831(2) of the Companies Act 2006) was not less than the aggregate of its called-up share capital and undistributable reserves.

Statutory Auditor
Address
Date

TABLE 8: Statement required when a private company wishes to re-register as a public company – previous balance sheet with non material qualification

Statement of the Independent Auditor to the directors of XYZ Limited for the purpose of s92(1)(b) and (c) of the Companies Act 2006

We have examined the balance sheet and related notes of XYZ Limited as at ... which formed part of the financial statements for the year then ended which were audited by [us]/[name of firm].[8]

Respective responsibilities of directors and auditors

The company's directors are responsible for the preparation of the balance sheet and related notes.

---

[7] Auditors may include a 'Bannerman Statement' as part of the opening section of their report (see **3.20**).
[8] Auditors may include a 'Bannerman Statement' as part of the opening section of their report (see **3.20**).

It is our responsibility to:

- report on whether the balance sheet has been properly prepared in accordance with the requirements of the Companies Act 2006; and
- form an independent opinion, based on our examination, concerning the relationship between the company's net assets and its called up share capital and undistributable reserves at the balance sheet date.

Qualified opinion concerning proper preparation of balance sheet

[We]/[Name of firm] audited the financial statements for the year ended … and expressed a qualified opinion regarding the proper preparation of the balance sheet in accordance with the requirements of the Companies Act 2006.

The matter giving rise to [our]/[the] qualification is not material for determining by reference to the balance sheet at … whether, at that date, the amount of the company's net assets (within the meaning given to that expression by s831(2) of the Companies Act 2006) was not less than the aggregate of its called-up share capital and undistributable reserves.

Statement on net assets

In our opinion, at … the amount of the company's net assets (within the meaning given to that expression by s831(2) of the Companies Act 2006) was not less than the aggregate of its called-up share capital and undistributable reserves.

Statutory Auditor
Address
Date

TABLE 9: Report for re-registration where new balance sheet prepared and is unqualified

Report of the Independent Auditor to the directors of XYZ Limited for the purpose of s92(1)(b) and (c) of the Companies Act 2006

We have audited the balance sheet and related notes of XYZ Limited as at … set out on pages … to … which have been prepared under the accounting policies set out therein.[9]

Respective responsibilities of directors and auditors

The company's directors are responsible for the preparation of the balance sheet and related notes.

It is our responsibility to:

- report on whether the balance sheet has been properly prepared in accordance with the requirements of the Companies Act 2006 that would have applied if it had been prepared for a financial year of the company with such modifications as are necessary by reason of that fact; and
- form an independent opinion concerning the relationship between the company's net assets and its called up share capital and undistributable reserves at the balance sheet date.

---

[9] Auditors may include a 'Bannerman Statement' as part of the opening section of their report (see **3.20**).

Opinion concerning proper preparation of balance sheet

In our opinion the audited balance sheet as at ... has been properly prepared in accordance with the requirements of the Companies Act 2006, which would have applied had the balance sheet been prepared for a financial year of the company.

Statement on net assets

In our opinion, at ... the amount of the company's net assets (within the meaning given to that expression by s831(2) of the Companies Act 2006) was not less than the aggregate of its called-up share capital and undistributable reserves.

Statutory Auditor
Address
Date

TABLE 10: Report for re-registration where new balance sheet prepared and has a non material qualification

Report of the Independent Auditor to the directors of XYZ Limited for the purpose of s92(1)(b) and (c) of the Companies Act 2006

We have audited the balance sheet and related notes of XYZ Limited as at ... set out on pages ... to ... which have been prepared under the accounting policies set out therein.[10]

Respective responsibilities of directors and auditors

The company's directors are responsible for the preparation of the balance sheet and related notes.

It is our responsibility to:

- report on whether the balance sheet has been properly prepared in accordance with the requirements of the Companies Act 2006 that would have applied if it had been prepared for a financial year of the company with such modifications as are necessary by reason of that fact; and
- form an independent opinion concerning the relationship between the company's net assets and its called up share capital and undistributable reserves at the balance sheet date.

Qualified opinion concerning proper preparation of balance sheet

[Except for [*describe area of non-compliance with CA 2006*] in our opinion the balance sheet and related notes as at ... have been properly prepared in accordance with the provisions of the Companies Act 2006, which would have applied had the balance sheet been prepared for a financial year of the company.][11]

[Because [*describe area of non-compliance with CA 2006*] in our opinion the balance sheet and related notes as at ... have not been properly prepared in accordance with

---

[10] Auditors may include a 'Bannerman Statement' as part of the opening section of their report (see **3.20**).
[11] Use this wording if the auditor has expressed a qualified opinion concerning the proper preparation of the balance sheet.

the provisions of the Companies Act 2006, which would have applied had the balance sheet been prepared for a financial year of the company.][12]

However, in our opinion this matter is not material for determining by reference to the balance sheet at ... whether, at that date, the amount of the company's net assets (within the meaning given to that expression by s831(2) of the Companies Act 2006) was not less than the aggregate of its called-up share capital and undistributable reserves.

Statement on net assets

In our opinion, at ... the amount of the company's net assets (within the meaning given to that expression by s831(2) of the Companies Act 2006) was not less than the aggregate of its called-up share capital and undistributable reserves.

Statutory Auditor
Address
Date

6.6 ALLOTMENT OF SHARES OTHERWISE THAN FOR CASH

6.6.1 *Legal background*

All companies may allot shares and receive payment for them in something other than cash. However, where the company concerned is a public company, during the six months prior to the allotment, it is necessary to obtain a report on the value of the asset to be received instead of cash.

This report should be prepared by independent accountants. This is either the company's auditors, or a firm suitably qualified to be the company's auditors, i.e., a registered auditor. The accountants are entitled to rely on an expert, who is not connected with the company, to make a valuation of part or all of the asset.

If the company's own statutory auditor is requested to undertake a valuation in accordance with s599 of the Companies Act 2006 the standards and guidance in APB Ethical Standard 5 (Revised) are applied (see **Chapter 2**).

The report should be addressed to the company and sent to the company secretary for distribution to the allottees. It should include the following information:

- the nominal value of the shares in question;
- any premium payable on them;
- a description of the consideration;

---

[12] Use this wording if the auditor has expressed an adverse opinion concerning the proper preparation of the balance sheet.

- a description of the part of the consideration valued by the independent accountants, the method used and the date of the valuation; and
- the extent to which the nominal value of the shares and any premium are to be treated as paid up by the consideration and in cash.

If the valuation was carried out by someone else, the independent accountants should give their opinion on whether that valuation is reasonable and provide details on the expert's qualifications, the method used, and the amount and the date of the valuation. The expert must be independent of the company.

Where the allotment of shares represents only part of the consideration for the asset, the report should apply to as much of the value as is attributable to the shares. It must state what valuations have been made to determine the proportion of the consideration and the reasons for and methods of that valuation.

6.6.2   Guidance

The accountants' work will consist of:

- either valuing the consideration themselves or assessing whether it is reasonable to accept an external valuation;
- confirming that the value of the consideration is not less than the total amount to be treated as being paid up on the shares, together with any premium; and
- considering whether there has been any change in the value of the asset since the valuation and confirming that it has not diminished. Where they have used an expert to provide the valuation it may be necessary to obtain written confirmation that there has been no diminution since the original valuation exercise.

The report, which must not be qualified, is shown in **Table 11**. If it were qualified the company registrars would be unable to issue the share certificates. This example is effective for reports made on or after 1 October 2009.

TABLE 11: Report where shares allotted other than for cash

Report of the Independent [Valuer] [Auditor] to XYZ Plc for the purposes of s593(1) of the Companies Act 2006

We report on the value of the consideration for the allotment to . . . [*name of allottee*] of . . . shares, having a nominal value of [. . .] each, to be issued at a premium of . . . pence per share. The shares and share premium are to be treated as fully paid up.

The consideration for the allotment to . . . [*name of allottee*] is [the freehold building situated at . . . [*address*]] and . . . [*number*] shares, having a nominal value of [. . .] each in Blue Chip plc.[13]

---

[13] Auditors may include a 'Bannerman Statement' as part of the opening section of their report (see **3.20**)

Basis of valuation

The freehold building was valued on the basis of open market value by [*name of expert*], a Fellow of the Royal Institution of Chartered Surveyors.

The shares in Blue Chip Plc were valued by us on . . . on the basis of the price shown in The Stock Exchange Daily Official List at . . .

Opinion

In our opinion:

- it is reasonable to accept the valuation made by [name of expert];
- the methods of valuation of the freehold building and of the shares in Blue Chip Plc were reasonable in all the circumstances; and
- there appears to have been no material change in the value of either part of the consideration since the date(s) at which the valuations were made.

On the basis of the valuations, in our opinion, the value of the total consideration is not less than the aggregate of the nominal value and share premium to be treated as paid up by the consideration.

Qualified independent person
Address
Date

6.7 TRANSFER OF NON-CASH ASSETS TO A PUBLIC COMPANY BY ONE OF ITS MEMBERS

6.7.1 *Legal background*

A similar report to that described in **6.6** above is required when a public company, in the first two years following its registration, purchases a non-cash asset from one of its members for a consideration of at least one-tenth of the nominal value of its issued share capital. The Act does not allow such a purchase without approval by an ordinary resolution of the company and the submission of a report by independent accountants.

This report must be prepared by independent accountants and must be made to the company in the six months preceding the allotment of shares.

As with the report made in **6.6** above, if the company's own statutory auditor is requested to undertake a valuation in accordance with s599 of the Companies Act 2006 the standards and guidance in APB Ethical Standard 5 (Revised) are applied (see **Chapter 2**).

Instead of being sent to the allottees it will be addressed to the company and sent to the members and will detail the asset to be purchased by the company, together with details of the valuation. Again this report must not be qualified.

An example report is set out in **Table 12**, and is effective for reports made on or after 1 October 2009.

TABLE 12: Report where non-cash assets are transferred to a public company by certain of its members

Report of the Independent [Valuer] [Auditor] to XYZ Plc for the purposes of section 599 of the Companies Act 2006

We report on the transfer of non-cash assets to XYZ plc ('the Company') by subscribers to the Company's memorandum of association.

The consideration to be received by the Company is [a freehold building situated at . . . [*address*]] ('the consideration to be received').

The consideration to be given by the Company is [number] shares, having a nominal value of [. . .] each in LMN plc ('the consideration to be given').[14]

Basis of valuation

The freehold building was valued on the basis of open market value by [name of expert], a Fellow of the Royal Institution of Chartered Surveyors.

The shares in LMN Plc were valued by us on . . . on the basis of the price shown in The Stock Exchange Daily Official List at . . .

Opinion

In our opinion:

- it is reasonable to accept the valuation made by [name of expert];
- the methods of valuation of the freehold building and of the shares in LMN Plc were reasonable in all the circumstances; and
- there appears to have been no material change in the value of either part of the consideration since the date(s) at which the valuations were made.

On the basis of the valuations, in our opinion, the value of the total consideration to be received by the Company is not less than the value of the consideration to be given by the Company.

Qualified independent person
Address
Date

---
[14] Auditors may include a 'Bannerman Statement' as part of the opening section of their report (see **3.20**)

7 REPORTS ON ACCOUNTS PREPARED BY ACCOUNTANTS

7.1 INTRODUCTION

For accounting periods ending on or after 30 March 2004 companies with a turnover of less than £5.6 million are exempt from the Companies Act requirement for an audit. Small groups whose total turnover falls below the £5.6 million threshold are also eligible for the exemption.

This limit has been steadily raised over recent years from £90,000 prior to August 1994, through £350,000 and most recently £1 million for periods ending between 26 July 2000 and 30 March 2004.

Charitable companies are excluded from making use of the increased exemptions until a full consultation has taken place. Audit exemption reports for small charities are covered in **Chapter 43**.

As a result of the increase in the audit exemption threshold there are a number of issues with which auditing practitioners have had to deal. Some of the considerations arising from the removal of many companies from the audit requirement are detailed in section **7.5**.

7.2 GUIDANCE

The original guidance on the form and content of reports issued by accountants who prepare accounts on behalf of clients was contained in Technical Release Audit 1/95 issued by the Audit Faculty of the ICAEW.

In April 2004, the Audit and Assurance Faculty of the ICAEW issued Audit 02/04, *Chartered Accountants' Reports on the Compilation of Financial Statements of Incorporated Entities* to supersede Audit 1/95 in relation to incorporated entities only. It was issued in response to the increasing number of companies that, since the increase in the audit threshold, no longer require statutory audit, but still require chartered accountants to compile their financial statements. In February 2005, Audit 01/05 *Chartered Accountants' Reports on the Compilation of Historical Financial Information of Unincorporated Entities* was published to supersede the remainder of Audit 1/95. However, where accountants of unincorporated entities are asked to compile a set of financial statements in full compliance with the provisions of UK GAAP they should follow the guidance in Audit 02/04.

The statement reminds accountants that the five fundamental ethical principles of integrity, objectivity, competence, performance and courtesy apply to compilation engagements as they do to audits. It also reminds them that no tests are required on the assertions underlying the information they are presented with and therefore reporting accountants can express no assurance on the financial statements.

7.3   INCORPORATED ENTITIES

7.3.1   Terms of engagement

Audit 02/04 states that there must be clear understanding between the client and the accountants regarding the terms of the engagement. An example engagement letter extract is provided, which is reproduced in **Table 1**.

In addition, accountants should consider whether it is appropriate to include a section on the limitation of the accountants' liability.

TABLE 1: Engagement letter extracts for the compilation of unaudited financial statements

Responsibilities of directors

As directors of the company, you are responsible for maintaining proper accounting records and for preparing financial statements which give a true and fair view and which have been prepared in accordance with the Companies Act 1985 ('the Act').

In preparing financial statements, you are required to:

(1)   select suitable accounting policies and then apply them consistently;

(2)   make judgements and estimates that are reasonable and prudent; and

(3)   prepare financial statements on a going concern basis unless it is inappropriate to presume that the company will continue in business.

You are responsible for keeping proper accounting records which disclose with reasonable accuracy at any time the financial position of the company and for ensuring that the financial statements comply with the Act. You are also responsible for safeguarding the assets of the company and hence for taking reasonable steps for the prevention and detection of fraud and other irregularities.

You are also responsible for determining whether in respect of each financial year, the company meets the conditions for exemption from audit, as set out in Section 249A [or 249AA] of the Act and for determining whether, in respect of that year, the exemption is not available for any of the reasons set out in Section 249B.

You have undertaken to make available to us, as and when required, all the company's accounting records and related financial information, including minutes of management and shareholders' meetings, necessary to carry out our work. You will make full disclosure to us of all relevant information.

Scope of the accountants' work

You have asked us to assist you in the preparation of the financial statements. We will compile the annual financial statements for your approval based on the accounting records maintained by you and the information and explanations given to us by you. We shall plan our work on the basis that no report is required by statute or regulation for the year, unless you inform us in writing to the contrary. In carrying out our engagement we will make enquiries of management and undertake any procedures that we judge appropriate but are under no obligation to perform procedures that may be required for assurance engagements such as audits or reviews.

You have advised us that the company is exempt from an audit of the financial statements. We will not carry out any work to determine whether or not the company is entitled to audit exemption. However, should our work indicate that the company is not entitled to the exemption, we will inform you of this.

Our work will not be an audit of the financial statements in accordance with Auditing Standards. Consequently, our work will not provide any assurance that the accounting records or the financial statements are free from material misstatement, whether caused by fraud, other irregularities or error and cannot be relied on to identify weaknesses in internal controls.

Since we have not carried out an audit, nor confirmed in any way the accuracy or reasonableness of the accounting records maintained by the company, we are unable to provide any assurance as to whether the financial statements that we prepare from those records present a true and fair view.

We have a professional duty to compile financial statements that conform with generally accepted accounting principles from the accounting records and information and explanations given to us. Furthermore, as directors, you have a duty to prepare financial statements that comply with the Act and applicable accounting standards. Where we identify that the financial statements do not conform to accepted accounting principles or if the accounting policies adopted are not immediately apparent this will need to be disclosed in the financial statements.

We have a professional responsibility not to allow our name to be associated with financial statements which may be misleading. Therefore, although we are not required to search for such matters, should we become aware, for any reason, that the financial statements may be misleading, we will discuss the matter with you with a view to agreeing appropriate adjustments and/or disclosures in the financial statements. In such circumstances where adjustments and/or disclosures that we consider appropriate are not made or where we are not provided with appropriate information, and as a result we consider that the financial statements are misleading, we will withdraw from the engagement.

As part of our normal procedures, we may request you to provide written confirmation of any information or explanations given by you orally during the course of our work.

Form of the accountants' report

We shall report to the Board of Directors, with any modifications that we consider may be necessary, that in accordance with this engagement letter and in order to assist you to fulfil your responsibilities, we have compiled, without carrying out an audit, the financial statements from the accounting records of the company and from the information and explanation supplied to us.

> **Liability provisions**
>
> We will perform the engagement with reasonable skill and care. The total aggregate liability to the Company and the Board of Directors, as a body, of whatever nature, whether in contract, tort or otherwise, of [name of accountants] for any losses whatsoever and howsoever caused arising from or in any way connected with this engagement shall not exceed [amount].

7.3.2 Directors' responsibilities

Although they have asked their accountants to compile the financial statements, directors are ultimately responsible for ensuring that the company maintains proper accounting records and for preparing financial statements which give a true and fair view and have been prepared in accordance with the Companies Act 1985. In addition directors are required to:

- select suitable accounting policies and then apply them consistently;
- make judgements and estimates that are reasonable and prudent; and
- prepare financial statements on a going concern basis unless it is inappropriate to presume that the company will continue in business.

They are also responsible for safeguarding the assets of the company and for taking steps for the prevention and detection of fraud and other irregularities.

7.3.3 Accountants' procedures

Accountants will plan their work, and this includes obtaining a general understanding of the business and operations of the company and the accounting principles and practices of the industry in which the company operates.

Accountants also consider whether the financial statements are consistent with their understanding of the company, but are under no obligation to perform procedures that may be required for an audit or review.

There is no mandatory requirement to document the work that has been carried out; however, adequate documentation will demonstrate that the work performed is of the requisite quality and has been performed in accordance with the terms of engagement. Accountants may use a disclosure checklist or software package to check that all relevant disclosures have been made.

Accountants will also consider obtaining written confirmation of oral representations made by management.

7.3.4 Misleading financial statements

Although accountants are not reviewing or auditing the financial statements, they may become aware that the financial statements are misleading. If this is the case, the matter should be discussed with management with a view to making adjustments or giving additional disclosures. If such amendments are not made, accountants should withdraw from the engagement.

If there are departures from accounting standards, but these have been adequately disclosed, the accountants may wish to highlight this in their compilation report.

7.3.5   *Approving financial statements*

The financial statements should be approved and signed by the directors before the accountants' report is signed.

The directors are statutorily responsible for their company's accounts. They are required to approve the accounts and the balance sheet should state the name of the directors signing the accounts on behalf of the board. Under s249B(4) of the Companies Act 1985, introduced by the audit exemption regulations, directors acknowledge, on the face of the balance sheet, their responsibilities for keeping accounting records and for preparing true and fair accounts as well as entitlement to exemption.

7.3.6   *Accountants' reports*

The aim of the accountants' report is for readers to draw comfort from the fact that the accounts have been compiled by a chartered accountant who is subject to the ethical and other guidance issued by the Institute. An example report is given in **Table 2**.

The financial statements must contain a reference to the fact that they are unaudited, either on the front cover or on each page of the financial statements.

TABLE 2: Example accountants' report

Chartered Accountants'/Accountant's Report to the Board of Directors on the Unaudited Financial Statements of XYZ Ltd

In accordance with the engagement letter dated [date], and in order to assist you to fulfil your duties under the Companies Act 1985, we have compiled the financial statements of the company which comprise [the Profit and Loss Account, the Balance Sheet, the Cash Flow Statement, the Statement of Total Recognised Gains and Losses] and the related notes from the accounting records and information and explanations you have given to us.

This report is made to the Company's Board of Directors, as a body, in accordance with the terms of our engagement. Our work has been undertaken so that we might compile the financial statements that we have been engaged to compile, report to the Company's Board of Directors that we have done so, and state those matters that we have agreed to state to them in this report and for no other purpose. To the fullest extent permitted by law, we do not accept or assume responsibility to anyone other

---

than the Company and the Company's Board of Directors, as a body, for our work or for this report.

We have carried out this engagement in accordance with technical guidance issued by the Institute of Chartered Accountants in England and Wales and have complied with the ethical guidance laid down by the Institute relating to members undertaking the compilation of financial statements.

You have acknowledged on the balance sheet for the year ended [date] your duty to ensure that the company has kept proper accounting records and to prepare financial statements that give a true and fair view under the Companies Act 1985. You consider that the company is exempt from the statutory requirement for an audit for the year.

We have not been instructed to carry out an audit of the financial statements. For this reason, we have not verified the accuracy or completeness of the accounting records or information and explanations you have given to us and we do not, therefore, express any opinion on the financial statements.

[We draw your attention to note x in the financial statements which discloses and explains a departure from applicable accounting standards. The company has not depreciated its goodwill held in the financial statements in the year and this is a departure from the Financial Reporting Standard for Smaller Entities and from the Companies Act 1985.]

Accountants
Address
Date

Abbreviated accounts

Where the company wishes to take advantage of the ability to file abbreviated accounts and the turnover of the company is such as to require no statutory report (below £5.6 million), the same wording as used in the report for the full accounts compiled for directors should be used in the abbreviated accounts that are filed (see **Table 2**). There is no other report to which reference needs to be made.

7.4   UNINCORPORATED ENTITIES

7.4.1   Scope of guidance

Technical Release Audit 01/05 is intended to give general guidance to accountants when they compile historical financial information for their clients, and covers situations where the request is by unincorporated entities for a specific purpose, such as for tax purposes, partnership accounts or for grant claims.

However, where a set of financial statements which comply fully with the provisions of UK GAAP for an unincorporated entity are requested, the guidance in Audit 02/04 should be followed (see **7.3**).

Audit 01/05 may be of use, however, when accountants compile historical financial information, other than financial statements, for incorporated entities.

7.4.2   Professional ethics

When compiling historical financial information for unincorporated entities, accountants are bound by all ethical and other guidance laid down by the ICAEW. They should not, therefore compile, or allow their names to be associated with, financial information which they consider to be misleading.

7.4.3   Accounting basis

Accountants are not required to test assertions underlying the information which they are compiling and therefore are not able to express any assurance on the financial information being compiled.

There is no statutory requirement for the financial information of unincorporated entities to give a true and fair view and it is acceptable to compile the information on an accounting basis other than full UK GAAP. The appropriate accounting basis should be discussed with the clients and clearly defined so that the accountants can compile the information.

The accounting basis, purpose and limitations of the information presented should be fully disclosed in a note to the financial information and referred to in the accountants' report.

7.4.4   Terms of engagement

As with compilations performed under Audit 02/04 there must be clear understanding between the client and the accountants regarding the terms of the engagement. An example engagement letter extract for the compilation of historical financial information under Audit 01/05 is provided in **Table 3**.

In addition, accountants should consider whether it is appropriate to include a section on the limitation of the accountants' liability.

TABLE 3: Engagement letter extracts for the compilation of historical financial information for unincorporated entities

Client's responsibilities

You will be responsible for the reliability, accuracy and completeness of the accounting records.

You have undertaken to make available to us, as and when required, all your accounting records and related financial information, including minutes of

---

management meetings, necessary to carry out our work. You will provide us with all the information and explanations relevant to the purpose and compilation of the financial information.

Scope of the accountants' work

You have asked us to assist you in the preparation of [insert type of information required] for [insert purpose]. We will compile the financial information for your approval based on the accounting records maintained by you and the information and explanations given to us by you.

We shall plan our work on the basis that no report is required by statute or regulation, unless you inform us in writing to the contrary. In carrying out our engagement we will make enquiries of [management] and undertake any procedures that we judge appropriate but are under no obligation to perform procedures that may be required for assurance engagements such as audits or reviews.

Our work will not be an audit of the financial information in accordance with Auditing Standards. Consequently, our work will not provide any assurance that the accounting records or the financial information are free from material misstatement, whether caused by fraud, other irregularities or error and cannot be relied on to identify weaknesses in internal controls.

Since we have not carried out an audit, nor confirmed in any way the accuracy or reasonableness of the accounting records maintained by the company, we are unable to provide any assurance as to whether the financial information that we prepare from those records presents a true and fair view.

We have a professional duty to compile financial information that conforms with generally accepted accounting principles selected by management as being appropriate for the purpose for which the information is prepared. The accounting basis on which the information has been compiled, its purpose and limitations will be disclosed in an accounting policy note to the financial information and will be referred to in our accountants' report.

We also have a professional responsibility not to allow our name to be associated with financial information which we believe may be misleading. Therefore, although we are not required to search for such matters, should we become aware, for any reason, that the financial information may be misleading, we will discuss the matter with you with a view to agreeing appropriate adjustments and/or disclosures in the financial information. In circumstances where adjustments and/or disclosures that we consider appropriate are not made or where we are not provided with appropriate information, and as a result we consider that the financial information is misleading, we will withdraw from the engagement.

As part of our normal procedures, we may request you to provide written confirmation of any information or explanations given by you orally during the course of our work.

You will approve and sign the financial information thereby acknowledging responsibility for it, including the appropriateness of the accounting basis on which it has been compiled, and for providing us with all information and explanations necessary for its compilation.

Form of the accountants' report

We shall report to you that in accordance with this engagement letter we have compiled, without carrying out an audit, the financial information from the accounting records of the entity and from the information and explanation supplied to us. The report should not be used for any purpose other than as set out in this engagement letter.

Liability provisions

We will perform the engagement with reasonable skill and care. The total aggregate liability to you, of whatever nature, whether in contract, tort or otherwise, of [name of accountants] for any losses whatsoever and howsoever caused arising from or in any way connected with this engagement shall not exceed [amount].

7.4.5   Client's responsibilities

The client is responsible for the reliability, accuracy and completeness of the accounting records of the entity and for disclosing all relevant information to the accountant.

7.4.6   Planning

Having agreed a basis and format for the financial information, the accountant will plan the engagement. The level of planning will vary depending on the complexity and completeness of the client's accounting records and the reporting accountant's experience of the business.

7.4.7   Procedures

As in **7.3.3** above, reporting accountants will obtain a general understanding of the operations of the entity, consider whether the financial information is consistent with their understanding of the business and check whether relevant disclosures have been made. In addition they will obtain written representations from management, particularly in relation to estimates and the reliability, accuracy and completeness of information provided to them.

The accountants are under no obligation to perform procedures that would be necessary to enable them to give assurance on the financial information.

There is no mandatory requirement to document the work carried out, although full documentation will assist with performing a good quality engagement.

7.4.8   Misleading financial information

Accountants compiling financial information for unincorporated entities have the same responsibilities towards misleading financial information as accountants working for incorporated entities (see **7.3.4**).

7.4.9 Approval of financial information

Although there is no statutory duty for the financial information of unincorporated entities to be signed or approved by the client, it is recommended that the client does sign the information to acknowledge their responsibility for it. An example wording is given in **Table 4.**

TABLE 4: Example wording for approval of financial information

In accordance with the engagement letter dated [. . .], I/we approve the financial information which comprises [state the financial information compiled]. I/we acknowledge my/our responsibility for the financial information, including the appropriateness of the accounting basis as set out in note [x], and for providing [the accountants] with all information and explanations necessary for its compilation.

7.4.10 Accountants' reports

As stated in **7.3.6** above, the aim of the accountants' report is to help users derive comfort from the fact that the financial information has been compiled by an accountant who is subject to the ethical and other guidance issued by the ICAEW. It also clarifies that an audit has not taken place. An example report wording for the compilation of financial information for unincorporated entities is given in **Table 5.**

TABLE 5: Example accountants' report for the compilation of financial information for unincorporated entities

Chartered Accountants'/Accountant's Report to [Entity] on Unaudited Financial Information

In accordance with the engagement letter dated [date] we have compiled the financial information of [the entity] which comprises [the Profit and Loss Account, the Balance Sheet, the Cash Flow Statement and, where relevant, the related notes] from the accounting records and information and explanations you have given to us.

The [financial information] has been compiled on the basis set out in note [x] to the [financial information]. The financial information is not intended to achieve full compliance with the provisions of UK Generally Accepted Accounting Principles.

This report is made to you in accordance with the terms of our engagement. Our work has been undertaken so that we might compile the [financial information] that we have been engaged to compile, report to you that we have done so, and state those matters that we have agreed to state to you in this report and for no other purpose. To the fullest extent permitted by law, we do not accept or assume responsibility to anyone other than the [addressee of this report], for our work or for this report.

We have carried out this engagement in accordance with technical guidance issued by the Institute of Chartered Accountants in England and Wales and have complied with the ethical guidance laid down by the Institute.

You have approved the [financial information] [where appropriate, insert period to which the financial information relates] and have acknowledged your responsibility

---

for it, for the appropriateness of the accounting basis and for providing all information and explanations necessary for its compilation.

We have not verified the accuracy or completeness of the accounting records or information and explanations you have given to us and we do not, therefore, express any opinion on the financial information.

Accountants
Address
Date

7.5 CONSIDERATIONS FOLLOWING THE INCREASE IN THE AUDIT EXEMPTION LIMIT

Introduction

Many companies who fulfil the size criteria for audit exemption (profit and loss, balance sheet or number of employees) are still required to have an audit. This may be because they are 'ineligible' under the legislation, such as public, banking and insurance companies, trade unions, employers' associations, certain companies that are members of groups and companies regulated under the Financial Services Act. An audit may also be required where the company's constitution requires it or where it is requested by the provider of finance.

Registered auditor status

It is an offence under s41 of the Companies Act 1989 for anyone to describe themselves as, or hold themselves out to be, a registered auditor when they are not. If an audit report is published with the financial statements, or otherwise made available to the public, the auditor who signed that report must be registered to avoid committing an offence. Practitioners should bear this is mind when deciding whether to renew their registered status.

Requirements when a company becomes exempt

Where clients become audit exempt, either as a result of changing exemption limits, or due to changes in their results and employee count, auditors should not continue to perform an audit without telling the client about the options open to them. Discussing these options will allow the auditor to sell the advantages of continuing with the annual audit process.

Engagement letters

Where there is a significant change in the nature of the services provided, a new engagement letter will be required. Therefore, when a client becomes audit exempt and takes advantage of that exemption a new engagement letter will be required, assuming the practitioner continues to act in some other capacity for that client. Where the client becomes exempt, but elects to continue with the audit process the ICAEW have stated that it is also desirable to issue a new engagement letter, regardless of whether the audit report is filed with the financial statements.

Resignation procedures

Where a client becomes audit exempt and an audit is no longer requested for non-statutory reasons, auditors do not, in theory, have to resign from office. There is a lack of clarity within the Companies Act 1985 as to whether an audit firm still engaged to an audit exempt client is required to issue an annual report even if the client is exempted from the requirement to have an audit.

Commentators' views on this matter have varied and therefore in order to avoid unnecessary risk auditors should resign from office when a client becomes audit exempt.

The Department of Trade and Industry have advised that audit exemption is not, in itself, an issue that should be brought to the attention of members or creditors. However, when an auditor ceases to hold office a section 394 statement should still be made and deposited at the company's registered office in the normal way. An example wording is set out in **Table 6**.

TABLE 6: Example section 394 statement for use when client becomes audit exempt

To the Directors of XYZ Limited

Dear Sirs

We hereby give notice, under s392 of the Companies Act, of our resignation as auditors to XYZ Limited as of .. [date]. In accordance with s519 of the Companies Act 2006, we confirm that there are no circumstances connected with our ceasing to hold office that we consider should be brought to members' or creditors' attention.

Yours faithfully

. . .

---

8 REPORTS TO THE FSA ON INVESTMENT BUSINESSES

8.1 LEGAL BACKGROUND

This Chapter covers the reporting requirements for auditors of investment business regulated by the Financial Services Authority (FSA).

The FSA took over the regulation of investment businesses previously regulated by the Securities and Futures Authority (SFA), the Investment Management Regulatory Organisation (IMRO) and the Personal Investment Authority (PIA) on 1 December 2001 (known as 'N2'). SFA, IMRO and PIA were previously Self Regulatory Organisations (SROs) under the Financial Services Act.

The FSA has High Level Standards, Regulator Processes and Redress Sourcebooks that apply to all FSA regulated firms.

8.2 TYPES OF REPORT

Two types of report made by auditors to the Regulator are covered in this chapter:

- opinions on client money and custody assets; and
- special ad hoc reports on regulatory matters of material significance.

Opinions on interim profits are covered in **Chapter 46**.

The requirement for auditors to report directly to the FSA on financial statements, financial resources and accounting records has been removed for periods ending on or after 31 December 2007. An investment business must still file a set of its annual financial statements with the FSA, which must be audited unless that business is exempt.

8.3 AUDITING STANDARDS AND GUIDANCE

The standards and guidance on reporting for this type of engagement are included in:

- Section B of Proposed Clarified ISA (UK and Ireland) 250 *The Auditor's Right and Duty to Report to Regulators in the Financial Sector* (see **8.6** below); and
- Practice Note 21 (Revised) *The Audit of Investment Businesses in the United Kingdom*.

During the process of issuing the original ISAs (UK and Ireland), the APB appended Section B to ISA 250, as there was no equivalent guidance in the existing International ISAs. Clarified ISA (UK and Ireland) 250 Section B *The Auditor's Right and Duty to Report to Regulators in the Financial Sector* was issued in October 2009 and is effective for the audit of financial statements for periods ending on or after 15 December 2010. The updated ISA (UK and Ireland) replaces Section B of ISA (UK and Ireland) 250. This chapter covers both the existing and clarified standards. As the clarified ISA (UK and Ireland) does not significantly amend the requirements of the existing ISA (UK and Ireland) this chapter is written on the basis of the existing requirements, and any changes to them included in the clarified ISA (UK and Ireland) are included and clearly indicated.

Practice Note 21 (Revised) was issued in December 2007 and updated earlier guidance to reflect the changes in regulatory arrangements and changes to Auditing Standards to that date. Further amendment is anticipated following the publication of the suite of Clarified ISAs (UK and Ireland). The Practice Note superseded Bulletin 2001/7, which dealt with the changes that occurred at N2. This chapter considers only the reports of auditors of investment businesses. Other aspects of the audits of investment businesses are covered in **Chapter 46**.

8.4 RESPECTIVE RESPONSIBILITIES

A regulated investment business's management are required to:

- prepare financial statements which give a true and fair view of the state of affairs and the profit or loss for the period;
- prepare statements of financial resources, both actual and required, as detailed by the appropriate FSA Rules;
- establish and maintain adequate accounting and other records and systems of control;
- ensure clients' assets are protected and the rules on clients' assets are followed; and
- ensure that the entity complies with laws and regulations that apply to its activities, and for preventing non-compliance and detecting any that occurs.

The entity's auditors are required to prepare a report to the FSA on an annual basis stating whether the business complied with the FSA Rules concerning client assets (including client money) at the relevant dates.

The auditors should always be aware of any changes to the FSA Rules during the period and the impact this will have on their report.

Details of the FSA Rules applicable to auditors are contained within section 3 of the *FSA Supervision Handbook*, available on www.fsa.gov.uk.

Auditors must also notify the FSA if they are removed from office, resign before the end of their term of office or not reappointed. Any matters relevant to the removal, resignation or non-reappointment should be included in this communication. If there are no such matters, this must also be stated.

8.5   CLIENT ASSETS

The main purpose of the FSA Rules in this area is to ensure that the investment business safeguards client assets, both in its day-to-day business and in the event of its insolvency. Chapters 6 and 7 of The FSA's Client Assets Sourcebook contains the FSA's rules with which an investment business must comply with client assets and client money. Auditors have to report on this compliance under Section 3.10 of the FSA's Supervision Manual.

Appendix 2 of the Practice Note sets out the relevant planning considerations for the categories of client assets, being:

● custody assets and collateral; and
● client money.

It also covers cases where there are no client assets. It is the auditors' responsibility to plan and perform their audit of these areas to be able to fulfil their reporting obligations.

Table 1 sets out the General Principles applicable to reporting on client assets taken from Practice Note 21.

TABLE 1: General Principles applicable to reporting on client assets

Auditors:

● agree the terms of the engagement with the investment business and record them in writing;
● comply with ethical guidance issued by their relevant professional body;
● familiarise themselves with the relevant rules contained in the FSA Handbook;
● take steps to ensure that any delegated work is directed, supervised and reviewed in a manner which provides reasonable assurance that such work is performed competently;
● plan the work to be undertaken so as to perform that work in an effective manner, taking into account their other reporting responsibilities;
● consider materiality and its relationship with the risk of material misstatement in the report to the FSA in planning their work and in determining the effect of their findings on their report;
● assess the objectivity and competence of other professionals on whose work they seek to rely and obtain sufficient appropriate evidence that such work is adequate for the purposes of the report;
● carry out procedures designed to obtain sufficient appropriate evidence on which to base their opinions;
● obtain written confirmation of appropriate representations from management before their report is issued;

- record in their working papers:
  - details of the engagement planning;
  - the nature, timing and extent of the procedures performed in relation to their auditors' report to the regulator, and the conclusions drawn; and
  - their reasoning and conclusions on all significant matters which require the exercise of judgement;
- undertake their work with an attitude of professional scepticism;
- address their report to the FSA explaining the basis of their work (including a statement of compliance with Practice Note 21) and express a clear opinion that complies with the requirements of the FSA rules;
- consider the matters which have come to their attention whilst performing their procedures and whether they should be included in a report to those charged with governance;
- report any matters of material significance they become aware of in the course of their work to the FSA without delay.

8.5.1   Custody assets and collateral

Custody assets and collateral ('client investments') may be any of the following, held by an investment business on behalf of a client:

- shares and stocks in the capital of a company;
- debentures;
- government and public securities;
- warrants or other instruments entitling the holder to subscribe for investments;
- certificates representing securities;
- units in a collective investment scheme;
- money-market instruments; or
- options, futures, swaps, forward rate agreements and any other derivative contracts.

In addition, arranging custody for a client as well as actually providing the custody is also covered by the legislation.

Accounting records

Auditors must consider whether the investment business has promptly recorded in its books and records all transactions undertaken by it in the period. This includes the purchase and sale of investments on behalf of its clients, as well as the movement of documents (including the business's own documents, due to the risk of mixing clients' documents with the investment business's own). Auditors should also consider whether records are in agreement with the statements sent out to clients, if reconciliations are carried out in accordance with the FSA Rules and whether other benefits accruing to clients, such as bonus or scrip issues, are correctly accounted for.

Evidence that the matters set out in **Table 2** are being properly carried out is likely to give auditors comfort in respect of these control objectives.

TABLE 2: Matters on which evidence is required in respect of accounting records

- that documents of title are recorded immediately on receipt;
- that documents of title are not released to clients, registrars, brokers, etc., without the records being amended;
- records are kept in respect of each document setting out date of receipt and despatch, the nature of the document, details of the investment to which it relates and the client to whom the investment belongs;
- that the statements are correct and regularly dispatched to clients;
- that client correspondence and queries are promptly and properly dealt with; and
- that bonus and scrip benefits are properly allocated to clients.

Accounting systems and controls

The Practice Note stresses the importance of the control environment to the effectiveness of the system of internal control that operates in the investment business. One element of this is to ensure that lapses in procedures are dealt with immediately, rather than ignored.

The auditors should consider the following areas in detail as part of their audit of client investments:

- safe custody and proper control of client investments including the sending of periodic statements;
- proper registration and segregation of client investments; and
- compliance with reconciliation requirements.

The appendix to the Practice Note gives details of the objectives to be tested and typical evidence to be gained by auditors in each of these areas.

8.5.2   Client money

Definition

Client money is defined by the FSA Rules as:

'(a)   that a firm receives or holds for, or on behalf of, a client in the course of, or in connection with, its MiFID business; and/or

(b)   which, in the course of carrying on designated investment business that is not MiFID business, a firm holds in respect of any investment agreement entered into, or to be entered into, with or for a client, or which a firm treats as client money in accordance with the client money rules.'

The definition of client money specifically includes the cash component of an ISA.

It is important for auditors to understand what constitutes client money for the particular investment business on which they are reporting. They need to be aware of the possibility that the management of the entity has not correctly identified what is client money.

Auditors should be aware that different types of clients are identified in the FSA Rules and although, in general, all money received from private clients must be treated as client money, there are certain limited exemptions to what is deemed to be 'client money'. Auditors should consult the relevant FSA Rules in individual cases.

In relation to banks, the application of client money rules is limited in certain respects. Where a bank holds the money of its investment business clients in accounts with itself, it is not considered to be holding client money. The client money rules will apply, however, if the bank passes the money outside the bank. Again, the auditor should refer to the FSA Rules.

Client bank accounts

All client money must be held in accounts at an approved bank, and the FSA rule books require investment businesses to perform a risk assessment on the bank prior to opening the accounts and regularly throughout the period of holding the account. The auditor must ensure that the investment business has adhered to all relevant rules pertaining to the client bank account including:

- ensuring the account is named so as to make it clear that the money in the account does not belong to the business;
- checking that the bank has no right of set off over the accounts; and
- ensuring that any interest accrued is paid into that account.

Auditors will request written confirmation of adherence to these rules from the bank.

Detailed audit objectives and examples of audit evidence in respect of:

- adequate accounting records;
- adequate systems and controls as regards:
    - proper holding of client money;
    - payment into and withdrawal from client bank accounts;
    - proper accounting for interest; and
- compliance with the relevant regulations at specified dates

are set out in an appendix to the Practice Note.

8.5.3 No client assets

Auditors must be aware of situations where investment businesses do not hold client assets, either by their own choice or under the terms of their authorisation by the Regulator. In these cases there should be controls to ensure that where client assets are received they are immediately returned to the investor.

Where no client assets are held, the FSA will require a report from the auditors that this is the case. Possible procedures for this purpose are detailed in **Table 3**.

> **TABLE 3: Procedures to verify that no client assets are held**
>
> - ensure that procedures are in place to train staff about the existence and importance of client assets;
> - enquire how settlements are made on clients' behalf;
> - review the investment business's cash book to ensure that no client money transactions pass through it;
> - review client files for indications that client assets may exist;
> - review client files for agreements on how custody is to be managed and review agreements with any custodians to ensure that money is not classed as, or treated as, client money;
> - if an investment business has no client assets because it does not act for private clients, review client lists to confirm that no private clients are included;
> - enquire how dividends, especially unclaimed dividends, and rights issues are dealt with (these should not be taken to the investment business's own profit and loss account even if not material);
> - ensure reviews occur at regular intervals to confirm that client money is not held;
> - enquire about the action taken if any client money is received; and
> - obtain representations from management that no client money is held.

8.5.4 Other audit considerations

The auditors must test compliance with certain of the FSA Rules at particular dates during the period under review. For example, reconciliations should be performed on a timely basis as laid down in the FSA Rules and this should be checked by the auditors. Other requirements may be tested at any time during the accounting period – for example, the use of appropriately designated client bank accounts.

8.5.5 Further guidance

Appendix 2 to Practice Note 21 (Revised) provides more detailed guidance on the work normally carried out in order to form an opinion on client assets in the auditors' report to the FSA. In particular, it provides guidance on the FSA's Client Assets Sourcebook (CASS) with which auditors are required to familiarise themselves.

The guidance sets out the relevant planning considerations and assists in determining the scope of work to be performed.

8.5.6 Reporting

Each FSA regulated firm falls into a prudential category which determines the opinions required in the auditors' report.

In all cases, however, the auditor is obliged by the FSA's rules to submit this report directly to the FSA. If it is not submitted within the stipulated timeframe, the auditors will be in breach of the FSA rules and are required to notify the FSA of that fact and provide an explanation.

The deadline for submitting a report on client money is four months after the end of the period on which auditors are reporting. This may not be the accounting reference date, as reports on client money and custody assets can be prepared at a different date to the accounting reference date.

Subsequent client asset reports may be submitted covering any period of up to 53 weeks from the date on which the previous report ended.

The main provisions of the rules set out by the FSA on submission of client money reports are:

- the report must contain the firm's FSA reference number and be marked for the attention of its normal supervisory contact;
- the coversheet contained in SUP 16 Ann 13R must be used;
- the report may be submitted by e-mail;
- the return may be faxed by the deadline;
- if the deadline is not a normal business day, then the report can be submitted by the next business day after the due date.

Table 4 gives an example auditors' report. The report is addressed to the FSA and:

- identifies the matters to which the report relates;
- addresses all matters that are required by the engagement letter;
- explains the basis of the auditor's work and in particular makes a statement of compliance with Practice Note 21;
- contains a clear expression of opinion that complies with the requirements of the FSA rules;
- includes the auditor's manuscript or printed signature;
- includes the auditor's address; and
- includes the date.

TABLE 4: Example auditor's report on client assets under SUP 3.10

Independent Auditor's report to the Financial Services Authority ('the FSA') in respect of ABC Limited for the year/period ended [date]

We report in respect of ABC Limited ('the firm') on the matters set out below.

Our report has been prepared in accordance with SUP 3.10.4R and is addressed to the FSA in its capacity as regulator under the Financial Services and Markets Act 2000.

Basis of opinion

We have carried out such procedures as we considered necessary for the purposes of this report having regard to Practice Note 21, 'The audit of investment businesses in the United Kingdom (Revised)' issued by the Auditing Practices Board.

Systems and controls procedures relating to client assets are subject to inherent limitations and, accordingly, error or irregularities may occur and not be detected. Such procedures cannot be proof against fraudulent collusion, especially on the part of those holding positions of authority or trust. Furthermore, this opinion relates only to the year/period ended on [date] and should not be seen as providing assurance as to any future position, as changes to systems or control procedures may alter the validity of our opinion.

Opinion

Either:

In our opinion:

- the firm has maintained systems adequate to enable it to comply with the custody rules, the collateral rules and the client money rules throughout the year/period [from ... to ...] since the last date at which a report was made [see note];
- the firm was in compliance with custody rules, the collateral rules and the client money rules [see note] at the date as at which the report has been made;
- [if applicable] in relation to the secondary pooling event during the period, the firm has complied with the rules in CASS 7.A (Client money distribution) in relation to that pooling event.

Or

The scope of the firm's permission did not allow it to hold [client money] [or] [custody assets].

The directors have stated that the firm did not hold [client money] [or] [custody assets] during the year/period. Based on review procedures performed, nothing has come to our attention that causes us to believe that the firm held [client money] [or] [custody assets] during the year/period.

Nominee companies [if applicable]

In our opinion, [name of nominee companies] subsidiaries of the firm which are nominee companies in whose name custody assets are registered, maintained throughout the year/period systems for the custody, identification and control of custody assets which:

(a)   were adequate and
(b)   included reconciliations at appropriate intervals between the records maintained (whether by the firm of the nominee company) and statements or confirmations from custodians or from the person who maintains the record of legal entitlement.

Registered Auditors
Date
Address

Note: the requirements of the Handbook that apply, and the wording of the opinion differ, depending on whether or not the firm holds both client money and assets or only one of these:

		MiFID Business
(i)	where the firm holds both client money and custody assets	CASS 6, CASS 7 apply Opinion refers to custody, collateral and client money rules
(ii)	where the firm holds custody assets but not client money	CASS 3 and CASS 6 apply Opinion refers to custody and collateral rules
(iii)	where the firm holds client money but not custody assets	CASS 3 and CASS 7 apply Opinion refers to collateral and client money rules

8.5.7   Qualified reports

In all cases where there are breaches, it is necessary to understand what the FSA Rules are trying to achieve. In the case of regulated investment business this is not only numerical accuracy. An overriding objective is to ensure that clients' assets are safeguarded.

Where there is doubt whether particular FSA Rules have been complied with it may be necessary to refer the matter to one of the technical advisory services of the professional bodies or to a member of the FSA supervision team who deals with the audit client.

The FSA allows auditors to classify some FSA Client Asset Rule breaches as 'trivial' and not report them. In order to classify breaches of the FSA Rules as trivial, auditors must carry out extra work and decide that:

- the breaches were minor in nature and would not cause concern to the FSA;
- no loss to the client has been incurred or would be caused by the breach; and
- the firm has immediately corrected the breach on discovery.

Even where breaches are reported, auditors may also wish to inform the FSA that the breaches have been put right and that they appeared not to cause, or were not likely to cause, any loss to a client. It is usual for auditors to inform the FSA of such matters by way of an accompanying letter.

Where auditors find evidence of breaches and have informed their client, the responsibility for corrective action lies with the management. The fact that corrective action has been taken will not remove the necessity for the auditors to consider qualifying their report on the matter where the breach is not trivial.

Where there is a breach of the FSA Rules the auditors' report should clearly indicate the specific requirement and how it has not been met so that it can be easily understood and evaluated by the FSA.

Once the auditors have informed their client that they intend to qualify their audit report, the client will immediately need to inform the FSA. Where the client does not inform the FSA the auditors should consider whether to do so themselves in a special report.

8.6 SPECIAL AD HOC REPORTS

Under the FSMA 2000 (Communications by Auditors) Regulations 2001 (SI 2001/2587) auditors of authorised firms, or auditors of an entity closely linked to an authorised firm has a statutory duty to communicate certain matters to the FSA relevant to the FSA's functions, which has come to their attention 'in the capacity of auditor' during their audit work.

Further regulations within the Financial Services and Markets Act 2000 clarify the matters to be reported and extend the application of the statutory duty to information to which auditors of a financial institution become aware in their capacity as auditors of other entities with close links to the financial institution.

8.6.1 Guidance

Guidance on the implications of and the procedures necessary under these regulations is contained in Section B of ISA (UK and Ireland) 250 *The Auditors' Right and Duty to Report to Regulators in the Financial Sector*. This includes guidance covering:

- the right and duty to report to regulators;
- material significance;
- procedures;
- reporting;
- communication with the regulator; and
- relationship with other reporting responsibilities.

Practice Notes have also been developed for each type of entity – for example, Practice Note 18 covers Building Societies, Practice Note 19 covers Banks and Practice Note 20 covers Insurers. These have all been supplemented by APB Bulletins 2001/4 to 2001/6 to take into account the introduction of FSA as a single regulator. Where entities are governed by more than one regulator, auditors should ensure that they follow the guidance in each relevant Practice Note.

8.6.2 Right and duty to report

Section B of ISA (UK and Ireland) 250 requires auditors to bring to the attention of the regulator information of which they become aware in the course of the work required to fulfil their audit responsibilities, which in their opinion is:

- relevant to the FSA's functions (such as breaches of FSA Rules or concerns about the fit and proper status of management); and

- of material significance to the FSA.

Auditors have a statutory duty to report certain other information, typically breaches of regulations which may come to their attention during their work. Auditors are not required to perform any additional procedures to search out these matters. This statutory duty applies only to information which comes to the auditor in their capacity as auditor. Guidance on what constitutes information gained in their capacity as auditor is given in the ISA (UK and Ireland).

The statutory duty to report to a regulator applies to information which comes to the attention of auditors in their capacity as auditors. If the information is discovered by someone not involved in the audit, but it is of relevance to the audit, and the work that it related to, it should be taken into account as if it were audit evidence. If the work is not relevant to the audit then it is unlikely that it will give rise to a duty to report.

Where information is discovered in the course of work performed for another client the auditors have no right to breach their duty of confidentiality in respect of it. However, they may choose to make enquiries during the audit of the regulated entity to establish whether the information can be substantiated from that source.

The guidance stresses that firms should ensure that they have suitable lines of communication so that any information which may give rise to a duty to report is brought to the attention of the partner responsible for the audit, usually by enquiries of other members of the firm as part of the audit planning and completion.

The statutory right to report to the FSA is not affected if the auditors cease to hold office. Hence, if they are aware of information, this may be reported either before or after ceasing to hold office.

Auditors may have a right to report certain matters direct to the regulator in addition to those which they have a duty to report. This right will usually be exercised where the auditors consider that doing so is necessary to protect the interests of those for whose benefit the regulator is required to act.

8.6.3 *'material significance'*

This is defined in ISA (UK and Ireland) 250 as being where the FSA is likely to investigate a matter because of its nature or potential financial impact. Material significance does not mean the same as materiality in the context of the audit of financial statements. Whilst an event may be trivial in its financial impact, it may be of a nature or type likely to change the perception of the FSA. Further guidance concerning each type of regulated entity is contained in the Practice Notes and supplementary APB Bulletins.

Under the Financial Services and Markets Act new statutory definitions are provided for matters giving rise to a duty to report. They are generally matters which the auditor has a reasonable cause to believe will, or may be, of material significance in determining whether:

- a person is a fit and proper person to carry on investment business; or
- disciplinary action or powers of intervention should be used to stop investors suffering loss.

Although the particular nature of the various sectors are considered in the legislation, in general the definitions incorporate the following terms:

- circumstances indicating that the regulated entity's authorisation could be revoked;
- there is, has been, or may have been, either:

  (i)   a failure to fulfil specified requirements; or
  (ii) a contravention of other provisions of the Rules which is likely to be of material significance to the FSA concerned for the exercise of its functions;

- there is a doubt as to the entity's status as a going concern; and
- the auditors conclude that their report on the entity's financial statements should include a qualified opinion.

Practice Note 21 gives additional guidance on the meaning of material significance in relation to investment businesses. It states that any breach of the FSA Rules may be reportable, whether an isolated or recurring breach, depending on size or significance, and auditors must use their judgement in determining whether a breach will be of material significance to the FSA. In doing so, auditors must consider both the facts of the matter and their implication.

Status of regulated entities, directors and senior management as fit and proper persons

When planning the audit, auditors must familiarise themselves with any guidance issued by the FSA on the information that the FSA takes into consideration when deciding whether the fit and proper requirement has been met.

Generally, the FSA assesses entities against three broad measures:

- honesty;
- competence; and
- solvency.

Although auditors cannot be expected to make judgements on competence, soundness of judgement and diligence, there may be persuasive evidence which calls the appropriateness of some of the entity's actions into question. Therefore, auditors should be alert for any indication of shortfalls in any of the following areas:

- probity, honesty, skill, care and integrity;
- attention to establishing satisfactory compliance arrangements;
- attention to compliance with notification requirements;
- observing appropriate standards of market practice; and
- openness with the FSA.

Any report on the fitness and propriety of the entity, or any of its directors or management, should be made to the FSA without prior reference to the directors of the entity.

Risk of loss – client assets

The auditor should report any identified deficiency in client assets which cannot be explained or accounted for, as well as any suspicions that misappropriation of assets may occur. Immediate action is required to ensure that the FSA can take appropriate action to protect client assets from future loss.

Risk of loss – financial position

Areas of material significance to the FSA will be those that indicate:

- the occurrence or possibility of a material loss to the regulated entity; or
- the breach, or likelihood of breach, by the entity of the requirements concerning the adequacy of its financial resource or solvency requirements.

A material loss to the business will include an event leading to a loss which is material in meeting the entity's solvency or capital adequacy requirements, or the requirement of a subsidiary, related or nominee company. This may include litigation against the entity, which may give rise to contingent liabilities and costs in defending the action.

An entity may be required to notify the FSA if its financial resources fall below a multiple of the financial requirement (e.g., 110 per cent). Failure to make this notification will also be regarded by the FSA as having material significance.

Compliance with requirements for the management of its affairs

Areas that auditors are likely to be aware of as a result of their work include:

- significant concerns over the internal control environment;
- disagreements or lack of evidence about amounts in the financial statements which cannot be resolved;
- material breaches of client asset rules and the rules requiring suitable systems in relation to client assets;
- evidence of business being conducted outside the entity's authorised scope; and
- significant matters affecting the regulated businesses' appointed representatives.

Doubt as to the entity's status as a going concern

Any doubt as to the entity's ability to continue to undertake investment business should be reported to the FSA.

8.6.4   Procedures

ISA (UK and Ireland) 250 stresses that neither the legislation nor the ISA (UK and Ireland) require auditors to perform any extra work to discover information that may give rise to a duty to report. The duty relates only to work performed to fulfil other reporting responsibilities where auditors must be alert to instances which would give rise to a duty to report.

Although there is no obligation to perform additional procedures, time must still be spent complying with the FSA Rules. When planning, time must be allocated to understanding the FSA Rules. Additionally, if matters which may give rise to the duty have been found, further procedures are necessary to assess whether the matter should be reported, and if so, how.

The duty does not only cover matters which are in the financial statements or are covered by the requirements of the auditors' standard report to the FSA, as there may be implications for the FSA's functions in any information discovered during the audit. For example, where information comes to light which could cast doubt on the fit and proper status of the management, this should be investigated and reported if appropriate, even though it is not a matter that the annual report to the FSA covers.

Closely linked entities

During planning, auditors should establish whether any closely linked entities exist, of which they are also auditor. A closely linked entity is a:

- parent undertaking;
- subsidiary undertaking;
- parent undertaking of a subsidiary undertaking; or
- subsidiary undertaking of a parent undertaking.

Where such entities exist and are commonly audited, auditors consider the significance of the entities and the nature of the issues that might arise which may be of material significance to the Regulator. The audit engagement partner should contact the audit engagement partner of the closely linked entity to inform them of the audit firm's responsibility to report to the FSA and notify them of circumstances which might be of material significance to the regulator. These would include:

- activities or uncertainties within the closely linked entity which might significantly impair the financial position of the regulated entity;
- money laundering; and

- if the closely linked entity is itself regulated, matters that the auditor of the closely linked entity are intending to report to its regulator.

Prior to completion of the audit, auditors of the regulated entity should obtain written confirmation that such circumstances do not exist from the other audit team. If circumstances do exist, further information may need to be obtained from the other auditors and the closely linked entity itself.

There is no duty for the auditors of the closely linked entity to make a report to the FSA, unless they are themselves regulated.

Planning

Section B of ISA (UK and Ireland) 250 extends ISA (UK and Ireland) 315 concerning the knowledge of the business, to cover the statutory provisions and the Rules.

As part of their assessment of the accounting systems and internal controls, auditors should consider the control environment, including the attitude of management to compliance with the relevant FSA Rules. Auditors should also assess whether the business is being conducted outside its authorisation as this could result in a need to report.

Supervision and control

ISA (UK and Ireland) 250 requires staff involved in regulated business audits to obtain a sufficient knowledge of what constitutes reportable matters to be able to identify them. Practice Note 21 states that as a basic minimum, the knowledge of all staff involved in the audit of a regulated business will extend to:

- the provisions of the Regulations concerning the auditors' duty to report to the regulators (FSMA 2000 (Communication by Auditors Regulations 2001));
- Part B of ISA (UK and Ireland) 250;
- Practice Note 21;
- the *FSA Principles for Business*; and
- the types of business which require authorisation by other regulatory authorities.

In addition, and depending on the individual's role in the engagement, understanding will be required of the *FSA Rules and guidance* relating to matters on which auditors are routinely required to report, in particular section 3 of the *FSA Supervision Manual*.

Other staff who are only involved in non-audit work for a regulated entity are not required to have a detailed knowledge of the FSA Rules nor to bring any information to the attention of the audit partner. However, there should be procedures in firms to ensure that any relevant relationship is notified to the partner responsible for the audit by other departments of the firm.

Identifying matters requiring a report

When auditors become aware of matters that they suspect may give rise to a report to the FSA, they should:

- obtain evidence to assess the implications for reporting;
- determine whether the matter is of material significance to the FSA; and
- consider whether the breach is criminal conduct that gives rise to criminal property, and therefore should be reported to the relevant authority.

It is necessary to perform these procedures in this order because not all matters may be of material significance and this may only be apparent once the matter has been investigated further. Minor breaches may be reportable if they indicate a general lack of compliance which calls into question the fit and proper status. Breaches which have been rectified and reported by the entity itself do not normally need to be reported by the auditors, but if they have not been rectified or reported then a report may be required.

It is not necessary to collect sufficient evidence to determine the full implications of the matter before deciding to report. It is only necessary that there are reasonable grounds. What constitutes reasonable grounds is a matter for professional judgement. Such a judgement will be based on:

- discussions with management and staff; and
- a review of correspondence and documents relating to the matter.

Certain matters, such as a loss of client money, may be so serious as to necessitate an immediate report to the FSA to prevent further losses being sustained.

The evidence obtained by the auditors should be documented so that their decision whether to proceed with a report can be clearly demonstrated should the need arise in the future.

Items reportable on an ad hoc basis

Appendix 6 to the revision to Practice Note 21 sets out a number of 'themes' within which 'relevant requirements' or matters of concern which may give rise to a statutory duty to report are likely to fall. These are reproduced in **Table 5**.

TABLE 5: Examples of items reportable on an ad hoc basis

- controllers, directors and senior management who may not be 'fit and proper';
- serious breaches of law/regulations;
- potential disciplinary action against the firm or directors;
- undertaking activities outside the scope of their permission;
- failure to comply with limitations or restriction on permission or individual requirements;
- false or misleading information given to the FSA or matters concealed;
- problems with another 'regulator', e.g. Office of Fair Trading (i.e. regards the Consumer Credit Act) or overseas regulators;
- breaches of prudential limits and/or any financial limits;

- significant actual or potential loss by investors, e.g. loss of customer assets or breach of client money rules; where there appear to be conflicts of interest; where there appears to be systemic abuse of advice or discretionary decisions; or as identified by complaints or by cases where a customer sues under s150 FSMA;
- failure to clearly allocate responsibilities between senior managers or to implement clear reporting lines;
- major systems and control weaknesses (including major reconciliation failures and backlogs);
- possible going concern issues; and
- adverse skilled person's report or qualified auditor's report.

Cumulative minor breaches

Minor breaches would not normally be of material significance to the FSA and give rise to an ad hoc report. However, ISA (UK and Ireland) 250 requires auditors of regulated entities to review whether the cumulative effect of a number of minor breaches is such as to give rise to a duty to report to the Regulator. Auditors may wish to seek legal advice on whether such a report would be necessary.

The facts and circumstances of their decision to report or not should be clearly documented in the audit work papers.

Reliance on other auditors

The same principles apply as in a statutory audit and these are discussed in **35.3**. Group auditors would have a responsibility to report matters arising from the regulated entity's own and the consolidated financial statements. If they do not audit one of the regulated subsidiaries, they are not responsible for reporting on that company, but they must assess the effect of any matter on the group. Where there are joint auditors each has a responsibility and there should be an exchange of information.

8.6.5 *Reporting*

ISA (UK and Ireland) 250 does not suggest a format for the report, only that it should be 'in a form and manner which will facilitate appropriate action'. The report should be made without delay and may be made orally, so long as it is followed up in writing. Normally, auditors should agree the report to the FSA with the directors before it is made and a copy of the report should be sent to the directors.

Where a statutory duty to report arises, auditors must report the matter, even if it has already been reported by another party, including the directors.

ISA (UK and Ireland) 250 notes that there may be occasions where it is not appropriate for the directors to be involved – for example, where the integrity of the directors is questioned. In such extreme cases, the guidance notes that speed is of the essence and that the auditors may wish to take legal advice.

Any evidence indicating money laundering with links to the proceeds of any crime that auditors discover must be reported to the appropriate authority. Under the Money Laundering Regulations 2007 and the Proceeds of Crime Act 2002 it is an offence not to do so. This is an extension of the requirements under the old Criminal Justice Act to report the proceeds of suspected terrorist or drug trafficking activities. It is also an offence to report suspicions to any other party. The FSA may require that such information is disclosed to them, but if the directors are implicated, the auditors must not inform them of the matter as this would amount to 'tipping off' (see **Chapter 12**). It will often be the case that matters that are required to be reported to the regulator will also lead to a report under the Money Laundering Regulations 2007 and the Proceeds of Crime Act 2002.

Auditors' right to report directly to regulators

Under the FSMA 2000, auditors are not held to breach any duty by communicating in good faith to the FSA, information or an opinion on a matter that they reasonably believe is relevant to any functions of the FSA. This only applies to information obtained as auditors. Auditors should ensure compliance with legislation relating to 'tipping off' (see **Chapter 12**).

In addition to the statutory duty to report directly, auditors have a right to do so where they believe the matter to be relevant to the regulator's function and the directors have not informed the regulator themselves. On discovery of such a matter, the auditors should inform the directors in writing that, in their opinion, it should be reported, and if they do not obtain evidence within a reasonable period that the directors have reported it, they should do so themselves. No examples are given in ISA (UK and Ireland) 250.

Auditors may wish to take legal advice before deciding on what, and in what form, to report. However, it is important to balance this against the need for prompt reporting to protect the interests of investors.

8.6.6   Form of report

Section B of ISA (UK and Ireland) 250 states that the report should include the following:

- the name of the regulated entity;
- the statutory power under which the report was made;
- a statement that it has been prepared in accordance with ISA (UK and Ireland) 250, Section B;
- a description of the context in which the report is given;
- a description of matters giving rise to the report;

- a request that the FSA confirms receipt of the report; and
- the name of the auditors making the report, the date of the written report and, if appropriate, the date of the oral report and the name of the person to whom it was made.

The description of the matter should give an indication of the extent of any discussions with the directors on the matter.

The context of the report will depend on several matters such as:

- the nature of the appointment from which the report derives;
- the interpretation of the relevant legislation;
- the extent to which the auditors have investigated the matter;
- whether the matter has been discussed with the directors; and
- whether steps have been taken to rectify the matter.

No example of the report is given in ISA (UK and Ireland) 250.

8.6.7   Communication by the regulator

The FSA may pass on to auditors any information which it considers relevant to their function. Auditors are bound by the confidentiality provisions set out in Part XXIII of the Financial Services and Markets Act 2000 (Public record, disclosures of information and co-operation). Communications of this nature must be treated as confidential by auditors and must not be disclosed to their client or any other party without the express permission of the FSA or the other party. The FSA will indicate if anyone at the client has been informed of the matter.

The FSA has confirmed that it will take the initiative in communicating with auditors. The most likely matters are those which may affect the opinion that the auditors give on the financial statements. However, auditors should not assume that no communication from the FSA means that there is nothing that may be materially significant.

Where information has been brought to their attention, the auditors may need to amend their approach, but there is no requirement to change the scope of their work or actively investigate the matter further, unless specifically requested to do so by the FSA.

8.6.8   Relationship with other reporting responsibilities

Where matters have been reported directly to Regulators, auditors should consider the implications for their report on the financial statements. These are most likely to give rise to contingencies or other uncertainties which should be disclosed in the financial statements.

9 REPORTS TO MANAGEMENT

9.1 INTRODUCTION

In addition to reporting under the Companies Act 2006, auditors may also report to management – for example, on the adequacy of the company's system of internal control and on possible improvements to the financial and accounting efficiency of the business. The timing, form and content of such reports should be covered in the engagement letter between the auditors and their client.

This Chapter considers such reports, particularly in the context of ISA (UK and Ireland) 260, *Communication of Audit Matters to those Charged with Governance*.

Clarified ISA (UK and Ireland) 260 was issued in October 2009 and is effective for the audit of financial statements for periods ending on or after 15 December 2010. At the same time the APB issued Clarified ISA (UK and Ireland) 265 *Communicating deficiencies in internal control*. This is discussed in **9.13** below.

The Clarified ISAs (UK and Ireland) are not applicable until the audits of financial statements for periods ending on or after 15 December 2010.

As the Clarified ISAs (UK and Ireland) add to the requirements of the existing ISAs (UK and Ireland) this chapter is written on the basis of the existing requirements, and changes to them included in the Clarified ISAs (UK and Ireland) are included and clearly indicated.

9.2 AUDITING STANDARDS

ISA (UK and Ireland) 260 provides guidance on:

- the purpose of the report;
- format of the report;
- report contents; and
- requirements for listed companies.

The clarified ISA (UK and Ireland) 260 gives additional guidance on the need for effective two-way communication, (see **9.7** below).

9.3 THOSE CHARGED WITH GOVERNANCE

ISA (UK and Ireland) 260 defines those charged with governance as including 'the directors (executive and non-executive) of a company or other body, the members of an audit committee where one exists, the partners, proprietors, committee of management or trustees of other forms of entity, or equivalent persons responsible for directing the entity's affairs and preparing its financial statements'.

Depending on the nature and circumstances of the entity, management, i.e., those persons who perform senior management functions, may include some or all of those charged with governance. These individuals are executive directors. Non-executive directors are not usually part of management.

9.4 AIMS OF REPORTS TO THOSE CHARGED WITH GOVERNANCE

ISA (UK and Ireland) 260 requires auditors to 'communicate audit matters of governance interest arising from the audit of the financial statements with those charged with governance'. These reports must be made on a sufficiently prompt basis to enable those charged with governance to take appropriate action.

The main purposes of such reports are to:

- ensure there is a mutual understanding of the scope of the audit and the respective responsibilities of the auditors and the client;
- share information to enable the parties to fulfil their responsibilities; and
- provide constructive observations to those charged with governance.

Those charged with governance are ultimately responsible for the financial statements, and although the ISA (UK and Ireland) concentrates on the form and content of auditors' communications with the client, there must be an effective two-way process for the audit of the financial statements to be concluded satisfactorily.

All reports should be relevant to the particular client, and auditors should consider the extent, form and frequency of their reports in accordance with the size and nature of the client. The attitude of those charged with governance and the importance of the issues to be raised will also affect the format and timing of the report. For example, reports of relatively minor matters to a small client may be best handled orally via a meeting or telephone conversation rather than with a formal written report. These considerations are considered further in **9.6** below.

All reports should be made promptly to allow those charged with governance to take appropriate action. The speed with which auditors report will depend on the nature of the issue arising, but matters relating to the qualitative aspects of the entity's accounting and financial reporting will usually be communicated prior to the approval of the financial statements.

9.5 ESTABLISHING EXPECTATIONS

At an early stage in their relationship auditors should agree the level of detail and timing of communication between themselves and those charged with governance. This will vary depending on the circumstances of the client. Auditors should also clarify that they will only report matters which they consider relevant to those charged with governance as a result of their normal audit procedures, and will not perform additional procedures specifically to determine other matters to report.

Such communication is often made in the engagement letter, (see **Chapter 21**). Auditors are required to set out that they are responsible for forming and expressing an opinion on the financial statements which have been prepared by those charged with governance and that the audit does not relieve those charged with governance of their responsibility for the financial statements.

9.6 FORM OF COMMUNICATION

The auditors' report should usually be made in writing. The format of the report will depend on factors such as:

- the size, operating structure, legal structure and communication process of the entity being audited;
- the nature, sensitivity and significance of the matters being communicated;
- statutory and regulatory requirements; and
- the arrangements made with the client at the outset of the engagement.

A written report would usually be produced even if its content is limited to an explanation of why there are no significant matters that the auditor wishes to report.

Clarified ISA (UK and Ireland) 260 requires that where matters are communicated orally, the discussion should be documented on the audit file, typically by including a copy of the minutes of the meeting at which the issue was discussed.

Typically auditors will discuss their findings with management or those with direct responsibility for an area before reporting them to those charged with governance. This should ensure that all facts are clarified as well as providing management with an opportunity to provide further explanations. Where it will aid the understanding of those charged with governance, the auditors will include details of comments made by management in their final communication.

9.7   EFFECTIVENESS OF COMMUNICATIONS

Although the ISA (UK and Ireland) focuses mainly on communications from the auditors to those charged with governance, clarified ISA (UK and Ireland) emphasises the importance of effective two-way communication. Such effective communication is important in order to:

- enable auditors to understand matters in the context of the entity's business and operations;
- develop a constructive working environment;
- obtain assistance in identifying appropriate sources of audit evidence; and
- allow those charged with governance to fulfil their responsibility to oversee the financial reporting process.

The responsiveness of those charged with governance to communications from auditors may be considered when assessing the effectiveness of the entity's control environment. This may also affect the auditor's assessment of the risks of material misstatements. Auditors may consider:

- the appropriateness and timeliness of actions taken by those charged with governance following the auditors' recommendations;
- how open those charged with governance appear to be when communicating with the auditors;
- the willingness of those charged with governance to meet with the auditors; and
- the ability of those charged with governance to comprehend the recommendations made by the auditor.

9.8   MATTERS TO BE COMMUNICATED

9.8.1   Definition

Auditors will communicate 'audit matters of governance interest' to those charged with governance. These are matters arising from the audit of financial statements and which, in the opinion of auditors, are both important and relevant to those charged with governance in their role of overseeing the financial statements and disclosure process. Only matters which have come to auditors' attention as a result of the audit will be reportable, and auditors are not required to perform additional procedures to identify matters of governance interest.

9.8.2   Listed companies

ISA (UK and Ireland) 260 states that for listed companies the auditors should, at least annually:

- disclose in writing and discuss as appropriate:

- all relationships between the audit firm and its related entities and the client entity and its related entities that may reasonably be thought to bear on the firm's independence and the objectivity of the audit engagement partner and audit staff; and
- the related safeguards that are in place;

- where it is the case, confirm in writing to the audit committee that, in their professional judgement, the firm is independent within the meaning of regulatory and professional requirements and the objectivity of the audit engagement partner and audit staff is not impaired.

9.8.3   Integrity, independence and objectivity

For all companies, listed and unlisted, Ethical Standard 1 requires that those charged with governance should be told of any significant facts and matters which may impact the auditors' objectivity and independence.

The communication should include the key issues considered by the engagement partner such as:

- the principal threats, if any, to objectivity and independence identified by the auditor;
- any safeguards implemented with an explanation of why they were thought to be effective;
- any independent partner review;
- the overall assessment of threats and safeguards;
- information about the general policies and processes employed by the audit firm to maintain independence and objectivity.

9.8.4   Planning information

The ISA (UK and Ireland) states that auditors of all entities, listed or unlisted, should inform those charged with governance of the nature, scope and limitations, if any, of the work they plan to perform. Matters that might be communicated in outline include:

- the concept of materiality and its application to the audit;
- the approach the auditors will use in relation to assessing and relying on internal controls;
- the extent, if any, that reliance can be placed on internal audit; and
- where relevant, the work to be performed by other auditors and how auditors intend to ensure the adequacy of the work of those other auditors.

These matters may be dealt with in the engagement letter, and where the audit team consider that there has been no change in this information from one year to the next there is no requirement to reproduce it. Instead the auditors need only to make those charged with governance aware that no change has taken place. In all cases auditors should ensure that those charged with governance are provided with a copy of the engagement letter.

9.8.5   Findings from the audit

The following areas as those that auditors should communicate to those charged with governance:

- the auditors' views on the qualitative aspects of the entity's accounting practices and financial report – this will include the auditors' opinions on the accounting policies used, the appropriateness of accounting estimates, the potential impact of uncertainties and apparent misstatements in other material issued with the financial statements;
- the final draft of the management letter for signature;
- uncorrected misstatements (see below);
- expected modifications to the auditor's report – to ensure that those charged with governance are aware of the proposed modification, that there are no disputed facts and that those charged with governance have an opportunity to provide further information so that a modification is no longer required;
- material weakness in internal control identified during the audit;
- written representations the auditors are requesting;
- matters specifically required by other ISAs (UK and Ireland) to be communicated to those charged with governance; and
- any other matters of governance interest.

Clarified ISA (UK and Ireland) 260 also introduces the requirement for auditors to explain, where relevant, why significant accounting policies, which are acceptable under the applicable financial reporting framework are not considered appropriate in the particular circumstances of the entity. Examples may include the effect of accounting policies in controversial or emerging areas where there may be a lack of guidance, areas where estimates are significant, or the effect of the timing of a transaction in relation to the period in which they are recorded.

The Clarified ISA (UK and Ireland) also makes explicit communication requirements where significant difficulties encountered during the audit such as:

- significant delays in management providing relevant information;
- an unnecessarily brief time within which to complete the audit;
- extensive unexpected effort required to obtain sufficient appropriate audit evidence;
- the unavailability of expected information;
- restriction imposed on auditors by management; and
- management's unwillingness to make or extend its assessment of the entity's ability to continue as a going concern when required.

It also explicitly requires auditors to communicate with those charged with governance significant matters discussed with management, unless all of those charged with governance are involved in managing the entity.

Unadjusted misstatements

Where auditors find uncorrected misstatements, they should report them to the entity's management to request that they be corrected. These misstatements should be clearly distinguished as either errors of fact or matters of judgement. There is no requirement to report those misstatements which are 'clearly trivial' or inconsequential whether taken individually or in aggregate.

Where any of these misstatements are not corrected by management they are reported to those charged with governance. If those charged with governance refuse to make any of the adjustments, auditors should discuss the matter with them and consider the implications for their report. Auditors should also obtain written representations from those charged with governance that explains why they have not been corrected.

Even where management have corrected the misstatements auditors may consider that including the details of the misstatement in their communications may assist those charged with governance with their role, including considering the effectiveness of the system of internal control.

Where matters previously reported have not been rectified by those charged with governance, auditors consider repeating the point. Failing to do so may lead to the auditor giving the impression that they are satisfied that the matter has been addressed.

Guidance on unadjusted misstatements is detailed in Clarified ISA (UK and Ireland) 450 *Evaluation of Misstatements Identified During the Audit* (see **Chapter 18**).

9.9 ADDRESSEES

Auditors should use judgement to determine to whom they communicate certain matters. This may be contrary to the arrangement agreed at the start of the audit if the matter is sufficiently important to require reporting directly to the board or governing body.

For listed companies and other entities where they have been constituted, reports will often be made to the audit committee. However, auditors and boards should understand that a report to the audit committee will only form part of the auditors' overall obligation to report to those charged with governance and additional reports to other parts of the client's organisation may also be required, such as reports direct to the remuneration or to individual departments. In any case it is important that the report is seen by those who have the authority to implement the recommendations included therein. If the report is presented in sections of varying importance, it may be appropriate for the more detailed matters to be referred directly to the division or branch to which they relate.

9.10 GROUPS

Where a parent undertaking is preparing group financial statements, auditors bring to the attention of those charged with governance any matters arising through the audit of the subsidiary entities which they judge to be of significance in the context of the group.

There is a statutory requirement for auditors of corporate subsidiaries in the UK to supply this information to parent company auditors. Where no statutory obligation exists (for example for non-corporate or overseas entities) permission may be needed from those charged with governance in the subsidiary entity before the auditors can release this information to the parent company auditors.

9.11 THIRD PARTIES

The report is solely for the use of the addressee. If the auditors wish to disclose its contents to a third party they should obtain permission from the client before releasing it. In practical terms, once the report has been sent, auditors have little control over it and it may be given to third parties without the knowledge of the auditors. The auditors should ensure that their report therefore contains the appropriate disclaimer, as shown in **Table 1**, so that any third parties who see the report understand it was not prepared for their benefit.

In the public or regulated sectors auditors may have a duty to submit a copy of their report to the relevant regulatory or funding bodies and therefore the disclaimer will not be appropriate. However, any communication with those charged with governance is confidential and the auditor will require prior consent from those charged with governance before sending a copy to the regulator or funding body.

Where reports are required by such third parties, auditors should show due consideration for the requirements of those bodies when compiling their reports. For example public sector bodies may be particularly interested in:

- misconduct, fraud or other irregularity;
- failure to maintain the requisite high standard of financial integrity by a member of the board; and
- expenditure which is considered to be extravagant or wasteful.

9.12   FORM OF REPORTS

The form of the report will depend on the type of organisation concerned. It may be appropriate to divide the report into sections, which cover significant and general points for senior management first, and then proceed to more specific, divisional points in subsequent sections. The ISA (UK and Ireland) does not include example wordings, but the report covering findings from the audit may typically be formed of a covering letter (see **Table 1**) and a schedule of points raised.

TABLE 1: Reports to management covering letter

Private & Confidential
The Directors
XYZ Plc
1 High Street
London W1

24 June 20XX

Dear Sirs

XYZ Plc

Following our recent audit of your company, we are writing to advise you of various matters which came to our attention.

We set out on the attached schedule the major areas of weakness which we noted, together with our recommendations. These recommendations have already been discussed with . . . and their comments have been included.

As the purpose of the audit is to form an opinion on the company's financial statements, you will appreciate that our examination cannot necessarily be expected to disclose all shortcomings of the system and for this reason, the matters raised may not be the only ones which exist.

We should appreciate your comments as to how you propose to deal with the matters raised in this letter. If you require any further information or advice, please contact us.

We have prepared this letter for your use only. It should not be disclosed to a third party and we can assume no responsibility to any person to whom it is disclosed without our written consent.

We would like to take this opportunity to thank you and your staff for your help and co-operation during the course of our audit.

Yours faithfully
ABC & Co

9.13 CLARIFIED ISA 265 COMMUNICATING DEFICIENCIES IN INTERNAL CONTROL TO THOSE CHARGED WITH GOVERNANCE AND MANAGEMENT

9.13.1 Background

In December 2007 the IAASB issued an Exposure Draft of a new standard, ISA 265, *Communicating deficiencies in internal control.* The original aim of the project was to define the term 'material weakness' as defined in ISA 315 (Redrafted) and to clarify auditors' responsibilities to evaluate whether material weaknesses have been identified based on the audit work performed. However, in the course of their work, the IAASB considered that the term 'material weakness' itself caused issues because any definition they would wish to apply to it would be contrary to that used by the US PCAOB in its Accounting Standard 5. For that reason the IAASB decided that the term 'material weakness' no longer be used in the ISAs, and all relevant ISAs undergo the necessary conforming changes.

In October 2009, the APB issued a Clarified ISA (UK and Ireland) 265 *Communicating Deficiencies in Internal Control to Those Charged with Governance and Management,* which is effective for audits of financial statements for periods ending on or after 15 December 2010.

9.13.2 Identifying and reporting deficiencies

Auditors are required to obtain an understanding of internal control sufficient to allow them to identify and assess risks of material misstatement and to plan audit procedures which address those risks. Auditors are not required to identify deficiencies with the sole purpose of reporting them to those charged with governance or management.

However, Clarified ISA (UK and Ireland) 265 sets out those deficiencies which, once identified, must be reported to those charged with governance and management. This does not preclude auditors from reporting any other deficiencies in internal control identified during the course of their work.

9.13.3 Significant deficiency

The Clarified ISA (UK and Ireland) has introduced a new classification which is based on the assumption that an important public interest consideration for audits is to ensure that non-trivial deficiencies in internal control be communicated to management or those charged with governance as appropriate. In order to make this reporting more meaningful, the Clarified ISA (UK and

Ireland) considers that deficiencies should be prioritised by auditors, so that only those matters deemed to be a 'significant deficiency' need to be reported to those charged with governance. All other deficiencies would be reported to management.

A deficiency in internal control exists when:

- a control is designed, implemented or operated in such a way that it is unable to prevent, or detect and correct, misstatements in the financial statements on a timely basis; or
- a control necessary to prevent, or detect and correct, misstatement in the financial statements on a timely basis is missing.

A deficiency is a 'significant deficiency' when, either in isolation or in combination with other deficiencies, it is of sufficient importance to merit the attention of those charged with governance. This will depend not only on whether a material misstatement has actually occurred, but also on the likelihood that a misstatement could occur, and the potential magnitude of the misstatement. Therefore significant deficiencies can exist without a misstatement having been identified.

Auditors may consider the following when determining whether a deficiency or combination of deficiencies in internal control constitutes a significant deficiency, the:

- likelihood of the deficiencies leading to material misstatement in the financial statements in the future;
- susceptibility to loss or fraud of the related asset or liability;
- subjectivity and complexity of determining estimated amounts, such as fair value accounting estimates;
- financial statements amounts exposed to the deficiencies;
- volume of activity that has occurred or could occur in the account balance or class of transactions exposed to the deficiency or deficiencies;
- importance of the controls to the financial reporting process; for example

  - general monitoring controls (such as oversight of management);
  - controls over the prevention and detection of fraud;
  - controls over the selection and application of significant accounting policies;
  - controls over significant transactions with related parties;
  - controls over significant transactions outside the entity's normal course of business;
  - controls over the period-end financial reporting process (such as controls over non-recurring journal entries);

- cause and frequency of the exceptions detected as a result of the deficiencies in the controls;
- interaction of the deficiency with other deficiencies in internal control.

All significant deficiencies should be reported on a timely basis and in writing to those charged with governance. Other deficiencies not considered to be significant deficiencies need not be reported in writing and the report should be made to management. In addition, management should also be notified in writing of any significant deficiencies reported to those charged with governance.

9.13.4 *Reporting of significant deficiencies*

When reporting significant deficiencies to those charged with governance, auditors should include in their written communication:

- a description of the deficiencies and an explanation of their potential effects; and
- sufficient information to allow those charged with governance and management to understand the context of the communication. In particular auditors should explain that the:
  - purpose of the audit was for the auditor to express an opinion on the financial statements;
  - audit included consideration of internal control relevant to the preparation of the financial statements in order to design audit procedures that are appropriate in the circumstances but not for the purpose of expressing an opinion on the effectiveness of internal control; and
  - matters being reported are limited to those deficiencies that the auditor has identified during the audit and that the auditor has concluded are of sufficient importance to merit being reported to those charged with governance.

Auditors may include suggestions for remedial actions and management's own responses as well as details of any steps taken to verify whether management's responses have been implemented.

Auditors may also include in their reports:

- an indication that if they had performed more extensive procedures on internal control more reportable deficiencies may have been discovered, or it may have been concluded that some of the reported deficiencies may not have needed to be reported; and
- an indication that the report has been provided for the purposes of those charged with governance only, and that it may not be suitable for other purposes.

10 FRAUD AND ERROR

10.1 INTRODUCTION

This Chapter covers the responsibility of auditors in relation to fraud. In recent years, well-publicised cases of major company fraud have focused the public attention on the auditors' responsibility in relation to fraud and illegal acts. This has in turn raised the question of the auditors' responsibility in terms of discovering and reporting them.

It is widely believed by the general public that the auditors' principal duty is to detect fraud. This is one of the components of the so-called 'gap' between the expectations of users of audit reports and the auditors' perception of their responsibilities.

This chapter does not cover non-compliance with law and regulations, which is covered in Chapter 11.

10.2 AUDITING STANDARDS

Clarified ISA (UK and Ireland) 240 *The Auditor's Responsibility to Consider Fraud in an Audit of Financial Statements* was issued in October 2009 and is effective for the audit of financial statements for periods ending on or after 15 December 2010. The updated ISA (UK and Ireland) replaces ISA (UK and Ireland) 240 which was published in December 2004. This chapter covers both the existing and Clarified ISAs (UK and Ireland). As the Clarified ISA (UK and Ireland) adds to the requirements of the existing ISA (UK and Ireland) this chapter is written on the basis of the existing requirements, and changes to them included in the Clarified ISA (UK and Ireland) are included and clearly indicated. The ISA (UK and Ireland) provides guidance on auditing fraud covering:

- the definition of fraud and error;
- the responsibilities of those charged with governance;
- auditors' responsibilities;
- assessment of the risks of material misstatement due to fraud;
- evaluating audit evidence;
- written representations;
- reports to management;
- communication with those charged with governance;
- communication with the authorities; and
- documentation.

10.3 DEFINITIONS

Auditors plan and perform audit procedures to reduce audit risk to an acceptably low level. As part of this process, the ISA (UK and Ireland) requires them to consider the risk of material misstatement in the financial statements due to fraud.

Misstatements can arise from either fraud or error. The main difference between fraud and error is whether the action that resulted in the misstatement was intentional or unintentional.

10.3.1 Fraud

Fraud is an intentional act by one or more individuals among management, those charged with governance, employees, or third parties, involving the use of deception to obtain an unjust or illegal advantage.

Although fraud has a wide legal definition, for the purpose of the ISA (UK and Ireland), auditors are only concerned with fraud that causes a material misstatement in the financial statements.

Fraudulent financial reporting involves intentional misstatements in financial statements to deceive the users of those financial statements. It may be a result of:

- falsification or alteration of records and documents;
- misappropriation of assets or theft;
- suppression or omission of the effects of transactions from records or documents;
- recording fictitious transactions;
- wilful misrepresentation of transactions or of an entity's state of affairs; or
- intentional misapplication of accounting policies.

Fraud often involves management override of controls using such techniques as:

- recording fictitious journal entries, particularly close to the end of the accounting period;
- adjusting assumptions and changing judgements used when performing accounting estimates;
- omitting, advancing or delaying recognition of items in the financial statements;
- concealing facts that could affect the amounts recorded in the financial statements;
- engaging in complex transactions which aim to misrepresent the financial position or performance of the entity; or
- altering records and terms related to significant and unusual transactions.

10.3.2 Error

Error is distinguished from fraud and is defined as unintentional mistakes in the financial statements. It may arise from:

- mathematical or clerical mistakes in the underlying records and accounting data;
- oversight or misinterpretation of facts; or
- unintentional misapplication of accounting policies.

As part of their assessment of an error, auditors should decide its cause and whether it was intentional or unintentional.

10.4 RESPONSIBILITIES OF THOSE CHARGED WITH GOVERNANCE

As stewards of the company, both those charged with governance and management have a fiduciary duty towards the owners of the company. Those charged with governance also have a statutory duty to maintain proper accounting records and prepare financial statements that give a 'true and fair view'. Those charged with governance are responsible for the prevention and detection of fraud and error. It is not possible to achieve absolute assurance against fraud and error, but the implementation and continued operation of adequate accounting and internal control systems may reduce the likelihood of such occurrences.

An additional responsibility is that, under s501 of the Companies Act 2006, it is a criminal offence to give auditors information or explanations which are misleading, false or deceptive.

Those charged with governance should take steps to prevent and detect fraud, and these may include:

- creating a culture of honesty and ethical behaviour, including setting a proper tone;
- developing an appropriate control environment;
- hiring, training and promoting appropriate employees; and
- requiring periodic confirmation by employees of their responsibilities and taking appropriate action in response to actual, suspected or alleged fraud.

10.5 AUDITORS' RESPONSIBILITIES

The position has not altered since the pronouncement of Lord Justice Lopes in *Re Kingston Cotton Mill Company (1896)* that an auditor 'is a watchdog ... not a bloodhound'. The auditors' responsibilities are thus very much tied in with the duty to report on financial statements and are restricted by the concept of 'reasonable assurance'.

ISA (UK and Ireland) 240 expects auditors to recognise that fraud or error may materially affect the financial statements when planning their work and when evaluating and reporting their findings.

Compliance with Auditing Standards will not guarantee that the financial statements are free from material misstatement. The risk of undetected misstatement will be higher with regard to those resulting from fraud or error due to:

- the inherent limitations of the accounting and internal control systems and the use of audit sampling to test them;
- the persuasive, rather than conclusive, nature of the evidence generally obtained by auditors;
- frauds sometimes taking place over a number of years but only being discovered when they become material;
- audit procedures which are planned to detect error may not be appropriate to detect fraud which does not immediately affect the financial statements; and
- frauds often involving collusion or intentional misrepresentations to auditors.

Often auditors are less likely to detect fraud perpetrated by management than fraud perpetrated by employees. This is because management are frequently in a position to directly or indirectly manipulate accounting records or override control procedures.

Because fraud or errors are subsequently discovered which were not detected by the audit it does not mean that the audit was defective. The guidance stresses that although auditors cannot prevent fraud and error the very fact that an annual audit is carried out may act as a deterrent.

10.5.1   Professional scepticism

Auditors should maintain an attitude of professional scepticism throughout the audit. Professional scepticism requires an enquiring mind and a critical questioning of the audit evidence, and is particularly important when considering the risks of material misstatement due to fraud. Even when management and those charged with governance have been found previously to be honest and trustworthy, a sceptical view should be maintained. However, as auditors are not trained to be experts in the authentication of documents, they will accept records and documents as genuine as long as there is no evidence to the contrary.

10.5.2 Engagement team discussion

ISA (UK and Ireland) 315 requires auditors to discuss any susceptibilities of the financial statements to material misstatement (see **22.3.3**), and ISA (UK and Ireland) 240 requires this discussion to include particular emphasis on those risks arising from fraud.

The discussion should include the engagement partner and key staff, and the engagement partner has a responsibility to ensure that those engagement team members not present at the discussion are informed of matters relevant to their work. Areas that the discussion would normally consider are set out in **Table 1**.

TABLE 1: Considerations for the engagement team discussion

- how and where they believe the financial statements may be susceptible to material misstatement due to fraud, how management could perpetrate and conceal fraudulent financial reporting and how assets of the entity could be misappropriated;
- circumstances that might be indicative of earnings management and how earnings may be managed fraudulently;
- the known external and internal factors affecting the entity that may create an incentive for management or others to commit fraud;
- management's involvement in overseeing employees with access to cash or other assets susceptible to misappropriation;
- any unusual or unexplained changes in behaviour or lifestyle of management or employees which have come to the attention of the engagement team;
- the important of maintaining an air of professional scepticism;
- types of circumstances that might be indicative of fraud;
- how an element of unpredictability will be incorporated into the nature, timing and extent of the audit procedures to be performed;
- the audit procedures selected to respond to the risk of fraud and whether some types of procedures are more effective than others;
- any allegations of fraud that have come to the auditors' attention; and
- the risk of management override of controls.

After the initial discussion it is important that the engagement team members continue to communicate and discuss their findings.

Where a small audit is being carried out entirely by the engagement partner, that partner must consider the susceptibility of the entity to fraud during the planning and execution of the work.

10.5.3 Risk assessment

ISA (UK and Ireland) 240 requires an assessment of the risk that fraud or error may lead to misstatement. It sets out the following areas for consideration.

Management and others within the entity

Auditors should enquire about the entity's:

- assessment of the risk that the financial statements may be materially misstated by fraud;
- process for identifying and responding to the risks of fraud in the entity including any specific risks of fraud that have been identified or account balances, classes of transactions or disclosures for which a risk of fraud is likely to exist;
- communication, if any, with those charged with governance regarding its fraud risk identification procedures; and
- communication, if any, to employees regarding its views on business practices and ethical behaviour.

Auditors should also ask those charged with governance, management and internal audit about any actual, suspected or alleged fraud affecting the entity. Where there is an internal audit department auditors should ask about the department's view of the risk of fraud, whether internal auditors have performed any procedures to detect fraud in the period and whether management and those charged with governance have responded satisfactorily to any findings resulting from those procedures.

Others to whom auditors may direct enquiries about fraud include:

- operating personnel not directly involved in the financial reporting process;
- employees with different levels of authority;
- employees involved in initiating, processing or recoding complex or unusual transactions and those who supervise or monitor such employees;
- in-house legal counsel;
- chief ethics officer or equivalent; and
- the person or persons who deal with allegations of fraud.

Those charged with governance

Those charged with governance have a duty to oversee the systems for monitoring risk, financial control and compliance with the law and this will include the entity's assessment of the risks of fraud and controls put in place to mitigate specific risks of fraud that have been identified. Auditors should understand how those charged with governance fulfil this responsibility, and this may give insight into the susceptibility of the entity to fraud, the adequacy of internal control and the competence and integrity of management.

Unusual or unexpected relationships

Any unusual results from analytical review work should make auditors consider the possibility of fraudulent financial reporting.

Other information

Any other information that comes to auditors' attention should be considered as a possible indicator of fraudulent financial reporting. The engagement team member discussion (see **10.5.2**) may be particularly useful in this respect. In addition, work performed as part of acceptance or reacceptance procedures, and work done for the entity in other capacities may be of use.

Fraud risks

After their work on understanding the entity and its environment is complete, auditors should consider whether it indicates that one or more fraud risk factor is present. Examples include the:

- need to meet expectations of third parties to obtain additional financing; or
- granting of significant bonuses if unrealistic profit targets are met.

Fraud risk factors may not necessarily indicate that a fraud has occurred or is likely to occur and auditors use their judgement to assess whether the existence of a fraud risk factor does actually affect the risk of material misstatement of the financial statements.

Fraud risk factors are generally classified as:

- an incentive or pressure to commit fraud, e.g., profitability being threatened by changes in the market;
- a perceived opportunity to commit fraud, e.g., the handling of large amounts of cash; and
- an ability to rationalise the fraudulent action, e.g., a known history of violations against laws and regulations.

10.5.4 *Identification and assessment of fraud risk*

As part of their work of identifying and assessing the risk of material misstatement at the financial statements and assertion level, auditors should assess the risks of material misstatement due to fraud. Fraud risks will automatically be significant risks (see **22.3.6**) and therefore auditors should evaluate the design of the related controls and determine whether they have been implemented.

The assessment of fraud risk is a three-stage process. Auditors use their professional judgement to:

- identify risks of fraud through risk assessment procedures;
- relate the risks of fraud to the assertions; and
- consider the likely size of the potential misstatement and the likelihood of the risk occurring.

Not all fraud risks will have related controls, as the entity's management and those charged with governance may believe that some risks are so remote that the implementation of controls to mitigate them is not necessary.

Revenue recognition

As material misstatement due to fraud often results in an understatement or overstatement of revenue, ISA (UK and Ireland) 240 states that auditors ordinarily assume that there are risks of fraud in revenue recognition. This means that these risks will be significant risks and the three-stage assessment noted above should be followed, together with consideration of associated controls.

The assumption that there are risks of fraud in revenue recognition may be rebutted, for example where there is a single type of simple revenue transaction, such as leasehold revenue from a single unit rental property.

10.5.5 Responses to fraud risk

Overall responses

Where the risk of material misstatement in the financial statements due to fraud has been identified, auditors will respond in ways that have an overall effect on how the audit is conducted. This means that professional scepticism will be increased in all areas which may lead to an increased need to corroborate explanations and representations, and take greater care when examining documentation in relation to material matters.

In their overall response to the risk of material misstatement due to fraud, auditors are required by ISA (UK and Ireland) 240 to pay particular attention to:

- the assignment and supervision of suitably experienced personnel and experts;
- the accounting policies used by the entity, particularly those related to subjective and complex areas; and
- the selection, nature and timing of audit procedures, including incorporating an element of unpredictability in their audit plan.

Responses at the assertion level

Auditors' responses to the risk of material misstatement from fraud at the assertion level may include changing the nature, extent and timing of tests planned. They will aim to obtain more relevant and reliable audit evidence and additional corroborative evidence. This may include a greater reliance on observation and inspection procedures or, where relevant, CAATs. Auditors may conclude that better quality evidence will be obtained by performing more, or all, of their procedures at the period end, rather than during an interim visit, unless the fraud risk has arisen from improper revenue recognition during an interim period, which may be best investigated earlier in the audit process. More extensive testing may also be suitable in response to the increased risk assessment.

Table 2 sets out possible audit procedures to address the assessed risks of material misstatement due to fraud.

TABLE 2: Example audit procedures to address the assessed risks of material misstatement due to fraud

- visiting locations or performing certain tests on a surprise or unannounced basis. For example, observing stock at locations where auditor attendance has not been previously announced or counting cash at a particular date on a surprise basis;
- requesting that stocks be counted at the end of the reporting period or on a date closer to period end to minimise the risk of manipulation of balances in the period between the date of completion of the count and the end of the reporting period;
- altering the audit approach in the current year. For example, contacting major customers and suppliers orally in addition to sending written confirmations, sending confirmation requests to a specific party within an organisation, or seeking more or different information;
- performing a detailed review of the entity's year end adjusting entries and investigating any that appear unusual as to nature or amount;
- for significant and unusual transactions, particularly those occurring at or near year end, investigating the possibility of related parties and the sources of financial resources supporting the transactions;
- performing substantive analytical procedures using disaggregated data. For example, comparing sales and costs of sales by location, line of business or month to expectations developed by the auditors;
- conducting interviews of personnel involved in areas where a risk of material misstatement due to fraud has been identified, to obtain their insights about the risk and whether, or how, controls address the risk;
- when other independent auditors are auditing the financial statements of one or more subsidiaries, division or branches, discussing with them the extent of work necessary to be performed to address the risk of material misstatement due to fraud resulting from transactions and activities among these components;
- if the work of an expert becomes particularly significant with respect to a financial statement item for which the risk of misstatement due to fraud is high, performing additional procedures relating to some or all of the expert's assumptions, methods or findings to determine that the findings are not unreasonable, or engaging another expert for that purpose;
- performing audit procedures to analyse selected opening balance sheet accounts of previously audited financial statements to assess how certain issues involving accounting estimates and judgements, for example a provision for sales returns, were resolved with the benefit of hindsight;
- performing procedures on account or other reconciliations prepared by the entity, including considering reconciliations performed at interim periods;
- performing computer-assisted techniques to test for anomalies in a population;
- testing the integrity of computer-produced records and transactions;
- seeking additional audit evidence from sources outside of the entity being audited.

Responses to management override of controls

The extent of the risk that management may use their position to override controls to manipulate accounting records and prepare fraudulent financial statements will vary from entity to entity. However, there will be some risk in all entities, and the ISA (UK and Ireland) deems this to be a significant risk (see **22.3.6**). Therefore, in accordance with ISA (UK and Ireland) 315 specific procedures should be planned and performed to address this risk. ISA (UK and Ireland) 240 requires auditors to:

- test the appropriateness of journal entries recorded in the general ledger and other adjustments made in the preparation of financial statements;
- review accounting estimates for biases that could result in material misstatement due to fraud; and
- obtain an understanding of the business rationale of significant transactions that the auditors become aware of that are outside the normal course of business for the entity, or that otherwise appear to be unusual given the auditors' understanding of the entity and its environment.

Auditors' assessment of the risk of material misstatement due to fraud may lead them to perform additional procedures to those set out above.

Journal entries

The financial reporting process is often manipulated by the recording of inappropriate or unauthorised journal entries or other adjustments. When considering which journals or adjustments to test, auditors consider:

- their assessment of the risks of material misstatement, which may indicate a type of class or adjustments for testing;
- whether there are effective controls over journal entries and adjustments;
- the nature of evidence that can be obtained, particularly when journal entries are made electronically;
- the typical characteristics of fraudulent journal entries, including entries:
  - made to unrelated, unusual or seldom-used accounts;
  - made by individuals who do not usually make journal entries;
  - recorded at the end of the period or as post-closing entries that have little or no explanation or description;
  - made either before or during the preparation of the financial statements; or
  - containing round numbers or consistent ending numbers;
- the nature and complexity of the accounts involved, as fraudulent entries may be made to accounts that:
  - contain transactions that are complex or unusual in nature;
  - contain significant estimates and period end adjustments;
  - have been prone to misstatements in the past;
  - have not been reconciled on a timely basis or contain unreconciled differences;
  - contain intercompany transactions; or
  - are otherwise associated with an identified risk of material misstatement due to fraud; and

- those journals processed outside the normal course of business.

Accounting estimates

Fraudulent financial reporting is often performed through intentional misstatement of accounting estimates. Therefore, the ISA (UK and Ireland) suggests that, when auditors are reviewing accounting estimates, they should consider whether the estimates indicate a bias on the part of the entity's management. Auditors may also perform a retrospective review of management judgements and assumptions in the prior year to see if any bias is indicated in the current period.

If a bias is indicated, auditors should consider whether the circumstances represent a risk of material misstatement due to fraud.

Business rationale of transactions

Auditors aim to understand the rationale of unusual business transactions in order to consider whether the transactions have been entered into to conceal fraudulent financial reporting or misappropriation of assets. Auditors should consider whether:

- the transaction appears overly complex;
- management has discussed the nature of, and accounting for, the transaction with those charged with governance;
- management is placing emphasis on the need for a particular accounting treatment;
- transactions involving related parties have been properly reviewed and approved by those charged with governance; and
- the transaction involves previously unidentified related parties or parties that do not have the substance to support the transaction without the assistance of the entity being audited.

10.6   EVALUATING AUDIT EVIDENCE

In accordance with ISA (UK and Ireland) 330, once audit evidence has been obtained, auditors should revisit their assessment of the risk of material misstatement and consider whether it remains valid or needs amendment. This includes the risk of material misstatement due to fraud. If the risk assessment requires amendment, further audit procedures may be required.

Auditors' overall analytical review procedures at the end of the audit should include consideration of whether there is an indication of material misstatement due to fraud. For example, uncharacteristically large amounts of income being reported in the last few weeks of the accounting period may indicate fraudulent activity.

Any misstatements discovered during the audit process should be considered as possible indicators of fraud. If fraud is indicated, auditors should reconsider the reliability of management representations.

Auditors must consider the severity of the fraud and its impact on their report. Where a suspected fraud has caused a misstatement that is not material to the financial statements, auditors consider its implications to the rest of their evidence. For example, a petty cash fraud perpetrated by a clerk is not likely to impact auditors' opinions. However, if the same fraud was perpetrated by management, auditors may consider that it is indicative of a more pervasive problem with the integrity of management.

10.7 AUDITOR UNABLE TO CONTINUE THE ENGAGEMENT

Clarified ISA (UK and Ireland) 240 states that there may be situations where auditors are required to question their ability to continue performing an audit. These may include:

- the entity does not take the appropriate action regarding fraud that auditors consider necessary in the circumstances, even where the fraud is not material to the financial statements;
- auditors' consideration of the risk of material misstatement due to fraud and the results of audit tests indicate a significant risk of material and pervasive fraud; or
- auditors have significant concerns about the competence or integrity of management or those charged with governance.

In such situations auditors should:

- consider whether it is appropriate to withdraw from the engagement;
- determine their professional and legal responsibilities, including responsibilities to report their inability to continue the engagement with the person or person who made the audit appointment or any relevant regulatory authority;

10.8 MANAGEMENT REPRESENTATIONS

ISA (UK and Ireland) 240 requires auditors to obtain written representations from management and those charged with governance that:

- it acknowledges its responsibility for the design, implementation and maintenance of internal controls to prevent and detect fraud;
- it has disclosed to the auditor the results of its assessment of the risk that the financial statements may be material misstated as a result of fraud;

- it has disclosed to the auditor its knowledge of fraud or suspected fraud affecting the entity involving:

  - management;
  - employees who have significant roles in internal control; or
  - others where the fraud could have a material effect on the financial statements; and

- it has disclosed to the auditor its knowledge of any allegations of fraud, or suspected fraud, affecting the entity's financial statements, communicated by employees, former employees, analysts, regulators or others.'

10.9 COMMUNICATION WITH MANAGEMENT AND THOSE CHARGED WITH GOVERNANCE

Where auditors have identified a fraud, or have indications that a fraud may exist, this should be communicated to an appropriate level of management as soon as possible.

If fraud is identified involving:

- management;
- employees who have significant roles in internal control; or
- others where the fraud could have a material effect on the financial statements,

auditors should communicate with those charged with governance as soon as practicable. Communication may be oral or in writing, having regard to the factors set out in section **8.5**.

If the integrity or honesty of management or those charged with governance is doubted, auditors consider seeking legal advice before continuing with their work.

In addition, auditors should inform those charged with governance about any material weaknesses in the design and implementation of internal controls to prevent and detect fraud, or other matters related to fraud which may have come to their attention.

10.10 COMMUNICATION WITH THE AUTHORITIES

The auditors' duty of confidentiality will be overridden by the requirements of the anti-money laundering regulations and the Proceeds of Crime Act 2002, which impose a duty on auditors to report all suspicions that a criminal offence giving rise to any direct or indirect benefit from criminal conduct has been committed. Further details are given in **Chapter 12**.

10.11   DOCUMENTATION

As part of their understanding of the entity as required by ISA (UK and Ireland) 315, auditors should document:

- the significant decisions reached during the engagement team discussion about the susceptibility of the entity's financial statements to material misstatement due to fraud (see **10.5.2** above); and
- the identified and assessed risks of material misstatement due to fraud at the financial statements level and at the assertion level.

Auditors should also document:

- their planned responses to the assessed risk of material misstatement due to fraud at the financial statements level and the nature, timing and extent of audit procedures planned, with those procedures linked back to the assessed risks of material misstatement due to fraud at the assertion level;
- the results from the procedures planned;
- communications about fraud made to management and those charged with governance; and
- if they have assessed that there is no risk of material misstatement due to fraud related to revenue recognition, their reasons for this conclusion.

11 CONSIDERATION OF LAW AND REGULATIONS

11.1 INTRODUCTION

This Chapter covers the responsibility of auditors in relation to illegal acts or non-compliance with laws and regulations. In recent years, well-publicised cases where major companies have not acted in accordance with the laws and regulations which apply to them have focused public attention on the auditors' responsibility for discovering and reporting upon such acts.

This chapter does not cover fraud and error, which are covered in **Chapter 10** or money laundering and the Money Laundering Regulations 2003 which is covered in **Chapter 12**.

11.2 AUDITING STANDARDS

In October 2009, the APB issued Clarified ISA (UK and Ireland) 250. The Clarified ISA (UK and Ireland) has two parts: Part A covers *Consideration of Laws and Regulations in an Audit of Financial Statements* and Part B covers *The Auditor's Right and Duty to Report to Regulators in the Financial Sector*.

Part A is based on International Clarified ISA 250, but Part B is composed entirely of UK and Ireland specific guidance.

The Clarified ISA (UK and Ireland) is applicable for the audits of financial statements for periods ending on or after 15 December 2010.

This chapter covers both the existing and clarified ISAs (UK and Ireland). As the clarified ISA (UK and Ireland) adds to the requirements of the existing ISA (UK and Ireland) this chapter is written on the basis of the existing requirements, and changes to them included in the Clarified ISA (UK and Ireland) are included and clearly indicated.

Part A of the ISA (UK and Ireland) contains guidance covering:

- types of law and regulation;
- auditor's consideration of compliance; and
- reporting non-compliance.

Part B of the ISA (UK and Ireland) is detailed in **Chapter 8**.

As with all ISAs (UK and Ireland), the text of the international ISA has been supplemented with additional guidance from a UK and Ireland perspective.

11.3 LEGAL AND REGULATORY FRAMEWORK

An entity's legal and regulatory framework is the laws and regulations to which it is subjected. The legal and regulatory framework will vary from entity to entity. Some laws and regulations will have a direct effect on the financial statements as they determine the amounts to be reported and disclosures in the financial statements. Examples of such laws and regulations include those governing taxation and pension rights.

Other laws and regulations do not have a direct effect on the amounts in the financial statements, but compliance with them is fundamental to the ability of the business to operate. These include compliance with the terms of an operating licence, compliance with regulatory solvency requirements or compliance with environmental regulations. Non-compliance with these laws and regulations will have an effect on the financial statements by calling the going concern assumption into doubt or requiring additional disclosure of matters in the accounts.

The amount of law and regulation that an entity is governed by will depend on the industry it operates in and its constitution. For example, some sectors are heavily regulated, such as banks or pharmaceutical companies, whilst others are only subject to 'general' laws such as health and safety regulations. The further removed the non-compliance is from what is reflected in the financial statements, the less likely the auditor is to recognise it.

11.4 MANAGEMENT RESPONSIBILITY

It is management's responsibility to ensure that the entity complies with law and regulations and that they establish procedures to prevent and detect non-compliance. To do this they would normally set up procedures whereby they:

- maintain a register of significant laws and regulations as they affect the entity;
- monitor relevant legal requirements and ensure operating procedures and conditions meet them;
- institute and operate an appropriate system of internal control;
- develop and publish within the entity relevant codes of conduct;
- ensure employees are properly trained and understand the relevant codes of conduct;
- monitor compliance with the code;
- engage legal advisers to assist in monitoring; and
- maintain a record of complaints.

In larger entities, these methods may be supplemented by the establishment of:

- a wide-ranging internal audit function;
- a legal department;
- a compliance department; and/or
- an audit committee.

In certain industries these compliance procedures may be imposed by regulations, such as the financial services sector.

Non-compliance with law and regulations may lead to financial penalties being imposed on an entity or a loss of its business. Therefore, the implications of any non-compliance, either suspected or actual, should be assessed using FRS 12, *Provisions, Contingent Liabilities and Contingent Assets* or IAS 37 of the same name, with regard to the inclusion and/or disclosure in the financial statements of such liabilities. In serious cases this may also affect the directors' consideration of going concern.

11.5 RESPONSIBILITY OF THE AUDITORS

The auditors have no responsibility for the prevention of illegal acts or duty to report them except in certain restricted circumstances. However, the annual audit and the auditors' right to report in the public interest may act as a deterrent. Auditors may also highlight areas where illegal acts could occur, and suggest practical solutions in their reports to management (see **Chapter 9**).

Under ISA (UK and Ireland) 200 auditors 'should plan and perform the audit with an attitude of professional scepticism recognising that the audit may reveal conditions or events that would lead to questioning whether an entity is complying with laws and regulations'.

The guidance goes on to stress that an audit cannot be expected to detect all possible non-compliance. There is always a risk that material misstatement arising from non-compliance will not be detected, but the level of risk will be affected by:

- whether the non-compliance can be captured by the system of internal controls and accounting system;
- the inherent limitations of the internal control system and the use of audit testing;
- the fact that auditors obtain evidence which is persuasive rather than conclusive; and
- non-compliance may involve concealment.

The risk will also be affected by management's ethos as regards compliance as well as consideration of any relevant codes of conduct. A review of management's procedures and controls together with relevant correspondence with those authorities responsible for regulation in industries where specific laws and regulations may be expected to have such a fundamental effect may be useful.

As part of their planning process, auditors should obtain a general understanding of the legal and regulatory framework applicable to the client and its industry. Auditors should also consider the procedures the entity follows to ensure that it complies with this framework. Procedures would include:

- using and updating existing knowledge of the entity's industry, regulatory and other external factors;
- enquiring of those charged with governance about the entity's policies and procedures for complying with laws and regulations;
- enquiring of those charged with governance as to the regulations that may be expected to have a fundamental effect on the operations of the entity;
- discussing the policies for identifying, evaluation and accounting for litigation claims with those charged with governance; and
- discussing the legal and regulatory framework with auditors of subsidiaries in other countries.

11.6 CONSIDERATION OF COMPLIANCE

11.6.1 *Laws with a direct effect on the financial statements*

Evidence should be obtained by the auditors of compliance with laws and regulations which have a direct effect on the financial statements under ISA (UK and Ireland) 250. Examples of such laws are:

- those which determine the form and content of an entity's financial statements – for example,Sch.1 to SI 2008/410, The Large and Medium-sized Companies and Groups (Accounts and Reports) Regulations 2008;
- those which determine when a company is prohibited from making a distribution – for example, s830 of the Companies Act 2006;
- those which oblige auditors to report in accordance with specific statutory requirements – for example, failure of a company to maintain proper accounting records, or disclosure of directors' remuneration; and
- financial reporting requirements for specific industries – for example, the Friendly and Industrial and Provident Societies Act 1968.

The Taxes Acts are a special case and the extent to which they need to be considered by auditors depends on whether that firm also acts as tax advisors. If they do not, their only consideration will be the material misstatement of the tax liability. Where auditors are also tax advisors, even though different people may be involved in each service, those responsible for the audit should inform the partner responsible for tax advice of any non-compliance they come across during the course of their work, in addition to assessing the effect of the matter on the financial statements.

Where laws determine the form and content of an entity's financial statements or, alternatively, are reportable on by auditors, the auditors have a responsibility to properly plan, perform and evaluate their audit with these in mind. In doing this, auditors must aim to give themselves a reasonable expectation of identifying non-compliance and any resulting misstatements in the financial statements which would be important to the user, although not necessarily material in quantitative terms. Auditors therefore must have regard to these laws when planning their audit, by understanding them and then testing compliance with them.

To identify instances of non-compliance with laws which have a direct effect on the financial statements, the ISA (UK and Ireland) requires auditors to:

- review correspondence with relevant authorities;
- make enquiries of those charged with governance to ascertain whether they are aware of any non-compliance; and
- obtain written confirmation from the directors that they have disclosed to the auditors all possible non-compliance, together with the consequences that may arise.

11.6.2   *Laws affecting the operations of the entity*

In addition, in the UK and Ireland, the auditor should plan and perform procedures which are designed to identify possible or actual instances of non-compliance with the laws and regulations within which the entity conducts its business and which are central to the entity's ability to continue operating. These may include environmental restrictions or non-compliance with terms of an operating licence.

11.7   MONEY LAUNDERING

Following the introduction of the Money Laundering Regulations 2003 and the Proceeds of Crime Act 2002, the scope of offences reportable by auditors to the relevant authorities has been considerably increased. Auditors should, therefore, be aware that instances of possible or actual non-compliance with laws and regulations discovered during the audit may incur obligations for partners and staff to report money laundering offences to the authorities. Further guidance is given in **Chapter 12**.

11.8   NON-COMPLIANCE

Auditors may receive specific information from testing which may alert them to the possibility that illegal acts have occurred. For example:

- investigation by government department;

- payment of fines or penalties;
- large payments for unspecified services or loans to consultants;
- excessive sales commissions;
- purchasing at prices significantly above or below market price;
- unusual payments in cash, cheques payable to bearer or transfers to numbered bank accounts;
- unusual transactions with companies registered in tax havens;
- payments for goods or services made to a country other than that where goods originated;
- existence of an accounting system or part of one which fails, whether by design or accident, to give an adequate audit trail;
- unauthorised or improperly recorded transactions; or
- media comment.

When auditors become aware of possible non-compliance, they should obtain an understanding of the nature of the act and the circumstances in which it has occurred, and sufficient other information to evaluate the possible effect in the financial statements.

Evaluating the effect on the financial statements involves considering:

- any contingent liabilities, such as fines;
- whether the going concern assumption is still appropriate; and
- the extent of required disclosure.

The consideration may involve matters outside the knowledge of the auditors and in these cases expert advice should be sought on the effect on the financial statements. ISA (UK and Ireland) 620 *Using the Work of an Expert* sets out the procedures that auditors should follow in such circumstances (see **36.4**).

Once auditors believe there is non-compliance, ISA (UK and Ireland) 250 requires them to:

- document their findings, including taking copies of original records which give rise to suspicions and make full notes of minutes of conversations with management on the subject if appropriate;
- report them direct to a third party if necessary; and
- discuss them with the directors, subject to consideration of the risk of 'tipping off', see **Chapter 12**.

Where management does not provide sufficient information about the suspected non-compliance to demonstrate that the entity is in fact complying, auditors should consider taking legal advice. In normal circumstances they would consult the entity's lawyers, but if they believe that it is not appropriate or they are unable to consult them, the auditors may obtain their own legal advice. If there is still insufficient information concerning the non-compliance then auditors should consider the implications for their report, and whether there is any obligation to report to third parties.

However, it is not just the effect on the audit report that should be considered. Auditors need to assess the reliability of management representations they have received in the light of the suspected non-compliance. This may be particularly important where the non-compliance includes:

- an apparent failure of specific control procedures;
- involvement of management; and
- any concealment of the act.

The guidance cites the example of a series of instances which, although financially immaterial, are 'symptomatic of management's probity' and cast doubt on the integrity of the financial statements.

11.9 REPORTING

11.9.1 Reporting to those charged with governance

The discovery of non-compliance should normally be reported to those charged with governance and where the non-compliance is believed to be intentional and material this report should be made as soon as is practicable.

The non-compliance should be reported to the next level of management who are not suspected of being involved. Where it is suspected senior management are involved it may be necessary to report the matter to the audit committee, or in the case of money laundering directly to the appropriate authority. Legal advice may be required if auditors believe that no higher authority exists or that their report may not be acted on. If money laundering or some other reportable event is suspected it may be appropriate to report suspicions directly to the relevant authority.

11.9.2 Reporting to owners/members

Where a non-compliance has a material effect on the financial statements, and it has not been adequately reflected in those financial statements, auditors should issue a qualified audit report.

If management have not given sufficient evidence for the auditor to conclude that the entity is free from non-compliance a limitation of scope opinion should be given. This will be either a disclaimer of opinion or a qualified opinion depending on the severity of the limitation.

If the auditor is unable to determine whether a non-compliance has occurred as a result of circumstances rather than management intervention, a limitation of scope opinion will also be suitable.

In all the above situations, and where there is the suspicion of money laundering, auditors must consider whether issuing their audit report would be considered to be 'tipping off' (see **Chapter 12**). In such a situation, auditors should obtain specialist legal advice.

Auditors should not refrain from qualifying their report or omitting an explanatory paragraph because the matter has since been corrected. They should base their assessment on the adequacy of the view given by the financial statements.

The consideration of the disclosure of the non-compliance will focus on going concern issues and contingencies. In particular:

- whether shareholders require the information to assess the performance of the directors;
- any potential consequences for the operational future of the company; and
- any contingencies such as fines or litigation costs.

The disclosure should be sufficient to provide a true and fair view enabling users to 'appreciate the significance of the information disclosed'. Normally full disclosure of the potential consequences will be necessary to give a true and fair view.

Where there is no specific disclosure requirement, auditors must assess the potential financial consequences and, in particular, have regard to whether non-compliance or its consequences are material to the financial statements and the probability of the act or its consequences recurring.

11.9.3   Reporting to third parties

Where auditors become aware of an actual or suspected non-compliance which gives rise to a statutory duty to report they should do so to the appropriate authority without delay. The guidance in Section B of ISA (UK and Ireland) 250, which covers reporting to regulators in such circumstances (see **Chapter 8**), should be adapted for non-regulated entities whose auditors are under a statutory duty to report, for example where they suspect money laundering.

ISA (UK and Ireland) 250 requires auditors who become aware of suspected or actual non-compliance to:

- consider if the matter should be reported to 'a proper authority in the public interest'; and where this is the case
- discuss the matter with the board and the audit committee, except in cases where they no longer have confidence in the integrity of the directors (see below).

Once they have reached a decision, auditors should then notify the directors in writing that they are of the opinion that the matter is reportable. If the directors do not report the matter themselves, or do not provide evidence that they have already reported the matter, the auditors should report directly. Auditors may take legal advice before making a decision on whether the matter needs to be reported.

Where auditors have lost confidence in the integrity of the directors as a result of the suspected or actual non-compliance, they may report extreme cases directly to the proper authority in the public interest, without discussing the matter with the board.

Reporting to third parties may lead to some concerns regarding the apparent breach of confidentiality and what is meant by the public interest. The guidance in the ISA (UK and Ireland) considers both in detail.

11.10   RESIGNATION

The guidance suggests that as a last resort, where auditors cannot obtain the necessary information, or have no opportunity to inform the shareholders, or where management refuse to issue financial statements, they should withdraw from the engagement.

12 MONEY LAUNDERING

12.1 BACKGROUND

Chapter 11 deals with laws and regulations and the need for auditors to take them into account in the course of their audits. One area which is of great concern to auditors in relation to this is money laundering. Until 1 March 2004 the specific duties of auditors in the UK to report money laundering suspicions extended only to the suspected proceeds of drug trafficking or terrorist funds. From that date new regulations, the Money Laundering Regulations 2003, were introduced which extended the Proceeds of Crime Act 2002 to accountants. This new legislation extended money laundering reporting to include possessing or any way dealing with, or concealing, the proceeds of any criminal conduct, where criminal conduct is defined as conduct which constitutes an offence in any part of the United Kingdom, or is an indictable offence in the Republic of Ireland.

The Serious Organised Crime and Police Act 2005, which was passed by Parliament in April 2005, made some changes to the Anti-Money Laundering reporting requirements. These are detailed below.

Updated regulations, the Money Laundering Regulations 2007, became effective from 15 December 2007. These changes introduced by the 2007 Regulations are set out in **12.2** below.

12.2 CONSEQUENCES FOR ACCOUNTANTS IN PRACTICE

In February 2004, the Consultative Committee of Accounting Bodies (CCAB) issued guidance for all accountants on meeting their obligations under the new Money Laundering Regulations entitled *Anti-Money Laundering (Proceeds of Crime and Terrorism), Second Interim Guidance for Accountants.* Under this guidance, accountants in practice must report any suspicions or grounds for suspicion to the Serious Organised Crime Agency (SOCA) into which the previous responsible body, the National Crime Intelligence Squad (NCIS) has been subsumed. Firms must:

- appoint a nominated officer (a money laundering reporting officer (MLRO)) to receive reports of suspicions from colleagues and pass them on to the SOCA;
- train partners and staff on the requirements of the legislation, and how to recognise and report money laundering suspicions;
- verify the identity of new clients and keep records of the evidence obtained; and

- establish appropriate internal procedures to prevent or halt money laundering.

Sole practitioners are not required to appoint a MLRO, but in other respects are recommended to follow the CCAB guidance.

In assessing whether an individual had knowledge or suspicion of money laundering which they should have reported, the courts are likely to take into account the level of skill and experience held by that individual, including any professional qualification. Wilful blindness will also be seen as having knowledge.

12.2.1   Changes in the 2007 Regulations

Where firms were already following the previous CCAB guidance, the introduction of the 2007 Regulations should not mean too many changes for auditors. The main areas for change are for firms which are not part of the practice assurance scheme run by the ICAEW or covered by the monitoring arrangements of another anti-money laundering supervisory authority, who will be supervised by HMRC. These will:

- need to have a risk assessment in place, and conduct their client due diligence on the basis of that assessment including:

  - simplified due diligence; and
  - enhanced due diligence;

- need to identify the beneficial owner of a client;
- be required to monitor, on an ongoing basis, their relationship with the client and have evidence of identity in place for all clients, even those which have been on the books for many years; and
- need to monitor their firm's compliance with the regulations.

12.3   AUDITORS' RESPONSIBILITIES

The Money Laundering Regulations 2003 extended to the Proceeds of Crime Act to all accountants. This chapter is concerned with how these regulations impact on the responsibilities of auditors specifically and outlines various sources of guidance which have been published.

Whilst the main guidance for auditors is set out in Practice Note 12 (Revised) (see **12.4**), further guidance is also available in Section B of ISA (UK and Ireland) 250, and this is covered in **12.5** below. In addition, **12.6** includes details of ICAEW guidance notes and useful information which was published in the original Practice Note 12, but which has not been reproduced in the revised version.

In the autumn of 2007, the CCAB issued a document containing anti-money laundering guidance for the accountancy sector. It was first issued by the ICAEW in October 2007 as Tech 05/07, and comments were requested. It was then reissued in December 2007 in its final form as Tech 07/07. Relevant guidance from the document is included throughout this chapter.

12.4 PRACTICE NOTE 12 (REVISED)

12.4.1 Introduction

Practice Note 12, *Money Laundering – Interim Guidance for Auditors in the United Kingdom* was originally issued in May 1997. It has undergone a continued programme of updates to ensure that it addresses new legislation as it is published. The most recent update, issued in March 2008, reflects the legislation effective at 31 January 2008. Recent legislation has a major impact on auditors' responsibilities to report money laundering suspicions. The Practice Note concentrates on the impact of the new legislation on auditors' responsibilities when auditing and reporting on financial statements; it does not provide general guidance on the legislation.

An Exposure Draft of a further update to Practice Note 12 was issued in March 2010. The Practice Note was updated following the publication of the suite of Clarified ISAs (UK and Ireland), and the APB stated that there had not been any substantial changes to the Practice Note. Comments were requested by 30 June 2010.

12.4.2 What is money laundering?

The widening of the definition of money laundering is illustrated by examples of offences set out in Appendix 1 to the Practice Note, an example of which is set out below.

Example

A subsidiary of a public company has guaranteed a £20,000 loan made by the bank to one of its directors. Such provision of guarantees for loans to directors are prohibited by s330 of the Companies Act 1985, and for subsidiaries of public companies such loans can give rise to criminal offences under s342(2) of the Act. If none of the exemptions set out in the Act apply and the company could not claim that it did not know the relevant circumstances at the time of the loan, the auditors would conclude that the director is in possession of the proceeds of the company's crime and make a report to their MLRO.

The appendix contains a number of situations where suspicions of money laundering may be reportable. With the frequently changing legislation surrounding money laundering, the Practice Note suggests that each case is assessed individually in relation to the current rules and independent advice obtained as necessary.

The Serious Organised Crime and Police Act 2005 states that it is no longer necessary for auditors to report money laundering suspicions where the suspect cannot be identified and the whereabouts of the proceeds are unknown. Commentators are assuming that this change also includes situations where an auditor knows that their client keeps records of suspected shoplifters or other minor criminals, but does not need to access those records for the purposes of the audit. The CCAB 2007 guidance states that if the whereabouts of the criminal property is known or information is held that might assist in locating the property, a report is still required.

As stated above, the definition of money laundering has been widened, but the scope of the audit has not been extended. Auditors are required to make a report when information comes to their attention in the normal course of their audit work. All incidences should be reported, not just those which are material to the financial statements. Failure to make a report is a criminal offence and auditors, both partners and staff, face criminal penalties if they breach the requirements. Auditors are not required to undertake any further work to determine whether an offence has been committed; the suspicion alone is reportable.

The CCAB 2007 guidance amends requirements for auditors who discover conduct overseas which would have been an offence if committed in the UK. Previously all such incidents were reportable, but now auditors are not required to report conduct giving rise to criminal property if it was:

- reasonably believed to have taken place outside of the UK;
- was lawful under the criminal law of the place where it occurred; and
- the maximum sentence if the conduct had occurred in the UK would have been less than 12 months.

Therefore when considering non-UK parts of a group audit, the UK parent company auditors will need to consider whether information obtained as part of the group audit procedures, such as discussions with subsidiary auditors or discussions with UK or non-UK directors, gives rise to a reportable offence.

The Serious Organised Crime and Police Act 2005 takes steps to remove the possession of proceeds of foreign actions which would be illegal in the UK, from the definition of money laundering. However, implementation of these changes are being delayed until further procedures are in place to ensure that reports of suspicious activities such as terrorism and organised crime are still received, wherever the underlying behaviour took place.

12.4.3 Procedures

Training

Firms are required to implement training programmes to ensure that their partners and staff are aware of the Proceeds of Crime Act 2002, the Money Laundering Regulations 2007, the Terrorism Act 2000 and the Serious Organised Crime and Police Act 2005.

Risk assessment

Professional firms are likely to have systems in place to minimise professional, client and legal risk. Money laundering risk assessment procedures will probably be integrated within these other systems.

Firms should assess each client in relation to their money laundering risk. Money laundering risk is the risk that:

- the client is involved in money laundering; or
- the firm may be used to launder money or provide the means to launder money, for example by handling client money.

From their considerations, firms can put together a simple matrix of money laundering risk and combine this with their client acceptance procedures to ensure that sufficient client due diligence work is performed.

Even where clients are only subject to simple due diligence and are considered low risk, firms should always gain an understanding of:

- who the client is;
- who owns the client (including its ultimate beneficial owners – see below);
- who controls it;
- the purpose and intended nature of their business relationship with the client;
- the nature of the client;
- the client's source of funds; and
- the client's business and economic purpose.

Client identification

Client identification procedures under the 2007 Regulations fall into a number of different areas:

- general client identification;
- simplified client due diligence;
- enhanced client due diligence;
- politically exposed person;
- identification of beneficial owner;
- third party reliance;
- ongoing monitoring; and
- electronic identification.

General client identification

Under the 2003 Regulations, firms were required to perform client identification procedures for new clients. The 2007 Regulations have extended that requirement to all new and existing clients.

Auditors must ensure that they have on file sufficient evidence to prove that the identity of the client has been verified and suitable evidence has been retained. The method of verification is not set out in the Regulations, but the CCAB 2007 guidance provides suggested evidence for companies and individuals, and this is reproduced in **Tables 1** and **2**.

TABLE 1: Example client identification procedures suggested by the CCAB guidance

For private companies and LLPs

If a representative of the company has been met face to face and the client has been assessed as normal money laundering risk:

- obtain full company search from Companies House (or equivalent information obtained through a commercial provider of registry information); or
- obtain certified copies taken from original documents evidencing details of incorporation or registration, registered office and list of directors and shareholders/members; and
- identify any shareholder/member in the entity holding more than 25 per cent of the equity (rights to either income, capital or voting), or if there is no holding over 25 per cent, the largest holding. This step should be repeated until the ultimate beneficial owners have been identified.

If no representative of the company has been met face to face and/or the client has been assessed as high money laundering risk:

- select individual(s) and entities that is/are capable of exercising significant influence over this entity either as an appointed director, or as a shadow director or equivalent, identify it/them according to whether a legal or natural person;
- select any shareholder/member in the entity holding more than 25 per cent of the equity (rights to either income, capital or voting), or where no holding over 25 per cent, the largest holding and identify it/them according to whether a legal or natural person. This step should be repeated until appropriate ultimate beneficial owners have been verified.

For all entities that are a money service business, verify HMRC registered number by obtaining a certified copy of their certificate.

For listed or regulated entities

Obtain either a printout from the relevant regulator's or exchange's website (and annotate), or obtain direct written confirmation from the regulator or exchange, to confirm the regulated or listed status of the entity (ensure that basic details of name, address, any membership or registration details, and any disciplinary details where applicable are provided).

TABLE 2: Example client identification procedures suggested by the CCAB guidance for individuals

If the individual has been met face to face and has been assessed as normal money laundering risk, obtain either:

- photo identity; or
- non-photo identity and proof of address (cannot be a PO Box) or date of birth.

If the individual has not been met face to face and/or has been assessed as higher money laundering risk, obtain either:

- photo identity and another piece of evidence; or
- non-photo identity, proof of address (no PO Boxes) or date of birth, plus an additional piece of evidence.

Suitable sources of evidence of identity are:

- photo identity:

  - valid passport;
  - valid photocard driving licence (full or provisional);
  - national identity card (issued by EEA member states and Switzerland);
  - firearms certificate or shotgun licence;
  - identity card issued by the Electoral Office for Northern Ireland.

- non-photo identity:

  - documents issued by a government department, incorporating the person's name and residential address or their date of birth, such as:

    - a current UK full driving licence old version (not provisional licence);
    - evidence of entitlement to a state or local authority funded benefit, tax credit, pension, educational or other grant;
    - documents issued by HMRC, such as PAYE coding notices and statements of account;
    - end of year tax certificates.

Suitable sources of evidence of address or date of birth are:

- instrument of a court appointment (such as a grant of probate, bankruptcy);
- current council tax demand letter or statement;
- current (within the last three months) bank statements, or credit/debit card statements issued by a regulated financial sector firm in the UK, EU or Joint Money Laundering Steering Group equivalent jurisdiction (but not statements printed off the internet);
- a file note of a visit by a member of the firm to the address concerned;
- an electoral register search showing residence in the current or most recent electoral year;
- a recent (last available) utility bill;
- valid photocard driving licence (full or provisional);
- a current UK full driving licence old version (not provisional licence);
- evidence of entitlement to a state or local authority funded benefit, tax credit, pension, educational or other grant;
- documents issued by HMRC, such as PAYE coding notices and statements of account;
- a firearms/shotgun licence;
- a solicitor's letter confirming a recent house purchase or land registry confirmation (auditors must also verify the previous address).

Client identification procedures should be applied when:

- a business relationship is established;
- an occasional transaction is carried out;
- there is a suspicion of money laundering or terrorist financing; or
- there are doubts about the veracity or adequacy of the documents or data previously obtained.

Simplified due diligence
Simplified due diligence means that the customer due diligence measures required on establishing a business relationship, carrying out an occasional transaction or doubting the veracity of documents previously obtained is not obligatory.

Clients who may be subject to simplified due diligence are:

- credit or financial institutions subject to the provisions of the money laundering directive or equivalent overseas requirements;
- companies listed on a regulated EEA market or equivalent overseas requirements; or
- UK public authorities and certain public authorities in the EU and EEA.

The right to simplified due diligence is revoked if a suspicion of money laundering or terrorist financing arises in relation to that client.

Enhanced client due diligence
Enhanced due diligence must be performed where auditors have assessed their clients as having a higher money laundering risk or where the client has not been physically present for identification purposes. The additional information to be gathered in these circumstances is set out in **Tables 1** and **2** above.

In addition, if a business relationship or occasional transaction is to be undertaken with a politically exposed person (see below) the firm must:

- provide approval from senior management before the relationship is established;
- take adequate measures to establish the source of wealth and funds which are involved; and
- conduct enhanced monitoring of any relationship entered into.

Politically Exposed Person
A Politically Exposed Person (PEP) is defined as a person 'who is or has, at any time in the preceding year been entrusted with a prominent public function by a state other than the United Kingdom, a community institution or an international body' or a family member or known close associate of such as person. PEPs must always be subject to enhanced due diligence.

Identification of beneficial owner

Under previous guidance it was prudent, but not obligatory to identify the beneficial owners of a client, that is any individual who owns more than 25 per cent of the shares or voting rights. Under the 2007 Regulations it is now a requirement for auditors to perform this investigation and document the results in their files.

Third party reliance

Under the new Regulations, auditors may now rely on third parties such as regulated credit or financial institutions, lawyers, other audit firms, external accountants, insolvency practitioners and tax advisors when completing their customer due diligence work. Any reliance is subject to the consent of the third party, and auditors will remain liable for any failures to comply with the requirements.

Ongoing monitoring

The 2007 Regulations contain a requirement for customer due diligence to be kept under review, although no prescribed periodic review is given. Where updates to a client's risk profile indicates that customer due diligence may require updating, additional work should be performed. In addition, the following should trigger a review of customer due diligence:

- at the start of new engagements and when planning for recurring engagements;
- when a previously stalled engagement restarts;
- whenever there is a change of control and/or ownership of the client;
- when there is material change in the level, type or conduct of business; and
- where any cause for concern, or suspicion, has arisen (in such cases, care must be taken to avoid making any disclosure which could constitute 'tipping off' (see **12.4.4** below)).

Electronic identification

Electronic resources are an acceptable part of client due diligence and can be used as stand alone evidence of verification of identity.

Engagement letters

For new clients, a form of pre-engagement communication may be of use in explaining the procedures being undertaken. The requirement for obtaining additional evidence of clients' identities may also be explained in the engagement letter for ongoing clients. The example in **Table 3** could be used for both purposes.

TABLE 3: Example client identification wording

Client identification

As with other professional services firms, we are required to identify our clients for the purposes of the UK anti-money laundering legislation. We are likely to request from you, and retain, some information and documentation for these purposes and/or to make searches of appropriate databases. If we are not able to obtain satisfactory evidence of your identity within a reasonable time, there may be circumstances in which we are not able to proceed with the audit appointment.

It may also be useful to include a paragraph similar to the example in **Table 4** to inform clients of auditors' responsibility to report suspicions or knowledge that a money laundering offence has taken place.

TABLE 4: Example money laundering reporting wording for engagement letter

Money laundering reporting

The provision of audit services is a business in the regulated sector under the Proceeds of Crime Act 2002 and, as such, partners and staff in audit firms have to comply with this legislation which includes provisions which may require us to make a money laundering disclosure in relation to information we obtain as part of our normal audit work. It is not our practice to inform you when such a disclosure is made or the reasons for it because of the restrictions imposed by the 'tipping off' provisions of the legislation.

Where a decision is taken to include paragraphs such as those in **Tables 3** and **4** in engagement letters, this should be done for all clients. Where the paragraphs are included in only some of the auditor's engagement letters, the inclusion of these paragraphs may be seen as 'tipping off'.

12.4.4   Tipping off

Previously, anyone who had knowledge or suspicion that a money laundering offence has occurred should be aware that various actions may mean that they breached the 'tipping off' requirements, that is disclosing information to any person or individual where doing so was likely to prejudice an investigation. Changes in legislation mean that this offence is now limited to people in the regulated sector. This includes auditors, external accountants, insolvency practitioners and tax advisers. Therefore auditors should:

- ensure that any further investigation consists only of steps that the auditor would have performed as part of their normal audit work;
- obtain clearance from their MLRO before any further investigation is performed;
- consider whether the wording of a qualified audit report will fall foul of the

tipping off regulations, consulting with the law enforcement agency for agreement as necessary;

- issue their report on a timely basis, as an unnecessary delay may be construed as tipping off; and
- take advice on the precise dating of the s394 statement if they decide to resign from the engagement in order to avoid tipping off.

12.4.5   Reporting to the MLRO and SOCA

Subject to the Privilege Reporting Exemption, introduced by the CCAB 2007 guidance (see **12.4.6** below), all suspicions or knowledge of money laundering offences must be reported to the firm's MLRO or, for sole practitioners, direct to the Serious Organised Crime Agency (SOCA). The MLRO must then report the matter 'as soon as is practicable' to SOCA, and at the latest up to one month after the audit report is signed. There is no de minimis limit for reporting, or provision for a report not to be made where the auditors consider that SOCA is already aware of the matter, so all incidences, however small, will warrant a report. The Serious Organised Crime and Police Act paved the way for the introduction of mandatory reporting forms, and the SOCA is currently reviewing its system for reporting including the use of 'standard' and 'limited intelligence value' reports. For sole practitioners making reports directly to the SOCA, the SOCA disclosure forms are available on its website *www.soca.gov.uk* and these can be submitted electronically.

Reporting to SOCA does not relieve auditors from other statutory duties such as reporting to the FSA for entities in the financial sector or other regulators for entities such as pension schemes and charities. The need to report to SOCA is likely to be a matter of 'material significance' to a regulator, and therefore will require to be reported to them. Again auditors should ensure that they do not breach tipping off regulations in making reports to regulators.

12.4.6   Privilege reporting exemption

Prior to the Money Laundering Regulations 2003 (Amendment) Order 2006, which came into force on 21 February 2006, only lawyers enjoyed exemption from reporting suspicions of money laundering formed in privileged circumstances. From that date a 'relevant professional adviser' can also be exempted from reporting in privileged circumstances. The exemption is only in relation to money laundering reports and no other legal professional privilege is extended.

A relevant professional adviser is an accountant, auditor or tax adviser who is a member of a professional body which:

- tests the competence of those seeking admission; and

- imposes and maintains professional and ethical standards, as well as imposing sanctions for non-compliance with those standards.

The exemption also extends to those in partnership with such an adviser, or employed by them.

If a relevant professional adviser obtains knowledge or suspicion of money laundering in privileged circumstances, they should still make a report to their MLRO, who in turn assesses whether they are exempted to report under s330(6) of the POCA. There is no exemption if the information is passed to him with the intention of furthering the criminal act. The details of the information and the consideration of whether to make a report should be fully documented by the MLRO.

Privileged circumstances

There are two types of privileged circumstances; those relating to legal advice and those to litigation.

In relation to legal advice, for a privileged circumstance to exist:

- there needs to be a confidential communication (written or oral) between the relevant professional adviser and his client, or a representative of the client, in which the client seeks or the relevant professional adviser gives legal advice;
- that communication must take place within the confines of a professional relationship between them, including an initial meeting which does not progress to a business relationship; and
- the communication must relate to legal advice (i.e., advice concerning the rights, liabilities and obligations or remedies of the client under the law).

Examples where relevant professional advisers may fall within privileged circumstances in relation to legal advice include:

- advice on taxation matters, where the tax adviser is giving advice on the interpretation or application of any element of tax law and in the process is assisting a client to understand his tax position;
- advice on the legal aspects of a take-over bid, for example on points under the Companies Act legislation;
- advice on duties of directors under the Companies Act;
- advice to directors on legal issues relating to the Insolvency Act 1986; and
- advice on employment law.

In relation to litigation, for a privileged circumstance to exist:

- there must be a confidential communication (written or oral) between the relevant professional adviser and the client or third party;
- the confidential communication must be made for the dominant purpose (i.e., the overriding purpose) of being used in connection with actual, pending or contemplated litigation.

Examples where relevant professional advisers may fall within privileged circumstances in relation to litigation include:

- assisting a client by taking a witness statement from him or from third parties in respect of litigation;
- representing a client, as permitted, at a tax tribunal; and
- when instructed as an expert witness by a solicitor on behalf of a client in respect of litigation.

Conducting audit work, routine book-keeping, accounts preparation or tax compliance assignments do not in themselves give rise to privileged circumstances.

12.4.7 Auditors' report on the financial statements

Where it is suspected that money laundering has occurred auditors should be wary about breaching the regulations relating to 'tipping off' when issuing their audit report. When considering the nature of their audit report, auditors should apply the concept of materiality, considering whether the disclosure of the:

- crime itself;
- consequences of the crime; or
- outcome of any subsequent investigation by police or other investigatory body

may have a material effect on the financial statements.

12.5 CONSIDERATION OF LAWS AND REGULATIONS

ISA (UK and Ireland) 250 requires auditors to gain an understanding of the legal and regulatory framework within which an entity operates and to plan and perform procedures designed to help identify possible or actual instances of non-compliance with those laws and regulations. As a result of this work, auditors may uncover evidence which creates a duty to report money laundering offences.

The Money Laundering Regulations 2003 have widened the scope of reportable offences to include the concealing, disguising, converting, transferring, removing, using, acquiring or possessing of property which constitutes or represents a benefit from any criminal conduct. Criminal conduct is defined as 'conduct which constitutes an offence in any part of the UK or would constitute such an offence if it occurred in any part of the UK'. As a result auditors are more likely to come into contact with matters that should be reported.

As the number of reportable incidences increase, so does the likelihood of auditors falling foul of the offence of 'tipping off'. Many of the procedures set out in ISA (UK and Ireland) 250 may constitute 'tipping off' if actioned where an incidence of money laundering is discovered or suspected. Examples include:

- discussing non-compliances with management or those charged with governance;
- issuing a qualified audit report;
- issuing a report to a regulatory authority; or
- resigning their position as auditors.

In such situations, auditors should discuss their actions with experts in SOCA.

12.6 OTHER GUIDANCE

In December 1999, the Institute of Chartered Accountants in England and Wales issued a set of guidance notes for auditors. They deal with the statute law, regulations and professional requirements in relation to the avoidance, recognition and reporting of money laundering. Although the guidance notes are based on the law and conditions existing in England and Wales prior to 1 March 2004, they outline a number of useful procedures which should be followed by every entity, covering:

- identification: obtaining evidence of the identity of prospective clients;
- records: keeping records of identity documents and of transactions;
- reporting: ensuring that all suspicions of money laundering are reported to the appropriate authorities; and
- training: training partners and staff, particularly in how to recognise suspicious transactions.

In order to ensure that a firm has sufficient knowledge of their new and existing clients, auditors should ask and document the answers to the questions in **Table 5**.

TABLE 5: Questions to ensure that the identity of a client is known

- is the prospective client who they claim to be?
- is enough known about their personal or business and financial background to be able to provide an effective service?
- if the client's premises are not visited, what is being taken on trust?
- are changes in the continuing clients' circumstances notified to the firm?

The guidance also indicates potential danger signals, which may point to underlying money laundering, and these are set out in **Table 6**.

TABLE 6: Money laundering danger signals

- the client is reluctant to provide details of identity and background, or is over-plausible. This may be of greater importance where the client is never met in person, or the client's premises are never visited;
- the client has no obvious reason for using a particular auditor. Other auditors may

---

be available nearer the client's base or the client is asking for services which are outside the normal remit of the firm;
- the client's transactions lack, or include steps which lack, apparent commercial purpose – for example, the structure of transactions appears unnecessarily complex, or there is no obvious commercial requirement for the number of subsidiaries, branches, trusts or nominees included in the client's structure;
- there is an inability to obtain convincing evidence as to the origins of the funds behind the financial and legal structure;
- the client asks its auditors to hold or transmit money or other assets, without giving a convincing reason for the auditor's involvement;
- the client comes from, or is introduced by a third party in, a country where drug production and trafficking may be prevalent. Similar caution should be exercised where the client has links with a country with an ineffective anti-money laundering system.

Where the laws on money laundering are considered to be central to the entity's operations auditors must assess compliance with them. Where the legislation is not central to the operations of the entity, auditors should consider whether the business is one of those which is more prone to involvement, either knowingly or unknowingly, in money laundering. Businesses which are conducted mainly in cash, such as auction houses and garages, may have a higher risk of being used by criminals to launder the proceeds of their activities.

The old Practice Note provided illustrative lists of factors which may give rise to an increased risk of involvement in money laundering, shown in **Table 7** and **Table 8**. The guidance stressed that the existence of one of these factors does not give rise to a suspicion that money laundering is occurring, but that auditors should be alert to circumstances in which a combination of factors may give rise to a suspicion. These factors remain relevant under the new regulations.

TABLE 7: Factors arising from action by the entity or its directors which may indicate an increased risk of money laundering

- complex corporate structure where complexity does not seem to be warranted;
- complex or unusual transactions, possibly with related parties;
- transactions with little commercial logic taking place in the normal course of business;
- transactions not in the normal course of business;
- transactions where there is a lack of information or explanations, or where explanations are unsatisfactory;
- transactions at an undervalue;
- transactions with companies whose identity is difficult to establish as they are registered in countries known for their commercial secrecy;
- extensive or unusual related party transactions;
- many large cash transactions when not expected;
- payments for unspecified services, or payments for services that appear excessive in relation to the services provided;
- the forming of companies or trusts with no apparent commercial or other purpose;
- long delays in the production of company or trust accounts;
- foreign travel which is apparently unnecessary and extensive.

TABLE 8: Factors arising from action by a third party which may indicate an increased risk of money laundering

- a customer establishing a pattern of small transactions and then having one or two substantially larger ones;
- unusual transactions or a pattern of trading with one customer that is different from the norm;
- unusual requests for settlement of sales in cash;
- taking out of single premium life assurance policies, with subsequent early cancellation and encashment;
- a customer setting up a transaction that appears to be of no commercial advantage or logic;
- a customer requesting special arrangements for vague purposes;
- unusual transactions with companies registered overseas;
- requests for settlement in bank accounts or jurisdictions which would be unusual for a normal commercial transaction.

---

13 GOING CONCERN

13.1 INTRODUCTION

Auditors' consideration of the going concern basis is an area that has recently been the subject of much debate. High profile cases where companies have collapsed with apparently inadequate warning in financial statements and audit reports have concentrated attention in this area. This is, however, a difficult area in which to set standards for auditors, being one involving more judgements than most others which auditors face.

Directors have a responsibility to prepare financial statements on the going concern basis unless it is inappropriate to do so. This involves an assessment of, and judgements about, the future. If they decide the basis is inappropriate, assets may need to be written down to recoverable amounts or reclassified, and liabilities restated to reflect changes in amount or date of maturity. Auditors must assess how directors have carried out this assessment on a realistic basis and that the consequences, where relevant, are reflected in the financial statements.

13.2 AUDITING STANDARDS

Clarified ISA (UK and Ireland) 570 *Going Concern* was issued in October 2009 and replaces ISA (UK and Ireland) 570 previously issued in December 2004. The Clarified ISA (UK and Ireland) is effective for the audit of financial statements for periods ending on or after 15 December 2010. This chapter covers both the existing and clarified ISAs (UK and Ireland). As the Clarified ISA (UK and Ireland) does not significantly amend the requirements of the existing ISA (UK and Ireland) this chapter is written on the basis of the existing requirements, and any changes to them included in the Clarified ISA (UK and Ireland) are included and clearly indicated.

ISA (UK and Ireland) 570 provides guidelines relating to the going concern basis covering:

- general requirements;
- the entity's responsibilities;
- the auditors' responsibilities; and
- audit conclusions and reporting.

As with all ISAs (UK and Ireland), the text of the international ISA has been supplemented with additional guidance from a UK and Ireland perspective.

Also in October 2009, the APB issued a revision to ISA (UK and Ireland) 700, *The Auditor's Report on Financial Statements* which updated the format of the auditor's report following the enactment of the Companies Act 2006 and a consultation process by the APB which considered improvements which could be made to the readability of auditor's reports, see **Chapters 3** and **4**. Examples of modified auditor's reports relating to going concern issues are provided in Bulletin 2009/2 *Auditor's Reports on Financial Statements in the United Kingdom*.

In response to the economic downturn, the APB issued Bulletin 2008/10 *Going Concern Issues During the Current Economic Conditions* in December 2008. This supplements Bulletin 2008/1 *Audit Issues when Financial Market Conditions are Difficult and Credit Facilities may be Restricted*, which provided more general guidance and is covered in **Chapter 37**. Bulletin 2008/10 is discussed in **13.10**.

Further guidance in relation to listed companies is provided in APB Bulletin 2009/4, *Developments in Corporate Governance Affecting the Responsibilities of Auditors of UK Companies*, which is discussed in **15.6.4**.

13.3 GENERAL REQUIREMENT

ISA (UK and Ireland) 570 requires auditors to consider, when forming an opinion on whether the financial statements present a true and fair view:

- the entity's ability to continue as a going concern; and
- any disclosures in the financial statements.

The guidance focuses on the auditors' responsibility to assess how the directors have satisfied themselves that the financial statements have been prepared on an appropriate basis.

It is implied therefore that the directors must make their assessment and, on the basis of this, decide what disclosure is necessary.

13.4 THE ENTITY'S RESPONSIBILITIES

Those charged with governance have the responsibility of determining whether the entity is a going concern and for preparing the financial statements on a going concern basis. Under the going concern assumption an entity will be assumed to continue in business for the foreseeable future without the intention or need to liquidate, cease trading or seek protection from its creditors. Assets and liabilities will, therefore, be recorded assuming that they will be traded or settled in the normal course of business.

Those charged with governance may be preparing their financial statements under either IFRS or UK accounting standards. The requirements governing going concern are the same under the two frameworks, except that if the period considered by the directors is less than one year from the date of approval of the financial statements disclosure of that fact must be made in the financial statements under FRS 18. There is no such requirement under IAS 1, where the relevant 12-month period runs from the balance sheet date.

When making their assessment, those charged with governance should be aware that:

- the outcome of an event is less certain the further it is likely to occur from the date the assessment is made;
- judgements can only be made on the basis of information available at the time. Subsequent events can contradict a decision which was reasonable at the time it was made; and
- any judgement will be affected by the size and complexity of the entity, its type of business and how susceptible its activities are to outside influences.

Auditors should also consider these factors when forming an opinion on the assessment made by those charged with governance.

Examples of events or circumstances which may cause doubt about the suitability of using the going concern assumption are given in **Table 1**. However, such circumstances may be mitigated, for example, the loss of a principal supplier may be mitigated by the availability of a suitable alternative supplier.

TABLE 1: Events or circumstances which may cause doubt over use of the going concern assumption

Financial

- net liability or net current liability position;
- necessary borrowing facilities have not been agreed;
- fixed-term borrowing approaching maturity without realistic prospects of renewal or repayments; or excessive reliance on short-term borrowings to finance long-term assets;
- major debt repayment falling due where refinancing is necessary to the entity's continued existence;
- major restructuring of debt;
- indications of withdrawal of financial support by debtors and other creditors;
- negative operating cash flows indicated by historical or prospective financial statements;
- adverse key financial ratios;
- substantial operating losses or significant deterioration in the value of assets used to generate cash flows;
- major losses or cash flow problems which have arisen since the balance sheet date;
- arrears or discontinuance of dividends;
- inability to pay creditors on due dates;

- inability to comply with the terms of loan agreements;
- reduction in normal terms of trade credit;
- change from credit to cash-on-delivery transactions with suppliers;
- inability to obtain financing for essential new product development or other essential investments;
- substantial sales of fixed assets not intended to be replaced.

Operating

- loss of key management without replacement;
- loss of key staff without replacement;
- loss of a major market, franchise, licence or principal supplier;
- labour difficulties or shortages of important suppliers;
- fundamental changes in the market or technology to which the entity is unable to adapt adequately;
- excessive dependence on a few product lines where the market is depressed;
- technical developments which render a key product obsolete.

Other

- non-compliance with capital or other statutory requirements;
- pending legal or regulatory proceedings against the entity that may, if successful, result in claims that are unlikely to be satisfied;
- changes in legislation or government policy expected to adversely affect the entity;
- issues which involve a range of possible outcomes so wide that an unfavourable result could affect the appropriateness of the going concern basis.

13.5 THE AUDITORS' RESPONSIBILITIES

Auditors' objectives are to:

- obtain sufficient appropriate audit evidence regarding the appropriateness of those charged with governance's use of the going concern assumption in the preparation of the financial statements;
- conclude, based on the audit evidence obtained, whether a material uncertainty exists related to events or conditions that may cast significant doubt on the entity's ability to continue as a going concern; and
- determine the implications for the auditor's report.

13.5.1 Planning the audit

As part of their gathering of knowledge of the business, auditors should remain alert for indications that the use of the going concern assumption may not be appropriate. They should continue to be mindful of any such circumstances throughout the audit and if they become aware of any events and related business risks which may indicate that the entity is not a going concern, they should perform the procedures set out in **Table 2.**

If such events or risks are identified, auditors should also consider their impact on the assessment of the risk of material misstatement (see **Chapter 22**).

TABLE 2: Audit work to be performed if events or circumstances are identified which indicate that the entity may not be a going concern

- review the entity's plan for future actions based on the going concern assessment, e.g. the use of the financial statements to secure funding;
- gather evidence to support or dispel the material uncertainty, including considering the plans of management and any mitigating factors; and
- obtain written representations from those charged with governance concerning:

  - their future plans;
  - their belief that the entity is a going concern; and
  - any relevant disclosures in the financial statements.

At the planning stage auditors may be able to review any preliminary assessment of going concern made by those charged with governance. If no preliminary assessment has been made, auditors should discuss going concern with the entity at this early stage to enable any further reviews and resolution of issues to be completed.

13.5.2 Evaluating the entity's assessment of going concern

ISA (UK and Ireland) 570 requires that auditors evaluate the entity's assessment of its ability to continue as a going concern.

Auditors' procedures will involve:

- holding discussions with those charged with governance;
- examining appropriate supporting documentation; and
- planning and performing procedures designed to identify any material matters which could impact on the entity's ability to continue as a going concern, including considering the process followed to make the assessment, the assumptions on which the assessment is based and plans for the future.

The issues auditors should consider may include the:

- period assessed by those charged with governance;
- system for identifying future risks;
- existence/quality of budgets or forecasts;
- appropriateness of assumptions;
- sensitivity of budgets;
- adequacy of borrowing facilities; and
- the entity's plans for resolving going concern problems.

The extent of the procedures carried out will depend on the headroom between financial requirements and the facilities available. The more demonstrably healthy the company, the less extensive the procedures need to be.

Borrowing facilities

The assessment of the going concern assumption also involves comparing available cash with requirements and assessing the 'headroom' available. For companies financed by debt, the assessment involves deciding what level of borrowing facilities may reasonably be expected to be available.

The ISA (UK and Ireland) highlights the need for auditors to make their own assessment of ongoing facilities. It notes that auditors may need to make an assessment of the intentions of the company's bankers, the most common provider of finance, where:

- there is a low margin of financial resources available;
- the company's facilities are shortly due for renewal;
- they are aware of previous difficulties in agreeing facilities and the bankers have imposed further conditions for continued lending;
- the directors have projected a significant deterioration in the cash position; or
- the company has recently breached or is likely to breach its borrowing covenants.

Such an assessment may include:

- reviewing correspondence between directors and their bankers; and
- meeting with the directors and bankers to clarify the latter's intentions.

The auditors may, despite the above, decide it is necessary to obtain confirmation from bankers of the existence and terms of facilities.

If they are neither able to satisfy themselves about the existence and terms of facilities or about the bankers' future intentions, auditors need to consider whether:

- there is sufficient disclosure of the uncertainty in respect of the facilities in the financial statements to give a true and fair view; and
- to refer to the matter in their audit report (see below).

Some possible procedures that auditors may consider where the situation is complex and headroom is tight are shown in **Table 3**.

TABLE 3: Possible audit procedures

Forecasts and budgets

Review cash flow forecasts and budgets, where available, from the expected date of approval of the financial statements. Perform sensitivity analysis on the key components of forecasts and budgets.

Consider the assumptions used in preparing the forecasts, for example:

- anticipated levels of sales;
- projected winning of new customers;
- expected cash collection performance;

- capital expenditure programme;
- timing of anticipated payments to Inland Revenue or Customs; and
- basis of payment terms to existing suppliers.

Assess reliability of directors' previous forecasting.

Borrowing facilities

Confirm the existence and terms of facilities.

Establish the date for renewal of facilities.

Assess the future intentions of lenders via discussion or correspondence.

Assess possible breaches of any borrowing covenants imposed by lenders.

Check for any arrears of interest on current borrowings.

Review the value of any assets granted as security for borrowings.

Review correspondence between directors and lenders.

Contingent liabilities

Consider possible exposure to contingent liabilities arising, for example, from:

- legal proceedings;
- guarantees or warranties; and
- retentions.

Assess potential intra-group guarantees (e.g., unlimited multilateral guarantees).

Review possible breaches of grant conditions leading to repayment of grants.

Financial risk

Review directors' assumptions about projected foreign currency exchange rates.

Consider exposure to major fixed-price contracts.

Financial adaptability

Assess entity's ability to adapt to unexpected events, for example:

- disposal of fixed assets;
- leasing;
- debt restructuring;
- share capital issue;
- financial support from group companies; and
- new sources of finance.

13.5.3 Period covered by auditors' review

Auditors should ensure that their procedures cover the same period of time considered by those charged with governance when they made their initial assessment of going concern. The ISA (UK and Ireland) states that where those charged with governance have considered a period shorter than 12 months from the balance sheet date, the auditor should ask management to extend their assessment period to cover the full 12 months. This is then supplemented by a UK and Ireland specific paragraph which states that this will usually be at least 12 months from the date of approval of the financial statements. The ISA (UK and Ireland) goes on to stress that the period considered will depend on:

- the entity's reporting and budgeting systems; and
- the nature of the entity, including its size and complexity.

Under ISA (UK and Ireland) 570, where the period considered by those charged with governance is less than 12 months from the date of approval of the financial statements disclosure of this fact should normally be made in the financial statements. Where those charged with governance do not make this disclosure in the financial statements, the auditors are required to do so within their report. **Table 5** gives an extract from a report where the financial statements have been prepared under UK GAAP. As the period considered by those charged with governance has not extended to 12 months from the date of approval of the financial statements there is a qualification arising from the failure to disclose this under FRS 18.

In this example there is no emphasis of matter paragraph required because no disclosure has been made about the 12-month period in the financial statements and all references to the elapsed period have been made in the qualified opinion.

When the entity is preparing financial statements under IFRS, there is an anomaly between the period those charged with governance are required to consider under IAS 1 (twelve months from the balance sheet date) and the period specified by ISA (UK and Ireland) 570 (twelve months from the date of approval of the financial statements). Therefore, the situation may arise where the requirements of IAS 1 are fulfilled, but those in ISA (UK and Ireland) 570 are not. In such circumstances the financial statements are unqualified as the accounting requirements have been met, but an emphasis of matter paragraph should be added to the auditor's report to draw attention to the fact that the requirements of ISA (UK and Ireland) 570 have not been fulfilled (see **Table 6**).

Where financial statements have been prepared under IFRS, and those charged with governance have refused to extend their assessment period to a period of more than 12 months from the balance sheet date (to comply with IAS 1) or 12 months from the date of approval of the financial statements (to comply with ISA (UK and Ireland) 570), the auditor should follow the example in **Table 7** which includes both a qualification and an emphasis of matter paragraph.

In contrast to **Table 5**, **Table 7** includes a case under IAS 1, where the qualification results from the fact that the correct period has not been considered, and here, an emphasis of matter refers to the inadequate disclosure which is not considered to be a matter for qualification under these rules.

The period under consideration may not have formal cash flow forecasts and budgets prepared for it, but this does not necessarily mean that the going concern assumption cannot be used. Although these are likely to provide the most persuasive evidence, alternative sources of evidence may be acceptable, such as:

- the state of the company's order book and its tendering activities;
- its relationship with its bankers (the company has renewed its arrangements with its bankers for a further year in this example);
- the stability of the work force; and
- the ability to reduce cash needs if work is not obtained.

13.5.4 Events after the period considered by those charged with governance

Auditors should enquire of those charged with governance if they are aware of any events or circumstances which may occur after their period of assessment has elapsed (i.e., after 12 months from the date of approval of the financial statements) which may impact the use of the going concern assumption. Events this far in the future are unlikely to be certain, but auditors should consider the impact of any such event which is made known to them up until the date of their audit report. However, auditors have no responsibility to design audit procedures to discover such events.

13.6 AUDIT CONCLUSIONS AND REPORTING

13.6.1 Entity considered not to be a going concern

ISA (UK and Ireland) 570 requires that auditors should document any concerns they have about the entity's ability to continue in operational existence. Concerns may arise not only from their evaluation of the entity's assessment, but also from other evidence or knowledge of the business obtained during the audit, together with any other information of which they may have become aware.

If there is a significant level of concern about the entity's ability to continue as a going concern auditors could disagree with the use of the going concern assumption in preparing the financial statements. If this is the case, auditors would draw the attention of those charged with governance to the need to obtain specialist advice.

Where the financial statements have been incorrectly prepared assuming the entity is a going concern, auditors would give an adverse opinion in their report, as shown in **Table 8**.

However, if those charged with governance have correctly prepared the financial statements using an alternative appropriate basis of preparation, and this has been adequately disclosed, the audit report can be unqualified. An emphasis of matter paragraph may be required in the audit report to draw readers' attention to the alternative basis.

If the alternative basis of preparation has not been adequately disclosed an adverse or disagreement opinion may be given (see examples in **Tables 8** and **9**). In extreme circumstances, where there are multiple significant uncertainties, a disclaimer of opinion may be suitable.

13.6.2   Inadequate disclosures

Auditors are required to consider whether the financial statements are required to include disclosures about going concern and whether those disclosures are adequate. For example if the period considered by those charged with governance is less than 12 months from the date of approval of the financial statements, this should be disclosed. Where it is not disclosed in the financial statements, auditors should make reference to it in the basis of audit opinion section of their report, as in the example extract in **Table 6**.

13.6.3   Those charged with governance not taking adequate steps

Where auditors are of the opinion that those charged with governance have not taken adequate steps to assess the reasonableness of the going concern assumption, they would give a qualified opinion. Such a qualification would be a limitation on the scope of the auditors' work as they are unable to obtain all the information and explanations which they consider necessary for the purpose of their audit. Depending on the severity of the limitation, the extract examples in **Tables 10** and **11** could be used.

13.6.4   Material uncertainty

If auditors consider that the use of the going concern assumption is correct but that there remains a material uncertainty, they should assess whether the financial statements:

- describe adequately the principal events or conditions that give rise to the uncertainty that the entity can continue in operation and the entity's plans to deal with these events or conditions; and
- state that the material uncertainty exists and that it may cast significant doubt on the entity's ability to continue as a going concern and, therefore, that it may not be unable to realise its assets and discharge its liabilities in the normal course of business.

If these disclosures are made, the audit report would be unqualified, but would contain an emphasis of matter paragraph to bring readers' attention to the matter. **Table 12** sets out an example emphasis of matter paragraph. To be content with the disclosures made in the financial statements, auditors should ensure that the financial statements include:

- a statement that the going concern basis has been used;
- a statement of relevant facts;
- the nature of the concern;
- the assumptions adopted by the entity;
- the entity's plans, where practicable, to resolve the concern; and
- details of any relevant actions taken by the entity.

Where the relevant disclosures are not made or are inadequate, the example in **Table 9** should be followed.

13.6.5   Example report extracts

Bulletin 2009/2 (see **Chapter 3**) sets out a number of extracts from example reports. A navigation aid is set out in **Table 4** below, together with reference to the example reports which follow.

13.   Going Concern

TABLE 4: Navigation aid for modified auditor's reports arising from going concern issues

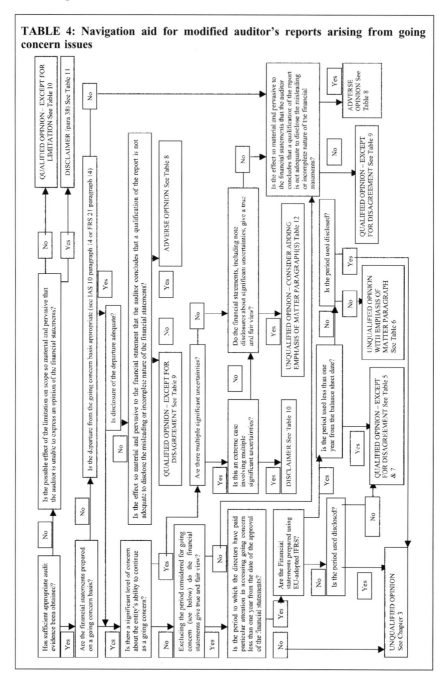

TABLE 5: Example of disagreement under UK GAAP where the requirements of FRS 18 have not been fulfilled and no disclosure of this fact is made

Qualified opinion arising from departure from FRS 18 'Accounting Policies'

In assessing whether it is appropriate to prepare the financial statements on a going concern basis the directors have paid particular attention to a period ending on 30 September 20X3 which is less than twelve months from the date of approval of the financial statements. This fact has not been disclosed in the financial statements, contrary to the requirements of Financial Reporting Standard 18 'Accounting Policies'.

Except for the absence of the disclosure referred to above in our opinion the financial statements:

- give a true and fair view of the state of the company's affairs as at [date] and of its profit [loss] for the year then ended;
- have been properly prepared in accordance with United Kingdom Generally Accepted Accounting Practice; and
- have been prepared in accordance with the requirements of the Companies Act 2006.

Opinion on other matter prescribed by the Companies Act 2006

In our opinion the information given in the Directors' Report for the financial year for which the financial statements are prepared is consistent with the financial statements.

Matters on which we are required to report by exception

We have nothing to report in respect of the following matters where the Companies Act 2006 requires us to report to you if, in our opinion:

- adequate accounting records have not been kept or returns adequate for our audit have not been received from branches not visited by us; or
- the financial statements are not in agreement with the accounting records and returns; or
- certain disclosures of directors' remuneration specified by law are not made; or
- we have not received all the information and explanations we required for our audit.

[*Signature*]
John Smith (Senior statutory auditor)
For and on behalf of ABC LLP, Statutory Auditor
Address
Date

TABLE 6: Example of emphasis of matter where entity has complied with IAS 1, but not ISA (UK and Ireland) 570

Emphasis of matter – Going concern

In forming our opinion, which is not qualified, we have considered the adequacy of the disclosures made in note x to the financial statements concerning the period used by the directors in assessing whether the going concern assumption is appropriate. In making their assessment the directors have considered the period up to 31 March 20X3 which is less than 12 months from the date of the approval of the financial statements and the directors have not disclosed this fact. International Standards on Auditing (UK and Ireland) required the auditors to draw this fact to the attention of readers of the financial statements.

TABLE 7: Example of disagreement under IFRS where the financial statements do not comply with the requirements of IAS 1 and inadequate disclosure of this fact is made

Qualified opinion arising from departure from IAS 1 'Presentation of financial statements'

In assessing whether it is appropriate to prepare the financial statements on a going concern basis the directors have paid particular attention to a period ending on 30 November 20X2 which is less than 12 months from the balance sheet date. This is contrary to the requirements of International Accounting Standard 1 'Presentation of financial statements'.

Except for the non-compliance with IAS 1 referred to above in our opinion:

- give a true and fair view of the state of the company's affairs as at 31 December 20.. and of its profit for the year then ended;
- have been properly prepared in accordance with United Kingdom Generally Accepted Accounting Practice; and
- have been prepared in accordance with the requirements of the Companies Act 2006.

Emphasis of matter – Going concern

In forming our opinion, we have considered the adequacy of the disclosures made in note x to the financial statements concerning the period used by the directors in assessing whether the going concern assumption is appropriate. In making their assessment the directors have considered the period up to 30 November 20X2 which is less than 12 months from the date of the approval of the financial statements and the directors have not disclosed this fact. International Standards on Auditing (UK and Ireland) required the auditors to draw this fact to the attention of readers of the financial statements. Our opinion is not further qualified in respect of this matter.

Opinion on other matter prescribed by the Companies Act

In our opinion the information given in the Directors' Report for the financial year for which the financial statements are prepared is consistent with the financial statements.

Matters on which we are required to report by exception

We have nothing to report in respect of the following matters where the Companies Act 2006 requires us to report to you if, in our opinion:

- adequate accounting records have not been kept or returns adequate for our audit have not been received from branches not visited by us; or
- the financial statements are not in agreement with the accounting records and returns; or
- certain disclosures of directors' remuneration specified by law are not made; or
- we have not received all the information and explanations we required for our audit.

[Signature]

John Smith (Senior statutory auditor)
For and on behalf of ABC LLP, Statutory Auditor
Address
Date

TABLE 8: Example adverse opinion

Adverse opinion

As explained in note x to the financial statements the company's financing arrangements expired and the amount outstanding was payable on 31 December 20X1. The company has been unable to re-negotiate or obtain replacement financing and is considering entering insolvency proceedings. These events indicate a material uncertainty which may cast significant doubt on the company's ability to continue as a going concern and therefore it may be unable to realise its assets and discharge its liabilities in the normal course of business. The financial statements (and notes thereto) do not disclose this fact and have been prepared on the going concern basis.

In our opinion, because of the omission of the information referred to above:

● do not give a true and fair view of the state of the company's affairs as at 31 December 20.. and of its profit for the year then ended; and
● have not been properly prepared in accordance with United Kingdom Generally Accepted Accounting Practice

In all other respects, in our opinion the financial statements have been prepared in accordance with the requirements of the Companies Act 2006.

Opinion on other matter prescribed by the Companies Act 2006

Notwithstanding our adverse opinion on the view given by the financial statements, in our opinion the information given in the Directors' Report for the financial year for which the financial statements are prepared is consistent with the financial statements.

Other matters on which we are required to report by exception

We have nothing to report in respect of the following matters where the Companies Act 2006 requires us to report to you if, in our opinion:

● adequate accounting records have not been kept or returns adequate for our audit have not been received from branches not visited by us; or
● the financial statements are not in agreement with the accounting records and returns; or
● certain disclosures of directors' remuneration specified by law are not made; or
● we have not received all the information and explanations we required for our audit.

[*Signature*]
John Smith (Senior statutory auditor)
For and on behalf of ABC LLP, Statutory Auditor
Address
Date

TABLE 9: Example of disagreement over non-disclosure of going concern problems

Qualified opinion arising from omission of information concerning going concern

The company's financing arrangements expire and amounts outstanding are payable on 19 July 20X2. The company has been unable to re-negotiate or obtain replacement financing. This situation indicates the existence of a material uncertainty which may cast significant doubt on the company's ability to continue as a going concern and therefore it may be unable to realise its assets and discharge its liabilities in the normal course of business. The financial statements (and notes thereto) do not disclose this fact.

Except for the omission of the information included in the preceding paragraph, in our opinion the financial statements:

- give a true and fair view of the state of the company's affairs as at 31 December 20.. and of its profit for the year then ended;
- have been properly prepared in accordance with United Kingdom Generally Accepted Accounting Practice; and
- have been prepared in accordance with the requirements of the Companies Act 2006.

Opinion on other matter prescribed by the Companies Act

In our opinion the information given in the Directors' Report for the financial year for which the financial statements are prepared is consistent with the financial statements.

Matters on which we are required to report by exception

We have nothing to report in respect of the following matters where the Companies Act 2006 requires us to report to you if, in our opinion:

- adequate accounting records have not been kept or returns adequate for our audit have not been received from branches not visited by us; or
- the financial statements are not in agreement with the accounting records and returns; or
- certain disclosures of directors' remuneration specified by law are not made; or
- we have not received all the information and explanations we required for our audit.

[*Signature*]
John Smith (Senior statutory auditor)
For and on behalf of ABC LLP, Statutory Auditor
Address
Date

TABLE 10: Example of limitation of scope

Qualified opinion arising from limitation in audit scope

The audit evidence available to us was limited because the directors of the company have prepared cash flow forecasts and other information needed for the assessment of the appropriateness of the going concern basis of preparation of the financial statements for a period of only nine months from the date of approval of these financial statements. We consider that the directors have not taken adequate steps to satisfy themselves that it is appropriate for them to adopt the going concern basis because the circumstances of the company and the nature of the business require that such information be prepared, and reviewed by the directors and ourselves, for a period of at least twelve months from the date of approval of the financial statements. Had this information been available to us we might have formed a different opinion on the financial statements.

Except for the financial effects of any adjustments that might have been found to be necessary had we been able to obtain sufficient evidence concerning the appropriateness of the going concern basis of preparation of the financial statements, in our opinion the financial statements:

- give a true and fair view of the state of the company's affairs as at 31 December 20.. and of its profit for the year then ended;
- have been properly prepared in accordance with United Kingdom Generally Accepted Accounting Practice; and
- have been prepared in accordance with the requirements of the Companies Act 2006.

Opinion on other matter prescribed by the Companies Act

In our opinion the information given in the Directors' Report for the financial year for which the financial statements are prepared is consistent with the financial statements.

Matters on which we are required to report by exception

In respect solely of the limitation on our work relating to the assessment of the appropriateness of the going concern basis of preparation of the financial statements, described above, we have not obtained all the information and explanations that we considered necessary for the purpose of our audit.

We have nothing to report in respect of the following matters where the Companies Act 2006 requires us to report to you if, in our opinion:

- adequate accounting records have not been kept or returns adequate for our audit have not been received from branches not visited by us; or
- the financial statements are not in agreement with the accounting records and returns; or
- certain disclosures of directors' remuneration specified by law are not made.

[*Signature*]
John Smith (Senior statutory auditor)
For and on behalf of ABC LLP, Statutory Auditor
Address
Date

TABLE 11: Disclaimer of opinion

Opinion: disclaimer on view given by financial statements

The evidence available to us to confirm the appropriateness of preparing the financial statements on the going concern basis was limited because the company has not prepared any profit or cash flow projections for an appropriate period subsequent to the balance sheet date. As a result, and in the absence of any alternative evidence available to us, we have been unable to form a view as to the applicability of the going concern basis, the circumstances of which, together with the effect on the financial statements should this basis be inappropriate, are set out in note x to the financial statements.

Because of the possible effect of the limitation in evidence available to us, we are unable to form an opinion as to whether the financial statements:

- give a true and fair view of the state of the company's affairs as at [date] and of its profit [loss] for the year then ended;
- have been properly prepared in accordance with United Kingdom Generally Accepted Accounting Practice; and
- have been prepared in accordance with the requirements of the Companies Act 2006.

Opinion on other matter prescribed by the Companies Act 2006

Notwithstanding our disclaimer on the view given by the financial statements, in our opinion the information given in the Directors' Report for the financial year for which the financial statements are prepared is consistent with the financial statements.

Matters on which we are required to report by exception

In respect solely of the limitation of our work referred to above we have not obtained all the information and explanations that we considered necessary for the purpose of our audit.

We have nothing to report in respect of the following matters where the Companies Act 2006 requires us to report to you if, in our opinion:

- adequate accounting records have not been kept or returns adequate for our audit have not been received from branches not visited by us; or
- the financial statements are not in agreement with the accounting records and returns; or
- certain disclosures of directors' remuneration specified by law are not made.

[*Signature*]
John Smith (Senior statutory auditor)
For and on behalf of ABC LLP, Statutory Auditor
Address
Date

TABLE 12: Example emphasis of matter paragraph

Emphasis of matter – Going concern

In forming our opinion, which is not qualified, we have considered the adequacy of the disclosures made in Note 1 of the financial statements concerning the company's ability to continue as a going concern. The company incurred a net loss of £x during the year ended ... and, at that date, the company's current liabilities exceeded its total assets by £y. These conditions, along with the other matters explained in note 2 to the financial statements, indicate the existence of a material uncertainty which may cast significant doubt about the company's ability to continue as a going concern. The financial statements do not include the adjustments that would result if the company was unable to continue as a going concern.

13.7   REGULATED ENTITIES

Where the entity is regulated it may be necessary to inform the regulator at an early stage of the intention to use an explanatory paragraph or qualify the audit report. This may lead to corrective action being requested by the regulator, which may serve to reduce the concerns that led to the proposal to include the explanatory paragraph or qualify the audit report.

13.8   GROUPS

The provisions of ISA (UK and Ireland) 570 apply to group financial statements as well as individual company ones. However, the going concern basis may be appropriate for a group, even though it may not be for one or more of the group companies on the grounds of materiality. Where this is the case auditors should ensure that they document their considerations, and those of the directors, fully.

13.9   PRELIMINARY ANNOUNCEMENTS

The Listing Rules of the Financial Services Authority require that the preliminary announcement of full year results include a reference to any qualification on those financial statements. The announcement should also be agreed with the auditors. Although there is no reference in these requirements to going concern, best practice suggests that auditors would not agree a preliminary statement that made no reference to significant concerns where these existed.

13.10   BULLETIN 2008/10

13.10.1   The need for guidance

As referred to above, Bulletin 2008/10 was issued in response to the severe economic conditions affecting the UK and Irish economies in the latter half of 2007. Conditions had aggravated since 2008/1 was published to justify a Bulletin solely covering going concern. Part of the reason for this was caused by the interaction with Financial Reporting requirements which had themselves developed since the last severe recession.

13.10.2   General principles

The guidance in 2008/10 is in the context of the framework provided by ISA (UK and Ireland) 570. It reiterates that the primary responsibility for the assessment is with management and re-emphasises this by including within the Bulletin as an appendix The Financial Reporting Council (FRC) publication *An*

Update for Directors of Listed Companies: Going Concern and Liquidity Risk ('Update for Directors'). The aim of this publication was to bring together existing guidance for directors in the context of both the current economic climate and developments in going concern and liquidity risk disclosures.

The requirements for these disclosures have changed since the original going concern guidance was developed as a result of the need to:

- disclose the principal risks and uncertainties facing the company in the Business Review contained in the Directors' Report; and
- to make additional disclosures relating to going concern and liquidity risk arising from changes to IFRS and UK GAAP.

An important principle underlying the Bulletin is that the recession in itself would not give rise to a material uncertainty that causes significant doubt and causes auditors to issue a report containing an emphasis of matter paragraph. It is only where there are matters which are specific to the entity that such an uncertainty would arise.

It is still therefore necessary for the process set out in ISA (UK and Ireland) 570 to be followed whereby management assess the applicability of the going concern assumption and makes disclosures regarding any uncertainty around it whilst the auditor assesses and evaluates what management has done and reports accordingly where there is a material uncertainty that causes significant doubt. Given the current circumstances it is anticipated that this process will be more involved and time consuming.

13.10.3   Detailed considerations

As well as reiterating the general principles of ISA (UK and Ireland) 570, the Bulletin goes into more detail about how the recession affects the various stages of this process and amongst other things makes the following points:

- the process directors go through to make the disclosures around risk referred to above will provide useful audit evidence;
- the need for the assessment by both the directors and auditors to start early. As this process will often result in Board papers or possibly in remediation plans so the earlier the issues are addressed the better;
- because the risks in relation to the entity not being a going concern are so pervasive they must be borne in mind throughout the audit;
- because the future outcome of implementing plans may be an important part of the assessment of going concern then specific representations relating to these matters may be needed;
- the understandability of disclosures is an important feature given that the disclosures may be made in numerous places in the financial statements;
- the extent of disclosure is not an indicator that there is a material uncertainty that causes significant doubt. A lengthy disclosure may be as a result of explaining why this is not the case; and

- the issue of facility renewal is likely to be problematic but need not result in significant doubt (see **13.10.4**).

13.10.4 Availability of finance

One impact of the economic conditions may be the limited availability of finance from both suppliers and customers as well as bank and other lenders. Companies often find themselves needing to renew facilities before the end of the period over which going concern is being assessed. In these cases bankers may be reluctant to confirm that facilities will continue to be available. This in itself is not a reason to doubt the ability of the entity to continue as a going concern.

The Bulletin refers to a number of reasons why a bank may be reluctant to confirm that a facility will be available in the future, including:

- the bank responding that in the current economic environment, as a matter of policy, it is not providing such confirmations to its customers and their auditors;
- the entity and its bankers are engaged in negotiations about the terms of a facility (e.g., the interest rate), so there is no evidence that the bank is reluctant to lend to the company; or
- the bank renewed a rolling facility immediately prior to the date of the issuance of the annual report and accounts and is reluctant to go through the administrative burden to confirm that facility will be renewed on expiry.

The absence of a confirmation on its own does not constitute a significant doubt. The Bulletin makes the point that there needs to be other reasons specific to the entity which lead to the belief that the bankers are refusing to confirm ongoing facilities.

Even in this event directors and auditors should consider whether alternative strategies or sources of finance are available. Auditors should assess the directors' plans for future action, including plans to liquidate assets, borrow money or restructure debt, reduce or delay expenditure or increase capital. Where alternative strategies are in place, auditors should consider whether these:

- are realistic;
- have a reasonable expectation of resolving the problem; and
- are likely to be put into place effectively by the directors.

If this is the case, auditors may decide it is unnecessary to include an emphasis of matter paragraph in their report.

One of the examples in the *Update for Directors* (Example 2) shows disclosures for a group which needs to renew facilities in the foreseeable future (i.e., before the end of the period the directors have to assess) but this does not give rise to a material uncertainty that causes significant doubt.

13.10.5 Smaller companies

In March 2009 the FRC issued *An Update for Directors of Companies who adopt the Financial Reporting Standard for Smaller Entities (FRSSE): Going Concern and Financial Reporting.* This adapts some of the messages in the *Update for the Directors of Listed Companies* for the smaller companies. In particular it refers to the different Financial Reporting framework that those companies operate under and points out that the FRSSE requires them to assess whether the use of the going concern basis of accounting is appropriate and to make disclosures of any material uncertainties.

13.10.6 Ethical issues

At a time of economic uncertainty, auditors may be asked to perform additional work to assist their clients. This may lead to self-review, management or advocacy threats which may jeopardise their objectivity and independence. Engagement which could lead to such threats may include:

- undertaking a review of the business with a view to advising the audited entity on restructuring options;
- advising on forecasts or projections, for presentation to lenders and other stakeholders, including assumptions; and
- advising the audited entity on how to fund its financing requirements, including any debt restructuring programmes.

Guidance on how to mitigate such risks is given in Ethical Standard 5, which is discussed in **Chapter 2**.

14 OTHER INFORMATION IN DOCUMENTS CONTAINING AUDITED FINANCIAL STATEMENTS

14.1 INTRODUCTION

Companies issue, because of legal requirement, custom or investor demand, other information as part of the annual report, which contains the audited financial statements. Some of this is interrelated to audited information while other parts of it are new. There is often confusion over the auditors' role in respect of this information.

14.2 AUDITING STANDARDS

Clarified ISAs (UK and Ireland) 720A *The Auditor's Responsibilities Relating to Other Information in Documents Containing Audited Financial Statements* and 720B *The Auditor's Statutory Reporting Responsibility in Relation to Directors' Reports* were issued in October 2009 and replace ISA (UK and Ireland) 720 previously issued in April 2006. The Clarified ISAs (UK and Ireland) are effective for the audit of financial statements for periods ending on or after 15 December 2010. This chapter covers both the existing and clarified ISAs (UK and Ireland). As the clarified ISAs (UK and Ireland) do not significantly amend the requirements of the existing ISA (UK and Ireland) this chapter is written on the basis of the existing requirements, and any changes to them included in the Clarified ISAs (UK and Ireland) are included and clearly indicated.

As with all ISAs (UK and Ireland), the text of the international ISAs have been supplemented with additional guidance from a UK and Ireland perspective.

In July 2008, the Audit and Assurance Faculty of the ICAEW issued a paper entitled *Assurance on Non-Financial Information: Existing Practices and Issues* which examines the types of information on which practitioners may be requested to provide external assurance reports and identifies areas for further consideration. This is covered in more detail in **Chapter 42**.

'Other information' is defined as the other financial and non-financial information, apart from the audited financial statements, that is contained in an entity's 'annual report' (for example, the chairman's statement, the operating and financial review, or any other financial summaries). However, it does not include other information which is released in conjunction with financial statements either of which the auditors have no knowledge or which has been issued without their consent. It does not address issues that may arise where financial information is extracted from the annual report and issued separately, or published in a different format (for example, on the Internet).

14.3   ISA (UK AND IRELAND) 720

ISA (UK and Ireland) 720 contains two sections:

- *Section A* 'Other Information in Documents Containing Audited Financial Statements' which applies to all 'other information' including the directors' report, and remains largely unchanged from the earlier version of the standard; and
- *Section B* 'The Auditor's Statutory Reporting Responsibility in Relation to Directors' Reports' which gives additional guidance on the requirement for auditors to report whether the information given in the directors' report is consistent with the financial statements. This requirement arose from changes to the Companies Act applicable to financial years beginning on or after 1 April 2005.

14.4   AUDITORS' RESPONSIBILITY

Auditors have a statutory responsibility to review the directors' report and, following the enactment of The Companies Act 1985 (Operating and Financial Review and Directors' Report etc) Regulations 2005, they are required to state in their report whether, in their opinion, the information given in the directors' report for the financial year for which the annual accounts are prepared is consistent with the financial statements.

To support this additional statement in their report, auditors must ensure that the documentation of their review of the directors' report includes:

- where the information in the directors' report is a direct extraction from the financial statements, agreement of the information to the financial statements;
- where the information is more detailed than that contained in the financial statements, agreement of the information to specific audit working papers or the client's financial records as appropriate;
- where the information in the directors' report has been prepared on a different basis from that in the financial statements, the documentation should include:
  - a consideration of whether there is adequate disclosure to enable an understanding of the differences between the information in the directors' report and that in the financial statements; and

- substantive testing of the reconciliation of the information to that contained in the financial statements.

ISA (UK and Ireland) 720 goes further and requires them to read the other information to make themselves aware of any apparent misstatement and identify any material inconsistencies with the audited financial statements. Where there are material inconsistencies or misstatements the auditors should seek to resolve them as the credibility of the audited financial statements and the related auditors' report may be undermined by such inconsistencies.

It is pointed out that when auditors read the other information they should do this in the light of their knowledge acquired during the audit and it stresses that they are not required to verify any of this information but to identify any inconsistencies or significant misstatements contained in it.

The other information should be read by a senior member of the audit team who can reasonably be expected to be aware of the more important matters arising during the audit and to have a general understanding of the entity's affairs.

In certain circumstances auditors may have a statutory or contractual obligation to report on aspects of this other information. For listed companies, this would include the auditors' review of the directors' statement of compliance with the Combined Code.

14.5 AUDITORS' CONSIDERATION OF OTHER INFORMATION

ISA (UK and Ireland) 720 requires that if as a result of their consideration of any 'other information', including the director's report, they identify inconsistencies or misstatements, the auditors should consider whether an amendment should be made to either the financial statements or the other information, and aim to resolve the matter through discussions with those charged with governance.

Misstatements and inconsistencies are defined as:

- *misstatement*: when the other information is stated incorrectly or presented in a misleading manner;
- *inconsistency:* when the other information contradicts, or appears to contradict, information contained in the financial statements.

An inconsistency may give rise to doubts over the conclusions drawn from evidence previously obtained and, in turn, over the audit opinion given.

14.5.1 Misstatements

If the material misstatement of fact concerns only the other information and does not affect the financial statements themselves, the audit report will not be qualified in this respect.

If auditors become aware that a material misstatement of fact exists, they should discuss the matter with management. If management refuse to amend the other information, the auditor should consider including an emphasis of matter paragraph in their audit report, describing the material misstatement.

14.5.2 Inconsistencies

If an inconsistency is found, the auditor should determine whether the financial statements or the other information require amendment.

If the directors' report is inconsistent with the financial statements the auditors have a statutory responsibility to comment on this in their report. Matters that may require resolution or reference within the auditors' report include:

- amounts or narrative appearing in the financial statements and the directors' report;
- the bases of preparation of related items appearing in the financial statements and the directors' report, where the figures themselves are not directly comparable and the different bases are not disclosed; and
- figures contained in the financial statements and a narrative interpretation of the effect of those figures in the directors' report.

An example of the wording where the directors' report is inconsistent with the financial statements is shown in **Table 1**.

TABLE 1: Extract from auditors' report where inconsistency between financial statements and directors' report

. . .

Opinion

In our opinion the financial statements:

- give a true and fair view, in accordance with United Kingdom Generally Accepted Accounting Practice, of the state of the company's affairs as at . . . and of its profit for the year then ended; and
- have been properly prepared in accordance with the Companies Act 1985.

Inconsistency between the financial statements and the directors' report

In our opinion, the information given in the seventh paragraph of the directors' report is not consistent with the financial statements. That paragraph states without amplification that 'the company's trading for the period resulted in a 10% increase in

---

profit over the previous period's profit'. The profit and loss account, however, shows that the company's profit for the period includes a profit of £Z which did not arise from trading but arose from the disposal of assets of a discontinued operation. Without this profit on the disposal of assets, the company would have reported a profit for the year of £Y, representing a reduction in profit of 25% over the previous period's profit on a like for like basis. Except for this matter, in our opinion, the information given in the directors' report is consistent with the financial statements.

Where there are inconsistencies between other information that is not in the directors' report and the financial statements, and these misstatements or inconsistencies have not been resolved through discussion with the directors, the auditors should consider requesting the directors to consult with a qualified third party, such as the entity's lawyers.

If, subsequently, the auditors still consider an amendment is necessary to the other information and the directors refuse to make it, the auditors should consider including in the audit report an explanatory paragraph describing the apparent misstatement or material inconsistency. If the amendment is necessary in the financial statements, the auditor should express a qualified or adverse opinion.

14.5.3 Matters of fact and judgement

Auditors should consider the nature of the inconsistency or misstatement that they consider exists. A distinction may be drawn between a matter of fact and one of judgement. It is more difficult for auditors to take issue with a qualitative statement, such as the directors' view of the likely out-turn for the following year, than a factual error. However, even here there may be circumstances in which auditors are aware that the expressed view of the directors is 'significantly at variance with the entity's internal assessment or is so unreasonable as not to be credible to someone with the auditors' knowledge'. In these circumstances, the guidance suggests that auditors may need to take legal advice, including advice on whether they would be protected by qualified privilege from a defamation claim if they were to refer to the matters in their report or subsequently in a resignation statement or at the annual general meeting.

This reflects an unsatisfactory legal position in that auditors may be aware of misleading information but are unable to disclose this in public.

Auditors may also choose to make use of their entitlement to be heard at a general meeting of the company as the business of the meeting would concern them as auditors.

Where they decide to resign from the assignment, under the Companies Act 1985 they should make a statement concerning their ceasing to hold office. Even in these cases legal advice must be taken about any intended comments.

14.6 ACCESS TO INFORMATION

ISA (UK and Ireland) 720 requires that all of the other information to be approved by the entity is present before an audit opinion is expressed, and that the auditors consider all the necessary evidence. This means that timely access to the information is required and that the auditors must see all the information that is to be included in the annual report, for example, the chairman's statement before they sign and date their report.

14.7 ELECTRONIC PUBLICATION

The Companies Act 1985 (Electronic Communications) Order 2000 allows companies to meet, subject to certain conditions, their statutory reporting obligations to shareholders by distributing their annual financial statements and certain other reports electronically, or to post their financial statements on their website and advise shareholders of this. The implications for the auditor's work and report are set out in section **3.15**.

14.8 STATUTORY INSTRUMENT 2005/1011

Statutory Instrument 2005/1011 implemented a requirement for auditors to make a positive statement that the information given in the directors' report is consistent with the financial statements. This requirement applies to all financial statements for periods commencing on or after 1 April 2005.

The change in the SI necessitated amendments to the auditor's report, and these are detailed in **3.5.1**.

To support this additional statement in their report, auditors must ensure that the documentation of their review of the directors' report includes:

- where the information in the directors' report is a direct extraction from the financial statements, agreement of the information to the financial statements;
- where the information is more detailed than that contained in the financial statements, agreement of the information to specific audit working papers or the client's financial records as appropriate;
- where the information in the directors' report has been prepared on a different basis from that in the financial statements, the documentation should include:
  - a consideration of whether there is adequate disclosure to enable an understanding of the differences between the information in the directors' report and that in the financial statements; and

- substantive testing of the reconciliation of the information to that contained in the financial statements.

Where auditors are unable to give this statement, the details of the inconsistency should be given in the opinion paragraph (see **Tables 1** and **2**).

15 CORPORATE GOVERNANCE

15.1 BACKGROUND

Corporate governance arrangements for listed companies have been subject to formal external scrutiny since the Cadbury Committee reported in 1992. Since then the Greenbury Committee focused on directors' remuneration and, subsequently, in June 1998, the Hampel Committee published its 'Combined Code'. This was derived from its own final report and those of the Cadbury and Greenbury Committees. At the same time the Stock Exchange issued an amendment to its Listing Rules regarding statements of compliance with the Combined Code.

The Stock Exchange then appended the Combined Code to the Listing Rules, although it does not form part of those Rules. From 1 May 2000, responsibility for the Listing Rules themselves, and the Combined Code, has fallen under the auspices of the Financial Services Authority. Under the Listing Rules, companies have to disclose in their Annual Report how they have applied the principles of the Code and whether or not they have complied throughout the accounting period with the best practice provisions.

The Combined Code has undergone a number of revisions since first being issued, the most recent being in June 2008 and which applies to accounting periods beginning on or after 29 June 2008.

The Listing Rules require that the auditors review compliance with 9 out of the 45 provisions of the Code. The relevant provisions of the current code on which auditors must report are set out in **Table 1**.

TABLE 1; Provisions of the Combined Code which auditors are required to review

C1.1

The directors should explain in the annual report their responsibility for preparing the accounts and there should be a statement by the auditors about their reporting responsibilities.

C2.1

The Board should, at least annually, conduct a review of the effectiveness of the group's system of internal controls and should report to shareholders that they have done so. The review should cover all material controls, including financial, operational and compliance controls and risk management systems.

C3.1

The Board should establish an audit committee of at least three, or in the case of smaller companies two, members, who should all be independent non-executive directors. The Board should satisfy itself that at least one member of the audit committee has recent and relevant financial experience. For listed companies below the FTSE 350, the company chairman may be a member of, but not chair, the audit committee provided they are considered independent on appointment.

C3.2

The main role and responsibilities of the audit committee should be set out in written terms of reference and should include:

- to monitor the integrity of the financial statements of the company, and any formal announcements relating to the company's financial performance, reviewing significant financial reporting judgements contained in them;
- to review the company's internal financial control and, unless expressly addressed by a separate Board risk committee composed of independent directors, or by the Board itself, to review the company's internal control and risk management systems;
- to monitor and review the effectiveness of the company's internal audit function;
- to make recommendations to the Board, for it to put to the shareholders for their approval in general meeting, in relation to the appointment, reappointment and removal of the external auditors and to approve the remuneration and terms of engagement of the external auditor;
- to review and monitor the external auditor's independence and objectivity and the effectiveness of the audit process, taking into consideration relevant UK professional and regulatory requirements;
- to develop and implement policy on the engagement of the external auditor to supply non-audit services, taking into account relevant ethical guidance regarding the provision of non-audit services by the external audit firm; and to report to the Board, identifying any matters in respect of which it considers that action or improvement is needed and making recommendations as to the steps to be taken.

C3.3

The terms of reference of the audit committee, including its role and the authority delegated to it by the Board, should be made available. A separate section of the annual report should describe the work of the committee in discharging those responsibilities.

C3.4

The audit committee should review arrangements by which staff of the company may, in confidence, raise concerns about possible improprieties in matters of financial reporting or other matters. The audit committee's objective should be to ensure that arrangements are in place for the proportionate and independent investigation of such matters and for appropriate follow-up action.

C3.5

The audit committee should monitor and review the effectiveness of the internal audit activities. Where there is no internal audit function, the audit committee should consider annually whether there is a need for an internal audit function and make a recommendation to the Board, and the reasons for the absence of such a function should be explained in the relevant section of the annual report.

C3.6

The audit committee should have primary responsibility for making a recommendation on the appointment, reappointment and removal of the external auditors. If the Board does not accept the audit committee's recommendation, it should include in the annual report, and in any papers recommending appointment or reappointment, a statement from the audit committee explaining the recommendation and should set out reasons why the Board has taken a different position.

C3.7

The annual report should explain to shareholders how, if the auditors provides non-audit services, auditors' objectivity and independence is safeguarded.

The tenth verifiable FRC Code provision, C1.2 on going concern, is covered by Listing Rule (LR) 9.8.6R(3) which separately states that the going concern statement made by the directors should undergo auditor review.

The other 39 Code provisions not included in the Listing Rule 9.8.10R Requirement for review must be read by auditors to ensure that any apparent misstatements or material inconsistencies with the audited financial statements are identified and resolved. This is in line with the requirements of ISA (UK and Ireland) 720.

The Listing Rules do not specifically require auditors to report on their review of the directors' statement. In the APB's view the statement of auditors' responsibilities avoids the need for a separate report dealing with the review of corporate governance matters.

15.2   GUIDANCE

In September 2006, the APB issued Bulletin 2006/5, *The Combined Code on Corporate Governance: Requirements of Auditors Under the Listing Rules of the Financial Services Authority and the Irish Stock Exchange* to provide guidance for auditors when reviewing a company's statement made in relation to the Combined Code.

The Bulletin replaces guidance in:

- APB Bulletin 2004/3, *The Combined Code on Corporate Governance: Requirements of Auditors Under the Listing Rules of the Financial Services Authority*; and
- APB Bulletin 2004/4, *The Combined Code on Corporate Governance: Requirements of Auditors Under the Listing Rules of the Irish Stock Exchange.*

This updated guidance reflects:

- The publication of *Internal Control: Revised Guidance for Directors on the*

Combined Code ('Turnbull Guidance') by the Financial Reporting Council in October 2005. However, this revised Turnbull Guidance made only a small number of changes to the original issued in 1999 and these are discussed in **15.6.3** below under the guidance on specific procedures relating to section 2.1 of the Combined Code;

- Revised listing rules published in July 2005, which changed the text of the rules, but not the substance of the requirements.

Further guidance for auditors is given in Bulletin 2002/2, *The United Kingdom Directors' Remuneration Report Regulations 2002*, which was issued following the publication of the publication of the Directors' Remuneration Report Regulations 2002 (see **15.6.2**).

Additionally, in December 2009, the APB issued Bulletin 2009/4 *Developments in Corporate Governance Affecting the Responsibilities of Auditors of UK Companies*. This new bulletin:

- updates and supersedes guidance in paragraphs 68 to 72 of Bulletin 2006/5 relating to the requirement for auditors to review the directors' statement on going concern (see **15.6.4**);
- provides guidance in relation to the corporate governance statements required by the Disclosure Rules and Transparency Rules of the Financial Services Authority (see **15.7.2**); and
- provides guidance for reporting on 'standard listed companies' (see **15.7.3**).

There is additional guidance issued by the APB in July 2001 for situations where auditors are requested to perform further work on internal control procedures to issue an opinion on their effectiveness. The Briefing Paper, *Providing Assurance on the Effectiveness of Internal Control* is covered in section **15.6.1.**

In September 2002 the APB issued a briefing paper, *Effective Communication between Audit Committees and External Auditors*, to assist audit committees' understanding of the changes introduced in the updated SAS 610. The briefing paper supersedes the 1998 Briefing Paper, *Communication between External Auditors and Audit Committees*. It is considered in **15.7**.

The guidance in the briefing paper has been written primarily with regard to the audit committees of listed companies but is also of relevance to other board members of listed companies, and directors of non-listed entities. It does not cover communications between external and internal auditors.

Guidance in this area was also supplemented in 2003 and 2004 with the publication of:

- an Audit and Assurance Faculty document *The Power of Three: Understanding the roles and relationships of internal and external audits and audit committees*; and
- seven ICAEW booklets containing guidance for audit committees.

These are considered in **15.10** and **15.11** below.

15.3   TERMS OF ENGAGEMENT

Bulletin 2006/5 contains an example of suitable paragraphs to include in an engagement letter with respect to the company's compliance with the Listing Rule (LR) 9.8.10R. This is reproduced in **Table 2** below. The example terms of engagement also include the paragraphs required following the publication of the Directors' Remuneration Report Regulations 2002 and the subsequent APB Bulletin 2002/2, *The United Kingdom Directors' Remuneration Report Regulations 2002.*

TABLE 2: Example terms of engagement

Review of the company's disclosures relating to corporate governance and going concern

Responsibilities of directors

As directors of the company you are responsible for ensuring that the company complies with the Listing Rules of the Financial Services Authority including rules LR 9.8.6R (3), (5) and (6) 'Additional information' and LR 9.8.10R 'Auditors report'.

Responsibilities of auditors

Listing Rule 9.8.10R states that 'A listed company must ensure that the auditors review each of the following before the annual report is published:

(1)   LR 9.8.6R (3) (statement by the directors that the business is a going concern); and

(2)   the parts of the statement required by LR 9.8.6R (6) (corporate governance) that relate to the following provisions of the Combined Code:

  (a)   C1.1;
  (b)   C2.1; and
  (c)   C3.1 to C3.7'

As we have agreed, we will carry out the review required of us by the Listing Rules having regard to the guidance published in APB Bulletin 2006/5. We are not required to form an opinion on the company's corporate governance procedures.

Having finalised our review we expect to communicate and discuss with you the factual findings of our review.

Scope of reviews

You will provide us with such information and explanations as we consider necessary. We may request you to provide written confirmation of oral representation which you make to us during the course of our reviews. We shall request sight of all documents or statements which are due to be issued with either the statement of compliance or the going concern statement and all documentation prepared by or for the Board in support of the company's statements.

As we have agreed we will attend the meeting of the audit committee [full Board] at which the Annual Report and Accounts, including the statement of compliance, are considered and approved for submission to the Board of directors.

Internal control

With respect to Code Provision C.2.1, our work will be restricted to:

(a) assessing, based on enquiry of the directors, the supporting documentation prepared by or for the directors and our knowledge obtained during the audit of the financial statements, whether the company's summary of the process the Board (and where applicable its committees) has adopted in reviewing the effectiveness of internal control appropriately reflects that process; and

(b) assessing whether the company's disclosures of the processes it has applied to deal with material internal control aspects of any significant problems disclosed in the Annual Report and Accounts appropriately reflects those processes.

As our work is not designed to:

● consider whether the Board's statements on internal control cover all risks and controls; or

● form an opinion on the effectiveness of the company's risk and control procedures; or

● assess whether the directors' decision as to what constitutes a significant failing or weakness, or whether the actions, taken or to be taken, will in fact remedy the significant failings or weaknesses identified by the directors,

our work on internal control will not be sufficient to enable us to express any assurance as to whether or not your internal controls are effective. In addition, our financial statement audit should not be relied upon to draw to your attention matters that may be relevant to your consideration as to whether or not your system of internal control is effective.

Going concern

With respect to the company's going concern statement our work will be restricted to a consideration of whether the statement provides the disclosures required by LR 9.8.6R (3) and is not inconsistent with the information of which we are aware from our audit work on the financial statements. We will not carry out the additional work necessary to give an opinion that the company has adequate resources to continue in operational existence.

Statement of auditors' responsibilities

Code provision C.1.1 requires among other things that there should be a statement in the Annual Report about the auditors' reporting responsibilities. As we have agreed we will incorporate a full description of our reporting responsibilities in our audit report on the financial statements.

Audit of directors' remuneration disclosures

The disclosures that quoted companies are required to make with respect to directors' remuneration are specified in:

● Paragraph 1 in Part I of Schedule 6 to the Companies Act 1985; and
● Schedule 7A to the Companies Act 1985.

The disclosures specified by paragraph 1 of Part I of Schedule 6 are required to be given in notes to the annual accounts whereas the disclosures specified by Schedule 7A are required to be given in the Directors' Remuneration Report.

With respect to the disclosures specified by Schedule 7A we are only required to report on that part of the Directors' Remuneration Report which contains the information required by Part 3 of that Schedule. You have agreed that the disclosures in the Directors' Remuneration Report that are required to be audited will be clearly and unambiguously identified as such. If the disclosures are not capable of being clearly described to our satisfaction we will need to set out all the particulars that we have audited within the auditors' report.

The Companies Act requires that we include in our report any required particulars omitted by the directors if we are reasonably able to do so.

The APB does recommend that, in order to clarify auditors' responsibilities, the:

- engagement letter explains the scope of the auditors' review; and
- auditors discuss the findings of their review with those charged with governance, prior to the publication of their report.

15.4 STATEMENT OF AUDITORS' RESPONSIBILITIES

Auditors have different responsibilities for different parts of the annual report. They are required to audit the financial statements, review the company's compliance with some aspects of the Combined Code and read all information in the annual report that is not subject to any other requirement. Code provision C1.1 requires auditors to include a statement about their reporting responsibilities within the annual report. This statement may either be within their audit report or be a separate statement within the annual report. The inclusion of such a statement of reporting responsibilities aims to reduce misunderstanding about the varying level of work undertaken on different elements of an annual report (i.e., auditing, reviewing or reading).

Table 3 sets out an example responsibility statement.

TABLE 3: Example auditors' responsibility statement

. . .

Respective responsibilities of directors and auditors

The directors' responsibilities . . .

Our responsibility is to . . .

We report to you our opinion . . .

We review whether the Corporate Governance Statement reflects the company's compliance with the nine provisions of the June 2008 FRC Code specified for our review by the Listing Rules of the Financial Service Authority, and we report if it does not. We are not required to consider whether the Boards' statements on internal control cover all risks and controls, or form an opinion on the effectiveness of the [company's][group's] corporate governance procedures or its risk and control procedures.

We read the other information . . .

Basis of audit opinion

We conducted our audit in accordance with . . .

15.5 AUDITORS' RESPONSIBILITIES FOR THE 'COMPLY OR EXPLAIN' STATEMENT

The Listing Rules require listed companies to include a two-part statement in their annual report relating to the FRC Code:

- ***Part one***: explaining how the company has applied the main and supporting principles of the FRC Code;
- ***Part two***: Either:

  - *Comply* – include 'a statement as to whether or not it has complied throughout the accounting period with the Code provisions set out in Section 1 of the Combined Code'; or
  - *Explain* – 'A company that has not complied with the Code provisions, or complied with only some of the Code provisions or (in the case of provisions whose requirements are of a continuing nature) complied for only part of an accounting period, must specify the Code provisions with which it has not complied, and (where relevant) for what part of the period such non-compliance continued, and give reasons for any non-compliance'.

Auditors have no responsibility to assess and comment upon a company's decision to depart from the provisions of the Code. The auditor is, however, required by LR 9.8.10R(2), to review nine of the ten objectively verifiable FRC Code provisions relating to accountability and audit as set out in **Table 1**.

15.6 PROCEDURES

Bulletin 2006/5 sets out a number of general procedures relating to the auditors' review of the statement of compliance, and specific procedures relating to each FRC Code provision that is to be reviewed.

15.6.1 General procedures

For the code provisions within the scope of their review, auditors should obtain appropriate evidence to support the compliance statement made by the company. Procedures they may undertake include:

- reviewing Board and relevant committee meeting minutes (e.g., audit or risk management committees);
- review of supporting documents prepared for the Board or committees;
- making enquiries of the directors or company secretary about the procedures used by the company to implement the Code provisions;
- attending meetings of the audit committee at which the annual report and accounts, including the statement of compliance, are considered and approved for submission to the Board of directors; and
- requesting written confirmation of representations made by directors during the review.

15.6.2 Non-compliance with the Code

Where auditors discover a non-compliance with a Code provision that is within the scope of their review, they should ascertain whether adequate disclosure of the failure has been made in the directors' statement of compliance. They need not perform any additional procedures in this respect, and as long as the non-compliance has been adequately disclosed, they need not refer to it in their audit report.

If the non-compliance is not adequately disclosed, the auditors should report this in the opinion section of their report. This does not, however, give rise to a qualified audit report. An example wording is given in **Table 4**.

TABLE 4: Example opinion paragraph where non-compliance is not adequately disclosed

Opinion

In our opinion:

- the financial statements give a true and fair view, in accordance with International Financial Reporting Standards (IFRSs) as adopted by the European Union, of the state of the company's affairs as at [date] and of its profit [loss] for the year then ended;
- the financial statements have been properly prepared in accordance with the Companies Act 1985 and Article 4 of the IAS Regulations;
- the information given in the Directors' Report is consistent with the financial statements.

Other matter

We have reviewed the Board's statement of compliance with the Combined Code set out on page [x] of the annual report. In our opinion, the Board's comments concerning [. . .] do not appropriately reflect our understanding of the process undertaken by the Board because [. . .].

15.6.3 Specific procedures – the nine verifiable code provisions

Responsibilities of directors and auditors (FRC Code provision C1.1)

Directors' responsibilities
Auditors should ensure that the directors' responsibility for preparing the accounts is explained in the annual report.

Auditors' responsibilities
Auditors have responsibilities to audit, review or read different parts of the annual report. These should be clarified by inclusion of a statement of auditors' responsibilities in the audit report or as a separate statement (see **Table 3**) and by inclusion of a paragraph in the engagement letter (see **Table 2**).

Internal Control (FRC Code provision C2.1)

Directors' responsibilities
Under the revision to the Turnbull Guidance issued in October 2005 boards were additionally recommended to 'confirm that necessary actions have been or are being taken to remedy any significant failings or weaknesses identified from [their review of the effectiveness of the system of internal control]' in their statement on internal control.

Auditors' responsibilities with respect to the directors' narrative statement
The annual report will contain a narrative statement about how the company has applied Code principle C2.1. This should, as a minimum, disclose that there is an ongoing process for identifying, evaluating and managing the significant risks faced by the company that is regularly reviewed by the Board. This statement is likely to vary significantly from company to company.

Auditors have no responsibility to review this narrative statement, but are expected to read it in line with the requirements of ISA (UK and Ireland) 720 to ensure that there are no apparent misstatements or inconsistencies with the audited financial statements.

However, in relation to the additional recommendation that the Board should confirm that actions have been or are being taken to remedy significant weaknesses, Bulletin 2006/5 recommends that auditors:

- review the documentation prepared to support the Board's statement in relation to any significant failings or weaknesses and consider whether or not this documentation provides sound support for the Board's statement;

- discuss actions already taken or about to be taken with directors; and
- consider the statement made in relation to their knowledge of the company obtained during the audit of the financial statements. This would include whether the directors have considered any material weaknesses in internal control reported to those charged with governance in accordance with ISA (UK and Ireland) 260 (see **Chapter 9**).

Auditors are not required, however, to assess the Board's decision as to what constitutes a 'significant' failing or weakness or whether the actions taken or planned will actually remedy the failure identified.

Auditors' review of compliance
Auditors are, as part of their review, required to assess whether the summary of the process given by the Board is supported by documentation and reflects the actual process that took place. Auditors' procedures will include:

- discussing the process used with the directors and comparing the understanding this provides with the statement made in the annual report;
- reviewing the documentation connected with the process and considering whether it supports the statement; and
- considering whether the statement is reasonable given the knowledge gained about the company during the audit of the financial statements.

Auditors should also consider whether the directors' statement covers the year under review and the period to the date of approval of the annual report and accounts, as recommended by the Turnbull guidance.

As their knowledge of the client is narrower than the directors', auditors are not expected to assess whether all risks and controls have been addressed or that risks are satisfactorily addressed by internal controls. However, if auditors discover a material weakness in internal control as part of their audit work, they should report it to those charged with governance as soon as possible so that it can be considered as part of the statement on internal control.

Significant problems in the annual report
The Turnbull guidance recommends that the internal control aspects of any 'significant problems' disclosed in the annual report and accounts are discussed in the Board's statement. Unfortunately, the term 'significant problem' is not defined, and in practice this is likely to be highly subjective and include both financial and non-financial items.

Auditors have a responsibility to:

- discuss the steps the directors have taken to identify 'significant problems' disclosed in the annual report and accounts; and
- assess whether the narrative disclosure of the process applied to deal with

any internal control aspects of these problems is an appropriate reflection of the actual process undertaken.

If auditors are aware of a significant problem in the annual report and accounts which has not been considered in the statement this should be brought to the attention of the directors. If the matter cannot be resolved, auditors should consider whether there is an impact on their report.

Failure to conduct a review
LR 9.8.6R (6)(b) requires the company to disclose if the Board has failed to conduct a review of the effectiveness of internal control. Auditors should consider whether this recommendation is met and whether the explanation given for the failure is consistent with their understanding.

Groups of companies
The review of effectiveness of internal control should be from a group perspective and where material joint ventures and associated companies have been excluded this fact should be disclosed. Using their knowledge of the client, auditors should assess whether any material joint ventures or associated companies have been excluded.

Non-executive Directors (FRC Code provision C3.1)

Auditors' procedures
The Bulletin recommends that auditors should:

- check the number of members of the audit committee complies with the Code requirements (at least three members, or two for smaller companies);
- obtain an understanding of the process used by the Board to determine:

  - if the audit committee are all independent non-executive directors; and
  - that at least one member of the audit committee has recent and relevant financial experience; and

- review evidence, such as minutes and other documentation, to support the above.

Auditors are not responsible for determining whether the directors are independent or whether a particular audit committee member has the relevant financial experience. However, if they have doubts over either of these areas, they should be communicated to the audit committee and Board.

Audit Committee (FRC Code provision C3.2)

Auditors' procedures
The Bulletin recommends that auditors should obtain a copy of the terms of reference of the audit committee and review whether the roles and responsibilities described therein reflect the recommendations of FRC Code provision C3.2.

Auditors are not responsible for considering whether the audit committee has fulfilled its roles and responsibilities.

Audit Committee Terms of Reference (FRC Code provision C3.3)

Auditors' procedures
Auditors should review whether:

- the terms of reference for the audit committee are posted on the company's website or otherwise made readily available; and
- a description of the work performed by the audit committee is included in a separate section of the annual report, and is not materially inconsistent with the information that the auditor has obtained in the course of their audit work.

Raising Staff Concerns (FRC Code provision C3.4)

Auditors' procedures
Auditors should review:

- supporting documentation to determine whether there is evidence that the audit committee has reviewed the arrangements and discuss the review with staff as necessary; and
- documentation supporting the company's arrangements for 'proportionate and independent' investigations.

Auditors are not responsible for considering whether the arrangements do allow 'proportionate and independent' investigations or whether follow-up action is appropriate, but rather should review the process undertaken to assure the audit committee that this is the case.

Internal Audit (FRC Code provision C3.5)

Auditors' procedures
The Bulletin states that auditors should perform the following procedures:

- hold discussions with the audit committee chairman and review supporting documentation to establish that the effectiveness of any internal audit function has been monitored and reviewed;
- where no internal audit function exists, review whether:
  - the audit committee has considered the need for an internal audit function;
  - there is documentation that this recommendation has been made to the Board; and
  - the reasons for not having an internal audit function are included in the relevant section of the annual report.

The auditor is not responsible for considering whether the internal audit function is effective or whether the reasons disclosed in the annual report for not having an internal audit function are reasonable.

Appointment, Reappointment and Removal of the External Auditor (FRC Code provision C3.6)

Auditors' procedures
Auditors should:

- review the terms of reference of the audit committee, or other documentation, to ensure that the audit committee has primary responsibility for making a recommendation on the appointment, reappointment and removal of auditors;
- review documentation of the audit committee's recommendation to the Board;
- where the Board has not accepted the audit committee's recommendation, review the annual report and any papers recommending appointment or reappointment of the auditors, to ensure inclusion of:

  - a statement from the audit committee explaining its recommendation; and
  - a statement from the Board setting out reasons why they have taken a different position from that recommended by the audit committee.

Non-audit activities (FRC Code provision C3.7)

Auditors' procedures
The Bulletin recommends that auditors should review whether the annual report includes a statement explaining how the objectivity and independence of the auditor is safeguarded if they provide non-audit services. Auditors should consider this statement and:

- notify the audit committee and Board if the audit committee has not fulfilled its responsibilities to review and monitor the independence and objectivity of the external auditor and to develop and implement policy on the engagement of the external auditors to supply non-audit services; and
- consider the requirements of ISA (UK and Ireland) 720 in relation to other information issued with audited financial statements if they believe the explanation is misleading. This will involve attempting to resolve differences with the Board, and considering the implications for their report if they are not able to do so.

15.6.4   Going concern

The requirement for directors to report that the business is a going concern is set out in the Listing Rules and detailed in *Going Concern and Liquidity Risk: Guidance for Directors of UK Companies 2009* issued by the Financial

Reporting Council in 2009 ('the FRC guidance'). The Listing Rules require the directors of all companies which have a premium listing (see **15.7.3** below) of equity shares, preference shares or securities convertible into equity shares to include in the annual report and accounts a statement that:

> the business is a going concern, together with supporting assumptions or qualification as necessary, as has been prepared in accordance with *Going Concern and Liquidity Risk: Guidance for directors of UK Companies 2009*, published by the Financial Reporting Council in October 2009.

The FRC guidance sets out three principles that directors should apply to determine whether it is appropriate to adopt the going concern assumption, see **Table 5**.

TABLE 5: Principles in the FRC Guidance

Principle 1: Assessing Going Concern

Directors should make and document a rigorous assessment of whether the company is a going concern when preparing annual and half-yearly financial statements. The process carried out by the directors should be proportionate in nature and depth depending upon the size, level of financial risk and complexity of the company and its operations.

Principle 2: The Review Period

Directors should consider all available information about the future when concluding whether the company is a going concern at the date they approve the financial statements. Their review should usually cover a period of at least 12 months from the date of approval of annual and half-yearly financial statements.

Principle 3: Disclosures

Directors should make balanced, proportionate and clear disclosures about going concern for the financial statements to give a true and fair view. Directors should disclose if the period that they have reviewed is less than 12 months from the date of approval of annual and half-yearly financial statements and explain their justification for limiting their review period.

Auditors' procedures

The Listing Rules require a listed company to ensure that the auditor reviews the going concern statement prior to publication of the annual financial report. Auditors have a responsibility to:

- review the documentation prepared by or for the directors which supports the use of the going concern assumption;
- evaluate the consistency of the documentation with their knowledge of the client obtained during their audit of the financial statements; and
- consider whether the directors' statement meets the disclosure requirements set out in the FRC guidance.

15.7 OTHER DISCLOSURES

15.7.1 Disclosures under the FRC guidance

ISA (UK and Ireland) 720 sets out the auditors' responsibilities in relation to other information in documents containing audited financial statements. This other information will include the FRC guidance disclosures.

These Auditing Standards require that where there is an inconsistency between the audited financial statements and the FRC guidance disclosures, the auditors determine which needs to be amended and seek to resolve the matter with those charged with governance.

If an amendment is needed to the audited financial statements and the entity refuses to make the amendment, auditors express a qualified or adverse opinion on the financial statements.

If the directors' disclosures are not balanced, proportionate or clear, auditors should consider including an 'other matter' paragraph describing the material inconsistency in their report.

If there is a material uncertainty about the ability of the company to continue as a going concern, but the going concern basis remains appropriate, the directors should disclose this fact. If the directors make this disclosure, the audit report will not be qualified but should contain an emphasis of matter paragraph. If the directors' disclosure is not balanced, proportionate or clear, an 'other matter' paragraph should be added to the auditor's report.

15.7.2 Disclosures under the 'Disclosure Rules and Transparency Rules'

European Directive 2006/46 requires that publicly traded companies include a Corporate Governance Statement in the annual report. In the UK this has been implemented through:

- section 7.2 of the Disclosure Rules and Transparency Rules (DTR) of the FSA;
- s496 of the Companies Act 2006; and
- SI 2009/1581 *Companies Act 2006 (Accounts, Reports and Audit) Regulations* 2009 ('the Regulations').

The FSA requirements are effective for financial years beginning on or after 29 June 2008 and include a new requirement for disclosure to include a description of the main features of the issuer's internal control and risk management systems in relation to the financial reporting process. Details of all the requirements relating to the Corporate Governance Statement are set out in **Table 6** below.

The Companies Act 2006 amendments are effective for financial years beginning on or after 29 June 2008 which had not ended by 27 June 2009.

TABLE 6: Disclosure Rules and Transparency Rules requirements relating to the Corporate Governance Statement

DTR 7.2.2R and 7.2.3R

Requirements relating to the Corporate Governance Code to which the issuer is subject which are satisfied by compliance with LR 9.8.6R (3) (the 'comply or explain' rule, see **15.5** above).

DTR 7.2.5R

New requirement requiring a description of the main features of the issuer's internal control and risk management systems in relation to the financial reporting process, see below.

DTR 7.2.6R

Takeover Directive disclosures regarding share capital which were first introduced in the *Large and Medium-sized Companies and Groups (Accounts and Reports) Regulations* 2008 and effective for financial years beginning on or after 20 May 2006.

DTR 7.2.7R

Description of the composition and operation of the issuer's administrative, management and supervisory bodies and their committees, which is also covered by adherence to provisions A.1.1, A.1.2, A.4.6, B.2.1 and C.3.3 of the Combined Code.

The disclosure requirements set out in the DTR may be fulfilled by including the Corporate Governance Statement:

- as a separate section of the directors' report; or
- in a separate report, which is either:

  - published together with the annual report; or
  - available on the company's website with its location cross-referenced in the director's report.

Wherever the disclosure is made, auditors are responsible for forming an opinion on whether the information in the Statement is consistent with the financial statements.

Where the disclosure is made in the directors' report auditors are not required to make specific reference to it in their report.

If the disclosure is made in a separate report, auditors are required to consider whether the information required by DTR Rules 7.2.5 and 7.2.6 is consistent with the financial statements and report in the opinion section of their report (see **Table 7**).

When there is no Corporate Governance Statement in the directors' report s498A of the CA 2006 requires auditors to ascertain whether or not such a statement has been prepared. If no statement has been prepared, this must be stated in the auditor's report.

If the Corporate Governance Statement is included in a document containing audited financial statements, the requirements of Section A of ISA (UK and Ireland) 720 apply (see **33.2**).

TABLE 7: Example auditor's report extract where the Corporate Governance Statement is a separate report rather than being included in the directors' report

Opinion on financial statements

In our opinion, the financial statements:

- give a true and fair view of the state of the company's affairs as at ... and of its profit [loss] for the year then ended;
- have been properly prepared in accordance with IFRSs as adopted by the European Union; and
- have been prepared in accordance with the requirements of the Companies Act 2006.

Opinion on other matters prescribed by the Companies Act 2006

In our opinion:

- the part of the Directors' Remuneration Report to be audited has been properly prepared in accordance with the Companies Act 2006;
- the information given in the Directors' Report for the financial year for which the financial statements are prepared is consistent with the financial statements; and
- the information given in the Corporate Governance Statement set out [on pages] [in *describe document*] [at *include web-address*] with respect to internal control and risk management systems in relation to financial reporting processes and about share capital structures is consistent with the financial statements.

Matters on which we are required to report by exception

We have nothing to report in respect of the following:

Under the Companies Act 2006, we are required to report to you if, in our opinion:

- adequate accounting records have not been kept, or returns adequate for our audit have not been received from branches not visited by us; or
- the financial statements and the part of the Directors' Remuneration Report to be audited are not in agreement with the accounting records and returns; or
- certain disclosures of directors' remuneration specified by law are not made; or
- we have not received all the information and explanations we require for our audit; or

---

● a Corporate Governance Statement has not been prepared by the company.

Under the Listing Rules, we are required to review:

● the directors' statement, [set out [on page ...]], in relation to going concern; and
● the part of the Corporate Governance Statement [on pages] [in *describe document*] [at *web-address*] relating to the company's compliance with the nine provisions of the [2006] [June 2008] Combined Code specified for our review.

[Signature]

[name] (Senior Statutory Auditor)

For and on behalf of ABC LLP, Statutory Auditor

[Address]

[Date]

15.7.3   Changes to the Listing Regime

From 6 October 2009 UK companies can join the Standard Listing Segment which was previously only available to overseas companies. If a company joins the Standard Listing Segment or migrates to it from the Premium Listed Segment they are no longer required to make the going concern statement required by Listing Rule 9.8.6(R) (3) or the corporate governance statement required by Listing Rule 9.8.6(R) (6). As auditors will no longer be required to review these statements, the section of the auditor's report dealing with matters set out by the Listing Rules to be reported on by exception can be removed.

15.8   OTHER MATTERS

15.8.1   Assurance on internal control

In March 1998 the APB issued a consultative document *Providing Assurance on Internal Control*, which proposes a framework for auditors to report privately to directors on internal controls. This follows a recommendation of the Hampel Committee that reports on internal controls should be private, rather than public, as this 'allows for an effective dialogue to take place and for best practice to evolve'.

The paper proposes eight 'basic principles', which the APB believes 'are applicable to all engagements involving the provision of assurance on internal control matters by reporting accountants'. These are shown in **Table 8** below.

The paper continues by providing example reports for both limited scope controls opinion engagements, such as those made by custodians' auditors and controls opinion engagements. Where the latter is performed, five 'additional basic principles' are proposed as shown in **Table 9**.

One of the examples given in the paper of a 'controls opinion' engagement is where reporting accountants report on the process undertaken by management in making an assertion regarding the adequacy of internal control. Such a report may be requested by audit committees to support their corporate governance disclosures concerning internal controls. The suggested report is shown in **Table 10**. It highlights that the reporting accountants are commenting on the process rather than the design, adequacy or effectiveness of the underlying internal controls.

TABLE 8: Basic principles for engagements providing assurance on internal control

The reporting accountants should:

- together with the appointing party, agree on the objective of the engagement and the nature of the assurance to be provided (i.e., issue an engagement letter);
- ensure that staff used on the engagement possess the necessary skills and experience;
- only allow reports that provide assurance on internal control to be included in documents containing other information when such other information is not in conflict with the matters covered by their report and they have no cause to believe it to be misleading;
- plan and conduct an engagement to provide assurance on internal control with an attitude of professional scepticism;
- obtain sufficient appropriate evidence on which to base the opinions expressed in their report;
- express a clear opinion about the subject matter in their report;
- include in their report:

    - the addressee;
    - a description of the engagement including identification of the subject matter;
    - an identification of the party responsible for the subject matter and a statement setting out the respective responsibilities of the responsible party and the reporting accountants;
    - identification of the standards under which the engagement was conducted;
    - their opinion;
    - the date;
    - their name;

- express a clear reservation or denial of opinion when they are unable to obtain sufficient appropriate evidence to support the assurance that the appointing party is seeking.

TABLE 9: Additional basic principles for controls opinion engagements

- reporting accountants should make a preliminary assessment to establish whether there is a reasonable basis for believing that assurance based on criteria can be established;
- the engagement letter should refer to the criteria or control objectives to be used for evaluating the subject matter;
- in conducting the engagement the reporting accountants should confirm their preliminary assessment that the criteria are suitable for evaluating the subject matter;
- reporting accountants should assess what would constitute a reportable deficiency

when both planning and conducting an engagement in order to reduce the risk of expressing an inappropriate opinion;

- the reporting accountants' report should identify the suitable criteria or control objectives used by the reporting accountants.

TABLE 10: Report concerning management process

To the Audit Committee of XYZ plc

The objective of this engagement is to report on whether the process followed by the directors in making their assertion (included on page ... of the XYZ plc Annual Report) concerning the system of internal control for the year ended 31 December 20 ... constitutes due and careful enquiry. The directors of the company are responsible for maintaining an adequate system of internal control.

Our responsibility is to express an opinion as to whether the directors' process constitutes due and careful enquiry sufficient for them to make the statement set out on page ... under the 'criteria for effectiveness' described in 'Internal control and financial reporting' issued by the Internal Control Working Group. This opinion is based on the evidence we obtained, that evidence being persuasive rather than conclusive in nature. In accordance with the terms of our engagement we have not examined either the design of the system of internal control or its operational adequacy. Accordingly we neither express nor imply opinions on any aspect of the company's system of internal control, other than the evaluation process undertaken by the directors.

This engagement has been undertaken in accordance with the United Kingdom Auditing Practices Board's [insert title of guidance yet to be decided] and accordingly included such procedures as we considered necessary in the circumstances.

In our opinion the directors have made their assertion concerning the system of internal control, referred to above, after due and careful enquiry.

Reporting Accountants
Address
Date

15.8.2 Directors' remuneration

Specific disclosure requirements were added to the Listing Rules regarding directors' remuneration as a result of the Greenbury Report and these have been incorporated into the Combined Code. The board of directors should report on:

- a statement of the company's policy on executive remuneration;
- the amount of each element in the remuneration package of each director by name, including basic salary, bonuses and benefits in kind;
- information on share options for each director;
- details of other long-term incentive schemes;
- details of elements of remuneration which are pensionable, other than basic salary; and
- information on directors' service contracts with notice periods in excess of

one year and the unexpired term of any service contract of a director who is seeking re-election at the forthcoming annual general meeting.

The second, third, fourth and fifth points are to be audited and if the company has not provided the information the auditors should provide it, so far as they are able, in their report on the annual financial statements.

Most recently, in August 2002, The Directors Remuneration Report Regulations (SI 2002/1986) received royal assent. These require directors to publish an annual Remuneration Report containing detailed narrative and numerical disclosures on directors' remuneration. The numerical disclosures must be audited. This applies for financial years ending on or after 31 December 2002.

Scope of auditors' work

Bulletins 2002/2 and 2004/3 note that auditors' work is limited to examining the specified disclosures of individual directors' remuneration contained within the Listing Rule and the corresponding Companies Act disclosures. In general, there should be little difficulty in carrying out appropriate procedures but the auditors may need to liaise with the company's pension advisers with regard to the disclosures concerning the valuation of pension benefits.

Where companies choose to disclose 'sufficient information to enable a reasonable assessment to be made of the values of the increase in accrued pension', auditors will need to assess whether there is any relevant information which will significantly affect the value of the benefits. When both considering the need for, and the audit of, such disclosures the APB recommend that auditors only take into account information of which they are aware from:

* their normal audit work on the financial statements; and
* reasonable enquiry of the directors and the company's pension advisers.

There is no statutory requirement to audit or review the narrative disclosures. However, Bulletin 2002/2 notes the requirement for auditors to read such 'other information' and if they become aware of any apparent misstatements or identify material inconsistencies with the financial statements to seek to resolve them with the directors.

Auditors' report

Bulletin 2002/2 stresses the importance of making sure that the information that forms the auditable part of the Remuneration Report is clearly distinguished from the unaudited part. It suggests that this be communicated to directors in the letter of engagement (see **15.3** above).

The Bulletin suggests that directors should be encouraged to clearly mark the disclosures that have been audited. If this is not done to their satisfaction, auditors should set out the particulars that have been audited within their audit report. **Table 12** in **Chapter 3** provides an example of an audit report for a quoted company where the auditable part of the remuneration report has been adequately distinguished from the unaudited part.

There is no requirement to report positively on the disclosures required by the Listing Rules or Schedule 7A.Where the disclosures do not comply with the Listing Rules, the auditors must state this in their report and provide the disclosures where they are reasonably able. Although the disclosures required by Schedule 7A are very similar to those required by the Listing Rules, they are not identical. Therefore it is possible for a company to comply with the Act, but not the Listing Rules. However, all of the disclosures in the Listing Rules that the auditors must review are also disclosable and auditable under Schedule 7A. Unlike under the previous regime, a situation should not arise where the accounts give a true and fair view but do not give the disclosures required by the Listing Rules.

As set out in APB Bulletin 2001/2 (see **Chapter 3**) reference in any audit report to 'the Listing Rules of the Financial Services Authority' may be replaced by 'the Listing Rules of the United Kingdom Listing Authority'.

15.8.3   Independent non-executives

As there is no precise definition of independence in respect of a non-executive director in the Combined Code, the Bulletin recommends that auditors should only establish that:

- an audit committee has been formed;
- the audit committee has written terms of reference; and
- the majority of members of the committee are independent non-executives as identified in the Annual Report.

The Bulletin notes that it is not for the auditors to consider whether directors are properly described as 'independent' non-executives.

The Code proposed by Higgs states that it is the responsibility of the Board as a whole to determine who is and who is not independent. It lists circumstances and relationships which could affect, or appear to affect, the directors' judgement.

15.8.4   Other matters

In addition to the specific audit procedures, auditors should read the entire statement of compliance (not just the specific paragraphs upon which they report) to ensure that the statement is consistent with their knowledge of the company. This should not involve actively searching for other matters that have not been properly disclosed in the compliance statement. However, if as a result of their review or as a result of their audit of the financial statements they have identified a non-compliance that has not been properly disclosed, they should request the directors to amend the compliance statement accordingly.

15.9 COMMUNICATION BETWEEN EXTERNAL AUDITORS AND AUDIT COMMITTEES

The Auditing Practices Board sees communication between external auditors and audit committees as an important element of corporate governance and in June 1998 issued an Audit Briefing Paper on the subject. The paper covers:

- understanding the audit committee role;
- designing communication to complement the audit committee role;
- communicating plans for conducting the audit;
- private communication between the auditor and audit committee; and
- communicating audit findings.

15.9.1 *Understanding the audit committee role*

The scope of these will differ depending on the terms of reference. The role will normally include:

- challenging management in respect of the financial reporting process;
- monitoring management's commitment to a sound control environment and a satisfactory system of internal control; and
- considering the arrangements for external audit and supporting the external auditors.

15.9.2 *Designing communication to complement the audit committee role*

Auditors should be frank and unambiguous in their communication with the audit committee. They should not play down sensitive issues and should ensure that all relevant and significant issues are brought to the committee and openly discussed. Reports to the committee should enable its members to assess management's response to issues raised.

Sometimes it may be necessary to bypass the management when direct contact with the audit committee may be a means of 'anticipating and facilitating the resolution of potentially contentious situations'. However, auditors should also beware treating communicating with the audit committee as satisfying their obligation to communicate certain matters to the full Board.

15.9.3   *Communicating plans for conducting the audit*

Auditors should discuss with the audit committee prior to the audit matters such as the nature and scope of the audit, the planned methods for carrying it out (covering such matters as the role of internal audit), the fees and the extent of other services provided.

15.9.4   *Private communication between the auditors and audit committee*

This may be required to discuss:

* observations on the overall control consciousness and operating style of management;
* the state of relationships between the auditors and management; and
* observations on the extent to which the spirit of good corporate governance is followed.

15.9.5   *Communicating audit findings*

At the completion of the audit, the auditors' discussion with the audit committee should cover:

* all matters on which they are required by regulation or standard to report, for example, actual instances of non-compliance with law or regulation discovered in their audit;
* the control environment;
* any differences between the auditors and management and how these have been resolved;
* significant adjustments made to the financial statements and any unadjusted amounts; and
* observations on other information to be published with the statements.

The auditors may also wish to discuss other matters such as presentation issues in respect of the Annual Report, operational and business risks and, in the public sector, findings in respect of regularity, value for money and probity.

15.10   PROVIDING ASSURANCE ON INTERNAL CONTROL

15.10.1   *Background*

As discussed in **15.5**, auditors of fully listed companies are required to review their clients' compliance with provision C2.1 of the Combined Code. The procedures that auditors perform to support the review required by the Listing

Rules are considerably narrower in scope than those that would be required to provide assurance on the effectiveness of internal control. Indeed, audit reports of fully listed companies make it clear that the auditors' responsibilities do not extend to considering whether the Board's statements on internal control cover all risks and controls, or to forming an opinion on the effectiveness of corporate governance or risk and control procedures.

However, auditors may be engaged, separately from the statutory audit, to report on such matters. There is increasing interest, not only from capital markets but also from regulators, in the effectiveness of companies' systems of internal control. There is therefore an expectation that greater demand will develop for either external or internal auditors to provide assurance on internal control. To contribute to developing a model of how practitioners might be able to express assurance on the reliability of internal control systems the APB published a Briefing Paper in July 2001 entitled *Providing Assurance on the Effectiveness of Internal Control.*

15.10.2 Framework

The paper sets out a framework for forming an opinion on the effectiveness of internal control, identifying the following three key processes that management undertakes in order to establish an effective system of internal control:

- risk identification and assessment, which is based on an understanding of the entity's business objectives;
- the design of the system of internal control, based on a knowledge of the applicable risks;
- system evaluation, to determine that the system actually operates in accordance with the system description.

The framework is reproduced in **Table 11**.

TABLE 11: Framework for forming an opinion on the effectiveness of internal control

The framework illustrates the management processes which practitioners will assess when engaged to provide assurance on the effectiveness of internal control.

15.10.3   *Providing assurance*

Practitioners will need to have a knowledge of the entity's business that is sufficient to enable them to identify and understand the events, transactions and processes that may, or ought to, have a significant effect on the entity's system of internal control. The extent of knowledge required will depend on the scope of each individual engagement. Depending on the needs of the entity, the starting point (other than the requisite knowledge of the business) of a particular engagement may be:

- the description of the system of internal control (in which case consideration of management's risk identification process and internal control design is not within the scope of the engagement);
- the 'applicable risks' (in which case consideration of management's risk identification process is not within the scope of the engagement); or
- the entity's business objectives.

If the entity's description of its system of internal control is sufficiently detailed, auditors are likely to be able to gather sufficient evidence to express a high level of assurance on engagements that consider whether a system operated in accordance with that description. However, the paper recognises that only a moderate level of assurance may be possible for engagements providing assurance on the applicable risks or the effectiveness of the design and operation of the system of internal control. This is because risk identification and assessment processes are highly judgemental as companies and their internal control needs will differ as a result of industry, size, culture and management philosophy. Therefore practitioners are unlikely to be able to obtain sufficient evidence concerning the completeness of the entity's 'applicable risks' or the effectiveness of the process that was used to determine them.

15.10.4   Narrative reports

The paper makes it clear that the scope of a control assurance engagement will have a large impact on the content of the report provided by the auditor. It is anticipated that reports will often be lengthy to communicate accurately to the addressee the various judgements the practitioners have made, the reasoning underpinning those judgements, and the context in which the opinion is given. There is a danger that short form reports expressing an assurance opinion that internal controls are 'effective' or 'adequate' will lead to misunderstandings and are not advocated by the paper.

An example of a narrative report providing assurance on the effectiveness of internal control is set out in **Table 12**. The example should be carefully tailored depending on the requirements of the engaging party and is not intended to be authoritative.

TABLE 12: Illustration of a narrative report providing assurance on the effectiveness of internal control

Date
The Audit Committee
XYZ Limited

Dear Sirs

Effectiveness of internal controls relating to the advertising revenues of XYZ Limited

In accordance with the arrangements set out in our letter dated ..., we are writing to summarise the outcome of our work in assessing the effectiveness of internal controls relating to the advertising revenues of XYZ Limited during the period ... to .... A separate report submitted to senior management contains a full description of the design of the system of internal control which, in the interests of brevity, has been excluded from this report.

Scope of the Engagement

Included in the scope of our engagement were the processes relating to:

- maintaining XYZ's competitiveness by keeping current with the advertisement presentation styles of its competitors;
- the booking in and recording of advertisements;
- the accuracy and timeliness of the inclusion of advertisements in the newspapers published by XYZ Limited;
- adherence of the advertisements to XYZ's 'Code of publication values';
- the processing of the related advertising revenues to the general ledger and the management accounts; and
- the collection and banking of cash and the recording of cash receipts.

As agreed we have not assessed the systems that control bank payments or the onward reporting and summarisation of general ledger information into either the management or statutory accounts.

Inherent Limitations of the Engagement

There are inherent limitations as to what can be achieved by internal control and consequently limitations to the conclusions that can be drawn from this engagement. These limitations include the possibility of faulty judgement in decision making, of breakdowns because of human error, of control activities being circumvented by the collusion of two or more people and of management overriding controls. Also there is no certainty that internal controls will continue to operate effectively in future periods or that the controls will be adequate to mitigate all significant risks which may arise in future. Accordingly we express no opinion about the adequacy of the system of internal control to mitigate future risk.

Companies and their internal control needs differ by industry, size, culture and management philosophy. When designing a system of internal control there are many options as to the nature and extent of controls that may be implemented. Internal controls, for example, may be preventive or detective in nature and may be performed by people or by information technology systems. There is a balance to be achieved between the cost of implementation of controls and the identified benefits derived from the controls. Consequently one company's internal controls system may be very different from another's in relation to similar business processes.

Decisions made in designing internal controls inevitably involve the acceptance of some degree of risk. As the outcome of the operation of internal controls cannot be predicted with absolute assurance any assessment of internal control is very judgemental.

Business Objectives

We discussed the business and control objectives of XYZ Limited relating to advertising revenues with the executive directors and senior management and understand them to be:

- to maximise revenues from advertisements placed in XYZ Limited newspapers by ensuring that the presentation of advertisements keeps pace with developments at its competitors, but without incurring the expense of being the brand leader;
- to ensure that all advertisements booked by customers are published accurately in accordance with each advertiser's requirements;
- to ensure that all advertisements placed in newspapers are invoiced in accordance with the appropriate rate card;
- to accept that a proportion of revenues may not be collectible as a result of credit risk, but given the low marginal cost of advertisements being published, to accept a level of uncollectible revenue of up to 2.5% of total revenue as a feature of the business;
- to ensure that the textual and pictorial content of advertisements adhere to XYZ's 'Code of publication values';
- to ensure that XYZ Limited is able to receive and process advertisements even when its computer systems are unavailable.

Work Performed

We performed our work during the period [date] to [date].

Our assessment of the effectiveness of internal controls was divided into four phases:

- understanding the business and management's business objectives in controlling advertising revenues;
- reviewing management's embedded risk identification processes and observing management's risk screening process that is intended to identify those risks (the 'applicable risks') that represent both a significant and likely risk to the business;
- assessing the effectiveness of the design of controls intended to control the applicable risks;
- testing the effectiveness of the operation of those controls during the period [date] to [date].

Understanding the business

To provide the necessary background information to carry out the engagement we obtained an understanding of the following:

- the trends in the financial results of the business, and the key performance measures used by management, together with comparisons to similar businesses;
- the systems used to process transactions and produce management information.

We also obtained an understanding of the background to the business, including its people, customers, suppliers and competitors, the key business processes and the current business environment.

Risk identification

We assessed both the effectiveness and results of management's ongoing processes for identifying and managing risks. This included obtaining an understanding of the overall control environment, the key performance measures used by management and management's processes designed to identify emerging risks.

Using these assessments and this background information about the business, we reviewed the adequacy of the listing of potential risks identified by management. The potential risks identified are set out in an appendix to this letter.

Risk screening

Risk screening is a process whereby all of the potential risks are evaluated by management, based on their assessment of the likelihood of the risk occurring and the potential impact of the risk. Risks meeting certain criteria are deemed to be applicable risks. The screening process was organised and facilitated by consultants skilled in this field. We observed and participated in risk screening meetings held at each division.

The process of risk screening involves a significant degree of judgement and the culmination of the process was the final screening meeting with the executive directors, which the audit committee also attended, on [date]. This meeting considered:

- the potential risks previously identified by line management and the executive directors;
- whether there were other risks requiring consideration;
- the likelihood and significance of each potential risk.

Risks were screened out from further consideration if they met one of the following three criteria:

- if the effect of the risk is capable of being quantified and its direct financial effect was less than a materiality level of £x;
- if an appropriate risk management strategy such as insurance effectively mitigates the risk;
- based on judgemental assessments of the likelihood and possible significance of the risk, if it was judged to be either unlikely to occur or not of high significance.

The detailed results of this screening process are set out in the appendix to this letter. This shows the risks identified, the results of the screening process and the reasons why risks were screened out from further consideration.

This resulted in the following list of applicable risks:

- the risk that advertising revenue may not be maximised because of a failure to monitor developments by competitors in the presentation of advertisements;
- the risk that advertisements may be published that do not meet XYZ's 'Code of publication values';
- the risk of inaccurate transfer of data between the editorial and billing system, and hence of incomplete billings;
- the risk that cheque receipts are not properly banked or are misappropriated;
- the risk that cash received at the front desk is not passed to the cashiers or is misappropriated;
- the risk that the editorial and billing systems are not available.

The risk screening processes were initially undertaken in [date]. During the period to [date] we updated our understanding of the business and its processes for any indications that there may be changes which would indicate that risks previously screened required more consideration, or for indications of new risks.

We have not considered the impact on the risks to the business arising from the changes in sales ledger and general ledger systems implemented in [date] and the associated personnel changes.

Controls designed to mitigate applicable risks

We assessed the design of the internal controls relating to each applicable risk. These controls comprise:

- specific controls – relating to the processing of individual transactions;

- pervasive controls – relating to the processing environment, access to systems, quality and training of personnel, physical safeguards etc.;
- monitoring controls – relating to performance of key reconciliations of account balances, management oversight of the key performance measures and other monitoring procedures.

For each individual applicable risk we assessed the effectiveness of the design of the specific, pervasive and monitoring controls. Apart from the exceptions described below, in all cases, we concluded that the controls were effectively designed. Details of the design of the internal controls relating to the applicable risks are set out in the report that we have previously sent to senior management.

Operation of controls

We tested whether the controls operated in accordance with their design during the period [date] to [date]. These tests consisted of reviewing evidence of the application of the controls, discussion with key personnel and evaluating the integrity of the information used to perform the controls. We did not test those specific controls where we found that both the related pervasive and monitoring controls were operating effectively.

Exceptions arising

Our work indicated that there were adequate controls over five of the six applicable risks. In the case of the risk relating to the availability of the editorial and billing systems we found that XYZ Limited does not have an appropriate plan in place to enable it to continue operating if these systems are not available. Whilst there have been no incidences of any problems arising in the period [date] to [date], we strongly recommend that management should develop and test a detailed plan for continuing operations in the event of a failure of these computer systems.

Conclusions

Our conclusions in relation to the internal controls over advertising revenue processing at XYZ Limited in the period [date] to [date] are as follows:

During the course of our work, as described above, nothing came to our attention to indicate that there are any risks, other than the applicable risks detailed in the section on risk screening above, that we consider should have been assessed as both likely to arise and having high impact.

In our opinion:

- except for the risk of non-availability of the editorial and billing systems, the design of the controls related to the applicable risks were in all cases effective to mitigate the applicable risks to an acceptable level;
- the monitoring and pervasive controls identified which related to the applicable risks (and which are described in the detailed report sent to management) were in all cases operating effectively during the period [date] to [date].

Limitation of use

This report is for the internal use of XYZ Limited only. It should not be made available to any third party without our prior written consent. We accept no responsibility to any other party who may gain access to this report.

Yours faithfully

15.11 EFFECTIVE COMMUNICATION BETWEEN AUDIT COMMITTEES AND EXTERNAL AUDITORS

In September 2002 the APB issued a briefing paper, *Effective Communication between Audit Committees and External Auditors*, to assist audit committees' understanding of the changes introduced in the updated SAS 610.

The guidance in the briefing paper has been written primarily with regard to the audit committees of listed companies but is also of relevance to other board members of listed companies, and directors of non-listed entities. It does not cover communications between external and internal auditors.

15.11.1 Introduction

The aim of the APB briefing paper is to assist audit committees understand the changes introduced in the update to SAS 610, *Communication of audit matters to those charged with governance*. It supersedes the 1998 Briefing Paper issued by the APB, *Communication between external auditors and audit committees*.

Although SAS 610 has itself been superseded, the guidance in the briefing paper is still relevant.

The Briefing Paper describes matters that are often covered in communications between auditors and audit committees and focuses on:

- establishing expectations of both parties;
- the scope of the audit;
- findings from the audit; and
- the independence of the auditors.

15.11.2 Establishing the expectations of both parties

The audit committee and auditors must have a clear understanding of each other's expectations. The auditors should understand how the audit committee operates and the committee's role in relation to identifying and managing business risks.

Auditors should agree with the committee the extent, format and frequency of the communications they will make at an early stage. Communication may be oral or in writing. The form of communication used will depend on a number of factors, but these will include:

- the size and activities of the company;
- the responsibilities of the audit committee;
- how the committee operates;

- legal and regulatory requirements; and
- how important the issues are.

Issues reported to the audit committee will normally be discussed with management in advance, and the audit committee should be given copies of management's comments to enable them to form a view about the adequacy of the response.

In some situations a private meeting may be the most appropriate way to communicate sensitive matters.

All communication should be made on a prompt basis to ensure that it remains relevant to the audit committee and to allow the committee to take appropriate action.

15.11.3   The scope of the audit

Ultimate responsibility for determining the nature and scope of work needed to express an opinion on the financial statements rests with the auditors. However, to gain an understanding of the scope of the audit work performed the audit committee may benefit from knowledge of:

- management's views on risk;
- the way auditors intend to address the risk of misstatement;
- the process for monitoring the effectiveness of the internal control system;
- the auditors' approach to assessing and relying on internal control;
- if the auditors will rely on internal audit;
- what work is to be undertaken by other firms of auditors;
- relevant developments in law, accounting standards, the Listing Rules, etc; and
- whether auditors review or audit interim financial statements.

15.11.4   Findings from the audit

Information provided by auditors may help the audit committee to:

- appraise the actions and judgements of management;
- monitor management's commitment to a satisfactory control environment;
- consider the adequacy and cost effectiveness of internal audit; and
- assess whether the directors have discharged their responsibility for the financial statements.

Auditors must comment on the following in communicating with those charged with governance to satisfy Auditing Standards:

- misstatements identified by the audit that have not been adjusted by management;
- material weaknesses in the accounting and internal control system;

- their views on the quality of the company's accounting practices and financial reporting; and
- expected modifications to the audit report.

Unadjusted misstatements

Other than those that are 'clearly trifling', auditors should ask management to adjust all misstatements identified. Where management have not made all the adjustments requested, the audit committee should be informed of the reasons why the adjustments have not been made and implications for the audit report. This may assist the committee in appraising the actions and judgements of management.

Material weaknesses in the accounting and internal control system

Information from auditors about material weaknesses in the accounting and internal control systems can help the audit committee perform aspects of its role such as:

- monitoring management's commitment to a sound system of internal control; and
- reviewing the scope and results of the audit and its cost effectiveness.

The directors are required by the Combined Code to review all controls and therefore their review will be broader in scope than the review undertaken by the auditors, who do not have to conclude on the effectiveness of internal controls. The auditors work will tend to focus on those controls that relate to amounts in the financial statements.

Quality of accounting practices and financial reporting

The auditors' observations in relation to the quality of the company's financial reporting may help the audit committee come to an assessment of the financial reporting process. The benefit is likely to be greater when discussions are held face to face, to avoid 'boilerplate' wording in written reports.

Discussions are likely to include:

- the appropriateness of the accounting policies applied;
- the timing of transactions and period in which they are recorded;
- the appropriateness of accounting estimates and judgements;
- effects of unusual transactions;
- effects of uncertainties;
- doubts over going concern;
- apparent misstatements in 'other information'; and
- overall clarity of information in the annual report.

Expected modifications to the audit report

Any anticipated modification to the audit report, such as a qualification or fundamental uncertainty should be discussed with the committee before the report is finalised. The audit committee may be able to assist with any disagreements between auditors and management.

15.11.5   The independence of the auditors

Audit committees have a duty to keep under review the independence and objectivity of auditors. At least annually listed company auditors must make a written statement of independence to the audit committee outlining any potential conflicts of interest and the safeguards that are in place to ensure that independence is maintained.

Audit committees should be informed of any possible difficulties in maintaining independence and objectivity prior to the proposed appointment or reappointment of auditors, and the committee may wish to establish its own safeguards in addition to those maintained by the auditors. Actions taken may include:

- ensuring a written confirmation is received from the auditors and understanding the impact of the information included therein;
- monitoring the quality and nature of the relationship with the auditor;
- considering whether the audit fee is reasonable for a high quality audit; and
- consider whether it is appropriate to obtain other services from the audit firm.

15.12   THE POWER OF THREE

In May 2003, the Audit and Assurance Faculty of the ICAEW published *The Power of Three: Understanding the roles and relationships of internal and external auditors and audit committees.* This guidance develops a number of principles that members of audit committees may wish to consider in order to help them gain a better understanding of the roles that both internal and external auditors play within an organisation and how their respective responsibilities can contribute to its overall governance. This is in line with the recommendation of the Smith report, for audit committees to play an active role in relationships with both internal and external auditors.

In order to assist with these relationships the paper provides a number of principles around the need:

- to understand the roles that both sets of auditors play in relation to those charged with governance;
- for an overall assurance framework to help organisations and audit

committees make the best use of the total resources that are available from both the internal and external auditors; and

- for continuous evaluation and improvement to ensure that the relationships are working effectively.

The Faculty believes their publication is relevant to both listed companies and to other types of entity.

The guidance complements the seven booklets for audit committees published by the ICAEW, in May 2003 and March 2004 (see **15.13** below).

15.13   ICAEW GUIDANCE BOOKLETS

In May 2003, the ICAEW published the first four booklets in a series of publications aimed at assisting non-executive directors on audit committees to gain an understanding of the proposals set out in the Smith report. Three further publications were issued in March 2004. The seven booklets are:

- *Working with your auditors*;
- *Company reporting and audit requirements*;
- *Reviewing auditor independence;*
- *Evaluating your auditors;*
- *Monitoring the integrity of financial statements*;
- *The internal audit function, and*
- *Whistleblowing arrangements.*

15.13.1   Working with your auditors

The Smith report requires that the audit committee acts as a 'body responsible for overseeing the company's relations with the external auditor'. The booklet outlines two aspects of this relationship:

- the audit committee ensures that appropriate plans are in place for the audit at the start of each audit cycle; and
- the audit committee reviews, with the external auditors, the findings of their work.

The booklet looks at how these aspects work in practice and how they relate to the requirements made of auditors by Auditing Standards.

15.13.2   Company reporting and audit requirements

This booklet provides a high level overview of reporting by listed companies and audit requirements, covering:

- the legal requirements and accounting and auditing standards;
- recommendations of codes and guidance; and

- the sources and authorities of those requirements and recommendations.

It does not, however, provide guidance on how to deal with specific situations and recommends making reference to the underlying guidance for detailed information.

15.13.3 Reviewing auditor independence

One of the elements of the audit committee's role laid down by the Smith report was the overseeing of auditor independence. Whilst the prime responsibility for remaining independent is the auditors', it may assist members of the audit committee to be familiar with the key elements of the applicable guidance.

This booklet is written in relation to audit engagements (although much of its contents may be relevant to the provision of other services), and contains:

- a summary of the key requirements for audit committees in respect of auditor independence that the Smith report sets out;
- an outline of the approach taken by auditors to achieving independence;
- appendices giving more information on the approach and setting out some of the general considerations for key areas referred to in the Smith report:

    (1) Analysis of threats to independence and available safeguards to be adopted.

    (2) Advantages of a threats and safeguards approach.

    (3) Non-audit services by auditors to their clients.

    (4) Rotation of audit partners.

    (5) Fee dependence on the client by the auditor.

    (6) Employment by the client of former audit partners and staff..

15.13.4 Evaluating your auditors

This booklet explains how proposals in the Smith report relating to the evaluation of auditors might be addressed by audit committees and how they relate to legal requirements and Auditing Standards. Practically, this will involve a structure for an annual appraisal and recommendation of external auditors, which is agreed by all concerned. Suggestions for this structure are set out in this booklet.

15.13.5 Monitoring the integrity of financial statements

One of the roles of the audit committee set out in the Combined Code is to monitor the integrity of the financial statements and any other formal announcements relating to the financial performance of the company. This booklet gives a high level overview of these provisions and the issues to consider, including the content of the financial statements and areas where judgement are required. However, it does not deal with individual situations.

15.13.6   The internal audit function

This publication sets out a brief background to internal audit and explains how an internal audit function may operate and how it may interact with the audit committee. This booklet is aimed at assisting audit committee members with the requirements set out in the Combined Code to assess the effectiveness of their internal audit function or determine whether an internal audit department is required.

15.13.7   Whistle-blowing arrangements

The Combined Code requires audit committees to ensure arrangements are in place whereby members of staff can raise any concerns about inappropriate activities or work practices ('whistle-blowing'). This publication provides background information on whistle-blowing and examples of how an audit committee can meet the requirements set out in the Combined Code.

16 REVIEW OF INTERIM REPORTS

16.1 INTRODUCTION

For entities listed on the London Stock Exchange and required to prepare consolidated annual accounts using International Financial Reporting Standards (IFRS) interim reports should be prepared to comply with IAS 34 *Interim Financial Reporting* as adopted by the European Union.

The Listing Rules require that listed companies produce a half yearly report which includes, as a minimum:

- a summarised profit and loss account;
- a balance sheet;
- a cash flow statement; and
- an explanatory statement.

In addition, the Accounting Standards Board's non-mandatory statement, *Interim reports*, recommends presentation of:

- a statement of total recognised gains and losses;
- associated notes; and
- a management commentary.

Companies may choose to have this statement reviewed by their auditors, and the Listing Rules state that where such a review has taken place it must be published with the interim report.

16.2 GUIDANCE FOR AUDITORS

The APB has issued guidance on these engagements in International Standard on Review Engagements (UK and Ireland) 2410, *Review of interim financial information performed by the independent auditor of the entity*. As with the ISAs, the ISRE is the text of the international version, supplemented by UK and Ireland specific guidance. The ISRE supersedes APB Bulletin 1999/4 and is effective for the reviews of interim financial information for periods ending on or after 20 September 2007.

16.3 GENERAL PRINCIPLES

Although a review engagement is different in scope to a full audit, auditors should comply with the ethical requirements relevant to the audit of the entity's annual financial statements and implement the same relevant quality control procedures such as leadership responsibilities, acceptance arrangements and monitoring. The same attitude of professional scepticism should be applied to an interim review as to a full annual audit.

16.4   ASSURANCE PROVIDED

The interim financial information will be significantly less in scope than that included in the annual financial statements. The work performed does not provide a basis for expressing a true and fair opinion or that the interim financial information is free from material misstatement. The procedures are designed so that the auditor can give an opinion that the interim financial information has been prepared in accordance with the applicable financial reporting framework. The review will not include:

- inspection, observation or confirmation of accounting records;
- obtaining corroborative evidence in response to enquiries; or
- other typical audit tests such as tests of controls or verification of assets and liabilities.

Where auditors have not audited the latest annual financial statements or have not reviewed the corresponding financial information in the preceding year, additional review procedures are likely to be necessary.

Additional guidance on cases where there are changes of auditor is given in **16.7** below.

16.5   ENGAGEMENT LETTERS

An engagement letter for the review, or a separate section in the main audit engagement letter, confirms the auditors' acceptance of the appointment and helps to avoid misunderstandings about the level of assurance provided by the review. It also clarifies the extent of the auditors' responsibilities for the review.

An illustrative engagement letter is shown in **Table 1** below.

TABLE 1: Example engagement letter for interim review report

Board of Directors XYZ PLC

Date

Dear Sirs

XYZ Plc Financial information for the six months ended 30 June 20..

We are providing this letter to confirm our understanding of the terms and objectives of our engagement to review the entity's interim balance sheet as at June 30 20.. and the related statements of income, changes in equity and cash flows for the six-month period then ended.

As directors of XYZ plc you are responsible under the [Companies Act 1985] [Companies Act 1990] for keeping proper accounting records. You are also responsible for presenting the half-yearly financial report in accordance with [International Accounting Standard 34, 'Interim Financial Reporting', as adopted by the European Union] [the Accounting Standards Board Statement 'Half-Yearly Financial Reports'] and the requirements of the Disclosure and Transparency Rules of the Financial Services Authority. *[The second sentence identifies the applicable financial reporting framework for the entity and should be amended as necessary.]*

For the purpose of our review you will make available to us all of the company's accounting records and all other related information, including minutes of directors', shareholders' and audit committee meetings and of all relevant management meetings that we consider necessary.

Our review will be conducted in accordance with International Standard on Review Engagements (UK and Ireland) 2410, 'Review of Interim Financial Information Performed by the Independent Auditor of the Entity' issued by the Auditing Practices Board with the objective of providing us with a basis for reporting whether anything has come to our attention that causes us to believe that the interim financial information is not prepared, in all material respects, in accordance with the [indicate applicable financial reporting framework, including a reference to the jurisdiction or county of origin of the financial reporting framework when the financial reporting framework used is not International Financial Reporting Standards]. Such a review consists of making inquiries, primarily of persons responsible for financial and accounting matters, and applying analytical and other review procedures and does not, ordinarily, require corroboration of the information obtained. The scope of a review of interim financial information is substantially less than the scope of an audit conducted in accordance with International Standards on Auditing (UK and Ireland) whose objective is the expression of an opinion regarding the financial statements and, accordingly we shall express no such opinion.

We expect to report on the interim financial information as follows:

[include text of sample report]

Responsibility for the interim financial information, including adequate disclosure, is that of management of the entity. This includes designing, implementing and maintaining internal control relevant to the preparation and presentation of interim financial information that is free from material misstatement, whether due to fraud or error; selecting and applying appropriate accounting policies; and making accounting estimates that are reasonable in the circumstances. As part of our review we will request written representations from management concerning assertions made in connection with the review. We will also request that where any document containing interim financial information indicates that the interim financial information has been reviewed, our report will also be included in the document.

A review of interim financial information does not provide assurance that we will become aware of all significant matters that might be identified in an audit. Further, our engagement cannot be relied upon to disclose whether fraud or errors, or illegal acts exist. However, we will inform you of any material misstatement that come to our attention.

[Insert additional information regarding fee arrangements and billings, as appropriate.]

This letter will be effective for future years unless it is terminated, amended or superseded (if applicable).

> Please sign and return the attached copy of this letter to indicate that it is in accordance with your understanding of the arrangements for our review of the financial statements.

16.6   PLANNING

As with any other engagement, auditors should plan their review so that it is carried out effectively. The planning process, which should focus on areas of potential risk of material misstatement, will include:

- updating the auditors' knowledge of the business;
- consideration of the company's organisation, accounting and control systems and operating characteristics; and
- consideration of the nature of its assets, liabilities, revenues and expenses.

The auditors' understanding of the entity and its environment should be sufficient to allow them to identify potential material misstatement and consider the likelihood of it occurring and to select the review procedures required.

Where auditors have previously been engaged to report on the most recent full financial statements, it will be sufficient for them to update their existing understanding of the business. Typical procedures implemented to do this are listed in **Table 2**.

TABLE 2: Example procedures to update the auditors' understanding of the entity and its environment

- reading the documentation, to the extent necessary, of the preceding year's audit and reviews of prior interim period(s) of the current year and corresponding interim period(s) of the prior year, to enable the auditor to identify matters that may affect the current period interim financial information;
- considering any significant risks, including the risk of management override of controls, that were identified in the audit of the prior year's financial statements;
- reading the most recent annual and comparable prior period interim financial information;
- considering materiality with reference to the applicable financial reporting framework as it relates to interim financial information to assist in determining the nature and extent of the procedures to be performed and evaluating the effect of misstatements;
- considering the nature of any corrected material misstatements and any identified uncorrected immaterial misstatements in the prior year's financial statements;
- considering significant financial accounting and reporting matters that may be of continuing significance such as material weaknesses in internal control;
- considering the results of any audit procedures performed with respect to the current year's financial statements;
- considering the results of any internal audit performed and the subsequent actions taken by management;
- reading management accounts and commentaries for the period;
- considering any findings from prior periods relating to the quality and reliability of management accounts;
- inquiring of management about the results of management's assessment of the

---

> risk that the interim financial information may be materially misstated as a result of fraud;
> - inquiring of management about the effect of changes in the entity's business activities;
> - inquiring of management about significant changes in internal control and the potential effect of any such changes on the preparation of interim financial information; and
> - inquiring of management of the process by which the interim financial information has been prepared and the reliability of the underlying accounting records to which the interim financial information is agreed or reconciled.

Where auditors have not previously been involved with the audit of the full year financial statements, they will have to perform more rigorous procedures, particularly in relation to:

- knowledge of the business;
- assessment of inherent risk;
- understanding the accounting systems; and
- verification of opening balances.

However, any work performed at the interim stage will reduce the year end workload.

The planning exercise should determine the extent of the review work required, if any, for the different parts of the business, such as divisions, subsidiaries and associates or joint ventures. The following factors will influence this decision:

- the materiality of, and risk of misstatement in, the financial information associated with each part of the business;
- the extent to which management control is centralised within the group, and therefore the degree to which central management have a detailed understanding of operations and financial information in those parts of the business; and
- the strength of the control environment including the group accounting and reporting processes.

Where other auditors are involved, the principal auditors should ensure that the work of the other auditors is adequate for the purposes of the review.

16.7 PROCEDURES AND EVIDENCE

The auditors' evidence will be obtained primarily through enquiry and analytical review procedures. In the context of the review of interim financial information, analytical procedures are:

- comparison with comparable information for the prior period – both interim and full;
- evaluation of the information by consideration of plausible relationships

between financial data and also between non-financial and financial data elements; and

- comparison of amounts and ratios with the auditors' expectations, based on their knowledge of the business.

The extent of the procedures necessary will be based on the auditors' assessment of the risk of material misstatement. In determining the procedures necessary, auditors should consider:

- the financial position and trading conditions of the company;
- their knowledge of the business derived through previous audits;
- their knowledge of the company's accounting systems;
- the extent to which an item is affected by management judgement;
- management's own assessment of risks and the controls in place; and
- the materiality of transactions and account balances.

The ISRE suggests various procedures that auditors may use as part of their review. These include:

- reviewing prior year matters which may have a material effect on the financial information;
- considering whether the financial information is prepared on a basis which is consistent with the previous period and with the stated accounting policies;
- reviewing significant consolidation adjustments for consistency with the previous period;
- reading the financial information and considering it in the light of matters which have come to their attention during the course of their review work, and reading the rest of the interim report to ensure there are no inconsistencies or misstatements;
- considering the disclosures;
- considering the going concern status of the entity and the disclosures of any significant uncertainties;
- obtaining management representations (see **16.12** below); and
- ascertaining whether the financial information has been approved by the directors and the audit committee.

Where auditors consider that there is a high risk of material misstatement they should carry out additional procedures in order to be able to issue an unmodified review report.

In addition, the ISRE requires auditors to obtain evidence that the interim financial information agrees or reconciles to the underlying accounting records. For consolidated group accounts it is sufficient to agree the financial information of group components to the consolidation working papers.

Auditors may perform many of the review procedures before or simultaneously with the entity's preparation of the interim financial information. In addition, for convenience, some of the procedures required for the full period audit may also be performed at the interim stage, for example reading minutes or procedures relating to unusual transactions in the period.

16.8   DOCUMENTATION

The auditors should record in their working papers:

- details of the planning of the engagement;
- the nature, timing and extent of the procedures performed and their conclusions; and
- their reasoning and conclusions on all significant matters which require the exercise of judgement.

16.9   SUBSEQUENT EVENTS

To ensure that any relevant subsequent events are properly dealt with in the financial information, auditors should make enquiries about events up to the date of the approval of the financial information.

16.10   GOING CONCERN

At the interim period end, directors should undertake a review of the going concern assessment they made at the previous full year end. In the light of the directors' review, auditors should consider whether any significant factors identified at the previous audit have changed to such an extent as to affect the appropriateness of the going concern presumption. Particular attention should be paid to the period since the sign off of the full financial statements.

Where auditors do not have significant concerns they should limit their enquiries to discussions with management about changes to cash flow and banking arrangements.

Where there are significant concerns the ISRE notes that additional procedures will be necessary and auditors should consider whether adequate disclosure has been made.

16.11   COMPARATIVE PERIODS

Where comparative financial information is presented auditors should consider whether the accounting policies used for the comparative interim report are consistent with those used for the current period. Where this is not the case appropriate adjustments and disclosures should be made. Auditors should also check that the comparatives used have been correctly extracted from the prior year's interim report.

Extra review procedures will be required where auditors did not review the corresponding prior year interim financial information. The Listing Rules require comparatives to be given and readers will have expectations that these comparatives have been reviewed on the same basis as the prior period figures. If auditors are unable to perform additional procedures on the comparatives, they should modify their report to indicate that the comparative figures have not been reviewed.

16.12   MANAGEMENT REPRESENTATIONS

As with the year end audit, auditors may obtain from directors written representations to confirm matters arising throughout the review. The confirmation should include an acknowledgement of the limited scope of the review and of the directors' responsibilities for the interim report and the completeness of the financial records and minutes.

An example representation letter is included in the ISRE and this is shown in **Table 3** below, which should be tailored to suit the circumstances of the review engagement.

16.13   OTHER INFORMATION

The other information in the interim report will often include:

- the management commentary;
- prospective information; and
- a chairman's statement.

TABLE 3: Illustrative management representation letter for review of interim financial information

[Entity Letterhead]

[To auditor]   [Date]

This representation letter is provided in connection with your review of the balance sheet of ABC Entity as of 31 March 20X1 and the related statements of income, changes in equity and cash flows for the three-month period then ended and a summary of the significant accounting policies and other explanatory notes for the purposes of expressing a conclusion whether anything has come to your attention that causes you to believe that the interim financial information does not give a true and fair view of (*or 'does not present fairly, in all material respects,'*) the financial position of ABC Entity as at 31 March 20X1, and of its financial performance and its cash flows in accordance with [indicate applicable financial reporting framework, including a reference to the jurisdiction or country of origin of the financial reporting

---

framework when the financial reporting framework used is not International Financial Reporting Standards].

We acknowledge our responsibility for the fair presentation of the interim financial information in accordance with [indicate applicable financial reporting framework].

We confirm, to the best of our knowledge and belief, the following representations:

- The interim financial information referred to above has been prepared and presented in accordance with [indicate applicable financial reporting framework].
- We have made available to you all books of account and supporting documentation, and all minutes of meetings of shareholders and the board of directors (namely those held on [insert applicable dates]).
- There are no material transactions that have not been properly recorded in the accounting records underlying the interim financial information.
- There has been no known actual or possible non-compliance with laws and regulations that could have a material effect on the interim financial information in the event of non-compliance.
- We acknowledge responsibility for the design and implementation of internal control to prevent and detect fraud and error.
- We have disclosed to you all significant facts relating to any known frauds or suspected frauds that may have affected the entity.
- We have disclosed to you the results of our assessment of the risk that the interim financial information may be materially misstated as the result of fraud.
- We believe the effects of uncorrected misstatements summarised in the accompanying schedule are immaterial, both individually and in the aggregate, to the interim financial information taken as a whole.
- We confirm the completeness of the information provided to you regarding the identification of related parties.
- The following have been properly recorded, and when appropriate, adequately disclosed in the interim financial information:

  - Related party transactions, including sales, purchases, loans, transfers, leasing arrangements and guarantees, and amounts receivable from or payable to related parties;
  - Guarantees, whether written or oral, under which the entity is contingently liable; and
  - Agreements and options to buy back assets previously sold.

- The presentation and disclosure of the fair value measurements of assets and liabilities are in accordance with [indicate applicable financial reporting framework]. The assumptions used reflect our intent and ability to carry out specific courses of action on behalf of the entity, where relevant to the fair value measurements or disclosure.
- We have no plans or intentions that may materially affect the carrying value or classification of assets and liabilities reflected in the interim financial information.
- We have no plans to abandon lines of product or other plans or intentions that will result in any excess or obsolete inventory, and no inventory is stated at an amount in excess of realisable value.
- The entity has satisfactory title to all assets and there are no liens or encumbrances on the entity's assets.
- We have recorded or disclosed, as appropriate, all liabilities, both actual and contingent.
- [Add any additional representations related to new accounting standards that are being implemented for the first time and consider any additional representations required by a new International Standard on Auditing (UK and Ireland) that are relevant to interim financial information.]

To the best of our knowledge and belief, no events have occurred subsequent to the balance sheet date and through the date of this letter that may require adjustment to or disclosure in the aforementioned interim financial information.

_____

(Senior Executive Officer)

_____

(Senior Financial Officer)

Auditors should read any information to be published with the interim financial information and consider whether it is materially inconsistent with the interim financial information or their knowledge of the client and its circumstances. The auditors should only allow their review report to be included where they consider that the additional information is not in conflict with their report and that it is not misleading.

Where there is an apparent misstatement or a material inconsistency between the other information and the financial information which cannot be resolved through discussion with the directors, the ISRE suggests that the auditors should consider taking legal advice and that they are likely to make reference to the matter in their review report.

16.14   EVALUATING MISSTATEMENTS

The ISRE requires auditors to assess misstatements individually and in aggregate to determine whether a material adjustment is required to the interim financial information. They are not required to aggregate any misstatements that are 'clearly trivial'.

16.15   COMMUNICATION

Auditors should report matters which will necessitate a material adjustment to the interim financial information to the relevant level of management as soon as possible. If management does not respond adequately, the matter should be escalated to those charged with governance. If those charged with governance do not make the relevant changes to the interim financial information, the auditors consider:

- whether to modify their report;
- the possibility of withdrawing from the engagement; and
- the possibility of resigning from the full audit.

If matters come to the attention of auditors which suggest that fraudulent activity has taken place, it should be reported to the appropriate level of management, unless management are involved in the fraud, and then the matter should be reported directly to those charged with governance.

16.16   REPORTING

The auditor should issue a written report at the end of their work, and **Table 4** gives the example report taken from the ISRE.

TABLE 4: Unmodified review report

Independent review report to XYZ plc

Introduction

We have been engaged by the company to review the condensed set of financial statements in the half-yearly financial report for the six months ended [date] which comprises [specify the primary financial statements and the related explanatory notes that have been reviewed.

We have read the other information contained in the half-yearly financial report and considered whether it contains any apparent misstatements or material inconsistencies with the information in the condensed set of financial statements.

Directors' responsibilities

The half-yearly report is the responsibility of, and has been approved by the directors. The directors are responsible for preparing the half-yearly financial report in accordance with the Disclosure and Transparency Rules of the United Kingdom's Financial Services Authority.

As disclosed in note X, the annual financial statements of the [group/company] are prepared in accordance with IFRSs as adopted by the European Union. The condensed set of financial statements included in this half-yearly financial report has been prepared in accordance with International Accounting Standard 34, 'Interim Financial Reporting', as adopted by the European Union.

Our responsibility

Our responsibility is to express to the Company a conclusion on the condensed set of financial statements in the half-yearly financial report based on our review.

Scope of review

We conducted our review in accordance with International Standard on Reporting Engagements (UK and Ireland) 2410, 'Review of Interim Financial Information Performed by the Independent Auditor of the Entity' issued by the Auditing Practices Board for use in the United Kingdom. A review of interim financial information consists of making enquiries, primarily of persons responsible for financial and accounting matters, and applying analytical and other review procedures. A review is substantially less in scope than an audit conducted in accordance with International Standards on Auditing (UK and Ireland) and consequently does not enable us to obtain assurance that we would become aware of all significant matters that might be identified in an audit. Accordingly we do not express an audit.

Conclusion

Based on our review, nothing has come to our attention that causes us to believe that the condensed set of financial statements in the half-yearly financial report for the six months ended ... is not prepared, in all material respects, in accordance with International Accounting Standard 34 as adopted by the European Union and the Disclosure and Transparency Rules of the United Kingdom's Financial Services Authority.

Auditor
Address
Date

16.16.1 Modification of the review report

The auditors' review report will be modified if they consider that there is or has been:

- a departure from the applicable financial reporting framework;
- a limitation on scope; or
- going concern or significant uncertainties.

Departure from applicable financial reporting framework

Where auditors conclude that the interim financial information has not been prepared in accordance with the applicable financial reporting framework and a material adjustment is required, they should issue a qualified or adverse opinion, depending on the severity of the departure.

Limitation on scope

Where auditors cannot finish their review because of a limitation on scope, they should write to the appropriate level of management or those charged with governance to set out the reasons why. They should also consider the implications for their report.

Auditors should not accept an engagement to review the interim financial information if they are aware that a limitation on scope would be imposed by management. If the limitation is imposed after the auditors have accepted the engagement, and management refuse all requests to remove the limitation, they would ordinarily issue a disclaimer of opinion and ensure that their report outlines the reasons for issuing such a report.

Going concern or significant uncertainties

If there are going concern issues, and these are adequately disclosed in the interim financial information, auditors do not qualify their report, but instead should add an emphasis of matter paragraph to highlight the material uncertainty relating to going concern.

If there is not adequate disclosure of any going concern issue in the interim financial information, auditors will issue a qualified or adverse conclusion.

Emphasis of matter paragraphs should also be used for other significant uncertainties which are disclosed in the interim financial information.

16.16.2 Prior period modifications

Where the prior period review report was modified or the audit report on the most recent financial statements was qualified and the matter has not been resolved, the review report should refer to the earlier modification or qualification and discuss the current status of the matter.

TABLE 5: Extract from review report with fundamental uncertainty

Review work performed

. . . .

Fundamental uncertainty

In arriving at our review conclusion, we have considered the adequacy of disclosures made in the financial information concerning the possible outcome of litigation against B Limited, a subsidiary undertaking of the company, for an alleged breach of environmental regulations. The future settlement of this litigation could result in additional liabilities and the closure of B's business, whose net assets included in the summarised balance sheet total £Y and whose profit before tax for the year is £Z. Details of the circumstances relating to this fundamental uncertainty are described in note X.

Review conclusion

On the basis of our review we are not aware of any material modifications that should be made to the financial information as presented for the six months ended 30 June 20.. .

16.16.3 Date of review report

The date the auditors sign their report should not be earlier than the date on which the directors approve the financial information.

16.17 COMPLETE SET INTERIM FINANCIAL INFORMATION

The Listing Rules of the UK and Irish Stock Exchanges require condensed half yearly financial reports to be prepared. However, on some occasions where the company is not listed on the UK or Irish Stock Exchanges, the interim financial information may comprise a complete set of general purpose financial statements prepared in accordance with a financial reporting framework designed to achieve fair presentation. The appendices to the ISRE provide example engagement letter paragraphs, representation letter paragraphs, review reports and modified review reports for such circumstances.

16.18   REQUESTS TO DISCONTINUE AN INTERIM REVIEW ENGAGEMENT

As a review of the interim statement is not mandatory, directors may request auditors to discontinue their review engagement if it becomes clear that a modified review report will be given.

If this is the case the auditors must inform the Audit Committee of this in writing. If, in the auditors' opinion, the company does not take appropriate action to address their concerns about the interim financial information, the auditors may request the directors discuss the issue with the company's brokers. The directors and brokers should then consider whether the matter should be reported to the Stock Exchange.

In such a case, the auditors should also consider whether as a result they should resign as the company's auditors. The ISRE suggests that they may consider taking legal advice in these circumstances. If they decide to resign the details of the issue should be included, after taking appropriate legal advice, in their s394 statement.

17   PLANNING

17.1   AUDITING STANDARDS

Clarified ISA (UK and Ireland) 300 *Planning an Audit of Financial Statements* was issued in October 2009 and replaces ISA (UK and Ireland) 300 previously issued in December 2004. The Clarified ISA (UK and Ireland) is effective for the audit of financial statements for periods ending on or after 15 December 2010. This chapter covers both the existing and Clarified ISAs (UK and Ireland). As the Clarified ISA (UK and Ireland) does not significantly amend the requirements of the existing ISA (UK and Ireland) this chapter is written on the basis of the existing requirements, and any changes to them included in the Clarified ISA (UK and Ireland) are included and clearly indicated. The ISA (UK and Ireland) provides guidance on the planning process covering:

- the role and timing of planning;
- involvement of key engagement team members;
- planning activities;
- documentation; and
- considerations for initial audit engagements.

As with all ISAs (UK and Ireland), the text of the international ISA has been supplemented with additional guidance from a UK and Ireland perspective.

17.2   PLANNING THE WORK

Planning is discussed in the context of recurring audits and is described as 'not a discrete phase of an audit, but rather a continual and iterative process that often begins shortly after (or in connection with) the completion of the previous audit and continues until the completion of the current audit engagement'. However, some planning activities will, by necessity, have to be completed at the beginning of the audit, such as understanding the legal and regulatory framework within which the entity operates and briefing the audit team.

The objectives of planning include:

- ensuring that appropriate attention is directed to important areas of the audit;
- ensuring that potential problems are identified;
- organising and managing the engagement properly;
- assisting with proper allocation of work to engagement team members;
- where appropriate, assisting with the coordination of work performed by other auditors or specialists;
- facilitating review; and
- enabling the audit to be performed in an effective and timely manner.

The guidance stresses that planning varies according to the size of the entity and complexity of the audit. In the case of a smaller audit where accountancy assistance is provided by the auditors, the audit plan should take account of any areas of audit risk identified, and evidence obtained, during that exercise.

17.3 PRELIMINARY ENGAGEMENT ACTIVITIES

In order to ensure that auditors have considered any events or circumstances which may affect their ability to plan to reduce the risk of material misstatement to an acceptable level, they should:

* perform client and audit engagement acceptance procedures in accordance with ISA (UK and Ireland) 220 *Quality Control for Audits of Historical Financial Information* (see **Chapter 20**);
* evaluate compliance with ethical and independence requirements (see **Chapters 2 and 20**); and
* establish the terms of the engagement, in accordance with ISA (UK and Ireland) 210 *Terms of Audit Engagements* (see **Chapter 21**).

The factors affecting client acceptance and ethical and independence issues should be continually re-evaluated during the audit as circumstances may change. However, the main element of this work should be performed before any other audit procedures are started and, for continuing engagements, this may be at the end of the prior year's audit.

17.4 THE OVERALL AUDIT STRATEGY

Auditors should set an overall strategy for the audit which assists with the development of the more detailed audit plan. This will involve:

* considering the scope of the engagement, i.e., what reporting requirements are there, what financial reporting framework is the client using, what group companies are covered;
* understanding reporting deadlines and key dates for communications with those charged with governance;
* ascertaining the nature, timing and extent of resources necessary to perform the engagement;
* consider the results of preliminary engagement activities and, where applicable, knowledge gained from elsewhere; and
* making initial assessments in relation to, for example:
  * appropriate materiality levels;
  * areas where there may be a higher risk of material misstatement;
  * the identification of material components and account balances;
  * possible reliance on the effectiveness of internal control; and

- identification of recent significant events in terms of the business and its industry.

Table 1 sets out a list of matters auditors may consider when determining their overall audit strategy.

TABLE 1: Matters to consider when determining the overall audit strategy

Scope of the audit engagement

- the financial reporting framework on which the financial information to be audited has been prepared, including any need for reconciliations to another financial reporting framework;
- industry specific reporting requirements such as reports mandated by industry regulators;
- the expected audit coverage, including the number of locations of components to be included;
- the nature of the control relationships between a parent and its components that determine how the group is to be consolidated;
- the extent to which components are audited by other auditors;
- the nature of the business segments to be audited, including the need for specialised knowledge;
- the reporting currency to be used including any need for currency translation for the financial information audited;
- the need for a statutory audit of standalone financial statements in addition to an audit for consolidation purposes;
- the availability of the work of internal auditors and the extent of the auditor's potential reliance on such work;
- the entity's use of service organisations and how the auditors may obtain evidence concerning the design or operation of controls performed by them;
- the expected use of audit evidence obtained in prior audits, for example, audit evidence related to risk assessment procedures and tests of controls;
- the effect of information technology on the audit procedures, including the availability of data and the expected use of computer-assisted audit techniques;
- the coordination of the expected coverage and timing of the audit work with any reviews of interim financial information and the effect on the audit of the information obtained during such reviews;
- the discussion of matters that may affect the audit with firm personnel responsible for performing other services to the entity; and
- the availability of client personnel and data.

Reporting objectives, timing of the audit and communications required

- the entity's timetable for reporting, such as at interim and final stages;
- the organisation of meetings with management and those charged with governance to discuss the nature, extent and timing of the audit work;
- the discussion with management and those charged with governance regarding the expected type and timing of reports to be issued and other communications, both written and oral, including the auditor's report, management letters and communications to those charged with governance;
- the discussion with management regarding the expected communications on the status of audit work throughout the engagement and the expected deliverables resulting from the audit procedures;
- communication with auditors of components regarding the expected types and

---

timing of reports to be issued and other communications in connection with the audit of components;

- the expected nature and timing of communications among engagement team members, including the nature and timing of team meetings and timing of the review of work performed; and
- whether there are any other expected communications with third parties, including any statutory or contractual reporting responsibilities arising from the audit.

Direction of the audit

- with respect to materiality:

  - setting materiality for planning purposes;
  - setting and communicating materiality for auditors of components;
  - reconsidering materiality as audit procedures are performed during the course of the audit;
  - identifying the material components and account balances;

- audit areas where there is a higher risk of material misstatement;
- the impact of the assessed risk of material misstatement at the overall financial statement level on direction, supervision and review;
- the selection of the engagement team (including, where necessary, the engagement quality control reviewer) and the assignment of audit work to the team members including the assignment of appropriately experienced team members to areas where there may be higher risks of material misstatement;
- engagement budgeting, including considering the appropriate amount of time to set aside for areas where there may be higher risks of material misstatement;
- the manner in which the auditor emphasises to engagement team members the need to maintain a questioning mind and to exercise professional scepticism in gathering and evaluating audit evidence;
- results of previous audits that involved evaluating the operating effectiveness of internal control including the nature of identified weaknesses and action taken to address them;
- evidence of the commitment of those charged with governance to the design and operation of sound internal control including evidence of appropriate documentation of such internal control;
- volume of transactions which may determine whether it is more efficient for the auditors to rely on internal control;
- importance attached to internal control throughout the entity to the successful operation of the business;
- significant business developments affecting the entity, including changes to information technology and business process, changes in key management and acquisitions, mergers and divestments;
- significant industry developments such as changes in industry regulations and new reporting requirements;
- significant changes in the financial reporting framework such as changes in accounting standards; and
- other significant relevant developments such as changes in the legal environment affecting the entity.

The completed audit strategy should clearly set out:

- the resources to deploy;
- the amount of resources to allocate to different audit areas;
- the timing of the deployment; and

- how the resources are managed, supervised and directed.

A smaller audit team is likely to be involved in the audits of small entities and this makes coordination and communication easier. Developing an audit strategy for small entities need not be a time-consuming or complex exercise, and a brief memorandum prepared at the completion of the previous audit and based on a review of the working papers may suffice.

17.5 DOCUMENTATION

ISA (UK and Ireland) 300 requires that auditors should document the overall audit strategy. This will act as a record of the key decision considered necessary to properly plan the audit and communicate significant matters to the engagement team.

Once the audit strategy has been formulated, the audit plan can be prepared to address the various matters identified in the overall audit strategy in detail. Documentation of the audit plan also acts as a record that the planning has been properly completed, which can be reviewed and approved before further work is undertaken.

The audit plan should contain:

- a description of the nature, timing and extent of planned risk assessment procedures sufficient to assess the risks of material misstatement in accordance with ISA (UK and Ireland) 315 (see **Chapter 22**);
- a description of the nature, timing and extent of audit procedures planned at assertion level for each material class of transactions, account balance and disclosure in accordance with ISA (UK and Ireland) 330 (see **Chapter 22**); and
- details of other audit procedures required by ISAs (UK and Ireland).

17.6 INITIAL AUDIT ENGAGEMENTS

Much of the planning for ongoing or initial engagements will be identical, however, first time auditors will not be able to draw on their knowledge of the client from earlier work. In addition to the procedures detailed above, the first time auditors act for a client, as part of planning they should also:

- perform the client acceptance procedures set out by ISA (UK and Ireland) 220;
- follow up any matters discussed with management or those charged with governance as part of the process followed to select them as auditors;
- communicate with the predecessor auditor to arrange review of their working papers (see **Chapter 38**);

- consider the audit procedures necessary to obtain sufficient appropriate audit evidence regarding opening balances (see **Chapter 31**);
- assign appropriately experienced audit firm personnel; and
- perform the procedures required by the firm's quality control systems, such as appointment of a technical or concurring partner.

17.7 CHANGES TO PLANNING DECISIONS DURING THE COURSE OF THE AUDIT

The ISA (UK and Ireland) explains that the planning decisions should be reviewed and, if necessary, revised as necessary during the course of the audit. The results of the audit tests or new information may lead to changes in the approach adopted or the assessment of risks and materiality and these should be formally documented.

17.8 DIRECTION, SUPERVISION AND REVIEW

The amount of time spent directing and supervising audit team members will depend on a number of factors including their experience and the complexity of the areas in which they are working. ISA (UK and Ireland) 220 gives further details on the direction, supervision and review of audit work (see **Chapter 20**). For areas of higher risk of material misstatement, the extent of direction and supervision may be increased.

Direction, supervision and review is not relevant where the audit work is carried out by the audit engagement partner who is sole practitioner. However, that individual must be content that the audit has been performed in accordance with ISAs (UK and Ireland), and a sole practitioner may plan to consult with an outside source on particularly difficult or complex areas.

17.9 COMMUNICATIONS WITH THOSE CHARGED WITH GOVERNANCE

Auditors may discuss elements of the planning with those charged with governance to improve the efficiency and effectiveness of the audit. However, the overall audit strategy and the audit plan remain the auditors' responsibility.

18 MATERIALITY AND THE AUDIT

18.1 AUDITING STANDARDS

Clarified ISA (UK and Ireland) 320 *Materiality in Planning and Performing an Audit* was issued in October 2009 and is effective for the audit of financial statements for periods ending on or after 15 December 2010. The updated ISA (UK and Ireland) replaces ISA (UK and Ireland) 320 issued in December 2004.

As part of the process of issuing the clarified ISAs (UK and Ireland), the APB also issued Clarified ISA (UK and Ireland) 450 *Evaluation of Misstatements Identified During the Audit.* Taken together these two Clarified ISAs (UK and Ireland) contain the equivalent guidance that was in the original ISA (UK and Ireland) 450.

This chapter covers both the existing and clarified ISAs (UK and Ireland). As the clarified ISAs (UK and Ireland) add to the requirements of the existing ISA (UK and Ireland) this chapter is written on the basis of the existing requirements, and changes to them included in the clarified ISAs (UK and Ireland) are included and clearly indicated.

As with all ISAs (UK and Ireland), the text of the international ISAs have been supplemented with additional guidance from a UK and Ireland perspective.

18.2 MATERIALITY

Both the original and Clarified ISAs (UK and Ireland) use similar definitions for materiality. The term 'materiality' is used in financial reporting frameworks in relation to the preparation and presentation of financial statements. Misstatements are considered to be material if they, individually or in aggregate, can be reasonably expected to influence the economic decisions of users of the financial statements. The Clarified ISA (UK and Ireland) reinforces the fact that materiality is determined both by the size and nature of an item judged in relation to the surrounding circumstances.

Auditors' determination of materiality is a matter of professional judgement and will be affected by the auditors' perception of the financial information needs of users of the financial statements. There is no mathematical definition of materiality, as it has both qualitative and quantitative aspects.

The concept of materiality is applied by auditors in both planning and performing the audit and when evaluating the effect of identified misstatements on the audit. Materiality judgements are also used when considering the effect of any uncorrected misstatements on the financial statements.

18.3   THE NEED TO CONSIDER MATERIALITY

Auditors plan and perform their audits so as to obtain reasonable assurance that the financial statements are free from material misstatement. However, whether an item is to be considered as material is a matter of professional judgement. The relationship of materiality to audit risk should also be considered.

The consideration of materiality should not simply be a matter of amount, the nature of the error should also be assessed. For example, if the auditors find an illegal payment of an otherwise immaterial amount this may lead to a material contingent liability, a material loss of assets or a material loss of revenue, and the effects on the audit report should be considered. Similarly, a failure to disclose a breach of regulatory requirements may result in the imposition of restrictions, which could impair a company's ability to operate.

Auditors also need to be aware of qualitative misstatements. For example, an inadequate description of an accounting policy which would mislead users of accounts is material to those users. Clarified ISA (UK and Ireland) 320 also states that auditors should remain alert for possible bias in management judgements particularly in relation to the entity's accounting practices.

The level of materiality may be influenced by:

- legal and regulatory requirements;
- the level of exposure of the financial statements;
- whether the company is using the financial statements to negotiate additional finance or a listing on the Stock Exchange; and
- the auditors' previous experience of the company.

Auditors may use a benchmark such as a percentage of turnover, net assets or profit before tax as a starting point for determining materiality, but such calculated benchmarks should be adjusted as necessary for the factors listed above and other qualitative factors to determine the value of materiality to be used when planning and performing the audit. Guidance on the use of benchmarks was introduced by the clarified ISA (UK and Ireland).

Clarified ISA (UK and Ireland) 320 states that for some classes of transactions, account balances or disclosures a misstatement of less than the materiality set for the financial statements as a whole could be expected to influence the decision making of users, and for these areas a lower materiality figure may be set.

The expected degree of accuracy of certain statutory disclosures, such as directors' emoluments, may make normal materiality considerations irrelevant.

In addition, Clarified ISA (UK and Ireland) 320 introduces the concept of 'performance materiality', being the amount or amounts set by auditors at less than the general materiality level, so that the probability of the aggregate of uncorrected and undetected misstatements exceeding materiality is reduced to an appropriately low level. Performance materiality may be set for some or all individual classes of transactions, account balances or disclosures, as a single figure for the financial statements as a whole, or as a combination of both. The level of performance materiality is a matter of judgement. It will depend on auditors' understanding of the entity and the nature and extent of misstatements identified in previous audits, which determine expectations relating to misstatements in the current period.

18.4   MATERIALITY AND AUDIT RISK

When planning the audit, auditors will assess the risk of material misstatement of the financial statements and plan how to respond to those risks throughout the audit. This risk assessment also helps auditors to continually assess whether the materiality assessment remains valid throughout the course of the audit.

Materiality is also considered when determining whether any significant risks exist (see **Chapter 22**).

The assessment of materiality helps auditors to determine the type and extent of testing required to reduce audit risk to an acceptably low level.

Materiality is used specifically in:

- *Planning the audit.* At this stage materiality assists the auditors in deciding what areas need to be addressed, where material misstatement is likely to occur and whether any significant risks exist, so that their approach is efficient and effective.
- *Planning individual audit procedures.* Materiality is used to determine what items to examine and whether to use sampling and the extent of testing to be carried out on the particular transaction class or account balance. This enables specific audit procedures to be selected to support the opinion whilst reducing to a low level the risk of giving an inappropriate opinion.

18.5   REVISION TO MATERIALITY ASSESSMENTS

Clarified ISA (UK and Ireland) 320 sets out additional guidance in relation to revisions to materiality assessments. If information comes to light during the course of the audit which would have influenced auditors' assessment of materiality had it been known when materiality was determined, the materiality level (or levels for particular classes of transactions, account balances or disclosures) should be adjusted. The amendment and the reason for it should be clearly documented on the audit file.

If materiality levels are lowered, auditors should consider whether performance materiality should also be decreased.

Where revisions are made to materiality, auditors should consider the implications for their audit approach and, if necessary, modify the nature, timing and extent of planned audit procedures. If their revised assessment results in a lower level of materiality, auditors may find it necessary to carry out more audit work.

18.6   UNCORRECTED MISSTATEMENTS

18.6.1   During the audit

Guidance on evaluating misstatements is set out in Clarified ISA (UK and Ireland) 450 *Evaluation of Misstatements Identified During the Audit.*

In evaluating whether the financial statements give a true and fair view auditors are required to assess the materiality of the aggregate of uncorrected misstatements. Uncorrected misstatements arise from:

* specific misstatements identified by the auditors, including those from a previous financial period to the extent that they impact on the current financial statements; and
* the auditors' best estimate of other misstatements which cannot be quantified specifically, i.e., projected errors.

The various errors found during the audit should be assessed in aggregate as the audit progresses to ensure that there is no material misstatement in the financial statements. If the auditors are of the opinion that these may be material, they will need to consider reducing audit risk by extending audit procedures or requesting management to adjust the financial statements. If no adjustment is made after such a request, they will need to consider the effect on their report.

Misstatements that are individually and in aggregate 'clearly trivial' can be omitted from this aggregation. If there is debate over whether an item is 'clearly trivial' the Clarified ISA (UK and Ireland) states that by generating such a debate the item cannot be considered trivial.

If the aggregate of uncorrected errors approaches materiality, auditors should consider whether undetected errors could make this total material. In such a situation they may perform additional procedures or request that the identified errors are adjusted.

18.6.2 At the completion phase

Once all audit tests have been completed and prior to evaluating the effect of uncorrected misstatements, Clarified ISA (UK and Ireland) 320 states that auditors should reassess their materiality judgements in light of the entity's actual financial results.

Auditors should then consider whether any uncorrected misstatements are material either individually or in aggregate.

Each individual misstatement should be evaluated to determine its effect on relevant account balances, transactions or disclosures. Auditors should also consider whether any materiality levels for each account balance, transaction or disclosure has been breached.

Where a number of immaterial misstatements have been identified within the same account balance or class of transactions, this may lead auditors to reconsider their assessment of the risk of material misstatement for that account balance or class of transactions.

Auditors should also be aware of areas where errors are likely to be material by their nature and without aggregation. An example would be the disclosure of directors' emoluments, where any error should be amended. US guidance, in the form of SEC Staff Accounting Bulletin 99, reiterates the importance of not discounting errors simply because they fall below the materiality threshold.

18.7 DOCUMENTATION

Clarified ISA (UK and Ireland) 450 set out a number of documentation requirements in relation to misstatements identified during the audit. However, these are not expected to give rise to significant changes from existing practice. The requirements are to clearly document on file:

- the amount below which misstatement would be regarded as clearly trivial;
- all misstatements accumulated during the audit and whether they have been corrected; and
- auditors' conclusions as to whether uncorrected misstatements are material individually or in aggregate, and the basis for that conclusion.

18.8 COMMUNICATION OF ERRORS

Where a material misstatement has been found, auditors should provide details to the appropriate level of management on a timely basis. Depending on the circumstances, auditors may also consider it necessary to bring the error to the attention of those charged with governance, in accordance with Clarified ISA (UK and Ireland) 260 (see **Chapter 9**).

18.9 WRITTEN REPRESENTATIONS

Auditors should obtain written representations from those charged with governance to confirm their opinion that uncorrected misstatements are immaterial both individually and in aggregate. This would be achieved by attaching a list of uncorrected misstatements to the representation letter.

Where those charged with governance have been requested to correct misstatements but have chosen not to do so, auditors should obtain a written representation as to their reasons for not making the adjustment.

19   DOCUMENTATION

19.1   AUDITING STANDARDS

Clarified ISA (UK and Ireland) 230 (Revised) *Documentation* was issued in October 2009 and is effective for the audit of financial statements for periods ending on or after 15 December 2010. The updated ISA (UK and Ireland) replaces ISA (UK and Ireland) 230 issued in January 2006. This chapter covers both the existing and Clarified ISAs (UK and Ireland). As the clarified ISA (UK and Ireland) adds to the requirements of the existing ISA (UK and Ireland) this chapter is written on the basis of the existing requirements, and changes to them included in the Clarified ISA (UK and Ireland) are included and clearly indicated. The ISA (UK and Ireland) provides standards on documentation covering:

- form of working papers;
- content of working papers;
- changes to audit documentation after the date of the auditor's report;
- assembly of the final audit file; and
- confidentiality, safe custody and retention of audit documentation.

As with all ISAs (UK and Ireland), in publishing ISA (UK and Ireland) 230, the APB has supplemented the text of the international ISA with additional guidance from a UK and Ireland perspective.

19.2   PURPOSE OF DOCUMENTATION

ISA (UK and Ireland) 230 requires that auditors should document matters which are important in providing audit evidence to support their opinion and evidence that the audit was carried out in accordance with ISAs (UK and Ireland).

Working papers are any material the auditors obtain, prepare or retain in the course of their audit. This may be in paper form but may also include, for example, film, scanned documents, computer discs or electronic files, including e-mail.

Working papers provide a record of supervision and review, the planning and performance of the audit by the staff and the evidence to support the audit opinion. They provide the individuals responsible for approving the audit report with the means to satisfy themselves that the work delegated has been properly performed. Other advantages of working papers are that they are seen as providing a source of reference that may be used in subsequent years and that they encourage a methodical approach.

19.3   FORM AND CONTENT

Working papers should be sufficiently complete and detailed so as to provide an overall understanding of the audit. They should contain information on planning the audit, the nature, timing and extent of the audit procedures performed and the results and conclusions from the procedures.

Working papers should be sufficient to allow an 'experienced auditor, having no previous connection with the audit' to be able to understand:

- the nature, timing and extent of the audit procedures performed to comply with the ISAs (UK and Ireland) and applicable legal and regulatory requirements;
- the results of the audit procedures performed, and the audit evidence obtained; and
- significant matters arising during the audit, the conclusions reached thereon, and significant professional judgements made in reaching those conclusions.

An experience auditor is an individual (whether internal or external to the firm) who has practical audit experience, and a reasonable understanding of:

- audit processes;
- ISAs and applicable legal and regulatory requirements;
- the business environment in which the entity operates; and
- auditing and financial reporting issues relevant to the entity's industry.

The ISA (UK and Ireland) states that it may be necessary for that experienced auditor to hold discussions with the auditors to obtain a detailed understanding.

Because of a wide variety of circumstances in which working papers have to be prepared and the many types of business transactions to which they relate, it is not practicable to lay down a standard form for their preparation suitable for each and every situation. How the relevant information can best be shown, what audit procedures need to be applied and how their results can best be summarised is a matter for the particular circumstances. They should, however, be set out in such a fashion that the salient facts are readily apparent.

Working papers should be designed for each assignment and the factors set out in **Table 1** will determine their extent.

TABLE 1: Factors affecting form and content and extent of working papers

- the nature of the engagement;
- the identified risks of material misstatement;
- the extent of judgement required in performing the work and evaluating the results;
- the significance of the audit evidence obtained;
- the nature and extent of exceptions identified;
- the need to document a conclusion or the basis for a conclusion not readily

---

determinable from the documentation of the work performed or audit evidence obtained; and
- the specific methodology and technology the auditors use.

The use of standardised working papers, such as checklists, specimen letters and a standard index may aid efficiency and control, but auditors should be aware of the dangers of following a standard approach mechanically. Professional judgement should be exercised when such aids are used.

If schedules have been drawn up by the client, auditors require evidence that they have been properly prepared before relying on them.

As indicated above the term 'working papers' refers to the record of all of the evidence that auditors consider necessary to collect in order to support an opinion. This may relate to the current year or be of a permanent nature, i.e., of continuing importance and as a result be filed separately. The specific nature will depend on the assignment. Examples of the content of working papers are shown in **Table 2**.

TABLE 2: Contents of working papers

- information on the legal nature of the client, including copies of important documents;
- information concerning the industry and the economic and legislative environments within which the entity operates;
- evidence of the planning process, including any changes;
- notes on the accounting and internal control systems including extracts from the entity's internal control manual;
- assessment of inherent and control risks at the financial statements and assertion level;
- consideration of and conclusions on the work of internal audit;
- analyses of transactions and balances, including significant ratios and trends;
- audit programmes showing the nature, timing and extent of the audit procedures performed in response to risks at the assertion level, and the conclusions thereon;
- evidence that the work performed by assistants was supervised and reviewed;
- an indication as to who performed the audit procedures and when they were performed;
- correspondence with other auditors, experts and third parties;
- details of audit procedures applied where components of the financial statements are audited by another auditor;
- correspondence with the entity, including reports to management and notes of discussions with management concerning audit matters;
- letters of representation from management;
- a summary of the significant aspects of the audit, the conclusions reached and how matters have been resolved and the views of those charged with governance; and
- copies of the approved financial statements and auditors' reports.

19.3.1   Documenting characteristics of items tested

The ISA (UK and Ireland) requires auditors to include in their documentation details of the identifying characteristics of the items or matters tested. The characteristics recorded will vary depending on the items being tested, but may specifically identify the actual items testing, e.g., for a detailed test of entity-generated purchase orders, auditors may identify the actual documents tested by providing their purchase order number, or alternatively, indicate the population as a whole, e.g., for a review of credit notes over a certain amount, auditors may document the scope of the procedure and the threshold value above which items were reviewed.

Recording the items tested at this level of detail allows the subsequent investigation of exceptions or inconsistencies as well as enabling the audit team to be accountable for its work.

Typically, however, copies of the entity's records will only be required when they are necessary for an experienced auditor to understand the work performed and the conclusions reached.

19.3.2   Judgement areas

ISA 230 requires that working papers should include the auditors' reasoning on all significant matters which require the exercise of judgement, together with the auditors' conclusions thereon.

The ISA (UK and Ireland) provides examples of items which would be deemed to be 'significant matters':

- matters that give rise to significant risks;
- results of audit procedures which indicate either that financial information could be materially misstated or that there is a need to revise auditors' previous assessment of the risks of material misstatement;
- circumstances where auditors have significant difficulty in performing their procedures; and
- findings that could result in a modification to the auditor's report.

In addition, the inclusion of the entity's ability to continue as a going concern as a 'significant matter' was introduced in the clarified ISA (UK and Ireland) 230, effective for the audit of financial periods ending on or after 15 December 2010.

The working papers should note the relevant facts at the time the judgement was reached. This is particularly important where it concerns a difficult area which may be questioned later with the benefit of hindsight. The ISA (UK and Ireland) suggests that use of a summary of significant matters cross-referenced to detailed working papers may aid consideration of these matters together with assisting with review of the work performed and conclusions reached. This may form part of a 'completion memorandum'.

The ISA (UK and Ireland) also requires auditors to document any discussion held with management and others, including those charged with governance, about significant matters.

Where auditors have found information that contradicts their final conclusion on a significant matter the inconsistency should be documented on file, together with an explanation of how the final conclusion was reached. This does not mean, however, that incorrect or superseded documentation should be retained on file.

19.3.3 Documentation of departures from ISAs (UK and Ireland)

Where it is necessary to depart from the requirements of the basic or essential procedures in an ISA (UK and Ireland), auditors are required to document the alternative procedures followed and the reasons for the departure. This does not apply to procedures that are not relevant to the engagement, e.g., auditors need not apply the standards in ISA (UK and Ireland) 510 regarding initial engagements for ongoing audits.

19.3.4 Identification of the preparer and reviewer of documentation

The performer of audit work should be clearly identified on each piece of documentation, including the date on which their work was performed. There is no requirement to provide on each piece of documentation evidence of who reviewed the audit work. The documentation should indicate, however, who reviewed each element of the audit work and when. This may be on a control sheet rather than by, for example, initialling and dating each sheet of documentation itself.

19.4 ASSEMBLY OF THE FINAL AUDIT FILE

ISA (UK and Ireland) 230 requires the final audit file to be assembled on a timely basis. The requirements of ISQC (UK and Ireland) 1 suggest this should be within 60 days of the date of the auditor's report (see **19.3.8**).

The final assembly of the audit file is an administrative process and should not involve any further audit work or the drawing of new conclusions. Only administrative changes can be made to the audit documentation, such as:

- deleting or discarding superseded documentation;
- sorting, collating or cross-referencing working papers;
- signing off completion checklists relating to the file assembly process; or
- documenting audit evidence that auditors have obtained, discussed and agreed with the relevant members of the audit team before the date of their report.

Other audit documentation must not be deleted or discarded before the end of the retention period.

19.5   CHANGES TO AUDIT DOCUMENTATION

ISA (UK and Ireland) 230 states that exceptional circumstances may arise which require auditors to perform new procedures after the date of the audit report or modify existing documentation, such as in response to comments received during monitoring inspections performed by internal or external parties. The ISA (UK and Ireland) requires auditors to record who made the changes and when, the consequential changes to documentation, the reasons for the changes and the effect on their previous conclusions.

19.6   CONFIDENTIALITY, CUSTODY AND OWNERSHIP OF WORKING PAPERS

Although ISA (UK and Ireland) 230 no longer contains specific requirements that auditors should adopt appropriate procedures for maintaining the confidentiality and safe custody of their working papers, these have been added to ISQC (UK and Ireland) 1 (see **20.3.8**), and so such procedures should still be in place. It is the auditors' responsibility to ensure that the audit working papers are kept safely. They should bear in mind that their work is strictly confidential.

The audit working papers are the property of the auditors. Papers relating to accountancy work will normally be the property of the client although this will depend on the particular circumstances. Certain papers may be made available to clients but care should be taken not to undermine the independence or validity of the audit process. Because of their confidential nature they should not be divulged to third parties without the client's permission, although some third parties, for example the Inland Revenue, may have a right of access in certain circumstances. However, whatever the circumstances, they should not be seen as a substitute for the client's accounting records.

Audit Regulation 3.08b states that 'A Registered Auditor must keep all audit working papers which auditing standards require for a period of at least six years. The period starts with the end of the accounting period to which the papers relate.' The actual length of time they are kept for will be a matter of judgement based on auditors' own needs, those of the client and any regulatory requirements. However, it suggests that prior to their destruction a review is carried out to ensure that there is no need to refer to them again.

In addition to maintaining the confidentiality and safe custody of their audit documentation and retaining their documents for the minimum period required by law, auditors should also have appropriate procedures for audit documentation that:

- protects its integrity; and
- enables its accessibility and retrievability.

This is particularly relevant for any audit evidence held electronically and means that audit firms should ensure that they retain at least one version of any, otherwise superseded, information technology applications required to access old audit documentation. This may include both proprietary word-processing or spreadsheet tools which may have been upgraded, or any internally developed audit tools which have become obsolete or have been replaced or revised. The ability to retrieve work papers and other documentation is also an issue if it was originally prepared on paper and has later been scanned or microfiched for storage.

It is important that auditors have procedures in place to ensure that the integrity of data is maintained when it is stored electronically such as introducing appropriate back-up routines and use of restricted passwords. When original paper documentation is scanned or fiched, auditors should ensure that the scanned copy is identical to the original, properly integrated in the audit file and able to be retrieved and printed.

19.7   ACCESS TO WORKING PAPERS

When a company becomes a target for potential purchasers, the purchaser's investigating accountants will frequently want access to the audit working papers to assist in their investigations. The granting of access to working papers in these circumstances involves issues of confidentiality and also the possibility that auditors may be alleged to have accepted an additional duty of care.

The Audit Faculty of the Institute of Chartered Accountants issued Audit *4/2003: Access to Working Papers by Investigating Accountants*, to attempt to facilitate the agreement of access to working papers in these situations. This supersedes Audit *3/95* of the same title. It recommends that access to papers is granted on the basis of client authorisation and 'release' letters. These seek to deal with confidentiality issues and limit as far as possible additional risks. The guidance has been updated due to the complexity of transaction funding, coupled with the emergence of different approaches such as vendor due diligence, which has resulted in an increase in the number and diversity of parties seeking to gain access to work papers.

The main area of change in the release letter is in relation to the indemnity sought by the auditors, which is now narrowed to an indemnity against loss caused by the breach by the purchasers or the investigating accountants of the terms of the letter, rather than any claims arising from any breach of the provisions of the access to the working papers. In many cases this amounts to the same thing because the purchaser and the investigating accountants agree that the auditors do not assume a duty of care, and agree not to disclose the contents of the working papers to anyone else. If they do disclose the working paper contents, they are in breach of the terms of the letter and the indemnity applies.

In addition, it is recommended that auditors include a disclaimer notice with the working papers and require such a notice to be attached to the investigating accountants' due diligence report.

19.7.1   Work paper ownership and access

The working papers of auditors are their legal property and they have the right to restrict or decline access to them. They would not provide access to their work papers or provide explanations on those papers until they have received:

- an authorisation letter signed by the vendor and the target company permitting the auditor to give access (**Table 3**); and
- a release letter signed by the prospective purchaser and its investigating accountant in which they agree that the auditors do not assume any duties or liabilities as a result of granting access (**Table 4**).

The release letter also requires the purchaser to indemnify the auditor for any loss suffered in the event of the purchaser or investigating accountant failing to comply with their obligations in the release letter.

In addition, to assist in excluding any other duty of care which may arise, and to reinforce the importance and purpose of audit working papers, the guidance suggests:

- attaching a 'notice' to the working papers when access is provided which summarises the characteristics, and records the exclusion of, liability (see Attachment 1 in the example letter in **Table 4**); and
- obtaining an undertaking from the purchaser and investigating accountants to include such a standard notice in the text of their due diligence report.

This assumes that the purchaser and investigating accountant will not allow the working papers to be viewed by another third party without written consent from the auditor. Whether this will be granted depends on the circumstances, and will usually be dependent on the signing of a formal release letter. In many cases the auditor controls access to the files by requiring the investigating accountants to view them on the auditors' premises.

Auditors would normally give access to all working papers. If some are withdrawn, they should inform the investigating accountants and purchaser that this is the case.

TABLE 3: Client authorisation letter

Private and Confidential

The Directors
[Vendor]
[Address]

The Directors
[The Company]
[Address]

[Date]

Dear Sirs

Proposed sales of [Company Limited ('the Company') by [XYZ plc] ('the Vendor') to [ABC plc] ('the Purchaser')

In relation to the proposed sale by the Vendor [of the ordinary shares of the Company] to the Purchaser ('the Proposed Transaction') in which you requested this firm to allow [the Purchaser and/or] the Purchaser's accountants [PQR & Co] ('the Investigating Accountants') access to this firm's working papers relating to the statutory audit[s] of the Company's [and its subsidiaries'] financial statements for the year ended 31 December 20XX ('the Audit Working Papers').]

[As you are aware, this firm has not yet completed this year's statutory audit[s] of the Company's [and its subsidiaries'] financial statements, and therefore, the Audit Working Papers for this year are incomplete. Further this firm is not able to give any opinion on those financial statements and has not done so. Nevertheless, I understand that the Purchaser and the Investigating Accountants still wish the Investigating Accountants to review such Audit Working Papers as are available to date.]

[In addition, you requested this firm to allow the Investigating Accountants to review the taxation returns and computations of the Company [and its subsidiaries], so far as in the possession of this firm, as submitted to and/or agreed with the UK Inland Revenue for each of the last [insert number] years[, working papers relating to those returns and computations] and copies of the correspondence and related documents passing between this firm and the UK Inland Revenue in respect of those returns and computations (together, 'the tax papers').

This firm's general policy is not to allow third parties to have access to the working papers in the possession of this firm. However, this firm is content to allow such access to the Audit Working Papers [and the Tax Papers] ([together] 'the Papers'), but only on the basis of the guidance contained in Technical Release 04/03 issued by the Institute of Chartered Accountants in England and Wales. In accordance with that guidance I am now writing to confirm your agreement to the terms set out in this letter and to secure the authorisation of the Company [and its subsidiaries] for that access.

As a condition of providing access to the Investigating Accountants and responding to any requests for information and explanations in relation to the Papers in the course of or in connection with their review of the Papers, this firm requires that the Purchaser and the Investigating Accountants agree to the terms of the letter enclosed.

As you will appreciate, the Audit Working Papers were created for the sole purpose of the statutory audit[s] of the Company's [and its subsidiaries'] financial statements

---

321

[and the Tax Papers were prepared and/or obtained for the purpose of calculating and agreeing the Company's [and its subsidiaries'] UK tax liabilities]. The Papers were not created for the purpose of the Proposed Transaction. Consequently, the information in the Papers should not be treated as suitable for the purposes of the Proposed Transaction. Furthermore, it is not this firm's function or responsibility to provide to the Purchaser or the Investigating Accountants any Papers that may come into existence, or information that may come to this firm's attention, after [date].

Accordingly, this firm requires the Vendor and its directors and the Company [(and its subsidiaries)] and [its] [their] directors to agree to the following conditions:

(a)   They each accept the risk, and do not and will not hold this firm responsible, if the Investigating Accountant's review of the Papers or any information or explanations that this firm gives to them in relation to the Papers or in connection with their review of the Papers:

(i)   results in or contributes to the termination or reduction of the interest of the Purchaser in, or to the alternation to the proposed terms of, the Proposed Transaction, or otherwise affects the Proposed Transaction or the prospects of its maturing into a binding transaction; or

(ii)   causes an action or proceeding to be brought at any time against the Vendor or its directors or the company [(or any of its subsidiaries)] or [its] [their] directors [respectively]; or

(iii) results in the Purchaser, the Investigating Accountants or any other person or entity using or misusing any confidential information obtained from a review of the Papers or from any information or explanations given by this firm.

(b)   They each accept that, to the fullest extent permitted by law, this firm owes them no duty of care or other obligation and has no liability to them, in relation to or in connection with the Proposed Transaction as a result of granting the Investigating Accountants access to the Papers or any information or explanations that this firm gives in relation to the Papers or in connection with the review by the Investigating Accountants of the Papers.

The audit of the financial statements of the [Company/Companies] was undertaken by and is the sole responsibility of this firm, that is [insert full, exact name of UK firm carrying out the audit]. In paragraph (a) and (b) above references to 'this firm', where appropriate in the context, shall have an extended meaning so that they include, in addition to [insert full, exact name of the UK firm carrying out the audit], [partners/directors/members], employees and agents of this firm [and any person or organisation associated with this firm through membership of the international association of professional service firms to which this firm belongs and their [partners/directors/members], employees and agents]. This letter is for the benefit of all those included within the reference to this firm and each of them may enforce in their own right all of the terms of this letter.

Please confirm that the Company [and its subsidiaries] authorise[s] this firm to allow access to the Papers and to give information or explanations on the terms described above by signing the enclosed copy of this letter on behalf of the Vendor and its directors and the Company and its directors [and its subsidiaries and their directors] and returning it to this firm marked for the attention of ....

Yours faithfully

....

ACKNOWLEDGEMENT

Acknowledged and agreed, for and on behalf of [Vendor] and the directors of [Vendor].

....
Director   Date

Acknowledged and agreed, for and on behalf of [the Company] and the directors of [the Company].

....
Director   Date

[Acknowledged and agreed, for and on behalf of [subsidiaries] and the directors of [subsidiaries].

....
Director   Date]

TABLE 4: Release letter to prospective purchaser and investigating accountants

(The Release Letter assumes a proposed purchase of a company and that both Audit Working Papers and Tax Papers are to be made available. It must be amended as appropriate for the circumstances of each transaction.)

Private and Confidential

[Purchaser]
[Address]
[Investigating Accountants]
[Address]

[Date]

Dear Sirs

Proposed Acquisition of [Company] Limited

1   In connection with the proposed acquisition by [ABC plc] ('the Purchaser') of [Company] Limited ('the Company') ('the Proposed Transaction') the Company [(and the subsidiary undertakings identified in Attachment 2)] [(together 'the Companies')] [has/have] requested this firm to allow [the Purchaser and/or] [name of Firm of Accountants] (the 'Investigating Accountants') access to this firm's working papers relating to the statutory audit[s] [(including the audits currently in progress)] of the financial statements of the [Company/Companies] for the year[s] ended [date] ('the Audit Working Papers') [and the taxation returns and computation of the [Company/Companies], so far as in this firm's possession, as submitted to and/or agreed with the UK Inland Revenue for each of the last [number] years[, working papers relating to those returns and computations] and copies of the correspondence and related documents passing between this firm and the UK Inland Revenue in respect of those returns and computations (together 'the Tax Papers')].[[The Company/Companies] [has/ have] authorised this firm at this firm's discretion to give information or explanations in relation to the Audit Working Papers [and the Tax Papers]]. The Audit Working Papers [and the Tax Papers together] are also referred to below as 'the Papers'.

2   The Purchaser and the Investigating Accountants should note that this firm has not reported on the [Company's/Companies'] financial statements for any period subsequent to [date] [nor have any tax liabilities of the [Company/Companies]

been agreed for any subsequent period to [date]] and significant events may well have occurred since [that date/those dates]. It is not this firm's function or responsibility to provide to the Purchaser or the Investigating Accountants any Audit Working Papers [or Tax Papers] that may come into existence, or information that may come to this firm's attention, at any point after [date].

3   This firm does not accept or assume responsibility to anyone other than the [Company/Companies] and the [Company's/Companies' respective] members as a body, for its audit work, for its audit report(s) or for the opinions it has formed. The statutory audit is undertaken in order that this firm might report to the [Company's/Companies' respective] members, as a body, in accordance with Section 235 of the Companies Act 1985. The audit procedures and the Audit Working Papers were designed and created solely for the purpose of enabling this firm to form and state an opinion to the [Company's/Companies' respective] members as a body, in accordance with the statutory requirements for audit, on whether the financial statements of [the Company/the Companies], which are the responsibility of the directors of the [the Company/the Companies], give a true and fair view of the state of affairs of [the Company/the Companies] as at the end of the relevant financial year and of the profit and loss for the period then ended. This firm's auditing procedures were designed to enable this firm to express an opinion on [the Company's/the Companies' respective] financial statements as a whole or not, for example and save where otherwise expressly stated, on individual account balances, financial amounts, financial information or the adequacy of financial, accounting or management systems. [The Tax Papers were prepared and/or obtained solely for the purpose of calculating and/ or agreeing [the Company's/the Companies'] tax liabilities.]

4   This firm's audit(s) of the [Company's/Companies'] financial statements, and the Audit Working Papers prepared or obtained in connection therewith, [was/ were] not planned or conducted in contemplation, or for the purpose, of the Proposed Transaction. [Nor were the Tax Papers.] Further, the scope of an audit is normally substantially narrower than an investigation on behalf of a potential purchaser. Moreover, there are a number of inherent limitations in audited financial statements [and the calculation or agreement of tax liabilities] as the Investigating Accountants will be able to advise.

5   Therefore, items of possible interest to the Purchaser may not have been specifically addressed for the purposes of the audit [or of calculating and agreeing [the Company's/the Companies'] tax liabilities]. The user of professional judgement and assessment of materiality for the purpose of this firm's audit [or of calculating and agreeing [the Company's/the Companies'] tax liabilities] means that matters may have existed that would have been assessed differently by the Purchaser or the Investigating Accountants for the purposes of the Proposed Transaction. This firm does not warrant or represent that the information in the Papers, or that information or explanations given by this firm in relation to the Papers or in connection with the review by the Investigating Accountants of the Papers, is appropriate for the purposes of the Purchaser or the Investigating Accountants. The Audit Working Papers were not created for, and should not be treated as suitable for, any purpose other than the Statutory Audit. [The Tax Papers were not created for, and should not be treated as suitable for, any purpose other than [calculating and agreeing [the Company's/the Companies'] tax liabilities.]

6   For the foregoing reasons, neither the Papers nor the information or explanations given by this firm in relation to the Papers or in connection with the review by the Investigating Accountants of the Papers can in any way serve as a substitute for other enquiries and procedures that the Purchaser and Investigating Accountants would (or should) otherwise undertake and judgements they must

make for the purpose of satisfying themselves regarding [the Company's/the Companies' respective] financial condition or for any other purpose in connection with the Proposed Transaction. No one should rely for any purpose whatsoever upon the Papers or any information or explanations that this firm may give in relation to them or in connection with the review by the Investigating Accountants of them.

7 This firm is prepared to grant the [Purchaser and/or the] Investigating Accountants access to the papers and at this firm's discretion to give information and explanations in relation to the Papers or in connection with the review by the Investigating Accountants of the Papers, on condition that the Purchaser and the Investigating Accountants acknowledge and accept the foregoing paragraphs (including that the position in respect of this firm's audit reports on the [Company's /Companies'] financial statements will remain as stated in paragraph 3 above following the grant of access to the Papers and giving of information and explanations in relation to the Papers) and agree to the following conditions upon which access to the Papers is granted and the explanations and information referred to are given:

(1) The Purchaser and the Investigating Accountants accept, agree and acknowledge:

(a) For the purposes of this letter, the expression 'the information' shall mean the Papers and any information and explanations given by this firm in relation to the Papers or in connection with the review by the Investigating Accountants of the papers;

(b) Where any information or explanation is given by this firm the onus shall be upon the Purchaser and the Investigating Accountants to verify any such information or explanation direct with [the Company/ the Companies] rather than seek to rely on this firm;

(c) to the fullest extent permitted by law, this firm owes no duty to them, whether in contract or in tort or under statute or otherwise (including in negligence) with respect to or in connection with the information or its provision or in relation to the audit reports on the [Company's/ Companies'] financial statements;

(d) if, notwithstanding the terms of this letter, they do rely upon any of the information or the audit reports on the [Company's /Companies] financial statements for any purpose, they will do so entirely at their own risk;

(e) they will not bring any actions, proceedings, or claims against this firm where the action, proceeding or claim in any way relates to or concerns or is connected with the use of or reliance on the information or the audit reports on the [Company's/Companies'] financial statements;

(f) to the fullest extent permitted by law, this firm has no liability to them for any loss or damage suffered or costs incurred by them, arising out of or in connection with the information or its use or the audit reports on the [Company's/Companies'] financial statements, however such loss or damage is caused;

(g) they will not refer to the information nor allow access to it or any report derived therefrom to any person or entity without this firm's prior written consent. (However the Investigating Accountants will not need to obtain such consent in order to disclose and discuss the same (i) with [the Company/the Companies] for the purpose of obtaining information or verification from [the Company/the Companies] in respect of any report to be prepared by the Investigating Accountants in connection with the Proposed

Transaction; (ii) with the Purchaser's legal advisers but then only on the basis that the firm will have no duty or liability to them; or (iii) otherwise as required by a Court or by statute.) Where this firm is willing to give written consent, this firm will require as a condition of such consent that the other person or entity agrees in writing to be bound by and to observe the terms set out in this letter, as if references to the Purchaser were a reference to the other person or entity.

(2) To the fullest extent permitted by law, the Purchaser agrees to indemnify and hold harmless this firm against all actions, proceedings and claims brought or threatened against this firm, and all loss, damage and expense (including legal expenses) relating thereto where such action, proceeding or claim has arisen out of or results from or is connected with the failure of the Purchaser, or any of its professional advisers or the Investigating Accountants to comply with the terms of this letter.

(3) Without limiting the obligation in paragraph 7(1)(g) above, the Purchaser and the Investigating Accountants agree to ensure that the notice attached as Attachment 1 to this letter is attached to any document obtained as a result of the Investigating Accountants' access to the Papers and is included in any note or report or other document in which they make reference to the information.

8   The audit of the financial statements of the [Company/Companies] was undertaken by and is the sole responsibility of this firm, that is [insert full, exact name of UK firm carrying out the audit]. In paragraph 7(1)(c) to (g) and 7(2) of this letter all references to 'this firm' (except for the first and the last two references in the paragraph 7(1)(g) shall have an extended meaning so that they include, in addition to [insert full, exact name of the UK firm carrying out the audit], [partners/directors/members], employees and agents of this firm [and any person or organisation associated with this firm through membership of the international association of professional service firms to which this firm belongs and their [partners/directors/members], employees and agents. This letter is for the benefit of all of those referred to in the previous sentence and each of them may enforce in their own right all of the terms of this letter.

9   This letter sets out the entire agreement as between the Purchaser and the Investigating Accountants and this firm in relation to the conditions upon which access to the Papers is given by this firm and upon which information and explanations in relation to the Papers or in connection with the review by the Investigating Accountants are given by this firm to the Purchaser and the Investigating Accountants. It replaces all prior agreements or understandings (if any) between or amongst the Purchaser, the Investigating Accountants and this firm in that regard.

10   The terms of the agreement shall be governed solely by English law, and the Courts of England and Wales shall have exclusive jurisdiction in respect of any dispute arising out of it or in connection with it. [The Purchaser, the Investigating Accountants, and this firm irrevocably waive any right to object to proceedings being brought in those Courts, to claim that the proceedings have been brought in an inappropriate forum, or to claim that those Courts do not have jurisdiction.]

11   Please confirm the agreement of the Purchaser and the Investigating Accountants to, and acceptance of, the provisions of this letter by signing, dating and returning to us a copy of this letter.

Yours faithfully

[Firm]

The Purchaser hereby acknowledges that it agrees to and accepts the provisions of this letter.

[Date]

_____

Director

The Investigating Accountants hereby acknowledge that they agree to and accept the provisions of this letter.

[Date]

_____

Director

Attachment 1 to Release Letter

Notice of the Auditor

1   [Firm name] ('the Auditor'), the auditor of [Company name] ('the Company'), has, on certain conditions, allowed [name of Investigating Accountants] ('the Investigating Accountants') to have access to the Auditor's working papers relating to the statutory audit of the Company's financial statements for the [year/period] ended [date] ('the Audit Working Papers').

2   The Auditor does not accept or assume responsibility to anyone other than the Company and the Company's members as a body, for its audit work, for its audit report or for the opinions it has formed. To the fullest extent permitted by law, the Auditor does not accept or assume responsibility to anyone as a result of the access given to the Audit Working Papers or for any information or explanation given to the Investigating Accountants in relation to the Audit Working Papers or in connection with the review by the Investigating Accountants of the Audit Working Papers.

3   The Audit Working Papers were not created for, and should not be treated as suitable for, any purpose other than the statutory audit. The statutory audit is undertaken in order that the Auditor might report to the Company's members, as a body, in accordance with Section 235 of the Companies Act 1985. The audit work of the Auditor is undertaken so that the Auditors might state to the Company's members those matters it is required to state to them in auditor's report and for no other purpose.

Attachment 2 to Release Letter

List of companies referred to in paragraph 1 for which access to the Audit Working Papers [and the Tax Papers] is to be provided.

19.7.2   Further explanations

If an auditor provides further explanation which extends to matters beyond the content of their work papers, they increase the risk of assuming a duty of care. In particular, auditors should take care not to give oral representations about matters arising after the date of the audit report.

If further explanations are sought, auditors are advised to re-emphasise the matters in the Notice in Attachment 1 to **Table 4** at the time, perhaps by reading this out, or circulating a copy of the Notice at the beginning of the meeting.

If matters outside the auditors' working papers are to be discussed, the auditors consider whether this is appropriate. If the risks can be managed they may wish to structure this as a separate engagement with appropriate liability protection in a separate engagement letter.

Auditors are recommended not to agree to any request by the investigating accountants to review or approve their due diligence report. Such requests do not give auditors any added protection and may serve to confuse auditors' roles in transactions.

19.7.3   Access for other parties

The example release letter in **Table 4** assumes a simple investment transaction where an existing corporate entity purchases a subsidiary of the vendor. There are other situations where the release letter may require amendment.

Syndicated financings

In syndicated financings the investigating accountants may be requested to provide copies of their investigation report, incorporating information derived from the audit working papers, to other parties who were not identified at the time the release letter was signed, and therefore could not be party to it. Providing this information without the auditors' consent would be in breach of paragraph 7(1)(g) of the release letter.

It might be appropriate for the lead bank or equity provider to sign a modified release letter containing the following paragraph:

> *This letter is addressed to [Lead Bank/Lead Equity Provider] for itself and on behalf of all [Banks/Equity Providers] listed in the [Loan/Equity Agreement] (together "the [Banks/Equity Providers"). By signing and accepting the terms of this letter, [Lead Bank/Equity Provider] warrants and represents that it has authority to accept the same on its own behalf and as agent for the [Banks/Equity Providers].*

The lead bank or equity provider may seek to amend paragraph 7(2) of the letter to seek to provide an indemnity for its own breaches only. If this is agreed, auditors should be aware of the risks of another bank or equity provider passing information on to another party.

Alternatively, each bank or equity provider should sign a release letter in its own right. This may be difficult where the draft investigating accountants' report is circulated to potential finance parties as a basis for their decision whether or not to go ahead with the finance. Technical Release Audit 4/2003 contains detailed guidance on this situation.

Flotations

Where access is provided in connection with a flotation, the auditors are advised to obtain a release letter signed by the:

- firm acting as reporting accountants;
- new company incorporated for the purpose of the float; and
- sponsor.

Auditors should obtain legal advice about limiting liability where no new company has been incorporated.

Where the reporting accountants are preparing an accountants' report (a short form report) there is no need to attach or refer to the Notice. Paragraph 7(3) of the Notice should be amended accordingly.

Vendor due diligence

Where a vendor has instructed a firm of accountants to prepare a due diligence report that will eventually be addressed to a purchaser, the auditors will require the vendor and the target company to sign an authorisation letter. The wording of that letter will be extended to include an indemnity from the vendor, as it is the vendor, rather than the purchaser, who will control the distribution of the due diligence report.

The auditors will also require a release letter signed by the investigating accountants, based on **Table 4**, but without the indemnity paragraph 7(2). Risks to unknown potential purchasers will be managed in much the same way as for financing syndicates above.

Alternatively auditors may be prepared to acknowledge that the investigating accountants will require permission to circulate their report to prospective purchasers, and replace paragraphs 7(1)(g) and 7(2) with **Table 5**.

TABLE 5: Alternative paragraph 7(1)(g) and 7(2) for use in vendor due diligence situations

'they will not refer to the Information nor allow access to it or any report derived therefrom to any person or entity without this firm's prior written consent. The Investigating Accountants may allow access to the Information or any part thereof, in the form of a report of Investigating Accountants incorporating or

---

referring to any part of the Information, to any prospective purchaser of the Company ("Prospective Purchaser") provided that the Investigating Accountants obtain the express prior agreement and acknowledgement of each Prospective Purchaser, addressed to this firm, that (a) this firm has, to the fullest extent permitted by law, no duty or liability and assumes no responsibility to the Prospective Purchaser or its professional advisers, whether in contract or tort or under statue or otherwise (including in negligence), with respect to or in connection with the Information or any part thereof the report and that (b) Prospective Purchaser will not disclose (including by reference or by copy, in whole or in part) any Information, including without limitation the report, to any other person or entity. Prior to the Investigating Accountants addressing to any party acquiring interest in the Company ("Purchaser") any report incorporating or referring to any part of the Information, the Investigating Accountants shall procure that Purchaser binds itself to this firm and accepts all the provisions of a letter in the terms of this letter (but adjusted to refer to Purchaser), together with an obligation in the following terms:

To the fullest extent permitted by law, Purchaser agrees to indemnify and hold harmless this firm against all actions, proceedings and claims brought or threatened against this firm and all loss, damage and expense (including legal expenses) relating thereto, where such action, proceedings or claim has arisen out of or results from or is connected with the failure of Purchaser, or any of its professional advisers or Investigating Accountants to comply with the terms of this letter.'

Where the vendor due diligence report is prepared by the same firm as the auditors, the firm may manage its risk relating to the purchaser or prospective purchaser by:

- requiring the purchaser to agree the terms of the release letter before agreeing to address the vendor due diligence report to them; or
- placing an obligation on the vendor to ensure that the purchaser signs the release letter.

Business refinancing where there is no acquisition

Where a firm of accountants are instructed to report to funders in respect of a proposed refinancing of the entity, it is recommended that auditors obtain a signed release letter from the funders and investigating accountants prior to releasing the audit working papers.

19.7.4 Investigating accountants from the same firm as the auditors

Where auditors and investigating accountants are from the same firm, there still remains a risk from releasing audit working papers to a purchaser.

In this situation, some firms will wish to amend the release letter so that it is addressed only to the purchaser. The indemnity may also be restricted to breaches by the purchaser only.

20 QUALITY CONTROL FOR AUDIT WORK

20.1 INTRODUCTION

This Chapter examines the area of quality control relating both to audit firms and to individual audits.

Under audit regulation, each RSB must ensure that its members have an adequate system of quality control (see **Chapter 2**).

20.2 GUIDANCE

Clarified International Standard on Quality Control (ISQC) (UK and Ireland) 1, *Quality Control for Firms that Perform Audits and Reviews of Historical Financial Information, and Other Assurance and Related Services Engagements* was issued in October 2009 and replaces ISQC (UK and Ireland) 1 previously issued in December 2004. It provides guidance on quality control for all audits and review work on historical information.

Clarified ISA (UK and Ireland) 220 *Quality Control for Audits of Historical Financial Information* was issued at the same time and will similarly replace the previous ISA (UK and Ireland). The Clarified ISA (UK and Ireland) provides guidance on quality control specifically for audits.

The Clarified ISQC (UK and Ireland) and the Clarified ISA (UK and Ireland) are effective for the audit of financial statements for periods ending on or after 15 December 2010. This chapter covers both the existing and clarified guidance. As the clarified guidance does not significantly amend the requirements of the existing ISQC (UK and Ireland) and ISA (UK and Ireland) this chapter is written on the basis of the existing requirements, and any changes to them included in the clarified guidance are included and clearly indicated.

As with other ISAs (UK and Ireland), the texts of the international ISA and ISQC have been supplemented with additional guidance from a UK and Ireland perspective.

In November 2002, the Audit and Assurance Faculty of the ICAEW issued *Audit Quality*, a publication which examines the components that make up a quality audit. This document is discussed in 20.6. This was followed in November 2006 by a discussion paper issued by the FRC entitled *Promoting Audit Quality*. Details of this paper are given in **20.7**.

The Financial Reporting Council published a study entitled '*The Audit Quality Framework*' in February 2008, which was designed to support effective communication between auditors, audit committees, preparers, investors and other stakeholders on audit quality. The paper is discussed at **20.8** below.

20.3 ISQC (UK AND IRELAND) 1: QUALITY CONTROL FOR FIRMS THAT PERFORM AUDITS AND REVIEWS OF HISTORICAL FINANCIAL INFORMATION, AND OTHER ASSURANCE AND RELATED SERVICES ENGAGEMENTS

20.3.1 Basic requirement

ISQC (UK and Ireland) 1 requires firms to establish a system of quality control which is designed to provide reasonable assurance that the firm and its personnel comply with professional standards and regulatory and legal requirements, and that reports issued by the firm or engagement partners are appropriate in the circumstances. The relevant ethical pronouncements with which auditors must comply are the APB's *Ethical Standards* (**Chapter 2**) and *Scope and Authority of Pronouncements* (**Chapter 1**).

The ISQC (UK and Ireland) is an overall quality standard from which the requirements for audits in ISA (UK and Ireland) 220 are derived. The APB's *Ethical Standards* share many requirements with the ISQC (UK and Ireland).

20.3.2 Elements of a system of quality control

The ISQC (UK and Ireland) sets out six areas which should be addressed by a firm's quality control policies and procedures, documented and communicated to the firm's personnel:

- leadership responsibilities for quality within the firm;
- ethical requirements;
- acceptance and continuance of client relationships and specific engagements;
- human resources;
- engagement performance; and
- monitoring.

These are discussed in greater detail below.

20.3.3   Leadership

From the very top of the organisation, the firm should establish policies which promote a culture of quality. The ISQC (UK and Ireland) states that this should be demonstrated practically, with actions and messages from all levels of the firm's management emphasising their commitment to quality. This should also be demonstrated in the firm's overall business strategy, which should promote the need for quality.

The firm's managing board of partners, or equivalent, will maintain ultimate responsibility for the quality of the work performed, but operational responsibility may be delegated to someone with sufficient and appropriate experience, ability and authority.

20.3.4   Ethical requirements

The firm should have procedures in place to provide it with assurance that its personnel comply with the APB's *Scope and Authority of Pronouncements* and *Ethical Standards* (see **Chapters 1** and **2**).

In relation to independence, the firm should ensure that it is able to:

- communicate its independence requirements to personnel and any others bound by them; and
- identify and evaluate threats to its independence and apply safeguards as necessary.

To adhere to these requirements, sufficient information must be held about the engagements undertaken by the firm, including the scope of the services provided to each client. Changes to the information should be notified to the person responsible for maintaining it on a timely basis.

Firms should also ensure that they have policies and procedures for informing the relevant individual when breaches of independence take place. The engagement partner and others who need to take action should be informed of the breach promptly.

In addition, the firm should obtain annual declarations of independence from all personnel who are required to do so by the Ethical Standards. Firms should set out criteria for rotation of senior personnel to ensure that no familiarity threat is created, and this should be in accordance with the requirements of the APB's Ethical Standards for audit engagements.

20.3.5   Client acceptance and continuance

The firm's policies should ensure that it:

- considers the integrity of each client;
- is competent and has the resources to provide the service; and
- can comply with ethical requirements.

The information should be gathered or reviewed at the commencement of the relationship with the client, when accepting recurring work in second or subsequent years or when accepting a new engagement from an existing client. Matters to be considered are set out in **Table 1**.

Where issues are discovered that cause concern, but the engagement continues, the issues, and their resolution should be fully documented.

TABLE 1: Matters to consider when accepting or reaccepting a client

Client integrity

- the identity and business reputation of the client's principal owners, key management, related parties and those charged with governance;
- the nature of the client's operations, including its business practices;
- information concerning the attitude of the client's principal owners, key management and those charged with governance towards such matters as aggressive interpretation of accounting standards and the internal control environment;
- whether the client is aggressively concerned with keeping the firm's fees as low as possible;
- indication of an inappropriate limitation in the scope of work;
- indications that the client might be involved in money laundering or other criminal activities;
- the identity and business reputation of related parties; and
- the reasons for the proposed appointment of the firm and non-reappointment of the previous firm (if relevant).

Firm resources and capabilities

- whether firm personnel have knowledge of relevant industries or subject matters;
- if firm personnel have experience with relevant regulatory or reporting requirements or the ability to gain the necessary skills and knowledge effectively;
- whether the firm has sufficient personnel with the necessary capabilities and competence;
- the availability of experts, if needed;
- whether individuals meeting the criteria and eligibility requirements to perform engagement quality control reviews are available, where applicable; and
- whether the firm can complete the engagement within the reporting deadline.

If the firm later discovers something that would have lead it to declining the engagement, they should take legal advice and consider resigning.

20.3.6 Human resources

Firms should have policies and procedures to ensure that they have sufficient capable, competent and committed staff. Policies should cover:

- recruitment;
- performance evaluation;
- capabilities;
- competence;
- career developments;
- promotion;
- compensation; and
- the number of staff needed.

Firms should allocate appropriately experienced and qualified staff to each engagement, together with an engagement partner whose responsibilities will be clearly defined and understood. The identity and role of the engagement partner should be communicated to key members of the client's management team and those charged with governance.

20.3.7   Engagement performance

ISQC (UK and Ireland) 1 requires firms to implement policies and procedures to provide it with assurance that its engagements are performed in accordance with professional and legal standards. The aim is to ensure consistently high quality engagements, and this can be accomplished through the use of manuals, software tools and standardised documentation as applicable.

The engagement team should be sufficiently briefed prior to commencing their work, adequately supervised throughout the engagement and their work reviewed by a more experienced team member.

Consultation

Policies should be in place which set out the requirement for consultation to take place on difficult or contentious matters and for that consultation, together with its conclusions, to be fully documented in order to enable an understanding of the matter and the results of the consultation.

Engagement quality control review

For certain engagements, the firm should implement engagement quality control reviews to ensure that significant judgements made by the engagement team undergo an objective evaluation. The policies for such reviews should:

- require reviews for audits of listed companies; and
- set out criteria against which all other work should be assessed to see if it requires a review.

When setting these criteria firms would consider the nature of the engagement, including the extent to which it involves a matter of public interest, any unusual circumstances or risks surrounding the work and whether a review is required by law.

The review should be completed before any report is issued.

Policies should also be developed to set out:

- the nature, extent and timing of the engagement quality control review;
- eligibility criteria for reviewers; and
- documentation requirements.

Nature, timing and extent of review
An engagement quality control review will usually involve discussions with the engagement partner, a review of the financial statements, consideration of the audit report and review of selected working papers. The engagement quality control review must be completed before the auditor's report is signed, however, documentation of that review may occur after the signing of the auditors' report.

Reviews of audits of listed clients include considering:

- the engagement team's evaluation of the firm's independence in relation to the specific engagement;
- significant risks identified during the engagement and the responses to those risks;
- judgements made, particularly with respect to materiality and significant risks;
- whether appropriate consultation has taken place on matters involving differences of opinion or other difficult or contentious matters, and the conclusions arising from those consultations;
- the significance of corrected and uncorrected misstatements identified during the engagement and the actions taken in relation to them;
- the matters to be communicated to those charged with governance and other parties such as regulatory bodies;
- whether working papers selected for review reflect the work performed in relation to the significant judgements and support the conclusions reached; and
- the appropriateness of the report to be issued.

Where the review is for an engagement other than the audit of a listed company, some or all of the above considerations will be relevant.

Eligibility of reviewers
The firm's policies should set out the technical qualifications, experience and authority required of quality control reviewers together with the extent to which the quality control reviewer can be consulted by the engagement partner during the audit without compromising the reviewer's objectivity. Procedures should be in place to allow replacement of the quality control reviewer where their ability to perform an objective review is impaired.

For the audit of the financial statements of listed companies, the reviewer should be sufficiently experienced to act as an engagement partner on listed audits.

For sole practitioners or small firms, suitably qualified external persons may be contracted to perform quality control reviews.

Review documentation
There should be documentation on file that the review occurred, that it was completed before the report was issued and that the reviewer is not aware of any unresolved matters that suggest that the conclusions of the engagement team were not appropriate.

Differences of opinion

There should be firm policies about resolution and documentation of differences of opinion within the engagement team. The firm's report should never be issued until any such differences have been resolved.

20.3.8 Engagement documentation

There should be policies and procedures for engagement teams to complete the assembly of final engagement files on a timely basis after the engagement reports have been finalised. For audits this is 'ordinarily not more than 60 days after the date of the auditor's report'.

Policies and procedures should also be established that are designed to maintain the confidentiality, safe custody, integrity, accessibility and retrievability of engagement documentation. For audits, these areas are detailed in the APB's Ethical Standards.

Clarified ISQC (UK and Ireland) 1 states that firms may implement controls to avoid alteration or loss of engagement documentation, whether on paper, electronic or using other media, including those that:

- ensure that details who created, changed or reviewed the working papers, and when that occurred, can be clearly seen;
- protect the integrity of the information, particularly if it is transmitted or shared with other members of the engagement team via the internet;
- prevent unauthorised changes to documentation; and
- allow access to the working papers to those that are authorised to have it.

Confidentiality, safe custody, integrity, accessibility and retrievability of engagement documentation may be improved by implementing further controls such as:

- the use of passwords to restrict access to electronic documentation to authorised users;
- appropriate back-up routines throuhout the engagement;
- procedures for distributing documentation to audit team members, retrieving it and collating it at the end of the engagement; and

- procedures for restricting access to, and ensuring proper distribution and storage of, hardcopy engagement documentation.

Where hardcopy documentation is scanned for storage and retention purposes, the following controls may be relevant:

- ensuring scanned copies reflect the entire content of the original paper documentation, including manual signature, cross references and annotation;
- integrating scanned copies into the engagement file, including indexing them and signing them off as necessary; and
- enabling the scanned copies to be retrieved and printed as necessary.

ISQC (UK and Ireland) is also amended to state that policies and procedures should be implemented to ensure that firms retain engagement documentation for the period required by law or regulation. Requirements for audit work papers are set out in **19.6**.

20.3.9 Monitoring

Each firm should have procedures to monitor their quality control policies and to ensure that they are complied with in practice. Evaluation of the system of quality control will include:

- analysis of:
  - changes in professional standards and regulatory and legal requirements;
  - written confirmation by staff of compliance with policies and procedures on independence;
  - continuing professional development and training; and
  - decisions related to acceptance and continuance of engagements;
- suggestions for corrective actions and improvements to the system;
- communication of weaknesses in the system to those in authority; and
- follow-up procedures to ensure that modifications are made as suggested.

Monitoring should also include a periodic review of completed engagements on a cyclical basis, typically with at least one engagement for each engagement partner in an inspection cycle (which should be no longer than three years). The monitoring inspector will be separate from the engagement partner or the quality control reviewer and may select engagements without prior notification. For small firms or sole practitioners, an external person may be engaged, or arrangements established with another small firm to provide personnel on a reciprocal basis.

The reviewer should consider whether any deficiencies found are:

- systemic, repetitive or significant which require prompt corrective action; or
- not indicative of failings in the firm's quality control system,

and an appropriate report should be given at the end of the work.

Where deficiencies are found, they should be communicated to the engagement partner and recommendations made for remedial action. Recommendations may include one or more of the following:

- taking action in relation to an individual engagement or member of personnel;
- informing those in charge of training and professional development;
- changing quality control policies and procedures; and
- disciplinary action against offenders.

Where an incorrect report is found to have been issued, firms should seek legal advice.

At least annually, a summary of the findings of the quality control review process should be provided to the managing board of partners, or equivalent. This should include details of the process undertaken, its conclusions and information about any systemic failures. Where the firm is part of a network of firms, this summary should also be sent to appropriate individuals in the network.

20.3.10   Complaints

ISQC (UK and Ireland) 1 also requires firms to have procedures for handling complaints or allegations that work performed does not comply with professional standards, or with the firm's own system of quality control, whether these arise from inside or outside the firm.

20.3.11   Documentation of quality control system

Firms are required to have sufficient documentation to provide evidence that their quality control system is operating effectively. The ISQC (UK and Ireland) does not set a standard form for this documentation, but points out that the content of documentation will vary depending on the size of the firm, the number of offices, and the nature and complexity of the firm's practice and organisation.

20.4   ISA (UK AND IRELAND) 220, QUALITY CONTROL FOR AUDITS OF HISTORICAL FINANCIAL INFORMATION

20.4.1   General requirement

ISA (UK and Ireland) 220 requires auditors to implement quality control procedures for the individual audit engagement. ISQC (UK and Ireland) 1 (see

20.3 above) sets out the detailed requirements for quality control systems for all reports on historical information, and ISA (UK and Ireland) 220 sets out the details of how those systems should be applied to audit engagements. The additional guidance concerns engagement partner responsibilities and is covered in **20.4.2**.

20.4.2 Engagement partner responsibilities

Where ISQC (UK and Ireland) 1 sets out the need for policies and procedures in relation to engagement partners, ISA (UK and Ireland) 220 gives more details of what these policies should cover:

- the direction, supervision and performance of the audit;
- ensuring the audit evidence supports the opinion given in the audit report;
- ensuring the team consults with experts on any contentious or difficult issues;
- determining that a quality control reviewer has been appointed as required;
- discussing significant matters with the quality control reviewer;
- the auditor's report being appropriate in the circumstances; and
- not issuing their report until the quality control review has been completed.

20.5 CONFLICTS OF INTEREST

The ICAEW's Business Law Committee has issued guidance on conflicts of interest and confidentiality. This follows from the decision in the case of *Prince Jefri Bolkiah* v *KPMG*.

The judgement stresses that where an accountant is acting as a fiduciary, he cannot act for clients with conflicting interests without their informed consent. Since the law is unclear about when accountants act as fiduciaries, consent should be obtained whenever where there is potential conflict. Such conflicts of interest could be wide ranging and could extend to audit clients who are competitors with one another in a particular market. This requirement does not apply to former clients, although duties of confidentiality will continue.

The guidance suggests additional paragraphs to be included in the engagement letter to deal with these issues. The paragraphs are set out in **Table 2**.

TABLE 2: Paragraphs to be included in an engagement letter where potential conflict of interest exists

Conflict and Confidentiality

You agree that we may reserve the right to act during this engagement for other clients whose interests are or may be adverse to yours, subject to the confidentiality requirements detailed here.

> We confirm that where you give us confidential information we shall at all times keep it confidential, except as required by law or as provided for in regulatory, ethical or other professional pronouncements applicable to our engagement.
>
> You agree that it will be sufficient compliance with our duty of confidence for us to take such steps as we in good faith think fit to preserve confidential information both during and after termination of this engagement.

Although these paragraphs leave accountants potentially liable for any actual breach of confidence, this is only where they do not take appropriate steps to keep confidential information secure. This means that the erection of 'Chinese Walls' may be avoided.

20.5.1   Chinese Walls

Where an accountant is not able to obtain consent from their client in line with the paragraphs in **Table 2**, it is possible for a Chinese Wall to be effective within a firm. The Prince Jefri ruling states that the Chinese Wall must have the characteristics noted in **Table 3** to be effective.

TABLE 3: Characteristics of an effective Chinese Wall

- the physical separation of the various departments in order to insulate them from each other (this may include details such as separate dining arrangements);
- training to emphasise the importance of not divulging confidential information;
- strict and defined procedures for when it is felt that the wall should be crossed and the maintaining of proper records where this occurs;
- monitoring of the effectiveness of the wall by compliance officers; and
- disciplinary sanctions where there has been a breach of the wall.

In addition, an effective Chinese Wall needs to be an established part of an organisation, not created on an ad hoc basis. Physical segregation would not create an effective barrier within a single department.

20.6   AUDIT QUALITY

In November 2002, the Audit and Assurance Faculty of the ICAEW published *Audit Quality* to provide detailed discussion and illustrations of good practice to facilitate audit quality.

The publication has a general introduction which considers the role of audit within the modern economy and business world, followed by detailed chapters covering:

- the need for strong leadership to champion audit quality throughout a firm;
- requirements for staff to have technical competence, professionalism and judgement underpinned by a clear ethical framework. The chapter also

considers the need for continued training and the development and retention of professional scepticism;

- managing client relationships to enable clear communications and an effective and efficient audit process;
- the need for a strong audit team, coupled with good communication and knowledge sharing amongst the team; and
- internal and external monitoring, on both formal and informal bases.

In addition, the publication examines the limitations of the audit, particularly in relation to fraud, whilst at the same time acknowledging that auditing must adapt to continue to meet the requirements of a changing business environment.

20.7 FRC DISCUSSION PAPER: PROMOTING AUDIT QUALITY

20.7.1 Background

The FRC issued the first of a series of discussion papers in November 2006, as part of a discussion of its objectives. By issuing this series of papers, the FRC wants to invite comments on whether it is correctly identifying the key issues on which to focus its attention and whether it is taking the correct steps to address those issues.

This first discussion paper, *Promoting Audit Quality*, addresses the FRC's objective of 'promoting and maintaining confidence in the audit process and the resulting audit report as a key component of the corporate reporting and governance regime and the effective operation of capital markets'. In order for this objective to be met, users of the financial statements must be able to rely on the audit report.

At a more fundamental level, the FRC is aware of concerns that the financial reporting regime in its entirety is not capable of meeting users' needs. However, given the widespread changes in recent years, they are keen to give users time to operate within the new environment before considering more wholesale changes. Therefore this discussion paper seeks opinions as to whether all appropriate steps are being taken within the existing legal and regulatory framework, and only after responses to this paper have been received by the FRC will they consider whether a discussion paper should be issued to consider the wider financial reporting regime.

This paper identifies the 'drivers' that are central to achieving a high quality audit and considers any threats to them.

20.7.2 Audit quality

Despite the recent changes aimed at improving audit quality, the discussion paper identifies the following concerns about audit quality which are still felt by commentators:

- changing business environment and increasing complexity of financial reporting, particularly in relation to the increasing requirement for estimates and valuations;
- audits possibly not detecting management fraud;
- relationships between executive management and auditors;
- lack of transparency in auditors' work and judgements; and
- an increasingly prescriptive approach to audit.

Against this background, the FRC have identified four main drivers of audit quality in the discussion paper. These are the:

- culture within the audit firm;
- skills and personal qualities of the audit partners and staff;
- quality of the audit process; and
- reliability and usefulness of audit reporting.

Audit firm culture

The discussion paper states that audit quality 'can be driven by audit firms creating an environment where achieving high quality is valued, invested in and rewarded'. It identifies a number of indicators that enhance audit quality, including respect for underlying auditing and ethical standards, partner and staff development systems and the promotion of consultation on difficult issues. Threats to quality oriented cultures include over-emphasis on winning and retaining audits or on non-audit services and excessive cost cutting in times of economic downturn.

Skills of partners and staff

The key drivers of audit quality in this area are subdivided into the skills required of partners and staff, the training provided to them and the appraisal process they undergo. Threats that may undermine quality in this area include failure to retain experienced staff, insufficient or ineffective training and lack of effective mentoring to develop the necessary personal characteristics.

Audit process

The discussion paper sets out the following characteristics of an effective audit process:

- an audit team appropriately structured for the engagement with relevant experience and knowledge;
- availability of high quality technical support;
- a well structured audit methodology which provides a good framework to

obtain sufficient appropriate audit evidence, ensures compliance with auditing standards, requires appropriate documentation and ensures effective review;

- objectives under ethical standards being achieved; and
- effective quality control procedures.

The paper identifies possible threats, including the increased use of computerised audit methodologies which may be over-prescriptive and reduce the importance of auditor judgement and a focus on producing documentation to the detriment of performing procedures properly.

Reliability of audit reporting

The discussion paper recognises that the structure of the audit report is specified by law and auditing standards and as such acts as 'a signal rather than a source of new information'. This means that confidence in the report is inextricably linked to the presumed quality of the audit process. This quality is best clarified through clear communication between the auditors and audit committees, as it is in this forum that auditors can provide further information about the process followed, key risks identified and issues found.

The FRC are aware that confidence in the audit report may be undermined by the concerns of some users and commentators. These concerns include whether auditors are fulfilling their responsibilities in relation to the adequacy of a company's accounting records and whether audit reports should contain more information about key issues.

20.7.3   Factors outside auditors' control

In addition, the discussion paper warns that some factors which affect audit quality will remain outside the control of auditors. It lists these as:

- the approach taken by management;
- contributions made by audit committees;
- the role of shareholders and commentators;
- litigation as a driver of audit quality;
- the approach of regulators; and
- pressures caused by tight reporting deadlines.

20.8   THE AUDIT QUALITY FRAMEWORK

In February 2008, the Financial Reporting Council issued its Audit Quality Framework to complement existing guidance in this area. The aim of the paper is to promote what the FRC sees as the key drivers of audit quality:

- the culture within the audit firm;
- the skills and personal qualities of audit partners and staff;

- the effectiveness of the audit process;
- the reliability and usefulness of audit reporting; and
- factors outside the control of auditors which affect audit quality.

For each key driver listed above, the paper outlines a number of indicators, the existence of which is a sign that the relevant key driver is in place. Some examples are listed in **Table 4**.

TABLE 4: Example indicators of key drivers of audit quality	
Driver	**Indicator**
Firm culture	• ensures robust system for client acceptance and continuation • creates an environment where achieving high quality is valued, invested in and rewarded
Skills of audit partners and staff	• junior staff provided with appropriate mentoring and training • partners and staff exhibit professional scepticism in their work
Effective audit process	• high quality technical support is available • collection of audit evidence is not inappropriately constrained by financial pressures
Reliability of reporting	• audit reports are written to be clear and unambiguous • auditors properly conclude as to the truth and fairness of the financial statements
Factors outside control	• audit committees that are active, professional and robust in dealing with issues identified during the audit • realistic reporting deadlines

The Financial Reporting Council recognises that the drivers and indicators of audit quality may change over time, and so they plan to review the Framework periodically.

21 ENGAGEMENT LETTERS

21.1 AUDITING STANDARDS

Clarified ISA (UK and Ireland) 210 *Terms of Audit Engagements* was issued in October 2009 and replaces ISA (UK and Ireland) 210 previously issued in December 2004. The Clarified ISA (UK and Ireland) is effective for the audit of financial statements for periods ending on or after 15 December 2010. This chapter covers both the existing and Clarified ISAs (UK and Ireland). As the Clarified ISA (UK and Ireland) adds to the requirements of the existing ISA (UK and Ireland) this chapter is written on the basis of the existing requirements, and changes to them included in the Clarified ISA (UK and Ireland) are included and clearly indicated.

ISA (UK and Ireland) provides guidance on engagement letters issued by auditors. The ISA contains guidance covering:

- agreeing terms of engagement in writing;
- respective responsibilities of auditors and those charged with governance;
- imposed limitations on audit scope;
- changes to the terms of the audit engagement;
- recurring audits; and
- changes in engagements.

In addition, Clarified ISA (UK and Ireland) 210 includes guidance on the preconditions for an audit (see **21.3** below).

As with all ISAs (UK and Ireland), the text of the international ISA has been supplemented with additional guidance from a UK and Ireland perspective.

In June 2008, the Financial Reporting Council issued guidance on auditor liability limitation agreements. It is outlined in **21.5** below.

21.2 PURPOSE

ISA (UK and Ireland) 210 requires that the auditor and the client should agree on the terms of the engagement and these terms should be recorded in writing.

The purpose of an engagement letter is to:

- define clearly the extent of the auditors' responsibilities;
- minimise the possibility of any misunderstanding between the client and the auditors; and
- provide written confirmation of the auditors' acceptance of appointment, the scope of the audit and the form of the report.

There may be occasions when an engagement letter is not appropriate, but the terms should still be agreed in some other form of contract.

It is important that the letter takes account of the relevant legislative requirements and should be tailored for each assignment.

The ISA (UK and Ireland) is primarily concerned with the audit of annual financial statements but the guidance to it notes that its principles can be applied to other audit related assignments, such as reporting on interim financial information or Combined Code compliance statements (see **Chapter 15** and **Chapter 16** for examples of appropriate engagement letters).

The guidance in the ISA (UK and Ireland) does not encompass other services such as tax and accounting and separate letters may be required for each such service. However, such services may be included in the audit engagement letter, but if so, the paragraphs must be clearly distinguished from those relating to the audit.

21.3   PRECONDITIONS FOR AN AUDIT

Guidance on preconditions for an audit was introduced in Clarified ISA (UK and Ireland) 210, published in October 2009, however audit firms are likely to be familiar with the procedures recommended by the Clarified ISA (UK and Ireland).

An auditor should only accept or continue with an audit when the basis upon which it is to be performed has been agreed. This will involve:

● establishing whether the preconditions for an audit are present; and
● confirming the understandings of the auditor and those charged with governance.

The preconditions for an audit are only present when the auditor can determine that the financial reporting framework to be applied by those charged with governance is acceptable and that those charged with governance understand and acknowledge their responsibility for:

● the preparation of the financial statements in accordance with that financial reporting framework;
● internal control systems that are adequate to ensure that financial statements can be prepared that are free from material misstatement; and
● providing the auditor with access to information relevant to the preparation of the financial statements, additional information requested by the auditor and individuals from whom the auditor may wish to gather audit evidence.

21.4 CONTENTS

An engagement letter should be sent to each new client as soon after the acceptance of the appointment as possible and certainly before the commencement of any audit work.

The principal contents of an audit engagement letter may vary for each client, but reference would generally be made to:

- the objective of the audit of the financial statements;
- those charged with governance's responsibility for the financial statements;
- the scope of the audit, including reference to applicable legislation, regulations or pronouncements of professional bodies to which the auditor adheres;
- the form of any reports or other communication of results of the engagement;
- the fact that because of the test nature and other inherent limitations of an audit, together with the inherent limitations of internal control, there is an unavoidable risk that even some material misstatement may remain undiscovered; and
- the need for unrestricted access to whatever records, documentation and other information requested in connection with the audit.

Auditors may also include:

- arrangements regarding the planning and performance of the audit;
- expectation of receiving written confirmation of oral representations made by management;
- agreement of management to make draft financial statements available to auditors on a timely basis;
- expectation that management will inform auditors of any facts that may affect the financial statements of which management may become aware during the period from the date of the auditor's report to the date the financial statements are issued;
- descriptions of any other letters or reports auditors expect to issue to the client;
- any confidentiality of other letters and reports to be issued and, where appropriate, the conditions, if any, on which permission might be given to make those reports available to others;
- basis on which fees are computed and any billing arrangements;
- complaint procedures;
- arrangements concerning the involvement of other auditors, experts or internal audit;
- for an initial audit, arrangements to be made with the predecessor auditor;
- a restriction of audit liability, where this is possible;
- a reference to any further agreements between auditor and client; and
- a request for the client to confirm acceptance of the terms of engagement.

An example engagement letter is shown in **Table 1**.

TABLE 1: Example terms of engagement for a non-listed company

Responsibilities of directors and auditors

1.1 As directors of the [company name], you are responsible for ensuring that the company maintains proper accounting records and for preparing financial statements which give a true and fair view and have been prepared in accordance with the Companies Act 2006 (**or other relevant legislation**). You are also responsible for making available to us, as and when required, all the company's accounting records and all other relevant records and related information, including minutes of all management and shareholders' meetings. We are entitled to require from the company's officers such other information and explanations as we think necessary for the performance of our duties as auditors.

1.2 We have a statutory responsibility to report to the members whether in our opinion the financial statements give a true and fair view and whether they have been properly prepared in accordance with the Companies Act 2006 (**or other relevant legislation**). In arriving at our opinion, we are required to consider the following matters, and to report on any in respect of which we are not satisfied:

(a) whether proper accounting records have been kept by the company and proper returns adequate for our audit have been received from branches not visited by us;

(b) whether the company's balance sheet and profit and loss account are in agreement with the accounting records and returns;

(c) whether we have obtained all the information and explanations which we consider necessary for the purposes of our audit; and

(d) whether the information in the directors' report is consistent with the financial statements.

In addition, there are certain other matters which, according to the circumstances, may need to be dealt with in our report. For example, where the financial statements do not give details of directors' remuneration or of their transactions with the company, the Companies Act 2006 requires us to disclose such matters in our report.

1.3 We have a professional responsibility to report if the financial statements do not comply in any material respect with applicable accounting standards, unless in our opinion the non-compliance is justified in the circumstances. In determining whether or not the departure is justified we consider:

(a) whether the departure is required in order for the financial statements to give a true and fair view; and

(b) whether adequate disclosure has been made concerning the departure.

1.4 Our professional responsibilities also include:

- a description in our report of the directors' responsibilities for the financial statements where the financial statements or accompanying information do not include such a description; and
- considering whether other information in documents containing audited financial statements is consistent with those financial statements.

Scope of Audit

2.1 Our audit will be conducted in accordance with the International Auditing Standards (UK and Ireland) issued by the Auditing Practices Board, and will include such tests of transactions and of the existence, ownership and valuation of assets and liabilities as we consider necessary. We shall obtain an understanding of the accounting and internal control systems in order to assess their adequacy as a basis for the preparation of the financial statements and to establish whether proper accounting records have been maintained by the company. We shall expect to obtain such appropriate evidence as we consider sufficient to enable us to draw reasonable conclusions therefrom.

2.2 The nature and extent of our procedures will vary according to our assessment of the company's accounting system and, where we wish to place reliance on it, the internal control system, and may cover any aspect of the business's operations that we consider appropriate. Our audit is not designed to identify all significant weaknesses in the company's systems but, if such weaknesses come to our notice during the course of our audit which we think should be brought to your attention, we shall report them to you. Any such report may not be provided to third parties without our prior written consent. Such consent will be granted only on the basis that such reports are not prepared with the interests of anyone other than the company in mind and that we accept no duty or responsibility to any other party as concerns the reports.

2.3 As part of our normal audit procedures, we may request you to provide written confirmation of certain oral representations which we have received from you during the course of the audit on matters having a material effect on the financial statements. In connection with representations and the supply of information to us generally, we draw your attention to s501 of the Companies Act 2006 under which it is an offence for an officer of the company to mislead the auditors.

2.4 In order to assist us with the examination of your financial statements, we shall request sight of all documents or statements, including the chairman's statement, operating and financial review and the directors' report, which are due to be issued with the financial statements. We are also entitled to attend all general meetings of the company and to receive notice of all such meetings.

2.5 The responsibility for safeguarding the assets of the company and for the prevention and detection of fraud, error and non-compliance with law or regulations rests with yourselves. However, we shall endeavour to plan our audit so that we have a reasonable expectation of detecting material misstatements in the financial statements or accounting records (including those resulting from fraud, error and non-compliance with law or regulations), but our examination should not be relied upon to disclose all such material misstatements or frauds, errors or instances of non-compliance as may exist.

2.6 (**Where appropriate**) We shall not be treated as having notice, for the purposes of our audit responsibilities, of information provided to members of our firm other than those engaged on the audit (e.g., information provided in connection with accounting, taxation and other services).

2.7 Once we have issued our report we have no further direct responsibility in relation to the financial statements for that financial year. However, we expect that you will inform us of any material event occurring between the date of our report and that of the Annual General Meeting which may affect the financial statements.

Other Services

3   You have requested that we provide other services in respect of ... The terms under which we provide these other services are dealt with in a separate letter. We will also agree in a separate letter of engagement the provision of any services relating to investment business advice as defined by the Financial Services Act 1986.

Fees

4   Our fees are computed on the basis of the time spent on your affairs by the partners and our staff, and on the levels of skill and responsibility involved. Unless otherwise agreed, our fees will be billed at appropriate intervals during the course of the year and will be due on presentation.

Applicable law

5   This [engagement letter] shall be governed by, and construed in accordance with [English] law. The Courts of [England] shall have exclusive jurisdiction in relation to any claim, dispute or difference concerning the [engagement letter] and any matter arising from it. Each party irrevocably waives any right it may have to object to an action being brought in those Courts, to claim that the action has been brought in an inconvenient forum, or to claim that those Courts do not have jurisdiction.

Complaints

6   We aim to provide you with a fully satisfactory service and [name] as engagement partner will seek to ensure that this is so. If, however, you are unable to deal with any difficulty through [him][her] then please contact [name]. We undertake to look into any complaints promptly and to do what we can to resolve the position. If you are still not satisfied you may of course take up the matter with [professional body] by whom we are regulated for audit purposes.

Agreement of terms

7   Once it has been agreed, this letter will remain effective, from one audit appointment to another, until it is replaced. We shall be grateful if you could confirm in writing your agreement to these terms by signing and returning the enclosed copy of this letter, or let us know if they are not in accordance with your understanding of our terms of appointment.

Yours faithfully

21.4.1   Recurring audits

Once agreed the letter will remain in force until it is replaced, but should be reviewed annually to ensure that it is appropriate to the client's circumstances. If a change has taken place then a new letter may need to be sent.

A new engagement letter may be appropriate when there is:

● any indication that the client misunderstands the objective and scope of the audit;

- any revised or special terms of the audit engagement;
- a recent change of management;
- a significant change in ownership;
- a significant change in the client's business;
- a change in the financial reporting framework adopted for the preparation of the financial statements; or
- a change in legal or professional requirements.

The guidance suggests that it may be appropriate to remind the client of the original letter when in the context of one of the above it is decided that a new letter is unnecessary.

21.4.2 Groups of companies

The ISA (UK and Ireland) does not deal with group or joint audits. However, accepted practice suggests that where the same firm of auditors is appointed for several companies within a group, they should consider whether separate letters should be sent to each Board. The decision will be influenced by:

- who appoints the auditors of the component;
- whether a separate audit report is to be issued on the component;
- whether the terms are the same for each component;
- legal requirements;
- the extent of any work performed by other auditors; and
- the degree of ownership by the parent.

Where a group letter is sent it should clearly identify the companies concerned and confirmation should be obtained from each Board.

Where joint auditors are appointed the audit engagement should be described in similar terms by each firm and that a joint letter be sent if there are no additional services provided by either party.

21.4.3 Changes in terms

The Clarified ISA (UK and Ireland) states that auditors 'shall not agree to a change in the terms of the audit engagement where there is no reasonable justification for doing so'. Although this new requirement is couched in stronger terms in line with the redrafting aims of the Clarity Project, its effect is equal to that in the existing ISA (UK and Ireland) that where auditors are requested to change the terms of the engagement before the audit has been completed, to one which 'provides a lower level of assurance, [they] should consider the appropriateness of doing so'. If they consider the changes appropriate, the auditors obtain written agreement to them.

Such situations arise from:

- changes in circumstances affecting the need for the service;

- misunderstandings as to the nature of the audit originally requested; or
- restrictions of the scope of the engagement.

Where auditors consider the changes inappropriate, normally because it may lead to the recipients of their report being misled in some way, they should consider their position and, if necessary, take legal advice. If they decide to withdraw from the engagement they should consider whether the reasons for this have to be notified to any party. For example, under the Companies Act 2006, outgoing auditors must send a notice of any circumstances which they consider should be brought to the attention of the members or creditors of the company.

21.5   LIABILITY LIMITATION

21.5.1   FRC guidance

Guidance on the use of auditor liability agreements was published by the Financial Reporting Council in June 2008. The guidance outlines the measures to improve auditor liability that are allowed under the Companies Act 2006, gives specimen clauses for use in agreements and explains the process to be followed for obtaining shareholder approval.

At present there are practical issues with introducing this into practice mainly caused by the US authorities' non-acceptance of these agreements and the unwillingness of major companies and auditors to implement them without acceptance by the US authorities.

The FRC have stated that the guidance will undergo a review in the second half of 2010.

21.5.2   Background

Prior to changes outlined in the Companies Act 2006, auditors were prohibited from entering into contractual arrangements that would have the effect of reducing or excluding their liability in relation to statutory audit work.

From 6 April 2008, when ss532 to 538 of the Companies Act 2006 came into force, auditors were permitted to limit their liability to their statutory audit clients as long as they obtain the agreement of the company and its shareholders.

21.5.3   Liability limitation agreements

A liability limitation agreement will limit the liability owed by the auditor in relation to negligence, breach of duty or breach of trust occurring during the course of the audit. In order for the liability agreement to be valid it must:

- cover only one financial year;
- be approved by a resolution of the company's shareholders, as follows:
  - for public companies, at a general meeting;
  - for private companies, by written resolution, if preferred; and
  - for group companies, by each company in the group, not just the holding company; and
- be 'fair and reasonable'.

The Courts can ultimately decide whether a liability limitation agreement is 'fair and reasonable'.

The actual limit on liability can be set out a number of different ways:

- based on the auditor's proportionate share of the responsibility for any loss;
- purely by reference to the 'fair and reasonable' test;
- a cap of liability (either in monetary terms or the basis of an agreed formula); or
- a combination of some or all of the above.

The FRC guidance sets out specimen 'principal terms' for each method of limiting liability above, together with example clauses which can be added to the relevant principal terms to form a liability limitation agreement.

The liability limitation agreement can be entered into at any time before the accounts for the year are approved. The existence of any such agreement and its principal terms must be disclosed in a note to the company's annual accounts.

PART 3
ACCOUNTING SYSTEMS AND
INTERNAL CONTROLS

22 AUDIT RISK ASSESSMENT

22.1 GUIDANCE

Three Clarified ISAs (UK and Ireland) provide guidance on the process involved in assessing the risk of material misstatement in an entity. These are:

- ISA (UK and Ireland) 200 *Overall Objectives of the Independent Auditor and the Conduct of an Audit in Accordance with International Standards on Auditing (UK and Ireland)*, which provides a general overview of the process;
- ISA (UK and Ireland) 315 *Identifying and Assessing the Risks of Material Misstatement Through Understanding the Entity and Its Environment*; and
- ISA (UK and Ireland) 330 *The Auditor's Responses to Assessed Risks*.

The Clarified ISAs (UK and Ireland) were issued in October 2009 and are effective for the audit of financial statements for periods ending on or after 15 December 2010. This chapter covers both the existing and Clarified ISAs (UK and Ireland). As the Clarified ISAs (UK and Ireland) do not significantly amend the requirements of the existing ISAs (UK and Ireland) this chapter is written on the basis of the existing requirements, and any changes to them included in the Clarified ISAs (UK and Ireland) are included and clearly indicated.

As with all ISAs (UK and Ireland), the text of the international ISAs have been supplemented with additional guidance from a UK and Ireland perspective.

In June 2001, the APB published a Consultation Paper on Aggressive Earnings Management. The paper aimed to alert directors, auditors and users of financial statements to the potential threat that increasing commercial and economic pressures may cause 'aggressive earnings management' and consequently increase audit risk.

In the United States, in January 2002 the American Institute of Certified Public Accountants (AICPA), released a detailed list of 'risk factors' that might also be helpful in planning the audit of a client's financial statements. These background considerations are covered in **22.5** below.

22.2 GENERAL OVERVIEW

ISA (UK and Ireland) 200 *Objective and General Principles Governing an Audit of Financial Statements*, provides a general overview of the audit risk assessment process.

Auditors are required to assess risks of material misstatement at the assertion level in order to determine the nature, timing and extent of further audit procedures necessary to obtain sufficient appropriate audit evidence which enables the auditor to express an opinion on the financial statements at an acceptably low level of audit risk. Audit risk is a function of the risk of material misstatement of the financial statements (i.e., the risk that the financial statements are materially misstated prior to audit) and the risk that auditors will not detect such misstatements ('detection risk').

Auditors determine what the risk of material misstatement is and seek to reduce their detection risk by performing audit tests based on that assessment. This involves focusing on what could lead to a misstatement at the assertion level and planning tests to address these areas.

Auditors also consider the risk of material misstatement at the overall financial statements level which may affect many assertions. This type of risk often relates to a failing in the control environment, such as management override of certain internal controls, and may be particularly indicative of a risk of fraud.

In addition, the risk of material misstatement at class of transaction, account balance and disclosure level should also be considered as this often determines the extent, nature and timing of audit tests at assertion level.

The components of audit risk

As stated above, audit risk is a function of the risk of material misstatement and detection risk. The risk of material misstatement is the entity's risk, and can be further broken down into:

- inherent risk; and
- control risk.

Inherent risk is the susceptibility of an assertion to material misstatement assuming that there are no related controls. The misstatement could be material either individually or when aggregated with other misstatements. This will vary depending on the nature of the assertion, transaction or account balance being considered. For example, items subject to complex calculations or accounting estimates are likely to have a higher inherent risk than others. External circumstances may create business risks which increase the inherent risk of some assertions, e.g., technological developments may render some stock obsolete, increasing the inherent risk of stock valuation.

Control risk is the risk that a material misstatement will not be prevented, or detected and corrected by the entity's internal control. The misstatement may be material either individually or when aggregated with other misstatements. There will always be some control risk as no internal control system is infallible.

Inherent and control risks may be assessed individually or using a combined assessment depending on the auditors' preferred methods and practical considerations.

Detection risk is the risk that the auditor will not detect a misstatement that exists in an assertion that could be material, either individually or when aggregated with other misstatements. Detection risk cannot be eliminated completely as auditors do not usually examine all of a class of transactions, account balance or disclosure. In addition, auditors may select the wrong audit procedure or misinterpret the results of a procedure.

For a given level of audit risk the level of detection risk bears an inverse relationship to the assessment of the risk of material misstatement. That is, the higher the risk of material misstatement, the less detection risk can be accepted and therefore more assurance is required from audit procedures, which are inevitably increased both in number and quality as a result.

22.3 ISA (UK AND IRELAND) 315

22.3.1 Guidance

ISA (UK and Ireland) 315 *Understanding the Entity and its Environment and Assessing the Risks of Material Misstatement* provides guidance on understanding the entity, including its internal control and using this understanding to assess the risks of material misstatement in the financial statements. The ISA contains guidance covering:

- risk assessment procedures and information about the entity and its internal control;
- understanding the entity;
- assessing the risks of material misstatement; and
- documentation.

22.3.2 Background

ISA (UK and Ireland) 315 requires auditors to identify and assess the risks of material misstatement, whether due to fraud or error, at the financial statements and assertion levels, through understanding the entity and its environment, including the entity's internal control, thereby providing a basis for designing and implementing responses to the assessed risks of material misstatement.

The risk assessment should be made at the financial statement and assertion levels, and ISA (UK and Ireland) 330 *The Auditor's Procedures in Response to Assessed Risks* (see below) sets out the auditors' responsibility to plan and perform audit procedures relating to these identified risks.

Further guidance in relation to the risk of material misstatement arising from fraud and error is set out in ISA (UK and Ireland) 240 *The Auditor's Responsibility to Consider Fraud and Error in an Audit of Financial Statements* (see **Chapter 10**).

22.3.3 Risk assessment procedures

Procedures

Although concentrated at the early stages of the audit, procedures to obtain an understanding of the entity, its environment and internal control, will be performed throughout the audit. Audit procedures designed and performed to obtain such an understanding are defined by the ISA (UK and Ireland) as 'risk assessment procedures'. Such procedures may also provide evidence about transactions, balances, disclosures or the operation of controls, although they were not specifically designed to.

The ISA (UK and Ireland) requires auditors to perform the following risk assessment procedures to obtain an understanding of different aspects of the entity and its environment:

- enquiries of management and others within the entity;
- analytical procedures; and
- observation and inspection.

Much information may come from management, but other directors or staff may be able to provide different perspectives which highlight the risk of material misstatement. For example, talking to sales personnel may uncover a change in sales trends or contractual arrangements with customers, or meeting with internal audit may highlight potential problems with the design or effectiveness of the internal control system.

Analytical procedures may identify unusual transactions or trends which may indicate material misstatements. At the risk assessment stage such analytical procedures tend to be at a high level and are therefore likely only to provide a broad initial indication of a misstatement which will require further investigation.

Observation and inspection may support management representations or may provide information directly. Procedures will normally include:

- observation of entity activities and operations;
- inspection of documents (such as business plans and strategies), records and internal control manuals;
- reading reports (such as quarterly management reports and minutes of directors' meetings);
- visits to the entity's premises; and

- tracing transactions through the information systems relating to financing reporting, i.e., walkthroughs.

Prior year information

For ongoing audits, information gained at the prior year's audit will be of use when performing risk assessment procedures in the current year. However, the ISA (UK and Ireland) requires auditors to determine whether changes have occurred since the previous audit that may affect the relevance of such information in the current audit. The continuing relevance of such information can be determined by performing system walkthroughs.

Information gathered during any interim review may also be relevant to the year end risk assessment procedures, but its ongoing accuracy should also be verified.

Engagement team discussion

ISA (UK and Ireland) 315 introduced a requirement for members of the engagement team to discuss the susceptibility of the entity's financial statements to material misstatement. This meeting is often combined with the fraud discussion outlined in **10.5.2**. The meeting should include all key members of the engagement team, but the exact participants, timing and extent of the meeting are matters of professional judgement. Typically such a discussion would include the engagement partner, audit manager and senior and tax manager, where such services are provided. More junior members of the engagement team may be included to enable them to gain a better understanding of how the results of the work assigned to them affect other aspects of the audit.

The engagement team must also consider whether experts assigned to the team, such as IT or valuation specialists, are including in the meeting.

The discussion should emphasise the need for professional scepticism and, in accordance with the requirements of ISA (UK and Ireland) 240 *The Auditor's Responsibility to Consider Fraud and Error in an Audit of Financial Statements* particular importance should be given to the susceptibility of the entity's financial statements to material misstatement due to fraud.

Further meetings may be held during the course of the engagement to allow team members to communicate and share information gained during the audit which may affect the assessment of risk or the audit procedures performed.

22.3.4 Understanding the entity, its environment and internal control

Detailed areas

The following areas should be included in auditors' understanding of the entity and its environment:

- industry, regulatory and other external factors, including the applicable financial reporting framework;
- nature of the entity, including:
  - its operations;
  - its ownership and governance structures;
  - the types of investment that the entity is making and plans to make, including investments in special-purpose entities; and
  - the way that the entity is structured and how it is financed to enable auditors to understand the classes of transactions, account balances, and disclosures to be expected in the financial statements;
- the selection and application of accounting policies;
- objectives and strategies and the related business risks that may result in a material misstatement of the financial statements; and
- measurement and review of the entity's financial performance.

Table 1 sets out examples of items that the auditor may consider in relation to the items above. Internal control is considered in **22.3.5** below.

Nature of the entity

A full understanding of the nature of entity, its operations, governance and the way it is structured will help to ensure that any risks relating to group structures or the need for consolidation are identified. Such knowledge will also assist with identifying related party transactions.

The ISA (UK and Ireland) also requires auditors to consider whether the accounting policies selected and applied by the entity are suitable given the business and its industry. Auditors should consider new financial reporting standards that may be relevant to the entity and situations where the entity has changed its accounting policies.

Objectives, strategies and related business risks

A business will define overall plans, or 'objectives' to respond to a variety of internal and external factors. To implement these objectives, practical 'strategies' are used. The risk that events or circumstances will mean that strategies cannot be implemented and objectives are not achieved is 'business risk'.

Business risk is a wider concept than the risk of material misstatement of the financial statements, but understanding business risk will increase the likelihood of identifying such risk. Whether a business risk will result in a risk of material misstatement will depend on the entity's circumstances. Examples of conditions that may indicate a risk of material misstatement are given in **Table 2**.

Smaller entities may not have formal, documented objectives and strategies. Therefore, to understand the business risk for such entities, auditors must make enquiries and observations of management.

TABLE 1: Example items to consider when gaining an understanding of the entity and its environment

Industry, regulatory and other external factors

- Industry conditions

  - the market and competition, including demand, capacity and price competition;
  - cyclical or seasonal activity;
  - product technology relating to the entity's products; and
  - energy supply and cost.

- Regulatory environment

  - accounting principles and industry-specific practices;
  - regulatory framework for a regulated industry;
  - legislation and regulation that significantly affect the entity's operations;

    - regulatory requirements;
    - direct supervisory activities;

  - taxation (corporation tax and other);
  - government policies currently affecting the conduct of the entity's business

    - monetary including foreign exchange controls;
    - fiscal;
    - financial incentives (e.g., grant programmes);
    - tariffs and trade restrictions; and

  - environmental requirements affecting the industry and the entity's business.

- Other external factors

  - general level of economic activity (e.g., recession or growth);
  - interest rates and availability of financing; and
  - inflation, currency revaluation.

Nature of the entity

- Business operations

  - nature of revenue sources (e.g., manufacture, wholesale, banking, insurance or other financial services, import/export trading, utilities, transportation and technology products and services);
  - products or services and markets (e.g., major customers and contracts, terms of payment, profit margins, market share, competitors, experts, pricing

---

policies, reputation of products, warranties, order book, trends, marketing strategy and objectives, manufacturing processes);

- conduct of operations (e.g., stages and methods of production, business segments, delivery or products and services, details of declining or expanding operations);
- alliances, joint ventures and outsourcing activities;
- involvement in electronic commerce including Internet sales and marketing activities;
- geographic dispersion and industry segmentation;
- location of production facilities, warehouses and offices;
- key customers;
- important suppliers of goods and services (e.g., long-term contracts, stability of supply, terms of payment, imports. methods of delivery such as 'just in time');
- employment (e.g., by location, supply, wage levels, union contracts, pension benefits, share option or incentive bonus arrangements and government regulation related to employment matters);
- research and development activities and expenditure; and
- transactions with related parties.

- Investments

  - acquisitions, mergers or disposals of business activities (planned or recently executed);
  - investment and dispositions of securities and loans;
  - capital investment activities, including investments in plant and equipment and technology and any recent or planned changes; and
  - investments in non-consolidated entities, including partnerships, joint ventures and special-purpose entities.

- Financing

  - group structure – major subsidiaries and associated entities, including consolidated and non-consolidated structures;
  - debt structure, including covenants, restrictions, guarantees and off-balance sheet financing arrangements;
  - leasing of property, plant or equipment for use in the business;
  - parent companies (local, foreign, business reputation and experience);
  - related parties; and
  - use of derivate financial instruments.

- Financial reporting

  - accounting principles and industry specific practices;
  - revenue recognition practices;
  - accounting for fair values;
  - stock (e.g., locations and quantities);
  - foreign currency assets, liabilities and transactions;
  - industry specific significant categories (eg loans and investments for banks, trade debtors and stock for manufacturers, research and development for pharmaceuticals);
  - accounting for unusual or complex transactions including those in controversial or emerging areas; and
  - financial statements presentation and disclosure.

Objectives and strategies and related business risks

- Existence of objectives relating to:

- • industry developments (a potential business risk might be that the entity does not have the personnel or expertise to deal with the changes in the industry);
- • new products and services (a potential related business risk might be that there is increased product liability);
- • expansion of the business (a potential business risk might be that the demand has not been accurately estimated);
- • new accounting requirements (a potential business risk might be incomplete or improper implementation or increased costs);
- • regulatory requirements (a potential business risk might be increased legal exposure);
- • current and prospective financing requirements (a potential business risk might be the loss of financing due to the entity's inability to meet requirements); and
- • use of IT (a potential business risk might be that systems and processes are incompatible).

- • Effects of implementing a strategy, particularly any effects that will lead to new accounting requirements (a potential business risk might be incomplete or improper implementation).

Measurement and review of the entity's financial performance

- • Key ratios and operating statistics
- • Key performance indicators
- • Employee performance measures and incentive compensation policies
- • Trends
- • Use of forecasts, budgets and variance analyses
- • Analyst reports and credit rating reports
- • Competitor analyses
- • Period-on-period financial performance (revenue growth, profitability, leverage)

TABLE 2: Example of conditions that may indicate a risk of material misstatement

- • operations in regions that are economically unstable, e.g., countries with significant currency devaluation or highly inflationary economies;
- • operations exposed to volatile markets, e.g., futures trading;
- • high degree of complex regulation;
- • going concern and liquidity issues including loss of significant customers;
- • constraints on the availability of capital and credit;
- • changes in the industry in which the entity operates;
- • changes in the supply chain:
- • developing or offering new products or services, or moving into new lines of business;
- • expanding into new locations;
- • changes in the entity such as large acquisitions or reorganisations or other unusual events;
- • entities or business segments likely to be sold;
- • complex alliances and joint ventures;
- • use of off-balance sheet finance, special purpose entities and other complex financing arrangements;
- • significant transactions with related parties;
- • lack of personnel with appropriate accounting and financial reporting skills;
- • changes in key personnel including departure of key executives;
- • weaknesses in internal control, especially those not addressed by management;

- inconsistencies between the entity's IT strategy and its business strategies;
- changes in the IT environment;
- installation of significant new IT systems related to financial statements;
- enquiries into the entities' operations or financial results by regulatory or Government bodies;
- past misstatements, history of errors or a significant amount of adjustments at period end;
- significant amount of non-routine or non-systematic transactions including intercompany transactions and large revenue transactions at period end;
- transactions that are recorded based on management's intent, eg debt refinancing, assets to be sold and classification of marketable securities;
- application of new accounting pronouncements;
- accounting measurements that involve complex processes;
- events or transactions that involve significant measurement uncertainty, including accounting estimates;
- pending litigation and contingent liabilities, e.g., sales warranties, financial guarantees and environmental remediation.

Measurement and review of financial performance

By understanding which areas management are keen to monitor and review, auditors can make assumptions about the areas which management perceive to be of relatively high risk. In turn, the existence of such performance measures may create a pressure on management, which may lead to motivation to misstate the financial statements.

Information used by management to monitor performance may include key performance indicators (both financial and non-financial), budgets, variance analysis, segment information and divisional, departmental or other level performance reports, and comparison of an entity's performance with that of competitors. Much of this information is likely to be internally generated and auditors must consider whether it is likely to be accurate and precise enough to detect material misstatement.

Although smaller entities may not have formal performance review procedures, management are still likely to focus on a number of performance indicators. Auditors can observe these in the same way as for larger entities.

22.3.5 *Internal control*

Components of internal control

ISA (UK and Ireland) 315 requires auditors to obtain an understanding of internal control relevant to the audit in order to identify types of misstatement and design audit procedures. Internal control is the process designed implemented and maintained to provide reasonable assurance about the achievement of the entity's objectives with regard to reliability of financial reporting, effectiveness and efficiency of operations and compliance with applicable laws and regulations.

Internal control consists of five components:

- the control environment;
- the entity's risk assessment process;
- the information system, including the related business processes, relevant to financial reporting and communication;
- control activities; and
- monitoring of controls.

Each of these is considered in detail below.

The design and implementation of internal control will vary from entity to entity and will differ depending on the entity's size and complexity. For smaller entities, the five components above may be blurred with an owner-manager taking sole responsibility for elements of each of them. Although the components of internal control may not be clearly distinguished in a smaller entity, their purpose will still stand.

Ordinarily, auditors will be concerned with those controls relevant to the preparation of financial statements. Controls over information not directly relevant to the financial statements may also be of concern to auditors if that information is used in the design or performance of an audit procedure, for example production statistics or controls, or pertains to the detection of non-compliance with laws and regulations. Therefore in assessing whether a control is relevant to the audit, auditors consider:

- materiality;
- the significance of the related risk;
- the size of the entity;
- the nature of the entity's business;
- the diversity and complexity of the entity's operations;
- applicable legal and regulatory requirements;
- the nature and complexity of the systems that are part of the entity's internal control; and
- whether, and how, a specific control, individually or in combination with others, prevents, or detects and corrects, material misstatement.

Once auditors have determined which controls are relevant to the audit they should evaluate the design of each control and determine whether it has been properly implemented. When evaluating the design of the control, auditors consider whether it is capable of preventing, detecting or correcting material misstatements. If a control is poorly designed it may lead to a weakness which should be reported to those charged with governance.

Obtaining an understanding of a control is not the same as testing its operating effectiveness. In order to obtain assurance that a control is mitigating the risk of material misstatement the control must be found to be operating effectively throughout the period. This is further explained in **Chapter 17.**

Control environment

ISA (UK and Ireland) 315 states that the auditor should obtain an understanding of the control environment and includes within the control environment the governance and management functions and the attitudes, awareness, and actions of those charged with governance and management concerning the entity's internal control and its importance in the entity. The control environment sets the tone of an organisation, influencing the control consciousness of its people.

When evaluating the design of the entity's control environment, auditors consider how the following elements have been incorporated:

- communication and enforcement of integrity and ethical values;
- commitment to competence;
- participation of those charged with governance, including their independence from management;
- management's philosophy and operating style, their approach to taking risk and attitude to financial reporting and financial reporting staff;
- organisational structure and how activities are planned, executed, controlled and reviewed;
- assignment of authority and responsibility; and
- human resources policies and practices, such as recruitment, training and evaluating.

In understanding the control environment, auditors must also consider whether the policies have actually been implemented. This will involve enquiries and corroboration using observation techniques or review of documents. For some controls documentary evidence may be limited. For example a commitment to ethical values is often demonstrated rather than documented. In smaller entities communication between management and other personnel may be particularly informal. In such situations auditors' observations will be important.

An entity's control environment has a pervasive effect on assessing the risk of material misstatement. Even the best documented and implemented internal control system will be rendered useless by a poor management attitude which allows control environment weaknesses and thinks little of overriding controls. However, the existence of a satisfactory control environment can be a positive factor when assessing the risk of material misstatement, and may allow auditors to have more confidence in the reliability of internally generated audit evidence.

The risk assessment process

The entity's risk assessment process is the way in which they identify the business risks that are relevant to financial reporting and determine actions to address those risks. Auditors are required to obtain an understanding of this process. This will involve considering how management identifies business risks, estimates their significance, assesses the likelihood of them occurring and determines actions to manage them.

The entity's process can assist the auditor in identifying risks of material misstatement, however, if auditors discover material risks which were not identified by the entity's process they consider whether there is a weakness which should be reported to those charged with governance.

The information system

Auditors are required to obtain an understanding of the information system insofar as it relates to financial reporting objectives. This will include gaining an understanding of the accounting system. The ISA (UK and Ireland) sets out the following areas that auditors should consider:

- the classes of transactions which are significant to the financial statements;
- the procedures by which transactions are initiated, recorded, processed and reported in the financial statements (these may be IT based or manual);
- the records supporting the above processes, held either electronically or manually;
- how other events are captured, i.e., those that are not normal transactions for the entity;
- the process used to prepare the financial statements from the accounting records; and
- controls surrounding journal entries, including non-standard journal entries used to record non-recurring, unusual transactions or adjustments.

Auditors should also be aware of whether and how controls are overridden and how incorrect processing of transactions is dealt with once it has been discovered. In addition, auditors should consider how information is transferred from the processing system to the general ledger or the financial reporting systems.

Auditors should also consider whether the entity's information system is suitable for its circumstances. This will involve gaining an understanding of the entity's business processes and how transactions originate during these processes.

As part of understanding the information system, auditors should also consider how the roles and responsibilities within the system are communicated to the individuals involved in the day-to-day running of that system. A risk of material misstatement may be reduced by the entity ensuring that all roles are set out in suitably detailed policy or financial reporting manuals.

Control activities

Auditors' risk assessment procedures performed to date will have provided a good indication of the areas where a risk of material misstatement exists. When assessing an entity's control activities, auditors will concentrate on those areas where material misstatements are more likely to occur.

In order to understand an entity's control activities auditors consider how a particular activity, individually or in conjunction with others, prevents, detects or corrects a material misstatement. Specific control activities may include:

- authorisation of payments;
- performance reviews;
- physical controls over assets; or
- segregation of duties.

Specifically, the ISA (UK and Ireland) requires auditors to consider how the entity has responded to risks arising from IT. Auditors should consider how control activities have responded to different risks posed by the advent of IT systems, and consider whether the integrity of the information and security of the data has been maintained.

IT controls can be categorised as 'general IT controls' or 'application controls'. General IT controls are policies and procedures that relate to many applications and assist with ensuring that the information system operates properly. Examples are controls over access to IT systems or development of new systems. Application controls typically operate at a more detailed level, can be preventative or detective in nature and aim to ensure the integrity of the accounting records. Examples include numerical sequence checks or checks to ensure that items are suitably authorised.

Monitoring of controls

ISA (UK and Ireland) 315 requires auditors to gain an understanding of what the entity does to monitor its own controls. This monitoring should encompass both the day-to-day operation of the controls and the overall design of the control system. Where the information used to monitor the controls is taken from the information system itself, auditors consider how the entity ensures it is reliable.

Where the entity has an internal audit function, auditors should obtain an understanding of:

- the nature of the internal audit function's responsibilities and how the internal audit function fits in the entity's organisational structure; and
- the activities performed, or to be performed by the internal audit function.

Further guidance can be found in **Chapter 39**.

Manual and automated elements of internal control

An entity's system of internal control is likely to include both manual and automated elements. For smaller companies there is likely to be a greater emphasis on manual procedures, but even for some large entities, elements of their internal control system may still rely heavily on manual intervention. The benefits and risks of using automated controls are set out in **Table 3**.

TABLE 3: Benefits and risks of using automated controls

Benefits – an entity is able to:

- consistently apply predefined business rules and perform complex calculations in processing large volumes of transactions or data;
- enhance the timeliness, availability and accuracy of information;
- facilitate the additional analysis of information;
- enhance the ability to monitor the performance of the entity's activities and its policies and procedures;
- reduce the risk that controls will be circumvented; and
- enhance the ability to achieve effective segregation of duties by implementing security controls in applications, databases and operating systems.

Risks

- reliance on systems or programmes that are inaccurately processing data, processing inaccurate data, or both;
- unauthorised access to data that may result in destruction of data or changes to data, including the recording of unauthorised or non-existent transactions or inaccurate recording of transactions. Particular risks occur where multiple users access a common database;
- the possibility of IT personnel gaining access privileges beyond those necessary to perform their assigned duties thereby breaking down segregation of duties;
- unauthorised changes to data in master files;
- unauthorised changes to systems or programmes;
- failure to make necessary changes to systems or programmes;
- inappropriate manual interventions; and
- potential loss of data or inability to access data as required.

Manual systems or elements of systems may be more suitable when judgement and discretion are required, such as for:

- large, unusual or non-recurring transactions;
- circumstances where errors are difficult to define, anticipate or predict;
- changing circumstances that require a control response outside the scope of an existing automated control; or
- monitoring the effectiveness of automated controls.

However, manual controls are generally less reliable than automated controls as they rely on people to perform them. Therefore, it cannot be assumed that a manual control has been applied consistently.

Limitations of internal control

Internal control, however well designed and implemented, can at best only provide reasonable assurance about achieving an entity's financial reporting objectives. Even automated controls are subject to some human involvement and, therefore, human error. There may have been errors at the programming stage, operatives may input data incorrectly and individuals receiving reports from the system may not understand the purpose of such reports.

In addition all controls are subject to override by collusion of one or more individuals. In smaller entities formal segregation of duties may be impossible, and the potential for override of controls by an owner-manager may be great.

22.3.6 Assessing the risks of material misstatement

Relating risks to assertions

Having gained an understanding of the entity, its environment and relevant controls, auditors relate the risks identified to the financial statements assertions. Further details of assertions are given in **24.2.2**. This means that each risk is considered in terms of the financial statements balance or balances it may affect and what that effect might be. For example a risk that goods may have been incorrectly invoiced to customers without being despatched may impact the existence and valuation of turnover and trade debtors.

Auditors then consider whether the risk is such that the effect on the financial statements would be material and then how likely it is that this will occur.

Auditors will next consider whether controls have been identified which are likely to prevent or detect and correct material misstatement arising from each risk. Often individual controls do not completely address a risk, but the controls within a particular process or system may together address an assertion. However, the less directly a control relates to an assertion, the less effective that control may be in preventing or detecting and correcting risks related to the assertion.

Once risks have been allocated to assertions and matched with controls, auditors can plan tests of control and substantive tests to gain their audit evidence.

Pervasive risks

Although many risks can be related to specific assertions, some risks may affect the financial statements as a whole, typically as a result of a weak control environment. Examples would be concerns about the integrity of the entity's management or untrained or inexperienced staff in a key accounting role.

In severe situations, the weakness of internal control may raise doubts about the auditability of the financial statements, for example unscrupulous management may lead to a very high risk of management misrepresentation in the financial statements or very poor accounting records may mean that insufficient audit evidence is available to support an unqualified audit opinion. In such cases auditors may issue a qualification or disclaimer of opinion, but if the situation is severe the only action available to the auditor is to resign.

Significant risks

As part of their risk assessment, auditors may decide that certain risks are 'significant risks'. Significant risks require special audit consideration as a result of the nature of the risk or the magnitude or likelihood of the error which may result. Significant risks often arise from non-routine transactions or judgemental matters as a result of:

● greater management intervention to specify the accounting treatment;
● greater manual intervention during data collection and processing;
● complex calculations or accounting principles, which may also be unfamiliar; and
● the difficulty of planning and implementing effective controls over non-routine transactions.

In determining whether a risk is a significant risk, the Clarified ISA (UK and Ireland) requires auditors to consider:

● whether the risk is a fraud;
● whether the risk is related to recent significant economic, accounting or other developments and, therefore, requires specific attention;
● the complexity of transactions;
● whether the risk involves significant transactions with related parties;
● the degree of subjectivity in the measurement of financial information related to the risk, especially those measurements involving a wide range of measurement uncertainty; and
● whether the risk involves significant transactions that are outside the normal course of business for the entity, or that otherwise appear to be unusual.

Having identified significant risks, auditors consider the controls, if any, in place to mitigate those risks. As such risks are often as a result of non-routine transactions there may not be controls specific to each risk, but rather general procedures for responding to such risks such as approval processes for any transaction falling outside of the standard accounting process.

If auditors wish to rely on the operating effectiveness of controls to mitigate a significant risk they will plan and perform tests of control. In addition, substantive procedures should be planned to address the significant risk. This is covered further in ISA (UK and Ireland) 330, which is discussed below.

Risks that cannot be mitigated by substantive procedures alone

At the risk assessment stage auditors should be aware of any risks which may not be mitigated by planning and performing substantive tests alone. Such risks are likely to arise in an environment where much of the entity's information is initiated, recorded, processed or reported electronically with little or no manual intervention. In such an integrated system, audit evidence may only be available electronically and its sufficiency and appropriateness will depend on the effectiveness of the controls over its accuracy and completeness. If such controls are not operating properly the potential for fictitious transactions to be created or existing transactions to be amended without detection may be large.

In such a situation auditors should plan and perform tests of control to satisfy themselves that controls are working to eliminate any risk of material misstatement. Due to the nature of such systems, the use of CAATs will be required (see **Chapter 23**).

22.3.7 Communicating with those charged with governance

Where auditors find material weaknesses in the design or implementation of internal control, or a risk of material misstatement which has not been addressed by one or more control, they should inform those charged with governance as soon as practical.

22.3.8 Documentation

ISA (UK and Ireland) 315 requires auditors to document:

- the engagement team's discussion about the likelihood of material misstatement arising from fraud or error and the significant decisions reached;
- their understanding of the entity and its environment, assessment of the component parts of internal control, risk assessment procedures and sources of their information;
- risks of material misstatement by financial statement area and assertion;
- significant risks; and
- risks that cannot be mitigated by substantive tests alone.

There are many techniques that may be used to document these areas:

- narrative descriptions;
- questionnaires;
- checklists; and
- flow charts.

These may be used in isolation or in combination. The extent and form of the documentation to support the assessment will depend on the complexity of the systems and the extent of the auditors' procedures required to assess them.

22.4 ISA (UK AND IRELAND) 330

ISA (UK and Ireland) 330 *The Auditor's Procedures in Response to Assessed Risks* provides guidance covering:

- overall responses;

- audit procedures responsive to risks of material misstatement at the assertion level;
- adequacy of presentation and disclosure;
- evaluating the sufficiency and appropriateness of audit evidence obtained; and
- documentation.

22.4.1   Overall responses

The first stage is for auditors to respond to any risks of material misstatement at the overall financial statements level. Responses may include:

- emphasising the need for professional scepticism;
- assigning more experienced audit staff;
- using specialists or experts;
- providing additional supervision; and
- incorporating further elements of unpredictability in the selection of audit tests.

Auditors may also decide to perform all audit procedures at the period end date rather than during any interim visit. Only if auditors have confidence in the effectiveness of the control environment may some audit procedures be performed at an interim date.

Where there are concerns about the control environment auditors are likely to use a substantive approach, rather than a combined approach which also relies on tests of control.

22.4.2   Responses at the assertion level

Procedures planned by auditors should link directly to their risk assessment. Auditors should consider:

- the significance of the risk;
- the likelihood that a material misstatement will occur;
- the characteristics of the class of transactions, account balance or disclosure involved;
- the nature of the specific controls used by the entity and in particular whether they are manual or automated; and
- whether the auditors expect to obtain audit evidence about related controls.

Auditors may plan to perform tests of controls alone, tests of controls combined with substantive procedures or follow a purely substantive testing route. The latter approach may be used where the risk assessment procedures have not identified any effective controls relevant to the assertion or because testing the operating effectiveness of controls would be inefficient. For smaller entities a fully substantive approach would probably be used as the number of control activities are likely to be limited.

Nature of procedures

The higher the auditors' assessment of risk, the more reliable and relevant the audit evidence must be. This will affect both the types of audit procedures performed and their mix. Where auditors have considered related controls in their assessment of material misstatement, they should test the effective operation of those controls. Where auditors use information produced by the entity's information system in their testing, the accuracy and completeness of that information should be verified. For example if analytical procedures include comparisons to budget data, the accuracy and completeness of the budget data should be considered.

Timing of procedures

The higher the assessed risk of material misstatement, the more likely auditors are to consider that performing substantive procedures at period end rather than at an interim date would be most effective. A disadvantage of performing all procedures at the period end is that auditors may lose the ability to identify and address significant matters at an early stage. Another strategy might be to perform procedures unannounced or at unpredictable times.

In considering when to perform their procedures, auditors consider:

- the control environment;
- when information is available;
- the nature of the risk, for example risks relating to the state of work in progress would be performed at the period end; and
- the period or date to which the audit evidence relates.

Extent of procedures

The extent of any audit procedure is a matter of judgement based on the materiality, the assessed risk and the degree of assurance the auditor plans to obtain. The use of CAATs may allow more extensive testing of electronic transactions and account files (see **Chapter 23**).

Tests of controls

Auditors should perform tests of control when:

- substantive procedures alone do not provide sufficient evidence; or
- the auditors' risk assessment includes the expectation that controls are operating effectively.

Typically, an enquiry will form part of auditors' testing of controls, but an enquiry will not be sufficient in itself and should be combined with other procedures such as observation, inspection or reperformance. The type of testing will be determined by the details of the control itself. For example some controls are documented and review of this documentation may provide evidence about the effective operation of the control. Others may not be documented, such as control activities performed by a computer, where the use of CAATs may be required.

Controls are generally tested throughout the period. Testing at one point in time only may be effective for some areas such as for controls over the entity's physical stock count at the period end. When testing has only covered part of the period, alternative audit procedures should normally be used for the remainder.

Relying on prior periods' assessments

If auditors plan to rely on evidence about the operating effectiveness of controls obtained in prior periods they should ensure, through observation or inspection, that the controls have not changed. If controls have changed, they must test the operating effectiveness of those controls in the current audit. Even if they have not changed, the ISA (UK and Ireland) requires that the operating effectiveness should be retested at least once every third audit. When there are a number of controls which are not being retested each year, a proportion of them should be tested at each audit.

In considering whether it is acceptable to rely on the testing carried out in prior periods, auditors consider:

* the effectiveness of other elements of internal control, including the control environment, the entity's monitoring of controls and risk assessment process;
* the characteristics of the control, including whether it is manual or automated;
* the effectiveness of general IT controls;
* the effectiveness of the control and its application by the entity, including the nature and extent of failures of the control in prior audits;
* whether the lack of change in a control is itself a risk, given changing circumstances elsewhere; and
* the risk of material misstatement and the extent of reliance placed on the control.

Where the operation of one or more controls is intended to mitigate a significant risk (see **22.3.6** above) evidence about the operating effectiveness of the control must be made in the current period.

Extent of tests of controls

Matters that auditors consider when deciding on the extent of tests of controls include:

* how frequently the control is performed during the period;
* the length of time during the audit period that auditors are relying on the operating effectiveness of the control;
* the quality of the audit evidence likely to be obtained;

- the extent to which other controls related to the assertion will provide audit evidence;
- the extent to which the control is relevant to the assessment of risk; and
- expected deviations in the control (although if this is too high, no reliance may be placed on the control).

The more auditors rely on the operating effectiveness of controls, the greater the extent of testing required.

Where controls are automated, auditors will not gain additional assurance from increasing the extent of testing of the control. The control should function consistently throughout the period unless the application is changed. Once auditors are content that the control is operating as intended, usually by testing it once only, testing should concentrate on ensuring that the application is not changed without appropriate change controls and testing.

Substantive procedures

Auditors should plan and perform substantive procedures for each material class of transactions, account balance and disclosure, regardless of their risk. In addition auditors are required by the ISA (UK and Ireland) to:

- agree the financial statements to the underlying accounting records; and
- examine material journal entries and other adjustments made during the course of preparing the financial statements.

Where the risk assessment process has identified a significant risk (see **22.3.6**) substantive procedures should be planned and performed in response to that risk. Substantive procedures may be analytical procedures or tests of detail. Substantive analytical procedures are generally more applicable to large volumes of transactions that tend to be predictable over time and suit gathering evidence about existence and valuation assertions. When designing substantive analytical procedures, auditors should consider:

- the suitability of using substantive analytical procedures given the assertions;
- the reliability of the data, whether internal or external, used to generate ratios and comparisons;
- whether the expected results are sufficiently precise to identify and material misstatement at the desired level of assurance; and
- the amount of any difference in recorded amounts from expected values that is acceptable.

If substantive procedures are performed at an interim date, auditors should perform further tests (either tests of control, substantive tests or a combination of both) to cover the remaining time to the period end. The decision whether it is worthwhile performing substantive procedures at an interim date will depend on the:

- control environment and other relevant controls;

- availability of information at the date of the interim procedure;
- the objective of the test;
- the assessed risk of material misstatement;
- the nature of the class of transactions or account balance and related assertions being tested; and
- the ability of the auditor to perform additional tests to cover the period between the interim testing and the period end.

If testing has occurred at an interim date and has detected misstatements, auditors would usually modify the assessment of risk and the nature, timing or extent of further audit procedures to be performed at the period end.

Relying on prior periods' work
Unlike for tests of control, it is not sufficient to rely on substantive procedures performed in prior periods to obtain evidence to address a risk of material misstatement in the current period. If any assurance is to be taken from work performed in prior periods, the audit evidence and related subject matter must not change fundamentally. An example would be where legal opinion was obtained about the structure of a securitisation in the prior period, and that securitisation has not changed.

Extent of substantive procedures
The greater the risk of material misstatement, the greater the extent of substantive procedures. Substantive procedures may also be extended if there are unsatisfactory results from the work performed on tests of control.

For tests of detail, the extent of testing is often thought of in terms of the sample size. ISA (UK and Ireland) 530 contains details on the use of sampling and other methods to select items for testing (see **Chapter 29**).

External confirmation procedures may be relevant in some situations and further details can be found in **Chapter 37**. Although external confirmations may provide relevant audit evidence relating to certain assertions, there are some assertions for which external confirmations provide less relevant audit evidence. For example an external confirmation provides more evidence about the existence of a debtors balance than they do about its recoverability.

22.4.3   Presentation and disclosure

The ISA (UK and Ireland) requires auditors to plan and perform procedures to determine that the presentation of, and disclosure within, the financial statements is in line with accounting standards and the requirements of the Companies Act 2006.

22.4.4   *Evaluating audit evidence*

Throughout the audit, auditors are required to evaluate whether their original assessment of the risk of material misstatement requires amending. For example, auditors may be required to amend their assessment as a result of:

- a higher level of misstatements being discovered than planned during the performance of substantive procedures;
- failures of the entity's controls during the period; or
- discrepancies coming to light as a result of the overall analytical review of the financial statements at the completion stage of the audit.

Changes to the assessment may require changes to the nature, timing and extent of the audit procedures.

At the completion of the audit procedures, auditors are required to conclude whether sufficient appropriate audit evidence has been obtained to reduce the risk of material misstatement in the financial statements to an acceptably low level. The factors influencing what constitutes sufficient appropriate audit evidence are set out at **24.2.1**. Where they conclude that the evidence obtained is not sufficient, auditors should attempt to gather further information. Where this is not possible, they should issue a qualified or disclaimer of opinion audit report.

22.4.5   *Documentation*

Auditors should ensure that the following are fully documented:

- overall responses to address the assessed risks of material misstatement at the financial statements level;
- nature, timing and extent of further audit procedures;
- linkage of those procedures with assessed risks at the assertion level;
- results of audit procedures; and
- where using evidence about the operating effectiveness of controls obtained in prior audits, the justification for relying on that work.

22.5   AUDITING IN AN ECONOMIC DOWNTURN

22.5.1   *Introduction*

In the United States there have been a number of high profile cases where companies have adopted aggressive accounting practices in an attempt to satisfy commercial demands. This may include selecting inappropriate accounting policies or stretching judgements about acceptable actions.

Such practices result in the misleading of stakeholders and may, at the extreme, constitute a criminal offence. The publication of the APB Consultation Draft, Aggressive Earnings Management and the AICPA's assessment of risk factors set out a number of issues of which auditors should be aware when planning and carrying out their work anywhere in the world.

22.5.2   The use of judgement

Whilst accounting standards attempt to narrow the opportunities for manipulating reported profits, it is unrealistic to expect standards to eliminate the need for judgement to be made in the preparation and audit of financial statements. Auditors are required to determine whether the judgements made by management are reasonable in the client's circumstances and, where necessary, these judgements and estimations are adequately disclosed.

In addition, when a difference is identified between the auditors' estimate and the amount included in the financial statements, auditors consider whether an adjustment will be required. This will be assessed on the grounds of materiality, which itself is a judgement influenced by a number of quantitative and qualitative factors which should be assessed in relation to the individual circumstances of the client.

22.5.3   Factors affecting financial reporting

The AICPA paper sets out a number of environmental factors which will affect financial reporting, and therefore may be the cause of increased use of aggressive or misleading accounting policies. Although these are written from a US perspective they are also relevant to the UK reporting environment. Auditors might consider each of the following when assessing risk and deciding the extent of audit procedures:

- difficult economic times such as the downturn in profitability of high tech, telecommunications and media;
- pressure from markets and investors to perform;
- complexity and sophistication of business structures and transactions formulated to meet specific reporting or economic objectives; and
- complex and voluminous accounting standards.

The other areas which the AICPA list as being worthy of additional auditor attention are:

- liquidity and viability issues where the changing business environment and market conditions can cause doubt about the going concern position of the client;
- changes in internal control if reduction in staff numbers reduces the effectiveness of separation of duties or other control procedures;

- unusual transactions outside of the entity's normal activities which may not be accounted for correctly;
- transactions with related parties which may increase in an attempt to achieve financial targets;
- transactions involving off balance sheet arrangements, such as those with Special Purpose Entities intended to shift assets or liabilities off balance sheet; and
- adequacy of disclosure to ensure that readers of financial statements are clearly informed of the range of possible effects of applying the accounting policies selected by management.

22.5.4   Warning signs

As they usually relate to areas of judgement, aggressive accounting methods are often difficult to discover. There are, however, a number of warning signs of which auditors should be aware during their work. Examples of these include:

- directors or management deciding many of the amounts for provisions rather than amounts being determined by others as part of the routine processing of the entity's accounting system;
- the final draft figure for earnings being significantly changed by journal entries generated at head office or non-standard journal entries being made close to the year end;
- contracts or transactions, especially undertaken close to the year end, the commercial rationale for which is unclear;
- earnings which are different from industry trends;
- directors or management unreasonably seeking to bring forward the reporting date, making it difficult for the auditors to obtain the required quantity and quality of audit evidence;
- a pattern whereby accounting policies or judgements and estimates made in the preparation of the financial statements are all biased in the direction that directors or management desire, or that are pushing the boundaries of acceptability; and
- delays in providing the auditors with the necessary information and explanations that they require to complete the audit by the due reporting date.

22.5.5   Auditors' actions

Whilst auditors should always maintain a high level of professional scepticism, in times of economic uncertainty their alertness to unusual or questionable circumstances should be increased. They can ensure that they are well placed to identify instances of aggressive earnings management by:

- understanding how the company is affected by changes in the current business environment;

- understanding the stresses on the company's internal control over financial reporting, and how they may impact its effectiveness;
- identify key risk areas, particularly those involving significant estimates and judgements;
- approach the audit with objectivity and scepticism, notwithstanding prior experiences with, or belief in, management's integrity;
- pay special attention to complex transactions, especially those involving potential substance over form issues;
- consider whether additional specialised knowledge is needed within the audit team;
- make management aware of identified audit differences on a timely basis;
- question the unusual and challenge anything that fails to make sense;
- foster open, ongoing communications with management and any audit committee, including discussions about the quality of financial reporting and any pressures to compromise on financial reporting issues; and
- when faced with grey areas, ensure that adequate corroboration of management's representations are obtained.

23 AUDITING IN AN INFORMATION SYSTEMS ENVIRONMENT

23.1 EXISTING GUIDANCE

Until December 1999, Auditing Guideline 407 *Auditing in a Computer Environment* provided guidance in this area. It was then withdrawn because, in the view of the APB, it was out of date but the guidance has not yet been replaced.

As there is now no extant guidance in the UK this chapter is based on ISA 401 *Auditing in a Computer Information Systems Environment*. This contains eight statements of 'basic principles and essential procedures', equivalent to the standards in an APB ISA (UK and Ireland), covering:

- consideration of the effect of the Information Systems (IS) environment on the audit;
- skills and competence;
- planning;
- risk assessment; and
- audit procedures.

23.2 BACKGROUND

The first requirement of the ISA is that the auditors should consider how an IS environment affects the audit. It notes the overall objective or scope does not change, but that the use of a computer may impact on:

- the procedures used to obtain a sufficient understanding of the accounting and internal control systems;
- the consideration of risk; and
- the design and performance of both tests of control and substantive procedures.

23.3 SKILLS AND COMPETENCE

ISA 401 requires that auditors have sufficient knowledge of IS to enable them to plan, direct, supervise and review the work performed. In some cases, it notes, specialist skills may be required to:

- obtain sufficient understanding of the effect of the IS on the accounting and internal controls system;
- determine the effect of the IS on the assessment of risk; and
- design and perform appropriate tests of control and substantive procedures.

Where an expert is used the auditors should consider the guidance in the relevant auditing standard – in the UK the appropriate guidance would be ISA (UK and Ireland) 620 *Using the Work of an Expert* (see **Chapter 39**).

23.4   PLANNING

It is essential that auditors obtain an understanding of the accounting and internal control system, which is sufficient to plan the audit and an effective audit approach (see **Chapter 22**). When planning parts of the audit which are affected by the IS environment, the ISA requires auditors to obtain an understanding of the significance and complexity of the IS activity and the availability of data for use in the audit.

This would include considering:

- materiality of the financial statement areas affected by the computerisation;
- complexity of the computer operation;
- organisation of the IS activities, in particular whether there is still adequate segregation of duties; and
- availability of data required by the auditors.

Auditors should also consider the impact of the IS on the assessment of inherent and control risk where there is significant computerisation within the entity. The areas where risk may differ from that associated with a manual system include:

- lack of transaction trails;
- uniform processing of transactions – clerical error is less of a risk in an IS environment but there is a risk of a programming error resulting in large numbers of similar transactions being incorrectly processed;
- lack of segregation of duties;
- potential to alter data without visible signs of this being done;
- lack of human involvement may mean that errors are not detected as quickly;
- automatic transactions carried out by the IS;
- potential for increased management supervision using analytical tools available via the IS; and
- potential for using computer assisted audit techniques.

23.5   ASSESSMENT OF RISK

ISA (UK and Ireland) 315 *Understanding the Entity and its Environment and Assessing the Risks of Material Misstatement*, requires that auditors consider the risk of material misstatement for the various assertions in the financial statements. Where there is an IS environment any pervasive or account-specific risks should be assessed.

23.6   AUDIT PROCEDURES

When auditors consider the procedures that are necessary to reduce risk to an acceptable level, in accordance with ISA (UK and Ireland) 315, the IS environment should be considered. Although its existence will not alter the auditors' specific objectives, the manner in which the evidence is obtained may alter, for example where computer-assisted audit techniques are required.

23.7   COMPUTER-ASSISTED AUDIT TECHNIQUES

ISA 401 does not provide any detailed guidance on computer-assisted audit techniques (CAATs), but we provide some background on them below.

Auditors may use CAATs to:

- examine the entity's computer files (audit software); and
- check the processing of data (test data).

CAATs may in some cases be the only way to obtain some of the required audit evidence or may improve the efficiency of the audit.

The main type of CAAT is an audit enquiry package. These may take various forms, including separate software packages or audit functions embedded in the client's software. This can be used to perform substantive tests, compliance tests and analytical review procedures including:

- reperforming calculations and casts, such as payroll calculations, calculations of royalties payable, casts of debtor balances, etc;
- selecting samples and checking the population for unusual conditions, such as duplicated items;
- testing items for certain conditions and printing out exceptions;
- comparing files at two points in time to detect records that have been added or deleted so that the reason and authority for these can be examined;
- creating information not otherwise available from or reported by the client's system; and

- proving certain figures in total by matching standing data with transaction data.

The choice between CAATs and manual audit techniques will depend on:

- whether there is any evidence of performance, as computers may not leave visible audit evidence, making manual testing impracticable;
- the cost-effectiveness of the CAAT and whether it can be used for other audit tests;
- whether the use of CAATs will be quicker and, if so, whether this is important;
- whether the relevant computer files are available, as some CAATs need to be carried out before ledgers for the relevant period are closed down;
- where CAATs are used by internal auditors, the extent that the external auditors are able to rely on them; and
- whether the data can be made available in a form capable of being interpreted by the computer auditors.

PART 4
EVIDENCE

24 AUDIT EVIDENCE

24.1 AUDITING STANDARDS

There are three ISAs (UK and Ireland) covering various elements of the subject of audit evidence. These are:

- ISA (UK and Ireland) 500 *Audit Evidence*;
- ISA (UK and Ireland) 501 *Audit Evidence – Specific Considerations for Specific Items*; and
- ISA (UK and Ireland) 505 *External Confirmations*

The Clarified ISAs (UK and Ireland) were issued in October 2009 and replace ISA (UK and Ireland) 300. They are effective for the audit of financial statements for periods ending on or after 15 December 2010. This chapter covers both the existing and Clarified ISAs (UK and Ireland). As the Clarified ISAs (UK and Ireland) do not significantly amend the requirements of the existing ISAs (UK and Ireland) this chapter is written on the basis of the existing requirements, and any changes to them included in the Clarified ISAs (UK and Ireland) are included and clearly indicated.

As with all ISAs (UK and Ireland), the text of the international ISAs have been supplemented with additional guidance from a UK and Ireland perspective.

24.2 ISA (UK AND IRELAND) 500

24.2.1 Concept of audit evidence

ISA (UK and Ireland) 500, *Audit Evidence* requires auditors to obtain sufficient appropriate audit evidence to be able to draw reasonable conclusions on which to base the auditor's opinion.

Audit evidence is obtained from a combination of tests of control and substantive procedures.

Audit evidence is defined as information used by the auditor in arriving at the conclusions on which the auditor's opinion is based. It may comprise:

- source documents and accounting records underlying the financial statement assertions; and
- corroborative information from other sources.

'Tests of control' are tests that test the suitability of design and effective operation of the accounting and internal control systems.

'Substantive procedures' are tests designed to detect material misstatement in the financial statements, and are of two types:

- tests of detail of transactions and balances; and
- analytical procedures.

Clarified ISA (UK and Ireland) 500 requires that auditors obtain audit evidence to determine the level of audit risk and to determine any significant risks (in accordance with Clarified ISA (UK and Ireland) 315), as well as in response to those assessed risks (in accordance with Clarified ISA (UK and Ireland) 330) (see **Chapter 22**).

24.2.2 Sufficient appropriate evidence

The ISA (UK and Ireland) contains a discussion on what 'sufficient appropriate evidence' means. Sufficiency is seen as a measure of the quantity of audit evidence, and appropriateness is a measure of its quality, including its relevance and its reliability.

Auditors are rarely able to rely on conclusive evidence, but use persuasive evidence which is supported by information from different sources. They seek reasonable, but not absolute, assurance that there are no material misstatements and may choose to rely on sample data, extracted either statistically or judgementally, in order to form their opinion on a particular balance or class of transaction. Reasonable assurance will be obtained when auditors have obtained sufficient appropriate audit evidence to reduce audit risk (i.e., the risk that auditors express an inappropriate opinion when the financial statements are material misstated) to an acceptably low level.

Audit evidence is cumulative in nature and the decision on whether there is sufficient appropriate evidence is a matter for the auditors' judgement and is influenced by:

- the assessment of the nature and degree of risk of material misstatement at both the financial statement level and at the account balance or transaction level;
- the nature of the accounting and internal control systems and the assessment of the control environment;
- the materiality of the item being examined;
- previous experience of the client and the auditors' knowledge of the business;
- the results of auditing procedures and work on preparing the financial statements; and
- the source and reliability of information available.

The reliability of audit evidence can be judged using the following general criteria:

- external evidence, for example, confirmation obtained from third parties, is generally more reliable than internal evidence;
- evidence from the entity's records and systems is generally more reliable when the related accounting and internal control system is satisfactory;
- evidence obtained directly by the auditors is generally more reliable than that obtained from the entity;
- evidence in the form of documents and written representations is generally more reliable than oral representations; and
- original documents are generally more reliable than photocopies, telexes or facsimiles.

Where auditors perform procedures on information produced by the entity, they should first satisfy themselves as to the accuracy and completeness of the information. For example, if auditors are verifying provisions against debtors outstanding at the year end, using an aged debts list prepared by the entity, they should first satisfy themselves that the listing is complete and correctly aged by checking invoices raised in the period for inclusion on the listing where appropriate and amounts on the listing back to dated invoices.

Where information to be used as audit evidence has been prepared using the work of an expert, such as actuarial calculations, valuations or engineering data, reference should be made to ISA (UK and Ireland) 620 (see **Chapter 39**).

Consistency is obviously important in deciding the sufficiency and appropriateness of the evidence obtained. Where evidence is inconsistent, for example, one piece of evidence leads auditors to believe a company owns an asset whilst another piece of evidence throws doubt on this, the auditors will need to consider what other procedures are necessary to resolve the inconsistency and ultimately what effect it has on their opinion. They also need to consider the relationship between the cost of obtaining evidence and its usefulness bearing in mind that the difficulty and expense of obtaining evidence is not a valid reason for not obtaining it.

24.2.3   Using assertions to gather audit evidence

ISA (UK and Ireland) 315 requires that auditors consider the risk of material misstatement is made at assertion level (see **Chapter 21**). When seeking to obtain audit evidence from audit procedures auditors should consider the extent to which the evidence supports the relevant financial statement assertions.

The term 'assertions' refers to the individual representations made by management and which make up the financial statements. The assertions considered by auditors are set out in **Table 1,** although the audit approaches of different firms may use different terminologies.

TABLE 1: Audit assertions

Assertions about classes of transactions and events for the period under audit

- Occurrence – transactions and events that have been recorded have occurred and pertain to the entity;
- Completeness – all transactions and events that should have been recorded have been recorded;
- Accuracy – amounts and other data relating to recorded transactions and events have been recorded appropriately;
- Cut-off – transactions and events have been recorded in the correct accounting period;
- Classification – transactions and events have been recorded in the proper accounts.

Assertions about account balances at the period end

- Existence – assets, liabilities and equity interests exist;
- Rights and obligations – the entity holds or controls the right to assets, and liabilities are the obligations of the entity;
- Completeness – all assets, liabilities and equity interests that should have been recorded have been recorded;
- Valuation and allocation – assets, liabilities and equity interests are included in the financial statements at appropriate amounts and any resulting valuation or allocation adjustments are appropriately recorded.

Assertions about presentation and disclosure

- Occurrence and right and obligations – disclosed events, transactions and other matters have occurred and pertain to the entity;
- Completeness – all disclosures that should have been included in the financial statements have been included;
- Classification and understandability – financial information is appropriately presented and described and disclosures are clearly expressed;
- Accuracy and valuation – financial and other information is disclosed fairly and at appropriate amounts.

24.2.4 Audit procedures

Auditors use audit procedures to:

- obtain an understanding of the entity and its environment and determine audit risk;
- test the operating effectiveness of controls; and
- detect material misstatements at the assertion level.

The objectives of testing the operating effectiveness of controls is to test the design of control systems by aiming to establish whether the system is capable of preventing and detecting material misstatement. When testing the operation of controls, auditors seek to establish whether the controls have operated for the whole of the period under review. Where controls are not effective, such testing may indicate the existence of audit risk.

Substantive procedures are planned and performed in order to determine audit risk and then in response to the risk of material misstatement assessed at the planning stage. Auditors use one or more of the types of audit procedure listed below.

The nature and timing of audit procedures will depend on the information available to auditors. Where information is held in electronic form, auditors may carry out Computer Assisted Audit Techniques (CAATs) (see **Chapter 23**).

Inspection of records or documents

This consists of examining records or documents whether internal or external, in paper form, electronic form or other media. It provides evidence of different degrees of persuasiveness depending on the nature and source of the documentation. The criteria used in assessing the reliability of evidence in general are noted at **24.2.1** above, and they should be applied to the type of evidence that can be obtained by inspection. For example, depending on the case, different degrees of reliability will apply to documentary evidence:

- created and provided by third parties;
- created by third parties and held by the entity; and
- created and held by the entity.

Some documentation will give direct evidence about existence, but may not provide evidence of ownership or value, for example share or bond certificates.

Inspection of tangible assets

This consists of physical examination of the assets. Again, the inspection of tangible assets provides evidence of their existence but alone is not sufficient to provide evidence of their ownership or value.

Observation

This consists of inspecting a particular process or procedure being performed by others. It is particularly useful where an internal control procedure does not leave an audit trail or for 'one off' procedures such as stocktakes. It is normally used in combination with other procedures.

Enquiry

This consists of seeking information from knowledgeable persons both inside and/or outside the entity. This may either be written or oral. Its reliability will vary depending on its source in a similar way to the evidence resulting from inspection.

An important part of the enquiry process is evaluation of the responses received, which may lead to amending the audit plan or performing additional audit procedures.

Enquiry alone is not sufficient to provide evidence of material misstatement or to confirm the effectiveness of controls. For example in relation to management intentions, in addition auditors should consider management's past history of carrying out is stated intentions and obtain written representation of oral responses.

Confirmation

Confirmation is a type of enquiry and involves obtaining information directly from a third party. For example a debtors' circularisation obtains confirmation of outstanding balances directly from the entity's debtors. Further information is provided in ISA (UK and Ireland) 505, *External Confirmations* (see **24.4**).

Recalculation

Recalculation involves checking the mathematical accuracy of documents or records, and may be done through the use of CAATs (see **Chapter 23**).

Reperformance

This describes the independent reperformance of calculations, for example, the calculations on a sales invoice or on a debtors' listing. Again, CAATs may be used to perform this task.

Analytical procedures

These involve the analysis of relationships between items of financial data both within the financial statements and between the financial statements and other internally and externally produced data. These are discussed in greater detail in **Chapter 25**.

24.3 ISA (UK AND IRELAND) 501

ISA (UK and Ireland) 501 *Audit Evidence – Additional Considerations for Specific Items* provides guidance on:

- attendance at stocktaking;
- enquiries about litigation and claims; and
- segment information.

24.3.1 *Attendance at stocktaking*

Further guidance on the audit of stocktakes in the United Kingdom is given by Practice Note 25, *Attendance at Stocktaking* (see **Chapter 37**).

ISA (UK and Ireland) 501 requires auditors to attend stock counts to obtain evidence about the existence and condition of the entity's stock, unless this is 'impracticable'. If they are unable to attend on the count date they should take or observe physical counts on another date and perform audit procedures on the transactions between the two counts. If auditors cannot attend, for example, due to the nature and location of the stock they should consider whether alternative audit evidence is available to support the existence and condition of stock at the period end date. If there is no suitable and adequate alternative, auditors would be required to give a limitation of scope opinion in their audit report.

If stock is held at a third party location, the ISA (UK and Ireland) requires auditors to perform one or both of the following:

- request confirmation from the third party as to the quantities and condition of stock held on behalf of the entity; and
- perform inspection or other audit procedures appropriate in the circumstances.

24.3.2   Enquiries about litigation and claims

The ICAEW statement on auditors' problems concerning contingencies arising from pending litigation against the entity upon which they are reporting is discussed in **37.3**. ISA (UK and Ireland) 501 provides some additional guidance about the audit procedures to be performed.

Auditors should perform audit procedures to determine whether a risk of material misstatement may arise from any litigation or claims made against the entity. This may involve reviewing board minutes, examining legal expense accounts or making enquiries of those charged with governance.

If a risk of material misstatement is discovered or suspected, auditors should seek to confirm the nature and estimated financial implications of the risk directly with the entity's legal advisors. Procedures for doing this, and an example pro forma letter are set out in section **37.3**.

If those charged with governance refuse to give permission for auditors to communicate with the entity's lawyers and sufficient appropriate audit evidence is not available from an alternative source, a limitation of scope opinion will be relevant.

24.3.3   Segment information

When segmental information is material to the financial statements, auditors should plan and perform procedures to confirm the presentation and disclosure of the information. This will usually involve discussion with those charged with governance about the techniques used to determine the segmental information and analytical techniques.

24.4 ISA (UK AND IRELAND) 505

24.4.1 Use of external confirmations

As stated above, audit evidence is more reliable when it is obtained from independent sources outside the entity. ISA (UK and Ireland) 505 *External Confirmations* provides guidance on using external confirmations to provide sufficient appropriate audit evidence at assertion level.

External confirmations are frequently used in connection with account balances and their components, such as debtors' circularisations, which are discussed in detail in section **37.2**. However, they need not be limited to this and may be used to confirm the terms of agreements or transactions an entity has with third parties. Examples of where external confirmations may be used are:

- bank balances and other information with bankers (see **Chapter 36**);
- stocks held by third parties at bonded warehouses for processing or on consignment;
- property title deeds held by lawyers or financiers for safe custody or as security;
- investments purchased from stockbrokers but not delivered at the balance sheet date;
- loans from lenders; and
- accounts payable and receivable balances.

The assertions covered by external confirmations will vary. For example in the case of goods held on consignment evidence will be obtained about existence and rights and obligations assertions, but not about the value. Confirmation about the completeness assertion can be obtained by contacting certain parties. For example, evidence about completeness of accounts payable balances can be obtained by circularising suppliers with a nil balance at the year end to determine whether all liabilities to them have been recorded. This means that external confirmation requests must be tailored to the specific audit objective.

All confirmation requests are usually sent on the entity's headed paper and contain the management's authorisation to disclose the information requested. Clarified ISA (UK and Ireland) 505 states that in order to have control over the process, auditors must design the confirmation request, determine the parties to contact and the information to be requested, send the requests themselves and make all follow up requests, where applicable. All responses should be sent directly to the auditors, not to the entity.

Auditors may use positive or negative confirmations, or a combination of both. Positive confirmations ask respondents to reply and either confirm information or provide data themselves. Negative confirmations ask for responses only in the event of a disagreement with the information provided in the request. There is an additional risk with negative confirmations that auditors will assume that information was correct when the respondent simply chooses not to respond. Clarified ISA (UK and Ireland) 505 states that auditors should not use negative confirmation requests as the sole substantive audit procedure to address an assessed risk of material misstatement unless:

- the risk of material misstatement has been assessed as low and the related controls have been assessed as operating effectively;
- the population subject to negative confirmation comprises a large number of small, homogeneous account balances, transactions or conditions;
- a very low exception rate is expected; and
- auditors are not aware of circumstances or conditions that would cause recipients of negative confirmation requests to disregard such requests.

With positive confirmations the response rate tends to be lower the more information auditors request. However, by requesting information from respondents, the value of audit evidence is greater than where they are asked only to confirm a balance included in the request. In order to obtain good quality responses auditors should consider to whom the confirmation request is addressed.

If those charged with governance refuse to allow auditors to obtain direct confirmations auditors should consider whether this is reasonable, whether alternative suitable audit evidence is available and whether a limitation of audit scope has arisen. Similarly where no response is obtained from a positive confirmation or where the response has not provided sufficient reliable evidence, auditors should perform alternative procedures. Where no response has been obtained they would normally first attempt to contact the recipient of the confirmation to elicit a response.

Clarified ISA (UK and Ireland) 505 requires that where auditors have doubts about the reliability of a response they should consider whether additional procedures are required. Doubts about the reliability of a response may arise because it was not received by the auditor directly or appeared not to come from the original intended confirming party. If a confirming party uses a third party to coordinate its response, auditors should perform procedures to confirm that the respondent was indeed authorised to respond on behalf of the original contact.

Once any alternative procedures have been performed, auditors evaluate whether the results in total have provided sufficient appropriate audit evidence, and where this is not the case, they consider the implications for their report.

25 ANALYTICAL PROCEDURES

25.1 AUDITING STANDARDS

Clarified ISA (UK and Ireland) 520 *Analytical Procedures* was issued in October 2009 and replaces ISA (UK and Ireland) 520 previously issued in December 2004. The Clarified ISA (UK and Ireland) is effective for the audit of financial statements for periods ending on or after 15 December 2010. This chapter covers both the existing and Clarified ISAs (UK and Ireland). As the Clarified ISA (UK and Ireland) does not significantly amend the requirements of the existing ISA (UK and Ireland) this chapter is written on the basis of the existing requirements, and any changes to them included in the Clarified ISA (UK and Ireland) are included and clearly indicated. The ISA (UK and Ireland) provides guidance on the use of analytical procedures covering:

- the nature and purpose of analytical procedures;
- use of analytical procedures in risk assessment;
- analytical procedures as substantive procedures;
- overall review at the end of the audit; and
- investigating unusual items.

As with all ISAs (UK and Ireland), the text of the ISA has been supplemented with additional guidance from a UK and Ireland perspective.

25.2 WHAT IS MEANT BY ANALYTICAL PROCEDURES?

Analytical procedures may be applied at the planning, execution and overall review stages of an audit. Analytical procedures are the examination and comparison of the financial and non-financial information of a business with internal and external information, for both the current and different periods. This is usually achieved by calculating ratios and trends and investigating fluctuations and inconsistencies. It may be described as the process of reviewing the figures to see if they make sense. Methods used range from simple comparisons to complex analyses using advanced statistical techniques. Analytical procedures may be applied to consolidated financial statements, financial statements of components, such as subsidiaries or divisions, and individual elements of financial information.

As well as comparing the current year information with that of prior periods, analytical review also includes comparisons with:

- budgets;
- estimates prepared by the auditors, such as depreciation; and
- similar industry information.

It also includes the consideration of various relationships among elements of financial information that are expected to conform to a predictable pattern based on the entity's experience, such as gross profit margin percentages, and between financial information and relevant non-financial information, such as payroll costs to number of employees. An example of this is shown in **Table 1**.

TABLE 1: Variable relationships

A company had 50 employees last year with total wages of £420,000 and 50 employees this year with a wage bill of £525,000, an increase of 25%. It is known that the annual pay rise was 12% and the level of business has remained approximately constant.

At first sight, the figures do not appear to make sense because the increase is substantially greater than expected. There may, however, be satisfactory explanations. For example, there may have been a change in sales mix with previously bought-in goods being replaced by goods manufactured in-house, resulting in substantial authorised overtime. This could be verified by looking at the sales figures for different products as well as the payroll. Alternatively, there could have been a switch to more skilled, and hence more expensive, labour; this could be verified from payroll and production records.

If no such explanation is available, it is possible that the payroll has been inflated by, for example:

(a)   misposting in the general ledger;
(b)   'dummy' employees on the payroll;
(c)   unauthorised overtime being paid; or
(d)   employees being paid at higher rates of pay than authorised.

The auditors may direct their substantive testing towards finding any errors of this nature.

Comparisons should also be made with other branches or divisions in the same line of business, which are part of the same company or group or with other companies within the same industry. It is often helpful to make comparisons on a monthly or quarterly basis where such figures are available. This can eliminate any distorting effects of seasonal trade and may enable auditors to distinguish genuine seasonal fluctuations from window dressing around the year end.

25.3   PROBLEMS IN PRACTICE

Although analytical procedures are a useful source of evidence there are certain pitfalls in relying on conclusions drawn from such comparisons. In particular, care must be taken that:

- *they are computed on a consistent basis for each period or location under review.* Where there is a change in the basis of the calculation of a ratio or in the relationships which make up the ratio, comparability may be lost. The ratio for the prior year may be restated to obtain a meaningful comparison. For example, if stock turnover is calculated using average stocks for the previous period, there is little point trying to make a comparison with a ratio for this year using year end stocks. Major changes in pricing policy and product lines may also render past relationships inconsistent with current results;

- *there ought to be a meaningful relationship between the items being compared.* For example, there is little point in comparing head office overheads with sales since there is unlikely to be any connection between them. Similarly there is little point in examining the relationship between sales and gross profit if stocks are valued by reference to a fixed gross profit ratio;
- *results and balance sheet values are not distorted by the effects of changing price levels.* For example, under historical cost accounting, assets acquired at different times are stated at different price levels. This means that any ratio involving fixed assets is affected by when the assets were purchased. Hence ratios such as return on capital employed and fixed asset turnover can be distorted and comparisons between different companies made meaningless unless they are carried out on a current cost basis;
- *they are not distorted by unusual items.* Such items are often first detected by means of analytical review procedures and once detected, they should be investigated separately and their effects removed from any ratios and trends;
- *they are not distorted by changes in accounting policy or accounting estimates.* It is necessary to adjust the figures for the prior year in order that comparisons can be made. It may also be useful to calculate the figures or ratios using the old accounting policy or estimate; this is not always possible but, if it is, it may give some indication of the effect, if any, of the change.

25.4 USE OF ANALYTICAL PROCEDURES IN RISK ASSESSMENT

Guidance relating to the use of analytical procedures as risk assessment procedures is set out in ISA (UK and Ireland) 315, *Identifying and Assessing the Risks of Material Misstatement through Understanding the Entity and its Environment.* That ISA (UK and Ireland) requires that auditors 'apply analytical procedures to assist in planning the nature, timing and extent of other audit procedures', including obtaining 'an understanding of the entity and its environment'.

The use of analytical procedures at the planning stage may also indicate aspects of the business of which the auditors are unaware but which they should take into account in planning their audit.

Analytical procedures at the planning stage are usually based on interim financial information, budgets and management accounts. For smaller entities such management information is often not extensive, and performance is monitored and controlled by less formal means. In such cases it is suggested that auditors extract information from the existing accounting records, such as VAT returns and bank statements, as well as any draft financial statements and then discuss variations with management.

25.5 ANALYTICAL PROCEDURES AS A SUBSTANTIVE PROCEDURE

There is no requirement for analytical procedures to be used as substantive procedures, and the decision whether to use them, and the extent of such use is a matter for auditors' professional judgement. Guidance on the nature, timing and extent of audit procedures in relation to assessed risks can be found in ISA (UK and Ireland) 330 (see **Chapter 22**).

Auditors should consider whether sufficient reliable information is available to apply analytical procedures and the results of any similar procedures already performed by the entity. In addition, when designing and performing analytical procedures, auditors should consider:

- the suitability of using substantive analytical procedures;
- the reliability of the data, whether internal or external, from which the expectation of recorded amounts or ratios is developed;
- whether the expected results are precise enough to show when a material misstatement has occurred; and
- the difference between expected and actual results which would be acceptable to the auditor.

Each item is considered in more detail below.

25.5.1 Suitability of using analytical procedures

Substantive analytical procedures are most effective when directed at high volumes of transactions that tend to be predictable over time. Where a financial statements amount is a result of few transactions, year-on-year comparisons are unlikely to be a useful source of evidence, as the components of the balance are likely to be different year on year.

In addition, if auditors note weak controls over an area, analytical procedures may be less conclusive than extensive detailed substantive tests. Similarly, an area with a historical problem of high error levels may be best tested using tests of detail as analytical procedures may show little or no trends for comparison purposes.

The ISA (UK and Ireland) notes that where material balances occur auditors would not rely on analytical procedures alone, instead coupling them with tests of detail. Tests of detail will also be required if a significant risk has been identified over a financial statements area or assertion at the planning stage.

25.5.2   Reliability of data

The reliability of data will depend on its nature, source and how it was obtained, i.e., direct from a third party or via the client. Auditors should consider:

- the source of the information available: information is normally more reliable when it is obtained from a source outside the entity;
- comparability of the information available: general industry data may need to be supplemented when the particular client deals only in a specialised area within the industry;
- nature and relevance of the information available: does the entity set attainable budgets, therefore making them a good benchmark for analytical procedures;
- controls over the preparation of the information: are budgets amended during the period to bring them closer in line to actual results? If so, this will lessen their use for comparative purposes;
- prior year knowledge and understanding: what data has been previously reliable and useful;
- whether the information has been produced internally: as noted above this will be less reliable than external information, but its reliability is enhanced if it is produced independently of the accounting system or there are adequate controls over its preparation; and
- whether controls over the preparation of the data are reliable.

25.5.3   Precision of expected results

Auditors must consider whether they can determine what the expected results of the analytical procedure will be with suitable precision before the test is performed. Precise expectations are required to allow auditors to determine when results indicate that a material misstatement has occurred. Auditors should consider:

- the accuracy with which the expected result can be determined. Some results can be more easily predicted than others, such as gross margins compared to discretionary expense payments;
- the degree to which information can be disaggregated. Results may be more easily predicted for individual sections of an operation;
- the availability of information; and
- the frequency with which a relationship is observed.

25.5.4   Acceptable differences

The amount of difference from expectation that auditors may accept without further investigation depends on the materiality of the item and the level of assurance they wish to derive from the procedure.

25.6 ANALYTICAL PROCEDURES IN THE OVERALL REVIEW AT THE END OF THE AUDIT

ISA (UK and Ireland) 520 requires that the auditors should also apply analytical procedures at or near the end of the audit when forming an overall conclusion as to whether the financial statements as a whole are consistent with the auditors' knowledge of the entity's business.

The results from this review should corroborate the results of the detailed audit testing, both in individual areas and in forming the final conclusion. They may also indicate areas where further work needs to be carried out.

Auditors should consider the following when carrying out such procedures:

* whether the financial statements adequately reflect the information and explanations previously obtained and conclusions previously reached during the course of the audit;
* whether the procedures reveal any new factors that may affect the presentation of, or disclosures in, the financial statements;
* whether analytical procedures applied when completing the audit, such as comparing the information in the financial statements with other pertinent data, produce results which support the overall conclusion that the financial statements as a whole are consistent with their knowledge of the entity's business;
* whether the presentation adopted in the financial statements may have been unduly influenced by the desire of those charged with governance to present matters in a favourable or unfavourable light; and
* the potential impact on the financial statements of the aggregate of uncorrected misstatements (including those arising from bias in making accounting estimates) identified during the course of the audit and the preceding period's audit, if any.

25.7 INVESTIGATING UNUSUAL ITEMS

ISA (UK and Ireland) 520 requires that, when analytical procedures identify fluctuations or relationships that are inconsistent with other relevant information or that differ from expected values by a significant amount, auditors should investigate and obtain adequate explanations and appropriate corroborative audit evidence.

Unexpected results may occur as a result of:

* actions of the client of which the auditors are unaware when they perform the review;

- external factors not controllable by the client of which the auditors are unaware when they carry out their review; or
- errors or omissions.

The investigation of unusual fluctuations will usually involve discussion between the client and the auditors. The auditors will then corroborate management's explanations by:

- comparing them with their existing knowledge of the business, either from previous years or obtained during the audit; or
- performing extra audit procedures to confirm the explanations received.

Where management are unable to offer any explanation the auditors should carry out additional work to identify the cause of the inconsistency.

Not all explanations are capable of verification; nevertheless the auditors may be able to decide on the reasonableness of those offered. For example, if a decrease in sales is attributed to a fall in demand, it may not be possible to verify this explanation directly nor quantify its effect (unless there are total market figures published and available in time for the audit). If the decrease is in line with the auditors' knowledge of the industry and prevailing market conditions, they may accept it as being reasonable. If the explanation cannot be verified, they must rely on other sources of evidence to satisfy themselves in this area.

25.8 RECORDING

Although the ISA (UK and Ireland) does not cover this area, there was a section in the APC Guideline 417 *Analytical Review*. This provides useful guidance on how analytical procedures should be recorded.

The recording of analytical procedures will normally contain:

- the information examined, the sources thereof and the factors considered in establishing its reliability;
- the extent and nature of material variations found;
- the sources and level of management from which explanations for material unexpected variations have been obtained;
- the verification of those explanations;
- any further action taken; and
- the conclusions drawn by the auditors.

It may also be helpful to compile a client profile in permanent working papers detailing key ratios and trends from year to year. This allows the auditors to establish a base of financial and non-financial information for use in subsequent years.

26 THE AUDIT OF FRS 17

26.1 BACKGROUND

FRS 17 *Retirement Benefits,* which was issued in 2000, deals with accounting by companies for the defined benefit and defined contribution schemes which provide pensions for their employees.

FRS 17 requires that for defined benefit schemes:

- scheme assets and liabilities are valued using specified methods;
- the surplus or deficit is recognised by the reporting entity as an asset or liability;
- the change in the defined benefit asset or liability (other than that arising from contributions to the scheme) to be analysed into specified components and recognised in the profit and loss account or the statement of total recognised gains and losses ('the STRGL'); and
- certain additional disclosures in the reporting entity's financial statements.

The full requirements of FRS 17 should be applied for accounting periods ending on or after 22 June 2003.

The recognition of pension fund assets and liabilities in companies' balance sheets or even in the notes to the balance sheet presents auditors with a number of problems. These include, for example, access to records and how far to rely on actuaries' valuations.

Guidance in this chapter is also relevant to IAS 19 which, in many ways, gives the auditor similar issues to FRS 17.

26.2 GUIDANCE

To deal with these new problems, in November 2001, the APB issued Practice Note 22 *The Auditors' Consideration of FRS 17 Retirement Benefits – Defined Benefit Schemes* ('the Practice Note').

This was followed in February 2002 by the issue of Technical Release Audit 1/02 *Practical Points for Auditors in Connection with the Implementation of FRS 17 'Retirement Benefits' – Defined Benefit Schemes*('the Technical Release') by the Audit and Assurance Faculty of the ICAEW. This is designed to supplement the Practice Note in certain areas and also to help auditors deal with practical issues they may encounter.

Although the Practice Note and Bulletin were issued prior to the APB adopting the ISAs (UK and Ireland) for the audit of periods beginning on or after 15 December 2004, the guidance within them remains relevant under the new regime. Where the guidance refers to the old SASs, this commentary also includes references to the relevant ISA (UK and Ireland).

26.3 RESPECTIVE RESPONSIBILITIES

The Practice Note makes clear that it is the directors' responsibility to develop procedures to enable the entity to comply with FRS 17 requirements. As directors may not have immediate access to the records of scheme assets, and are unlikely to possess the expertise to value the scheme liabilities, they may need to involve others in the process:

- the scheme trustees to value the scheme assets; and
- a qualified actuary to value the scheme liabilities.

Auditors' objectives are to consider the appropriateness of the steps taken by directors to satisfy themselves that the amounts and disclosures made in the financial statements are sufficiently reliable. Auditors are especially concerned whether directors have devoted sufficient resources to this process.

The Practice Note emphasises that it is not the auditors' role to 'second guess' actuaries' work in valuing scheme liabilities. Auditors should, however, assess whether the procedures taken by directors are appropriate and whether the FRS 17 accounting entries and disclosures are consistent with their knowledge of the reporting entity.

The Practice Note stresses the need for auditors to satisfy themselves that they are independent and objective when the audit firm provides other services to a client. This is especially important when such services directly affect the client's financial statements. Where an audit firm provides actuarial services to a client for FRS 17 purposes, this could constitute a threat to auditors' objectivity and independence. Where the audit firm concludes that it cannot adopt safeguards to address this problem, the firm would be unable to accept both engagements.

26.4 PLANNING

When planning, auditors should assess the process by which directors intend to comply with FRS 17 in preparing their financial statements. Auditors' discussions with directors are likely to cover:

- who is responsible for the process;
- the arrangements to identify the schemes where FRS 17 is significant;
- who is valuing the scheme assets;

- the arrangements to identify significant matters affecting the actuarial valuation;
- who is valuing the scheme liabilities;
- how the actuarial assumptions are to be developed and approved;
- whether there is a realistic co-ordinated timetable (allowing time for auditors to complete their work on retirement benefits); and
- whether procedures exist to enable effective communication between all parties.

The Technical Release highlights the potential problem where auditors discover at the planning stage that directors have taken no steps to comply with FRS 17 requirements. In these circumstances auditors should consider whether the necessary information can be obtained at short notice (for example, by employing actuaries other than those of the pension scheme).

26.4.1   Risks of material misstatement

Auditors and directors should also discuss the risk of material misstatement in the financial statements arising from FRS 17 requirements.

TABLE 1: Examples of risks of material misstatement in relation to FRS 17

The risks below may not necessarily exist in every case, nor is this table intended to be an exhaustive list of all possible risks.

General

- directors may not have allocated sufficient resources to the FRS 17 process compliance.

Completeness of retirement benefit arrangements

- directors may not be aware of all schemes (for example, information about overseas schemes may not be well documented).

Subsidiaries

- directors of subsidiary entities may not fully understand the FRS 17 requirements.

Scheme changes

- scheme actuaries may not have been advised of important changes to schemes (for example, changes in benefit structures).

Consistency

- the treatment of scheme assets and liabilities related to bulk transfers may be inconsistent (leading to cut-off errors).

Actuarial assumptions

- key assumptions may be inconsistent (for example, the discount rate and the

---

expected return on assets) or may be inappropriate (for example, benefit improvements).

Timetable

- the timetable for valuing scheme assets and liabilities may not be compatible with the entity's reporting timetable.

Surpluses

- directors may not have considered the recoverability of a surplus or may argue that it will be used for future benefit improvements (and therefore should not be accounted for in full).

Deficits

- the entity may be in breach of loan covenants when the deficit is taken into account and this may bring the entity's going concern into question.

Distributable profits

- the impact of any deficits in the group on distributable profits may not have been considered.

Actuarial updates

- changes since the most recent full actuarial valuation may give rise to imprecise liability calculations.

Source data

- actuaries may use incomplete or inaccurate source data (for example, in respect of membership records).

Asset values

- a timely, appropriate report on scheme assets may not be provided by trustees (for example, investments may be incomplete).

Multi-employer schemes

- it may be possible to allocate assets and liabilities to an individual reporting entity within the scheme and this may not have been identified.

Measurement and disclosure

- there may be a misallocation between the profit and loss account and the STRGL.

Deferred taxation

- directors may have failed to consider the allocation of deferred tax between the profit and loss account and the STRGL.

26.4.2   Communication

Effective communication between all the parties involved in FRS 17 compliance is essential to ensure a common understanding of what has to be done by each party and the timetable for its completion.

With the permission of directors, auditors communicate with actuaries at the audit planning stage to:

- inform actuaries of their intention to use their work as audit evidence;
- discuss the scope of their work, for example:

  - steps to produce the valuation within the reporting timescale,
  - procedures to establish the validity and completeness of the source data used in the valuation,
  - the possible variation in the liability and costs estimated by actuaries,
  - the impact of any significant events on the valuation,
  - the extent to which a fuller or more recent valuation may be required;

- ascertain the form and content of any reports to be issued in respect of FRS 17;
- confirm that actuaries:

  - will follow the FRS 17 requirements and their own professional guidance,
  - will include all the retirement benefits payable under schemes they have been engaged to advise upon,
  - understand the timetable for the preparation and audit of the financial statements,
  - will advise auditors of any matters occurring between the reporting entity's balance sheet date and the completion date of the valuation which would have a material effect on the valuation of scheme liabilities,
  - are content for directors to supply auditors with copies of the actuaries' draft or final FRS 17 reports.

Although actuaries are not professionally obliged to agree an engagement letter with directors, any terms of reference for their work may assist auditors in understanding the scope of their work.

For most FRS 17 purposes, actuaries can often update the most recent scheme valuation to reflect current conditions. Where significant changes have taken place, however, they may lead to material changes in the value of liabilities (for example, the impact of large bulk transfers or major new early retirement programmes). In such cases, auditors have to discuss the issues with directors and actuaries to determine whether actuaries need to carry out any additional work.

The entity auditors may also contact scheme auditors, fund managers or investment custodians who may be valuing the scheme assets.

Where the reporting entity prepares consolidated financial statements, there may be a large number of schemes. This may therefore involve a number of different trustees and actuaries with whom auditors may have to communicate. In practice, some responsibility passes to the subsidiary auditors, although it is important to establish that they are familiar with FRS 17 requirements (especially in the case of overseas subsidiaries). The reporting entity may appoint a lead actuary to communicate with the actuaries of the various schemes and collate FRS 17 information.

The Technical Release identifies a number of steps which auditors may take in respect of overseas schemes.

TABLE 2: Steps in respect of overseas schemes

- consider how, if at all, the principles of FRS 17 apply to the overseas schemes (for example, pension schemes being state run);
- review the year end reporting timetable;
- determine whether overseas accounts staff are familiar with FRS 17 requirements;
- enquire if it is possible to communicate with overseas actuaries; and
- assess whether there are material schemes within overseas joint ventures or associates.

26.4.3   Materiality

ISA (UK and Ireland) 320 *Audit Materiality* accepts that there may be different materiality considerations depending on the aspect of the financial statements being considered. Auditors may judge, for example, that the expected degree of accuracy for note disclosures is lower than for the figures included in the primary financial statements. The level at which an omission or misstatement is material would therefore be higher.

This may be the case in the transitional period to full FRS 17 compliance. In the first two years, auditors' judgements of materiality relating to note disclosures may be based primarily on the relative significance of amounts in the context of the reporting entity's balance sheet. Auditors should recognise, however, that note disclosures in the first two years will be the basis for the comparative figures in the financial statements in the third year.

26.5 AUDIT EVIDENCE

26.5.1 *Understanding the schemes involved*

Given the potential material impact which FRS 17 could have on an entity's financial statements, it is important for auditors to understand which schemes are involved and the general nature of their provisions.

Auditors should therefore obtain from directors an understanding of the scheme rules which could have a significant influence on the entity's FRS 17 compliance (for example, the details of obligations to pay retirement benefits).

There could, however, be other benefits payable not covered in the scheme rules, for example:

- legal obligations to pay retirement benefits arising from informal agreements rather than formal contracts; and
- statutory requirements overriding the original scheme provisions.

Auditors should also take care to ensure that they receive the most up-to-date copy of the scheme rules.

Auditors may perform other procedures during their work which may help identify obligations to pay retirement benefits (for example, the review of board minutes or communications with employees).

26.5.2 *Scheme assets*

Scheme assets normally comprise one or more of the following:

- quoted securities;
- unquoted securities;
- unitised securities;
- insurance policies;
- loans and debt instruments; and
- freehold and leasehold properties.

Auditors may be able to obtain satisfactory evidence in respect of scheme assets without carrying out procedures on scheme asset records. Where there is a short period between the most recent scheme year end and the reporting entity's year end, and audited scheme financial statements are available, auditors may be able to obtain sufficient audit evidence by:

- asking directors to reconcile the scheme assets valuation at the scheme year end date with the assets valuation at the reporting entity's date being used for FRS 17 purposes;
- obtaining direct confirmation of the scheme assets from the investment custodian; and

- examining the key reconciling items (for example, contributions paid, benefits paid and estimated investment returns).

26.5.3 Using the work of the scheme auditors

Where the above reconciliation is not possible, it may be necessary to carry out procedures directly on the records of scheme assets. Although entity auditors could perform this work themselves (with the permission of directors and the scheme trustees), it may be more cost-effective to ask directors to arrange with the scheme trustees for the scheme auditors to carry it out, because of their familiarity with the scheme assets and accounting records. Entity auditors use the work of the scheme auditors in accordance with ISA (UK and Ireland) 600 *Using the Work of Another Auditor* (see **Chapter 39**).

Scheme auditors need to perform additional procedures to those carried out in the audit of the scheme financial statements if:

- the scheme and reporting entity have different accounting periods. This could involve additional procedures to update their work on the audit of the scheme to the reporting entity's balance sheet date. Where the period between the different period ends is short and the scheme period end precedes that of the entity, the entity auditors may be able to obtain sufficient appropriate audit evidence of the scheme assets at the entity period end by reviewing major movements in scheme assets since the scheme period end; and
- the scheme and reporting entity have the same accounting period but the scheme financial statements will be audited at a date later than that of the reporting entity. Arrangements may be necessary to supply the entity auditors with the evidence they require on a timely basis.

The entity auditors, with the permission of directors and scheme trustees, also need to communicate with the scheme auditors at the planning stage of the audit to:

- confirm in writing the nature and extent of the scheme auditors' work;
- agree the materiality to be applied;
- agree a timetable for scheme auditors to report to the entity auditors and the manner in which they are to report (entity auditors, where practicable, require scheme auditors to provide a report of factual findings resulting from the specified procedures).

26.5.4 Multi-employer schemes

A multi-employer scheme is one where a number of employers participate in a single defined benefit scheme. Sometimes there is no clear allocation of scheme assets to specific employers and it may be difficult to attribute a reasonable share of the assets and liabilities to each employer. In this situation, FRS 17 requires that these are treated defined contribution schemes provided certain disclosures are made.

Auditors should ask directors and others (for example actuaries) about how they concluded that the scheme was a multi-employer arrangement. An allocation of assets and liabilities may be possible where different employers within the scheme contribute at different rates.

Auditors should also understand the principal provisions of these schemes and those circumstances (for example, wind up of the scheme) which could cause a scheme deficit and:

- a liability or contingent liability for the reporting entity; or
- possible going concern problems for the entity.

26.5.5   Scheme liabilities

The Practice Note covers the actuaries' role in determining scheme liabilities either by a full actuarial valuation (see **Chapter 44**) or an annual update. Auditors will need to use the work of actuaries as audit evidence for FRS 17 purposes. The principles of ISA (UK and Ireland) 620 *Using the Work of an Expert* are followed closely by the Practice Note in setting out auditors' work (see **Chapter 39**).

26.5.6   Competence and objectivity of the actuary

Auditors should consider whether actuaries are members of the Institute of Actuaries, Faculty of Actuaries or Society of Actuaries. Where a foreign actuary is involved in FRS 17 work, these three bodies can advise on the acceptability of the standards of overseas actuarial professional bodies.

Actuaries' objectivity should also be evaluated, particularly where they are employees of, or related to, the reporting entity.

26.5.7   The actuary's work as audit evidence

Under ISA (UK and Ireland) 620, auditors need to consider a number of matters to evaluate the appropriateness of actuaries' work for FRS 17 purposes, including:

- the source data used;
- the assumptions and methods used; and
- the results of actuaries' work in the light of auditors' knowledge of the business and results of other audit procedures.

Actuarial source data is likely to include:

- scheme member data (for example, classes of member and contribution details); and
- scheme asset information (for example, values and income and expenditure items).

Directors are responsible for the source data used by actuaries. Auditors should discuss with directors and actuaries what has been done to establish that the data is relevant, reliable and sufficient. Where auditors have concerns over the scope of such procedures, they may wish to perform their own procedures.

The nature, timing and extent of any additional procedures depends on:

- the nature of the data and its sensitivity to the actuarial valuation;
- the source of the data and the extent to which it has already been subjected to audit procedures (for example, by entity auditors or the internal auditors); and
- actuaries' approach to verify the completeness and validity of the data.

26.5.8   Actuarial assumptions

Actuarial assumptions are estimates of future events that will affect the valuation of the scheme liabilities and the reporting entity's costs of retirement benefits (for example, mortality rates, termination rates, retirement age and changes in salary and benefit levels). FRS 17 states that the assumptions are the ultimate responsibility of directors but should be set upon advice given by actuaries.

Auditors will not have the same expertise as actuaries and are unlikely to be able to challenge the appropriateness and reasonableness of the assumptions. Auditors can, however, through discussion with directors and actuaries:

- obtain a general understanding of the assumptions and review the process used to develop them;
- compare the assumptions with those which directors have used in prior years; and
- consider whether, based on their knowledge of the reporting entity and the scheme, and on the results of other audit procedures, the assumptions appear to be reasonable and compatible with those used elsewhere in the preparation of the entity's financial statements.

26.5.9   Assessing the results of the actuary's work

There is no prescribed form for actuaries' reports on the results of their work. The pensions scheme figures required for FRS 17 are normally provided in a letter or written report. Actuaries may also provide a commentary on other matters, such as:

- the movements since the previous valuation in the figures required for inclusion in the balance sheet and the profit and loss account;
- the possible variation in the valuation of the scheme liabilities and the implications for the financial statements and the audit; and
- the sensitivity of the results, funding level, scheme maturity and investments to variations in the source data and assumptions.

Auditors should obtain copies of all written communications from actuaries to directors concerning the findings of their work.

Auditors should also discuss with directors whether actuaries have indicated that:

- any matters have occurred in the period from the reporting entity's balance sheet date up to the date on which the valuation was completed that would have a material effect on the valuation; or
- there was a departure from relevant professional requirements or guidance issued by their professional body.

Auditors may request actuaries to:

- provide specific confirmation on the above points;
- comment on the degree of precision attaching to the valuation and factors giving rise to potential material misstatement;
- indicate whether the FRS 17 amounts and disclosures in the financial statements adequately reflect the results of their work.

Where the results of actuaries' work is inconsistent with other audit evidence, auditors should discuss the inconsistency with the directors and actuaries. Additional procedures, such as requesting directors to obtain evidence from another actuary, may assist in resolving the inconsistency.

26.5.10   Valuation of scheme liabilities and materiality

The defined benefit asset (or liability) is based on the surplus (or deficit) of the value of the scheme assets over the value of scheme liabilities.

Generally accepted actuarial techniques may give a range of acceptable values. Auditors may be faced with a large range arising from an unusual event (for example, the outcome of a recent court case, which could potentially have a significant effect on the scheme, cannot be established with certainty before the approval of the financial statements).

Both the Practice Note and the Technical Release stress the need for auditors to check that financial statements contain sufficient disclosures about the actuarial assumptions. Auditors may, in exceptional circumstances, consider a fundamental uncertainty, explanatory paragraph in their report where the uncertainty caused by the range is unusually large.

26.5.11 Disclosures

The Practice Note makes clear that, where auditors have concerns regarding the disclosures in the financial statements or in the OFR, they should discuss their views with directors. If this does not lead to the matter being resolved, auditors may decide to communicate their concerns to those charged with governance (in accordance with ISA (UK and Ireland) 260 *Communication of Audit Matters to those Charged with Governance*) and consider the effect on their audit opinion (see **Chapter 9**).

26.5.12 Going concern

When evaluating going concern, directors consider all relevant information of which they are aware at the time they approve the financial statements, including events known or expected to occur more than a year beyond the date on which they approve the financial statements (for example, a scheme is inadequately funded to a significant extent and the defined benefit liability to be recognised in the balance sheet may be material). In these circumstances, auditors would:

- enquire into the expected timing of the cash flows likely to arise as result of this liability and how directors would fund these payments; and
- consider whether the recognition of the defined benefit liability may cause the reporting entity to breach any existing loan covenant.

Under ISA (UK and Ireland) 570 *Going Concern* auditors should assess how directors have satisfied themselves that the going concern basis and any related disclosures are appropriate.

26.5.13 Recognition in the profit and loss account and the STRGL

The change in the defined benefit asset or liability is required to be analysed into a number of specified components. The nature, timing and extent of auditors' procedures in relation to these components depend on the materiality of the amounts involved and the risk of material misstatement of the financial statements.

TABLE 3: Profit and Loss Account and STRGL disclosures

Auditors should consider the following procedures in respect of Profit and Loss Account and STRGL disclosures:

Items charged to operating profit (current service cost, past service cost, gains and losses on settlements and curtailments)

- discuss with directors and actuaries the factors affecting current service cost (for

---

example, a scheme closed to new entrants may see an increase year on year as a percentage of pay with the average age of the workforce increasing).

Items charged/credited to finance costs/income (expected return on scheme assets, interest on scheme liabilities)

- consider whether the interest costs reflect an average of the liabilities at the beginning of the year and movements during the year;
- ensure that the discount rate reflects the appropriate high quality corporate bond rate at the start of the year and is the same as the rate at which the scheme liabilities were measured at the end of the previous year;
- compare the expected return with market indices when dealing with quoted fixed interest and index-linked securities;
- consider discussing with directors and actuaries whether the equity risk premium (in a scheme with a majority of equities) is being over-estimated in the current year (where the actual return shows a consistent pattern, for example, always less than the expected return).

Items recognised in the STRGL (actuarial gains and losses, comprising: actual return less expected return on scheme assets, experience gains and losses arising on scheme liabilities, effects of changes in assumptions underlying scheme liabilities)

- discuss with directors and actuaries the underlying reasons for actuarial gains and losses (for example, employee turnover rates or unexpected changes in salaries/ medical costs).

26.5.14   Expected return on scheme assets and discount rate

Auditors should pay particular attention to the amounts to be disclosed as the expected return on scheme assets and the rate used to discount the scheme liabilities.

TABLE 4: Expected return on scheme assets and discount rate

Auditors should consider the following procedures in relation to expected return on scheme assets and discount rate:

- consider directors' judgement of the expected long term rate of return for each category of scheme assets and the current rate of return on a high quality corporate bond of equivalent currency and term to the scheme liabilities;
- review directors' discussions with actuaries to select a discount rate;
- review the 5-year historical table of the amounts recognised in the STRGL to help identify any systematic bias in the assumptions about the expected rate of return;
- obtain explanations from directors and actuaries to support the expected rate of return for all significant asset categories and consider whether any changes are consistent with, for example, changes in investment strategy; and
- discuss the choice of discount rate and get explanations for any change in the rate.

26.5.15   Disclosures

Auditors should consider the disclosures in the entity's financial statements where the reporting entity has more than one defined benefit scheme and whether disaggregation is required for the financial statements to give a true and fair view.

TABLE 5: FRS 17 disclosures for an entity with more than one defined benefit scheme

Auditors should consider the following procedures for an entity with more than one defined benefit scheme:

- consider if disclosure has been made for each scheme or in groupings (helpful groupings may be based on the geographical location of the schemes and whether the schemes are subject to significantly different risks; and
- assess whether aggregated disclosure causes surpluses and deficits of different schemes being 'netted-off' or important information about arrangements whose costs are significantly different or more volatile compared with others being 'lost' by the presentation of averaged rates or aggregated values.

26.5.16   Distributable profits

Auditors should be aware of the potential problem arising where the individual financial statements of the reporting entity show a defined benefit liability so large that it reduces realised profits below that needed to cover any intended distribution.

ISA (UK and Ireland) 250 Part A *Consideration of laws and regulations in an audit of financial statements* requires auditors to obtain sufficient appropriate audit evidence about compliance with those laws and regulations relating directly to the preparation of, or the inclusion or disclosure of specific items in, the financial statements. This will include, for example, section 263 of the Companies Act 1985 (for a limited company), which specifies that a distribution cannot be made except out of profits available for the purpose.

If auditors become aware that there may be insufficient realised profits to make a proposed distribution, they normally discuss their concerns with directors and advise them of the potential consequences of making a potentially unlawful distribution. Directors and auditors may wish to consult their respective legal advisers. If directors are unable to dispel auditors' concerns and do not modify the proposed distribution, auditors should consider the implications of this disagreement for their report. This may result in auditors issuing a qualified or adverse opinion.

However, where companies have taken advantage of the transitional arrangements in FRS 17 only to make disclosures, ICAEW Technical Release 01/02 explains that the first time a company will need to take into account the effect of an FRS 17 deficit is in the declaration of interim dividends during the period in which FRS 17 is to be adopted in full (i.e., periods beginning on or after 1 January 2005). Furthermore, at the time of writing, there is no formal guidance on the extent to which a pension asset or liability recognised in accordance with FRS 17 affects distributable reserves. Where there is doubt as to the legality of any proposed dividend, companies should seek appropriate legal advice.

26.5.17 *Management representations*

ISA (UK and Ireland) 580 *Management Representations* requires auditors to obtain written confirmation of management representations on matters material to the financial statements when those representations are critical to obtaining sufficient appropriate audit evidence. Management representations cannot, however, be a substitute for other audit evidence.

Examples of typical representations which may be obtained by entity auditors are shown in Table 6.

TABLE 6: Typical management representations

- actuarial assumptions underlying the valuation of scheme liabilities are consistent with the entity directors' knowledge of the business;
- all significant retirement benefits, including any arrangements that:

  - are statutory, contractual or implicit in the employer's actions,
  - arise in the UK and the Republic of Ireland or overseas,
  - are funded or unfunded,
  - are approved or unapproved,
  - have been identified and properly accounted for; and

- all settlements and curtailments have been identified and properly accounted for.

26.6 SMALLER ENTITIES WITH INSURED SCHEMES

The Practice Note is intended to apply to auditors of all reporting entities and all types and sizes of defined benefit scheme (although some of the guidance may be more relevant to auditors of entities with significant and complex retirement benefit arrangements). These entities usually have well-resourced actuaries available but are often also subject to tight reporting deadlines (for example, listed companies).

The situation for smaller reporting entities is often quite different. Their retirement benefit arrangements may often be less complex and they generally enjoy a more relaxed reporting timetable. This may allow more time for directors and actuaries to comply with FRS 17 and allows auditors more time to obtain the necessary audit evidence.

A smaller reporting entity's occupational pension scheme is, however, sometimes administered by an insurance company with the only scheme asset an insurance policy (a 'fully insured scheme'). Scheme actuaries will usually be an employee of the insurance company and directors will probably ask the insurance company and its in-house actuary to provide the information for FRS 17 compliance.

In such circumstances, auditors should consider whether:

- the insurance company will be able to supply directors with values of the scheme assets and liabilities as at the entity balance sheet date, where it differs from the scheme year-end date;
- it will be appropriate for them to communicate with the insurance company's actuary;
- the basis to be used by the insurance company to value the insurance policies will represent 'the best approximation to fair value' under FRS 17: a surrender value will not be appropriate unless the trustees have decided to surrender the policy or wind up the scheme;
- 'earmarked' insurance policies (for example, deferred annuity policies), excluded from the accounts of the scheme in accordance with statutory exemptions, will have been valued and included in the fair value of scheme assets to comply with FRS 17; and
- evidence will be available to support the basis for valuing the insurance policy as at the entity year balance sheet date.

Where the insurance company is unable to provide a valuation of an insurance policy as at the reporting entity balance sheet date, directors might decide to adjust the most recently obtained valuation for contributions received and benefits paid, also allowing for investment returns. The basis of this approach would need to be clearly disclosed in the notes to the financial statements.

The fact that auditors are not able to discuss matters with actuaries does not of itself give rise to a need to qualify the auditors' opinion on the financial statements as the auditors may be able to obtain sufficient appropriate evidence by:

- discussing the matters with directors; and
- reviewing any correspondence between directors and actuaries.

27 AUDIT OF ACCOUNTING ESTIMATES

27.1 AUDITING STANDARDS

Clarified ISA (UK and Ireland) 540 *Auditing Accounting Estimates, Including Fair Value Accounting Estimates, and Related Disclosures* was issued in October 2009 and replaces ISA (UK and Ireland) 540 previously issued in December 2004. The Clarified ISA (UK and Ireland) is effective for the audit of financial statements for periods ending on or after 15 December 2010.

The Clarified ISA (UK and Ireland) incorporates the guidance which was previously included in ISA (UK and Ireland) 545, *Auditing Fair Value Measurements and Disclosures*. The guidance relating to the audit of fair values is detailed in **Chapter 28**.

This chapter covers both the existing and Clarified ISAs (UK and Ireland). As the Clarified ISA (UK and Ireland) adds to the requirements of the existing ISA (UK and Ireland) this chapter is written on the basis of the existing requirements, and any changes to them included in the Clarified ISA (UK and Ireland) are included and clearly indicated.

As with all ISAs (UK and Ireland), the text of the ISA has been supplemented with additional guidance from a UK and Ireland perspective.

27.2 ACCOUNTING ESTIMATES

ISA (UK) 540 requires that auditors should obtain sufficient appropriate audit evidence regarding the accounting estimates material to the financial statements on which to base their audit opinion.

Accounting estimates are approximations which are deemed necessary because there is no precise means of measurement for a particular item in the financial statements. Examples include:

- stock provisions;
- bad debt provisions;
- depreciation;
- accrued revenue;
- deferred taxation provisions;
- provision for a loss from a lawsuit;
- profits or losses on construction contracts in progress; and
- warranty claim provisions.

The estimates in the financial statements are the responsibility of management and result from uncertainties regarding the outcome of events that have occurred, or are likely to occur. They involve the use of judgement and consequently the audit evidence available is less conclusive than with other items. When faced with estimates auditors must use their judgement in assessing the sufficiency and appropriateness of the evidence.

The processes involved in determining the estimate will depend on the nature of the item. For example, establishing an accrual for rent will involve taking the quarterly rental and apportioning it over the period concerned. On the other hand, establishing a provision for a slow moving stock item involves examining sales of the item over the period and since the year end, the costs associated with selling the item and the estimated selling price. In some cases specialist knowledge may be required to make an estimate, such as the amount of damages payable in a legal case.

27.3 ASSESSING THE RISK OF AUDIT ESTIMATES

When determining the risk assessment relating to audit estimates, Clarified ISA (UK and Ireland) 540 requires auditors to consider the:

- requirements of the financial reporting framework relating to the relevant accounting estimates;
- processes used by management to identify accounting estimates; and
- procedures management uses to quantify accounting estimates, including:
  - the method, and where applicable, the model used to determine the value of the estimate;
  - relevant controls;
  - whether an expert has been used;
  - the assumptions underlying the estimate;
  - whether there has been, or ought to have been, a change from the prior period in the methods used by management; and
  - whether, and if so, how management has assessed the effect of estimation uncertainty.

In considering management's assessment of estimation uncertainty, auditors may determine:

- whether management has considered alternative assumptions or outcomes by performing a sensitivity analysis to determine the effect of changes in the assumptions on an accounting estimate;
- how management quantifies the estimate when the sensitivity analysis suggests alternative outcomes; and
- whether management monitors prior period's accounting estimates and responds appropriately to their findings.

As part of their risk assessment, the Clarified ISA (UK and Ireland) requires auditors to reconsider accounting estimates made in the prior period and determine whether their accuracy, or otherwise, compared to actual results may indicate a risk of material misstatement.

In addition to assessing whether management have considered estimation uncertainty, auditors are also required by the Clarified ISA to perform their own evaluation of estimation uncertainty. Where any accounting estimates are deemed to have a high level of estimation uncertainty, auditors should consider whether these give rise to significant risks.

27.4   AUDIT PROCEDURES

The ISA (UK and Ireland) requires that auditors should obtain sufficient audit evidence as to whether an accounting estimate is reasonable in the circumstances and when required, is appropriately disclosed. To this end, auditors should adopt one, or a combination, of the following approaches in the audit of an accounting estimate:

(a)   review and test the process used by management to develop the estimate;
(b)   test the operating effectiveness of the controls over how management made the accounting estimate together with appropriate substantive procedures;
(c)   develop their own estimate to compare to the estimate generated by management; or
(d)   review subsequent events which confirm the estimate made.

The review of subsequent events may remove the need for the auditors to obtain other evidence to support an accounting estimate. For example, if an estimate is made concerning an insurance claim for loss of profits after a fire and is provisionally settled during the audit, this will provide evidence on the estimate and means that the auditors may reduce the attention they give to the process by which management derive the estimate. An estimate may become an accrual where it is fully supported by the subsequent evidence, for example, an estimate in respect of legal fees incurred before the year end becomes an accrual when those fees are rendered.

Where accounting estimates give rise to significant risks, auditors should evaluate:

• whether the significant assumptions used by management are reasonable;
• whether management intend and are able to carry out any courses of action required by those assumptions; and
• how management have considered alternative assumptions and why they have been rejected.

The final item above was introduced by Clarified ISA (UK and Ireland) 540.

The Clarified ISA also requires auditors to obtain evidence concerning management's decision whether or not to recognise the estimate in the financial statements and if the measurement basis used for that estimate is in accordance with the requirements of the applicable financial reporting framework.

27.4.1 Testing management's methods

Testing management's methods and models for determining accounting estimates may be an effective audit tool when:

- the estimate is derived from a routine processing of data by the entity's accounting system;
- previous experience of similar estimates has shown that management's processes have been effective; and
- the accounting estimate is based on a large population of items of a similar nature, which individually are not significant.

Testing how management made the accounting estimate may involve:

- testing the reliability, accuracy, completeness and relevance of the data on which the estimate is based. This may be internal or external data supplied by experts;
- recalculating the estimate or assessing the validity of the model used (see **Table 1**);
- considering the process used to assess or review the calculated amount before approving it for use in the financial statements.

Where a model is used to determine the accounting estimate, auditors may consider the procedures in **Table 1**.

TABLE 1: Audit procedures to assess the validity of models used to determine accounting estimates

Auditors may test whether:

- the model is validated prior to use, with periodic ongoing reviews. This should include evaluation of:
  - the theoretical soundness and mathematical integrity of the model;
  - the consistency and completeness of the model's inputs with market practices; and
  - the model's output as compared to actual transactions;
- appropriate change control policies and procedures exist to eliminate the risk of unauthorised changes being made;
- the model is periodically calibrated and tested for validity;
- necessary adjustments are made to the output of the model to reflect changing assumptions in the market place; and
- the model is adequately documented including its applications and limitations, key parameters, required inputs and results of any validation analysis performed.

In addition, if the financial reporting framework does not set out a fixed method for determining a particular accounting estimate, auditors may consider:

- management's rationale for selecting the method used;
- whether management have applied any criteria set out in the financial reporting framework when selecting the chosen method;
- if the method is appropriate given the nature of the asset or liability being estimated; and
- if the method is appropriate in relation to the business, industry and environment in which the entity operates.

27.5 EVALUATION OF RESULTS

The ISA (UK and Ireland) requires that the auditors should make a final assessment of the reasonableness of the accounting estimate based on the auditors' knowledge of the entity and its industry and whether it is consistent with other evidence obtained during the audit and subsequent events.

If the auditors believe management's estimate to be unreasonable and management refuses to revise its estimate, the difference between management's estimate and the auditors' estimate must be considered with all other misstatements in assessing whether the effect on the financial statements is material.

27.6 DISCLOSURE

Auditors are required to obtain sufficient evidence as to whether disclosure of the accounting estimate in the financial statements is in accordance with the applicable financial reporting framework. Where accounting estimates give rise to significant risks, the Clarified ISA (UK and Ireland) also requires auditors to evaluate the adequacy of the disclosure of the estimation uncertainty and they may need to require additional details be provided in the notes to the financial statements.

28 AUDITING FAIR VALUE

28.1 INTRODUCTION

Certain financial assets and financial liabilities may be presented or disclosed at fair value in the financial statements. The fair value used may arise from the initial recording of that asset or liability or from a subsequent change in its value. In the UK the use of fair value accounting may be governed by Sch. 1 to SI 2008/410, The Large and Medium-sized Companies and Groups (Accounts and Reports) Regulations 2008 under the Companies Act 2006 or by UK or International Financial Reporting Standards. These rules are distinct from the alternative accounting rules that are also available under the Companies Act 2006.

The measurement of fair value can be simple, for example if assets are bought and sold in an active and open market, or more complex. Examples of fair values that can be difficult to determine include investment properties or complex financial derivatives. In these cases an estimation of fair value may be achieved by using the work of an expert valuer or a valuation model.

28.2 GUIDANCE

Clarified ISA (UK and Ireland) 540 *Auditing Accounting Estimates, Including Fair Value Accounting Estimates, and Related Disclosures* was issued in October 2009 and incorporates the guidance previously issued in ISA (UK and Ireland) 545 *Auditing Fair Value Measurements and Disclosures* issued in December 2004 together with more general guidance on the audit of accounting estimates. The Clarified ISA (UK and Ireland) is effective for the audit of financial statements for periods ending on or after 15 December 2010. This chapter covers both the existing guidance in ISA (UK and Ireland) 545 and Clarified ISA (UK and Ireland) 540. As the Clarified ISA (UK and Ireland) 540 does not significantly amend the requirements of the ISA (UK and Ireland) 545 this chapter is written on the basis of the existing requirements, and any changes to them included in the Clarified ISA (UK and Ireland) are included and clearly indicated.

In October 2009, the APB issued Practice Note 23 (Revised) *Auditing Complex Financial Instruments – Interim Guidance* which provides additional guidance to that in ISA (UK and Ireland) 545. It is detailed in **28.9** below.

In October 2008 the IAASB published a paper entitled *Challenges in Auditing Fair Value Accounting Estimates in the Current Market Environment*. The proposed update to Practice Note 23 incorporates the issues raised in the IAASB paper and supplements APB Bulletin 2008/1 *Audit Issues when Financial Market Conditions are Difficult and Credit Facilities may be Restricted* (see **Chapter 37**).

28.3   UNDERSTANDING THE ENTITY'S PROCESS

It is the responsibility of those charged with governance to establish procedures to allow the determination of fair values as necessary. This determination of procedures is often delegated to the entity's management, although responsibility remains with those charged with governance. This process may be simple, such as consulting published price quotations, or more complex involving assumptions and uncertainty.

In accordance with ISA (UK and Ireland) 315 *Understanding the Entity and its Environment and Assessing the Risk of Material Misstatement* auditors are required to gain an understanding of the process adopted by management and the related control activities in order to assess the risk of material misstatement (see **Chapter 22**). The risk of material misstatement should be assessed at the assertion level to allow the auditor to determine the nature, extent and timing of their audit tests.

When obtaining an understanding of the entity's fair value process auditors may consider the areas set out in **Table 1**.

TABLE 1: Areas to consider when gaining an understanding of an entity's fair value process

- the relevant control activities over the process used to determine fair value measurements, including, for example, controls over data and the segregation of duties between those committing the entity to the underlying transactions and those responsible for the valuation;
- the expertise and experience of those persons determining the fair value measurements;
- the role that information technology has in the process;
- the types of accounts or transactions requiring fair value measurements or disclosures (e.g., whether the accounts arise from the recording of routine and recurring transactions or whether they arise from non-routine or unusual transactions);
- the extent to which the entity's process relies on a service organisation to provide fair value measurements or the data that supports the measurement. When an entity uses a service organisation, auditors should refer to ISA (UK and Ireland) 402 *Audit Considerations Relating to Entities Using Service Organizations* (see **Chapter 37**);
- the extent to which the entity uses the work of experts in determining fair value measurements and disclosures;
- the significant management assumptions used in determining fair value;
- the documentation supporting management's assumptions;

> - the methods used to develop and apply management assumptions and to monitor changes in those assumptions;
> - the integrity of change controls and security procedures for valuation models and relevant information systems, including approval processes; and
> - the controls over the consistency, timeliness and reliability of the data used in valuation models.

If auditors consider that the risk of material misstatement identified is a significant risk that requires special audit considerations, they should refer to ISA (UK and Ireland) 315.

There may only be limited control activities that can be effective in relation to fair value as fair value determinations often involve subjective judgements by management. As fair value measurements become more complex the likelihood of effective controls decreases whilst the risk of material misstatement increases.

28.4   EVALUATING THE ENTITY'S APPROACH

The auditor uses their knowledge of the business and financial reporting requirement to assess whether the fair value approach used by the entity is appropriate and consistently applied. For example knowledge of a client's business and future plans will assist with assessing the valuation applied to research and development work.

Auditors should pay particular attention to management's intentions, for example whether the intentions relied upon as part of the fair value process are realistic and relevant. Auditors may:

- consider management's past history of carrying out its stated intentions with respect to assets or liabilities;
- review written plans and other documentation, including budgets and minutes as appropriate;
- consider management's stated reasons for choosing a particular course of action;
- consider management's ability to carry out a particular course of action given the entity's economic circumstances, including the implications of any contractual commitments; and
- consider whether the course of action is allowed by UK or International Accounting Standards as relevant.

When a valuation method is not determined by statute or accounting standards, auditors should consider whether management's reasons for selecting a particular valuation method is appropriate. They should consider whether:

- management has sufficiently evaluated and appropriately applied any criteria that have been provided in accounting standards to support the selected method;

- the valuation method is appropriate to the item being valued; and
- the valuation method is appropriate for the business, industry and environment in which the entity operates.

The selected valuation method should be applied consistently, both for like assets and year on year. Where the valuation method has been changed in the period, auditors consider whether the change is justified either as a result of a change to the financial reporting rules or a change in the entity's circumstances, and whether the new method of valuation is more appropriate.

28.5 USING THE WORK OF AN EXPERT

Where valuation methods are complex or specialised, auditors may require the assistance of an expert when assessing the entity's methods and procedures. Where an expert is used, the auditor should refer to ISA (UK and Ireland) 620, *Using the Work of an Expert* (see **Chapter 39**).

In accordance with ISA (UK and Ireland) 620, the auditor should assess the expert's work. This will involve obtaining an understating of the significant assumptions and methods used, and considering whether they are appropriate, complete and reasonable given the auditors' knowledge of the business and the results of other audit procedures.

28.6 AUDIT PROCEDURES

Once the risk of material misstatement has been assessed, auditors should plan and perform their audit procedures. Procedures are likely to vary widely as a result of the many different types of fair value measurements that may occur. The three main types of procedure are:

- testing the entity's assumptions, the valuation model and the underlying data;
- developing independent fair value estimates to corroborate the entity's valuation; and
- considering the effect of subsequent events.

For some valuations it may merely be a case of consulting the same third party pricing data that the entity has used: for other areas the work performed will be more complex.

Whatever procedure is used, auditors should consider the results of their testing in relation to the rest of the evidence gained during the audit, for example is the discount rate used reasonable given the interest rates on borrowings by the entity.

28.6.1   Testing the entity's assumptions, model and data

When assessing an entity's fair value measurements, auditors may evaluate whether:

- the assumptions used by management are reasonable;
- the fair value measurement was determined using an appropriate model; and
- management used relevant information that was reasonably available at the time.

Assumptions

Auditors assess whether the assumptions used by the entity provide a reasonable basis for the fair value measurements and disclosures in the financial statements. To provide a reasonable basis the assumptions must be relevant, reliable, neutral, understandable and complete.

The assumptions will vary depending on the asset or liability being valued and the valuation method used, for example where discounted cash flows are used assumptions will be required about the level of cash flows, the period over which they are measured and the discount rate applied.

Auditors should concentrate on significant assumptions, i.e., those that cover matters that materially affect the fair value measurement, and this will typically include those which are:

- sensitive to variation or uncertainty, such as long-term interest rates; and
- susceptible to misapplication or bias.

The auditor should encourage the entity to perform a sensitivity analysis on their fair value measurements, and should consider performing the analysis themselves if it is not completed by the entity.

Assumptions are often interdependent and should be assessed both individually and in conjunction with each other. Sometimes assumptions which appear reasonable on their own may not be consistent with others used in the same valuation. Assumptions should be consistent with:

- the general economic environment and the entity's economic circumstances;
- the plans of the entity;
- assumptions made in prior periods, if appropriate;
- past experience of the entity, although past experience may not be indicative of future conditions or events;
- other matters relating to the financial statements, for example assumptions used by management in other accounting estimates, whether fair value or not; and
- if applicable, the risk associated with the cash flows.

Auditors should obtain written confirmation of representations made by management or those charged with governance regarding the reasonableness of significant assumptions.

Model

Where a valuation model is used, auditors review the model and evaluate whether it is appropriate and the assumptions used are reasonable.

Data

The auditor should plan and perform audit procedures to determine whether the data used in deriving the fair value measurement is accurate, complete and relevant. They should also consider whether the fair value measurement has been properly calculated using that data and the entity's assumptions.

Typical audit procedures will include:

- verifying the source of the data;
- mathematical recalculation of the valuation; and
- reviewing the information for internal consistency.

28.6.2   Independent fair value estimates

Instead of testing the assumptions, model and data as stated above, auditors may choose to attempt to corroborate the entity's fair value measurement by using their own model to generate a valuation. Typically they would use the entity's assumptions and data in this model, and would, therefore, be required to plan and perform procedures to verify these as discussed in **28.6.1** above.

Alternatively, auditors could use their own model and assumptions, but they would still be required to understand the assumptions applied by the entity in order to consider how their valuation differs from that prepared by the entity.

28.6.3   Subsequent events

Transactions and events that appear after the period end, but before the completion of the audit, may provide evidence about fair value measurements. An example would be the sale of an investment property after the period end. Care should be taken, however, that the post balance sheet events may no longer reflect events at the balance sheet date, e.g., a property value may vary considerably month on month in a time of volatile markets.

28.7 DISCLOSURES

Auditors are required to consider whether the disclosures made about fair values are in accordance with the requirements of statute and financial reporting standards. This will include considering whether any additional information given voluntarily is appropriate and not misleading.

Auditors must also ensure that, where a change in valuation methods has occurred in the period, the details and reasons for this change have been properly disclosed.

28.8 COMMUNICATION WITH THOSE CHARGED WITH GOVERNANCE

As the assumptions used in fair value measurement can often have significant effects on the financial statements, auditors may choose to include details of the assumptions, the degree of subjectivity involved in their formulation and the relative materiality of items measured at fair value in their communications with those charged with governance.

28.9 PRACTICE NOTE 23 (REVISED)

28.9.1 Background

In October 2009, the APB issued a revision to Practice Note 23 *Auditing Complex Financial Instruments – Interim Guidance*. The revision widens the scope of the original Practice Note which was issued in April 2002, and covers other complex financial instruments, as well as derivatives. In addition the revision incorporates guidance relevant to the current difficult financial market conditions, which necessitates consideration of valuations and financial statement disclosures about risks and uncertainties relating to financial instruments. The Practice Note was issued as interim guidance because:

- relevant accounting standards were currently under review; and
- conforming changes will be required to the Practice Note once the new ISA (UK and Ireland) 540 becomes effective for the audit of entities with accounting periods ending on or after 15 December 2010.

28.9.2 Complex financial instruments

New financial instrument products are being developed all the time, but typical examples are derivatives (including option contracts, futures and swaps) and notes or security instruments involving:

- contracts with one or more optional or conditional characteristic embedded within them; and/or
- underlying risk exposures which are not apparent from the form of the financial instrument (sometimes described as a 'host contract').

Values of complex financial instruments can be volatile and this increases their risk. There is often further risk due to the complex nature of the activities, which management sometimes do not fully understand.

However, the use of complex financial instruments can reduce some risks such as exposure to exchange rates, interest rates and commodity prices, by leveraging risks or providing a hedge to compensate for losses.

The guidance in the Practice Note is intended to be helpful for audits of entities with different levels of use of complex financial instruments, ranging from banks with high levels of trading to entities with a low number of foreign currency transactions.

28.9.3   Responsibilities

Management and those charged with governance are responsible for establishing a suitable control environment over complex financial instruments to ensure that they are able to make the relevant assertions about the existence, completeness and value of those financial instruments in their financial statements. Auditors are responsible for obtaining sufficient audit evidence to satisfy themselves that management's assertions give a true and fair view and are prepared in accordance with the applicable financial reporting framework.

Auditors may need special skills or knowledge to plan and perform auditing procedures for certain assertions about complex financial instruments and this may require the assistance of an expert from within or external to the firm. Difficult areas include the:

- operating characteristics and risk profile of the industry;
- instruments used by the entity and their characteristics;
- methods of valuing the complex financial instruments; and
- requirements of relevant legislation, regulations and applicable accounting standards.

The audit team may need to make use of the experience of an expert, from within or external to the firm, with the necessary skills or knowledge to help plan and perform the audit procedures. In periods of economic uncertainty use of an expert may be required where previously it was not considered necessary (eg where valuation methods have moved away from observable market prices and have become more complex).

The requirements of ISQC (UK and Ireland) 1 and ISA (UK and Ireland) 220 require that an engagement quality control reviewer is appointed for all audits of financial statements of listed entities and those other audits that fall within the procedures laid down by the firm. Typically other audits where the appointment of an engagement quality control reviewer is required would include those with unusual circumstances or risks. Auditors should consider whether the complex financial instruments or the market conditions surrounding the financial instruments would require such a review to take place.

28.9.4 *Understanding the entity*

Auditors must understand the type of financial instruments the entity is using and its objectives and strategies for using them, for example to eliminate risk or maximise income. The entity may use service organisations such as asset managers to initiate the purchase or sale of complex financial instruments. If so, auditors should have regard to ISA (UK and Ireland) 402 (see **Chapter 37**).

ISA (UK and Ireland) 315 requires that auditors obtain an understanding of internal control relevant to the audit. Internal control will consist of:

- the control environment, in relation to complex financial instruments, of particular relevance are:
  - the level of knowledge and experience of management and those charged with governance;
  - strength, or lack of, direction from management and those charged with governance;
  - segregation of duties and the assignment of personnel; and
  - whether or not the general control environment has been extended to those responsible for complex financial instrument activities;
- the entity's risk assessment process, including the assessment of operational risk, valuation risk, market risk, credit risk and settlement risk;
- the information system relevant to financial reporting and communication, particularly whether it is sophisticated enough to handle complex financial instruments with minimal manual intervention;
- control activities, including whether the entity's control activities remain capable of preventing, detecting and correcting material misstatements, even at times when the entity may have changed the way it uses financial instruments or the market conditions have deteriorated, leading to an increase in risk; and
- monitoring of controls, including ensuring that dealers are properly authorised and prices are independently verified.

As part of assessing internal control, auditors may consider the role of internal audit and whether they have sufficient knowledge and skill to cover complex financial instruments. Skills in this area are typically quite different to those required in other parts of the business.

When considering the risk of material misstatement in relation to complex financial instruments, auditors should consider:

- the business purpose of the entity's financial instrument activities;
- the complexity and features of the financial instruments used;
- whether the transaction involves the exchange of cash;
- the entity's experience in the field of complex financial instruments;
- whether the financial instrument includes an embedded derivative;
- whether risk is affected by external factors such as a declining market;
- whether the complex financial instrument is traded nationally or across borders; and
- the strength of the entity's control environment.

The nature and use of some complex financial instruments may increase the likelihood of fraud risk factors related to them, and this may be more marked when financial market conditions are difficult. Incentives to engage in fraudulent financial reporting may include protection of personal bonuses, hiding management error, avoiding breaching borrowing limits or avoiding reporting catastrophic losses.

28.9.5   Reliance on controls

Where auditors' assessment of risk includes an expectation that controls are operating effectively, they are required to perform tests of those controls. In determining the level of testing required in relation to complex financial instruments, auditors should consider the:

- importance of the complex financial instrument activities to the entity;
- nature, frequency and volume of complex financial instrument transactions;
- potential effect of any identified weaknesses in control procedures;
- types of control activities being tested;
- frequency of performance of these control activities;
- evidence of performance.

Key areas for evaluation are listed in **Table 2**.

TABLE 2: Key areas to be evaluated as part of testing control activities

Procedures may include evaluating whether:

- complex financial instruments have been used in accordance with the agreed policies, guidelines and within authority limits;
- appropriate decision-making processes have been applied and the reasons behind entering into selected transactions are clearly understandable;
- the transactions undertaken were within the policies for complex financial instrument transactions, including terms and limits and transactions with foreign or related parties;
- the transactions were undertaken with counterparties with appropriate credit risk;
- complex financial instruments are subject to appropriate timely measurement, and reporting of risk exposure, independent of the dealer, including regular review

---

and challenge of the valuation of transactions, the appropriateness of valuation models and variations in profit and loss;
- counterparty confirmations have been sent;
- incoming confirmation from counterparties have been properly matched and reconciled;
- early termination and extension of transactions are subject to the same controls as new transactions;
- designations, including any subsequent changes in designations, are properly authorised;
- designations, including any subsequent changes in designations, as hedging are properly authorised;
- transactions have been properly recorded and are entered completely and accurately in the accounting records, and correctly processed in any subsidiary ledger through to the financial statements; and
- adequate security has been maintained over passwords necessary for electronic fund transfers.

28.9.6   Audit procedures

Auditors are required to perform substantive procedures for each material class of transaction, account balance and disclosure. In addition, when a significant risk has been identified, they are required to perform substantive procedures that are specifically responsive to that risk.

Materiality may be difficult to determine for complex financial instruments where their impact on the balance sheet is small, but their relative risk is high, and will vary depending on the complexity of the financial instruments entered into.

In addition, auditors may have difficulty in assessing materiality for an entity using complex financial instruments, particularly if their valuation is likely to be volatile. Some assets may become liabilities between the initial assessment of materiality and the year end date. Where auditors become aware of information during the course of their audit which would have caused them to assess materiality differently, they should revise their assessment of materiality accordingly.

Auditors may need to make use of management representations to gain appropriate evidence in relation to some aspects of complex financial instrument transactions, including management's objective in entering into such transactions and whether all such transactions have been disclosed, conducted at arm's length and at market value.

In designing substantive procedures, auditors consider:
- the appropriateness of the accounting treatment;
- the involvement of a service organisation;
- interim audit procedures performed and market movements since the date at which they were performed;

- routine and non-routine transactions; and
- procedures performed in other audit areas such as cash receipts and payments.

The use of analytical procedures may be difficult as the complex interplay of the factors from which these instruments are derived often masks any unusual trends that might arise. Volatile markets also make meaningful comparisons difficult.

Existence, rights and obligations

In relation to existence and rights and obligations, substantive tests are likely to involve obtaining confirmations from the holder or, or counterparty to, the financial instrument and inspecting the underlying agreement.

Completeness

Substantive tests for completeness may include:

- sending zero balance confirmations to potential holders or counterparties to complex financial instruments;
- reviewing brokers' statements for the existence of complex financial instruments;
- reviewing unresolved reconciliation items; and
- inspecting other documentation, such as loan or equity agreements or sales contracts for embedded derivatives.

Valuation

It is management's responsibility to estimate the value of the financial instrument and auditors are required to test the valuation model used. Where quoted market prices are available, these are generally considered to provide sufficient evidence. Otherwise auditors are required to assess the valuation, and may:

- assess the reasonableness and appropriateness of the model used by the entity, including whether the variables and assumptions used are reasonable and consistently applied;
- recalculate the value using their own or a third party model;
- compare the value with recent transactions;
- consider the sensitivity of the valuation to changes in variables and assumptions; and
- inspect supporting documentation for subsequent realisation or settlement of the instrument after the balance sheet date.

It would not normally be sufficient to rely on a broker quote obtained from the institution that initially sold the instrument without further verifying that quote. This may be done by supplementing the quote with quotes from other brokers or from pricing services.

If management obtain valuations of complex financial instruments directly from third parties such as banks and other financial institutions, auditors should consider the:

- competence and objectivity of the third party, and their independence from the audited entity; and
- appropriateness of the valuation, the model used and its sensitivities.

Disclosure

Auditors consider whether complex financial instruments are presented in conformity with relevant legislation, regulations and the applicable financial reporting framework. Their judgement will be based on whether, in their opinion:

- the accounting policies selected and applied are in keeping with the relevant financial reporting framework;
- disclosure is adequate to ensure that the entity is in full compliance with the current disclosure requirements;
- the information presented in the financial statements is classified and summarised in a appropriate and meaningful manner; and
- the financial statements show a true and fair view.

Auditors are also required to consider whether information in the Directors' report relating to the use of financial instruments by the company is consistent with their knowledge of the client and their activities.

28.9.7   Evaluating audit evidence

The assertions relating to the audit of complex financial instruments may be based on highly subjective assumptions or be particularly sensitive to changes in underlying assumptions. This can make the evaluation of audit evidence challenging and management bias, whether intentional or unintentional can be difficult to detect. Examples of indicators of possible management bias with respect to accounting estimates relating to financial instruments include:

- changes in accounting estimate, or the method for making it, where management has made a subjective assessment that there has been a change in circumstances;
- use of an entity's own assumptions for fair value accounting estimates when they are inconsistent with observable market place assumptions;
- selection or construction of significant assumptions that yield a point estimate favourable for management objectives; and
- selection of a point estimate that may indicate a pattern of optimism or pessimism.

28.9.8   Management representations

Depending on the volume and complexity of financial instrument activities, management representations sought to support other evidence obtained by auditors may include:

- management objectives with respect to complex financial instruments, for example, whether they are used for hedging, asset/liability management or investment purposes;
- those relating to the financial statements disclosures concerning complex financial instruments, for example that:
  - the records reflect all complex financial instrument transactions;
  - the assumptions and methodologies used in the complex financial instrument valuation models are reasonable;
  - all embedded derivative instruments have been identified;
- whether all transactions have been conducted at arm's length and at market value;
- the terms of transactions;
- whether there are any side agreements associated with any complex financial instruments;
- whether the entity has entered into any written options;
- if applicable, the appropriateness of the basis used by management to overcome the presumption relating to the use of fair values; and
- whether subsequent events require adjustment to the valuations and disclosures included in the financial statements.

28.9.9   Considerations in difficult market conditions

When financial market conditions are difficult it can lead to the severe curtailment or even cessation of trading in certain complex financial instruments. This makes valuation of such instruments difficult, because:

- values may fluctuate rapidly; and
- there is no ready market to obtain valuations from.

In such situations, the degree of estimation increases, and this leads to an increased risk of material misstatement.

Even where a market remains, in times of economic difficulty it is important for management and auditors to examine the continuing appropriateness of models and assumptions, which may have been determined when markets were healthier.

In such difficult times, there may also be an increased risk in relation to fraudulent financial reporting. Market instability may lead to unexpected losses, and financial difficulties may create pressures on management who are concerned about the solvency of the business. This may lead to fraudulent activities to protect personal bonuses, hide management error, avoid breaching borrowing limits or avoid reporting catastrophic losses.

In auditing fair value accounting estimates, auditors may therefore need to consider whether the circumstances give risk to increased fraud risks.

29 AUDIT SAMPLING

29.1 AUDITING STANDARDS

Clarified ISA (UK and Ireland) 530 *Audit Sampling* was issued in October 2009 and replaces ISA (UK and Ireland) 530 previously issued in December 2004. The Clarified ISA (UK and Ireland) is effective for the audit of financial statements for periods ending on or after 15 December 2010. This chapter covers both the existing and Clarified ISAs (UK and Ireland). As the Clarified ISA (UK and Ireland) does not significantly amend the requirements of the existing ISA (UK and Ireland) this chapter is written on the basis of the existing requirements, and any changes to them included in the Clarified ISA (UK and Ireland) are included and clearly indicated. ISA (UK and Ireland) 530 provides guidance on sampling covering:

- use of sampling;
- risk assessment;
- design of the sample;
- sample size;
- selecting the sample;
- performing audit procedures;
- errors; and
- evaluating results.

As with all ISAs (UK and Ireland), the text of the ISA has been supplemented with additional guidance from a UK and Ireland perspective.

29.2 USE OF SAMPLING

> When designing audit procedures, the auditor should determine appropriate means for selecting items for testing so as to gather sufficient appropriate audit evidence to meet the objectives of the audit procedures. ISA (UK and Ireland) 530.

The ISA (UK and Ireland) recognises that auditors do not normally examine all of the information available but reach conclusions on, for example, account balances using audit sampling.

In the ISA (UK and Ireland), audit sampling is defined as 'the application of audit procedures to less than 100 per cent of items within a population of audit relevance such that all sampling units have a chance of selection in order to provide the auditors with a reasonable basis on which to draw conclusions about the entire population'. It does not include procedures where individual items which have a particular significance are examined, e.g., all items over £10,000, as here auditors are testing part of the population in its entirety and cannot use the results to draw conclusions about the rest of the population. Similarly, procedures such as walk-through tests are not sampling.

Auditors may use either tests of control or substantive procedures in their work. When performing tests of control, auditors identify a characteristic or attribute which indicates that a control has been implemented. This may be the signing of a purchase order or the completion of a credit check for new customers. The presence or absence of these attributes is then tested by auditors. Audit sampling for tests of control is generally appropriate when application of the control leaves audit evidence of performance, such as an approval stamp or the initials of an authorised person.

Substantive procedures can be broken down into substantive analytical procedures and tests of detail. Audit sampling will only relate to tests of detail.

29.3 RISK ASSESSMENT

ISA (UK and Ireland) 530 states that 'the auditor should use professional judgement to assess the risk of material misstatement ... and design further audit procedures to ensure that this risk is reduced to an acceptably low level'.

A population will have a risk of material misstatement as assessed by the auditor at the planning stage. The level of risk of material misstatement will have a direct bearing on the sample size used. Where there is a high risk of material misstatement the number of items tested from the population will be greater than in situations where the risk of material misstatement has been assessed as low. A higher sample size will result in lower sampling risk, increasing auditors' confidence levels that the population does not contain a material misstatement. Other factors will also affect sample sizes (see **29.5** below).

29.3.1 Sampling risk

Where sampling is used, auditors must accept a risk that the sample is not representative of the population from which it is drawn and that they may draw the wrong conclusion from the test.

Sampling risk may result in:

- a population such as a file of reconciliations, which is acceptable, being rejected because the sample happens to pick a large proportion of the items in error. This normally results in additional, unnecessary audit work but should not affect the validity of the final audit conclusion; or
- a population, which contains a material error, being accepted as satisfactory because the sample happens not to select any of the items that contain errors. This risk is more serious because there is the possibility that an unqualified audit report is issued when the financial statements contain material misstatement (although auditors should organise their other audit procedures so that it is, in fact, unlikely that such an error escapes detection).

Sampling risk does not only affect substantive procedures; tests of control may result in:

- too high an assessment of control risk, because the error in the sample is greater than that in the population; or
- too low an assessment of control risk, because the error in the sample is less than the error in the population as a whole.

Sampling risk may be reduced by using a rational (possibly a statistical) basis for planning, selecting and testing the sample and for evaluating the results. This will ensure that auditors have adequate assurance that the sample is representative of the population from which it is drawn.

29.3.2 Non-sampling risk

Non-sampling risk arises from factors that cause the auditor to reach an incorrect conclusion and is not related to the size of the sample. For example auditors may plan unsuitable audit procedures or misinterpret audit evidence and fail to recognise an error.

29.4 DESIGN OF THE SAMPLE

29.4.1 Deciding whether to sample

When designing audit procedures, the auditor must decide whether to:

- select all items in a population (100 per cent examination);
- select specific items; or
- use audit sampling.

Selecting all items

This is most appropriate for tests of detail, for example where the population constitutes a small number of large value items or where CAATs are used to test or reperform all the transactions in the period.

Selecting specific items

The decision to select specific items from population will be based on the auditor's knowledge of the client, the assessed risk of material misstatement and the characteristics of the population itself. Items selected may include:

- high value or key items (i.e., those which are themselves material, or have some other characteristic);
- all items over a certain amount;
- items to obtain information; and
- items to test control activities.

Audit sampling

Audit sampling may be applied to a class of transactions or account balances. Either non-statistical or statistic approaches may be used (see **29.9**).

29.4.2 Designing the sample

When designing an audit sample, the auditor should consider the objectives of the audit procedure and the attributes of the population from which the sample will be drawn.

When designing an audit sample the auditor should also consider the sampling and selection methods (ISA (UK and Ireland) 530)

Objectives

Auditors choose the audit procedures that are most likely to achieve the stated audit objectives. Once the procedures have been decided they design the most appropriate form of sampling. This involves identifying conditions that are to be regarded as errors. For example, in a test of controls operating over purchases, non-compliance with the approval procedures may be assessed as an error. By contrast the types of errors on a substantive test on sales invoices might be arithmetical inaccuracy and/or a failure to reflect them properly in the books of account.

Population

Auditors need to ensure that they are extracting the sample from the appropriate population to test the specific audit objectives. This is more difficult when the audit objective is testing for understatement, such as the understatement of creditors, as the sample is chosen from a related population. The relevant population for such a test of understatement might be suppliers' statements, post-period payments or a list of all suppliers during the period, rather than unpaid invoices. In these cases auditors need to take steps to ensure that the chosen population is complete, such as choosing suppliers' statements from a list taken from the purchase ledger.

The sampling unit is any of the individual items that make up the population and will vary according to the nature of the audit test. The auditors define the sampling unit in order to obtain an efficient and effective sample to achieve their audit objective. For example, when testing the validity of debtors the sampling unit is the individual customer balances or invoices.

Stratification

By dividing a population into discrete sub-populations, sample sizes can be reduced without increasing sampling risk. Populations are often subdivided by monetary value, meaning greater audit effort can be directed to larger value items. However, the results of audit procedures performed on a stratified population can only be projected to items in the same stratum; other items will have to be tested separately.

Value-weighted selection

When sampling for tests of details, auditors may define the sampling unit as the monetary unit that makes up the population, e.g., each £1 of the balance. Auditors will then test the balance containing the £1 sampling unit. This means that larger balances have more chance of being selected for testing than smaller ones.

29.5 SAMPLE SIZE

In determining the sample size, the auditor should consider whether sampling risk is reduced to an acceptably low level.

Sample size is affected by the level of sampling risk that auditors are willing to accept. The lower the acceptable risk, the greater the sample size will need to be.

Examples of some factors affecting sample sizes, taken from the ISA (UK and Ireland), are shown in **Table 1** and **Table 2**.

TABLE 1: Some factors influencing sample size for substantive tests

Factor	*Impact on sample size*
Inherent risk[1]	The higher the assessment of inherent risk, the more audit evidence is required to support the auditors' conclusion.
Control risk[2]	The higher the assessment of control risk, the greater the reliance on audit evidence obtained from substantive procedures.
	A high control risk assessment may result in the decision not to perform tests of control and reliance entirely on substantive procedures.
Detection risk[3]	Sampling risk for substantive tests is one form of detection risk. The lower the sampling risk the auditors are willing to accept, the larger the sample size.
	Other substantive procedures may provide audit evidence regarding the same financial statement assertions and reduce detection risk. This may reduce the extent of the auditors' reliance on the results of the substantive procedure using audit sampling.
	The lower the reliance on the results of a substantive procedure using audit sampling, the higher the sampling risk auditors are willing to accept, and, consequently, the smaller the sample size.
Tolerable error rate	The higher monetary value of the tolerable error rate, the smaller the sample size and vice versa.

Factor	Impact on sample size
Expected error rate	If errors are expected, a larger sample usually needs to be examined to confirm that the actual error rate is less than the tolerable error rate.
Population value	The less material the monetary value of the population to the financial statements, the smaller the sample size that may be required.
Numbers of items in population	Virtually no effect on sample size unless population is small.
Stratification	If it is appropriate to stratify the population this may lead to a smaller sample size.

Notes

[1] Inherent risk is the susceptibility of an account balance or class of transactions to material misstatement, either individually or when aggregated with misstatements in other balances or classes, irrespective of related internal controls (see **Chapter 22**).

[2] Control risk is the risk that a misstatement that could occur in an account balance or class of transactions. The misstatement could be material, either individually or when aggregated with misstatements in other balances or classes, and would not be prevented, or detected and corrected on a timely basis, by the accounting and internal control systems (see **Chapter 22**).

[3] Detection risk is the risk that auditors' substantive procedures do not detect a misstatement that exists in an account balance or class of transactions, which could be material, either individually or when aggregated with misstatements in other balances or classes (see **Chapter 22**).

TABLE 2: Some factors influencing sample size for tests of controls

Factor	Impact on sample size
Sampling risk	The greater the reliance on the results of a test of control using audit sampling, the lower the sampling risk the auditors are willing to accept and, consequently, the larger the sample size.
	The lower the assessment of control risk, the more likely the auditors are to place reliance on audit evidence from tests of control.
Control risk	A high control risk assessment may result in a decision not to perform tests of control.
Tolerable error rate	The higher the tolerable rate the lower the sample size and vice versa.
Expected error rate	If errors are expected, a larger sample usually needs to be examined to confirm that the actual error rate is less than the tolerable error rate. High expected error rates may result in a decision not to perform tests of control.
Number of items in population	Virtually no effect on sample size unless population is small.

29.6 SELECTING THE SAMPLE

ISA (UK and Ireland) 530 requires auditors to select items for the sample with the expectation that all sampling units in the population have a chance of selection. In other words, all items in the population must have an opportunity of being selected although this need not be equal. For example, auditors will often choose samples so as to give higher value items a greater chance of selection.

The three most common methods of selecting a sample are:

- random selection, where each item has an equal chance of selection, using random number tables or CAATs;
- systematic selection, using a constant interval between selections and a randomly selected starting point. Where this method is being used it is important that the population is not structured in such a way that the sampling interval used corresponds to a particular pattern in the population; and
- haphazard selection, so long as there is no bias in the selection.

29.7 PERFORMING AUDIT PROCEDURES

Auditors perform the planned procedures on each item in the sample. If any item selected is not appropriate a replacement item should be chosen. However, auditors should consider whether the unsatisfactory item indicates an error. If procedures cannot be completed on a sample item, for example the supporting documentation has been lost, alternative audit procedures should be considered for that item. If no alternative procedures are possible, the item should be considered to be an error.

29.8 ERRORS

ISA (UK and Ireland) 530 requires auditors to consider the sample results, the nature and cause of any errors identified, and their possible effect on the particular audit objective and other areas of the audit.

Before evaluating the results of a sample, auditors need to establish whether a matter detected is an error. There may be instances where such a matter does not meet the criteria for an error that were set in the planning of the test. For example, a substantive test of the validity of debtors may indicate that there has been a misposting between customer accounts. This does not lead to a misstatement of the total trade debtor balance; therefore in evaluating the sample it may be inappropriate to consider that this is an error. However, there may be implications for other areas of the audit, such as the recoverability of debtors.

The qualitative aspects of the error also need to be considered, particularly the nature and cause of the error, as they may have implications for other audit areas. It may be that all the errors fall within a particular time period or are at one location, in which case it may be possible to identify the extent of the error in the rest of the population. For example, if the member of staff who inputs the sales invoices on to the system was away from work for a month and the replacement was entering the net amount of the invoice instead of the gross amount, an exercise could be undertaken to quantify the extent of the error by comparing the total of that month's gross and net sales.

29.8.1 *Tolerable misstatement*

This is the maximum error that is acceptable to the auditors, if they are to conclude that their audit objectives have been achieved. This is not necessarily the same as materiality, which relates to the financial statements as a whole rather than a particular balance or class of transactions, although it is the application of performance materiality in the case of substantive testing (see **Chapter 18**). The tolerable misstatement may be the same amount or an amount lower than performance materiality. Where tests of control are being performed, the tolerable level of error will be the maximum rate of failure of an internal control that the auditors are prepared to accept.

29.8.2 *Expected error*

Before a test is performed an error may already be expected. Here, a larger number of items may need to be tested to conclude that the actual error in the population is not greater than the planned tolerable error. This may be the case where previous years' audit tests have produced errors or the review of the internal controls indicates this.

29.8.3 *Projecting errors*

For tests of details, the auditor should project monetary errors found in the sample to the population, and should consider the effect of the projected error on the particular audit objective and on other areas of the audit.

When projecting errors found in the sample for tests of detail to the population from which it was drawn, the method used must be consistent with that used to select the sample. Projection commonly involves extrapolating the errors in the sample and estimating any further error not detected due to the imprecision of the methods used.

To assess whether errors in the population might exceed the tolerable error, the projected population error (net of adjustments made by the entity) should be compared with the tolerable error, taking into account the results of other audit procedures relevant to that financial statement assertion.

Where the projected errors exceed the tolerable error, auditors reassess sampling risk and if they conclude that it is unacceptable (for example, they have insufficient confidence in the results of the sample) they should consider:

- extending their own audit procedures; or
- performing alternative procedures (which may involve reviewing a client's exercise to investigate errors).

This will enable them to conclude on the test and may result in identifying the need for an adjustment to the financial statements.

Anomalous errors, i.e., errors which arise from an isolated event that has not recurred other than on a specifically identifiable occasion, may be excluded when projecting errors to the population. This is because anomalous errors will not be representative of the population as a whole. However, their effect still needs to be considered in addition to the projection of non-anomalous errors.

Projection of errors is not appropriate for tests of control. On discovering errors in a test of control, auditors should consider whether the error is indicative of a general weakness in the control system.

29.9   EVALUATING RESULTS

Auditors should assess the results of the sample tested to determine if the objectives of the test have been met.

For tests of control, a high incidence of errors may lead auditors to increase their assessment of the risk of material misstatement. For tests of detail, high error rates may indicate that a class of transactions or an account balance is materially misstated.

Auditors should use judgement where the projected error in a sample, plus any anomalous error which was not subject to projection, is close to their assessment of tolerable error. Auditors should be aware that sampling risk may mean that selection of a different sample may have provided an error which was greater than tolerable error. Auditors should consider the results of other audit procedures when assessing whether an adjustment to the financial statements is required.

If auditors determine that test objectives have not been met, they may:

- request those charged with governance to investigate identified errors and the potential for further errors and to make any necessary adjustments; and/ or

- modify the nature, timing and extent of further audit procedures. For example in the case of tests of controls, the auditor might extend the sample size, test an alternative control or modify related substantive procedures; and/or
- consider the effect on the audit report.

29.10 STATISTICAL AND NON-STATISTICAL SAMPLING

There are several similarities between statistical and non-statistical sampling. Both:

- examine less than the total population to reach a conclusion about the population;
- involve sampling risk;
- provide approximate, not exact, knowledge about the population;
- perform the same audit steps; and
- require audit judgement.

One major difference between statistical and non-statistical methods is that a statistical sample must be selected using an appropriate statistical basis from the population while, although desirable, this is not essential for non-statistical methods.

Not every audit sample is worth performing on a rigorous statistical basis. Non-statistical sampling may be used whenever auditors conclude that the additional costs of statistical sampling, such as set-up time, are in excess of the benefits to be obtained, for example, objectivity of sample selection and evaluation. Non-statistical sampling may be preferable in situations where the statistical selection is difficult to make because the records are not readily accessible or are in a form that makes it difficult to make a valid statistical selection. For example, at the physical stocktaking, when selecting items for test counting from floor to stock sheet there is no list of the population from which a statistical sample can be taken. In these cases, statistical sample sizes can still be used to get an idea of an appropriate sample size.

When using non-statistical methods, auditors also need to be satisfied that the selection is appropriate to obtain a reasonable conclusion and that they have not used these methods to exclude difficult items. Non-statistical sampling does not automatically solve problems or turn documents with errors into correct documents. Every item selected should be audited (and not replaced if not found). For example, a missing invoice should be investigated rather than inspecting the next available invoice. A conclusion about the population should be drawn from the sample evidence.

Approximate sample sizes should be generated for a population whether statistical or non-statistical methods are used. The sample size will depend on a number of factors such as population size, materiality and identified risk, and these will remain identical whichever sampling approach is used.

Statistical sampling is more likely to be used whenever auditors conclude that the benefits are greater than the costs. Examples of this include situations where:

- the set-up time and selection time are reasonable in relation to the time required to test the selected items and follow up on discrepancies (more likely to be true for larger tests than for smaller ones);
- the most extensive part of the test is a representative selection, not the selection of material or unusual items;
- records of the entire population are reasonably accessible for the purpose of making the selection (although even if they are not readily accessible, statistical sampling could be desirable if it is likely that a non-statistical selection would yield an inappropriate conclusion because of a failure to include inconvenient records in the selection); and
- the selection of the statistical sample can be effected easily, perhaps with the aid of computer-assisted techniques.

Even where the approach adopted does not meet the criteria for statistical sampling, elements of the statistical approach may still be used, for example the use of random selection of items to be tested using computer-generated random numbers.

30 MANAGEMENT REPRESENTATIONS

30.1 AUDITING STANDARDS

Clarified ISA (UK and Ireland) 580 *Written Representations* was issued in October 2009 and is effective for the audit of financial statements for periods ending on or after 15 December 2010. The updated ISA (UK and Ireland) replaces ISA (UK and Ireland) 580 issued in December 2004. This chapter covers both the existing and Clarified ISAs (UK and Ireland). As the Clarified ISA (UK and Ireland) adds to the requirements of the existing ISA (UK and Ireland) this chapter is written on the basis of the existing requirements, and changes to them included in the Clarified ISA (UK and Ireland) are included and clearly indicated.

The ISA (UK and Ireland) provides guidance on the need to gain written confirmation of management representations and covers:

- management responsibilities;
- representations by management as audit evidence;
- documentation of representations; and
- refusal to provide written representations.

As with all ISAs (UK and Ireland), the text of the ISA has been supplemented with additional guidance from a UK and Ireland perspective.

In November 2002, the Audit and Assurance Faculty of the ICAEW issued an Explanatory Note on Management Representation Letters (Audit 04/02). The aim of the Note is to help auditors increase the usefulness of management representation letters as audit evidence by suggesting methods to ensure that representations are reliable. The Explanatory Note is detailed in **30.8** below.

30.2 REQUIREMENT TO OBTAIN WRITTEN CONFIRMATION

During the course of their audit, auditors receive oral representations from management in response to particular enquiries. ISA (UK and Ireland) 580 requires that auditors obtain written confirmation of appropriate representations from management before they issue their report. In this context, management includes senior management, the directors and members of the audit committee.

Written confirmations may be in the form of:

- a representation letter from management;

- a letter from the auditors outlining their understanding of management's representations, duly acknowledged and confirmed by management; or
- minutes of meetings of the board of directors at which such representations are approved.

30.3 ACKNOWLEDGEMENT OF DIRECTORS' RESPONSIBILITY

ISA (UK and Ireland) 580 requires auditors to obtain evidence that those charged with governance acknowledge their collective responsibility for the fair presentation of the financial statements in accordance with the applicable financial reporting framework, and has approved the financial statements. This applies to all financial statements, not only those prepared by the auditors on behalf of the directors.

In addition, management are also required to provide written representation that:

- they have provided auditors with all relevant information and access agreed in the terms of the audit engagement; and
- all transactions have been recorded and are reflected in the financial statements.

This last representation may refer to a threshold amount agreed with the auditor or to state that all transactions that may have a material effect on the financial statements have been recorded.

The requirements in relation to the representations listed above have been strengthened in the Clarified ISA. In addition, the Clarified ISA (UK and Ireland) states that if management does not provide written representations acknowledging its responsibilities, auditors are required to disclaim an opinion on the financial statements.

The use of language to the effect that the representations are made to the best of management's knowledge and belief does not invalidate the representation as long as, during the audit, auditors have found no evidence that the representations are incorrect.

This acknowledgement can be achieved by the auditors receiving:

- relevant minutes from the directors' meeting;
- a written representation from the directors; or
- a signed copy of the financial statements which incorporates a statement of directors' responsibilities.

The last of these is generally included either in the directors' report or in a separate statement. A signed copy of the financial statements, however, is not, by itself, sufficient appropriate evidence to confirm other representations made throughout the audit.

In group situations, acknowledgement of the directors' responsibilities applies to the group financial statements as well as those of the parent undertaking.

The failure by management to provide the relevant representation about their responsibilities will lead to a disclaimer of opinion.

30.4 REPRESENTATIONS BY MANAGEMENT AS AUDIT EVIDENCE

In addition to the written confirmations of representations concerning the management's responsibilities in **30.3** above, ISA (UK and Ireland) 580 requires auditors to obtain them for matters material to the financial statements when other appropriate audit evidence cannot reasonably be expected to exist. It is suggested that auditors discuss these matters with those responsible for providing the written confirmation before they sign it to reduce the possibility of misunderstanding.

The auditors should assess the reasonableness of the representations on material matters. This may be achieved by:

- obtaining corroborative evidence from inside or outside the entity;
- assessing the representations for any inconsistency with other audit evidence obtained; and
- considering whether the individuals who made the representations can be expected to be well-informed on the matter.

To address concerns that auditors may be over-relying on written representations, Clarified ISA (UK and Ireland) 580 reasserts that, although written representations provide necessary audit evidence, they support other audit evidence obtained and do not on their own provide sufficient appropriate audit evidence about any of the matters with which they deal. Where no other evidence is available it could lead to a qualification to the auditor's report because of a limitation of scope.

This also applies to cases where there is a genuine limitation of scope and the auditors do not expect any other evidence to be available. For example, where auditors are appointed after the end of the reporting period and are unable to find any means of verifying material quantities of stock, management representations could never be sufficient evidence on their own to support quantities.

There will, however, be instances when no supporting evidence is available and cannot reasonably be expected to be available, and where written confirmation of the representation will constitute acceptable evidence. For example, when auditing a deferred tax provision auditors may need to accept representations about management's intentions in regard to future capital spending. Similarly, where the carrying value of one particular line of stock can only be supported by a proposed future marketing programme, representations concerning this are likely to be an essential part of the audit evidence. In such cases the auditors should ensure that nothing conflicts with the representations and that, when combined with other evidence, it supports an unqualified opinion.

In exceptional cases a matter may be so significant that the auditor makes reference to the representation in the audit report.

An example of a management representation letter from management to the auditors is shown in **Table 1** at **30.7**. It should be tailored for the circumstances of each client.

When consolidated financial statements are being produced there will be representations which are relevant to the group, in addition to those for the parent undertaking. Such representations may be obtained from either the directors of the parent undertaking or directly from those of the subsidiary. The method chosen will depend on the decision-making structure of the group. For example, where the parent company directors, or a proportion of them, are involved in the operational management of the subsidiary, the representations may be obtained directly from them by virtue of their day-to-day involvement.

30.5   CONTRADICTORY AUDIT EVIDENCE

Where there is a contradiction between the representation and other audit evidence, auditors should investigate the circumstances through discussions with management and other substantive procedures, and where necessary, reconsider the reliability of other representations and the competence, integrity, ethical values or diligence of management.

30.6   BASIC ELEMENTS OF A MANAGEMENT REPRESENTATION LETTER

The auditors need to ensure that when they request a management representation letter that it:

- is addressed to them;
- contains specified information, i.e., additional paragraphs may be needed;
- is appropriately dated; and
- is signed by someone with the appropriate level of authority.

In most cases, it will be appropriate for the chairman and the secretary to sign the letter on behalf of the Board based on the best of their knowledge and belief and having made appropriate enquiries of other members of management. Often the letter is discussed by the Board of directors before they approve the financial statements to ensure that all members are aware of the representations on which the auditors intend to rely in expressing their opinion on those financial statements.

The letter will normally be dated on the date of the audit report.

Where there is a delay in completing the audit after the date of receipt of the representation letter, auditors should consider whether there is a need to obtain further representations in respect of the intervening period and also whether they should extend their post balance sheet event review.

30.7 REFUSAL TO PROVIDE WRITTEN CONFIRMATION

ISA (UK and Ireland) 580 requires that where management refuses to provide the auditors with written confirmation of the representations, the auditors should consider whether this leads to a limitation of scope requiring either a qualified opinion or a disclaimer of opinion.

This will mean that the auditors need to reconsider any representations that they have relied on during the course of their audit.

TABLE 1: Example letter of representation

ABC & Co 1 High Street London

Dear Sirs

Financial Statements at 31 March 20..

We confirm to the best of our knowledge and belief, and having made appropriate enquiries of other directors and officials of the company, the following representations given to you in connection with your audit of the company's financial statements for the year ended 31 March 20 . . .

We acknowledge as directors our responsibility under the Companies Act 2006 for preparing the financial statements which give a true and fair view and for making accurate representations to you. All the accounting records have been made available to you for the purpose of your audit and all the transactions undertaken by the company have been properly reflected and recorded in the accounting records. All other records and related information, including minutes of all management and shareholder's meetings have been made available to you.

We confirm that we believe that the effects of the uncorrected financial statements misstatements listed in the attached schedule are not material to the financial statements, either individually or in aggregate.

The legal claim by XYZ Limited has been settled out of court by a payment of £ . . . . No further amounts are expected to be paid and no similar claims have been received or are expected to be received.

In connection with deferred tax not provided, the following assumptions reflect the intentions and expectations of the company:

capital investment of £ . . . is planned over the next three years;

there are no plans to sell revalued properties; and

we are not aware of any indications that the situation is likely to change so as to necessitate the inclusion of a provision for tax payable in the financial statements.

The company has not had, or entered into, at any time during the period any arrangement, transaction or agreement to provide credit facilities (including loans, quasi-loans or credit transactions) for directors or to guarantee or provide security for such matters.

There have been no events since the balance sheet date which necessitate revision of the figures included in the financial statements or inclusion of a note thereto.

We confirm that the above representations are made on the basis of enquiries of management and staff with relevant knowledge and experience (and where appropriate, of inspection of supporting documentation) sufficient to satisfy ourselves that we can properly make each of the above representations to you.

As minuted by the board of directors at its meeting on ....

Chairman _____

Secretary _____

30.8 AUDIT 4/02: MANAGEMENT REPRESENTATION LETTERS, EXPLANATORY NOTE

In November 2002, the Audit and Assurance Faculty of the ICAEW issued an Explanatory Note on *Management Representation Letters* (Audit 04/02). The guidance was issued following a recent High Court decision concerning the audit of Barings Futures (Singapore) Pte Ltd (BFS) by Deloitte & Touche (D&T).

The guidance in the Note supplemented SAS 440 *Management Representations* and is still relevant under ISA (UK and Ireland) 580. It does not, however, constitute an Auditing Standard in its own right.

30.8.1 The case

Deloitte & Touche faced a claim in damages following their audit of BFS, and attempted to defend themselves by stating that management representations provided to them were recklessly fraudulent, as they were made by a director of BFS who had little knowledge of Nick Leeson's activities, despite being nominally his reporting superior.

However, their claim failed because they could not prove that the director signed the representation letter whilst:

- knowing that the statements were untrue; and
- knowing that he had no reasonable grounds for making the statements.

Despite Deloitte & Touche not winning their argument, the Judge did state that if they had been successful he would have held BFS vicariously liable for the director's actions.

30.8.2 *Increasing the usefulness of representation letters as audit evidence*

The Explanatory Note re-emphasises the requirement that auditors should discuss the contents of the representation letter with management, so that they understand what they are being asked to sign. Auditors should also consider whether the person signing the letter is in a position to enable them to sign the letter in full knowledge of the matters contained therein.

The Note suggests adding the following statement to all management representation letters to focus the attention of those signing the letter on whether proper enquiries have been made:

'We confirm that the above representations are made on the basis of enquiries of management and staff with relevant knowledge and experience (and, where appropriate, of inspection of supporting documentation) sufficient to satisfy yourselves that we can properly make each of the above representations to you.'

Auditors may also ask signatories what enquiries have been made of management and staff and how they went about this process. Where signatories have themselves obtained written representations from others, for example in relation to complex or specialist areas such as financial instruments, these may be attached to the management representation letter itself and referred to in the letter. Auditors may also wish to impress upon their clients that it is an offence under s501 of the 2006 Companies Act to knowingly or recklessly make a misleading or false statement to the company's auditors.

31 OPENING BALANCES AND COMPARATIVES

31.1 AUDITING STANDARDS

Clarified ISA (UK and Ireland) 510 *Initial Engagements – Opening Balances and Continuing Engagements – Opening Balances* and Clarified ISA (UK and Ireland) 710 *Comparative Information – Corresponding Figures and Comparative Financial Statements* were issued in October 2009 and replace ISA (UK and Ireland) 300 previously issued in December 2004. The Clarified ISAs (UK and Ireland) are effective for the audit of financial statements for periods ending on or after 15 December 2010. This chapter covers both the existing and Clarified ISAs (UK and Ireland). As the Clarified ISAs (UK and Ireland) do not significantly amend the requirements of the existing ISAs (UK and Ireland) this chapter is written on the basis of the existing requirements, and any changes to them included in the Clarified ISAs (UK and Ireland) are included and clearly indicated.

As with all ISAs (UK and Ireland), the text of the international ISAs have been supplemented with additional guidance from a UK and Ireland perspective.

31.2 AUDITORS' RESPONSIBILITIES

ISAs (UK and Ireland) 510 and 710 require auditors to obtain sufficient evidence to ensure that accounts derived from the previous financial statements are:

- free from material misstatement; and
- incorporated appropriately in the current financial statements.

In the UK, auditors have no statutory responsibility to report specifically on corresponding or comparative amounts.

They do, however, have to report that the financial statements have been properly prepared under the Companies Act and as corresponding amounts are required by the Companies Act, this requirement imposes a responsibility to ensure that these amounts have been correctly extracted and, where appropriate, properly restated to achieve consistency and comparability.

31.3 OPENING BALANCES

As part of their audit evidence, auditors should confirm under ISA (UK and Ireland) 510 that:

- opening balances have been appropriately brought forward;
- opening balances are free from material error or misstatement; and
- appropriate accounting policies are consistently applied, or where there are changes these are adequately accounted for and disclosed.

Evidence may be obtained by:

- for incoming auditors, reviewing the predecessor auditor's working papers to obtain evidence regarding the opening balances;
- evaluating whether audit procedures performed in the current period provide evidence relevant to the opening balances; or
- performing specific audit procedures to obtain evidence regarding the opening balances.

Where such evidence cannot be obtained, auditors should consider the implications for their report. An example of the report is shown in **Table 1**.

TABLE 1: Unable to obtain evidence regarding opening balances

Extract from independent auditors' report to the shareholders of XYZ Ltd

Scope of audit

A description of the scope of an audit of financial statements is [provided on the APB's web-site at *www.frc.org.uk/apb/scope/UKNP*]/[set out [on page x] of the Annual Report].

Qualified opinion arising from limitation in audit scope

The evidence available to us was limited because we were not appointed auditors of the company until [*date*] and in consequence it was not possible for us to perform the auditing procedures necessary to obtain sufficient appropriate audit evidence as regards [*specify and evaluate the balances involved*] included in the preceding years' financial statements at £ . . . .. Any adjustment to [*these figures*] would have a consequential effect on the profit for the year ended 31 December 20 . . .

Except for any adjustments that might have been found to be necessary had we been able to obtain sufficient evidence concerning [*specify the balances involved*] as at 1 January 20 . . . in our opinion the financial statements:

- give a true and fair view of the state of the company's affairs as at [date] and of its profit [loss] for the year then ended;
- have been properly prepared in accordance with United Kingdom Generally Accepted Accounting Practice; and
- have been prepared in accordance with the requirements of the Companies Act 2006.

Opinion on other matter prescribed by the Companies Act 2006

In our opinion the information given in the Directors' Report for the financial year for which the financial statements are prepared is consistent with the financial statements.

Matters on which we are required to report by exception

In respect solely of the limitation on our work relating to [*specify balances involved*]:

- we have not obtained all the information and explanations that we considered necessary for the purpose of our audit; and
- we were unable to determine whether proper accounting records had been maintained.

We have nothing to report in respect of the following matters where the Companies Act 2006 requires us to report to you if, in our opinion:

- returns adequate for our audit have not been received from branches not visited by us; or
- the financial statements are not in agreement with the accounting records and returns; or
- certain disclosures of directors' remuneration specified by law are not made.

[*Signature*]
John Smith (Senior statutory auditor)
For and on behalf of ABC LLP, Statutory Auditor
Address
Date

31.3.1   Continuing auditors

Where their previous report was unqualified and their current audit has not cast any doubt on the opening balances, auditors may limit their procedures to ensuring that:

- the opening balances have been brought forward correctly; and
- the accounting policies have been consistently applied, or if there has been a change in policy that this is accounted for and disclosed properly.

In cases where the previous report was qualified, auditors should, in addition to those procedures noted above, consider whether the matter giving rise to the qualification has been resolved and properly dealt with in the current financial statements. Even if it is resolved it may still give rise to a qualification (see **31.4.1** below).

31.3.2   Incoming auditors

The guidance to the ISA (UK and Ireland) suggests that the sufficiency and appropriateness of the evidence incoming auditors require depends on:

- the entity's accounting policies;
- whether the previous financial statements were audited, and if so, whether the report was qualified;

- the nature of the opening balances and the risk of misstatement in the current financial statements; and
- the materiality of the opening balances relative to the current financial statements.

This means that in general more evidence is expected to support balances from previous years which affect the current year's results, for example, stock or debtors, where these are material. Where the level of activity has increased significantly and the relative importance of these figures is diminished, less evidence would be necessary.

Incoming auditors must carry out more extensive procedures than continuing auditors and these will include:

- consultations with management and review of the previous period's accounting records and control procedures; and
- substantive procedures on the opening balances, if other procedures on the current period to confirm the opening position do not provide sufficient evidence.

In situations where the previous financial statements were not audited, because of entitlement to audit exemption (see **Chapter 7**), and where auditors are unable to obtain sufficient appropriate evidence from alternative procedures, they should consider the implications for their report. This will usually lead to a qualification, or in rare cases a disclaimer, on the basis of a limitation of scope depending on the effect of the unaudited figures on the financial statements. An example of such a qualified report where the company took advantage of audit exemption in the previous year is shown in **Table 2**.

TABLE 2: Extract from example report where previous year's figures are unaudited (subject to audit exemption report)

To the shareholders of XYZ Limited

Scope of audit

A description of the scope of an audit of financial statements is [provided on the APB's web-site at *www.frc.org.uk/apb/scope/UKNP*]/[set out [on page x] of the Annual Report].

Qualified opinion arising from limitation in audit scope

The evidence available to us was limited because we were appointed auditors during the year and we have been unable to carry out auditing procedures necessary to obtain adequate assurance regarding the opening balances and comparative figures because the financial statements for the year ended 31 December 20 . . . were unaudited. Any adjustments to the opening balances would have a consequential effect on the profit for the year. In addition, the amounts shown as corresponding amounts for the year ended 31 December 20 . . . may not be comparable with the figures for the current period.

Except for any adjustments that might have been found to be necessary had we been able to obtain sufficient evidence concerning the opening balances as at 1 January 20 . . . in our opinion the financial statements:

- give a true and fair view of the state of the company's affairs as at [date] and of its profit [loss] for the year then ended;
- have been properly prepared in accordance with United Kingdom Generally Accepted Accounting Practice; and
- have been prepared in accordance with the requirements of the Companies Act 2006.

Opinion on other matter prescribed by the Companies Act 2006

In our opinion the information given in the Directors' Report for the financial year for which the financial statements are prepared is consistent with the financial statements.

Matters on which we are required to report by exception

In respect solely of the limitation on our work relating to opening balances:

- we have not obtained all the information and explanations that we considered necessary for the purpose of our audit; and
- we were unable to determine whether proper accounting records had been maintained.

We have nothing to report in respect of the following matters where the Companies Act 2006 requires us to report to you if, in our opinion:

- returns adequate for our audit have not been received from branches not visited by us; or
- the financial statements are not in agreement with the accounting records and returns; or
- certain disclosures of directors' remuneration specified by law are not made.

[*Signature*]
John Smith (Senior statutory auditor)
For and on behalf of ABC LLP, Statutory Auditor
Address
Date

31.4 COMPARATIVES

As with opening balances, auditors should obtain evidence that comparatives are not materially misstated. ISA (UK and Ireland) 710 requires that evidence is obtained to confirm that:

- accounting policies are consistent, or if there has been a change that this is properly accounted for and disclosed;
- the comparative figures agree with those in the previous financial statements and are free from material error in the context of the current financial statements; and
- where comparatives have been adjusted because of material errors and misstatements that this is properly disclosed.

Where auditors are unable to obtain such evidence, they should consider the implications for their report.

The ISA (UK and Ireland) states that written representations received from management should cover both the current and all comparative periods as reaffirmation is needed that representations made previously about comparative information are still relevant. Auditors are also required to obtain a written representation regarding any restatement made to correct a material misstatement in prior period financial statements that affect the comparative information.

For continuing auditors, as long as they have no concerns about prior year items, procedures are normally restricted to ensuring that the comparatives have been correctly brought forward and disclosed.

31.4.1   *Qualified reports*

The effect that a qualified report has on the report in the subsequent period will depend on:

- the nature of the qualification; and
- whether the matter has been resolved and correctly reflected in the financial statements.

The reasons for the qualification in one period may have knock-on effects into the next. The effect of a qualification on a subsequent period depends on whether or not the matter has been resolved:

(a)   when the matter is unresolved, and is material in the context of the current period's opening balances as well as comparatives, auditors should qualify the current period audit report in respect of opening balances and comparatives;

(b)   where the matter is unresolved and does not effect the opening balances, but is material to the comparatives shown in the current financial statements, auditors should qualify their report in respect of the comparatives; and

(c)   where the matter has been resolved, but is material to the current period, the auditors should include an emphasis of matter paragraph in their report on the current period explaining how it has been dealt with.

In (a) the qualified opinion would describe the matter and its effect on the current and preceding years' figures. An example of this would be where in a previous year the company had made a provision for the permanent diminution in value of a fixed asset which the auditors did not believe was necessary. In subsequent years they would qualify their report in respect of the consequential understatement of the depreciation charge and corresponding understatement of the asset and give an 'except for' opinion.

A further example would be a disagreement over the necessity for a provision against a debtor. **Table 3** shows the opinion paragraph that would be appropriate.

Where an auditors' report on the previous year contained a limitation of scope disclaimer covering all aspects of the report, it would be unlikely that they could satisfy themselves on the profit and loss account or the cash flow statement in the next year, even if they obtained sufficient evidence that the balance sheet for that year showed a true and fair view.

TABLE 3: Preceding period was qualified and the matter has not been resolved

Extract from independent auditor's report to the shareholders of XYZ Ltd

Qualified opinion arising from disagreement about accounting treatment

Included in the debtors shown on the balance sheet of 31 December 20 . . . and 31 December 20 . . . is an amount of £Y which is the subject of litigation and against which no provision has been made. In our opinion, full provision of £Y should have been made in the year ended 31 December 20 . . . reducing profit before tax for the year ended 31 December 20 . . . and net assets at 31 December 20 . . . and 31 December 20 . . . by that amount.

Except for the financial effect of not making the provision referred to in the preceding paragraph, in our opinion the financial statements:

- give a true and fair view of the state of the company's affairs as at [date] and of its profit [loss] for the year then ended;
- have been properly prepared in accordance with United Kingdom Generally Accepted Accounting Practice; and
- have been prepared in accordance with the requirements of the Companies Act 2006.

Opinion on other matter prescribed by the Companies Act 2006

In our opinion the information given in the Directors' Report for the financial year for which the financial statements are prepared is consistent with the financial statements.

Matters on which we are required to report by exception

We have nothing to report in respect of the following matters where the Companies Act 2006 requires us to report to you if, in our opinion:

- adequate accounting records have not been kept or returns adequate for our audit have not been received from branches not visited by us; or
- the financial statements are not in agreement with the accounting records and returns; or
- certain disclosures of directors' remuneration specified by law are not made; or
- we have not received all the information and explanations we required for our audit.

[*Signature*]
John Smith (Senior statutory auditor)
For and on behalf of ABC LLP, Statutory Auditor
Address

Date

Where this occurs it normally affects areas such as stock and work in progress or debtors and creditors at the beginning of the period, uncertainty about which directly affects the profit and loss account and the cash flow statements. Where the effect is material either a qualification or disclaimer on the grounds of limitation of scope is needed depending on the effect of the limitation on the audit procedures and the significance of the amounts involved to the financial statements. An example of such a disclaimer is shown in **Table 4** of **Chapter 4**.

An example of (b) might be a limitation of scope in respect of the accounting records kept in the first six months of the year which had been destroyed by a fire but which had not led to a qualification in respect of the balance sheet. In the subsequent year there would be an 'except for' opinion in respect of the corresponding profit and loss figures as the auditors would still not have sufficient evidence on them.

Similarly, if there was a change in auditors in the previous period and that previous report contained the limitation of scope shown in **Table 6** of **Chapter 4**, the subsequent report will refer to this, as shown in **Table 4** below.

Situation (c) would result from a fundamental uncertainty which was not properly disclosed in the previous financial statements resulting in a disagreement which has now been resolved.

TABLE 4: Previous qualification not affecting opening balances

Extract from independent auditors' report to the shareholders of XYZ Ltd

Scope of audit

A description of the scope of an audit of financial statements is [provided on the APB's web-site at *www.frc.org.uk/apb/scope/UKNP*]/[set out [on page x] of the Annual Report].

Qualified opinion arising from limitation in audit scope

However, the evidence available to us was limited in relation to the comparatives in the current year's financial statements which are derived from the financial statements for the year ended 31 December 20 . . . In our report on those financial statements we stated that, because we were appointed auditors on 30 June 20 . . . it was not possible for us to perform the auditing procedures necessary to obtain sufficient appropriate audit evidence concerning the quantities and condition of certain stock and work in progress included in the balance sheet at 31 December 20 . . . at £ . . . . . Any adjustment to this figure would have a consequential effect on the profit for the year ended 31 December 20 . . . and, consequently, our opinion on the financial statements for the year ended 31 December 20 . . . was qualified because of this limitation in audit scope. Accordingly the amounts shown as cost of sales and profit for the year ended 31 December 20 . . . may not be comparable with the figures for the current period.

Except for the financial effects of any such adjustment, if any, as might have been determined to be necessary had we been able to satisfy ourselves as to the quantities and condition of stock and work in progress as at 31 December 20 . . . in our opinion the financial statements:

- give a true and fair view of the state of the company's affairs as at [date] and of its profit [loss] for the year then ended;
- have been properly prepared in accordance with United Kingdom Generally Accepted Accounting Practice; and
- have been prepared in accordance with the requirements of the Companies Act 2006.

Opinion on other matter prescribed by the Companies Act 2006

In our opinion the information given in the Directors' Report for the financial year for which the financial statements are prepared is consistent with the financial statements.

Matters on which we are required to report by exception

In respect solely of the limitation on our work relating to stock and work in progress:

- we have not obtained all the information and explanations that we considered necessary for the purpose of our audit; and
- we were unable to determine whether proper accounting records had been maintained.

We have nothing to report in respect of the following matters where the Companies Act 2006 requires us to report to you if, in our opinion:

- returns adequate for our audit have not been received from branches not visited by us; or
- the financial statements are not in agreement with the accounting records and returns; or
- certain disclosures of directors' remuneration specified by law are not made.

[*Signature*]
John Smith (Senior statutory auditor)
For and on behalf of ABC LLP, Statutory Auditor
Address
Date

In contrast, where auditors issue a qualified report because of disagreement over an accounting policy, but this no longer exists following a change in accounting policy, which has been properly disclosed and adjustments made to the prior year, no qualification is necessary as the matter has been resolved and dealt with correctly.

Where an issue over which there was a disagreement has been resolved but not satisfactorily, for example, where the disagreement over the accounting policy was resolved by adjusting the current year's figures when the auditors considered a prior year adjustment was required, then both current period and comparatives would be qualified on the basis of disagreement.

For audits under the Companies Act 2006 there is no direct requirement to report on comparatives, apart from the fact that they are a 'disclosure requirement' under relevant UK law. Any qualification should therefore be in terms of this requirement. If corresponding amounts are presented solely as good practice, the audit report reference should be made as an explanatory paragraph.

The guidance to the ISA (UK and Ireland) considers what auditors should do when they become aware of a material misstatement which affects the previous financial statements, which had an unqualified audit opinion. If the previous financial statements have been revised (see **Chapter 5**) the auditors need to ensure that the comparatives agree with the revised financial statements. Where the previous year's financial statements have not been reissued but the comparatives adjusted, no qualification is necessary as long as the matter is properly disclosed. Where no adjustment or disclosure has been made the auditors need to consider whether the misstatements in the opening balances will give rise to misstatements in this period's financial statements or whether the comparatives are materially misstated. Both of which, in the absence of adjustments, will lead to qualifications as discussed above.

31.5   INCOMING AUDITORS – COMPARATIVES

Where the comparative figures have been audited by other auditors, the new auditors assume responsibility for them as part of the financial statements as a whole. They should assess them in the light of their knowledge of the client and the previous financial statements.

If the comparative figures have not been audited, for example, advantage had been taken of the audit exemption regulations, auditors should ensure that the financial statements clearly disclose the fact that the comparatives are unaudited, but also need to ensure that they are not aware of any possible material misstatement in those figures. For accounts under the Companies Act, where additional procedures are not feasible, inability to do this will inevitably lead to a qualification of the comparatives on the basis of scope limitations as discussed above.

32 RELATED PARTIES

32.1 INTRODUCTION

In October 1995, the Accounting Standards Board issued FRS 8 on related parties. This introduced a substantial increase in the scope and amount of disclosure of transactions with related parties from those already required by the Companies Act. At the time of its exposure commentators noted that an accounting standard of this nature would make auditors' task more difficult and called for guidance. Since that date a number of versions of guidance for auditors have been issued, the most recent being Clarified ISA (UK and Ireland) 550 *Related Parties* which was issued in October 2009 and is effective for the audit of financial statements for periods ending on or after 15 December 2010.

The updated ISA (UK and Ireland) replaces ISA (UK and Ireland) 550 issued in December 2004. This chapter covers both the existing and Clarified ISAs (UK and Ireland). As the Clarified ISA (UK and Ireland) adds to the requirements of the existing ISA (UK and Ireland) this chapter is written on the basis of the existing requirements, and changes to them included in the Clarified ISA (UK and Ireland) are included and clearly indicated.

In anticipation of the introduction of the requirements of the revised and redrafted ISA 550 into UK GAAP, the Audit and Assurance Faculty of the ICAEW issued an Exposure Draft of a practical guide to the audit of related parties in September 2008. *The Audit of Related Parties in Practice* is considered in **32.11** below.

FRS 8 requires certain disclosures of related party transactions, and the auditors' task is to obtain reasonable assurance that the disclosures made are complete and accurate. The nature of related party transactions makes them difficult to identify, and auditors may thus be faced with a high level of risk that they will not detect related party transactions which should be, but are not disclosed in the financial statements.

In addition, the definitions of related parties in the FRS are not easy to apply in practice. In deciding whether parties are related, it is necessary to consider the substance of the relationships either between individuals and the reporting entity or between different individuals. For example, members of a director's immediate family may be related parties if they are influenced or subject to influence by that director. In preparing financial statements directors must address the question of whether related party relationships exist in such circumstances and auditors must judge the reasonableness of this assessment. This may involve auditors in areas that are outside their normal areas of expertise.

For accounting periods beginning on or after 1 January 2005, the consolidated financial statements of listed companies must be prepared under IFRS. Under IFRS, the disclosure of related parties is made in accordance with the requirements of IAS 24.

In November 2003, and following the very public failures of a number of companies who made use of so called 'business empires' and off-balance sheet arrangements, such as Special Purpose Entities, the APB published a study exploring some of the pitfalls of auditing these arrangements. The issues contained in the study are discussed in **32.13**.

32.2 AUDITING STANDARDS

ISA (UK and Ireland) 550 provides guidance covering:

- the existence and disclosure of related parties;
- evidence relating to transactions with related parties;
- disclosures relating to control of the entity;
- management representations;
- communication with those charged with governance; and
- documentation.

The Clarified ISA (UK and Ireland) was updated following a number of corporate scandals where fraudulent financial reporting arose through the involvement of related parties. The revision focuses guidance on the identification and assessment of risk of material misstatement associated with related party relationships and transactions and on performing appropriate procedures to respond to such risks. The guidance takes an increasingly risk-based approach to the difficult issue of identifying related party relationships and transactions not disclosed to auditors by management or those charged with governance.

32.3 GENERAL REQUIREMENT

Auditors have a responsibility to perform audit procedures to identify, assess and respond to the risks of material misstatement arising from the entity's failure to appropriately account for or disclose related party relationships, transactions or balances in accordance with the requirements of the financial reporting framework. In order to do this, auditors need firstly to understand, as part of their knowledge of the business, the relevant disclosure requirements in legislation and accounting standards.

Auditors' understanding of related parties should be sufficient to:

- recognise fraud risk factors; and

- conclude whether the financial statements are fairly presented and are not misleading.

Many related party transactions are in the normal course of business and may carry no higher risk of material misstatement of the financial statements than similar transactions with unrelated parties. However, related party transactions may be difficult to detect due to:

- reticence on the part of the directors to disclose sensitive transactions;
- accounting systems not being designed to identify these transactions;
- a lack of controls over such transactions; and
- the complexity of the definition of a related party in FRS 8.

In certain instances, related party transactions may be concealed in whole, or in part, from auditors for fraudulent purposes. ISA (UK and Ireland) 240 *The Auditor's Responsibility to Consider Fraud in an Audit of Financial Statements* (see **Chapter 10**) provides guidance on the auditors' responsibility to consider fraud and error in financial statements and this includes fraudulent related party transactions.

The auditors' risk of not detecting related party transactions is compounded when transactions are:

- without charge;
- not self-evident to the auditors;
- with a party that auditors could not reasonably know was a related party; or
- actively concealed by the directors.

Directors are responsible for the identification and disclosure of related party transactions. However, in addition to their responsibility to ensure that the disclosures are complete and accurate, auditors should consider the effect they may have on other items within the financial statements, such as the tax liability. They must also be aware that the reliability of evidence may be reduced if it is obtained from related parties and also that transactions with them may be motivated by considerations other than ordinary business, such as window dressing.

Clarified ISA (UK and Ireland) 550 requires that the audit team discussion required by ISA (UK and Ireland) 315 (see **Chapter 22**), also includes consideration of fraud or error that may arise as a result of related party relationships and transactions.

32.4 MATERIALITY

FRS 8 requires the materiality of the transaction to the related party, where that party is a director or an entity controlled by an individual, to be considered in addition to that of the reporting entity. This may prove difficult for auditors to assess where they are not in full possession of the facts concerning the director's affairs. This additional assessment is not required by IAS 24.

This difficulty does not arise where companies are complying with the FRSSE (see **3.12.3**) as, when applying this, materiality only needs to be considered from the point of view of the entity itself.

32.5   EXISTENCE AND DISCLOSURE OF RELATED PARTIES

ISA (UK and Ireland) 550 requires auditors to assess the risk of undisclosed material related party transactions when planning their audit.

As part of their initial risk assessment procedures in accordance with ISA (UK and Ireland) 315, auditors will make enquiries of management regarding:

- the identity of related parties, including changes from prior periods;
- the nature of relationships with those related parties; and
- whether any transactions were entered into with those related parties during the period, and if so, the type and purpose of those transactions.

The Clarified ISA (UK and Ireland) requires that auditors are also required to gain an understanding of controls in place over related party transactions by understanding controls over the:

- identification, accounting and disclosure of related party relationships and transactions;
- authorisation and approval of significant transactions and arrangements with related parties; and
- authorisation and approval of significant transactions and arrangements outside the normal course of business.

As transactions between related parties may not be at arm's length, there may be an actual or perceived conflict of interest. For this reason many entities will require that such transactions are authorised by those charged with governance. This means that such transactions are often recorded in the minutes of meetings of for example, meetings of directors. This is less likely for owner-managed entities where procedures are often less formalised.

Relevant information about related parties should be shared with the whole audit team as part of the meeting held during planning (see **22.3.3**).

32.5.1   *Responses to assessed risks*

Undisclosed related parties

Auditors should remain alert to indicators of the existence of related parties and related party transactions when inspecting records and documents throughout the audit. ISA (UK and Ireland) 550 requires auditors to inspect the following documents for indications of unidentified related parties:

- bank and legal confirmations obtained as part of the auditors' procedures;
- minutes of meetings of shareholders and of those charged with governance; and
- such other records or documents considered necessary by auditors.

Auditors will also review prior year working papers to determine names of known related parties.

In addition, **Table 1** sets out other documents that auditors are likely to view as part of their audit procedures which may uncover previously undisclosed related parties.

TABLE 1: Records or documents that auditors may inspect to uncover related parties

- third party confirmations obtained by the auditor (in additional to bank and legal confirmations);
- entity income tax returns;
- information supplied by the entity to regulatory authorities;
- shareholder registers to identify the entity's principal shareholders;
- statements of conflicts of interest from management and those charged with governance;
- records of the entity's investments and those of its pension plans;
- contracts and agreements with key management or those charged with governance;
- significant contracts and agreements not in the entity's ordinary course of business;
- specific invoices and correspondence from the entity's professional advisors;
- life insurance policies acquired by the entity;
- significant contracts re-negotiated by the entity during the period;
- internal auditors' reports; and
- documents associated with the entity's filings with a securities regulator (such as prospectuses).

Where there is an indication of an increased risk of material misstatement in relation to related parties, the auditors should perform additional tests to those listed as appropriate. Many of these procedures, such as review of prior year working papers, will often need to be carried out in any case as part of the auditors' planning to gain sufficient knowledge of the business.

If previously unidentified related parties are discovered, they should be reported to all members of the audit team immediately, as this information could affect the results of work they are performing or have already performed, including the assessment of the risk of material misstatement, which may need revision. Auditors should also make enquiries of management to determine all transactions with the newly identified related party so that they can be evaluated.

If non-disclosure of the related party by management appears intentional it may be indicative of a risk of material misstatement due to fraud, and auditors should evaluate the implications for the audit and their report. It may also cast doubt over other representations made by management.

The extent of substantive testing required to obtain sufficient audit evidence following the procedures in **Table 1** will vary depending on the auditor's assessment of the entity's internal control over related party transactions. When assessing the control activities auditors should concentrate on controls over the authorisation and recording of related party transactions.

Auditors should also be aware of related party transactions which may not be included in the information provided by the entity. **Table 2** sets out a number of circumstances where auditors may wish to investigate further if they become aware of them during other audit testing.

TABLE 2: Examples of unusual circumstances

- transactions which have unusual terms such as very low interest rates;
- transactions which appear to lack a logical business rationale, such as the sale of an asset for what appears to be less than market value;
- transactions in which substance differs from form;
- transactions processed or approved in a non-routine manner or by personnel who do not ordinarily deal with such transactions, for example, a sale authorised by the chief executive rather than the sales manager;
- high volume or significant transactions with certain customers or suppliers compared to others;
- unrecorded transactions such as the receipt or provision of management services at no charge; and
- unusual transactions which are entered into shortly before or after the end of the reporting period, such as a large sale just before the year end which is later cancelled.

If auditors discover significant related party transactions which had not previously been identified by management or disclosed to the auditor, Clarified ISA (UK and Ireland) 550 requires that auditors consider whether other such related party relationships or transactions exist. If the non-disclosure appears intentional, and is therefore indicative of a risk of material misstatement due to fraud, auditors should evaluate the implications for the audit as a whole.

Related party transactions outside the entity's normal course of business

If auditors discover related party transactions which appear outside the entity's normal course of business, Clarified ISA (UK and Ireland) 550 requires that they:

- inspect the underlying contracts to determine whether the:

  - business rationale, or lack thereof, is indicative of fraudulent activity;
  - terms are consistent with management's explanations; and

- transactions have been appropriately accounted for; and
- obtain evidence that the transactions have been appropriately authorised and approved.

The Clarified ISA (UK and Ireland) also requires that any such significant related party transactions outside the entity's normal course of business are treated as giving rise to a significant risk.

Arm's length transactions

If management assert that a related party transaction has been conducted on terms equivalent to an arm's length transaction, Clarified ISA (UK and Ireland) 550 requires that auditors should obtain evidence to support that assertion.

In order to verify their assertion, management may:

- compare the terms of the related party transaction with those of an identical or similar transaction with an unrelated party;
- engage an external expert to determine a market value and confirm market terms and conditions for the transaction; or
- compare the terms of the transaction with broadly similar transactions in the open market.

Evaluating the information provided by management may include:

- considering the appropriateness the processes undertaken by management to support their assertion;
- verifying internal or external data used as evidence by management;
- evaluating whether assumptions used by management are reasonable.

32.6 EVIDENCE

The reliability of the audit evidence regarding related parties may be of concern when it is either:

- limited, such as an instruction from one group company to another to pay a management charge; or
- created by the related party, such as the confirmation of a loan.

In order to assess reliability where evidence is limited, the guidance suggests that auditors should consider:

- discussing the matter with management;
- confirming the terms and amount of the transaction with the related party; and
- corroborating the explanation with the related party.

Where the evidence is created by the related party, auditors should consider:

- inspecting any additional evidence held by the related party; or

- confirming explanations with persons associated with the transaction such as lawyers and bankers.

32.7   MATERIALITY

With related parties it is particularly important for auditors to consider not just the monetary amount of any misstatements, but also their nature. A misstatement of a related party transaction may be significant to users of the financial statements even if its monetary value is low, depending on the nature of the relationship with the related party.

32.8   CONTROL DISCLOSURES

In addition to the disclosure of related party transactions, FRS 8 and IAS 24 require disclosure relating to the control of the entity. ISA (UK and Ireland) 550 expects auditors to obtain appropriate evidence in this respect usually via enquiry of management and it is suggested that this representation may be confirmed with the ultimate controlling party if considered appropriate.

32.9   REPRESENTATIONS FROM THOSE CHARGED WITH GOVERNANCE

ISA (UK and Ireland) 550 requires auditors to obtain written confirmation from those charged with governance that information concerning related parties and control provided to them is complete and that the disclosures in the financial statements regarding related party transactions are adequate. A paragraph on directors' interests is already included in the example representation letter shown in **Chapter 30** and this needs to be extended to cover other related parties and control.

Where an entity requires its management and those charged with governance to confirm their interests in writing, the auditors should inspect these documents. In such cases the guidance suggests that the confirmations may be jointly addressed to the company and the auditors.

32.10   COMMUNICATION WITH THOSE CHARGED WITH GOVERNANCE

Examples of items which auditors may report in their communications with those charged with governance in respect of related party transactions include:

- intentional or unintentional non-disclosure of related parties or significant related party transactions, which may alert those charged with governance to relationships and transactions of which they had not previously been aware;
- significant related party transactions which have not been appropriately authorised and approved, which may give rise to suspected fraud;
- disagreements with management regarding the accounting for and disclosure of significant related party transactions;
- non-compliance with laws and regulations which prohibit or restrict certain types of related party transactions; and
- difficulties in identifying the party that ultimately controls the entity.

32.11   DOCUMENTATION

Clarified ISA (UK and Ireland) 550 introduces a formal requirement for the names and nature of the relationship with all related parties be documented on the audit file.

32.12   REPORTING

If auditors are unable to obtain sufficient appropriate evidence on related party matters or the disclosures are not adequate, they should consider the implications for their report.

Where the auditors believe that there is more information which could have been obtained but they have been unable to do so, this is a limitation of scope which could lead to a qualified or disclaimed opinion as set out in **4.2.2**. For example, such a report would be appropriate where they suspect a related party transaction but have not been able to obtain all the evidence to which they are reasonably entitled to determine the matter.

In instances where auditors have sufficient evidence to know that the disclosure is incorrect or they consider the disclosures inadequate because the directors are unwilling to disclose information, they should consider giving a qualified or adverse opinion on the basis of disagreement (see **4.2.4**). Where the disclosures are required by the Companies Act, auditors are obliged to include the missing information in their report. The requirement of ISA (UK and Ireland) 700 to give details of all substantive factors that give rise to the disagreement and their implications for the financial statements imposes a similar requirement in respect of disclosures required by FRS 8.

32.13 THE AUDIT OF RELATED PARTIES IN PRACTICE

32.13.1 Introduction

In September 2008, the Audit and Assurance Faculty of the ICAEW issued an Exposure Draft of a paper entitled *The Audit of Related Parties in Practice*. The aim of the paper is to provide practical advice to auditors on how best to plan for the change in audit requirements which the likely introduction of ISA 550 in the UK will bring.

The paper voices concerns that auditors have previously seen their work in relation to related parties and related party transactions as a mere check on disclosures made under IAS 24 or FRS 8, rather than focusing on this as an area where material misstatement may occur as a result of fraud or error. ISA 550 (Revised and Redrafted), and therefore Proposed Clarified ISA (UK and Ireland) 550, aims to redress this balance by including procedures to identify, assess and respond to risks of material misstatement associated with related parties. It focuses on fraud risk factors linked to related party transactions, and creates a stronger parallel to the requirements of ISA 240. It recommends that there is focus on and an understanding of the controls in place in respect of related parties, and that auditors inspect documents for evidence of undisclosed related parties.

The Audit and Assurance Faculty Exposure Draft highlights common pitfalls when auditing related parties and related party transactions, and provides suggestions to improve audit quality in this area. It emphasises the importance of proper planning in this area, involving the whole audit team.

32.13.2 The five point action plan

The Exposure Draft contains a five point plan highlighting specific areas where existing audit work on related parties and related party transactions could be enhanced to improve the quality of the audit. It is reproduced in **Table 3**.

TABLE 3: The Five Point Action Plan

(1) Plan your work on the audit of related parties and related party transactions thoroughly

- Plan the audit of related parties and related party transactions
- Where possible obtain a list of related parties from clients or compile a list based on discussions with clients and knowledge of the business
- Update previous knowledge of related parties and related party transactions
- Ensure that the client understands what a related party is and why the relevant disclosure requirements are necessary
- Speak to the right person 'in authority' at the client who can answer your questions

---

- Plan for specific related party issues or concerns, such as those raised by audit team members, to be considered and reviewed by suitably experienced staff on the audit team
- Brief all audit team members about related parties and related party transactions and the risks of material misstatement due to fraud or error that could result from the entity's related party transactions
- Ensure that all staff are informed about changes to related party relationships throughout the engagement.

(2) Focus on the risk of material misstatement that might arise from related party transactions

- Understand the business, including the nature, size and complexity of the business and transactions
- The use of family trees and group structures can help to identify related parties and understand relationships between client and related parties
- Follow up potential related party indicators and issues identified
- Consider fraud risk and the risk of undisclosed related parties and related party transactions
- Consider materiality
- Emphasise the importance of the audit team remaining alert for related parties and related party transactions as the audit proceeds
- Discuss awareness of related party relationships with others within the firm involved in providing services to the client, eg tax/accounting/corporate finance departments

(3) Understand the internal controls in the entity to identify related parties and record related party transactions

- Understand the controls, if any, that management has put in place to identify, account for and disclose related party transactions and to approve significant transactions with related parties, or significant transactions outside the normal course of business
- If few or no processes are in place for dealing with related party relationships and related party transactions, seek to obtain an understanding of related party relationships and related party transactions through inquiry of management

(4) Design procedures to respond to risks identified

- Perform procedures to confirm/identify related party relationships not yet identified including:

  - Inspecting bank and legal confirmations
  - Inspecting minutes of meetings of shareholders and management

- On becoming aware of any undisclosed related parties perform appropriate substantive audit procedures as set out in the application material to ISA 550 (Revised and Redrafted)
- Consider any arm's length assertions and obtain evidence to support them
- Consider the use of corroborative evidence such as third party confirmations
- Consider significant related party transactions outside the normal course of business
- Document the identity and, if unclear, the nature of related parties
- Document risk assessment and any additional procedures performed
- Obtain a management representation letter
- Communicate any significant matters to management those charged with governance

(5) Perform completion procedures

> - Ensure that the disclosures on related party transactions are appropriate
> - Consider implications of work performed and findings for the audit opinion.

32.14 IMPROVING THE AUDITING OF ENTITIES UNDER COMMON CONTROL

32.14.1 Introduction

This study, published in November 2003, explores some of the pitfalls involved when auditing horizontal groups (or 'business empires') and off-balance sheet arrangements, which have featured prominently in a number of recent business collapses.

While such horizontal groups are legitimate they are not required to present consolidated financial statements. Consequently, financial statements of components of the empire may be misleading if there is inadequate disclosure of the effect of transactions with other parts of the empire.

Under UK Accounting Standards, 'Common control is deemed to exist when both parties are subject to control from boards having a controlling nucleus of directors in common'. Therefore, issues of common control are not limited to large listed companies, and they often feature in smaller family businesses.

Obtaining sufficient audit evidence concerning the proper disclosure of related party transactions can be difficult for auditors, and this is compounded when directors seek to avoid making the disclosures required by Accounting Standards. Indeed company law does not require those who control related entities to provide information to those who audit the companies that they control. Even when one firm is appointed to all the entities subject to common control, their duty of confidentiality may restrict them auditing the entities as if they were a single group.

33 OTHER INFORMATION IN DOCUMENTS CONTAINING FINANCIAL STATEMENTS

33.1 INTRODUCTION

In October 2009 the APB issued Clarified ISA (UK and Ireland) 720 in two parts. Section A *The Auditor's Responsibilities Relating to Other Information in Documents Containing Audited Financial Statements* is based on ISA 720 published by the IAASB as part of its Clarity Project (see **Chapter 2**). Section B *The Auditor's Statutory Reporting Responsibility in Relation to Directors' Reports* has no international equivalent and as such contains only UK and Ireland specific guidance. Together these sections will replace SAS 470 *Overall Review of Financial Statements*, for which an ISA (UK and Ireland) replacement was never published.

The Clarified ISA (UK and Ireland) is effective for the audit of financial statements for periods ending on or after 15 December 2010. This chapter covers both the existing and clarified guidance. As the Clarified ISA (UK and Ireland) does not significantly amend the requirements of the existing guidance this chapter is written on the basis of the existing requirements, and any changes to them included in the Clarified ISA (UK and Ireland) are included and clearly indicated.

33.2 ISA (UK AND IRELAND) 720, SECTION A

33.2.1 Scope

Section A of ISA (UK and Ireland) 720 *The Auditor's Responsibilities Relating to Other Information in Documents Containing Audited Financial Statements* contains guidance covering:

- reading other information;
- material inconsistencies; and
- material misstatements of fact.

The guidance in section A applies to all other information included in documents containing audited financial statements, including the directors' report. Further guidance in relation to the directors' report is set out in Section B (see **33.3** below).

33.2.2 Reading other information

ISA (UK and Ireland) 720 states that the objective of the auditor is to 'respond appropriately when documents containing audited financial statements and the auditor's report thereon include other information that could undermine the credibility of those financial statements and the auditor's report'.

The overall review will include all material published as part of the financial statements, either contained in the physical document or, where financial statements are published on a website, incorporated with the financial statements by means of hyperlinks. Further information on the electronic publication of financial information can be found in **Chapter 3**. Other information included in the review, does not encompass:

- press releases or covering letters accompanying the document;
- information included in analyst briefings; or
- other information contained on the entity's website.

This overall review involves reading the 'other information' and should be carried out in the final phase of the audit, once other evidence has been obtained. Such a review requires a person with 'appropriate levels of experience and skills'. As with other parts of the audit, auditors consider materiality when performing this review. The review complements their other evidence and is not intended to be the only procedure that the auditors carry out in order to give their opinion. No verification of any of the other information is required.

Auditors should obtain the other information as soon as possible to allow time for any inconsistencies to be resolved.

In performing such a review the auditors may need to consider whether:

- the financial statements reflect the results of the audit;
- the review provides new information which affects the presentation of or disclosures in the financial statements;
- when compared with other available data, the information in the financial statements is as expected;
- the presentation of information in the financial statements is fair; and
- the aggregate of unadjusted misstatements, found during the current and previous years' audits, have any effect on the financial statements.

33.2.3 Material inconsistencies

Where auditors discover an inconsistency they should first determine whether it is the financial statements or the other information that require amendment.

If auditors determine that the financial statements require amendment and those charged with governance refuse to make the change a modified report should be issued.

If it is the other information that requires amendment and those charged with governance refuse to make this change, auditors should either:

- include an 'Other Matters' paragraph in their report describing the material inconsistency; or
- withhold the auditor's report; or
- withdraw from the engagement.

The decision on which course of action should be taken should be based on legal advice.

In addition, auditors have the right to be heard at any general meeting of the members on matters that concern the auditor and to make a statement to members on ceasing to hold office.

33.2.4   Material misstatement of fact

If auditors discover a material misstatement of fact in the other information (rather than an inconsistency between it and the financial statements) they should have regard to the nature of the misstatement and discuss it with those charged with governance. The Clarified ISA (UK and Ireland) also requires auditors to request those charged with governance to consult their legal counsel on the matter. If management refuses to correct the error, auditors may consult their own legal advisors and resort to one of the actions listed in **33.2.3** above.

If the matter is actually one of judgement (such as the view of those charged with governance of the likely course of business in the following year) it is more difficult to take issue with it than one of factual error. Although auditors cannot substitute their judgement for that of those charged with governance, there may be situations where the judgement of those charged with governance is so unreasonable or at variance with the auditors' knowledge of the client to make it not credible.

33.3   ISA (UK AND IRELAND) 720, SECTION B

33.3.1   Guidance

This section of ISA (UK and Ireland) 720 was originally published as a separate document and consists entirely of UK and Ireland specific guidance and it extends the guidance in Section A to the directors' report.

33.3.2   Procedures

Much of the information in the directors' report is likely to be extracted or directly derived from the financial statements and as such should be directly comparable with them. If however, the financial information in the directors' report has been prepared on a different basis auditors should consider whether there is adequate disclosure of the differences to aid the understanding of readers.

Auditors should document the procedures they have undertaken to assess whether the information in the directors' report is consistent with the financial statements, including verifying the reconciliation of the information in the report with the financial statements.

33.3.3   Inconsistencies

If inconsistencies are found between the information in the directors' report and the financial statements, auditors should ask those charged with governance to resolve them.

If amendment of the directors' report is required, but those charged with governance refuse to make the amendment, auditors should describe the inconsistency in their report.

If those charged with governance refuse to make a required amendment to the financial statements, auditors will express a qualified or adverse opinion on the financial statements.

Details of any inconsistencies and their resolution should be documented on the audit file.

34 SUBSEQUENT EVENTS

34.1 INTRODUCTION

Clarified ISA (UK and Ireland) 560 *Subsequent Events* was issued in October 2009 and replaces ISA (UK and Ireland) 560 previously issued in December 2004. The Clarified ISA (UK and Ireland) is effective for the audit of financial statements for periods ending on or after 15 December 2010. This chapter covers both the existing and Clarified ISAs (UK and Ireland). As the Clarified ISA (UK and Ireland) does not significantly amend the requirements of the existing ISA (UK and Ireland) this chapter is written on the basis of the existing requirements, and any changes to them included in the Clarified ISA (UK and Ireland) are included and clearly indicated. The ISA (UK and Ireland) provides standards on the audit of post balance sheet events covering:

- events between the period end and the date of the audit report;
- events between the date of the audit report but before the financial statements are issued; and
- events discovered after the financial statements have been issued but before they are laid before members.

As with all ISAs (UK and Ireland), the text of the international ISA has been supplemented with additional guidance from a UK and Ireland perspective.

34.2 AUDITING STANDARDS

ISA (UK and Ireland) 560 states that 'the auditor should consider the effect of subsequent events on the financial statements and on the auditor's report'.

Subsequent events are those events (favourable or unfavourable) which occur between the balance sheet date and the date when the financial statements are authorised for issue.

Relevant events are those which:

- provide additional evidence on conditions existing at the balance sheet date, for which an adjustment should be made to the financial statements; or
- concern conditions which did not exist at the balance sheet date, but require disclosure because of their materiality. However the financial statements would not be adjusted for these events.

The ISA (UK and Ireland) also considers the situation where facts are discovered after financial statements are laid before members, and this is covered in **34.6** below.

34.3 BEFORE THE DATE OF THE AUDIT REPORT

The auditor should perform audit procedures designed to obtain sufficient appropriate audit evidence that all events occurring between the date of the financial statements and the date of the auditor's report that require adjustment of, or disclosure in, the financial statements have been identified.

It is important that auditors review matters of which they may have become aware during the course of their work and which may be susceptible to change after the period end. This review may be carried out in addition to those specific procedures which are necessary to confirm certain account balances, such as inventory cut-off or payments to creditors, although these procedures may be extended as part of this review.

The guidance provides some examples of procedures that may be performed as near as practicable to the date of the audit report. These are:

- enquiring into procedures that management has established to identify subsequent events;
- reviewing minutes of meetings of members, directors, and audit and executive committees held since the period end and enquiring about any matters discussed at meetings for which minutes are not available;
- reading the latest available information concerning the entity, including the accounting records and any management accounts;
- making enquiries of the entity's legal counsel concerning litigation and claims; and
- making enquiries of management as to whether any subsequent events have occurred which might affect the financial statements.

The extent of these procedures will depend on the length of the period between the balance sheet date and the date of the audit report. The type of procedures undertaken will also depend on whether management accounts and minutes of meetings since the balance sheet date have been prepared. If this is not the case auditors are more likely to inspect underlying books and records and require more detailed written representations from management or those charged with governance.

Some examples of specific enquiries that auditors might make of the management are provided and include:

- the current status of items involving subjective judgement or which were accounted for on the basis of preliminary data – for example, litigation in progress;
- whether sales of fixed assets are planned or have occurred;
- whether new commitments, borrowings or guarantees have been entered into;

- whether the issue of new shares or debentures or an agreement to merge or liquidate has been made or is planned;
- whether any assets have been appropriated by government or destroyed, for example, by fire or flood;
- whether there have been developments regarding risk areas and contingencies;
- whether any unusual accounting adjustments have been made or are contemplated; and
- whether any events have occurred or are likely to occur which might bring into question the appropriateness of accounting policies used in the financial statements – for example, any that would bring the validity of the going concern assumption into question.

One area which is the frequent subject of specific enquiries by auditors is the appropriateness of the going concern assumption and this is considered in **Chapter 13**, 'Going concern'.

Under any circumstances, auditors will request a written representation from those charged with governance, in accordance with ISA (UK and Ireland) 580, that all events occurring subsequent to the date of the financial statements and which require adjustment or disclosure have been adjusted or disclosed.

Where a part of the entity is audited by other auditors, the principal auditors should consider the other auditors' procedures for reviewing subsequent events up to the date planned for the principal auditors' report.

When the auditor becomes aware of an event which materially affects the financial statements, they should consider whether the events are properly accounted for and adequately disclosed in the financial statements.

34.4   BEFORE THE FINANCIAL STATEMENTS ARE ISSUED

There is occasionally a period of some time between the date of signature of the auditors' report and the issue of the financial statements. This will normally be caused by the time taken to print and process the financial statements. More rarely it may be because the statements are held back for issue with another document.

Once their report has been dated the auditors have no responsibility to perform procedures to review subsequent events. However, until the financial statements have been issued they can reasonably expect management to inform them of any events discovered which may affect the financial statements.

If the auditors become aware of subsequent events before the issue of the financial statements, they should establish whether the financial statements need amendment, discuss the matter with the directors and consider the implications for their report.

Dual dating

Clarified ISA (UK and Ireland) 560 introduces the concept of dual dating where events occur subsequent to the signing of the audit report which require amendment to an element of the financial statements. This concept is not permitted by some laws, regulations or financial reporting frameworks covered by the International ISA, but the UK and Ireland specific guidance in the Clarified ISA (UK and Ireland) does not restrict its use.

In such as situation, the date of the auditor's report should be presented as:

[Date of auditor's report], except as to Note Y, which is as of [date of completion of audit procedures restricted to amendment described in Note Y].

Failure to amend financial statements

If the financial statements are not amended, the auditors should consider the implications for their report and issue a qualified report if the original report has not been issued to the entity. When the original report has been issued, the auditors should request management not to issue the financial statements; but if these are issued, the auditors need to take action to prevent reliance on the audit report and may need to take legal advice.

34.5   REVISING OR WITHDRAWING FINANCIAL STATEMENTS

In situations where auditors become aware of events after the financial statements have been issued, if the facts would have led them to issue a different report they should consider whether the financial statements need amendment and consider the implications for their report. Where events have occurred after the date of the audit report, but before the financial statements have been issued there is no statutory procedure, but this normally involves attempting to have management withdraw the statements and, failing this, taking legal advice. This is a difficult area in which to give specific guidance, as much will depend on the circumstances.

In such circumstances auditors may wish to make use of their power under the Companies Act to address the general meeting at which the members consider the financial statements. The possibility of withdrawing their audit report is also one that is sometimes raised. However, it appears that this may not legally be effective.

35 THE AUDIT OF SMALL BUSINESS

35.1 INTRODUCTION

The area of small business audits has been one which has exercised many minds over the last 20 years. The need for audits for small business has been the subject of much of the debate, although this has abated since the introduction of audit exemption regulations (see **Chapter 7**). As a result of these – and following subsequent changes to the exemption limits – small companies with turnover of less than £6.5 million and meeting the small criteria in s477(2) of the Companies Act 2006 do not require an annual audit. There are, however, many small businesses which still require an audit because they do not qualify for the exemptions and even some which fall within the exemptions but for which its shareholders or some third party, for example a lender, requests an audit. The focus of the issue has changed more recently to how to perform such audits.

35.2 EXISTING GUIDANCE

In June 1997, Practice Note 13 *The Audit of Small Business* was issued by the Auditing Practices Board. This followed recognition in *The Audit Agenda* that although SASs must apply so that every audit 'provides a uniform and reliable quality of assurance', some guidance is necessary on the characteristics of 'owner-managed companies, including small businesses and how the SASs can be applied to them'. The objective of the guidance is to give helpful, realistic and practical advice on the way in which the audit of small businesses can be cost-effectively combined with the accountancy work which is normally also undertaken by the auditors of small businesses. As with other practice notes, the guidance is presented on a standard-by-standard basis. Although the Practice Note was issued prior to the APB adopting the ISAs (UK and Ireland) for the audit of periods beginning on or after 15 December 2004, the guidance it contains remains relevant under the new regime. Where the guidance refers to the old SASs, this commentary also includes references to the relevant ISA (UK and Ireland). In September 2007, the APB issued Practice Note 26, *Guidance on Smaller Entity Audit Documentation* to provide assistance to auditors of small businesses on applying the documentation requirements contained within ISAs (UK and Ireland). It is detailed in **35.10** below. In July 2009, the APB issued an Exposure Draft of a revision to Practice Note 26, and this is discussed in **35.10.6** below.

35.3 CHARACTERISTICS OF SMALL BUSINESSES

The definition of a 'small business' cannot be a solely quantitative one, i.e., by reference to some measure of the size such as turnover. It also depends more upon qualitative characteristics.

The Practice Note defines as small any business in which:

(a) there is a concentration of ownership and management in a small number of individuals (or one individual); and

(b) one or more of the following are also found:

- few sources of income and uncomplicated activities;
- simple record-keeping; or
- limited internal controls and potential for management override.

A restriction on the number of managers that an entity has may mean that there is only limited management time to devote to such matters as formal internal control procedures. However, this lack of formality may not necessarily mean an increased risk of fraud or error. Indeed, supervisory controls exercised on a day-to-day basis by the owner-manager may also have a significant beneficial effect.

On the other hand, owner-managers may have the ability to override controls, and this may have an adverse effect on the control environment and lead to an increased risk of misstatement. Auditors must assess this based upon their knowledge of the attitude and motives of the owner-manager. The Practice Note states that in auditing small businesses, as with any other audit, auditors should not assume that management is dishonest, but likewise should not assume unquestioned honesty.

Where a business has few sources of income and simple record-keeping procedures this may make it easier to acquire, record and maintain knowledge of the business. Accounting populations may be very easily analysed and many analytical review tests may be simple to perform, with easily corroborated explanations for any variations found. Analytical review procedures may, as a result, significantly reduce the amounts of tests of detail to be performed.

By contrast small businesses may have very informal accounting systems and completeness of records may therefore be a specific audit risk.

35.4 THE RELATIONSHIP BETWEEN SMALL BUSINESSES AND THEIR AUDITORS

Because they do not employ many people, small businesses often engage auditors to provide additional services such as accounting, advising on accounting and computer systems, taxation and other matters such as the preparation of budgets and forecasts and assisting with obtaining finance.

This in-depth involvement with a small business will allow auditors to keep their knowledge of the business up to date and help them to plan and conduct the audit as efficiently as possible.

Where assistance with the keeping of accounting records and the preparation of financial statements is given, auditors are able to use the information gained as audit evidence, which may reduce the need for separate audit procedures.

The Practice Note points out that provision of other services must always be limited by the knowledge that the client value of an audit derives from its objectivity. Auditors must always strive therefore to ensure that their relationship with small business does not prejudice their ability to form an objective opinion. To maintain this independence they must ensure that they do not take over the role of management. This is a particular problem where management are not aware of the nature and extent of their own responsibilities in certain areas (for example, choice of accounting policies and preparation of financial statements), which they may otherwise regard as part of the audit.

35.5 RESPONSIBILITIES

35.5.1 SAS 110 Fraud and Error/ISA (UK and Ireland) 240 The Auditor's Responsibility to Consider Fraud in an Audit of Financial Statements

The Practice Note sees the tendency of small businesses to be controlled by a single individual as making them more susceptible to the risk of fraud and error described in SAS 110 and ISA (UK and Ireland) 240. Auditors' knowledge of the owner-manager's general attitude to control issues and the way they exercise supervisory control will have a significant influence on their approach.

Examples of conditions or events typical of, but not exclusive to, small businesses, which may increase the likelihood of fraud or error or be indicative that it is occurring include the following set out in **Table 1** below:

TABLE 1: Conditions which may indicate fraud or error

- the owner-manager has a specific motive to distort the financial statements, and has the ability to do so;
- there is confusion between personal and business transactions;
- the owner-manager's lifestyle is inconsistent with their remuneration;
- the owner-manager has not taken any holiday for a long period;
- there have been frequent changes in professional advisers;
- the audit start date is repeatedly delayed;
- there are demands to complete the audit in any unreasonably short period of time;

- accounting records are unavailable or have been lost;
- significant level of cash transactions with inadequate documentation;
- numerous unexplained aspects of audit evidence (e.g., differences with third-party confirmations, etc.);
- inappropriate use of accounting estimates;
- unusual transactions around the year end with a material effect on profit;
- unusual related party transactions; and
- excessive fees for agents or consultants.

35.5.2 SAS 120 Consideration of Law and Regulations/ISA (UK and Ireland) 250 Part A Consideration of Laws and Regulations in an Audit of Financial Statements

The laws and regulations governing small companies tend to be largely identical to those of larger entities. The difference anticipated by Practice Note 13 is the fact that small businesses tend to have less complicated activities, and thus are subject to a less complex regulatory environment. However, auditors must assess each situation on its own merits.

35.5.3 SAS 130 The Going Concern Basis in Financial Statements/ISA (UK and Ireland) 570 Going Concern

As discussed in **Chapter 13**, SAS 130 and ISA (UK and Ireland) 570 *Going Concern* contain features which allow them to be applied more easily to smaller businesses (or at least those with uncomplicated circumstances) in that the directors' assessment of going concern:

- does not have a minimum period;
- may be informal in nature; and
- does not have to be in great detail.

The Practice Note points out that where auditors assist an owner-manager with the assessment of going concern and the production of projections and budgets they must ensure that the owner-manager is aware that he remains responsible for this information and the reasonableness of the assumptions on which the information is based.

35.5.4 SAS 140 Engagement Letters/ISA (UK and Ireland) 210 Terms of Audit Engagements

One way of ensuring that owner-managers are aware of their responsibilities in areas such as going concern, as mentioned above, and their responsibilities for financial statements, even when these have been prepared by the auditors, is to ensure that this is stated in the engagement letter.

35.5.5   SAS 150 Subsequent Events/ISA (UK and Ireland) 560 Subsequent Events

Because of the lack of reporting deadlines often associated with small companies the length of time to be considered in a subsequent events review will often be greater.

In addition, accounting records and minutes may not have been written up since the year end and the auditors may need to rely on representations from the owner-managers. Here a representation letter, dated when the financial statements are approved and which ensures that the entire period since the year end has been covered, becomes increasingly important.

When the meeting at which the financial statements are approved is immediately followed by the annual general meeting (as is often the case with small companies) SAS 150 and ISA (UK and Ireland) 560 state that the interval is so short as to not require separate consideration.

35.6   PLANNING, CONTROLLING AND RECORDING

35.6.1   SAS 200 Planning/ISA (UK and Ireland) 300 Planning an Audit of Financial Statements

The basic considerations relating to planning are identical to entities of all sizes; however, planning the audit of a small business need not be a complex or time consuming exercise.

Where accountancy work is being performed the planning process must be properly co-ordinated in order to gain the most benefit from effort and cost. Planning should also be reconsidered as the accountancy work progresses.

Planning the audits of smaller businesses may also be easier in that much of the information may be obtained from:

- discussion with the owner-manager; and
- the knowledge of the audit engagement partner who is often involved in the provision of other services and will have some first-hand knowledge.

35.6.2 *SAS 210 Knowledge of the Business/ISA (UK and Ireland) 315 Understanding the Entity and its Environment and Assessing the Risks of Material Misstatement*

Often the provision of other services to small businesses enables auditors to gain additional information about the client's accounting system, activities, management style, plans for the future, etc. However, this information may be obtained incidentally, and therefore it is important to document such findings so that they can be taken into account when planning and conducting the audit.

The Practice Note states that documentation must be of a level sufficient to:

- facilitate proper planning of the audit; and
- enable any change of responsibility within the audit firm (either partner or staff) to occur smoothly.

35.6.3 *SAS 220 Materiality and the Audit/ISA (UK and Ireland) 320 Audit Materiality*

The levels of materiality used for the preparation of financial statements by auditors and the audit work itself are likely to be different as management will want to ensure that their accounting records are as accurate as possible, which involves a greater degree of accuracy than would be necessary to give an unqualified audit opinion.

In the case of small businesses, draft financial statements may not be available on which to assess planning materiality. Therefore it is important for any initial judgements to be revisited once the final figures are available.

To focus auditors' attention on the more significant financial statement items, while determining the audit strategy, materiality is generally assessed by reference to some measure of the size of the business. One method is to use a percentage of a figure in the financial statements, such as:

- profit or loss before tax (adjusted, if appropriate, for the effect of any abnormal levels of items of expenditure such as directors' remuneration);
- turnover; or
- balance sheet total.

If an entity is at or near 'break-even' point, as may more often be the case with small businesses, assessing materiality as a percentage of pre-tax results alone may be inappropriate and lead to excessive audit work.

35.6.4 SAS 230 Working Papers/ISA (UK and Ireland) 230 Documentation

The guidance in Practice Note 13 on documentation has been updated by the issue of Practice Note 26. For further guidance see section **35.10** below.

35.6.5 SAS 240 Quality Control for Audit Work/ISA (UK and Ireland) 220 Quality Control for Audits of Historical Financial Information and ISQC 1 Quality Control for Firms that Perform Audits and Reviews of Historical Financial Information, and Other Assurance and Related Service Engagements

While the general principles set out in the SAS, ISA (UK and Ireland) and ISQC apply, the Practice Note points out that the requirements relating to quality control on individual audits are mostly only relevant to engagements where some of the work is delegated to one or more assistants. When small business audits are carried out entirely by the audit engagement partner (or a sole practitioner), questions of direction and supervision of assistants and review of their work do not arise.

35.7 ACCOUNTING SYSTEMS AND INTERNAL CONTROL

35.7.1 SAS 300 Accounting and Internal Control Systems and Audit Risk Assessments/ISA (UK and Ireland) 315 Understanding the Entity and its Environment and Assessing The Risks of Material Misstatement and ISA (UK and Ireland) 330 The Auditor's Procedures in Response to Assessed Risks

In applying SAS 300 *Accounting and Internal Control Systems and Audit Risk Assessment,* control risk is invariably assessed as high and therefore it is extremely unlikely that the audit of a small business will involve 'tests of controls'. In many small businesses there will be no formal system of internal control. This does not make such businesses 'unauditable' as it only raises the possibility of a risk of error. Such a risk may be offset by a number of factors and the absence of error may be established by reference to evidence obtained externally to the company. In fact, as explained above, a strong control environment will more often than not offset the potential problems that could result from lack of formal internal controls. Even where controls exist, they will not generally be ones that are easy to test. Thus it is rarely cost-effective to plan to rely on them. SAS 300 para 26 acknowledges that in these circumstances audit evidence may have to be obtained entirely through substantive procedures.

As small businesses tend to have few internal controls, the assessment of audit risk will often depend entirely on the assessment of inherent risk, as the risks identified here cannot be mitigated by a strong control environment. Therefore it is important that the assessment of inherent risk is performed carefully and in possession of full knowledge of the client, its business and trading position.

In addition, the risks of small businesses are often mitigated by the auditors' providing of other services, such as accountancy, and this should also be taken into account.

Auditors may also be involved in advising the client about their accounting systems and this may supply them with sufficient knowledge for the planning of the audit. Even if this is not the case the accounting systems of small businesses will usually be simple, informal and easily documented in short narrative notes.

35.8   EVIDENCE

35.8.1   SAS 400 Audit Evidence/ISA (UK and Ireland) 500 Audit Evidence, 501 Audit Evidence – Additional Considerations for Specific Items and 505 External Confirmations

Although the SAS and ISAs (UK and Ireland) recognise that audit evidence may be obtained from a number of sources (such as tests of control and substantive procedures), where segregation of duties is limited and evidence of supervisory control is lacking, evidence may be obtained entirely from substantive procedures. This would often be the case for small businesses.

As mentioned above, gaining assurance from accountancy procedures may lead to a reduction in the level of other audit procedures. This assurance may be gained through:

● examining prime documentation which supports a transaction or balance;
● calculating a balance for inclusion in the financial statements; or
● posting entries in the accounting records.

While the work may not be performed by those directly involved with the audit, it is important to ensure that the accountancy work is planned with the needs of the audit in mind.

While accountancy work may provide much of the assurance required, there will always be a need for some additional audit procedures in areas where it is unable to give assurance, for example, on the recovery of debtors, the valuation and ownership of stock, the carrying value of fixed assets and investments and the completeness of creditors. For convenience this work may be carried out at the same time as the accountancy work.

In the case of small businesses the completeness assertion may cause auditors particular problems. The two main reasons for this are:

- the owner-manager occupies a dominant position and may be able to ensure that some transactions are not recorded; and
- the business may not have internal control procedures that provide documentary evidence that all transactions are recorded.

Practice Note 13 states that auditors should plan and conduct the audit with an 'attitude of professional scepticism', and should not accept representations from management as a substitute for other audit evidence that would be expected to be available. However, unless the audit reveals evidence to the contrary, auditors are entitled to accept representations as truthful and records as genuine.

35.8.2   *SAS 410 Analytical Procedures/ISA (UK and Ireland) 520 Analytical Procedures*

The use of analytical review procedures when planning the audit of a small business may be limited due to lack of reliable information such as interim or monthly financial reports. Therefore analytical procedures at the planning stage may be more worthwhile once some of the accountancy work is completed. In some cases, a brief review of the general ledger or discussions with the owner-manager may prove sufficient.

When the activities of a business are uncomplicated and the number of variables to be considered is limited, analytical procedures may often be a very cost-effective way of obtaining audit assurance.

Such analytical review may also provide effective evidence regarding completeness, where expected results can be predicted with a reasonable degree of precision and confidence.

Practice Note 13 states that all auditors are required to perform a final analytical review to assess whether the financial statements are consistent with their knowledge of the business. However, due to the relative simplicity of small businesses many of the procedures performed are very similar to those used as substantive procedures. These may include:

- comparison to prior year;
- comparison to budget or forecast;
- review of trends in ratios;
- consideration of whether any changes in business are adequately reflected; and
- enquiry into unusual and unexplained features of the financial statements.

35.8.3   SAS 430 Audit Sampling/ISA (UK and Ireland) 530 Audit Sampling and other Means of Testing

The smaller populations normally encountered in small businesses may occasionally make it feasible to test:

- the whole population; or
- some part of the population – for example, all items above a given amount – applying analytical procedures to the balance of the population, if it is material.

Where auditors decide to sample a population, the same underlying principles apply to a small business as to a larger one.

35.8.4   SAS 440 Management Representations/ISA (UK and Ireland) 580 Management Representations

An important issue in respect of audit evidence in relation to completeness is that of acceptance of management representations. In many smaller businesses, the accounting system is often controlled by one or two individuals and the auditors may have difficulty in obtaining sufficient reliable evidence to assure themselves of the completeness of populations. This is particularly the case with cash businesses but may also apply to service industries or in businesses where stock is not purchased for specific customers. Auditors may also need to rely on representations when establishing that all expenditure is a valid charge on the business, given the confusion between the company and the owner in many small companies.

On their own, representations as to the completeness and accuracy of the accounting records cannot be sufficient. They may only be used if they are supported by or support the results of substantive tests of transactions and analytical review of costs and margins (or possibly one of them).

35.8.5   SAS 450 Opening Balances and Comparatives/ISA (UK and Ireland) 510 Initial Engagements – Opening Balances and Continuing Engagements – Opening Balances and ISA (UK and Ireland) 710 Comparatives

A small business which is a limited company may find itself in the position where its comparatives are taken from preceding period financial statements which were covered by the exemption from audit conferred on small companies.

Auditors will still need to obtain sufficient assurance about the opening balances and comparatives. Some information may be easily available (such as cash and debtors), but where they are unable to obtain the required evidence, they must consider qualifying their audit report. This issue is discussed in more detail above where a suitable report for use for these purposes is set out (see **Chapter 31**).

35.8.6 SAS 460 Related Parties/ISA (UK and Ireland) 550 Related Parties

Small businesses are as likely as larger businesses to enter into related party transactions, and the disclosures are identical. However, auditors of small businesses are more likely to be closely involved in the preparation of the financial statements, and will probably have a relatively detailed knowledge of the businesses' transactions, enabling them to identify those that are disclosable.

Where a small business is preparing accounts under the FRSSE, then the auditors' assessment of whether a related party transaction involving an individual related party is material is from the company's point of view only (see **3.12.3**).

35.9 REPORTING

35.9.1 SAS 600 Auditors' Reports on Financial Statements/ISA (UK and Ireland) 700 The Auditor's Report on Financial Statements

The modifications needed for auditors' reports either under the FRSSE or Sch 8 of the Companies Act 1985 are discussed in more detail above (see **3.12.3**).

35.9.2 SAS 610 Reports to Directors or Management/ISA (UK and Ireland) 260 Communication of Audit Matters with those Charged with Governance

Small businesses will often have simple, informal accounting systems and the scope for detailed internal control procedures based on segregation of duties will be limited. This is not necessarily a weakness, as the accounting system in place may be suitable for the size and complexity of the business and the degree of owner-manager involvement. Auditors must, therefore, ensure that recommendations to management are relevant and realistic to their business.

In addition, if management has not acted upon points made in previous management letters as the suggestions are not practical or cost-effective, auditors are likely to gain little from repeating the same recommendations again. However, they should continue to check that the recommendations remain valid.

35.10   PRACTICE NOTE 26

35.10.1   Background

Practice Note 26, *Guidance on Smaller Entity Audit Documentation* is aimed at auditors of companies that are exempt from audit, but have chosen to have a voluntary audit. It provides guidance on the application of the documentation requirements set out in the ISAs (UK and Ireland) for the audits of such entities.

Since the publication of the ISAs (UK and Ireland), there has been comment that the burden of documentation put on auditors of small companies has increased, particularly in relation to ISA (UK and Ireland) 315 *Understanding the Entity and its Environment and Assessing the Risks of Material Misstatement*. Practice Note 26 provides examples of documentation where work papers have been prepared to meet the requirements of the ISAs (UK and Ireland), but without documenting the entirety of auditors' understanding of the entity and matters related to it. The illustrative examples are not, however, mandatory. An Exposure Draft of a revision to Practice Note 26 was issued in July 2009 and is detailed in **35.10.6** below.

35.10.2   The purpose of audit documentation

ISA (UK and Ireland) 230 requires auditors to prepare audit documentation that provides:

* a sufficient and appropriate record of the basis for the auditor's report; and
* evidence that the audit was performed in accordance with ISAs (UK and Ireland) and applicable legal and regulatory requirements.

In addition good documentation serves a number of purposes, including:

* assisting the audit team to plan and perform the audit;
* assisting members of the audit team to fulfil their review responsibilities;
* enabling the audit team to be accountable for its work;
* retaining a record of matters of continuing significance to future audits; and
* enabling an experienced auditor to conduct quality control reviews or external inspections as required.

These remain relevant irrespective of the size of the entity.

35.10.3   Special considerations for smaller entities

A number of factors will influence the nature and extent of documentation required for a small company:

* the qualitative indicators of a simple entity:

- ownership is concentrated in a small number of individuals who are actively involved in managing the business;
- the operations are uncomplicated;
- business processes and accounting systems are simple; and
- internal controls are relatively few and may be informal;

- the characteristics of a smaller entity audit team and the way they carry out their work, including:

  - the provision of accounting and business related advice;
  - relatively small team size; and
  - the use of proprietary audit systems.

Concentration of ownership and management

For small entities there are often few owners, who are typically involved in the day to day running of the company, and this means that documentation of ownership is typically brief. Particular care should be taken, however, when documenting family and other close relationships which may impact auditors' risk assessment in respect of related parties.

Uncomplicated operations

Typically smaller entities have a limited range of products or services and a limited number of locations. This means that documentation of auditors' understanding of their operations is likely to be simple and relatively brief. Such documentation may be in free-form narrative notes or by completing a structured form.

Simple accounting systems

For small companies accounting systems are typically uncomplicated, with few, if any, personnel solely engaged in record keeping. There are likely to be no documented descriptions of accounting policies and procedures and limited opportunities for segregation of duties.

Small entities will typically use well known accounting systems, and previous knowledge of that system can help auditors focus on areas of risk.

Limited and informal controls

For the audit of smaller entities most of the audit evidence will typically come from substantive tests of detail. However, there is still a requirement for auditors to document their understanding of the entity's system of internal control relevant to the audit.

Both size and economic considerations mean that internal controls are usually limited in such operations, but the direct control that management is able to exert will be an important feature of the control environment. Therefore, the extent and nature of management's involvement is likely to be a key aspect of auditors' documentation, including whether the dominant position of management may be abused, leading to an override of controls.

Professional relationship between auditors and small entity clients

It is common for audit firms to provide non-audit services to smaller clients. The provision of such services can help auditors gain further understanding of the entity and keep their knowledge up to date. Auditors must keep in mind the need to maintain objectivity throughout their work.

The Practice Note lists the following considerations associated with providing non-audit services:

- to achieve completeness of audit documentation, information, gained as a result of the provision of other services, which is used as audit evidence needs to be incorporated or cross-referenced into the audit documentation;
- auditors' assessment of their objectivity and independence is documented, including a description of the threats identified and the safeguards applied to eliminate or reduce the threats to an acceptable level; and
- the respective responsibilities of directors (or equivalent) and auditors are documented in an engagement letter. This is particularly important where the audit firm is involved in the preparation of the financial statements.

Small audit team

Whatever the size of the audit team, even if it is an audit partner working alone, the documentation must be sufficient to enable an experienced auditor, having no previous connection with the audit, to understand the audit approach adopted, the audit evidence obtained, and the significant matters arising during the audit and the conclusions reached thereon.

If the audit team size increases, further documentation may be useful in enabling the team to obtain an appropriate understanding of the entity.

Use of proprietary audit system

Where the auditor of a small entity operates in a small practice, proprietary audit systems are likely to be used. Such systems are designed to deal with a wide variety of situations and must be tailored or adapted to meet each client's circumstances.

Sections of such systems relating to documenting the client, its operations and controls are usually checklists or blank spaces for narrative notes. Audit team members should be adequately trained before using such tools to ensure that they do not prepare excessive and, therefore, costly audit documentation.

35.10.4   Audit documentation requirements in the ISAs (UK and Ireland)

The Practice Note lists the documentation requirements set out in each ISA (UK and Ireland) on an ISA by ISA basis. The table is not reproduced here.

35.10.5   Assembling the final audit file

Chapter 19 sets out the procedures for assembling the final file, including document retention requirements and how to deal with the situation where documentation requires amendment after the date of the auditor's report.

35.10.6   Exposure Draft

An Exposure Draft of a revision to Practice Note 26 was published in July 2009 and comments were requested by 30 September 2009. The Exposure Draft was issued following the publication of the Exposure Drafts of the Clarified ISAs (UK and Ireland) in April 2009 and updates the current Practice Note to incorporate changes to audit documentation requirements set out in the Clarified standards. The overall structure of the Practice Note and the guidance on the special considerations in the documentation of a smaller entity audit are largely unchanged from the previous version.

36   BANK CONFIRMATIONS

36.1   INTRODUCTION

This chapter reviews the confirmations that auditors may obtain from banks. These are generally of two types:

- bank reports for audit purposes, confirming balances, interest and other account information; and
- confirmations of ongoing facilities.

36.2   GUIDANCE

Practice Note 16 *Bank Reports for Audit Purposes* contains guidance on the form of the request letters and has been agreed with the British Bankers Association (BBA). In October 2005 the APB issued a Consultation Draft of a revision to Practice Note 16 and a second draft of this revision was issued in July 2007 which reflected further discussion between auditors and banks. The final update to Practice Note 16 was issued in December 2007 and is effective for accounting periods commencing on or after 26 December 2007. In August 2008, the APB issued further practical guidance on the implementation of the updated version of Practice Note 16, setting out the differences between it and the earlier version in tabular form.

In September 2002, the ICAEW's Audit and Assurance Faculty published Technical Release 3/02, *Bank Reports for Audit Purposes: Explanatory Note*, to assist auditors and banks in the prompt processing of requests for bank reports. The explanatory note was prepared by the British Bankers' Association and the CCAB and does not form an update or amendment to Practice Note 16, *Bank Reports for Audit Purposes*, but rather provided additional, non-mandatory guidance. The revision to Practice Note 16, issued in December 2007, incorporates this guidance.

36.3   AUTHORITY

Customers have to give explicit authority to their banks before any information can be released to their auditors and the BBA has asked that, where possible, this takes the form of an ongoing standing authority rather than as a separate authority each time information is requested.

A single authority can cover several entities, for example in group situations, provided that each entity is specified, together with the relevant authorised signatures. An example of such a letter is shown in **Table 1** below.

TABLE 1: Example of authority to disclose letter

XYZ Bank plc

(Parent Company Ltd, Subsidiary 1 Ltd, Subsidiary 2 Ltd)

I/we authorise XYZ Bank plc, including all branches and subsidiaries to provide our auditors ABC & Co any information that they may request from you regarding all and any of our accounts and dealings with you.

Authorised signatory

The Practice Note clarifies that banks do not need a new authority to disclose information to auditors each time they are asked for confirmation of bank details. However, auditors are responsible for ensuring that standing authorities remain up to date, e.g., they cover all relevant entities or are amended if the auditor changes its name or status.

36.4   DISCLAIMERS

The request letter indicates that the process of obtaining a confirmation does not create any contractual or other duty between the bank and the auditors. In addition, the bank may include a disclaimer stating that their response is given solely for the purposes of the audit and creates no responsibility to the auditors.

The APB is of the view that neither the statement in the request letter nor the disclaimer in the bank's reply significantly impairs the value of the confirmation. This is because the information supplied by a bank ought not to be regarded as inaccurate simply because legal action cannot be taken against the bank supplying it. Therefore, auditors can rely on this evidence as long as it is not:

- clearly wrong;
- suspicious; or
- inconsistent in itself or in conflict with other evidence gathered in the course of the audit.

36.5   BANK CONFIRMATION PROCESS

The Practice Note suggests that as part of their planning process, auditors consider the need for a bank report as part of their assessment of risk. Given the importance of cash and its susceptibility to fraud it is likely that auditors will conclude that sufficient audit evidence cannot be obtained without receiving a bank report. In some rare circumstances where banking transactions and relationships are very simple, auditors may determine that sufficient evidence is available from other sources. Having decided to obtain a bank report, auditors:

- determine the date by which the bank report is needed;

- determine whether confirmation is needed for additional information such as trade finance transactions and balances;
- decide what type of report to use (see **36.5.3** below);
- make arrangements for obtaining the necessary information to be included in the request. This will include the main account sort code and number for each legal entity, and any other references required for additional information;
- check that the relevant authorities to disclose information are valid; and
- ascertain where to send the request.

36.5.1 Timing of requests

The December 2007 Practice Note recommends that auditors submit their requests for information at least one month before the period end date, an increase from the 14-day timescale set out in the original Practice Note. Where this notice is provided, banks will endeavour to provide the information within one month of the confirmation date. However, where auditors submit an Incomplete Information Request (see **36.5.3** below), the bank's response period may increase. The Practice Note also recommends that additional time is allowed at busy times of the year, i.e., for December or March year ends.

Where auditors of listed clients or other entities with a tight reporting deadline require a faster response, auditors should use the Fast Track Template set out in **Table 4** below.

36.5.2 Information required

The Practice Note asks auditors to provide the names of all the entities covered by the request, together with the main account and sort code of the principal entity or the holding company. The aim of this is to aid the identification of the customer by the bank as entity names are often similar and identification is sometimes problematic. Banks will still be responsible for identifying all other relevant accounts.

This contradicts earlier guidance which warned against providing such information. The APB are of the opinion that where account details are taken from bank statements, this does not diminish the value of the evidence.

It notes that there are clients with more complex relationships with their bankers and that in such cases auditors may require supplementary information about trade finance or derivative and commodity trading transactions. The decision on whether supplementary information is necessary will be based on the auditors' knowledge of the business and discussions with directors and management.

Where such information is requested, auditors are required to supply a sample facility account number.

36.5.3 Type of report

The December 2007 Practice Note introduced three alternative templates to reflect auditors' planning decisions as to the nature and timing of the information sought.

The Standard (**Table 2**) and Fast Track (**Table 3**) templates specify:

- the names of all legal entities covered by the request, together with the main account sort code and number of each entity listed;
- reference to a sample facility account number for any additional information required. This will enable the bank to identify the units providing specialist services which need to be consulted. A full listing of all transactions or balances is not required;
- the date for which the auditor is requesting confirmation and the date at which the report request is made;
- a statement that neither the auditor's request or the bank's response will create a contractual relationship between the bank and the auditor; and
- the auditor's contact details.

The template for Fast Track Requests is the same as the Standard but it also allows the auditor to explain the need for such an approach and provide the date by which a reply is needed.

The Incomplete Information Request (**Table 4**) contains:

- the names of all legal entities covered by the request, together with the main account number and sort code of the parent company and of as many group entities as can be obtained by the auditor;
- the period end date for which the auditor is requesting confirmation;
- the date at which the report request is made;
- a statement that neither the auditor's request or the bank's response will create a contractual relationship between the bank and the auditor; and
- the auditor's contact details.

TABLE 2: Example Standard Request

Please note – Complete **section 6** only where additional information is required.

In accordance with the agreed practice for provision of information to auditors, please forward information on our mutual client(s) as detailed below on behalf of the bank, its branches and subsidiaries. This request and your response will not create any contractual or other duty with us.

1. BANK NAME AND ADDRESS

2. AUDITOR CONTACT DETAILS

Name and address of auditor

Contact Number

Contact Name

Email address

Period end date (DD/MM/YYYY)   Date of request (DD/MM/YYYY)

3.   COMPANIES AND OTHER BUSINESS ENTITIES

Company	Main account sort code	Main account number

4.   AUTHORITY TO DISCLOSE INFORMATION

Authority already held and dated   Or   Authority Attached
(DD/MM/YYYY)

5.   ACKNOWLEDGEMENT

Please complete this section if an acknowledgement is required.

Acknowledgement   By email   Reference
required   number to be
                                             quoted

OR   By post   (template
                                             attached)

6.   ADDITIONAL INFORMATION REQUIRED

Trade Finance   One of the facility account numbers

Derivative & Commodity Trading   One of the facility account numbers

TABLE 3: Example Fast Track Request

Please note – Complete **section 6** only where additional information is required.

In accordance with the agreed practice for provision of information to auditors, please forward information on our mutual client(s) as detailed below on behalf of the bank, its branches and subsidiaries. This request and your response will not create any contractual or other duty with us.

1. BANK NAME AND ADDRESS

2. AUDITOR CONTACT DETAILS

Name and address of auditor

Contact Number

Contact Name

Email address

Period end date (DD/MM/YYYY)

Date response required (DD/MM/YYYY)

Date of request (DD/MM/YYYY)

Reason for fast track request

3. COMPANIES AND OTHER BUSINESS ENTITIES

Company	Main account sort code	Main account number

4. AUTHORITY TO DISCLOSE INFORMATION

Authority already held and dated   Or   Authority Attached
(DD/MM/YYYY)

5. ACKNOWLEDGEMENT

Please complete this section if an acknowledgement is required.

Acknowledgement   By email   Reference
required   number to be
                                     quoted

OR   By post   (template
                                 attached)

6. ADDITIONAL INFORMATION REQUIRED

Trade Finance   One of the facility account numbers

Derivative & Commodity Trading   One of the facility account numbers

TABLE 4: Example Incomplete Information Request

Please note – Complete **section 6** only where additional information is required.

In accordance with the agreed practice for provision of information to auditors, please forward information on our mutual client(s) as detailed below on behalf of the bank, its branches and subsidiaries. This request and your response will not create any contractual or other duty with us.

1. BANK NAME AND ADDRESS

2. AUDITOR CONTACT DETAILS

Name and address of auditor

Contact Number

Contact Name

Email address

Period end date (DD/MM/YYYY)

Date response required (DD/MM/YYYY)

We confirm that there are exceptional circumstances that require us to ask for this request to be processed on the basis of incomplete account numbers, sort code and facility account numbers for all companies in the group and/or a facility account number for additional information. We understand that this may result in the search taking longer to complete than the standard request

3. COMPANIES AND OTHER BUSINESS ENTITIES

Company	Main account sort code	Main account number

4. AUTHORITY TO DISCLOSE INFORMATION

Authority already held and dated   Or   Authority Attached
(DD/MM/YYYY)

5. ACKNOWLEDGEMENT

Please complete this section if an acknowledgement is required.

Acknowledgement required   By email   Reference number to be quoted

OR   By post   (template attached)

6. ADDITIONAL INFORMATION REQUIRED

Trade Finance   One of the facility account numbers

Derivative & Commodity Trading   One of the facility account numbers

36.5.4   Where to send the request

To better reflect banks' working practices, the Practice Note states that requests for bank reports should be sent to regional centres, rather than to individual branches. Addresses for regional centres to which bank requests should be sent on are published on the BBA website, *www.bba.org.uk*.

Also on the site are contact details or preferred contact methods for auditors to follow up bank requests. This information may also be included in the acknowledgement letter sent by the bank (see **36.5.5**).

36.5.5 Acknowledgement letters

The Bank Acknowledgement of Auditor Request form which was introduced by interim guidance issued during the process of updating Practice Note 16 has been replaced by a section of each bank report request template, which allows auditors to select if they wish to receive an acknowledgement from the bank.

Such acknowledgements should be provided within five working days of receipt. A list of those banks which do not provide acknowledgements is posted on the BBA website, together with contact details for pursuing enquiries.

36.5.6 Other issues

Other issues highlighted by the Practice Note are:

- minor omissions or amendments to a bank report may be communicated by telephone or e-mail, although auditors may request written confirmation of these changes; and
- a bank has the right to decline to give information about accrued interest or charges as this is not within the scope of the guidance agreed between the British Bankers' Authority and the Auditing Practices Board.

36.5.7 Non-BBA Banks

Where banks are not members of the BBA, auditors should follow the same procedures. A full list of BBA banks can be found on the BBA website, *www.bba.org.uk*. If auditors are not able to obtain a satisfactory reply they should consider whether this leads to a limitation of scope.

36.6 CONFIRMATION OF ONGOING FACILITIES

As part of their consideration of 'going concern' (see **Chapter 13**), auditors will carry out a review of the ability of ongoing bank facilities to meet the entity's future cash needs. Where they consider existing banking facilities to be critical to the continuing operation of the entity, they may need to obtain a letter from the bank as to their intentions.

36.6.1 Procedures

As part of the reply to the standard request for a bank report for audit purposes, the auditors will have received details of any overdrafts and loans repayable on demand, specifying agreed facilities and dates of review. Where such facilities are in the process of being reviewed or they are to be reviewed within the time frame of the 'foreseeable future', and where the auditors consider their renewal as critical to their opinion, they may have to enter into correspondence with bankers to obtain confirmation.

Such correspondence should always be within the framework set out above for supplementary requests. This should encourage the banks to use standard disclaimers, which do not significantly impair the value of a response as audit evidence.

Table 5 contains suggested wording for a letter from the auditors to the bank requesting comfort as to the continuation of facilities, while **Table 6** provides an example of a letter from the bank to the auditors indicating their intentions concerning the facilities. It is suggested that this wording constitutes the minimum level of comfort acceptable from the bank.

In both cases, it is important to ensure that the client is made aware that such confirmation is being sought.

TABLE 5: Comfort letter request

The Manager XYZ Bank Plc

Dear Sir

X Limited

We refer to your above named customer's instructions given in the authority

.... already held by you and to your reply to our Standard Request for Bank Report for Audit Purposes dated

....

For the purpose of our audit, as part of a request for supplementary information, we would ask you to confirm that, based on the information provided to you by the company (specific documents should be listed) and subject to unforeseen circumstances, you see no reason why the company's facilities will not be renewed on existing terms when they fall due nor are you aware of any reason why such facilities will not continue to be made available (specify timing, e.g., six months after that date).

Yours faithfully

TABLE 6: Bank's response to comfort letter request

ABC & Co

Dear Sirs

X Limited

We refer to your letter of .... requesting confirmation as to continuing facilities.

The company's facilities are due for renewal on ..... No decision has been reached as to whether the facilities will be renewed and we will continue to monitor the situation in the light of information which is supplied to us. Renewal of the facility will be considered on the agreed renewal date.

Yours faithfully

36.6.2   Level of reliance to be placed on reply

A satisfactory reply from the bank does not absolve the auditors from properly considering the going concern position of a client company by reference to primary audit evidence. Further reference should be made to the matters discussed in **Chapter 13**.

37 OTHER OPERATIONAL ISSUES

37.1 INTRODUCTION

This chapter covers various guidance issued by the ICAEW and APB covering:

- debtors' confirmations;
- pending legal matters;
- paid cheques;
- stocktaking;
- service organisations;
- auditing derivative financial instruments;
- auditing when financial market conditions are difficult; and
- XBRL tagging of information in financial statements.

37.2 DEBTORS' CONFIRMATIONS

Guidance in this area comes from ICAEW Statement 901 – *Verification of Debtor Balances: Confirmation by Direct Communication* and the statement is directed towards the verification of trade debtors and is not intended to relate to debts from group companies or other special debts.

Further guidance is given in ISA (UK and Ireland) 505, External Confirmations (see **Chapter 24**).

As part of their procedures the auditors may decide to carry out a circularisation of the company's trade debtors to enable them to form an opinion as to the adequacy of the system of internal control over sales and its operation in practice. It will be a confirmation that the cut-off procedures are operating and should provide evidence as to whether the balances are genuine, accurately stated and not in dispute.

The auditors cannot approach the debtors directly as only the client can authorise third parties to divulge information to the auditors but generally, if asked, the management will authorise the circularisation. Where the client refuses, the auditors need to consider whether they are able to obtain sufficient alternative evidence and the implications for their report.

Where a circularisation is performed on a sample basis it may not provide sufficient evidence on its own, but may influence the extent of any other tests carried out.

There are two methods that can be used when requesting information from the debtor. These are:

- *positive*: where the debtor is requested to confirm the accuracy of the balance shown or state in what respect he disagrees; or
- *negative*: where the debtor only replies if the amount stated is disputed.

In either case the reply should be sent directly to the auditors. The choice of method will be a matter for the auditors' judgement, but there are certain factors which may influence this decision, including:

- the strength of the system of internal controls;
- whether there are any suspicions of irregularities;
- the number and size of accounts;
- whether there are amounts which are likely to be in dispute; and
- the number of bookkeeping errors.

Where there are doubts about the accuracy of the sales ledger or where there is a small number of large balances, more confidence will be gained from a positive circularisation. However, if errors are not expected or there is a large number of small balances then a negative one may be more appropriate.

In most cases, a sample of debtors' balances based on the complete population will be tested. However, the following should be considered when selecting the sample:

- old, unpaid accounts;
- accounts written off during the period;
- accounts with credit balances;
- accounts with nil balances; and
- accounts which have been paid by the date of the examination.

The request is usually accompanied by a statement of the account, either the normal monthly statement if the circularisation is carried out at the same time as these are sent out, or a specially printed one if the circularisation is at any other time. Where a positive response is required a pre-paid reply envelope is normally included.

The request may be as a specially prepared letter or as an attachment to the statement. The ICAEW Statement does not provide an example of such a letter, but one for a positive circularisation is shown in **Table 1**.

Where requests are returned as undelivered they should be sent to the auditors, who will need to consider what action to take.

When the positive method is used and replies are not received auditors should make every effort to ensure that some response is obtained. It may be that a member of the client's staff can be used to do this, but auditors will need to ensure that the clearance procedure is properly performed. It may be necessary to use other audit tests to provide evidence of the validity of the debtor where no reply is received in a positive circularisation, as every item selected must be concluded upon.

The responses may indicate inaccuracies in the part of the population that is not tested and further work may be necessary.

37.3   PENDING LEGAL MATTERS

ICAEW Statement 903 – *The Ascertainment and Confirmation of Contingent Liabilities Arising from Pending Legal Matters* covers the auditors' problems concerning contingencies arising from pending litigation against the company upon which they are reporting. Further guidance is also given in ISA (UK and Ireland) 501 Audit Evidence – Additional Consideration for Specific Items (see **Chapter 24**).

TABLE 1: Example of positive debtors' circularisation letter

XYZ Plc Industrial House
Anytown

Name & Address

Dear Sir As part of their normal audit procedures, we have been requested by our auditors, ABC & Co, to ask you to confirm direct to them the balance on your account at 31 December 20..... This request is made for audit purposes only and remittances should be sent to us in the normal way.

According to our records the balance at that date in our favour was as shown by the enclosed statement of your account. If the balance is in agreement with that shown by your records, please sign the confirmation below and return it in the enclosed reply-paid envelope to ABC & Co. Please do this even if the account has been settled.

If the balance is not in agreement with that shown by your records will you please send the confirmation to our auditors showing, if possible, details of the items making up the difference.

Your co-operation in this matter is greatly appreciated.

Yours faithfully

XYZ Plc
ABC & Co
1 High Street
London

....

Dear Sirs

We confirm that according to our records a balance of £ .... was owing by us to XYZ Plc at 31 December 20.....

Name of company or _____ individual:
_____

Signed: _____
Position held: _____
Items making up difference if any: _____

It suggests procedures the auditors may use to verify the existence of claims, although they will not necessarily provide sufficient evidence of the likely amount that the company may be responsible for. These include:

- reviewing the system of recording claims and the procedure for bringing these to the attention of management;
- discussing with management arrangements for instructing solicitors;
- examining Board minutes and correspondence for potential claims;
- examining bills from solicitors or estimates of unbilled charges;
- obtaining a list of matters referred to solicitors with estimates of the possible ultimate liabilities; and
- obtaining written representations that there are no further matters of which the directors are aware.

Auditors may decide that they wish to obtain confirmation of these matters directly from the solicitors involved. This should be done with the client's authority and the Statement recommends that the letter should come from the client with a request that a copy of the reply be sent directly to the auditors.

The auditors may choose to make a non-specific enquiry, i.e., to enquire if there are any matters which are not listed of which the directors are aware, as this serves as a confirmation that the information received from the directors is complete. However, the Law Society has advised solicitors that it is unable to recommend them to comply with requests for information that are more widely drawn than the specific enquiry shown in **Table 2**.

The ICAEW considers that there may be circumstances in which non-specific enquiries are appropriate; however, it does not discuss how the opposing stands may be reconciled.

The correspondence and the other procedures adopted by the auditors may mean that undisclosed liabilities become apparent and it may be necessary to discuss these with management and their solicitors before considering the effect on their audit report.

TABLE 2: Extract from a letter to company solicitors requesting information on pending litigation

'In connection with the preparation and audit of our accounts for the year ended ... the directors have made estimates of the amounts of the ultimate liabilities (including costs) which might be incurred, and are regarded as material, in relation to the following matters on which you have been consulted. We should be obliged if you would confirm that in your opinion these estimates are reasonable.

Matter

Estimated liability including costs'

Where there are matters which are being dealt with by solicitors but the auditors are unable to take photocopies of documents because of legal privilege, they should prepare file notes of the evidence they have reviewed.

There are occasions when solicitors do not reply directly to requests on the grounds that letters written concerning the merits of litigation involving a client would be discoverable by the other party to the litigation.

The Audit Faculty of the ICAEW has issued Audit 2/95 an addendum to 3.903 dealing with this. They identify and make the following recommendations in two cases:

- *When solicitors refuse to write to auditors or clients* where it is advised that auditors should meet with the solicitors to discuss the matter and agree a file note that the auditor considers adequate to support the treatment of the matter in the financial statements.
- *When solicitors are prepared to write only to the clients* where the auditors should read and make notes of the relevant contents but will generally not photocopy the letter.

The file notes concerned in either of these cases must be non-specific and may only indicate that evidence has been obtained and the matter considered. Any fuller note may itself be discoverable.

37.4   PAID CHEQUES

Changes in legislation and audit practices have made it less important for auditors to review paid cheques returned to entities by their clearing bank.

37.4.1   Existing guidance

Guidance in this area was updated in February 2009 with the publication of the ICAEW's Audit and Assurance Faculty Technical Release AAF 1/09 *Paid Cheques*. The guidance encourages auditors to:

- consider using alternative procedures;
- advise their clients to adopt more rigorous controls over cheque payments; and
- use cost-effective methods of examining paid cheques where they consider it to be necessary.

The statement does not provide detailed procedural guidance.

37.4.2   Audit evidence

Where adequate controls exist over purchasing and cheque payments it may not be necessary to examine returned cheques. In cases where controls are weak auditors may want evidence that:

- there has been no fraudulent endorsement of cheques;
- cheques are properly recorded and controlled; and
- the cash book accurately reflects details of them.

With regard to purchase ledger items, other forms of evidence may be sufficient such as the reconciliation of supplier statements. Evidence on other items may be obtained from analytical review or examination of supporting evidence.

Additionally the entity may use other forms of payment, such as electronic funds transfers, standing orders or direct debits.

37.4.3   Cheques Act 1992

Further controls against fraudulent endorsement comes from the Cheques Act 1992, which means that cheques crossed 'account payee' cannot be transferred by way of endorsement. Many banks now pre-print their cheques with this, which greatly reduces the risk and, in turn, the auditors' need to examine paid cheques.

37.4.4   Obtaining paid cheques

Where auditors decide that they need to review paid cheques they should aim to choose the most cost-effective method of obtaining this evidence. Discussions with the client and their bank will normally be necessary as to the most appropriate method. Options include:

- returning all paid cheques to the client;
- providing the auditors with an agreed number of paid cheques directly, the selection being left to the bank;
- providing photocopies of paid cheques;
- extracting cheques before they are stored and forwarding them to the auditors directly; and
- providing specific paid cheques at the auditors' request.

Where paid cheques are to be sent to the auditors directly by the bank, authority will have to be provided by the client.

37.5   STOCK

37.5.1   Introduction

The APB published Practice Note 25, *Attendance at Stocktaking* in January 2004 to supersede Auditing Guideline 405 which was some 20 years old. The Practice Note sought to give guidance on the application of SAS 300*Accounting and Internal Control Systems and Audit Risk Assessment* and SAS 400*Audit Evidence*, when determining the existence of stock but is equally as relevant to the ISA (UK and Ireland) equivalents.

The Practice Note covers:

- assessment of risks and internal controls;
- audit evidence;
- audit procedures before, during and after the stocktake;
- work in progress;
- the use of experts; and
- stock held by third parties.

Further guidance on the audit of stock is given in ISA (UK and Ireland) 501 Audit Evidence, Additional Considerations for Specific Items (see **Chapter 24**).

37.5.2   Assessment of risks and internal controls

ISA (UK and Ireland) 315 states that auditors should use professional judgement to ascertain levels of audit risk. Example factors to consider when assessing risks relating to existence of stock are set out in **Table 3**.

TABLE 3: Example risk factors relating to existence of stock

- Reliability of accounting and stock recording systems including, in relation to work in progress, the systems that track location, quantities and stages of completion.
- Timing of stocktakes relative to the year end date, and the reliability of records used in any roll forward of balances.
- Location of stock, including stock on consignment and items held at third-party locations.
- Physical controls over stock, and its susceptibility to theft or deterioration.
- Objectivity, experience and reliability of the stock counters and of those monitoring their work.
- Degree of fluctuation in stock levels.
- Nature of stock, for example, whether specialist knowledge is needed to identify the quantity, quality and/or identity of stock items.
- Difficulty in carrying out the assessment of quantity, for example, whether a significant degree of estimation is involved.

The assessment of risk should also include consideration of frauds that influence stock levels. These may include the risk of false sales involving the movement of stock to another location, movement of stock to sites with different stocktaking dates, using inappropriate estimation techniques, or amendment or falsification of stock count sheets.

37.5.3   Audit evidence

Where stock is material or there is a risk of material misstatement, auditors will normally attend a stocktake. As well as giving evidence about the existence assertion, attending a stocktake may also provide evidence in respect of completeness and valuation of stock.

The main sources of evidence for the existence of stock are:

- evidence from audit procedures which confirm the reliability of the accounting records upon which the amount in the financial statements is based;
- evidence from tests of control over stock, including the reliability of stock counting procedures; and
- substantive evidence from the physical inspection tests undertaken by the auditors.

The amount and type of evidence required depends on the auditors' risk assessment.

Entities may or may not maintain detailed stock records. Where these are kept auditors should check that these records are up to date, that adequate stocktaking procedures are used, and that all material differences between physical and book stock are investigated and corrected.

Where no continuous stock records are maintained, the year-end stock figure will be derived from a full year-end stock count. In this situation it would be preferable for stocktaking to be completed at the year-end date but, where necessary, the count may be on a different date and updated for stock movements between that date and year-end.

In both situations attendance at the stocktake would be beneficial, either to confirm that accurate stock records are maintained or, where no stock records exist, to ensure that the count to determine year-end stock is accurate.

37.5.4   Audit procedures before, during and after the stocktake

Table 4 outlines example procedures that may be used before, during and after the stocktake. It does not provide an exhaustive list.

TABLE 4: Example audit procedures

Before the stocktake:

- performing analytical procedures and discussing findings with management;
- discussing client stocktaking arrangements and instructions with management;
- familiarisation with the nature and volume of the stock, the identification of high value items, the method of accounting for stock and the conditions giving rise to obsolescence;
- considering the location of the stock and assessing the implications of this for stock control and recording;
- considering the quantity and nature of work in progress, the quantity of stock held by third parties and whether expert valuers or stocktakers will be required;
- reviewing the system of internal control and accounting relating to stock;
- considering any involvement of internal audit; and
- considering the results of previous stocktakes and reviewing prior year work papers.

During the stocktake:

- ascertain whether client staff are following instructions;
- perform test counts to ensure that procedures and internal controls relating to the stocktake are operating effectively. Counting should be checked in both directions, i.e., from physical stock to stock sheet and vice versa;
- request recounts where results are not satisfactory;
- copy extracts of stocktaking records for subsequent testing;
- check the sequence of stock count records;
- consider whether the procedures for identifying damaged, obsolete and slow moving stock operate properly;
- ensure that stock held for third parties is separately identified and accounted for;
- consider the adequacy of cut-off procedures to ensure stock movements are included or excluded from the year end stock figure as necessary.

After the stocktake:

- follow up details of last serial numbers of goods inwards and outwards records to check cut-off;
- check copies of stock sheets are correctly reflected in final stock figures;
- review whether continuous stock records have been adjusted to the amounts physically counted and that differences have been investigated;
- follow up queries and notify senior management of serious problems encountered during the stocktake.

Some entities used computer-assisted techniques to perform stocktakes, for example, using hand held scanners. This may lead to there being no stock sheets, no physical count records and no paper records available at the time of the count. In such circumstances the auditors should consider the IT environment surrounding the stocktake and consider the need for specialist assistance to evaluate the techniques used and the controls in place.

37.5.5   Work in progress

Management may use accounting systems and internal controls to determine the completeness and accuracy of records of work in progress, and there may not be a stocktake. However, auditors may still find it beneficial to observe the work in progress as it may help with understanding the entity's control systems and processes and with determining the stage of completion of construction or engineering work in progress.

37.5.6   The use of experts

Auditors should determine whether expert help is required prior to attending the stocktake. Assistance may be required to substantiate quantities (e.g., a quantity surveyor) or to determine the nature and condition of specialist stock.

Where management involve a specialist third party stocktaker, common practice for farms, petrol stations and public houses, this does not eliminate the need for auditors to obtain audit evidence as to the existence of stock.

37.5.7   Stock held by third parties

If stock is located in public warehouses or with other third parties, the auditors normally obtain direct confirmation relating to quantities and ownership in writing from the custodian. If such stock is material auditors should consult ISA (UK and Ireland) 402 *Audit Considerations Relating to Entities Using Service Organisations* to ascertain how to obtain sufficient audit evidence (see **37.6**).

37.6   SERVICE ORGANISATIONS

Clarified ISA (UK and Ireland) 402 *Audit Considerations Relating to An Entity Using a Service Organisation* was issued in October 2009 and is effective for the audit of financial statements for periods ending on or after 15 December 2010. The updated ISA (UK and Ireland) replaces ISA (UK and Ireland) 230 issued in December 2004. This discussion covers both the existing and Clarified ISAs (UK and Ireland). As the Clarified ISA (UK and Ireland) adds to the requirements of the existing ISA (UK and Ireland) this section is written on the basis of the existing requirements, and changes to them included in the Clarified ISA (UK and Ireland) are included and clearly indicated.

The ISA (UK and Ireland) provides guidance on the procedures necessary to assess the impact of a reporting entity's use of a service organisation. As with all ISAs (UK and Ireland), the text of the ISA has been supplemented with additional guidance from a UK and Ireland perspective.

ISA (UK and Ireland) 402 *Audit Considerations Relating to an Entity Using a Service Organisation*, contains guidance covering:

- understanding the services provided by a service organisation;
- responding to assessed risks of material misstatement;

- subservice organisations;
- fraud and uncorrected misstatements; and
- reporting.

37.6.1 Identification and assessment

Auditors are required to identify whether the reporting entity uses service organisations and then to consider the impact of this on the client's internal control, their assessment of the risk of material misstatement and their procedures. The guidance notes that the outsourcing of an activity by an entity does not relieve its directors of their responsibilities nor does it alter those of the auditors. As not all outsourced activities have a significant effect on the reporting entity's financial statements auditors need to assess initially whether those activities are relevant to the audit and if so their effect on audit risk.

Service organisations undertake a wide variety of activities including:

- information processing;
- maintenance of accounting records;
- facilities management;
- maintenance of safe custody of assets, such as investments; and
- initiation or execution of transactions on behalf of the entity.

Services provided by a service organisation will be relevant when those services, and the controls over them, effectively form part of the entity's information system relevant to financial reporting. Controls at the service organisation may be relevant to the audit, such as controls over the safeguarding of assets. A service organisation's services will be part of the entity's information system if those services affect any of the following:

- the classes of transactions that are significant the user entity's financial statements;
- the procedures by which the user entity's transactions are initiated, recorded, processed, corrected as necessary, transferred to the general ledger and reported in the financial statements;
- the related accounting records, supporting information and specific accounts in the user entity's financial statements;
- how the user entity's information system captures events and conditions, other than transactions, that are significant to the financial statements;
- the financial reporting process used to prepare the financial statements; and
- controls surrounding recurring and non-recurring journal entries.

Auditors should obtain and document an understanding of the contract terms, whether agreed orally or in writing, and the way in which the reporting entity monitors the service organisation's activities so that it can meet its fiduciary and other legal responsibilities. This will assist the auditors in their consideration of the impact of the arrangement on the assessment of inherent risk (see **37.6.3**).

37.6.2 Considering the responsibilities of those charged with governance

Outsourcing all or part of their accounting records does not diminish the responsibilities of those charged with governance in relation to those records. Therefore, for each material element of the accounting records maintained by a service organisation, auditors should obtain and document an understanding of the way the accounting records are maintained and how those charged with governance ensure the accounting records meet any relevant legal obligations. Under UK company law those charged with governance must retain ownership of the accounting records and allow auditors to access them at any time.

The guidance states that auditors should assess whether the arrangements for maintaining all or part of the entity's accounting records by a service organisation has any effect on their reporting responsibilities in relation to accounting records.

The guidance notes that the wording of UK company law is such that it requires companies to keep records rather than cause them to be kept, and thus the wording of the contract with the service organisation will need to be reviewed to determine whether the entity retains ownership of those records. It is suggested that the auditors may wish to seek legal advice where there is any doubt on this matter.

37.6.3 Assessing risk

Inherent risk will be affected by:

- the nature of the services provided and their significance to the user entity (the clarified ISA (UK and Ireland) extends this to the impact on the user entity's internal control);
- the nature and materiality of the transactions processed or the financial reporting processes affected;
- the degree to which authority is delegated to the service organisation;
- the arrangements for ensuring quality of the service provided including the contractual terms;
- whether the activities involve assets which are susceptible to loss or misappropriation;
- the reputation for integrity of those responsible for direction and management of the service organisation; and
- whether, if the service organisation maintains all or part of a user entity's accounting records, the arrangements affect the user auditors' reporting responsibilities in relation to accounting records arising from law or regulation.

Auditors will consider these factors and assess inherent risk by financial statement assertion.

If, as a result of their assessment of inherent risk, the auditors decide that they expect to be able to rely on the operation of controls to reduce the extent of substantive procedures, they should then make an assessment of the control risk for material financial statement assertions. Auditors should consider controls operated by the service organisation as well as those operated by the client over the information provided by the service organisation.

A number of factors are relevant to the auditors' assessment of control risk, including:

- the extent and nature of controls operated by the user entity's personnel;
- undertakings by the service organisation for the operation of internal controls, and whether such controls are adequately specified, having regard to the size and complexity of the activities undertaken by the service organisation;
- actual experience of adjustments to, or errors and omissions in, reports received from the service organisation;
- the way in which the user entity determines whether the service organisation complies with its contractual undertakings; and
- whether the service organisation provides information on the design and operation of systems of controls, possibly accompanied by reports from its external auditors.

Where the maintenance of accounting records has been outsourced, the following particular risk factors require consideration by the reporting entity's auditors:

- the knowledge and expertise of the service organisation's staff in matters relevant to the client's business;
- the practicality of control by the entity's management and the nature of controls actually implemented; and
- the use of quality assurance processes by the service organisation.

Examples of ways in which different activities undertaken by service organisations can affect the risk of misstatement are given in **Table 5**.

TABLE 5: Characteristics of service organisation activities which may increase risk

Outsourced Accounting Functions

Degree of risk	Characteristics	Examples
High	<ul><li>Complex transactions</li><li>Those undertaking accounting work need extensive business or specialist knowledge</li><li>Delegated authority to initiate and execute transactions</li></ul>	<ul><li>Maintenance of both accounting records and preparation of budgets and control reports</li><li>Accounting records of retail business</li></ul>

Degree of risk	Characteristics	Examples
	• Effective controls only possible on 'real time' basis • Reversal of outsourcing costly/difficult • High cost of performance failure (eg misleading management reports leading to poor decision making • High proportion of finance functions outsourced	
Medium	• Some business knowledge needed but parameters for necessary judgements can be identified and agreed in advance • Transactions can be initiated but execution requires approval from entity • Execution of transactions on instruction from entity • Analytical techniques insufficient for adequate degree of control • Discrete functions outsourced	• Outsourcing of accounting records by a supplier of raw materials • Credit control • Leasing arrangements
Low	• Little requirement for judgement in processing transactions • Non-complex transactions • Little business knowledge required • Analytical control techniques effective • Effects of failure can be contained • Easy to rearrange/find alternate service organisations • Low proportion of discrete functions outsourced	• Processing salary payments • Preparation of invoices • Data entry

Outsourced Accounting Functions

Degree of risk	Characteristics	Examples
High	• Transactions can be initiated on a discretionary basis • Entity does not maintain and cannot generate independent records of assets and interests, dividends or other income • Complex financial instruments	• Discretionary trading, same custodian

Degree of risk	Characteristics	Examples
	• Custody and investment management undertaken by two separate entities but records are not independently generated, or one combined report is provided to the entity	
Medium	• Combination of custody and execution of transactions/ collection of income but entity maintains or can generate (for example by reference to Extel) independent records of income • Custody and investment management undertaken by two unrelated entities which maintain independently generated records (ie derived from different source data) and report separately direct to the entity	• Custodian responsible for collection of dividends and reporting of income: entity reviews information • Independent custodian and investment manager
Low	• Entity initiates and maintains records of transactions • Separation of execution and custody functions • Low frequency of transactions and/or counterparties • Non-complex financial instruments • Analytical control techniques effective	• Custody of assets only • Execution of investment transactions pursuant to entity's instructions

If auditors are unable to ascertain sufficient information about the operation of controls at the service organisation from the user entity, Clarified ISA (UK and Ireland) 402 requires that they perform one or more of the following procedures:

• obtain a type 1 report on the description and design of controls, or a type 2 report on the description and design of controls and their operating effectiveness, if available;

• contact the service entity, through the user entity, to obtain specific information;

• visit the service organisation and perform procedures that will provide the necessary information about controls; or

• use another auditor to perform those procedures for them.

Type 1 and type 2 reports are prepared under International Standards on Assurance Engagements (ISAE) 3402 (see **Chapter 42.8**).

37.6.4   Designing procedures and audit evidence

The ISA (UK) requires auditors to use their understanding of the arrangement to:

- assess whether they can obtain sufficient appropriate audit evidence on the relevant financial statement assertions from the records held at the reporting entity; and if not
- determine effective procedures to obtain audit evidence either by direct access to the records kept by the service organisation or through information obtained from the service organisation or its auditors.

Where auditors require evidence concerning balances representing assets held by or transactions undertaken by the service organisation, they may consider the efficiency and effectiveness of the following procedures:

- inspecting records and documents held by the reporting entity;
- establishing the effectiveness of controls;
- obtaining representations to confirm balances and transactions from the service organisation;
- performing analytical review procedures on the records maintained by the reporting entity or the returns from the service organisation;
- inspecting records and documents held by the service organisation;
- requesting the service organisation auditor or the reporting entity's internal audit function to perform specified procedures; and
- reviewing information from the service organisation and its auditors concerning the design and operation of its controls systems.

Where a report from the service organisation's auditors or from the reporting entity's internal auditors is being used by the auditors, they should consider the scope of the work performed and assess whether the report is sufficient and appropriate for its intended use. This will include ascertaining whether the external auditor is competent and suitably independent from the service organisation.

The nature of the activities undertaken by the service organisation may mean that the evidence may not be regarded as independent for audit purposes. In such circumstances, auditors need to assess carefully the nature and source of information available to them in order to establish the most effective way to obtain evidence sufficient to support an independent opinion on its financial statements. This may involve auditors requesting access to the staff and records of the service organisation in order to do their own testing.

If the service organisation themselves outsource some of their activities to another service organisation, auditors should consider whether those activities are relevant to the audit of the user entity's financial statements. If they are the requirements of ISA (UK and Ireland) 402 should be applied to their operations as well.

37.6.5 Fraud, non-compliance with laws and regulations and uncorrected misstatements

ISA (UK and Ireland) requires auditors to enquire of management of the user entity whether the service organisation has reported to them any incidences of fraud, non-compliance with applicable laws and regulations and uncorrected misstatements affecting the financial statements of the user entity. Terms of the contract between the user entity and the service organisation may require that such disclosure is made.

If such incidents have been reported, auditors should consider any impact they may have on the nature, timing and extent of their audit procedures.

37.6.6 Reporting

If the auditors of the reporting entity decide that they need access to the service organisation's records in order to form an opinion on the financial statements and they are unable to obtain this evidence, the ISA (UK and Ireland) requires them to:

- include a description of the factors leading to the lack of evidence in their report; and
- qualify their opinion or issue a disclaimer of opinion on the financial statements.

The guidance notes that auditors are unlikely to be able to obtain sufficient evidence if the following conditions exist:

- the reporting entity does not maintain adequate records of, or controls over, the activities undertaken by the service organisation; and
- no report from the service organisation's auditors concerning the operation of the system of controls has been made available; and
- the auditors are unable to carry out tests that they consider appropriate at the service organisation or it has not been possible for these tests to be carried out by the service organisation's auditors.

Examples of qualifications arising from limitations in scope are shown in **Table 4** and **Table 6** in **Chapter 4**.

37.7 AUDITING DERIVATIVE FINANCIAL INSTRUMENTS

37.7.1 Introduction

In April 2002 the APB issued Practice Note 23, based on the International Auditing Practice Statement (IAPS) on planning and performing the audit of derivative financial instruments, with amendments as necessary to reflect the Financial Reporting framework in the United Kingdom and the Republic of Ireland.

The Practice Note focuses on auditing derivatives held by end users. This may include banks and other financial sector entities where they are the end users. An end user is one that enters into a financial transaction for the purpose of hedging, asset/liability management or speculating.

FRS 13, *Derivatives and Other Financial Instruments*, defines a derivative financial instrument as a financial instrument that derives its value from the price or rate of some underlying item. Underlying items may be equities, bonds, commodities, interest rates, exchange rates or stock market and other indices. Derivative financial instruments include:

- futures;
- options;
- forward contracts;
- interest rate and currency swaps;
- interest rate caps, collars and floors;
- forward interest rate agreements;
- commitments to purchase shares or bonds;
- note issuance facilities; and
- letters of credit.

For many, the use of derivatives reduces exposure to change in exchange rates, interest rates and commodity prices. However, the characteristics of the derivatives may also result in increased business risk in some entities, which will, in turn, increase audit risk. These features include:

- little or no cash outflow/inflow is required until maturity of the transaction;
- no principle balance or other fixed amount is paid or received;
- potential risks and rewards can be substantially greater than the current outlays; and
- the value of the entity's asset or liability arising from the derivative may exceed the amount (if any) that the derivative is recognised at in the financial statements. This is because the UK and Republic of Ireland financial reporting framework does not allow derivatives to be shown at their fair value in the financial statements.

37.7.2 Responsibilities

As with any other item in the financial statements, the consultation draft states that it is management's responsibility to ensure that the preparation and presentation of the value of derivatives given in the financial statements is correct. In relation to derivatives, management are also responsible for:

- maintaining a system which will ensure that:

- only authorised individuals can participate in the derivative market,
- the use of derivatives is within the entity's agreed risk exposure levels;
- risk and financial control is monitored; and
- the entity is in compliance with applicable laws and regulations; and

- ensuring that the accounting system is able to report reliably on derivatives.

The purpose of an audit of financial statements is not to provide assurance on the adequacy of the entity's risk management related to derivatives or the controls over them. Rather the auditors' responsibility is to consider whether management's disclosures about derivatives in the financial statements are materially in accordance with all relevant legislation and accounting standards.

It is therefore important that clients are aware of this limitation on auditors' responsibilities. The engagement letter may set out these responsibilities in order to avoid any misunderstanding.

Auditors may need specialist skills or knowledge to ensure that they have the relevant professional competence to service a client holding derivative instruments. This knowledge will include:

- the operating characteristics and risk profile of the industry in which the entity operates;
- the derivative financial instruments used by the entity, and their characteristics;
- the entity's information system for derivatives, including services provided by a service organisation. This may require specialist knowledge about computer applications where significant information about these derivatives are transmitted, processed, maintained or accessed electronically;
- the methods of valuing the derivative; and
- the requirements of relevant legislation, regulations and applicable accounting standards for derivatives.

If this knowledge is not readily available within the audit team, auditors may seek the assistance of an expert from outside the team or outside the firm as necessary. This is more likely where the derivatives are particularly complex or valuations are based on complex pricing models. The consultation draft considers the knowledge of the business required in greater depth, looking in turn at general economic factors, the industry and the entity itself.

Auditors should understand how derivative activities are linked to the entity's day-to-day business activities. For example, because of the economic conditions that affect the price of the entity's raw materials, the entity may enter into a forward contract to hedge the cost of its stock.

37.7.3 Risks

The consultation draft considers the types of risk which auditors should consider when planning their audit procedures. The key financial risks are identified as:

- *Market Risk* relating to unfavourable changes in the value of the derivative on the market, together with related areas of *Price Risk* (including interest rate risk and foreign exchange risk) and *Liquidity Risk* that the instrument cannot be sold or disposed of;
- *Basis Risk* relating to changes in the Basis, or difference between the price of the hedged item and the related hedging instrument;
- *Credit Risk* that the customer or counterparty will not settle the obligation in full. This also includes *Settlement Risk*, that one party to the hedge will settle whilst the other fails;
- *Solvency Risk* that the entity will not have the funds available to honour outgoings as they fall due; and
- *Legal Risk*, relating to potential losses from legal or regulatory action.

These factors should be considered by auditors when assessing their client's inherent risk. Factors which might affect the auditors' assessment of inherent risk relating to the holding of derivatives include:

- the economics and business purpose of the entity's derivative activities. The auditors should understand the purpose of the activities. Different inherent risks will arise from derivatives held to reduce risk (hedging) or to increase profits (speculating);
- the complexity of the derivative's features. The more complex a derivative is, the more difficult it will be to determine its value, introducing increased valuation risk;
- whether the transaction giving risk to the derivative involved the exchange of cash. Derivatives not involving cash exchange at inception, or with irregular or end of term cash flows are often difficult to identify;
- an entity's experience with the derivative. Use of complex derivatives without sufficient expertise will increase inherent risk;
- whether the derivative is an embedded feature of an agreement. Management are less likely to identify embedded derivatives leading to a completeness issue;
- external factors affecting valuation, such as market fortunes or interest rate volatilities;
- whether the derivative is traded on national exchanges or across borders. Risk will be increased as a result of exchange rate changes or where cross border exchanges are subject to different laws and regulations.

Many derivatives have the associated risk that a loss may exceed the amount, if any, of the value of the derivative recognised on the balance sheet (off-balance sheet risk). In some cases the potential losses may be enough to cause significant doubt on the ability of the entity to continue as a going concern. Auditors should consider any sensitivity analyses or value-at-risk analyses performed by the entity as part of their evaluation of management's assessment of the entity's ability to continue as a going concern.

37.7.4 Types of audit procedures

When selecting audit procedures auditors should consider the following issues set out by the consultation draft:

- the assessed level of inherent risk;
- the accounting method used, i.e., if hedge accounting is used different procedures will be relevant to assess whether this is suitable;
- the sophistication of the accounting system used to record derivatives;
- the control environment in place;
- the role of internal audit;
- the use of service organisations; and
- the efficiency of using control procedures to reduce substantive testing.

The consultation draft continues to detail suggested substantive procedures which can be used to test derivative financial instruments.

37.7.5 Materiality

Particular care should be taken when assessing materiality for the testing of derivatives. As derivatives have little or no recorded balance sheet value, materiality should not be based on these values alone.

Despite their low financial recorded value errors in this area may give rise to high value misstatements. Auditors should be aware of this risk and assess materiality accordingly.

37.7.6 Other areas

Auditors usually obtain confirmation of oral representations from the board of directors. As a result of the often complex nature of derivative activities, auditors may prefer to obtain representations about derivatives from those responsible for the derivatives activity within the entity.

Auditors may consider the following areas for inclusion in a representation letter:

- management's objectives when entering into derivative activities, i.e. whether the derivatives are for hedging or speculation purposes;
- disclosures required by FRS 13;
- whether all transactions have been conducted at arm's length and at market value;
- the terms of derivative transactions;

- whether there are any side agreements associated with any derivative instruments; and
- whether the entity has entered into any written options.

When reporting to those charged with governance, the Practice Note sets out the following areas which the auditor may report:

- material weakness in the design or operation of the accounting or internal control systems;
- lack of management understanding of the nature or extent of the derivative activities or the related risks;
- a lack of formal policies covering the purchase, sale and holding of derivatives; and
- a lack of segregation of duties.

37.8 AUDITING WHEN FINANCIAL MARKET CONDITIONS ARE DIFFICULT

37.8.1 Introduction

In January 2008, the APB issued Bulletin 2008/1 *Auditing issues when financial market conditions are difficult and credit facilities may be restricted* in response to developments in the financial markets commonly termed 'the credit crunch'.

As financial markets are characterised by difficult trading conditions made worse by a reduction in liquidity, entities with exposure to the financial markets through debt, equity, derivative and leveraged finance activities may experience a significant difficulty both trading in and valuing certain investments. This in turn will lead to an increased risk of material misstatement in the financial statements.

Even for those businesses outside the financial sector, the effect may be felt through:

- reduced liquidity making it expensive or impossible to replace finance arrangements that have expired, which may lead to going concern issues; and
- an increased difficulty in valuing investments where there has been a curtailment or cessation in market trading.

The Bulletin does not establish any new requirements, but pulls together guidance in the APB's other material into one place.

37.8.2　Risk assessment

As part of their risk assessment procedures, auditors should consider the impact of current market conditions on their client. **Table 6** sets out the risk factors identified in Bulletin 2008/1 and updated by Bulletin 2008/10 (see **Chapter 13**).

TABLE 6: Example factors that may increase the risk of material misstatement in financial statements when financial market conditions are difficult and credit facilities may be restricted

Going concern:

- obtaining external financing

  - entity has experienced difficulty in the past in obtaining external finance facilities and/or complying with the related terms and covenants
  - finance facilities are due for renewal in the next year but haven't yet been agreed
  - management have no plans for alternative arrangements should current facilities not be extended
  - borrowing agreements or executory contracts include clauses relating to debt covenants or subjective clauses (e.g., a 'material adverse change clause') that may trigger repayment
  - entity has breached some of the terms or covenants giving rise to the risk that the facilities may be withdrawn or not renewed
  - terms or covenants of renewed financing are changed and more difficult to comply with (e.g., increased interest rates or charges)
  - finance facility is secured on assets (e.g., properties) that have decreased in value below the amount of the facility
  - for financial institutions, reduced deposits from retail customers or reduced availability of funding from wholesale financial markets
  - there are significant doubts about the financial strength of the entity's bankers
  - financing is provided by a syndicate of banks and other financial institutions and there are concerns about the viability of one or more of the members of the syndicate

- management plans to overcome financing difficulties include disposal of assets

  - plans developed prior to current market conditions have not been updated
  - lack of evidence that management can sell the assets at the values included in the plan

- entity provides significant loans or guarantees

  - guarantees may be called in
  - borrowers may be unable to make payments

- entity dependent on guarantees provided by another party

  - guarantor no longer able/prepared to provide the guarantee

- future cash flows

  - reduction in cash flows resulting from unfavourable economic conditions
  - customers taking longer to pay
  - terms or covenants of renewed financing are changed and become more difficult to comply with

---

- entity is subject to margin calls as a result of a decrease in fair market value of financial instruments that it holds
- entities have issued loans (or received borrowings) having an introductory period during which favourable terms are in force which revert to normal market rates in the forthcoming year

- entity dependent on key supplier

  - suppliers facing financial difficulties not able to provide essential goods/services
  - entity unable to find alternative suppliers

Fair values

- fair values are affected by current market conditions

  - entity needs to change valuation model and/or management's assumptions to reflect current market conditions
  - active market no longer exists, requiring use of a model for valuation purposes
  - inputs to a model are not based on observable market inputs but rather are based on the entity's own data
  - impairment of non-financial assets held at fair value (e.g., properties)
  - suspension of external valuation indices triggering a need for alternative valuation approaches
  - entity uses an external pricing service for fair value measurements that needs to change its valuation model and/or assumptions to reflect current market conditions
  - entity does not have necessary expertise to undertake valuations

Other risk factors

- impairment of assets other than those held at fair value (e.g., need for increased doubtful debts provisions)
- impairment of the carrying value of purchased goodwill
- pension obligations of an entity increased by reduction in values of assets in a related defined benefits pension scheme
- hedging arrangements no longer effective
- effects on accounting for Special Purpose Entities and other off balance sheet arrangements

Where a risk is identified as a result of these market factors, auditors should pay particular attention to:

- the partner's involvement in the direction, supervision and performance of the audit in line with the requirements of ISA (UK and Ireland) 220 (see **Chapter 20**);
- the capabilities and competence of the audit team, particularly where fair value is an issue (ISA (UK and Ireland) 220);
- consultation with other professionals on difficult and contentious matters, again particularly in relation to fair values (ISA (UK and Ireland) 220); and
- the nature and timing of communication with those charged with governance in accordance with ISA (UK and Ireland) 260 (see **Chapter 9**).

37.8.3 Going concern

Market conditions may limit the credit available to clients, and therefore past experience of obtaining finance cannot be a guarantee of an entity's ability to obtain financing in the future.

In line with the requirements of ISA (UK and Ireland) 570 (see **Chapter 13**) auditors may:

- obtain confirmation of bank facilities from the bank and make an independent assessment of the likely course of action of the bank. This is particularly relevant where the entity has a low margin of financial resources available to it; and
- consider whether any inability to obtain sufficient audit evidence about the extent of finance and the intentions of the bank need to be disclosed in the financial statements in order to give a true and fair view or otherwise referred to in the auditor's report as either an explanatory paragraph or a qualified opinion.

In December 2008, the APB issued Bulletin 2008/10 *Going Concern Issues During the Current Economic Conditions* to specifically address these issues. The Bulletin is discussed in **13.10**.

37.8.4 Fair values

Poor market conditions may either:

- impair the value of investments; or
- make their valuation more difficult through lack of current market values.

Where auditors decide there is a significant risk relating to fair values they should consider whether the assumptions used by management to assess those fair values are reasonable. Auditors should ensure that the assumptions reflect current market conditions and information. It may be necessary to consult with experts in this regard (see **Chapter 39**).

Where there is severe curtailment or even cessation of market trading in certain investments, auditors should consider whether any alternative valuation method applied by management can be demonstrated to be more appropriate.

Auditors should also pay particular attention to the disclosure of material risks and uncertainties related to fair value measurements and ensure that they properly reflect the current market conditions and the situation of the entity. This includes disclosures under IFRS 7 *Financial Instruments: Disclosures* or SSAP 29 *Intangible Assets*.

37.8.5 Disclosures in the directors' report

Directors of companies affected by the downturn in market conditions are likely to make reference to this in their report. In line with the requirements of ISA (UK and Ireland) 720 (see **Chapter 14**) auditors should consider whether the information given in the Directors' Report is consistent with the financial statements.

If there is an omission of information in the Directors' Report which, in the auditors' opinion, should be included, they should bring this to the attention of those charged with governance.

37.8.6 Auditor's report

Auditors are required to add an emphasis of matter paragraph to their report if a note to the financial statements includes:

- discussion of a material matter regarding a going concern issue; or
- any other significant uncertainty the resolution of which is dependent on future events, which may include uncertainties relating to the valuation of financial instruments.

In determining whether an uncertainty is significant, auditors consider the:

- risk that the estimate included in the financial statements may be subject to change;
- range of possible outcomes; and
- consequences of those outcomes on the view shown in the financial statements.

37.8.7 Ethical issues

In difficult market conditions, auditors may be asked to undertake work that involves making judgements and taking decisions where credit facilities are restricted. Such decisions are the responsibility of the entity's management and by involving themselves in this way, auditors may jeopardise their objectivity and independence.

37.9   XBRL TAGGING OF INFORMATION IN FINANCIAL STATEMENTS

37.9.1 Background

In February 2010, the APB issued Bulletin 2010/1, *XBRL Tagging of Information in Audited Financial Statements – Guidance for Auditors*. This was in response to the joint statement by HMRC and Companies House made in September 2009, that the Company Tax Return, including the supporting statutory accounts and tax computations showing the derivation from those accounts of the entries in the Company Tax Return, must be delivered electronically using the Inline XBRL (iXBRL) format. This requirement is mandatory for accounting periods ending on or after 31 March 2010 where the tax return is submitted to HMRC after 31 March 2011.

XBRL stands for Extensible Business Reporting Language and it is a computer-based language for the electronic communication of business data. It works by tagging individual items of information with machine-readable codes which are drawn from a library of codes referred to as a 'taxonomy'. The use of XBRL allows data to be more easily accessed, manipulated and reviewed. Inline XBRL uses tags which can still be read by the human eye, for example by hovering the computer mouse over the tagged item.

37.9.2 Auditors' involvement

Aspects of XBRL tagging can be automated, but there is likely to remain an element of judgement over which tag to map to which piece of data.

However, there is no requirement in the HMRC statement for an audit of the data or the XBRL tagging and the ISAs (UK and Ireland) do not impose a general requirement on the auditor to check the tagging. In addition, because the XBRL tag is just a machine-readable rendering of the data in the financial statements it does not constitute 'other information' as defined in ISA (UK and Ireland) 720 Section A, and the requirement to read the other information with the purpose of identifying material inconsistencies or material misstatement is not invoked (see **Chapter 14**).

There is a possibility that regulators may impose a requirement for companies to obtain assurance from auditors on XBRL-tagged data in the future.

However, some companies may wish to engage an audit or accountancy firm to:

- perform the tagging exercise;
- perform an agreed upon procedures engagement to provide assurance about the tagging process;
- provide advice on the selection of individual tags;
- supply accounts preparation software that automates the tagging; or
- train management in XBRL tagging.

If such non-audit services are provided by the company's auditor, they must consider whether any possible threats to independence and objectivity arise. Particular care must be taken not to take decisions that are the responsibility of the management of the entity and suitable safeguards should be put in place.

Although there is currently no audit requirement in relation to XBRL tagging, firms should carefully consider how services provided either to set up a system for XBRL tagging or to tag data on behalf of a client may become a self-review threat if an audit requirement is introduced in future years. If XBRL becomes integrated into accounting systems it may be difficult to separate tagging from accounting services. In such situations, the prohibition in Ethical Standard 5 that auditors of listed companies (or significant affiliates of listed companies) cannot provide accounting services to those clients will apply (see **2.5.5**).

38 CHANGE OF AUDITORS

38.1 INTRODUCTION

There are three main ways in which auditors can cease to hold office under the Companies Act 2006 ('the Act'):

- removal (ss510-513), where the auditor is removed by the company by ordinary resolution at a general meeting;
- resignation (ss516-518), where the auditor deposits a notice in writing at the company's registered office; or
- failure to reappoint auditors (ss514-515) which occurs when a company proposes a resolution (either written or at a general meeting) the effect of which is to appoint a person as auditor in place of the outgoing auditor whose term of office has expired, or is due to expire.

Under the Act, each of these methods of ceasing to hold office require certain statements to be made by the auditors and the company. These are set out in **38.2** below.

Once auditors have been replaced, the incoming auditors may wish to use information gathered by the outgoing auditor. Under the Act, and for periods commencing on or after 6 April 2008, the outgoing auditor is required to provide access to relevant information where the newly appointed auditor makes a written request for such access.

Following this change in the law, the Audit and Assurance Faculty of the ICAEW issued Technical Release AAF 01/08 *Access to Information by Successor Auditors* to provide guidance in this area. This is discussed in **38.3** below.

38.2 STATEMENTS ON CESSATION OF OFFICE

38.2.1 The Companies Act 2006 requirements

The Act sets out the requirements which auditors and companies must comply with when auditors cease to hold office. The Act's cessation requirements are effective when the auditor ceases to hold office on or after 6 April 2008. For Limited Liability Partnerships the requirements of the Companies Act 1985 remain in place.

This chapter details the procedures that auditors are required to complete when they cease, for any reason, to hold office.

The nature and timing of these procedures depends on the following factors:

- the reason for the cessation of the appointment;
- if the company is a 'major audit client', that is a listed client or one where there is or likely to be major public interest; or
- if the company is quoted.

The Companies Act 2006 requires two separate reports to be made:

- in all cases, a public statement of circumstances under s519 surrounding auditors' cessation of appointment which must be deposited at the company's registered office and Companies House; and
- a private statement under s522 detailing the reasons for the cessation as auditors which must be deposited with the appropriate audit authority either the ICAEW or the Professional Oversight Board, a part of the FRC.

An additional change brought about by the Companies Act 2006 is that failure to comply with the requirements of either s519 or s522 is now a criminal offence.

Table 1 sets out a flowchart to assist in determining when s519 and s522 letters are required and to whom they must be delivered.

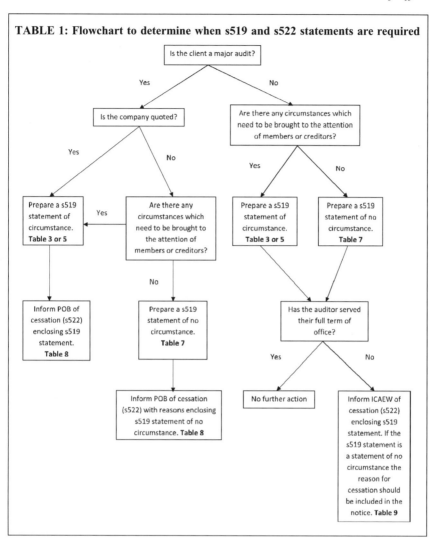

TABLE 1: Flowchart to determine when s519 and s522 statements are required

38.2.2   Section 519 statements

Section 519 of the Act requires auditors ceasing to hold office to deposit a statement of the circumstances connected with the cessation of office at the company's registered address. For unquoted companies, if the auditor considers that there are no circumstances that need to be brought to the attention of members a statement of no circumstances must be delivered. For quoted companies, the auditor must deposit a statement of circumstances connected with his ceasing to hold office. A statement of no circumstance cannot be made. This is a new requirement introduced by s519(3) of the Companies Act 2006.

The s519 statement of circumstance or no circumstance must be deposited at the companies registered office as follows:

Reason for cessation of appointment	Timeframe for delivery of s519 statement
Removal/Not reappointed	Up to 14 days after ceasing to hold office
Failure to seek reappointment	At least 14 days before the end of the time allowed for next appointing an auditor
Resignation	Must accompany the notice of resignation

Where circumstances are set out in the s519 statement, the company may apply to the court if it believes the auditor is using the s519 statement to secure needless publicity for a defamatory matter. The application to the court must be made by the company within 14 days of receiving the statement.

In addition to sending the s519 statement of circumstances or no circumstances to the company's registered address, the auditors must also send it to the Registrar of Companies.

For a statement of circumstances, the auditor must wait 21 days after depositing it at the company's registered office before sending the statement to the Registrar of Companies to allow time for the company to apply to court. If no application is made, the s519 statement must be delivered to the Registrar of Companies within a further 7 days. Therefore, the auditor has 28 days in total to deliver the s519 statement to the Registrar.

A statement of no circumstances can be delivered to the Registrar at the same time as it is deposited to the company's registered office.

As s519 statements regarding the circumstances connected with cessation of office are on public record and are likely to come under scrutiny by a wide range of interested parties they are sensitive in nature. Therefore where there are circumstances surrounding their cessation as auditors that need to be brought to attention of members/creditors (which is always the situation in respect to a quoted company) auditors must give due consideration towards the wording of their statements. In practice procedures may be put in place to ensure that all such statements are reviewed by a senior member of the firm before being submitted to the company.

Similarly, s519 statements of no circumstance can be similarly sensitive where information may have been accidentally missed by the audit team. Again an approval procedure may provide an extra level of assurance that important information has not been omitted.

Example s519 statements, together with the relevant covering letters are shown in **Tables 2** to **7**.

TABLE 2: Example covering letter to the company following resignation

[Name]

[Company]

[Address]

Dear Sir

[Company name]

Following our recent interview with [name], we are now writing to confirm our resignation as auditors of the above named company as from [date].

We attach notice of our resignation under s516 of the Companies Act 2006 ('the Act'). We also attach a statement as required by s519 of the Act detailing circumstances connected with our resignation which we consider should be brought to the attention of members and/or creditors of the company. We will be submitting a copy of this statement to the Registrar of Companies as required by s521 of the Act. [*Major audit clients only*: We will also be notifying the Professional Oversight Board of our resignation under s522 of the Act.]

We would like to take this opportunity to remind you of the company's obligations under the Act which are outlined in Appendix A to this letter.

Yours faithfully

Auditor

Appendix A: Guidance on the Company's Responsibilities on Resignation Statements

CA2006 Ref	**Requirements**
Section 517(1)	You should, within 14 days of receiving our notice of resignation, send a copy of the notice to Companies House.
Section 520(1), (2) & (3)	Where our statement under s519 details circumstances connected with our resignation which we consider should be brought to the attention of members and/or creditors of the company, you should, within 14 days of receiving the statement, either: (a) send a copy of it to every person who is entitled to be sent copies of the accounts, or (b) apply to the court. If you apply to the court, you should notify us that you have done so.
Section 523(1), (2) & (3)	Where we have resigned before the end of our term of office, you should notify [the Professional Oversight Board *if listed*/ The Institute of Chartered Accountants in England and Wales *if not listed*] ('the appropriate audit authority'). Within 14 days of receiving our s519 statement, you should notify the appropriate audit authority that we have ceased to hold office as auditors and include a copy of the s519 statement of circumstances.

Contact details for notification under s523

Notifications can be sent by letter or e-mail as follows:

[Change of Auditor Notifications

Quality Assurance Department
ICAEW
Metropolitan House
321 Avebury Boulevard
Milton Keynes
MK9 2FZ
By e-mail to auditorchange@icaew.com.

Or for major audit clients

Change of Auditor Notifications
Professional Oversight Board
5th Floor, Aldwych House
London
WC2B 4HN

By e-mail to auditorchange@frc-pob.org.uk]

TABLE 3: Example statement of circumstances under s519 following resignation

[Date]

Statement under s519 Companies Act 2006

We hereby give notice, under s516 of the Companies Act 2006, of our resignation as auditors to [company name] as of [date].

In accordance with s519, we detail the following circumstances connected with our ceasing to hold office as auditors of [company name] which we consider should be brought to the attention of members and/or creditors of the company.

LIST OF CIRCUMSTANCES

Auditor

TABLE 4: Example covering letter to the company following removal or failure to seek reappointment

[Name]

[Company]

[Address]

Dear Sir

[Company name]

Consequent upon our [removal from office/not being reappointed] as auditors of the company, we attach the statement required by s519 of the Companies Act 2006 ('the Act').

This statement details circumstances connected with our ceasing to hold office as auditors which we consider should be brought to the attention of members and/or creditors of the company. We will also be submitting a copy of this statement to the Registrar of Companies as required by s521 of the Act. [*Major audit clients only*: We will also be notifying the Professional Oversight Board of our ceasing to hold office under s522 of the Act.]

We would like to take this opportunity to remind you of the company's obligations under the Act which are outlined in Appendix A to this letter.

Yours faithfully

Auditor

Appendix A: Guidance on the Company's Responsibilities on s519 Statements

CA2006 Ref	Requirements
[Section 512(1)]	[(*For removal only*) You should, within 14 days of passing the resolution, notify Companies House of our removal as auditors.]
Section 520(1), (2) & (3)	Where our statement under s519 details circumstances connected with ceasing to hold office which we consider should be brought to the attention of members and/or creditors of the company, you should, within 14 days of receiving the statement, either:
	(a) send a copy of it to every person who is entitled to be sent copies of the accounts, or
	(b) apply to the court.
	If you apply to the court, you should notify us that you have done so.
Section 523(1), (2) & (3)	Where we have ceased to hold office before the end of our term of office, you should notify [the Professional Oversight Board *if listed*/The Institute of Chartered Accountants in England and Wales *if not listed*] ('the appropriate audit authority').
	Within 14 days of receiving our section 519 statement, you should notify the appropriate audit authority that we have ceased to hold office as auditors and include a copy of the section 519 statement of circumstances.

Contact details for notification under s523

Notifications can be sent by letter or e-mail as follows:

[Change of Auditor Notifications
Quality Assurance Department
ICAEW
Metropolitan House
321 Avebury Boulevard
Milton Keynes
MK9 2FZ
By e-mail to auditorchange@icaew.com.

Or for major audit clients

Change of Auditor Notifications
Professional Oversight Board
5th Floor, Aldwych House
London
WC2B 4HN
By e-mail to auditorchange@frc-pob.org.uk]

TABLE 5: Example statement of circumstances under s519 following removal or failure to seek reappointment

[Date]

Statement under s519 Companies Act 2006

Consequent upon our [removal/not being reappointed] as auditors on [date] under s[510/514] Companies Act 2006 and in accordance with s519, we detail the following circumstances connected with our ceasing to hold office as auditors of [company name] which we consider should be brought to the attention of members and/or creditors of the company.

LIST OF CIRCUMSTANCES

Auditors

TABLE 6: Example covering letter to the company accompanying statement of no circumstance

[Name]

[Company]

[Address]

Dear Sir

[Company name]

Consequent upon our [resignation/removal from office/not be reappointed] as auditors of the company, we attach a statement as required by s519 of the Companies Act 2006 ('the Act')

This statement indicates there are no circumstances connected with our ceasing to hold office as auditors which we consider should be brought to the attention of members and/or creditors of the company. We will also be submitting a copy of this statement to the Registrar of Companies as required by s521 of the Act.

[We also attach notice of our resignation under s516 of the Companies Act 2006 ('the Act').]

We would like to take this opportunity to remind you of the company's obligations under the Act which are outlined in Appendix A to this letter.

Yours faithfully

Auditor

Appendix A: Guidance on the Company's Responsibilities on s519 Statements

---

CA 2006 Ref	Requirements
Section 517(1)	[(*For resignation only*) You should within 14 days of receiving our notice of resignation, send a copy of the notice to Companies House.]
[Section 512(1)]	[(*For removal only*) You should, within 14 days of passing the resolution, notify Companies House of our removal as auditors.]
Section 523(1), (2) & (3)	Where we have ceased to hold office before the end of our term of office, you should notify [the Professional Oversight Board *if listed*/The Institute of Chartered Accountants in England and Wales *if not listed*] ('the appropriate audit authority').
	Within 14 days of receiving our s519 statement, you should notify the appropriate audit authority that we have ceased to hold office as auditors and include a copy of the s519 statement of no circumstances.

Contact details for notification under s523

Notifications can be sent by letter or e-mail as follows:

[Change of Auditor Notifications
Quality Assurance Department
ICAEW
Metropolitan House
321 Avebury Boulevard
Milton Keynes
MK9 2FZ
By e-mail to auditorchange@icaew.com.

Or for major audit clients

Change of Auditor Notifications
Professional Oversight Board
5th Floor, Aldwych House
London
WC2B 4HN
By e-mail to auditorchange@frc-pob.org.uk]

TABLE 7: Example statement of no circumstance

[Date]

Statement under s519 Companies Act 2006

Consequent upon our [resignation/removal from office/not being reappointed] as auditors on [date] under s[516/510/514] Companies Act 2006 and in accordance with s519, we confirm that there are no circumstances connected with our ceasing to hold office as auditors of [company name] which we consider should be brought to the attention of members and/or creditors of the company.

38.2.3 Section 522 statements

A s522 statement is effectively a cover letter sent to the appropriate audit authority along with a copy of the s519 statement.

Auditor's responsibilities

The auditor must notify the appropriate audit authority that he has ceased to hold office where:

- in the case of a major audit, the auditor ceases to hold office for any reason, or
- in the case of an audit that is not a major audit, the auditor ceases to hold office before the end of his term of office, i.e., he has resigned or been removed.

The notice must be accompanied by a copy of the s519 statement of circumstance or no circumstance deposited by him at the company's registered office.

When a s519 statement of no circumstance has been deposited, the notice to the appropriate audit authority must also be accompanied by a statement of the reasons for the auditor ceasing to hold office. This is a new requirement under s522 CA 2006.

The notification to the appropriate audit authority must take place at the same time as the auditor deposits the s519 statement at the company's registered office.

Company's responsibilities

Where the auditor ceases to hold office before the end of his term of office, the company will also have a duty to notify the appropriate audit authority that the auditor has ceased to hold office. The company must make a statement of the reasons the auditor has ceased to hold office and enclose a copy of the s519 statement made by the auditor where circumstances have been brought to the attention of members or creditors. This notice must be given within 14 days of the deposit of the s519 statement at the company's registered office (s523 CA 2006).

Appropriate authority

The appropriate audit authorities who should be notified are as follows:

Major audit	**The Professional Oversight Board**
Audit that is not a major audit	Institute of Chartered Accountants in England and Wales

Term of office

For a listed company the term of office ends at the conclusion of the accounts meeting following the appointment. For most listed companies this will be the AGM (CA 2006 s491). If the auditors' cessation from office takes place before this date then it will be treated as either a removal from office or resignation, as appropriate.

For a private limited company the term of office ends 28 days after the accounts filing deadline or 28 days after the accounts for the previous year are sent to the company's members, if this is earlier. This is a key date for non-major audits. For a non-major audit, if auditors cease to hold office:

- on this date, then it will be treated as failure to reappoint and no s522 statement is required;
- before this date then it will be treated as either a removal from office or resignation, as appropriate, and a s522 statement to the ICAEW will be required; and
- after this date then in most situations the auditor will be deemed to have been reappointed and cessation will be treated as either a removal from office or resignation, as appropriate, and a s522 statement to the ICAEW will be required.

EXAMPLE

An auditor is appointed to perform the audit of a non-major private company for the year ended 30 April 2008. The period for appointing auditors to perform the audit for the year ended 30 April 2009 ends on 28 March 2009 (i.e. filing deadline of 28 February 2009 plus 28 days) or, if earlier, 28 days after the April 2008 accounts are sent to members. Assuming the accounts are filed on the accounts filing date of 28 February 2009, the auditor's term of office expires on 28 March 2009. If the auditor ceases to hold office on 28 March 2009, a s522 statement to ICAEW is not required. However, if the auditor ceases to hold office before or after this date, a s522 statement to the ICAEW will be required.

Example s522 statements

Table 8 sets out an example statement.

TABLE 8: Example covering letter to the Professional Oversight Board (major audit clients only)

Change of Auditor Notifications

Professional Oversight Board
5th floor, Aldwych House
71-91 Aldwych
London
WC2B 4HN

Dear Sir

[Company name and number]

We hereby give notice that we ceased to hold office as auditors of [company name] ('the company') on [date]. The company's last audited accounts were for the year ended [date]. The company's registered office address is:

[address]

We enclose a copy of the [statement of circumstances/statement of no circumstance] prepared under s519 of the Companies Act 2006 which was deposited at the company's registered office today.

If you wish to discuss this matter further please contact: [Responsible individual] [Contact details]

Yours faithfully

[Auditors]

The letter in Table 8 should be addressed to the ICAEW for non-major audit clients.

38.3 ACCESS TO INFORMATION BY SUCCESSOR AUDITORS

38.3.1 Changes introduced by the Act

The European Union's Statutory Audit Directive states that:

> where a statutory auditor or audit firm is replaced by another statutory auditor or audit firm, the former statutory auditor or audit firm shall provide the incoming statutory auditor or audit firm with access to all relevant information concerning the audited entity.

When the Companies Act 2006 was introduced it brought this requirement from the Statutory Audit Directive into Sch. 10 of the Act under the rules of the Recognised Statutory Bodies, as follows:

> the Body must have adequate rules and practices designed to ensure that ... a person ceasing to hold office as a statutory auditor makes available to his successor in that office all relevant information which he holds in relation to that office.

The ICAEW, together with the Scottish and Irish Institutes have enacted this by redrafting Audit Regulation 3.09 to read:

> When a Registered Auditor (the "predecessor") ceases to hold an audit appointment and another Registered Auditor (the "successor") is appointed the predecessor must, if required in writing by the successor, allow the successor access to all relevant information held by the predecessor in respect of its audit work. .... Any information obtained by the successor is for the purposes of its audit and must not be disclosed to a third party unless the successor is required to do so by a legal or professional obligation.

The aim of the updated Audit Regulation is to maintain the effectiveness, including cost effectiveness, and efficiency of the audit process and to reduce the actual or perceived risk of changing auditors.

These changes are effective for the audits of financial periods commencing on or after 6 April 2008.

38.3.2 Technical Release AAF 01/08

In response to the change in the Act and the corresponding amendment to Audit Regulations, the Audit and Assurance Faculty of the ICAEW issued Technical Release AAF 01/08, *Access to Information by Successor Auditors*. AAF 01/08 provides practical guidance on the application of the additional guidance provided alongside the revision to Audit Regulation 3.09.

Background

Before the change to Audit Regulations it was unusual for predecessor auditors to share audit working papers with their successors due mainly to liability concerns. Access is now compulsory and the Regulation states that its purpose or object is not to involve one auditor in liability for another's audit work.

Information requested

As well as the current year's audit work papers, information requested by a successor auditor may include permanent information on any standing or systems audit file as well as prior year audit papers if these are relevant. AAF 01/08 suggests that successor auditors ask for the most recent audit working papers in the first instance and then, if their review suggests it is necessary, ask for older papers in another request.

As well as the papers relating to the standard audit, the following are set out in the 2006 Act as areas where a registered auditor may be required to perform specific functions, and therefore, for which access to working papers can be requested:

- a company applying to re-register as a public company (s92);
- a statement on summary financial statements issued by a quoted company (s428);
- abbreviated accounts (s449);
- when a private company makes a payment out of capital for the redemption or purchase of its own shares (s714);
- when a distribution is to be made by a company and the audit report was qualified (s837); and
- when initial accounts are prepared for a proposed distribution by a public company (s838).

There is no requirement for successor auditors to make a request to see work papers from predecessor auditors and they must, as part of their planning process, decide if such access is required and the areas to cover and amount of information to request.

There are specific references to reviewing a predecessor's audit work in ISA 510 (opening balances), ISA 710 (comparatives) and ISA 300 (planning), and information is likely to be necessary in these areas.

An example request letter from successor to predecessor is set out in **Table 9**.

TABLE 9: Specimen letter from the successor requesting access

[Predecessor firm]
[Address]

For the attention of [Name of Senior Statutory Auditor]

Dear Sirs

Provision of information pursuant to Audit Regulation 3.09 relating to the audit of [audit client]

This firm was duly appointed statutory auditor (as defined by s1210 of the Companies Act 2006 ('the Act')) on [date] to [company] ('the Company') [and its UK subsidiaries as listed in the schedule to this letter (together 'the Companies')].

Pursuant to paragraph 9(3) of Sch. 10 to the Companies Act 2006 and Audit Regulation 3.09, and in accordance with Technical Release AAF 01/08 issued by the Institute of Chartered Accountants in England and Wales, we request for the purposes of our audit work, access to the following information:

[*Set out information necessary at this stage, noting the guidance under Audit Regulation 3.09 that wherever possible a request framed simply as a request for 'all relevant information held by the predecessor and concerning the audited entity' or 'all relevant information held by the predecessor in relation to the office of auditor' should be avoided. The successor should strive to identify the information required, or the type of information required, as precisely as possible.*]

[*Where the request is for access to audit working papers and subsequent interim review working papers, insert where applicable*:

[The working papers in respect of your audit report on the financial statements of the [Company/Companies] relating to [insert period between the beginning of the last financial statements on which the predecessor reported and the date of cessation of the predecessor's appointment]].

[Where in your capacity as auditor you conducted a review of interim financial information subsequent to the audit report referred to above, this request includes a request for access to the working papers relating to that review also.]

We may also request explanations from you in connection with our consideration of the above information, and on the same basis.

[We/the Company will meet reasonable costs that you will incur in giving access/ providing copies, provided that a maximum amount is agreed first.]

> We look forward to receiving your confirmation letter in response to this request, which should be addressed for the attention of [name of successor engagement partner].
>
> Yours faithfully
>
> [Successor]
>
> **[Schedule of UK subsidiaries to which this letter applies in addition to the Company**
>
> Company 2 Limited
> Company 3 Limited
> . . .]

Audit files may contain information in a number of formats such as text, electronic file, sound or image and they may be kept in hard copy or electronic format, or a mixture of the two. Allowing another auditor access to information may mean that the successor auditor may gain access to the proprietary audit software of the outgoing auditor. If this is the case the successor cannot use the intellectual property or copyright of the software in any way. Predecessor auditors may prefer to make paper copies of work papers for the incoming auditor to review.

Care should also be taken where audit files also contain other documents relating to the client such as tax working papers. Papers to which the successor auditor has no right of access should be removed from the file before the successor auditor commences their review.

Where successors require access to tax papers, the Technical Release suggests that this would be best done directly from the client.

Relevant period

The period for which relevant information is normally requested would be in respect of any audit report relating to a period falling between the beginning of the last financial statement on which the predecessor reported and the date of cessation of the predecessor's audit appointment.

Example: An auditor resigns from an audit on 1 March 2010. The last accounting period for which they acted as auditor was the year ended 31 December 2009. The successor auditor can request access to relevant working papers for any reports prepared by the predecessor in the period 1 January 2009 to 1 March 2010.

The request for information can be made by the immediate successor only.

Liability

In order to ensure that there is no involvement of one auditor in liability for the other's work an exchange of letters as set out in **Tables 9** and **10**, should be undertaken. These letters should also be copied to the audit client.

Copying

There is no obligation to allow successor auditors to copy work papers, but it would be usual to allow extracts of the papers to be copied. The predecessor and successor should come to an agreement about what it is reasonable to copy prior to the meeting. Typically this would include documents such as the breakdown of analyses of financial statements figures and documentation of the client's systems and processes.

The Technical Release suggests that predecessors check through any document that the successor asks to copy and to keep a log of documents that have been copied on the audit file.

Timing

A request for relevant information may be made by a successor once the successor has formally been appointed to the audit client and will typically be made soon after appointment when the incoming auditor commences their planning.

Access should be granted by the predecessor on a timely basis, with regard to:

- the point at which the predecessor's audit file will be complete as ISA (UK and Ireland) 230 allows up to 60 days from the date of the audit report for the audit file to be completed; and
- the successor's reporting timetable.

The predecessor should also provide oral or written explanations in response to any further questions by the successor following the review of the work papers on a timely basis.

In providing such explanations, the predecessor should remember that:

- its obligation does not extend beyond relevant information;
- explanation should be given a factual or evidential reference point; and
- an internal written note or record of the request made and the explanation given should be put on file.

Location

The location where access is to be granted will be decided by the predecessor and will usually be their premises. The predecessor should be mindful of the confidentiality of other clients' information where access is granted at the predecessor's office.

Costs

Some recovery of the predecessor's costs of providing access may be reasonably recovered, but the legislation is silent on this point. Excessive charging may, however, be seen as a barrier to competition and choice, and it would not be reasonable to include an element of profit.

It may be reasonable to charge the successor auditor for the cost of:

- copying documents;
- paying someone to make the copies;
- retrieving documents from archive sources; and
- paying someone to attend to such retrieval and to provide documents for inspection by the successor.

Confidentiality

The predecessor is not breaching client confidentiality by allowing the successor access to its working papers. However, as a matter of courtesy a letter would be sent by the predecessor to the successor prior to granting access, in line with the example in **Table 10**.

TABLE 10: Specimen letter to predecessor responding to the successor's request for access

[Successor firm]

[Address]

Dear Sir

Provision of information pursuant to audit regulation 3.09 relating to the audit of [audit client]

We refer to your letter dated [date] following your appointment as statutory auditors of [company] ('the Company') [and its UK subsidiaries listed in the schedule to your letter (together 'the Companies')].

We confirm we will provide access to the information requested, namely:

[This should reflect the information set out in the successor's request letter. The successor should have identified the information required, or the type of information required, as precisely as possible.]

We understand that you may also request explanations from us in connection with your consideration of the above information, and on the same basis.

In accordance with the guidance under Audit Regulation 3.09 and Technical Release AAF 01/08 issued by the Institute of Chartered Accountants in England and Wales this letter sets out the basis on which the information and explanations (if any) are to be provided. Should you request or we provide any supplementary information to that set out above, such provision will be made on the same basis.

This access is provided to you:

(a)   solely in your capacity as duly appointed statutory auditors (as defined by s1210 of the Companies Act 2006 ('the Act')) of the [Company/Companies];

(b)   solely because we are required to give you access to information pursuant to paragraph 9(3) of Sch. 10 to the Act and Audit Regulation 3.09.

The provision of access does not and will not alter any responsibility that we may have accepted or assumed to the [Company/Companies] or the [Company's/respective Companies'] members as a body, in accordance with the statutory requirements for audit, for our audit work, for our audit report or for the opinions we have formed in the course of our work as auditors.

To the fullest extent permitted by law we do not accept or assume responsibility to you or to anyone else:

(a)   as a result of the access given;
(b)   for the information to which we provide access;
(c)   for any explanation given to you;
(d)   in respect of any audit work you may undertake, any audit you may complete, and audit report you may issue, or any audit opinion you may give.

Where access is provided to audit [and interim review] working papers, those papers were not created or prepared for, and should not be treated as suitable for, any purpose other than the statutory audit that was the subject of our audit report [and respectively the interim review we carried out]. The statutory audit was planned and undertaken solely for the purpose of forming and giving the audit opinion required by the relevant statutory provision to the persons contemplated by that statutory provision. [The interim review was planned and undertaken solely for the purpose of meeting the requirements of the relevant standard.] The statutory audit [and the interim review] [was/were] not planned or undertaken, and the working papers were not prepared in contemplation of your appointment as statutory auditor or for the purpose of assisting you in carrying out your appointment as statutory auditor.

Neither you nor anyone else should rely on the information to which access is provided or any explanations given in relation to that information. The information cannot in any way serve as a substitute for the enquiries and procedures you should undertake and the judgements that you must make for any purpose in connection with the audit for which you are solely responsible as the auditor.

If notwithstanding this letter you rely on the information for any purpose and to any degree, you will do so entirely at your own risk.

[We will remove/have removed from the audit working papers all material in respect of which legal professional privilege is asserted.]

[Thank you for your confirmation that you/the Company will meet the reasonable costs that we will incur in giving access. [As already agreed] these will not exceed £x.]

In accordance with the guidance issued under Audit Regulation 3.09:

(a)   you should refuse to accept an additional engagement, such as to act as an expert witness or to review the quality of our audit work, where the engagement would involve the use of the information obtained by you under the Regulation;
(b)   you should not comment on the quality of our audit work unless required to do so by a legal or professional obligation; and
(c)   the information should not be disclosed beyond persons who have a need to access the information where to do so is a necessary part of your audit work, nor should the information be disclosed to a third party including the [Company/Companies] (although this does not prevent you discussing the information with the [Company/Companies] where to do so is a necessary part of your audit work, or providing information to any third party if that is required of you by a legal or professional obligation).

In the event that access to information involves your having access to any intellectual property of ours or any material in which we have copyright, we do not grant permission to you to use or exploit that intellectual property or copyright and you must respect the same at all times.

When in this letter we refer to ourselves, we include [any person or organisation associated with this firm through membership of the international association of professional service firms to which this firm belongs,] our [and their] partners, directors, members, employees and agents. This letter is for the benefit of all those referred to in the previous sentence and each of them may rely on and enforce in their own right all of the terms of this letter.

Yours faithfully

[Predecessor]

cc The Company/Companies

Money laundering

In accordance with the Anti-Money Laundering Guidance for the Accountancy Sector issued by the CCAB (see **Chapter 12**):

- any money laundering report and papers recording the predecessor's consideration of apparently suspicious activities should not be provided to the successor unless the predecessor has clear advice that it would be lawful to do so; and
- if any information provided to the successor causes the successor to conclude that there are money laundering suspicions that need to be reported to the Authorities, they should make that report whether or not they are aware of any report already made by the predecessor.

39   RELIANCE ON OTHERS

39.1   INTRODUCTION

This chapter examines situations where auditors rely on others for part of the audit evidence. It examines reliance on:

- internal audit;
- other auditors; and
- experts.

39.2   INTERNAL AUDIT

39.2.1   Auditing Standards

Clarified ISA (UK and Ireland) 610 *Using the Work of Internal Auditors* was issued in October 2009 and is effective for the audit of financial statements for periods ending on or after 15 December 2010. The updated ISA (UK and Ireland) replaces ISA (UK and Ireland) 610 issued in December 2004. This chapter covers both the existing and Clarified ISAs (UK and Ireland). As the Clarified ISA (UK and Ireland) adds to the requirements of the existing ISA (UK and Ireland) this chapter is written on the basis of the existing requirements, and changes to them included in the Clarified ISA (UK and Ireland) are included and clearly indicated.

The ISA (UK and Ireland) provides guidance covering:

- the effect of internal audit on external audit procedures;
- understanding of internal audit;
- assessment of internal audit;
- evaluating specific internal audit work.

As with all ISAs (UK and Ireland), the text of the international ISA has been supplemented with additional guidance from a UK and Ireland perspective.

39.2.2   Effect of internal audit on external audit procedures

Internal audit is defined by the ISA (UK and Ireland) as 'an appraisal activity established within an entity as a service to the entity' and states that its functions include 'amongst other things, monitoring internal control'. It requires that external auditors consider the activities of this function and their effect, if any, on external audit procedures, although it does not relieve them of any of their responsibilities.

The activities of an internal audit function may include:

- review of the accounting and internal control systems;
- examination of financial and operating information;
- review of the economy, efficiency and effectiveness of operations;
- review of the compliance with laws, regulations and other external requirements and with management policies and directives; and
- special investigations.

Some of these activities will concern non-financial information and as such will not generally be of direct relevance to the external auditors. The level of precision that internal auditors work to may also be higher than that of the external auditors who are primarily concerned with material misstatement in the financial statements, but some of the methods used will be common.

Some entities will sub-contract the internal audit function to a third party but as this is still within the control of the entity, the external auditors may consider its impact on their own procedures.

39.2.3 Understanding and assessment of internal audit

External auditors should obtain a sufficient understanding of internal audit activities to identify and assess the risks of material misstatement of the financial statements and to design and perform further audit procedures.

Where an internal audit function is effective, external auditors may be able to reduce the extent of their own testing. However, they will not be able to rely solely on the work of internal audit to the extent of performing no additional testing themselves. Additionally, if internal audit is effective this may be a consideration in the external auditor's assessment of the entity's control environment and risk assessment.

Where internal audit is relevant to the risk assessment, the external auditor must obtain an understanding of the internal audit function and then carry out an assessment of the function. The ISA (UK and Ireland) sets out the criteria the auditors should use. External auditors should concentrate on the:

- organisational status of internal audit, including its ability to be objective and the level of management that it reports to;
- scope of the function, including the nature of assignments and whether management acts on its reports;
- technical competence of the persons performing the work; and
- application of due professional care, including whether the work is properly planned, supervised, reviewed and documented.

Coordination of the timing of the two auditors' work is best achieved by regular meetings throughout the year. This will normally ensure that the external auditors are made aware of any relevant matters as they come to light. The process also works in reverse, particularly at the end of the external audit when there may be matters in the report to management which are of concern to the internal audit.

39.2.4 Evaluating specific internal audit work

Where the external auditors use specific internal audit work 'they should evaluate and perform audit procedures on that work to confirm its adequacy for the external auditor's purposes'. This evaluation procedure may include consideration of whether:

- the work is carried out by adequately trained, proficient internal auditors;
- the work of assistants is properly supervised, reviewed and documented;
- sufficient appropriate evidence is obtained to give a reasonable basis for the conclusions reached;
- appropriate conclusions are reached;
- any reports are consistent with the results of the work performed;
- any exceptional or unusual matters found by internal audit are properly resolved; and
- any changes are required to the external auditors' procedures as a result of the work of the internal auditors.

Typical audit procedures employed by the external auditor may include:

- examination of items already examined by internal audit;
- examination of other similar items; or
- observation of internal audit procedures.

Table 1 gives examples of two scenarios and details the reliance that may be placed on the work of an internal audit department in each situation.

If the external auditors conclude that the internal auditors' work is not adequate for their purposes, they should consider what additional procedures of their own are necessary in order to have sufficient appropriate evidence to form an opinion.

TABLE 1: Evaluating internal audit work

Case A

An internal audit function is staffed by a number of qualified accountants. Reports go to the audit committee. Their programme of work consists of among other things, systems checks and periodic audits of branch returns. External auditors receive reports as and when produced.

Case B

Internal audits are carried out on a part time basis by the controller of one subsidiary. Work is mainly of an ad hoc nature, looking at problem areas both in terms of control and efficiency and producing reports for the finance director.

> **Extent of reliance**
>
> Based upon the facts set out above, the possible extent of reliance in Case A would appear to be far greater than in Case B. The auditors may seek to rely on work performed on the internal controls systems by internal audit together with some of the checks carried out during the audits of branch returns.
>
> In contrast, in Case B the opportunities for reliance on internal audit would be greatly reduced. Some reliance may be possible in areas reported on which have relevance to the external audit. However, because of the status of the internal audit and its method of operation there would probably be less reliance and a greater level of procedures in the relevant area.

39.3 OTHER AUDITORS

39.3.1 Auditing Standards

Clarified ISA (UK and Ireland) 600 *Special Considerations – Audits of Group Financial Statements (Including the Work of Component Auditors)* was issued in October 2009 and is effective for the audit of financial statements for periods ending on or after 15 December 2010. The updated ISA (UK and Ireland) replaces ISA (UK and Ireland) 230 issued in December 2004. This section covers both the existing and Clarified ISAs (UK and Ireland). As the Clarified ISA (UK and Ireland) adds to the requirements of the existing ISA (UK and Ireland) this chapter is written on the basis of the existing requirements, and changes to them included in the Clarified ISA (UK and Ireland) are included and clearly indicated.

The ISA (UK and Ireland) provides guidance covering:

* acceptance as principal auditors;
* overall audit strategy and audit plan;
* professional experience of other auditors;
* procedures of principal auditors;
* consolidation process;
* subsequent events;
* co-operation between auditors; and
* documentation.

As with all ISAs (UK and Ireland), the text of the international ISA has been supplemented with additional guidance from a UK and Ireland perspective.

Following research on the views of practitioners on how group audits are carried out in practice, the Audit and Assurance Faculty issued an eight point plan setting out practical guidance for increasing the quality of group audits in November 2005. This is detailed in **39.3.9** below.

39.3.2   *Definitions*

The Clarified ISA (UK and Ireland) uses the term 'component auditors' to refer to the auditors of one or more subsidiary companies who report to the group engagement team.

The ISA (UK and Ireland) does not deal with joint auditors.

In the context of the UK Companies Act, the term 'components' encompasses companies, joint ventures and branches which form part of a group.

39.3.3   *Acceptance as group auditors*

ISA (UK and Ireland) 600 requires that, before deciding to act for a particular organisation, the group engagement partner should consider whether sufficient appropriate audit evidence can reasonably be expected to be obtained in relation to the consolidation process and the financial information of the components on which to base the group opinion.

In order to do this, auditors should consider:

● the group structure including how the financial reporting system is organised;
● the industry and the regulatory, economic and political environments in which the significant components' business activities take place;
● the use of service organisations;
● a description of group-wide controls;
● the complexity of the consolidation process;
● whether any of the component auditors are from outside the group engagement partner's firm or network;
● whether the group engagement team will have unrestricted access to the management and those charged with governance of both the group and the components as well as the component auditors;
● whether the group engagement team will be able to perform necessary work on the financial information of the components.

This is intended to ensure that the group engagement team are sufficiently involved with the rest of the group, albeit not directly with the components' audit. If they feel that they are not sufficiently involved they should either not accept appointment or take appropriate action to ensure that they have sufficient involvement. The final three requirements above were included in the Clarified ISA (UK and Ireland) 600 as part of the move to achieve greater consistency in group audit practices.

39.3.4   The group engagement team's procedures

Understanding the group

Auditors are required to identify the risk of material misstatement through obtaining an understanding of the entity and its environment. The ISA (UK and Ireland) requires the group engagement team to perform procedures to increase their understanding in a number of areas, including:

- group-wide controls, including internal audit functions;
- the consolidation process, including

  - matters relating to the applicable financial reporting framework;
  - the group's processes for ensuring complete, accurate and timely financial reporting by the components;
  - the process for recording consolidation adjustments;
  - the consolidation adjustments required by the applicable financial reporting framework; and
  - procedures for monitoring, controlling, reconciling and eliminating intra-group transactions and unrealised profits, and intra-group account balances.

From this work, the group engagement team should determine which components are likely to be significant and assess the risks of material misstatement in the group financial statements.

Clarified ISA (UK and Ireland) 600 requires group auditors to formulate an overall audit strategy and audit plan for the group as a whole. This will include determining:

- the materiality level for the group financial statements as a whole;
- any materiality level to be applied to particular classes of transactions, account balances or disclosures which are lower than the general materiality level;
- materiality for individual components; and
- the threshold above which misstatements cannot be regarded as clearly trivial to the group financial statements.

Understanding the component auditors

Clarified ISA (UK and Ireland) 600 requires the group engagement team to consider the professional competence of the component auditor in the context of the assignment including whether they understand, and will comply with, the ethical requirements that are relevant to the group audit. There are various factors that affect the group engagement team's assessment of the component auditors, including:

- previous experience of their work;
- any affiliation of the other firm;
- membership of relevant professional bodies; and

- discussions with the component auditors.

Responding to assessed risk

The type of audit procedures to be performed in relation to components and the level of involvement the group engagement team will have in the component auditor's work will depend on the:

- significance of the component;
- identified significant risks of material misstatement of the group financial statements;
- group engagement team's evaluation of the design of group-wide controls and determination whether they have been implemented; and
- group engagement team's understanding of the component auditor.

Where individual components are not significant, either in terms of size or a significant risk of material misstatement, the Clarified ISA (UK and Ireland) 600 requires only that analytical procedures at group level need be performed. The group engagement team may supplement this as required with additional procedures relating to the component, performed either by the group engagement team or the component auditor on their behalf.

The ISA (UK and Ireland) requires that the group engagement team obtain sufficient appropriate audit evidence that the work of the component auditors is adequate for the group engagement team's purposes. This involves, as part of the initial planning by the group engagement team, discussing with the component auditors what use is to be made of the component auditors' work and informing them of any specific areas which the group engagement team want addressed. Additionally, the group engagement team advise and obtain representations from the component auditors concerning compliance with:

- the independence requirements of both the entity (parent) and the component (subsidiary); and
- the relevant accounting, auditing and reporting requirements.

The group engagement team may use a consolidation questionnaire or checklist, to be completed by the component auditors, to provide audit evidence or may review the component auditors' working papers. The choice of method will depend on the circumstances of the particular case and may also depend on the assessment of the competence of the component auditors.

There may be situations where it is decided not to use any of the methods outlined above because of evidence previously obtained that acceptable quality control policies and procedures are complied with in the conduct of the component auditors' practice. This will most commonly be the case where the component auditors are affiliated to the group engagement team. The group engagement team will be able to rely more readily on an associated firm as the component auditors than where the component auditors are an independent firm. The quality control procedures of a national or international association should

ensure that the work performed by the associate will be of a similar standard to
that of the group engagement team (see **Table 2**).

Communication with the component auditor

The group engagement team should communicate with the component auditor
on a timely basis, setting out the work to be performed, what use is to be made
of that work and what form reports back to the group engagement team should
take. The Clarified ISA (UK and Ireland) states that the group audit team
should:

- request that the component auditor confirms that they will cooperate with
  the group auditor;
- set out the ethical requirements that are relevant to the group audit;
- set out relevant materiality levels and thresholds;
- identify risks of material misstatement to the group financial statements that
  are relevant to the component auditor; and
- provide a list of related parties prepared by group management, and any
  other related parties of which the group engagement team are aware.

In return the component auditor is required by ISA (UK and Ireland) 600 to
communicate the following matters back to the group engagement team:

- whether they have complied with ethical requirements that are relevant to
  the group audit, including independence and professional competence;
- whether they have complied with the group engagement team's
  requirements;
- identification of the financial information of the component on which the
  component auditor is reporting;
- information on instances of non-compliance with laws and regulations that
  could give rise to a material misstatement of the group financial statements;
- a list of uncorrected misstatements of the financial information of the
  component (the list does not need to include those misstatements below the
  level of 'clearly trivial' communicated to the component auditor by the
  group auditors);
- indicators of possible management bias;
- any identified significant deficiencies in internal control at component level;
- other significant matters that the component auditors have, or expect to,
  communicate to those charged with governance; and
- any other matters relevant to the group audit, including the component
  auditor's overall conclusion or opinion.

Evaluating audit evidence

The group engagement team should consider the significant findings of the
component auditors. To do this they may use the methods noted above. They
may also decide that discussions are needed between the two auditors and the
management of the component. The group engagement team should also request
copies of any reports to the management of the component by the component

auditors. As a result the group engagement team may decide that additional procedures are necessary, performed by either the group engagement team or the component auditors.

The group engagement team should document any review of component auditors' work that they undertake.

39.3.5   Co-operation between auditors

Component auditors are required to co-operate with the group engagement team.

TABLE 2: Reliance on other auditors

A & Co audit the parent company of a group, XYZ Plc, which has two subsidiaries, U Limited and W Limited.

U Limited is audited by the local office of A & Co. W Limited is audited by a smaller practice. U Limited and W Limited are both significant to the group accounts.

The degree of reliance that A & Co would be able to place on work of the component auditors would differ.

For the audit of U Limited, assuming this was carried out in accordance with common procedures and that their local office was subject to national quality control procedures, there would be no need for a comprehensive review of U Limited's audit.

In contrast for W Limited, they would not be able to rely on this and may need to carry out a full-scale review.

For UK subsidiaries (of a UK group), the component auditors have a statutory duty to communicate such information and explanations as may be reasonably required by the group engagement team. Where there is no such obligation, the component auditors should obtain the permission of the component's management before giving such assistance.

Where the component auditors have been unable to conclude on a matter, or feel that there is something that should be brought to the attention of the group engagement team, they should do so bearing in mind their statutory obligation as noted above.

There is no complementary obligation, but the group engagement team may inform component auditors of such matters if they consider it appropriate after due consultation with those charged with governance at the parent entity.

39.3.6   The consolidation process

The group engagement team is required by ISA (UK and Ireland) 600 to design and perform further audit procedures to respond to the risk of material misstatement of the group financial statements arising from the consolidation process. The group engagement team's evaluation of the appropriateness, completeness and accuracy of the consolidation adjustments may include:

- evaluating whether significant adjustments appropriately reflect the events and transactions underlying them;
- determining whether significant adjustments have been correctly calculated, processed and authorised by group management and, where applicable, component management;
- determining whether significant adjustments are properly supported by documentation; and
- checking reconciliations and eliminations of intra-group transactions and balances.

39.3.7   Reporting to those charged with governance

When considering what to include in their report to those charged with governance, the group engagement team will consider deficiencies in internal control:

- identified by the group engagement team that affect the whole group;
- identified by the group engagement team that affect components; and
- identified by component auditors that affect components.

If fraud has been identified by the group engagement team or informed to the group engagement team by any of the component auditors, this should be reported to management of the group on a timely basis.

39.3.8   Reporting considerations

Reliance on the work of component auditors does not relieve the group engagement team of any of their own responsibilities in reporting on the consolidated financial statements. They have sole responsibility for their report and should not refer to the component auditors in it.

There are two instances when the group engagement team should consider the implications of the component auditors' work on their own report. These are when:

- adequate evidence about the work of the component auditors cannot be obtained and the group engagement team have not been able to perform additional procedures in respect of these financial statements; or
- the component auditors intend to issue a qualified report or one containing additional explanatory material.

39.3.9   Documentation

Clarified ISA (UK and Ireland) 600 requires the group engagement team to include the following in their audit documentation:

- an analysis of components, indicating those that are significant, and the type of work performed on the financial information of the components;
- the nature, timing and extent of the group engagement team's involvement in the work performed by the component auditors on significant components including, where applicable, the group engagement team's review of relevant parts of the component auditors' audit documentation and conclusions thereon; and
- written communications between the group engagement team and the component auditors about the group engagement team's requirements.

39.3.10   Promoting Best Practice in Group Audits

In November 2005, the Audit and Assurance Faculty of the ICAEW published *Promoting Best Practice in Group Audits*, to provide practical guidance on increasing the quality of group audits. The guidance was based on the findings of research commissioned by the Faculty which sought the views of practitioners on how group audits are carried out in practice and looked for examples of good practice in firms.

The publication focuses on an eight point plan which deals with the challenges of project management, communication between auditors and dealing with the technical issues that specifically arise in relation to group audits. The eight point plan is set out below.

The Eight Point Plan

The Audit and Assurance Faculty's research concentrated on:

- establishing how group audits are currently handled;
- identifying best practice;
- providing practical guidance on the pitfalls to avoid; and
- providing a gap analysis of current practice and the main requirements of the ISA (UK and Ireland) 600 version proposed at the time of publication.

The eight point plan covers a range of issues which the Faculty believes are important to get right in order to make group audits as effective as possible. The key area is good project management with open lines of communication being established with other auditors. The plan is set out in **Table 3**.

TABLE 3: The Eight Point Plan

1. Get organised

- start early and establish clear milestones
- provide very clear instructions and requirements for deliverables to other auditors; an example of possible documentation to send to other auditors is set out in **Table 4**
- get audit committee and management buy-in to the audit process and ensure they understand their responsibilities
- consider asking for information on planning and risk assessment, including fraud risk, prior to the year end
- keep in regular contact with the key group parties
- use more telephone and conference calls rather than relying solely on letters and e-mail
- where appropriate, visit other auditors and subsidiary management

2. Analyse the group structure

- focus attention on the more unusual corporate structures
- if there are doubts about the group structure, verify it against publicly available information
- consider whether to accept an engagement where the group auditor is only directly responsible for a minority of the total group
- understand the accounting framework applicable to each component and any local statutory reporting requirements

3. Focus on the quality of other auditors

- consider the qualifications, independence and competence of other auditors up front, along with their quality control procedures
- for related auditors (those who have common quality control policies and procedures), group auditors may be able to rely on those common policies and procedures, particularly where they also adopt the same audit methodology
- for unrelated auditors, or related auditors where the group auditor is unable to rely on common policies and procedures, consider:

    - visiting the other auditor
    - requesting that the other auditor completes a questionnaire or representation
    - obtaining confirmation from a relevant regulatory body and/or
    - discussing the other auditor with colleagues from their own firm

- for an other auditor based overseas, consider whether they have enough knowledge and experience of ISAs (UK and Ireland)

4. Focus the group audit on high risk areas

- group auditors need to ask for enough information from other auditors to form their own conclusions on significant risks arising in components that affect the group financial statements. Focus attention on the five warning signs identified by respondents to the research:

    - recently acquired components
    - jurisdictions with under-developed financial reporting regimes
    - components which are 'just below the radar'
    - components that have a history of reporting late and
    - components that have had big swings in their profits

- consider the risks arising from the consolidation process itself, including the use of journals and incomplete information relating to adjustments between accounting frameworks or to align accounting policies
- discuss fraud risks with other auditors as appropriate

5. Understand internal controls across the group

- request details of material weaknesses in internal control identified by other auditors
- communicate material weaknesses in group-wide controls and significant weaknesses in internal controls of components to group management and those charged with governance of the group

6. Ensure staff understand the technical complexities of group audits and know when to bring in specialist help

- consider areas of particular concern, where it is important that practitioners are aware of the main issues and bring in expertise where it is needed:
  - differing accounting frameworks and policies
  - intra group transactions and balances
  - fair values in acquisitions
  - capturing post-balance sheet events
  - intangibles
  - the basis and calculation of share options and bonuses
  - deferred tax

- plan early any specialist involvement, for example the use of a tax expert to deal with international tax issues or a valuation expert for share options

7. Review other auditors' working papers

- group and other auditors should cooperate as regards sharing of information unless prohibited by law. Appropriate use of hold harmless letters may be used to manage risk
- get group management to obtain the consent of subsidiary management to communicate with the group auditor to deal with concerns about client confidentiality and sensitivity
- consider whether holding discussions with or visiting other auditors could deal with secrecy and data-protection issues

8. Review and update procedures, training and tools

- provide formal training on group audits to supplement on-the-job experience
- review standard questionnaires, if any, for effectiveness
- make sure that training materials and manuals are updated to reflect the new ISA (UK and Ireland) 600 in good time

---

TABLE 4: Possible documentation to send to other auditors

This is not a definitive list and should be tailored to the circumstances of the individual group.

Referral instructions

Including:

- timetable for the work;
- details of each of the components within the group together with required scope of work, arrangements for coordination of work at the planning stage and during the audit, including the group auditor's involvement in their work;
- any other known related parties;
- level of materiality and threshold for 'clearly trivial' misstatements;
- details of scope of work required for each component;
- details of specific risks and areas of focus for the group audit, including fraud risks and specific procedures required including work to be done on intra-group transactions and balances and the work to be done on subsequent events;
- description of any group-wide controls including any testing by the group auditor relevant to the work of other auditors, work by internal audit; and
- details of the applicable financial reporting framework, auditing standards and any other statutory reporting responsibilities, including group accounting policies and applicable laws and regulations.

Letter from other auditor acknowledging instructions

Including:

- the use that will be made of their work and that they will perform the work required;
- confirmation of independence and, for unrelated firms, of whether the quality control system complies with ISQC (UK and Ireland) 1 and any relevant issues noted in recent monitoring reports;
- confirmation of understanding of the applicable financial reporting framework and auditing standards.

Specimen reports to group auditor

Including:

- template for planning memorandum to describe proposed audit approach;
- template for clearance memos, summary memoranda and/or questionnaires to report findings including significant accounting, financial reporting and auditing matters including accounting estimates and related judgements, going concern matters;
- template for specimen management letter/report to those charged with governance of components including details of any material weaknesses in internal control and/or for reporting such issues to the group auditor;
- template for reporting uncorrected misstatements;
- template for reporting any actual fraud or information obtained that indicates a fraud may exist, including any suspected or alleged fraud affecting the component and any instances of non-compliance with laws and regulations that may have a material effect on the group financial statements;
- subsequent events review sign-off; and
- confirmation of independence including details of fees for non-audit services.

39.4   EXPERTS

39.4.1   Auditing Standards

Clarified ISA (UK and Ireland) 620 *Using the Work of an Auditor's Expert* was issued in October 2009 and replaces ISA (UK and Ireland) 620 previously issued in December 2004. The Clarified ISA (UK and Ireland) is effective for the audit of financial statements for periods ending on or after 15 December 2010. This section covers both the existing and Clarified ISAs (UK and Ireland). As the Clarified ISA (UK and Ireland) does not significantly amend the requirements of the existing ISA (UK and Ireland) this chapter is written on the basis of the existing requirements, and any changes to them included in the Clarified ISA (UK and Ireland) are included and clearly indicated.

The ISA (UK and Ireland) provides guidance covering:

- using the work of an expert;
- competence and objectivity of the expert;
- the expert's scope of work;
- assessing the work of the expert.

As with all ISAs (UK and Ireland), the text of the international ISA has been supplemented with additional guidance from a UK and Ireland perspective.

39.4.2   Using experts

Auditors are required to determine whether it is necessary to use an auditor's expert to assist in obtaining appropriate audit evidence. Auditors may consider the following, when deciding whether or not to use an expert:

- whether those charged with governance have used an expert in preparing the financial statements;
- the nature and significance of the matter, including its complexity;
- the risks of material misstatement in the matter; and
- the expected nature of audit procedures planned to respond to assessed risk.

ISA (UK and Ireland) 620 requires that when using the work performed by an expert, auditors should obtain sufficient appropriate audit evidence that such work is adequate for the purposes of the audit.

The term 'expert' refers to a person or a firm possessing specialist skills or knowledge in a field other than auditing and accounting. They are usually members of another profession such as surveyors, actuaries or engineers.

Where the firm of auditors employs the experts full-time they will still need to assess aspects of their work as if the experts were third parties with regard to the work and its results, although they may not need to consider the experts' skills and competence for each assignment. Auditors, however, need to have regard to the related ethical guidance when deciding if they can use employees of their firm as experts on an audit assignment. They must ensure that their objectivity and independence is not impaired, which would be the case where 'in house' experts are required to value an asset or a liability of the client company for inclusion in its balance sheet.

The types of evidence that auditors may obtain from experts will usually be a report, opinion or valuation, such as:

- valuation of an asset, for example property;
- determination of the quantity of an asset, for example minerals;
- determination of amounts using specialised techniques, for example actuarial valuation;
- measurement of work completed on contracts in progress; and
- legal opinions on interpretations of agreements.

Although the work of an expert may be used, the auditor retains sole responsibility for the audit opinion.

39.4.3   Competence and objectivity of experts

When planning to use the work of experts, auditors should assess the objectivity and professional qualifications, experience and resources of the experts.

The objectivity of the experts will be impaired if they are either employed by the entity or related to it in some way (for example, they are a shareholder). The Clarified ISA (UK and Ireland) states that where 'a proposed auditor's expert is an individual who has played a significant role in preparing the information that is being audited, that is, if the auditor's expert is a management's expert' there are no safeguards that can be applied to reduce the threats to objectivity to an acceptable level.

39.4.4   The experts' scope of work

The nature, scope and objectives of the auditor's experts' work may vary considerably depending on the circumstances. Therefore, these matters should be agreed before the experts commence their work and may be best clarified in writing.

The letter of instruction should contain details of:

- the objectives and scope of the experts' work;
- the specific matters that the report is to cover;
- the intended use of the experts' work;
- the extent of the experts' access to the appropriate records; and
- information regarding the assumptions and methods intended to be used by the experts.

The letter of instruction may also contain details regarding access to, and retention of, each other's working papers and the expected method and frequency of communication between the auditor and the experts.

39.4.5 Assessing the work of experts

The auditors should assess the appropriateness of the experts' notes as audit evidence regarding the financial statement assertions being considered. This will involve assessment of:

- the source data used;
- the assumptions and methods used;
- the reasons for any changes in these from those used in the prior period;
- when the expert carried out the work; and
- the results of the work in the light of the auditors' knowledge of the business.

The auditors should ensure that the data used by the expert is sufficient, relevant and reliable and may consider reviewing or testing this data.

The experts' assumptions will not usually be challenged by the auditors as they do not have sufficient expertise, but they do need to understand the assumptions and consider whether they are reasonable given the auditors' knowledge of the business and the results of the other audit procedures.

Where the results of the experts' work are inconsistent with evidence obtained by the auditors, they should try to resolve this by discussion with the management. If they are unable to resolve the inconsistencies they will need to consider the implications for their audit report.

When the auditors are satisfied with the work of the experts there is no need for them to refer to this in their report.

39.4.6 Applying the guidance in practice

The different considerations in assessing the competence, objectivity and results of experts' reports may be seen by comparing the respective audit approaches to property carried in the accounts at valuation, which are supported by various levels of expert report. In summary, these are:

- full external valuation;
- valuation supported by limited review or a 'desk top' update by external valuers of a previous valuation;
- internal valuation by qualified directors supported by a full valuation report; or
- internal valuation by qualified directors not supported by a report.

External valuations

Where a valuation has been carried out by external experts, the auditors must:

- assess the competence and objectivity of the experts;
- agree on the scope of the work of the experts; and
- evaluate the findings of the experts.

Where the valuation is material to the accounts it will inevitably be the case that the auditors will need to discuss the valuation with the valuers.

Valuation supported by limited external evidence

In this case, there will be either a report or descriptive correspondence from external valuers, which must be assessed using the principles set out above. In particular, any limitations or qualifications should be examined to assess whether they undermine evidence already obtained. For example, a 'desk top' update is always qualified on the grounds that no site inspections have been carried out. If it is known that a site has been closed and severe dilapidation has taken place the auditors would question that valuation. If such an update assumes the same 'portfolio' but some sites have been sold, this must also cause the value to be questioned.

Internal valuation supported by full report

Where the directors are qualified valuers and support their valuation by a report setting out the assumptions that they have made in arriving at the figures (particularly in terms of rentals and yields), the auditors must initially assess this report using the same principles as they would for an external valuation. In assessing the other assumptions they may need to seek additional external evidence to support some of the assumptions (which the directors may in fact be able to provide). Where the effect is material, it will be necessary either to seek advice from other professionals or to use internal expertise to assess, for example, the reasonableness of assumptions concerning yields.

Auditors should avoid carrying out 'quasi-valuations' of their own. This course contains pitfalls, for example, using 'general' tables of yields as the only supporting evidence, as they cannot be easily attributed to a specific property. They should also be aware that special inducements can mean that quoted rentals are often in excess of the 'true rental'.

Unsupported internal valuations by qualified directors

In such cases the directors must be made to state their valuation and the underlying bases in writing. Where this is carried out the auditors will then assess it in the same way as at **39.4.5** above. If the directors are unable or unwilling to support their valuation the auditors must consider its materiality to their opinion.

39.4.7   Using the work of an actuary with regard to insurance provisions

Bulletin 1998/2 *Using the Work of an Actuary with Regard to Insurance Technical Provisions* was issued to provide guidance in the interpretation of SAS 520 in this particular situation. Although SAS 520 has been updated by ISA (UK and Ireland) 620, the guidance in the Bulletin remains relevant.

The Bulletin notes that auditors should consider the independence of the actuaries, their knowledge of the portfolio of business for which provision is being made and their experience of the market in which the insurer operates. When planning their audit, auditors should obtain information about the actuaries' approach to calculating the provisions in order to be able to assess their work.

Using their knowledge of the business and other evidence obtained in the course of their audit, auditors should consider whether the assumptions and methods of the actuaries are reasonable. If they are not satisfied that the actuaries' work provides sufficient appropriate evidence they should consider the implications for their report.

40 REPORTING IN ACCORDANCE WITH GLOBAL INVESTMENT PERFORMANCE STANDARDS (GIPS)

40.1 GLOBAL INVESTMENT PERFORMANCE STANDARDS (GIPS)

Global Investment Performance Standards (GIPS) are voluntary ethical standards, which aim to ensure fair representation and full disclosure of an investment firm's performance history. GIPS were drafted by a committee of investment professionals representing countries throughout the world. Although this is a voluntary code, the acceptance of the GIPS as the global standard is expected to be widespread, and it has become increasingly common for investment managers to receive requests to provide information on historic performance results to prospective clients based on the standards set down in the GIPS, or an equivalent local standard.

40.2 REPORTING IN ACCORDANCE WITH GIPS

The Standards recommend that a firm's claim to be calculating and presenting performance history in compliance with GIPS is 'verified'. The Audit Faculty of the ICAEW have issued Technical Release Audit 1/00 *Guidance for Reporting in Accordance with Global Investment Performance Standards* to assist reporting accountants who are requested to report in accordance with the GIPS framework.

The Technical Release does not make reference to the term 'verification' since it is the Institute's view that the term implies a degree of checking and accuracy which is not consistent with the work to be performed as set out in the GIPS. The primary purpose of the work is to ensure that a firm has adhered to the standards set out in the GIPS. The suggested procedures attempt to strike a balance between ensuring the quality, accuracy and relevance of any performance statement and the cost to the investment firm of commissioning the independent review.

Section III of the GIPS set out the scope and purpose of the review and the procedures required (see section **40.4**).

A report will be issued for the whole firm, as a GIPS review cannot be completed for a single composite. A composite is an aggregation of a number of portfolios into a single group that represents a particular investment objective or strategy.

The Technical Release is not mandatory when an accountant is asked to perform a review of a report of compliance, but if alternative procedures and reports are used, no reference should be made to the Technical Release in any report.

40.3 ENGAGEMENT LETTERS

To ensure that there is clear understanding of the scope and purpose of the engagement, the terms of the accountants' engagement should be agreed in writing. The engagement letter should include:

- the respective responsibilities of the investment management firm and the reporting accountants;
- the scope of the work which will be performed;
- the nature of the report;
- the agreed use of the report and the extent the report may be made available to the investment firm's existing and prospective clients;
- a reference to the likely need for client representations;
- an explanation of the limitations of the work to be performed; and
- limitations to the reporting accountants' liability.

The reporting accountant should exclude liability in respect of any loss or damage caused by the acts of the employees or directors of the investment firm. Liability to third parties or regulators should also be excluded, and reporting accountants would normally obtain a limitation in aggregate of any liability.

An example engagement letter is set out in **Table 1**.

TABLE 1: Engagement letter

The Directors
XYZ Asset Management

Dear Sirs

Following our recent meeting when you invited us to report on your policies over performance presentation and calculation of XYZ Asset Management ('the firm') for the period [date] to [date], we are writing to set out our proposed responsibilities, our understanding of the work to be performed, and the terms and conditions upon which we offer to perform such work.

Respective responsibilities of principals and reporting accountants

As the principals of XYZ Asset Management you are responsible for the design, implementation and maintenance of procedures that ensure that performance is reported in accordance with Global Investment Performance Standards (GIPS). You

---

will describe the policies adopted in your business to ensure GIPS compliance in a report. It is our responsibility to form an independent opinion on whether these policies, insofar as they affect our opinion, were complied with in compiling composite reports for the period [date] to [date] and to report our opinion to you. This will include considering whether your statement appropriately reflects the extent to which processes and procedures designed to calculate and report in compliance with GIPS were followed during the period. Because reporting qualified compliance with GIPS is not envisaged, if there are material deficiencies in compliance or significant exceptions we will not issue an opinion. Instead we will draw these matters to your attention.

Scope of work

The work we shall perform will be conducted in accordance with the framework set out in the guidance issued by the Audit Faculty of the Institute of Chartered Accountants in England and Wales (Technical Release AUDIT 1/00) and included in Section III of GIPS. Our work will include obtaining an understanding of the policies and procedures in operation, enquiry of management, review of documents supplied to us and tests of certain specific procedures designed to ensure compliance with GIPS. Our work will be planned in advance. [In developing our plan we shall liaise with your Internal Audit Department to ensure that our work is properly coordinated with theirs.]

We shall not be responsible for a review of the compliance with policies beyond the period reported upon or for the identification of changes not disclosed by management.

Use of report

Our report will be addressed to you as principals of the company although we understand that you may wish to make the report available to existing or prospective clients using the reporting company's services, and we consent to the report being provided to them at their request for their information only. However, we will not accept any liability/responsibility to those parties or to any other party to whom this report is shown or into whose hands it may come. You may not provide our report or copies thereof to any other third party. You agree to indemnify us against any liabilities, losses, expenses or other costs that we reasonably incur in connection with any claims against us by any such existing or prospective clients or any other third party. You agree not to use our report or references to it in material disseminated to the general public without our express written permission. In any cases where marketing literature is prepared which will refer either to us or to our report, you will seek our consent to those references in advance and we reserve the right to refuse.

Management representations

We may seek written representations from management in relation to matters for which independent corroboration is not available. We will also seek confirmation from you that any significant matters of which we should be aware have been brought to our attention.

Complaints procedure
[*Include relevant complaints procedures*]

Limitations of work

Procedures designed to address specified assertions are subject to inherent limitations and, accordingly, errors or irregularities may occur and not be detected. Such procedures cannot guarantee protection against fraudulent collusion especially on the part of those holding positions of authority or trust. Furthermore, our opinion will be based on historical information and the projection of any information or conclusions, contained in our opinion, to any future periods is subject to the risk that changes in procedures or circumstances may alter their validity.

Our work on the underlying accounting systems used to produce valuation information for performance calculation purposes will be restricted to a review of the design of processes and procedures to meet the input data requirements of GIPS and no detailed testing of those processes and procedures will be undertaken. Consequently, our work will not include tests of transactions in respect of any particular customer or composite. We will not carry out any independent examination work nor express an opinion on either the net asset value or the change in net asset value of any individual portfolio or composite.

Fees

Our fees will be based on the degree of skill involved, the experience of staff engaged and the time necessarily occupied on the work.

Limitation of liability

We accept no duty of care and deny any liability to anyone other than the firm. We will not be liable for any loss or damage caused by or arising from any fraudulent acts, fraudulent omissions, misrepresentations or wilful default on the part of the firm, its principals, employees or agents.

Any liability of our firm, its partners and staff from actions found against us to pay damages for losses arising as a direct result of breach of contract or negligence on our part in respect of services provided in connection with or arising out of the engagement set out in this letter (or any variation or addition thereto), whether in contract, negligence or otherwise shall in no circumstances exceed £x in aggregate: such amount including all legal and other costs which we may incur in defending any actions against us.

Applicable law

This engagement letter shall be governed by, and construed in accordance with, English law. The Courts of England shall have exclusive jurisdiction in relation to any claim, dispute or difference concerning the engagement letter and any matter arising from it. Each party irrevocably waives any right it may have to object to an action being brought in the Courts, to claim that the action has been brought in an inconvenient forum, or to claim that those Courts do not have jurisdiction.

Acknowledgement and acceptance

We shall be obliged if you will acknowledge receipt and your acceptance of this letter by [date].

Yours faithfully
Reporting Accountant

40.4   THE REPORTING ACCOUNTANTS' REVIEW

Guidance on the work to be undertaken by reporting accountants is included in GIPS section III, which is reproduced in **Table 2**. Professional judgement will be required to determine the nature, timing and extent of tests to be carried out. The reporting accountant may wish to place reliance on the work of the investment firm's own internal audit department or on the work of a local or previous reviewer, and the reporting accountant should consider the level of reliance that can be placed on evidence provided by such sources.

The level of work to be performed on the underlying accounting systems of the investment manager is restricted by GIPS to obtaining an understanding of the methods and policies used to record portfolio valuation information for performance calculation purposes. Because the underlying accounting records are not expected to be tested, let alone audited, the reporting accountant's opinion must explain the limitations of the review in this regard.

Therefore, it is likely that in the first year that GIPS are implemented the investment manager will rework their historical data to ensure that it conforms with the GIPS requirements. The principals' statement must make reference to this fact, and the accountants' report should state that it is corrected information, not information available for the first time, with reporting accountants ensuring that the status of the information is fully disclosed by the principals.

The reporting accountants will normally obtain written representations from the principals of the investment manager. Matters likely to be covered by the representation letter include:

- that any fraudulent or illegal acts, irregularities or uncorrected errors attributable to the client or its employees have been disclosed to the reporting accountants; and
- that the reporting accountants have been informed of all known instances of non-compliance with the policies in place.

TABLE 2: 'Verification' procedures outlined by GIPS

Pre-verification procedures

Knowledge of the firm: obtain samples of the firm's investment performance reports, and other available information regarding the firm, to ensure appropriate knowledge of the firm.

Knowledge of GIPS: understand the requirements and recommendations of GIPS, including any updates, reports or clarification of GIPS published by the Investment Performance Council, the body responsible for oversight of GIPS.

Knowledge of the performance standards: be knowledgeable of country-specific performance standards, laws and regulations applicable to the firm, and determine any differences between GIPS and the country-specific standards, laws and regulations.

Knowledge of firm policies: determine the firm's assumptions and policies for establishing and maintaining compliance with all applicable requirements of GIPS. As a minimum, reviewers must determine the following policies and procedures of the firm:

- investment discretion. The reviewer must receive in writing the firm's definition of investment discretion and the firm's guidelines for determining whether accounts are fully discretionary;
- definition of composites according to investment strategy. The reviewer must obtain the firm's list of composite definitions with written criteria for including accounts in each composite;
- timing of inclusion of new accounts in the composites;
- timing of exclusion of closed accounts in the composites;
- accrual of interest and dividend income;
- market valuation of investment securities;
- method for computing time-weighted portfolio return;
- assumptions on the timing of capital inflows/outflows;
- method for computing composite returns;
- presentation of composite returns;
- timing of implied taxes due on income and realised capital gains for reporting performance on an after tax basis;
- use of securities/countries not included in a composite's benchmark;
- use of leverage and other derivatives; and
- any other policies and procedures relevant to performance presentation.

Knowledge of valuation basis for performance calculations: understand the methods and policies used to record valuation information for performance calculation purposes. In particular, reviewers must determine that:

- the firm's policy on classifying fund flows (e.g., injections, disbursements, dividends, interest, fees, taxes, etc.) is consistent with the desired results and will give rise to accurate returns;
- the firm's accounting treatment of income, interest and dividend receipts is consistent with cash account and cash accruals definitions;
- the firm's treatment of taxes, tax reclaims and tax accruals is correct and the manner used is consistent with the desired method (i.e., gross – or net-of-tax return);
- the firm's policies on recognising purchases, sales and the opening and closing of other positions are internally consistent and will produce accurate results; and
- the firm's accounting for investment and derivatives is consistent with GIPS.

Verification procedures
Definition of the firm: determine that the firm is, and has been, appropriately defined.

Composite construction: ensure that

- the firm has defined and maintained composites according to reasonable guidelines in compliance with GIPS;
- all of the firm's actual discretionary fee-paying portfolios are included in a composite;
- the manager's definition of discretion has been consistently applied over time;
- at all times, all accounts are included in their respective composites and no accounts that belong in a particular composite have been excluded;

- composite benchmarks are consistent with composite definitions and have been consistently applied over time;
- the firm's guidelines for creating and maintaining composites have been consistently applied; and
- the firm's list of composites is complete.

Non-discretionary accounts: obtain a listing of all firm portfolios and determine on a sampling basis whether the manager's classification of the account as discretionary or non-discretionary is appropriate, by referring to the account agreement and the manager's written guidelines for determining investment discretion.

Sample account selection: obtain a listing of open and closed accounts for all composites for the years under examination. Reviewers may check compliance with GIPS using a sample of a firm's accounts. Reviewers should consider the following criteria when selecting the sample accounts for examination:

- number of composites at the firm;
- number of portfolios in each composite;
- nature of the composite;
- total assets under management;
- internal control structure at the firm (systems of checks and balances in place);
- number of years under examination; and
- computer applications, software used in the construction and maintenance of the composites, the use of external performance measurers and the calculation of performance results.

Account review: for selected accounts, determine

- whether the timing of the initial inclusion in the composite is in accordance with the policies of the firm;
- whether the timing of exclusion from the composite is in accordance with the policies of the firm for closed accounts;
- whether the objectives set forth in the account agreement are consistent with the manager's composite definition as indicated by the account agreement, portfolio summary and composite definition;
- the existence of the accounts by tracing selected accounts from account agreements to the composites;
- that all portfolios sharing the same guidelines are included in the same composite; and
- that shifts from one composite to another are consistent with the guidelines set forth by the specific account agreement or with documented guidelines of the firm's clients.

Performance measurement calculation: determine whether the firm has computed performance in accordance with the policies and assumptions adopted by the firm and disclosed in its presentations. In doing so, reviewers should

- recalculate rates of return for a sample of accounts in the firm using an acceptable return formula as prescribed by GIPS (i.e., time-weighted rate of return); and
- take a reasonable sample of composite calculations to assure themselves of the accuracy of the asset weighting of returns, the geometric linking of returns to produce annual rates of return and the calculation of the dispersion of individual returns around the aggregate composite return.

Disclosures: review a sample of composite presentations to ensure that the presentations include the information and disclosures required by GIPS.

Maintenance of records: maintain sufficient information to support the review report. The reviewer must obtain a representation letter from the client firm confirming major policies and any other specific representations made to the verifier during the examination.

40.5   THE REPORTING PACKAGE

The reporting package should comprise a report by the investment management firm concerning the policies they are claiming to comply with, and a report by the reporting accountants setting out the scope of their work and their opinion.

40.5.1   Report by the investment management firm

The report by the principals of the investment management firm should include:

- a statement of responsibility;
- representation that the whole firm has complied with GIPS for the whole period;
- the firm's policies as required by GIPS;
- details of significant changes to the policies during the period; and
- a statement that the procedures supporting the policies have been reviewed, and the extent to which the policies and procedures have been followed during the period.

A pro forma for the principals' report is given in **Table 3**.

TABLE 3: Principals' report

Report by the principals of XYZ Asset Management

Responsibilities of the principals
As the principals of XYZ Asset Management we are responsible for:

- the identification of policies relating to the presentation and calculation of investment performance in order to comply with the Global Investment Performance Standards (GIPS);
- the design, implementation and maintenance of procedures to provide reasonable assurance on an ongoing basis that the policies are followed.

We have reviewed the procedures [in operation during the period/applied retrospectively] to support the following policies and disclosures.

XYZ Asset Management Firm-wide GIPS assertions

XYZ Asset Management ('the firm') has complied [retrospectively] with the requirements of the Global Investment Performance Standards (GIPS) on a firm-wide basis in its application of processes and procedures to calculate and present composite reports and in compiling the performance results of each to the firm's composites for the periods from [date] to [date]. For the purpose of complying with GIPS, the firm has been defined as XYZ Asset Management. In particular, the following policies required by GIPS have been complied with in compiling composite reports for the period [date] to [date].

All of the firm's actual, discretionary, fee-paying portfolios are included in appropriate composites defined according to the investment strategy or investment objective. The firm's list and description of composites is available on request. The list of composites represents all of the composites of the firm for the period from [date] to [date].

The firm's policies for defining, creating and maintaining composites have been consistently applied.

Composites include new portfolios at the start of the next performance measurement period after the portfolio comes under management [or define alternative basis].

Composites exclude terminated portfolios after the last full performance period the portfolios were under management, but composites continue to include terminated portfolios for all periods prior to termination.

Accounting systems are designed to ensure input data requirements of GIPS have been complied with when computing portfolio returns.

Portfolio returns are calculated according to time-weighted total return methodology, with a minimum of [quarterly] valuation and accrual of income [for fixed income securities].

Portfolio returns within the composites are weighted using [beginning of period market values].

Composite returns for the required period are presented with all required disclosures.

.... (Principal's Signature)

40.5.2   Report by the reporting accountants

The reporting accountants' report should be addressed to the principals of the investment management firm, not the existing or prospective clients of that firm.

The reporting accountants' report should contain statements that:

- the report is intended for the use of the principals (the reporting accountant may wish to state that the report may be made available to third parties but without giving rise to any liability or duty to them);
- detail the scope of the report and the respective responsibilities of the principals and reporting accountants;
- the work performed is substantially less in scope than that of an audit and therefore no independent examination has taken place or any opinion expressed on the net asset values or change in net asset values of any individual portfolios or composites;
- no detailed testing of the processes and procedures relating to input data requirements has been performed, and work may have been limited to a review of the design of those processes and procedures;
- individual composite reports have not been subject to a detailed examination, and accordingly no opinion is expressed on them; and
- the report refers to a certain period, and the validity of the conclusions included may not be appropriate to future periods.

An example report is given in **Table 4**.

TABLE 4: Reporting accountants' report

Report by the independent reporting accountants to the principals of XYZ Asset Management

Use of this report

This report is intended solely for the use of the principals of XYZ Asset Management ('the firm') and for the information of its existing and prospective clients, without giving rise to any liability or duty on our part to such clients. The attention of existing and prospective clients of the firm is drawn to the engagement letter dated [date], which includes provisions relating to the scope of our responsibilities and the limitation of our liability, a copy of which is attached.

[*include more detail here on engagement terms if the engagement letter is not attached.*]

Scope

This report covers solely the application of the Global Investment Performance Standards (GIPS) by the firm, defined in your report, attached as [Appendix X] to this report. GIPS applies to the investment performance presentation and calculations operations carried out by the firm and does not extend to any other business or operation of XYZ Asset Management.

Our work was based upon obtaining an understanding of the policies and procedures applied by management in compiling performance reports for the period [date] to [date], assessment of whether such policies and procedures were appropriate to achieve compliance with GIPS, enquiry of management, review of documents supplied to us, and testing of such policies and procedures to confirm their operation. [Certain processes and procedures, as explained in the principals' report, were not in operation throughout the composite return period, but were applied retrospectively in order to bring the firm into compliance with GIPS in reporting performance for that return period.]

Individual composite presentations and returns calculations have not been subject to a detailed examination and accordingly we do not express an opinion on individual composite reports, including any such reports which may become attached to this report.

Our work on the underlying accounting system used to produce valuation information for performance calculation purposes was restricted to a review of the design of processes and procedures to meet the input data requirements of GIPS and no detailed testing of those processes and procedures was undertaken. Our work did not include tests of transactions in respect of any particular customer or composite and we have not carried out any independent examination of, and do not express an opinion on the net asset value or the change in net asset value of, any individual portfolio or composite.

Respective responsibilities of principals and the reporting accountant

Your responsibilities as principals are set out in the attached engagement letter and in your report attached hereto. The policies described in your report are designed to achieve compliance with GIPS and are your responsibility as principals of XYZ Asset Management. It is our responsibility to form an independent opinion, based on work

---

we have carried out, on whether these policies are designed to calculate and present performance reports in compliance with GIPS, and to ensure the composite construction requirements of GIPS have been complied with in compiling composite reports for the reporting period [date] to [date], and to report our opinion to you.

[*include principals' responsibilities here if not in principals' report.*]

Basis of opinion

Our review was conducted in accordance with the framework for reporting set out in the guidance issued by the Audit Faculty of the Institute of Chartered Accountants in England and Wales, Technical Release AUDIT 1/00, and procedures set out in Section III of GIPS, dated April 1999.

Procedures designed to address specific policies are subject to inherent limitations and, accordingly, errors or irregularities may occur and not be detected. Such procedures cannot guarantee protection against fraudulent collusion or misrepresentation especially on the part of those holding positions of authority or trust. Furthermore, this opinion is based on historical information and the projection of any information or conclusions to any future periods would be inappropriate.

Opinion

Based on the above, in our opinion:

- in compiling composite reports for the period from [date] to [date] the firm has complied, in all material respects, with all composite construction requirements of GIPS on a firm-wide basis;
- in compiling composite reports for the period [date] to [date] the firm's processes and procedures were designed to calculate and present composite reports in compliance with GIPS in conformity with policies set out by the principals in their report attached hereto.

Chartered Accountants   Address

Date

40.5.3   Material weaknesses

An investment management firm either complies with or does not comply with GIPS, and thus 'except for' opinions will be meaningless. If any material deficiencies are found, a reporting accountant will refuse to give any report.

However, an investment manager may have non-material deficiencies which, in the opinion of the reporting accountant, are not significant enough to render compliance invalid and where the issuing of an unmodified report will be appropriate.

41 AUDITING IN AN E-COMMERCE ENVIRONMENT

41.1 INTRODUCTION

E-commerce (electronic commerce) has seen unprecedented growth in the past couple of years, and few businesses have been left untouched by the advent of the Internet and the opportunities and risks resulting from the advance of the World Wide Web. E-commerce is the buying and selling of goods and services and the transfer of funds through digital communications. It also includes inter-company and intra-company functions, such as marketing, finance, manufacturing, selling and negotiating that enable commerce and use electronic mail, Electronic Data Interchange (EDI), file transfer, fax, video conferencing or interaction with a remote computer.

Whether clients have set up exclusively to take advantage of e-commerce opportunities (the so-called 'dot.com' businesses), or have expanded into e-commerce from a more traditional market place base, the different operating environment associated with e-commerce will require auditors to consider different audit risks and approaches.

Guidance in this area comes from a limited number of sources. In September 2000, the Audit and Assurance Faculty of the ICAEW issued, jointly with the Faculty of Information Technology, a guidance paper entitled *Implications of e-commerce for Auditors and Business Advisors*. This guidance paper sets out the main issues that an auditor or external adviser faces, and highlights the risks to which a business involved in e-commerce is exposed and the issues auditors may face, together with practical guidance on dealing with them.

In 2001 the APB issued Bulletin 2001/3, *E-business: Identifying financial statement risks* to provide additional guidance for auditors.

41.2 INVOLVEMENT IN E-COMMERCE

Businesses may be split between those who use e-commerce as an extension to their existing business, such as a hotel which takes reservations online, and those which are dependent entirely on e-commerce for their survival, such as a software vendor that sells only by clients downloading from its website. Auditors must be aware of this distinction, as entities of each type will have both different business models and audit risks resulting from e-commerce.

41.3 KNOWLEDGE OF THE BUSINESS

As with all entity types, auditors of businesses involved in or using e-commerce need to have sufficient knowledge of both the entity and its industry to enable them to understand the interaction of the events, transactions and practices with the financial statements and their effects on the audit. The auditors' knowledge of the industry in which their client is involved (e.g., selling books, travel and tourism or computer software) will help them to assess the impact of e-commerce on the business and also on their audit risk.

The growth of e-commerce may, however, have a significant impact on an entity's traditional business environment. To assess the impact of these changes auditors require appropriate IT skills and knowledge of the Internet. Understanding the business now involves not only understanding the business and the entity's business strategy, but also:

- understanding the e-commerce strategy and business model;
- understanding the technology; and
- assessing the IT skills and IT knowledge of its personnel.

The impact of e-commerce on an entity's business depends on the extent of its use. At the most basic level an entity may use its website as a static marketing tool with no connection to its internal systems. A more sophisticated e-commerce business may use its site to allow customers access to product information, place orders and make payments electronically. The most sophisticated user may provide an extranet to allow external parties to have direct selective and controlled access to its own systems through secure Internet pathways.

The types of enquiries an auditor may make of an entity which uses e-commerce together with the associated potential risks are set out in **Table 1**.

TABLE 1: Enquiries to be made of an e-commerce client to discover risk

Question	Potential risk
Is there a sufficient level of technical skill available, either within the entity or engaged by management (i.e., subcontractors)?	Lack of technical skill may mean that the website and any links into the entity's system are not developed or maintained to be sufficiently robust to handle a high volume of transactions. This may lead to excessive system 'down time' and loss of sales.
Is e-commerce a new business for the entity, or does it impact on traditional business channels?	E-business may provide additional growth opportunities for the entity. For some entities, entry into e-commerce may be the only way to ensure the continuation of the business.
Have the cost implications of electronic trading been fully evaluated by management and is the use of e-commerce supported by a justifiable business case?	Management may not have fully evaluated the costs and benefits of e-commerce. High set up costs may be poorly invested and cash receipts may be delayed, with an impact on profitability and cash flow.
What is the nature of the e-commerce business model (given that there is no standard for e-commerce businesses and the Internet based model is likely to vary significantly from that of the related 'traditional' business)?	A poorly constructed or ill thought-out business model may lead to failure to properly identify likely costs and business risks. If risks are unidentified they cannot be effectively controlled by management.
Have security issues been addressed by management?	Failure to address security issues could lead to corruption of a website or linked systems. This is particularly relevant where transactions initiated by customers impact directly on the financial statements. This may also lead to loss of confidence and loss of sales.
Has the entity's integration of Web applications with accounting systems been addressed business-wide to avoid unnecessary complexity?	Overly complex or poorly integrated systems and controls are likely to be less effective in controlling security risks and may lead to accounting systems breakdowns.
Has management considered e-commerce implementation difficulties and their resolution, and have past problems been properly dealt with?	Poorly developed implementation plans may lead to unforeseen additional cost, delay and loss of orders. Management attitude to resolving problems in the past may indicate a control weakness.

Question	Potential risk
Is there an appropriate structure to measure the performance of e-commerce activities?	Failure to incorporate different performance measures into management reporting may lead to an inability to track business, trading and cost trends and take steps to mitigate associated risks promptly.
Have any concerns been expressed by management over the number of customers connecting to the business via the Internet, for example insufficient numbers to achieve the anticipated efficiencies or the ability of the entity's technology to deal with unexpectedly high levels of demand?	Where insufficient business is being generated there may be a going concern risk. Where systems are unable to cope with high demand there may be a loss of sales and customer goodwill. If systems are unable to cope with high demand, controls may also be breached.
How does management ensure control is maintained over transaction processing carried out by a service organisation?	Depending on the nature of the e-commerce operations that are outsourced, risks may include those related to maintenance of accounting records, completeness of income, credit risk and understatement of liabilities.
How are the authenticity and integrity of trading partners verified?	Retail customers may not be who they claim to be and use stolen credit card details to order goods and services. This may create a credit risk as banks may force retailers that do not make adequate checks to pay the full cost of fraudulent transactions. There is also risk of repudiation of contract.
Are there appropriate systems in place to ensure that the level of goods returned are monitored and recorded?	There is typically a higher level of returns of items purchased remotely than in a traditional retail environment. There is a risk that revenue is incorrectly recognised where returns are not recorded correctly.
How have management ensured that electronic contracts are legally binding?	Failure to ensure that electronic contracts are legally binding introduces the risk of repudiation, which affects credit risk and the risk of goods being returned.

Another area to consider is the extent to which the entity's industry is currently affected by e-commerce. In assessing this, auditors must be aware that some industries' involvement in e-commerce will be relatively mature, such as computer software and hardware suppliers, but in other cases there may be little experience to date. In addition, an entity may be adversely affected by the use of e-commerce in its, or a related, industry. Part of assessing knowledge of the business involves discovering the effects of external factors on the industry on which it operates. E-commerce may have wide-ranging effects. For example, the client may act as an intermediary between producer and consumer, and may be made redundant by the use made of the Internet by the producer to sell its product.

41.4 E-FRAUD

E-fraud is not new, nor is it fundamentally different from other types of fraud. What distinguishes it is the speed in which the e-commerce environment changes, meaning that both the opportunities for fraud and the procedures required to intercept it must change as quickly.

Parties intent on fraud will seek out and exploit weak controls. Many e-businesses, faced with fast growth, may be exposed by control systems which have not expanded at a rate to match the growth of the business.

Other reasons why auditors should pay particular attention to the possibility of fraud during the planning and execution of their audit include:

● the geographical remoteness of their customers and/or suppliers, of whom they are less likely to have built up a full knowledge;
● the ease with which anyone dealing with the business can assume a false identity;
● the increase in dealing with contractors and third parties over whom the entity has little or no control; and
● the increase in electronic documentation making the usual identification techniques, such as manual signatures, redundant.

41.5 LAW AND REGULATIONS

41.5.1 Relevant regulations

Businesses involved in e-commerce need to be aware of a number of relevant laws and regulations. Some of the main legislation relevant to e-business is set out in **Table 2**. In some cases, a business must take positive action to ensure that it complies with the regulations to avoid prosecution.

As this is an area in which legislation and regulations change rapidly, auditors must be aware of amendments and additions in order to fulfil the requirements of ISA (UK and Ireland) 250 Section A *Consideration of law and regulations in an audit of financial statements*. Areas where changes are likely include:

● taxation;
● privacy;
● intellectual property;
● cryptography;
● digital signatures; and

- acceptable business practices.

In addition, the laws and regulations governing an e-commerce entity are further complicated by the easy ability of such businesses to trade in many jurisdictions without having a presence and to move locations to avoid legal requirements.

TABLE 2: Laws and regulations of importance to businesses involved in e-commerce

The Data Protection Act 1998

This Act makes it necessary for most businesses to notify the Data Protection Commissioner if personal data is being processed electronically, or in a structured manual system. A business is also expected to have strong controls in place. A number of specific guidelines relate to websites, in particular to the collection of personal data and the use of 'cookies' (bookmarks which remember details about a site visited).

Computer Misuse Act 1990

Makes unauthorised access to a computer (including hacking) a criminal offence.

Copyright Design and Patents Acts

In many circumstances this makes copying software outside the terms of the licence a criminal offence. Criminal action may also result in a civil claim for damages.

Electronic Communications Act 2000

Allows for the eventual removal of obstacles in other legislation to electronic publication, such as the need for manual records or documentation. For example, the Act has a provision for the legal recognition of electronic signatures.

Regulation of Investigatory Powers Act 2000 (RIP Act)

Gives security services such as the police and MI5 the right to examine Internet traffic from any source which poses a security threat. This is likely to have most impact on Internet Service Providers (ISPs).

Health and Safety (Display Screen Equipment) Regulations 1992

Employers have a number of responsibilities for the safety of users who 'habitually use VDU screens as a significant part of their normal work'. Penalties for non-compliance include improvement notices, prohibition, fines and imprisonment.

41.5.2 Commercial law

Auditors will need to be aware of the legal framework in which transactions are taking place. Where transactions occur, for example over the Web, between buyers and sellers in different countries, the law in one of the countries must govern the transaction. However, there may be a number of complicating factors in identifying the appropriate framework. These include whether the supplier is based in the country from which the goods are issued, or whether the entity's website is hosted in a different country to that in which the entity itself is registered. In addition, some countries are passing legislation that allows an aggrieved customer to apply the law of the land in which they themselves are domiciled.

What constitutes a valid contract will also vary from country to country. In some countries both parties must sign a written agreement before a valid contract is said to exist. In the United Kingdom some agreements are required to be signed on paper, such as consumer credit agreements, but most do not. In addition, the Electronic Communications Act 2000 recognises digital signatures in other circumstances. These are all factors of which auditors must be aware when planning and executing their audit procedures.

41.5.3   Taxation

The main area of concern is the identity of the jurisdictions where taxation is levied. The customer, the ISP, the website and the supplier may all be located in different countries. Different taxes may need to be applied to the goods being ordered. Auditors need an awareness of these taxes and their impact on the financial statements.

41.6   AUDIT RISK

41.6.1   Issues relating to e-commerce

As stated in **41.3** above, an entity's involvement in e-commerce and use of the Internet may be at various levels of sophistication. The degree of sophistication will have a corresponding impact on the assessment of audit risk. Common business risks arise in the following areas:

- the identity and nature of relationships with e-commerce trading partners;
- the integrity of transactions;
- electronic processing of transactions and electronic record keeping;
- system reliability;
- privacy issues;
- returns of goods and product warranties; and
- taxation and regulatory issues.

Auditors must determine how the entity has applied its control framework to cover these risks.

In addition, e-commerce businesses may not have the controls to mitigate some of these risks because they may have experienced rapid growth and do not have either the human or physical resources to develop proper controls. This is because there is a temptation for businesses to ignore these constraints and attempt to grow, without due attention to the systematic risks in an e-commerce environment. Management's view of acceptable risk levels is significant to the security, completeness and reliability of the financial information produced.

Section **41.2** sets out the difference between entities which make use of e-commerce and those where e-commerce is central to their business, the 'dot.com' entities. For these businesses, auditors should also consider risks arising from:

- the lack of a traditional asset base;
- the accounting treatment of costs incurred to establish an infrastructure and the ongoing investment in web technology;
- cash flow information and business plans based on subjective judgements without a proven basis; and
- market pressure to achieve expectations leading to inappropriate judgements, for example.

41.6.2 Assessing risk

The advent of e-commerce has required a shift in the assessment of audit risk and the way auditors plan their audit procedures to reduce that risk to an acceptable level. In particular, the assessment of controls may assume a far greater importance as it may not be possible to obtain sufficient assurance without placing reliance on them.

It is management's responsibility, as in other areas, to identify e-commerce business risks and address them through the implementation of appropriate security and internal control measures. If the risks are not ultimately mitigated by adequate control procedures, the auditors must assess the affect on their audit and ultimately whether the entity is auditable.

When assessing the adequacy of the control environment for a business using e-commerce, auditors must use their knowledge of the business. In general, the greater the level of reliance the entity places on e-commerce and the Internet, the stronger and more complex the control environment will need to be. For example, where an entity's website is only used to provide information about the entity, without third-party interactive access, security controls need to be less extensive than those where the website is used to collect transaction information and process transactions with customers.

A further area of risk arises where a client moves away from direct physical control over the corporate data, for example:

- a third party may perform some or all of the recording and processing of accounting data. This may be the ISP, an Application Service Provider (ASP) who provides on-line access to standard packages for which a metered charge is made, or a Value Added Network (VAN) which provides the platform for electronic data interchange (EDI) for entities with incompatible hardware or software;

- data may originate from different parts of the world, and may be subject to different levels of controls depending on its origin;
- receipts and payments may be automated via BACS and other electronic funds transfer (EFT) methods;
- documents such as orders and invoices may be automated, making controls, such as authentication controls, more difficult to implement.

Management must ensure that third parties have sufficient controls to ensure the integrity and validity of their processing and the information they supply. Auditors will consider management's assessment of third-party controls when deciding what audit work is necessary.

Auditors may need to seek extra assurances from third parties or from third-party reviewers or auditors. They need to take particular care when assessing authorisation controls over payments and authentication controls over orders received which ensure that only valid transactions are actioned.

41.6.3   Accounting risks

The new business practices of dot.com entities also give rise to new accounting issues. These may have an impact on the assessment of audit risk. Typical accounting issues to consider include:

- the treatment of costs incurred to set up and improve web pages;
- ongoing maintenance costs;
- timing and recognition of sales revenue; and
- recognition and treatment of unusual transactions such as those involving barter arrangements.

41.6.4   Assessing the control environment

As explained above, it is likely that auditors will seek to place an increasing level of reliance on the controls over systems including those exercised by third parties. Auditors' assessments of the control environment extend to both the electronic and physical environment.

In establishing which controls may be relied upon, auditors consider a number of areas, the main ones being:

- the entity's security measures; and
- system reliability and authentication of financial records.

Security measures

Sophisticated measures such the encryption of data will not be successful if they operate within a generally insecure IT environment. Auditors must therefore address whether the environment meets basic security requirements before evaluating more detailed security measures. Typically, in fast growing areas such as e-commerce, management is focused on developing ways of carrying out transactions rather than building in safeguards and controls.

There are three acknowledged components to security. These are:

Confidentiality – a commercial organisation has a legal duty to ensure that its information is secure. E-commerce has effectively opened up corporate data to the whole world, requiring a business to protect against breaches of confidentiality and ensure that confidential information is not published on the Internet.

Integrity – this means ensuring that data is accurate, authorised, kept secure and not duplicated. This is likely to have a direct impact on financial data, as electronic and automatic handling of data may mean an increased risk of duplicate entries or incorrect order amounts not being noticed and corrected.

Dependence – the need for technical support is now 24 hours a day, meaning that a business's back up and recovery procedures need to be fully tried and tested to ensure that there is no break in continuity of service and processing. This may include service level agreements with ISPs to guard against financial loss during excessive 'down-time'.

Encryption-based security

The use of encryption techniques results in a number of further risks. If encryption keys are lost information may not be accessible at a later date. This can pose both a business and an audit risk. Therefore, auditors should consider how encryption keys are safeguarded and their ability to access data and documents for testing as necessary. Where auditors are given copies of encryption keys they should have suitable internal procedures in place to make sure these are stored securely.

Ultimately, the use of encryption-based security does not absolve management from its responsibilities under company law to allow auditors access to data or to maintain adequate accounting records.

As part of their engagement letter, auditors should make clear that the establishment of appropriate security and controls, the addressing of encryption risk and the maintenance of audit access to documents and records is the responsibility of management.

System reliability and authentication of financial records

Audit procedures for traditional business activities tend to focus on controls over recording and storage. For entities involved in e-commerce the focus should be on the validity of the transaction – that is, those controls that apply to the actual initiation of transactions, such as the placing of an order by a customer, which generally prompt all other steps in processing the transaction. System controls, which ensure the integrity of the transaction at the time of its execution, are those controls that ensure that a transaction is accurate, valid and complete. The controls that auditors will be aiming to establish as present and working are likely to be those that:

- determine duplicate or fictitious identities;
- distinguish between browsing and order placement;
- validate all external inputs;
- prevent duplications or omissions;
- ensure that the payment is processed before the goods are despatched;
- address the causes of transaction failure, such as computer crashes or authentication problems which may lead to loss of information or interruption of service to customers;
- prevent incomplete processing;
- ensure details distributed to different systems are processed correctly and that multiple activities do not cause system breakdown; and
- ensure that records are properly entered and retained and that accounts balance both before and after transactions.

Auditors must also assess how the entity maintains the accessibility, integrity and retention of e-commerce records through real-time record keeping. Auditors will look for evidence of controls which act as a 'buffer' between the external 'shop front' interface and the accounting records of the entity to give comfort that financial data cannot be easily corrupted by those outside the organisation using the website.

As electronic records are more easily destroyed or altered, either unintentionally or maliciously, than their manual counterparts, auditors should consider the controls and policies in place to ensure ongoing security of information. They should also be aware of how system-based security measures such as digital signatures, electronic date stamps and record integrity checks are utilised to ensure data integrity.

Other control areas

Other controls auditors may consider include those designed to:

- ensure that all orders received will result in a valid sale not capable of repudiation;
- ensure that returned goods are correctly recorded; and
- establish privacy in accordance with legislative requirements.

41.7   AUDIT EVIDENCE

41.7.1   Difficulties in obtaining evidence

For entities with significant involvement in e-commerce, auditors may not be able to audit 'round the computer' – that is, verify inputs and outputs, and effectively bypass the processing that occurs in between. In a number of cases there is no alternative but to audit 'through the computer'. For example, although physical goods may be dispatched there is often very little conventional external audit evidence as the ordering and all the intervening steps are carried out 'on-line'. In addition, electronic records may not be as robust as physical records, which may present particular problems.

The audit trail available in e-commerce entities is therefore likely to vary significantly from that in the more traditionally organised industries. The two most common types of audit trail are access and transaction logs.

Although these logs are likely to be of significant use to auditors of an e-business, where a VAN or extranet is used there is a strong chance that the entity will not have access to some or all of them. Also in these cases, even where management has access, the level of detail included in them is likely to be such that it dissuades management from using them to control the business.

When using external processing auditors must be satisfied that a complete history exists of all events during the period and that the logs are a full list of all transactions processed. Therefore, they should suggest that service level agreements with external parties include the ability to retrieve and review audit trails or logs on demand, either for a particular date or range of dates. This should include an 'unusual activity log', which includes details of items such as apparently duplicated or very large orders.

41.7.2   Use of specialists

Auditors invariably require special skills to audit these systems. For each client auditors need to assess whether they possess the relevant skills within the practice to understand the business, assess risk and perform appropriate testing or, alternatively, how they may acquire such skills. This may involve using IS auditing specialists to perform evaluations of systems and carrying out computer-based tests of controls and computer-aided substantive audit procedures.

Where an external specialist is used, the guidance in ISA (UK and Ireland) 620 should be followed (see section **37.4**).

Although an e-commerce business may have complex computer systems they may not interface with accounting systems, which may be very simple and therefore require limited specialist skills to audit. An example is a vendor of computer software with complex search and download facilities on their site, but where payment for the download is made by credit card, the details of which are re-keyed and the cash collected by normal bank credit.

41.7.3 Types of evidence

Tests of control

Where, as is likely, auditors of e-commerce entities place significant reliance on the proven effective operation of controls, an IS audit specialist or an auditor with the requisite IT systems and e-commerce knowledge should be involved in the design and implementation of these tests.

The main objectives in assessing any internal controls remain the assessment of:

- the design of controls – that the accounting and internal control systems are capable of preventing or detecting material misstatements; and
- the operation of controls – that the systems exist and have operated effectively throughout the relevant period.

For e-commerce systems, auditors typically concentrate their efforts on the controls in place to ensure the security and authenticity of the originating transaction, such as the sales order received. Then they assess the reliability of the process within the computer system to prompt all the other steps in processing the whole transaction automatically. Typical controls over security and authenticity of inputs are detailed in section **41.6.4** above.

Because of the power and complexity of systems, there may be many effects of processing to which auditors must be alive. For example, where automatic processing of sales orders is linked directly to the accounting system it may affect auditors' consideration of matters such as:

- the completeness and accuracy of transaction recording;
- the timing of recognition of sales revenues; and
- recognition and recording of disputed transactions.

If there are doubts in these areas auditors may need to consider the reviews the client undertakes to ensure, for example, that items are reflected in the correct accounting period rather than the period in which the order is placed or that all resulting transactions are recorded by the automated system.

As the system's controls are likely to be so central to the process of collecting evidence and gaining assurance, auditors need to be sure that there is no possibility that these controls can be overridden. Where overrides occur auditors should review the appropriate reports to determine why they occurred and whether they received the required authorisation.

Where tests of controls are unable to provide sufficient evidence to reduce the amount of substantive tests, auditors may be able to obtain adequate audit evidence from increasing the number of substantive procedures planned. However, given the importance of effective controls for this type of entity, the successful operation of controls may be so central to the ability of the financial statements to show a true and fair view, that auditors have no alternative but to issue a qualified audit opinion.

Substantive procedures

ISA (UK and Ireland) 500 *Audit Evidence* requires auditors to consider the level of assurance required from substantive procedures following the assessment of relevant tests of controls. Whilst the level of assurance from substantive procedures may be reduced by planning and performing extensive work on the reliability of controls, the use of substantive procedures can never be eliminated.

Analytical review

Substantive procedures may comprise tests of detail, analytical procedures, or a combination of both. Particular issues exist when planning to use analytical procedures in the audit of e-commerce clients.

For these clients (especially for 'dot.com' companies) the traditional relationships between the financial statements' account balances may no longer be appropriate. The relationship between costs and revenues may be completely different and certain balances may disappear completely. For example, eliminating parts of the distribution network such as wholesalers will have a major effect on the commonly examined relationships. The impact may be on some, or all, of the following:

- stocks held;
- trade creditors;
- trade debtors;
- ratio analysis;
- forecasts and budgets;
- going concern considerations.

The problems are likely to be acute in early years of an e-commerce operation where the effect of constant change and, sometimes, fast growth, may mean that a different approach is needed each year. Auditors need to be aware of these changes and to adjust their analytical review procedures accordingly.

Where traditional analytical methods are no longer relevant, different non-financial measures may have to be used. These may include:

- website hits/impressions per week/month;
- percentage increase in subscriber base;
- incidence of returned goods compared to sales;
- direct costs per unit of each sale;

- advertising/marketing cost as a percentage of revenue; or
- burn rate – cash resources compared to monthly expenditure.

ISA (UK and Ireland) 520 *Analytical Procedures* requires analytical review at both the planning and overall review stage of the audit. For analytical review at the planning stage, given the speed of change it may be preferable to investigate trends and result with reference to management budgets and forecasts for the period, rather than making comparisons with prior year figures.

41.7.4 Materiality

Materiality benchmarks are often established in relation to turnover levels for traditional entities. However, for e-businesses it is increasingly unlikely that there is a performance history that can be reliably used to establish materiality. Therefore, auditors may have to extend their assessment beyond quantitative measures.

41.7.5 Other performance indicators

For e-commerce entities, financing from third parties is often obtained on the basis of non-financial measures and projections such as the number of registered users or the number of 'hits' on a website. Entities may also publish this data with their financial statements. These non-financial indicators should be clearly presented to ensure that they do not mislead readers, who may not be aware of uncertainties as to the accuracy or meaning of the figures.

This data will be part of the 'other information' read by auditors in line with ISA (UK and Ireland) 720 *Other information in documents containing audited financial statements* (see **Chapter 14**).

41.7.6 Work papers

As clients move increasingly to a paperless office, auditors are increasingly keen to follow the same route for their audit work papers. There are a number of unresolved issued in this area. These include the need to ensure safe and secure storage and prevent unauthorised changes to data. In addition, the use of electronic sign offs is an area of concern upon which no official guidance has yet been issued.

41.8 GOING CONCERN

Many e-commerce start-ups have reported significant losses in early phases. Therefore, auditors should be alert to the risk of business failure and should use their professional judgement to assess the appropriateness of the going concern assumption. They should have regard to non-recurring events, break-even forecasts and the entity's business plans. In particular, they should consider the business's arrangements to ensure the viability of continued activity.

Auditors should also consider the impact of e-commerce on the ability of an entity to continue as a going concern even when that entity is not itself involved in e-business. Risks may arise as a result of the entity falling behind developments in the industry or by the industry itself being rendered obsolete by e-commerce.

41.9 CERTIFICATION

As discussed above, the rapid growth of the Internet has prompted many reliability, security and privacy issues. The publicity given to these risks has created an environment of scepticism around trading on the Internet, both in the business-to-business (B2B) and the business-to-consumer (B2C) markets.

E-commerce entities are therefore keen to promote their businesses as having adequate systems to meet the security needs of their customers and suppliers. One way to do this is to gain a certification of security for their systems and display this on their website.

There are a number of certification schemes operated by trade associations and consumer groups. Some are self-certifying, but some, such as the WebTrust seal marketed by the ICAEW, require independent verification of the procedures put in place by the e-business to minimise the effect and occurrence of security breaches. With some schemes regular verification is required to maintain the seal. There is no common standard applied by all certification bodies, but the DTI is encouraging an environment in which seal providers subscribe to a minimum set of standards.

It is therefore important for the auditor and customer to understand the assurance that the seal provides and, more importantly, what it does not. Often clicking on the seal itself will provide much of this information. If the external auditor has been involved in awarding a WebTrust seal to the client, the work performed for this task will have provided a detailed knowledge of the security issues and the controls in place to mitigate them. This will be of relevance to their assessment of audit risk.

42 REPORTS FOR SPECIAL PURPOSES AND TO THIRD PARTIES

42.1 INTRODUCTION

Managing auditors' own risk has become increasingly important in recent years and one major area of concern is reliance by parties other than those with whom the auditor has contractual relations. For example where loans and other facilities are made available to businesses, the extent to which the auditor is responsible to the lender is often ambiguous. This becomes more difficult and potentially more dangerous where auditors have an obligation to report to other third parties, for example Regulatory Authorities. Managing the terms under which third parties can, or more importantly cannot, place reliance on reports is an area in which increasing guidance has been produced. This chapter provides an overview of this guidance and covers a number of areas where it is likely to happen.

42.2 DEVELOPMENT OF GUIDANCE

In November 2000, the Consultative Committee of Accountancy Bodies (CCAB) issued a Statement which contains guidance aimed at helping all parties involved in financing arrangements. This addresses issues such as the appropriate form of report, firms' duties of care and reporting in connection with covenants in loan agreements and other facilities.

The Statement was reissued by the Audit and Assurance Faculty of the ICAEW as Technical Release 4/00 *Firms' reports and duties to lenders in connection with loans and other facilities to clients and related covenants*. Audit 4/00 replaced Practice Note 4 issued by the Auditing Practices Board, *Reliance by Banks on Audited Financial Statements*. The guidance deals with non-statutory audits and reviews and is, therefore, of greater relevance to those companies taking advantage of the increase in the statutory audit exemption threshold (see **7.1**).

The guidance also deals with reports on client's compliance with loan covenants, including the scope of work to be performed and the format of the report to be given.

The Statement is based on current law governing duties of care, and notes that the ongoing review of company law may necessitate revision of this statement in due course.

Since 2001 a number of further publications have been issued addressing various aspects of liability to third parties. The main additional guidance is contained in:

- ICAEW Technical Release Audit 1/01: *Reporting to Third Parties* (see **42.9** below);

- ICAEW Technical Release Audit 2/01: *Requests for References on Clients' Financial Status and their Ability to Service Loans* (see **42.9** below);

- ICAEW Technical Release AAF 01/06: *Assurance Reports on Internal Controls of Service Organisations Made Available to Third Parties* (see **42.8** below);

- ICAEW Technical Release AAF 03/06: *The ICAEW Assurance Service on Unaudited Financial Statements* (see **42.7** below); and

- ICAEW Technical Release AAF 04/06: *Assurance Engagements: Management of Risk and Liability* (see **42.3** below).

In 2005, the Audit and Assurance Faculty completed a study of the legal cases involving claims by third parties against auditors. The review, *Audit liability: Claims by third parties*, was conducted in conjunction with the law firm Simmons & Simmons and summarises the key matters arising from the relevant cases. It is considered in **42.10** below.

The joint ICAEW/Association of British Travel Agents (ABTA) working group has developed a package of reporting arrangements, designed to help ABTA regulate its members and be consistent with the new AUDIT1/01 framework. These form Technical Release AUDIT 2/02, new arrangements for reporting to the ABTA.

In 2003 further guidance was issued by the ICAEW to develop the guidance in Audit 1/01 for specific circumstances:

- Audit 2/03: New Arrangements for Reporting to the Civil Aviation Authority (CAA) in connection with the Civil Aviation (Air Travel Organisers' Licensing) Regulations 1995;

- Audit 3/03: Public Sector Special Reporting Engagements – Grant Claims (see **Chapter 48**);

- Audit 4/03: Access to Working Papers by Investigating Accountants (see **Chapter 19**); and

- Audit 5/03: Reporting to Regulators of Regulated Entities (see **Chapter 48**).

On the international stage, the IAASB has reissued ISA 920 as International Standard on Related Services (ISRS) 4400, *Engagements to Perform Agreed-Upon Procedures Regarding Financial Information*. This is discussed in **42.11** below.

Following the publication of the other Technical Releases listed above, the ICAEW published AAF 04/06, *Assurance Engagements: Management of Risk and Liability* in November 2006. The general principles in this guidance are based on the IAASB's *International Framework for Assurance Engagements* and ISAE 3000, *Assurance Engagements other than Audits or Reviews of Historical Financial Information.* This is considered in the next section as it provides general guidance which can be applied to all cases.

In July 2008, the Audit and Assurance Faculty of the ICAEW issued a paper to stimulate discussion about how new assurance services could strengthen markets by increasing credibility of information. The paper, entitled *Assurance on Non-Financial Information: Existing Practices and Issues* is considered in **42.10** below.

42.3 GENERAL GUIDANCE

AAF 04/06 provides principles for reporting accountants to consider in relation to managing their risk and liability when agreeing to undertake assurance engagements and providing assurance reports to third parties. It does not seek to provide detailed advice on the planning and conduct of the work involved in such engagements or how to manage risk and liability in particular circumstances. Such detail will be provided in other technical releases which will cross-refer to this over arching guidance.

42.3.1 Accepting an engagement

Reporting accountants should have appropriate engagement acceptance procedures to assess the risks associated with taking on a particular engagement. Reporting accountants should consider the:

● purpose for which the work is being sought;
● party or parties seeking to benefit from the work, whether they are directly party to the engagement or not yet identified;
● use that will be made of the work; and
● professional competence of the engagement team.

42.3.2 Managing professional liability

AAF 04/06 outlines the following arrangements into which reporting accountants may enter:

● a tri-partite or multi-partite engagement contract with the client and the third parties, accepting that they owe a duty of care not only to the client but also to those third parties. Provisions to limit liability may be appropriate;
● an engagement with the client, with the option for third parties to join the duty of care if they accept the relevant terms of the engagement letter. Again liability may be limited;
● an engagement with the client alone, but allowing access to the audit report for third parties as long as they:

- acknowledge in writing that the reporting accountant owes them no duty of care; and
- agree in writing that no claims will be brought against the reporting accountant in relation to the assurance report; and

- an engagement with the client alone, disclaiming any liability or duty to others by notice in the assurance report. This may be in conjunction with the client indemnifying the reporting accountant if a third party makes a claim against the reporting accountant, although such indemnities may not be commercially attractive or reliable if the client is not financially stable.

Alternatively if the risks are too high or reporting accountants are unable to reach acceptable terms with the client or third parties, reporting accountants may decline to accept the engagement.

42.3.3   Agreeing the terms of the engagement

Reporting accountants must manage their relationship with the client and any third party, and clarify that any assurance engagements are separate from statutory audit engagements. Depending on the type of contractual arrangement agreed upon (see **42.3.2**), reporting accountants will need to agree specific terms with all parties to the engagement and record them in writing in the engagement letter. The engagement letter should include details of the purpose of the report to be issued, its agreed use and any accompanying disclosure restrictions setting out the extent to which, the context in which, and the basis on which the report may be made available by the client to the third parties.

It is often useful to include a draft pro forma report as an appendix to the engagement letter.

42.4   DUTIES TO LENDERS

As set out above, the position of the auditor in relation to the provider of loans and other facilities can be ambiguous. Technical Release 4/00 *Firms' reports and duties to lenders in connection with loans and other facilities to clients and related covenants* provides guidance in relation to various aspects of the relationship of auditors with providers of finance to their clients.

42.4.1   Case law

The guidance issued in Technical Release 4/00 is based on case law. In his judgement in the case of *Caparo Industries plc v Dickman(1990) 2 WLR 353,* Lord Bridge stated that a duty of care to a third party will exist if the person who owes the duty of care is aware:

- of the transaction to be undertaken by the third party;

- that the advice given will be passed to the third party, either directly or indirectly; and
- that it is likely that the third party will rely on that information in deciding whether to enter into the transaction.

Since this judgement, banks and other lenders have sought to document a direct and sufficient relationship between themselves and their customer's auditors so as to be able to rely on statutory audit reports.

42.4.2   Duties of care for the statutory audit report

An auditor's duty of care in respect of their audit report would not normally be expected to extend beyond that owed to their client. However, the general trend of authorities since *Caparo* makes it clear that, unless there is an effective disclaimer, an auditor may owe a duty of care to a lender or other third party. The test is whether the auditor, in making the statements in their audit report, assumed a responsibility to a lender who may subsequently be given a copy of those statements. The important issue is not whether the auditor in question intended to assume the responsibility towards the third party, but rather whether a reasonable auditor would have assumed the responsibility in those circumstances.

Therefore, auditors must be aware that they may inadvertently accept responsibility unless steps are taken to limit their exposure. Auditors may assume responsibility without their knowledge by the client having discussions with the lender, or the lender being passed a set of the most recent audited financial statements, if it is deemed that a reasonable auditor would assume such responsibility.

Lenders will seek to establish a relationship with the auditors. In this regard, certain banks have included a clause in the conditions attached to a loan, which requires the auditor of the borrower to provide written acknowledgement to the bank that the bank may rely on the audited financial statements of the borrower in connection with the facilities offered. Where auditors are aware, or are in receipt, of a request to provide acknowledgement, they should not let it go unanswered.

In addition, banks may write directly to auditors stating that they do intend to rely on audited financial statements in connection with a proposed transaction. In this situation, a duty of care will be created unless the auditor vigorously denies it. A firm should normally disclaim all responsibility in this situation in writing. An example response is shown in **Table 1**.

TABLE 1: Example disclaimer of responsibility to lenders for audit or review reports

[Lender plc]

Dear Sirs

XYZ plc – [Loan/transaction reference]

We acknowledge receipt of your letter of 31 March 20.., in which you state your intention to rely on the financial statements of XYZ plc for the year ended 31 December 20.. and our audit [review] report thereon, in connection with the above-mentioned loan agreement.

Our audit [review] of the financial statements was neither planned nor conducted for the purpose of (or in contemplation of) the loan agreement (and transaction) referred to above. In particular, the scope of our work was set, and judgements made, by reference to our assessment of materiality in the context of the financial statements taken as a whole, rather then in the context of your needs. For this reason, our work would not necessarily have addressed or reflected matters in which you may be primarily interested as lenders. Therefore, we cannot accept any responsibility to you in relation to our report and disclaim all liability to you in connection therewith (and your lending decision in relation to the proposed transaction and any other actions you may take).

Should you require any specific assurances from us regarding any matters in which you may be primarily interested as a lender, we should be happy to discuss them with you in the context of an engagement between ourselves, Lender plc and XYZ plc which would be entirely separate from our audit [review] of XYZ plc's financial statements.

Yours faithfully

cc. XYZ plc

42.4.3   Draft accounts

The courts have held that reliance on draft audited accounts was not actionable, since a reasonable auditor would not intend such reliance to occur. However, there may be circumstances in which a duty of care may arise and care must be taken, therefore, when circulating draft audited accounts. The status of the accounts must be clearly stated and the giving of assurances or representations about the reliability of the accounts (or whether the final position is likely to differ greatly from that shown in the draft) should be avoided.

42.4.4   Disclaimer of responsibility

Disclaimers of responsibility can only be relied upon if they pass the reasonableness test set out in s2 of the Unfair Contract Terms Act 1977. If the disclaimer is not reasonable it will be void.

Disclaimers can be worded to pass the reasonableness test and are therefore an effective way of limiting an auditor's liability to lenders and other third parties who seek to claim reliance on a report. They may also be useful in avoiding any doubt that a firm does not have a duty of care to a lender or third party to whom a report is shown or a reference to a report is made.

However, it is important to note that a disclaimer of responsibility does not exempt an auditor or an accountant issuing a review report from carrying out their work in accordance with Auditing Standards or other applicable standards.

42.4.5   The Contracts (Rights of Third Parties) Act 1999

The Contracts (Rights of Third Parties) Act 1999 came into force on 11 November 1999 and applies to all contracts entered into after 10 May 2000. Under the Act, a third party to a contract has the right to enforce a term of that contract if it confers a benefit or right to the third party. This equates to a partial abolition of the concept of 'privity of contract', which has been a central feature of the English law of contract for more than 100 years.

Therefore, if a reference is made to the provision of a set of financial statements to a lender, or to a lender requiring the financial statements for a specific purpose, within a contract between an auditor and their client, a benefit may have been conferred upon the lender.

Audit engagement letters should state clearly that they do not confer any rights on any third party and that, for the avoidance of doubt, any rights conferred on third parties pursuant to the Contracts (Rights of Third Parties) Act 1999 shall be excluded.

The Act does not apply to Scotland, which has long recognised the concept of *ius quaesitum tertio*, a right vested in and secured to a third party in and by a contract between two parties. Accordingly, a third party has the right to enforce a contract between two parties if the intention to confer a benefit on that third party can be gathered from the terms of the document.

42.4.6   Separate engagements to provide specific assurances to lenders

If a firm decides that it is able to provide specific assurances to a lender, it should be the subject of a separate engagement between the firm, the client and the lender. There should be a separate engagement letter in place for this work, normally the subject of separate financial arrangements.

A firm should also consider whether entering into such an agreement with both client and lender could present it with a conflict of interest. Reference should be made to the ethical guidance of the Institute which governs the firm.

42.5 COVENANTS IN AGREEMENT FOR LOANS AND OTHER FACILITIES

Agreements for certain financing arrangements often contain a number of covenants with which the borrower is expected to comply. Typically, the directors of the borrower are required to prepare a periodic statement or report, a 'Statement of Covenant Compliance', to confirm continuing compliance with the covenant terms agreed when arranging the finance.

Imposed covenants will be either financial or non-financial. Non-financial covenants tend to be more common and take the form of commitments by the borrower as to its future actions. Financial covenants may also need to be maintained by the borrower. These will often be financial statement ratios, the intention of which is to provide the lender with some assurance as to the continuing financial condition of the business.

A list of common financial and non-financial covenants is given in **Table 2**. In specialised industries, lenders may require the maintenance of industry key performance indicators (KPIs), which are derived from management information outside the financial statements, such as room occupancy rates for hotels or pollution levels for heavy industry.

TABLE 2: Common covenants for borrowings

Financial

- cash flow to total debt service;
- dividend cover;
- minimum share capital and reserves;
- PBIT-based interest cover;
- gearing;
- cash flow-based interest cover;
- net current assets/borrowings;
- proportion of debtors below certain days outstanding;
- current ratio;
- quick asset ratio;
- EBITDA;
- gross profit margin;
- rent roll ratios.

Non-financial

- first charge over specified assets;
- audited annual accounts within a specified period;
- cross default clauses;
- monthly management accounts within a specified period;
- restrictions on changes to ownership;
- restrictions on additional borrowings (from other sources);
- maintenance of adequate fire, theft and other insurances;
- restrictions in mergers/acquisitions;

- restrictions on asset disposals;
- no capital expenditure beyond certain limits without approval;
- compliance with environmental laws and regulations;
- compliance with other laws and regulations;
- no redemption of preference shares while loans outstanding;
- charges over key-man insurance;
- key-man critical illness policy;
- limits on directors' remuneration.

42.5.1   The lender's requirement for evidence of covenant compliance

The lender will require from the directors of the borrower, a written confirmation that they have complied with all covenants for the period under review. This confirmation should set out the computation of the relevant financial covenants for the applicable accounting date. Simple calculations of gearing and interest cover are often self-evident and can easily be re-performed by the lender to ensure compliance. However, where information for covenants is not readily available to the lender, or it is not contained in the borrower's financial statements, the lender may require a report from the borrower's auditors.

Auditors are not compelled to accept such an engagement, as they cannot be bound to comply with the terms of an agreement to which they are not party. Therefore, if auditors become aware that a client is negotiating a loan or other facility, it is good practice to enquire whether the draft loan agreement seeks to place any reporting obligations on them.

Where a requirement to report is found, auditors should write to the lender to clarify the basis of preparation. This is particularly important if the lender approaches the auditor directly, rather than through the borrower. An example letter for this purpose is set out in **Table 3**.

TABLE 3: Example letter to lender setting out basis on which reports under a loan agreement will be provided

[Lender plc]

Dear Sirs

XYZ plc – [Loan Agreement Reference]

XYZ plc has provided us with a copy of [and you have written to us in connection with], the Loan Agreement referred to above, Clause X of which contemplates that reports will periodically be provided to you by the auditors of XYZ plc in connections with XYZ plc's compliance with certain covenants.

As auditors of XYZ plc, we confirm that, provided that XYZ plc authorises us to do so and you sign an engagement letter with us substantially in the attached form, we will report to you on the following matters:

- whether the financial information contained in the Statement of Covenant

---

Compliance prepared by the directors of XYZ plc has been accurately extracted from the sources identified therein and, where applicable, agrees with the underlying accounting records;

- whether the calculations shown in the Statement, made in accordance with Clause X of the loan agreement, are arithmetically accurate; and
- where the elements and composition of the financial information contained in the Statement are the subject of objective accounting definition in the Loan Agreement, or have subsequently been agreed by Lender plc and XYZ plc, whether the financial information is presented in compliance with the relevant definitions and agreement.

As regards our audit work on XYZ plc's financial statements for future periods, our work will be carried out in accordance with our statutory and professional obligations and will not be planned or conducted in contemplation of your requirements or any matters which might be set out in the Loan Agreement. In particular, the scope of our audit work will be set and judgements made by reference to our assessment of materiality in the context of the audited accounts taken as a whole, rather than in the context of your needs. For this reason, our work will not necessarily address or reflect matters in which you may be primarily interested as lenders. Therefore, we cannot accept any responsibility to you in relation to our audit opinions and disclaim all liability to you in connection therewith.

Yours faithfully

cc. XYZ plc
Enc. Form of engagement letter [see Table 4]

42.5.2 The firm's duty of care when reporting on the directors' statement of covenant compliance

Auditors accepting an engagement to report on compliance with covenants acknowledge a duty of care to the lender. Firms will use their established risk management techniques to control this duty. One key method of achieving this is to issue an engagement letter which limits the use of the report to the intended addressee of the report, includes a disclaimer of responsibility to all other parties and specifies liability limits.

In addition, an engagement letter normally includes an exclusion of liability to the lender in respect of their normal audit or review report. This ensures that no responsibility to lenders is assumed for these reports.

Firms must consider whether the engagement is between themselves and the lender, or if it is a separate engagement between themselves and their client. In either case, a separate engagement letter is sent. An example wording is set out in **Table 4**.

The example wording also includes clauses excluding liability in respect of any loss or damage caused by, or arising from, fraudulent acts, misrepresentation or concealment on the part of the client entity, its directors, employees or agent, and excluding all liability to third parties.

TABLE 4: Example engagement letter

[Lender plc]

[Other addressees as provided for in the second paragraph of the letter]

Dear Sirs

XYZ plc – [Loan Agreement reference]

Under the terms of Clause [X] of the agreement dated [date] between XYZ plc and Lender plc ('the Loan Agreement'), the Directors of XYZ plc are required to procure that their auditors report to you in connection with the Directors' Statement of Covenant Compliance ('the Statement'), prepared in accordance with Clause [X] of the Loan Agreement. At the request of the Directors of XYZ plc, we are writing to set out our understanding of the work you wish us to perform and the terms and conditions upon which we are prepared to provide such a report for your use. A copy of this letter is being sent to the Directors of XYZ plc to confirm their authorisation and understanding of the basis on which we will report to you.

[This engagement letter is addressed to Lender plc, as lead manager/arranger of the facility/syndication agreement, and to each of the other lenders participating in the facility/syndication agreement whose names, as set out in Attachment 1, have been notified to us by Lender plc as having validly authorised it to accept this engagement letter on their behalf. By signing and accepting the terms of this engagement letter, Lender plc confirms that it will ensure that it receives prima facie authority from each other lender identified in Attachment 1, as participating in the facility/syndication agreement authorising it to enter into this engagement letter on the relevant lender's behalf.]

Respective responsibilities of directors and auditors

The Directors of XYZ plc are responsible for ensuring that XYZ plc complies with all of the terms and conditions of the Loan Agreement including each of the Covenants set out in Clauses [X] to [X] thereof. Under Clause [X] thereof, the Directors are responsible for preparing their Statement of Covenant Compliance. Our responsibility is to prepare a report to you on the computation of those financial covenants which pertain to accounting matters as identified below.

We are auditors of XYZ plc and have audited the annual accounts of XYZ plc ('the audited accounts') and reported to its members in accordance with our responsibilities under the Companies Act on [date]. Our audit of the accounts of XYZ plc was not intended to address compliance with financial covenants or other matters in which the addressees of this letter may be primarily interested. In particular, the scope of our audit work was set and our judgements made by reference to our assessment of materiality in the context of the audited accounts taken as a whole, rather than in the context of the report contemplated in this letter. Accordingly, we do not acknowledge any responsibility, and deny any liability, to the addressees of this letter in relation to the audited accounts.

Basis of report

Our work will be conducted in accordance with the framework for reporting in connection with loan covenants set out in guidance issued by the Consultative Committee of Accountancy Bodies and published as Audit Technical Release 4/00 by the Institute of Chartered Accountants in England and Wales [*or alternative CCAB member*]. We will read the Statement prepared by the Directors. Our work will be based on obtaining an understanding of the compilation of the Statement and by enquiry of management, reference to the Loan Agreement, comparison of the financial information in the Statement to the sources from which it was obtained and re-computation of the calculations in the Statement. [The specific procedures that we have agreed to conduct are set out in the Appendix to this letter.] Other than as set out herein, we will not carry out any work by way of audit, review or verification of the financial information nor of the management accounts, accounting records or other sources from which that information is to be extracted for the purpose of providing you with our report.

Use of report

Our report will be provided solely for your use in connection with the Loan Agreement and should not be made available to any other party without our written consent. The report is confidential to you and will be provided only for the purpose of your assessment of XYZ plc's compliance with the terms of Clause [X] of the Loan Agreement. We accept no liability to any other party who is shown or gains access to our report.

Obligations and liabilities

We undertake that we will exercise reasonable professional skill and care in the performance of our work as set out in this letter in accordance with applicable professional standards. This engagement is undertaken subject to certain terms excluding liability where information is or has been misrepresented to us, or withheld or concealed from us, and providing for our aggregate liability to the addressees of this letter and XYZ plc to be limited to a maximum aggregate amount of £[X] and subject to that cap, to the part of any loss suffered which is proportional to our responsibility.

It is agreed that the allocation between addressees of the limit of liability specified above will be entirely a matter for the addressees, who shall be under no obligation to inform us of it, provided always that if (for whatever reason) no such allocation is agreed, no addressee shall dispute the validity, enforceability or operation of the limit of liability on the ground that no such allocation was agreed.

Our detailed Terms of Business are set out in the attachment to this letter which shall apply as if set out in full herein.

Acknowledgement and acceptance

We will be grateful if, having considered the provisions of this letter together with the attachments and having concluded that they are reasonable in the context of all the factors relating to our proposed engagement, you will indicate your agreement to these arrangements by signing and returning to us the enclosed copy of this letter.

Yours faithfully

The terms and conditions contained in this letter and the attached Terms of Business are agreed and accepted on behalf of Lender plc by:

.... (authorised person)

Authorised and accepted on behalf of XYZ plc by:

.... (authorised person)

42.5.3   The firm's consideration of acceptance of the engagement

Before accepting the engagement the auditor must ensure that the respective responsibilities of the borrower and the auditor are clearly defined. It is the responsibility of the directors of the borrower to prepare the financial information and the Statement of Covenant Compliance, and the auditors' responsibility is to report on that information to the extent that it relates to financial and accounting matters.

The Statement of Covenant Compliance will normally set out the calculations of financial ratios, etc., as provided for under the loan agreement. The loan agreement will usually require the borrower to comply with the covenants at all times during the period being reported upon, but the auditors' report will only refer to compliance at specific dates. A firm would not normally accept an engagement which requires confirmation of compliance with covenants over an extended period of time, or for which confirmation that the borrower will comply with covenants in the future based on prospective information is required.

Firms should also consider carefully the implications of accepting an engagement to report on a Statement of Covenant Compliance based on financial covenants whose terms are imprecise.

42.6   ENGAGEMENTS TO REPORT ON COVENANT COMPLIANCE

42.6.1   Scope of work performed

The scope of work will vary from engagement to engagement and should be agreed with both the client and the lender. Typical procedures will include:

- reading the relevant clauses of the loan agreement and gaining an understanding of the operation of the covenants;
- reading the directors' Statement of Covenant Compliance;
- agreeing the financial information in the Statement to the sources from which it has been extracted;
- re-computing the calculations and ratios set out in the Statement in order to ascertain their arithmetical accuracy; and
- obtaining a representation from the client as to the completeness of disclosure in the Statement.

Firms will not undertake procedures to confirm the reliability of the financial information in the Statement nor of the sources from which the data has been extracted. In addition, they will not report on non-financial information in the Statement, such as directors' judgements on future business trends.

An example representation letter is provided in **Table 5**.

TABLE 5: Example representation letter

[Auditors' name and address]

Dear Sirs

[Loan Agreement Reference]

In connection with your proposed report in accordance with the arrangements set out in your letter of [date], we are writing to confirm to the best of our knowledge and belief the following representations we have made to you and on which you need to rely in providing your report on the Statement of Covenant Compliance ('the Statement') to Lender plc.

We are responsible for preparing the Statement, accurately reflecting the matters contained therein at the relevant dates.

The Statement is complete and accurate and reflects all matters of significance relating to Lender plc's assessment of XYZ plc's compliance with the Covenants set out therein as at the relevant dates and all significant matters relevant to that assessment have been brought to your attention.

Throughout the period since [date] the Company has at all times been in compliance with the terms of the Loan Agreement or, if not, all such instances of non-compliance have been notified to Lender plc in accordance with the terms of the Loan Agreement. Copies of such notifications have been made available to you.

[No events have occurred subsequent to [date of last audited financial statements] that would have required adjustment to, or disclosure in, the audited financial statements had their approval by the Board been deferred until the date of this letter.]

Yours faithfully

.... (signature of authorised person on behalf of XYZ plc)

42.6.2   The report

The report should be prepared in accordance with the engagement letter. The report will:

- identify the addressees who can rely on it;
- contain a statement concerning the scope of the report and the respective responsibilities of the directors and auditors;
- refer to the Statement of Covenant Compliance;
- set out the basis for the report;
- provide a description of the procedures undertaken (either in the body of the report or in an appendix);
- report on the arithmetical accuracy of the extraction and calculation of the financial information within the Statement; and
- where the elements and composition of the financial information in the Statement are the subject of objective accounting definition in the loan agreement, or have been subsequently agreed by the parties, report whether

the financial information is presented in compliance with the relevant definitions and agreement.

An illustrative form of report is given in **Table 6**.

TABLE 6: Example report

[Lender plc]

[Other addressees as provided for in the engagement letter]

Dear Sirs

XYZ plc – [Loan Agreement reference]

We refer to the above-mentioned agreement ('the Loan Agreement'). Under the terms of Clause [X] thereof, XYZ plc is required to comply with specified financial covenants and to supply the addressees of this letter with information in connection therewith reported upon by its auditors.

The directors of XYZ plc have prepared a Statement of Covenant Compliance ('the Statement'), a copy of which is appended to this letter.

This report letter is provided pursuant to, and must be read in conjunction with, our engagement letter dated [date] and is subject to the terms and limitations set out therein.

Basis of report

Our work was conducted in accordance with the framework for reporting in connection with loan covenants set out in guidance issued by the Consultative Committee of Accountancy Bodies [and published as Audit Technical Release 4/00 by the Institute of Chartered Accountants in England and Wales, *or alternative CCAB member*]. We have read the attached Statement prepared by the Directors. Our work was based on obtaining an understanding of the compilation of the Statement by enquiry of management, reference to the Loan Agreement, comparison of the financial information in the Statement to the sources from which it was obtained and re-computation of the calculations in the Statement. [The specific procedures we performed are set out in the Appendix to this letter.] For the purpose of providing you with this letter, other than as set out herein, we have not carried out any work by way of audit, review or verification of the financial information nor of the management accounts, accounting records or other sources from which that information has been extracted.

Report

Based solely on the procedures described above, we confirm that:

- the financial information contained in the accompanying Statement has been accurately extracted from the sources identified therein and, where applicable, agrees with the underlying accounting records;
- the calculations shown in the Statement made in accordance with Clause [X] of the Loan Agreement are arithmetically accurate; and
- the financial information in the Statement is presented in compliance with the relevant accounting definitions as to its elements and composition set out in Clause [X] of the Loan Agreement [and as agreed between Lender plc and XYZ plc and confirmed to us in a letter dated [date]].

Our report as set out herein is confidential to the addressees of this letter and should not be made available to any other party without our written consent. It is provided solely for the purpose of your assessment of XYZ plc's compliance with the terms of [Clause [X] of] the Loan Agreement. We accept no liability to any other party who is shown or gains access to this letter.

Yours faithfully

cc. XYZ plc

42.7 DUTIES OF CARE FOR NON-STATUTORY AUDITS OR REVIEWS

42.7.1 Background

Small companies which take advantage of the statutory audit exemption may still decide to have their financial statements reviewed for other purposes. The review report will not be on the public record and the firm performing the review will include a restriction on the use of its report, requiring written consent to be obtained before the report can be given to any third party. In August 2006, the Audit and Assurance Faculty of the ICAEW issued guidance in this area in AAF 03/06 *The ICAEW Assurance Service on Unaudited Financial Statements*. AAF 03/06 uses the IAASB's *International Framework for Assurance Engagements* as its reference as well as other guidance and standards on similar types of assurance engagements.

In an assurance engagement accountants express a conclusion on the financial statements, in those covered by AAF 03/06 the accountants give a negative form of conclusion on the unaudited financial statements. This is known as a limited assurance engagement, as opposed to reasonable assurance engagements where positive assurance is given, usually in terms of a true and fair view. The giving of a conclusion separates assurance engagements from compilation reports where no conclusion is given on the information compiled, or agreed upon procedure reports, where the report is purely factual. This is illustrated in **Table 7**.

TABLE 7: Rules of engagement

	Assurance Engagement			**Agreed Upon**
Type of engagement	**Reasonable Assurance**	**Limited Assurance**	**Compilation Engagement**	**Procedures Engagement**
Level of assurance/ type of conclusion	Positive opinion, usually 'true and fair'	Negative opinion, guidance given in AAF 03/06	Confirm facts of compilation only, no conclusion given	Purely factual, no conclusion given

42.7.2 Accepting the engagement

The terms of the engagement should be agreed in writing. Example engagement letter wording is given in **Table 8**. The assurance report may be received by people not party to the engagement and accountants should assess the risks of litigation arising from third parties prior to accepting the engagement. The engagement letter should be suitably worded to ensure that no liability is assumed to any third party.

TABLE 8: Example extracts from an engagement letter for limited assurance engagement

Scope of our work

You have asked us to report to you on a limited assurance basis on the unaudited financial statements of the company. We shall plan our work on the basis that the company is not required by statute or regulation to have an audit of its financial statements for the year ended [date], unless you inform us in writing to the contrary. In carrying out this engagement we will make enquiries, perform analytical procedures and assess the consistency of application of your accounting policies in accordance with Generally Accepted Accounting Practice in the United Kingdom ('UK GAAP'). We will perform limited examination of evidence relevant to certain balances and disclosures in the financial statements where, after performing the above work, we become aware of matters that might indicate material misstatements in the financial statements.

Our work will be undertaken and our report will be made in accordance with AAF 03/06 issued by the Institute of Chartered Accountants in England and Wales.

Our conclusion on the unaudited financial statements cannot be regarded as providing assurance on the adequacy of the company's systems or on the incidence of fraud, non-compliance with laws and regulations or weaknesses in internal controls. Engaging us to perform this assurance engagement on the unaudited financial statements does not relieve the directors of their responsibilities in these respects.

You have advised us that the company is exempt from an audit of the financial statements. We will not carry out any work to determine whether or not the company is entitled to audit exemption. However should our work indicate that the company is not entitled to the exemption, we will inform you of this.

Our work will not be an audit of the financial statements in accordance with International Standards on Auditing (UK and Ireland). Consequently, it does not include a comprehensive assessment of the risk of material misstatement, a consideration of fraud or of laws and regulations, to the gaining of an understanding of, or the testing of, internal control in accordance with International Standards on Auditing (UK and Ireland). It does not include the gathering of evidence in relation to all material areas of the financial statements and in respect of all relevant assertions.

Since we will not carry out an audit nor confirm the accuracy or reasonableness of the accounting records maintained by the company, we can only provide a limited assurance report as to whether the financial statements present a true and fair view.

Furthermore, as the Board of Directors, you have a duty to prepare financial statements that comply with the Companies Act 2006 and applicable accounting standards. Where we identify that the financial statements do not conform to UK

GAAP or if the accounting policies adopted are not immediately apparent this will need to be disclosed in the financial statements.

We have a professional responsibility not to be associated with financial statements which may be false or misleading. Therefore, although we are not required to search for such matters, should we become aware, for any reason, that the financial statements may be misleading, we will discuss the matter with you with a view to agreeing appropriate adjustments and/or disclosures in the financial statements. In circumstances where adjustments and/or disclosures that we consider appropriate are not made or where we are not provided with appropriate information, and as a result we consider that the financial statements are misleading, we will withdraw from the engagement.

Basis of the accountants' report

Our report is prepared on the following basis:

- our report is prepared solely for your confidential use. It may not be relied upon by anyone else; and
- except to the extent required by court order, law or regulation, or where required in any court proceedings in which you may be involved, our report must not be made available, copied, referred to or recited to any other person, or included in any other document, nor may you make reference to us or the services, without our prior written permission.

Liability provision

We (that is, [name of firm]), will perform the engagement with reasonable skill and care and we acknowledge that in respect of liability (if any) on our part to the Company for losses, damages, costs or expenses ('losses') caused by our breach of contract, negligence, fraud or other deliberate breach of duty, the following provisions will apply:

- we will not be liable if such losses are due to the provision of false, misleading or incomplete information or documentation or due to the acts or omissions of any person other than us, except where, on the basis of the work normally undertaken by us within the scope set out in these terms of engagement, it would have been reasonable for us to discover such defects;
- we will accept liability without limit for the consequences of our own fraud or other deliberate breach of duty and for any other liability which it is not permitted by law to limit or exclude; and
- subject to the previous provisions of this liability paragraph, our total aggregate liability whether in contract, tort (including negligence) or otherwise, to the Company, for losses arising from or in connection with the work which is the subject of these terms (including any addition or variation to the work), shall not exceed in aggregate the amount of [£agreed amount].

The Company and the directors of the Company will not bring any claims or proceedings against any of our individual partners, members, directors or employees. This clause is intended to benefit such partners, members, directors and employees who may enforce this clause pursuant to the contracts (Rights of Third Parties) Act 1999 ('the Act'). Notwithstanding any benefits or rights conferred by this agreement on such partners, members, directors or employees by virtue of the Act, we and the directors of the Company may together agree in writing to vary or rescind the agreement set out in this letter without the consent of any such partners, members, directors or employees. Other than as expressly provided in this paragraph, the provisions of the Act are excluded.

Any claims, whether in contract, negligence or otherwise, must be formally commenced within [years] after the party bringing the claim becomes aware (or ought reasonably to have become aware) of the facts which give rise to the action and in any event to later than [years] after any alleged breach of contract, negligence or other cause of action. This expressly overrides any statutory provision which would otherwise apply.

As part of their risk management process, accountants should consider whether there are third parties who may seek to rely on their report. Depending on circumstances, and similar to the general guidance for managing professional liability set out in **42.3.2** above, accountants may:

- accept that they owe a duty of care to the third parties and enter into a tri-partite or multi-partite engagement contract with the client and the third parties. Provisions to limit liability may be appropriate;
- proceed with an engagement with the client alone, but allowing access to the report for third parties as long as they:
  - acknowledge in writing that the reporting accountant owes them no duty of care; and
  - agree in writing that no claims will be brought against the reporting accountant in relation to the assurance report;
- engage with the client alone, disclaiming any liability or duty to others by notice in the assurance report. This may be in conjunction with the client indemnifying the reporting accountant if a third party makes a claim against the reporting accountant; or
- decline to accept the engagement.

42.7.3   Reliance by third parties

During the performance of the engagement, or after the report has been issued, accountants may become aware of third parties, such as banks or lenders, who may request sight of the report. In such cases, accountants may decline the request, or access may be agreed if the third party acknowledges in writing that they owe the accountant no duty of care.

When accountants become aware that a third party has obtained a copy of their report they should consider writing to the third party informing them that they did not undertake the work for the use of third parties and that they do not accept any responsibility to them and that all liability is denied.

42.7.4   Reporting

Accountants' reports help addressees derive comfort from the involvement of an independent accountant. They also assist in clarifying the scope of the engagement and ensuring that readers are aware that a full audit has not taken place. **Table 9** includes an example report to directors. **Table 10** shows a report addressed to directors and third parties.

TABLE 9: Example accountants' report to directors

Accountants' independent assurance report on the unaudited financial statements of [entity name]

To the Board of Directors of [entity name] ('the Company')

We have performed certain procedures in respect of the Company's unaudited financial statements for the year ended [date] as set out on pages [x] to [x], made enquiries of the Company's directors and assessed accounting policies adopted by the directors, in order to gather sufficient evidence for our conclusion in this report.

This report is made solely to the Company's directors, as a body, in accordance with the terms of our engagement letter dated [date]. It has been released to the directors on the basis that this report shall not be copied, referred to or disclosed, in whole (save for the directors' own internal purposes or as may be required by law or by a competent regulator) or in part, without our prior written consent. Our work has been undertaken so that we might state to the directors those matters that we have agreed to state to them in this report and for no other purpose. To the fullest extent permitted by law, we do not accept or assume responsibility to anyone other than the Company and the Company's directors as a body for our work, for this report or the conclusions we have formed.

Respective responsibilities

You have confirmed that you have met your duty as set out in the directors' statement on page [x]. You consider that the Company is exempt from the statutory requirement for an audit for the year. Our responsibility is to form and express an independent conclusion, based on the work carried out, to you on the financial statements.

Scope

We conducted our engagement in accordance with the Institute of Chartered Accountants in England & Wales Interim Technical Release AAF 03/06. Our work was based primarily upon enquiry, analytical procedures and assessing accounting policies in accordance with Generally Accepted Accounting Practice in the UK[/the Financial Reporting Standard for Smaller Entities]. If we considered it to be necessary, we also performed limited examination of evidence relevant to certain balances and disclosures in the financial statements where we became aware of matters that might indicate a risk of material misstatement in the financial statements.

The terms of our engagement exclude any requirement to carry out a comprehensive assessment of the risks of material misstatement, a consideration of fraud, laws, regulations and internal controls, and we have not done so. We are not required to, and we do not, express an audit opinion on these financial statements.

Conclusion

Based on our work, nothing has come to our attention to refute the directors' confirmation that in accordance with the Companies Act 2006 the financial statements give a true and fair view of the state of the Company's affairs as at [date] and of its profit [/loss] for the year then ended and have been properly prepared in accordance

---

with Generally Accepted Accounting Practice in the UK [/the Financial Reporting Standard for Smaller Entities].

Name of firm
Chartered Accountants
Location
Date

TABLE 10: Example accountants' report to directors and other parties

Accountants' independent assurance report on the unaudited financial statements of [entity name]

To the Board of Directors of [entity name] ('the Company') and [Third party]

We have performed certain procedures in respect of the Company's unaudited financial statements for the year ended [date] as set out on pages [x] to [x], made enquiries of the Company's directors and assessed accounting policies adopted by the directors, in order to gather sufficient evidence for our conclusion in this report.

This report is made solely to the Company's directors, as a body, and to [third party], [as a body], in accordance with the terms of our engagement letter dated [date]. It has been released to the directors and [third party] on the basis that this report shall not be copied, referred to or disclosed, in whole (save for the directors' own internal purposes or amongst the directors and [third party] or as may be required by law or by a competent regulator) or in part, without our prior written consent. Our work has been undertaken so that we might state to the directors and [third party] those matters that we have agreed to state to them in this report and for no other purpose. To the fullest extent permitted by law, we do not accept or assume responsibility to anyone other than the Company and the Company's directors as a body and [third party] [as a body] for our work, for this report or the conclusions we have formed.

Respective responsibilities

The Company's directors have confirmed that you have met their duty as set out in the directors' statement on page [x]. They consider that the Company is exempt from the statutory requirement for an audit for the year. Our responsibility is to form and express an independent conclusion, based on the work carried out, to the Company's directors and [third party] on the financial statements.

Scope

We conducted our engagement in accordance with the Institute of Chartered Accountants in England & Wales Interim Technical Release AAF 03/06. Our work was based primarily upon enquiry, analytical procedures and assessing accounting policies in accordance with Generally Accepted Accounting Practice in the UK[/the Financial Reporting Standard for Smaller Entities]. If we considered it to be necessary, we also performed limited examination of evidence relevant to certain balances and disclosures in the financial statements where we became aware of matters that might indicate a risk of material misstatement in the financial statements.

The terms of our engagement exclude any requirement to carry out a comprehensive assessment of the risks of material misstatement, a consideration of fraud, laws, regulations and internal controls, and we have not done so. We are not required to, and we do not, express an audit opinion on these financial statements.

Conclusion

Based on our work, nothing has come to our attention to refute the directors' confirmation that in accordance with the Companies Act 2006 the financial statements give a true and fair view of the state of the Company's affairs as at [date] and of its profit [/loss] for the year then ended and have been properly prepared in accordance with Generally Accepted Accounting Practice in the UK [/the Financial Reporting Standard for Smaller Entities].

Name of firm
Chartered Accountants
Location
Date

42.8 REPORTS ON INTERNAL CONTROLS OF SERVICE ORGANISATIONS

42.8.1 Background

Many entities use service organisations to perform various tasks for them. These services may vary from performing a certain task, such as preparing the payroll, to replacing entire business units. Many of the functions undertaken by service organisations affect an entity's financial statements and so auditors may seek information about the control procedures put in place by the service organisation.

Reporting accountants may be asked by service organisations to provide a report on their internal controls which they can supply to their customers and the customers' auditors.

In June 2006 the Audit and Assurance Faculty of the ICAEW issued AAF 01/06 *Assurance Reports on Internal Controls of Service Organisations Made Available to Third Parties* specifically in relation to financial service activities, including:

- custody;
- investment management;
- pension administration;
- property management;
- fund accounting; and
- transfer agency.

The guidance may be applied to other areas, such as payroll processing, but further considerations may be required.

AAF 01/06 replaces the original guidance in this area contained in AUDIT 4/97 *Reports on Internal Controls of Investment Custodians Made Available to Third*

Parties, FRAG 21/94 (Revised) and is effective for periods ending on or after 31 March 2007.

In December 2007, the IAASB issued an Exposure Draft of ISAE 3402, *Assurance Reports on Controls at a Third Party Service Organization*. Further details are given in **42.8.6** below.

42.8.2   Responsibilities of the service organisation

The directors of the service organisation are required to identify control objectives and the controls procedures which they consider appropriate to ensure that these control objectives are met. Their key responsibilities are:

- accepting responsibility for internal control;
- evaluating the effectiveness of the service organisation's controls procedures using suitable criteria;
- supporting their evaluation with sufficient evidence, including documentation; and
- providing a written report of the effectiveness of those control procedures for the relevant period.

The appendices to AAF 01/06 include a list of detailed control objectives for the financial services activities listed in **42.8.1** above. The list is not exhaustive and the directors of the service organisation are responsible for considering whether the objectives are sufficient for their organisation. The directors are required to make a statement in their report that they have referred to the examples in the appendices.

Service organisations are also responsible for:

- providing the reporting accountants with access to appropriate service organisation resources, such as service organisation personnel, systems documentation, contracts and minutes of management or audit committee meetings;
- disclosing to the reporting accountants any significant changes in control procedures that have occurred since the service organisation's last examination or within the last 12 months if the service organisation has not previously engaged reporting accountants to issue an assurance report;
- disclosing to the reporting accountants and the affected customers any illegal acts, fraud, or uncorrected errors attributable to the service organisation's management or employees that may affect its customers and the entity's whistle-blowing arrangements;
- disclosing to the reporting accountants any relevant design deficiencies in control procedures of which it is aware, including those for which the directors believe the cost of corrective action may exceed the benefits;
- disclosing to the reporting accountants all significant instances of which it is aware when control procedures have not operated with sufficient effectiveness to achieve the specified control objectives; and

- providing the reporting accountants with a letter of representation.

42.8.3 Accepting the engagement

As with other reports where third parties may be seeking to place reliance on their report, reporting accountants may:

- accept that they owe a duty of care to the third parties and enter into a tri-partite or multi-partite engagement contract with the client and the third parties. Provisions to limit liability may be appropriate. A multi-partite engagement contract may be difficult where the service organisation has numerous customers;
- engage with the service organisation with the ability for its customers to be afforded the same duty of care agreed between the reporting accountant and the service organisation if they subsequently accept the relevant terms of the engagement letter, including any limitations on liability;
- proceed with an engagement with the client alone, but allowing access to the report for third parties as long as they:
  - acknowledge in writing that the reporting accountant owes them no duty of care; and
  - agree in writing that no claims will be brought against the reporting accountant in relation to the assurance report;
- engage with the client alone, disclaiming any liability or duty to others by notice in the assurance report. This may be in conjunction with the client indemnifying the reporting accountant if a third party makes a claim against the reporting accountant; or
- decline to accept the engagement.

Reporting accountants will always disclaim liability to the auditors of the service organisation's customers, as auditors will have responsibility for their own audit report.

Example extract terms of engagement are shown in **Table 11**.

TABLE 11: Extracts of example engagement letter paragraphs for assurance reports on internal controls of service organisations

Responsibilities of directors

The Board of Directors ('the Directors') of [entity name] in relation to which the reporting accountant's assurance report is to be provided ('the Organisation') are and shall be responsible for the design, implementation and operation of control procedures that provide adequate level of control over customer's assets and related transactions. The Directors' responsibilities are and shall include:

- acceptance of responsibility for internal controls;
- evaluation of the effectiveness of the service organisation's control procedures using suitable criteria;

- supporting their evaluation with sufficient evidence including documentation; and
- providing a written report ('Directors' Report') of the effectiveness of the service organisation's internal controls for the relevant financial period.

In drafting this report the Directors have regard to, as a minimum, the criteria specified within the Technical Release AAF 01/06 issued by the Institute of Chartered Accountants in England & Wales ('the Institute') but they may add to these to the extent that this is considered appropriate in order to meet customers' expectations.

Responsibilities of reporting accountants

It is our responsibility to form an independent conclusion, based on the work carried out in relation to the control procedures of the Organisation's [ ] function carried out at the specified business units of the Organisation [located at [ ]] as described in the Directors' Report and report this to the Directors.

Scope of the reporting accountants' work

We conduct our work in accordance with the procedures set out in AAF 01/06, issued by the Institute. Our work will include enquiries of management, together with tests of certain specific control procedures which will be set out in an appendix to our report.

In reaching our conclusion, the criteria against which the control procedures are to be evaluated are the internal control objectives developed for service organisations as set out within the AAF 01/06 issued by the Institute.

Any work already performed in connection with this engagement before the date of this letter will also be governed by the terms and conditions of this letter.

We may seek written representations from the Directors in relation to matters on which independent corroboration is not available. We shall seek confirmation from the Directors that any significant matters of which we should be aware have been brought to our attention.

Inherent limitations

The Directors acknowledge that control procedures designed to address specified control objectives are subject to inherent limitations and, accordingly, errors or irregularities may occur and not be detected. Such procedures cannot guarantee protection against fraudulent collusion especially on the part of those holding positions of authority or trust. Furthermore, the opinion set out in our report will be based on historical information and the projection of any information or conclusion in our report to any future periods will be inappropriate.

Use of our report

Our report will, subject to the permitted disclosures set out in this letter, be made solely for the use of the Directors of the Organisation, and solely for the purpose of reporting on the internal controls of the Organisation, in accordance with these terms of our engagement.

Our work will be undertaken so that we might report to the Directors those matters that we have agreed to state to them in our report and for no other purpose.

Our report will be issued on the basis that it must not be recited or referred to or disclosed, in whole or in part, in any other document or to any other party, without the express prior written permission of the reporting accountants. We permit the disclosure of our report, in full only, to customers [of the Organisation using the

Organisation's [financial services] ('customers') [(as defined in appendix [ ] to this letter,] and to the auditors of such customers, to enable customers and their auditors to verify that a report by reporting accountants has been commissioned by the Directors of the Organisation and issued in connection with the internal controls of the Organisation without assuming or accepting any responsibility or liability to them on our part.

To the fullest extent permitted by law, we do not and will not accept or assume responsibility to anyone other than the Directors as a body and the Organisation for our work, for our report or for the opinions we will have formed.

Liability provisions

We will perform the engagement with reasonable skill and care and acknowledge that we will be liable to the Directors as a body and Organisation for losses, damages, costs or expenses ('losses') suffered by the Directors as a body and the Organisation as a result of our breach of contract, negligence, fraud or other deliberate breach of duty. Our liability shall be subject to the following provisions:

- we will not be so liable if such losses are due to the provision of false, misleading or incomplete information or documentation or due to the acts or omissions of any person other than us, except where, on the basis of the enquiries normally undertaken by us within the scope set out in these terms of engagement, it would have been reasonable for us to discover such defects;
- we accept liability without limit for the consequences of our own fraud or other deliberate breach of duty and for any other liability which it is not permitted by law to limit or exclude;
- subject to the previous provisions of this Liability paragraph, our total aggregate liability, whether in contract, tort (including negligence) or otherwise, to the Directors as a body and the Organisation, arising from or in connection with the work which is the subject of these terms (including any addition or variation to the work), shall not exceed the amount of [to be discussed and negotiated].

To the fullest extent permitted by law, the Organisation agrees to indemnify and hold harmless [name of reporting accountants] and its partners and staff against all actions, proceedings and claims brought or threatened against [name of reporting accountants] or against any of its partners and staff by any persons other than the Directors as a body and the Organisation, and all loss, damage and expense (including legal expenses) relating thereto, where any such action, proceeding or claim in any way relates to or concerns or is connected with any of [name of reporting accountants]'s work under this engagement letter.

The Directors as a body and the Organisation agree that they will not bring any claims or proceedings against any of our individual partners, members, directors or employees. This clause is intended to benefit such partners, members, directors and employees who may enforce this clause pursuant to the Contracts (Right of Third Parties) Act 1999 ('the Act'). Notwithstanding any benefits or rights conferred by this agreement on such partners, members, directors or employees by virtue of the Act, we and the Directors as a body may together agree in writing to vary or rescind the agreement set out in this letter without the consent of any such partners, members, directors or employees. Other than as expressly provided in this paragraph, the provision of the Act are excluded.

Any claims, whether in contract, negligence or otherwise, must be formally commenced within [years] after the party bringing the claim become aware (or ought reasonably to have become aware) of the facts which give rise to the action and in any event no later than [years] after any alleged breach of contract, negligence or other cause of action. This expressly overrides any statutory provision which would otherwise apply.

This engagement is separate from, and unrelated to, our audit work on the financial statements of the Organisation for the purposes of the Companies Act 2006 (or its successor) or other legislation and nothing herein creates obligations or liabilities regarding our statutory audit work, which would not otherwise exist.

[*Appendix*
List of customers to whom the assurance report may be made available.]

Reporting accountants may become aware of third parties other than the service organisation's customers who may request sight of the report. In such cases, accountants may decline the request, or access may be agreed if the third party acknowledges in writing that they owe the accountant no duty of care.

42.8.4   Reporting accountant's procedures

Reporting accountants will read the directors' description of the controls procedures and undertake procedures to determine whether that description is a fair presentation. Procedures may include:

- discussing aspects of the control framework and relevant control procedures with management and other personnel;
- determining who the customers are and how the services provided by the service organisation are likely to affect the customers;
- reviewing standard terms of contracts with the customers to gain an understanding of the service organisation's contractual obligations;
- observing the procedures performed by the service organisation's personnel;
- reviewing the service organisation's policy and procedure manual and other systems documentation; and
- performing walkthrough tests on selected transactions and control procedures.

Reporting accountants should consider whether the control procedures are suitably designed. Their assessment may include:

- considering the linkage between the control procedure and the associated control objectives;
- considering the ability of the control procedures to prevent or detect errors; and
- performing further procedures such as enquiries of personnel, inspection of documentation and observation of control procedures to determine whether they are adequately designed and operated as prescribed.

Where reporting accountants become aware that the control objectives are incomplete or inappropriate they discuss their findings with the directors and request that the directors amend their report accordingly. If the directors refuse to make suitable amendments, reporting accountants will highlight this fact in their report.

42.8.5 Reporting

The engagement performed by the reporting accountant is a reasonable assurance engagement, that is sufficient evidence is obtained to allow them to express a positive conclusion on the directors' report (see **Table 7**).

The report concludes on the fairness of the description and the design and operating effectiveness of controls procedures over a specified period. An example report is given in **Table 12**.

TABLE 12: Example report on internal controls of service organisations

To the directors of [name of entity]

Use of report

This report is made solely for the use of the directors, as a body, of [name of entity], and solely for the purpose of reporting on the internal controls of [name of entity], in accordance with the terms of our engagement letter dated [date] [and attached as appendix [ ]].

Our work has been undertaken so that we might report to the directors those matters that we have agreed to state to them in this report and for no other purpose. Our report must not be recited or referred to in whole or in part in any other document nor made available, copied or recited to any other party, in any circumstances, without our express prior written permission.

We permit the disclosure of this report, in full only, by the directors at their discretion to customers [of [name of entity] using [name of entity]'s [financial services] ('customers'),] and to the auditors of such customers, to enable customers and their auditors to verify that a report by reporting accountants has been commissioned by the directors of [name of entity] and issued in connection with the internal controls of [name of entity], and without assuming or accepting any responsibility or liability to customers or their auditors on our part.

To the fullest extent permitted by law, we do not accept or assume responsibility to anyone other than the directors as a body and [name of entity] for our work, for this report or for the conclusions we have formed.

Subject matter

This report covers solely the internal controls of [name of entity] as described in your report as at [date]. Internal controls are processes designed to provide reasonable assurance regarding the level of control over customers' assets and related transactions achieved by [name of entity] in the provision of [outsourced activities] by [name of entity].

Respective responsibilities

The directors' responsibilities and assertions are set out on page [ ] of your report. Our responsibility is to form an independent conclusion, based on the work carried out in relation to the control procedures of [name of entity]'s [ ] function carried out at the specified business units of [name of entity] [located at [ ]] as described in your report and report this to you as the directors of [name of entity].

Criteria and scope

We conducted our engagement in accordance with International Standard on Assurance Engagement (ISAE) 3000 and the Institute of Chartered Accountants in England & Wales Technical Release AAF 01/06. The criteria against which the control procedures were evaluated are the internal control objectives developed for service organisations as set out within the Technical Release AAF 01/06 and identified by the directors as relevant control objective relating to the level of control over customers' assets and related transactions in the provision of [outsourced activities]. Our work was based upon obtaining an understanding of the control procedures as described on page [ ] to [ ] in the report by the directors, and evaluating the directors' assertions as described on page [ ] to [ ] in the same report to obtain reasonable assurance so as to form our conclusion. Our work also included tests of specific control procedures, to obtain evidence about their effectiveness in meeting the related control objectives. The nature, timing and extent of the tests we applied are detailed on pages [ ] to [ ].

Our tests are related to [name of entity] as a whole rather than performed to meet the needs of any or any particular customer.

Inherent limitations

Control procedures designed to address specific control objectives are subject to inherent limitations and, accordingly, errors or irregularities may occur and not be detected. Such control procedures cannot guarantee protection against (among other things) fraudulent collusion especially on the part of those holding positions of authority or trust. Furthermore, our conclusion is based on historical information and the projection of any information or conclusions in this report to any future periods would be inappropriate.

Conclusion

In our opinion, in all material respects:

- the accompanying report by the directors describes fairly the control procedures that relate to the control objectives referred to above which were in place as at [date];
- the control procedures described on pages [ ] to [ ] were suitably designed such that there is reasonable, but not absolute assurance that the specified control objective would have been achieved if the described control procedures were complied with satisfactorily [and customers applied the control procedures contemplated]; and
- the control procedures that were tested, as set out in the attachment to this report, were operating with sufficient effectiveness for us to obtain reasonable, but not absolute, assurance that the related control objectives were achieved in the period [x] to [y].

Name of firm
Chartered Accountants
Location
Date

42.8.6   ED ISAE 3402

In December 2007, the IAASB issued an Exposure Draft of ISAE 3402, *Assurance Reports on Controls at a Third Party Service Organization*. Its aim is to enhance the consistency of auditor performance in relation to such reports as there had not previously been a specific standard on this topic. Comments were requested by 31 May 2008.

42.9   REPORTS TO OTHER THIRD PARTIES

42.9.1   Introduction

The Audit and Assurance Faculty increased the scope of the original guidance on reporting to lenders to other third parties by publishing two further Technical Releases: Audit 1/01, *Reporting to third parties* and 2/01 *Requests for references on clients' financial status and their ability to service loans.*

The aim of Audit 1/01 is to establish the same type of approach as set out in Audit 4/00 for all special reporting engagements. Firms should be on their guard to avoid circumstances that may result in a duty of care for the statutory audit report becoming established with a third party without sufficient disclaimers being put in place.

The guidance in Audit 2/01 is only appropriate where there is no need to perform any work, research or investigation to produce the reference. If further work is required, then a formal engagement should be agreed under Audit 1/01.

42.9.2   Audit 1/01: Reporting to third parties

Accountants have no obligation to sign reports requested by third parties such as trade bodies or regulators, but may wish to do so in order to assist their clients. Accountants should endeavour to become familiar with third parties' demands for customised reports as early as possible in the relationship with their client so that appropriate engagement terms can be negotiated.

Technical Release Audit 1/01 aims to help accountants to manage their risk in relation to providing such reports. However, it does not cover corporate finance engagements, reports made under UK company legislation, which will be covered by Practice Note 8, reports relating to public sector entities or requests for references, which are covered by Audit 2/01.

The Technical Release sets out, under a number of headings, the process accountants should follow in response to requests from third parties. The process is illustrated by the flowchart in **Table 13**.

TABLE 13: Process for responding to requests from third parties

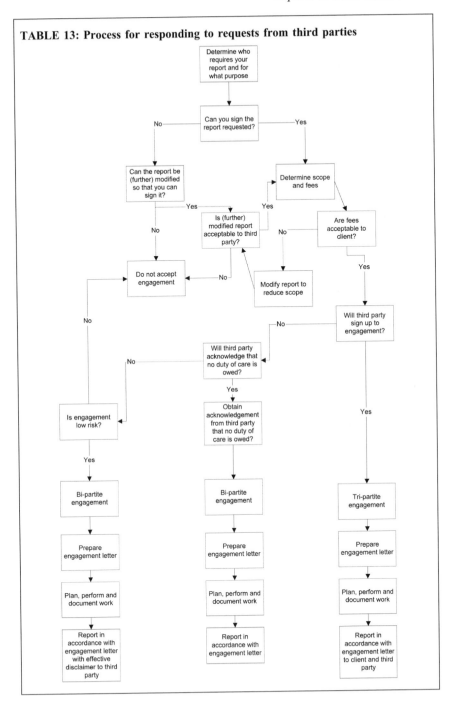

Determine who will rely on the accountants' work and for what purpose

When accountants become aware that a report has been requested, and will be relied upon, by a third party there is a risk that the accountant will owe that third party a duty of care unless an effective disclaimer is put in place. Therefore the accountant must determine the identity of the third party and details of the reliance they wish to place on the report, as well assessing the extent of loss the third party could suffer if they relied on the report and it proved to be misleading.

Once accountants have an understanding of the risks involved they can decide whether to:

- contract with the third party for the engagement and accept that they have a duty of care to the third party and limit liability if appropriate;
- contract with their client for the engagement and ensure that the third party confirms in writing that no duty of care exists before allowing them access to the report;
- contract with their client but disclaim or limit liability or duty to the third party in their report; or
- not accept the engagement.

If accountants regard a report as high risk they should only agree to provide the report if the third party either is a party to the engagement contract or has acknowledged that the accountants owe no duty of care to them in writing. Accountants should not allow their reports to be provided to third parties unless the extent of their liability to that party is clear.

Consider the form of the report requested by the third party

Accountants are not bound by any form of report agreed between the client and the third party without the accountants' consent. The form of report requested by the third party may not be appropriate for the accountant, and the accountant should not accept arguments that the form of the report cannot be changed (even where the report is of a 'standard' format in a pre-printed form).

Accountants should be wary of the following:

- wording giving an opinion on a matter as a statement of fact when that matter, by its nature, is inherently uncertain or a matter of judgement;
- the use of the term 'true and fair' when financial information is not prepared under the framework of Financial Reporting Standards;
- 'fair and reasonable' opinions, which are usually associated with investment banks making recommendations to shareholders in respect of transactions;
- wording that might suggest that the third party is able to rely on the statutory audit of the client;
- opinions that are open-ended or otherwise cannot be supported by the work carried out by the accountants;
- opinions which accountants do not have the necessary competence to provide, such as actuarial opinions or property valuations;
- opinions on matters beyond the accountants' knowledge and experience, particularly in relation to the detailed and specific operation circumstances of the client;
- wording that is open to interpretation;

- reports on internal controls where there are inadequate criteria for a sound control system;
- reports without addressees;
- reports on financial information which is not explicitly approved by the client;
- qualifications in covering letters only; and
- opinions which would impair the accountants' independence.

Accountants must only sign reports if they have performed sufficient work to support the statements they are asked to make. In some circumstances, such as reports on future solvency or performance of the client, statements cannot be supported by any amount of work, and accountants should refuse to sign such reports. Instead an agreed upon procedures form of report may be given, see below.

Agree the work to be performed and the form of the report to be given

In agreeing the work to be performed and form of report, accountants must make clear to clients and third parties that these engagements are separate from the statutory audit engagement and will be subject to separate terms and a separate fee. The terms for the report to third parties may include a limitation of liability.

The accountant must agree the form of report that is appropriate and the timescale in which it is to be delivered. The timescale must be realistic in relation to the amount of work the accountant will need to perform to provide the required opinion.

No UK auditing standards cover the forms of report which may be given, though some guidance is available in international standards. International standards break the types of report down into four types:

- *high level of assurance*, where a conclusion is expressed in positive terms;
- *moderate level of assurance*, requiring performance of limited procedures and possibly involving the provision of negative assurance in the style of 'nothing has come to our attention . . . ';
- *agreed upon procedures,* which involves performing certain defined procedures on factual information and reporting findings without any form of opinion on the implications of the work done; and
- *compilation engagements,* which involve preparing financial information on behalf of clients.

Where reports are to be given to third parties an agreed upon procedures report is usually most suited to the requirements of the client and the third party. Accountants must consider the level of risk of giving the type of report requested by the third party (even after appropriate liability limits are set) and consider whether the engagement should be accepted.

Agree appropriate terms of agreement

The accountant should agree terms of engagement in writing with both the client and third party. If the third party refuses to sign an engagement letter, the accountant should either refuse to provide a report, or do so only subject to a disclaimer of liability to the third party. Disclaimers must be reasonable to be effective. An example disclaimer notice is given in **Table 14**:

TABLE 14: Example disclaimer notices

Where the third party does not sign the engagement letter:

Our Report is prepared solely for the confidential use of [client name] and solely for the purpose of [details]. It may not be relied upon by [client name] for any other purpose whatsoever. Our Report must not be recited or referred to in whole or in part in any other document. Our report must not be made available, copied or recited to any other party [without our express permission]. [Accountant name] neither owes nor accepts any duty to any other party and shall not be liable for any loss, damage or expense of whatsoever nature which is caused by their reliance on our report.

Where the third party signs the engagement letter:

Our Report is prepared solely for the confidential use of [client name] and [name of third party], and solely for the purpose of [details]. It may not be relied upon by [client name] or [name of third party] for any other purpose whatsoever. Our Report must not be recited or referred to in whole or in part in any other document. Our Report must not be made available, copied or recited to any other party [without our express written permission]. [Accountant name] neither owes nor accepts any duty to any other party and shall not be liable for any loss, damage or expense of whatsoever nature which is caused by their reliance on our Report.

Example engagement letter extracts for an agreed upon procedures engagement are set out in **Table 15**.

TABLE 15: Example extracts from an engagement letter for an agreed upon procedures engagement

Services to be provided

We will complete the specified limited scope procedures set out below:

(describe the nature, timing and extent of the procedures to be performed, including specific reference, where applicable, to the identity of the documents and records to be read, individuals to be contacted and parties from whom confirmations will be obtained.)

The above procedures will be performed solely for your purposes. You are responsible for determining whether the scope of our work specified above is sufficient for your purposes.

Upon completion of the procedures we will provide you with a report of our findings in the form of that attached to this letter, solely for your information. Our report is not to be used for any other purpose or disclosed to any other third party without our

---

consent. [We consent to the report being released to [third party name] provided that [third party name] acknowledges in writing that we owe no duty of care to [third party name] and we will not be liable to [third party name] for any reliance it chooses to place on the report.]

We have agreed that, under this engagement, we will not perform an audit or any verification procedures other than those which are specified in the scope section above. [If we were to perform additional procedures or if we were to perform an audit or any more limited review, other matters might come to our attention that would be reported to you.] Our report will not extend to any financial statements of the Company taken as a whole.

Audit work

Our audit work on the financial statements of the Company is carried out in accordance with our statutory obligations and is subject to a separate engagement letter. Our audit report is intended for the sole benefit of the Company's shareholders as a body, to whom it is addressed, to enable them to exercise their rights in general meeting. Our audits of the Company's financial statements are not planned or conducted to address or reflect matters in which anyone other than such shareholders as a body may be interested.

We do not, and will not, by virtue of this report or otherwise, assume any responsibility whether in contract, negligence or otherwise in relation to our audits of the Company's financial statements; we and our employees shall have no liability whether in contract, negligence or otherwise to [third party name if addressee to this letter, or to] any [other] third parties in relation to our audits of the Company's financial statements.

Scope of our work

The scope of our work and the procedures we shall carry out in preparing our report, together with the limitations inherent therein, are outlined above. If the scope and procedures do not meet your requirements, please tell us so that we can discuss a different scope or additional or alternative procedures. [You should understand that there is no guarantee that these procedures will result in the identification of all matters which may be of interest to you.]

Our work will be based primarily on internal management information and will be carried out on the assumption that information provided to us by the management of the Company is reliable and, in all material respects, accurate and complete. We will not subject the information contained in our reports and letters to checking or verification procedures except to the extent expressly stated. This is normal practice when carrying out such limited scope procedures, but contrasts significantly with, for example, an audit. Even audit work provides no guarantee that fraud will be detected. You will therefore understand that the Services are not designed to and are not likely to reveal fraud or misrepresentation by the management of the Company. Accordingly we cannot accept responsibility for detecting fraud (whether by management or by external parties) or misrepresentation by the management of the Company.

Any engagement letter should include the following:

- an unambiguous description of the scope of work and form of report to be given;
- a description of the client's obligations and responsibilities;

- a statement that the engagement is separate from the statutory audit and that no duty of care will arise in relation to the statutory audit;
- if agreed, an appropriate liability cap;
- details of the addressee for the report, together with details of restrictions on who is entitled to see and rely on the report; and
- a copy of the report that will be provided.

Example wording for a liability cap is set out in **Table 16**.

TABLE 16: Example liability cap

The aggregate liability, whether to [client name] or [third party name] or any other party, of whatever nature, whether in contract, tort or otherwise, of [Accountant's name] for any losses whatsoever and howsoever caused arising from or in any way connected with this engagement [and this transaction] shall not exceed [amount] (including interest).

Perform the work

The work for a third party report is separate to that for the statutory audit, and the audit team should put together a separate working paper file for this engagement.

Report

The report should reflect the terms set out in the engagement letter, and should not include undefined terms such as 'review' without specifying what the terms mean.

Accountants should not modify the wording of their reports at the client's or third party's request unless the modification is appropriate and they have the opportunity to perform any additional work that is required to support the change in wording. If a different form of report is required to that set out in the engagement letter, the accountants should either reissue their terms of engagement or refuse to report, giving their reasons in writing.

Illustrative contents of a report of factual findings for an agreed upon procedures engagement are set out in **Table 17**.

TABLE 17: Illustrative contents of a report of factual findings for an agreed upon procedures engagement

These include:

- addressee;
- identification of the applicable engagement letter and specific information to which the agreed upon procedures have been applied;
- a statement that the procedures performed were those agreed with the client (and third party, if applicable);
- identification of the purpose for which the agreed upon procedures were performed;

- a listing of the specific procedures performed;
- a description of the accountants' factual findings, including sufficient details of errors and exceptions found;
- a statement that the procedures performed do not constitute either an audit or a review;
- a statement that had the accountants performed additional procedures, an audit or a review, other matters might have come to light that would have been reported;
- a statement that the report is restricted to those parties that have agreed to the procedures performed;
- a statement that the report relates only to the matters specified and that it does not extend to the entity's financial statements taken as a whole; and
- the date of the report.

42.9.3 Audit 2/01: Requests for references on clients' financial status and their ability to service loans

Accountants may be asked to provide references to banks, building societies and a range of other bodies about their clients' financial position, ability to pay debts as they fall due or service a loan. This is particularly relevant for individuals or small businesses that may not have audited accounts. Audit 2/01 provides guidance on how reporting accountants can manage their risks effectively when asked to perform such procedures.

The guidance is only appropriate where the accountant does not have to perform any additional work, research or investigation to give the reference. Where extra procedures have to be performed the guidance in Audit 1/01 should be followed.

The main issues

Third parties would like accountants to confirm that their client will have sufficient future income to service a loan or other commitment. However, no amount of enquiry can provide accountants with the assurance required to give such a confirmation.

Reporting on the present solvency of a client is only possible if the accountant is engaged to report on accounts, computations and projections as at a stated date. It is likely that the costs involved in producing such a report will be prohibitive to any third party.

References covered by Audit 2/01 require no extra work, and therefore incur no fee. This avoids the possibility of an implied contract. The fact that no extra work has been performed is stated in the reference.

Accountants may legitimately refuse to give a reference if they think the risks of doing so are too high, e.g. if the amounts involved are judged to be too large.

Unincorporated entities

Lenders who are entering into agreements with individuals and other unincorporated small borrowers, will not have audited reports to consider when making their lending decision. Accountants can, however, supply information that might be useful to a lender. This will include:

- the length of time the accountant has acted for the client;
- the net income or profits declared to the Inland Revenue; and
- a statement that the accountant has no reason to suppose that the client would have entered into a commitment which they would not expect to fulfil.

The third item above is a matter of judgement and will be based on the accountants' past experience of the client and the client's attitude to commercial obligations. Where accountants have insufficient knowledge of their client (for example, they have only just started to act) or there is any doubt about the judgement, they can decline to comment.

If the accountants' knowledge of the client is out of date, this will also be noted in the report.

Reporting

Accountants should report in a manner suitable for the particular circumstances. Third parties may provide a standard form of report, but accountants should amend the wording if necessary to reflect any limitations to the information requested.

Accountants should ensure that all technical terms are sufficiently defined, and should refer the third party to information provided directly by the client if this is more appropriate.

An example report is given in **Table 18**.

TABLE 18: Example of an accountants' reference in connection with a lending application made by an individual or other small borrower

Without responsibility

[Name of lender]

[Address]

Dear Sirs

REFERENCE IN CONNECTION WITH THE LENDING APPLICATION MADE BY [name of client and application reference, as appropriate]

Our above named client has approached us for a reference in connection with the proposed loan by you of [amount] [repayable by monthly instalments of amount over number years].

We have acted in connection with our client's [personal/business/corporate tax] affairs since [date]. However, it should be noted that our knowledge of our client's affairs may not be fully up to date. In addition, we have not carried out any specific work with regard to this statement.

Our client's net income [insert definition] declared by our client to the Inland Revenue as at [date] amounted to [amount]. (To be adapted for borrowers who are not individuals)

(Income/profits for previous years and identification of those agreed with the Inland Revenue may be added)

Whilst we have no reason to believe that our client would enter into a commitment such as that proposed which our client did not expect to be able to fulfil, we can make no assessment of our client's continuing income or future outgoings.

Whilst the information provided above is believed to be true, it is provided without acceptance by [Accountant's name] of any responsibility whatsoever, and any use you wish to make of the information is, therefore, entirely at your own risk.

Yours faithfully

Signed ....
Dated ....

42.10 ASSURANCE ON NON-FINANCIAL INFORMATION

42.10.1 Background

In July 2008, and as part of its re:Assurance initiative, the Audit and Assurance Faculty of the ICAEW issued a paper entitled *Assurance on Non-Financial Information: Existing Practices and Issues*. The aim of the initiative is to promote dialogue about different types of external assurance and discussing where new assurance services could strengthen markets by increasing credibility of information.

This paper looks at the types of non-financial information on which external assurance reports are currently provided and considers future potential additions to that list. It also discusses some of the practical challenges which practitioners may face when working in this area.

42.10.2 Non-financial information

There are a number of areas where entities currently report on non-financial information, and these include:

● statements and information contained in the annual report, such as the enhanced business review, corporate governance statements and information on risk management policies, internal controls or wider operating data;

- corporate responsibility reporting on environmental, economic and social performance;
- reports to Regulators on matters such as risk exposures, pricing policies or compliance with regulatory requirements; and
- reporting on public interest concerns, for example, quality of service provision, carbon emissions or the conduct of public competitions.

Demand for credible information in these areas is growing, and therefore there has been an increasing requirement for practitioners to provide assurance reports.

42.10.3 Current practices and guidance

International Standard on Assurance Engagements (ISAE) 3000 *Assurance Engagements other than Audits or Reviews of Historical Financial Information*, published by the IAASB, covers all aspects of assurance engagements including:

- engagement acceptance;
- agreeing the terms of engagement;
- planning and performing the engagement;
- using the work of experts;
- obtaining evidence;
- considering subsequent events;
- documentation; and
- preparing the external assurance report.

Corporate responsibility

Corporate responsibility reports provide non-financial information on the social, economic and environmental performance of an organisation. There is no generally accepted framework or standard for preparing a corporate responsibility report, however, the sustainability reporting guidelines issued by the Global Reporting Initiative (GRI) are the best-known global voluntary code for sustainability reporting.

Information in the annual reports and accounts

Non-financial information in the annual reports and accounts may be included in:

- the enhanced business review (the 'EBR');
- corporate governance statements; and
- disclosures in the audited accounts.

There is no requirement for the disclosures in the EBR to be audited, but auditors are required to report whether the other information in the directors' report (the EBR) is consistent with the accounts (see **Chapter 14**).

Auditors are only required to review the corporate governance statements relating to nine of the 48 Combined Code provisions (see **Chapter 15**). The other provisions are included in the 'other information' requirements set out in **Chapter 14**.

Qualitative information included in the accounts is covered by the auditor's opinion on the financial statements.

Regulatory reporting

Many regulatory bodies require information from the entities that they regulate in order to perform their duties, but the nature and volume of the information required varies significantly from Regulator to Regulator. Practitioners should ensure that they are fully conversant with the requirements of the relevant Regulator prior to accepting an engagement to provide assurance on such information.

Where Regulators request reports on non-financial information the form of report made by the regulated entity and the nature of external assurance requirements will be set out by the Regulator.

Other reports

Other areas where practitioners may be asked to report on non-financial information are:

- the assessment of circulation figures by media owners;
- the application of quality assurance standards in relation to information security or customer service; and
- the administration of public competitions and telephone voting.

There is no external framework of guidance to assist practitioners with this type of engagement, but ISAE 3000 should be helpful, and ISO 9000 may also provide some useful guidance on quality assurance.

42.10.4   Considerations for practitioners

By providing external assurance reports, practitioners are enhancing the credibility of non-financial information by:

- following rigorous ethical standard covering independence;
- following a defined framework and standards which cover the whole assurance engagement; and
- having the relevant skills and experience in carrying out assurance engagements, following professional standards, complying with CPD and training requirements and having internal quality control procedures in place.

When accepting such an engagement, practitioners should:

- consider the motivations and purpose behind the request to ensure that they are able to meet this need;
- understand the needs of the users of the non-financial information;
- be clear about what the information is that they are reporting on and why it is needed;
- have agreed criteria by which they can measure the information; and
- clearly communicate these considerations in their report to help to avoid any expectation gap.

Skills

Practitioners' auditing experience may be valuable when carrying out assurance engagements on non-financial information. They are used to applying professional judgement and are familiar with assessing materiality, understanding the business and obtaining sufficient appropriate evidence.

Specialists can be consulted or a multi-disciplinary team can be used where practitioners have less experience in assessing qualitative, rather than quantitative, information or have a lack of in-depth technical knowledge, such as in engineering or surveying.

Subjective information

Compared to financial information, established measurement conventions do not exist for non-financial information. In such situations it may not be possible to establish consistent measurement criteria that are acceptable to all interested parties, and practitioners must consider whether the criteria used are relevant to the needs of the intended users of the information.

A reference to the measurement criteria used should be made in the external assurance report so that the basis of the practitioners' conclusion is clear.

Information from third parties

Reported non-financial information may include data sourced from third parties, such as retail statistics, average market prices etc. In line with the requirements of ISA (UK and Ireland) 402, *Audit Considerations Relating to Entities Using Service Organisations* (see **Chapter 27**), practitioners should consider whether the bodies producing this information have suitable controls and procedures in place to ensure that the information produced is accurate. This assurance may be in the form of an external assurance report on their operations (see **42.8** above). If any such evidence is lacking, practitioners may exclude the associated data from the scope of their assurance report.

Evidence

Practitioners need to be aware that non-financial information is often qualitative, and therefore it is often difficult to determine criteria against which to measure the information. Evidence may also be harder to obtain as there is likely to be less documentation to support disclosure and third-party verification is likely to be less readily available. In addition, determining materiality can be difficult in areas which are less quantitative in nature.

Control environment

Internal controls related to non-financial business activities and operations are not always well monitored or documented and may not be as robust as those related to financial reporting. Therefore, at the planning stage of the engagement, practitioners consider how they will obtain evidence that the information is robust enough to express an opinion on.

42.11   AUDIT LIABILITY: CLAIMS BY THIRD PARTIES

In June 2005, the Audit and Assurance Faculty of the ICAEW, in conjunction with the law firm Simmons & Simmons, published a review of the legal cases involving claims by third parties against auditors. It sets out the key matters arising from the cases of which auditors in practice should take note.

All the cases have in common an institution seeking assurance or reassurance from a company's auditors as to that company's financial strengths at a particular point in time, whether by reference to its audited accounts or by means of some other independent confirmation from the auditors that the company is financially sound.

As stated in **42.3** above, the case law surrounding auditors' duty of care was set out in the *Caparo v Dickman* judgement. That case set out that there would only be sufficient grounds to establish a duty of care to a third party where:

- the work produced was required for a purpose made known to the auditor; and
- the auditor knew, or should have known, that its work would be communicated to the non-client party for that purpose; and
- the auditor, knew or should have known, that its work would be likely to be relied upon by that third party for that purpose, without independent enquiry.

The main categories of cases where the application of these principles has been considered in the paper are:

- potential investors;
- creditors and lenders;
- regulators and trade bodies; and
- affiliates/associates of the audit client.

42.11.1   Potential investors

A duty of care to potential investors may occur other than in written form. In *ADT v Binder Hamlyn*, ADT, the potential investor, argued that a duty of care had been created when the audit partner made a comment in a meeting that the firm stood by its earlier unmodified audit opinion. ADT stated that they made further investment in Britannia Securities Group plc as a result of this affirmation and therefore sought damages from Binder Hamlyn when that investment lost money. By orally restating the true and fair opinion to the potential investor, the audit partner had assumed a duty of care to ADT which did not exist from the earlier audit report itself, as this had been prepared only with the shareholders of Britannia in mind.

An important element of the *Caparo* decision is whether the third party would have had another way of obtaining the assurance it sought from the auditor. In *Barker v Grant Thornton*, where potential investors are suing the auditor, no duty of care was found to exist as it was reasoned that it would have been practical for the investor to have instructed investigating accountants to obtain the necessary assurance for them rather than rely on the statutory audit report. In addition, Grant Thornton had already specifically disclaimed responsibility to the investor.

In *Yorkshire Enterprises Ltd v Robson Rhodes*, however, as the auditors were aware that they were completing the audit promptly because the financial statements were to be passed on to venture capitalists, it was not judged reasonable to require the investors to instruct their own investigating accountants. In addition, Robson Rhodes had not specifically disclaimed responsibility to Yorkshire Enterprises.

Two other cases set out in the study, *Electra Private Equity Partners v KPMG* and *Man Nutzfahrzeuge Aktiengesellschaft and Others v Ernst & Young and Others* demonstrate that auditors may have a duty of care to a third party not by what they said or did when auditing the financial statements, but merely on the basis of what they were told during the audit, for example that the audited financial statements were to be relied upon as the basis of a proposed sale. Such cases make the use of a disclaimer of the type recommended by Audit 1/03.

Another case where actuaries were sued by a potential investor in a client highlights the need for caution when auditors or other professional advisors are asked to provide copies of their reports to third parties. Although the courts eventually found for the actuaries, the absence of a statement clarifying that no responsibility was being assumed to the third party in providing a copy of the report caused a lengthy protraction of the case.

42.11.2   Creditors and lenders

The same principles apply to those that lend money rather than invest in a company. The case of *Royal Bank of Scotland v Bannerman Johnstone Maclay* it was sufficient that auditors should have been aware that a lender would rely on audited financial statements to create a duty of care. This case is discussed in **Chapter 3**.

42.11.3   Regulators and trade bodies

In a similar manner, in *Andrew & Others v Kounnis Freeman*, the auditors ought to have known that the audited financial statements which they forwarded to the Civil Aviation Authority (CAA) would be relied upon by the CAA in determining whether to renew a company's ATOL licence, and by sending the audited financial statements they assumed a duty of care.

In another case audited financial statements were forwarded by the client to ABTA and IATA. In addition they were sent to the provider of bond facilities to the travel agent. A travel agent is required to hold such bonds in order to be a member of ABTA and IATA. A duty of care was found to exist between the auditor and the bond provider, despite the auditor not knowing who would be providing the bond facilities. In this situation it was sufficient that the auditor, with experience of clients in the travel business, should be aware that a bond provider would be required and that this provider would need sight of the audited financial statements.

42.11.4   Affiliates or associates of the audit client

As well as separate third parties pursuing claims against auditors, there are situations where a claim is made by entities affiliated or associated with the audit client. In *Barings plc (in administration) and Others v Coopers & Lybrand and Others*, Barings sought damages from the auditors of one of its own indirect subsidiaries. It was judged that Coopers & Lybrand knew that their audit report on the subsidiary would be required to allow directors of the parent company to prepare group financial statements which showed a true and fair view. In addition, the auditors of the subsidiary had liaised directly with the auditors of the parent company, reporting to them any matters of significance so that they could inform the parent company management. Both these matters created a duty of care between the subsidiary auditors and the parent company, independent of the duty of care the subsidiary auditors had to their own client.

42.12 ISRS 4400

International guidance in the area of reports to third parties is provided by International Standard on Related Services (ISRS) 4400, *Engagements to Perform Agreed-Upon Procedures Regarding Financial Information*. ISRS 4400 was previously issued by the IAASB as ISA 920 and contains guidance on auditors' professional responsibilities when an engagement to perform agreed-upon procedures is undertaken.

In an agreed-upon procedures engagement, auditors will carry out procedures of an audit nature on which they and the entity, together with any relevant third parties, have agreed, and report on their findings. This report will be factual in nature and no assurance is expressed.

ISRS 4400 contains detailed guidance on:

- defining the terms of the engagement;
- planning,
- documentation;
- procedures and evidence; and
- reporting.

PART 5
SPECIALIST AUDITS

43 CHARITIES

43.1 LEGAL BACKGROUND

There are a number of different regulators with responsibility for charities throughout the UK, and each is at a different stage in establishing its regulatory regime. The Charity Commission regulates charities in England and Wales, the Office of the Scottish Regulator regulates charities registered in Scotland and also, to some extent, English or Welsh charities operating in Scotland. Northern Ireland is currently establishing its own Charity Commission. This chapter mainly addresses the regime governing English and Welsh charities.

The main laws that relate to a charity's financial statements and audit are:

All charitable companies	Companies Act 2006
Charities in England and Wales	Charities Act 1993 (as amended by the Charities Act 2006)
All charities registered in Scotland with the Office of the Scottish Charity Regulator (OSCR)	Charities and Trustee Investment (Scotland) Act 2005
Non-company charities in Northern Ireland	Charities Act (Northern Ireland) 1964

By virtue of an order under s77 of the Charities Act 2006, the audit regimes of companies and non-company charities are now identical if the company elects for exemption from audit under the Companies Act.[1] Larger company audits continue to be performed under the Companies Act regime. Charitable companies (if they elect for exemption from the Companies Act audit requirement) are therefore now subject to the same independent examination and audit regime, depending upon their gross income and gross assets, as all other charities.

By virtue of The Charities Act 2006 (Charitable Companies Audit and Group Accounts Provisions) Order 2008, charitable parent companies of small groups are required to prepare accounts and be audited under both the Companies Act 2006 and the Charities Act 1993. As a result, the audit requirement and trustees' responsibilities need to reflect the legal requirements of both pieces of legislation.

Charities that are subject to alternative legislative requirements to the Charities Act (such as the Companies Act for larger charities that are limited companies),

---

[1] The option to elect for audit exemption is only available to small charitable companies. Under the Companies Act, a small company is one which meets at least 2 of the following 3 criteria: income under £6.5m, gross assets under £3.26m and average number of employees for the year less than 50.

or alternative SORPS to the Charities' SORP (for example, Registered Providers of Social Housing) should follow the accounting and auditing requirements in the alternative legislation or SORP. For charities which are limited companies, the DTI consider the SORP to be indicative of the accounting practices necessary for charities to produce financial statements which show a true and fair view. This chapter deals mainly with charities applying the Charities SORP or subject to the Charities Act 1993 accounting and auditing requirement.

In charitable companies the directors are also the charity trustees and the term 'trustees' has been used throughout to refer to both.

Furthermore, charities established in Scotland register separately as Scottish charities. The Charity Accounts (Scotland) Regulations 2006 apply to all charities with a financial year that begins on or after 1 April 2006. The exemptions applicable to Scottish charitable corporations, local authority trusts, and registered housing associations as contained in statutory instruments 1993/1624, 1995/645 and 2000/49, and the exemption orders in 1993 and 2005 for designated religious bodies also continue to apply for accounting periods commencing before 1 April 2006. The OSCR Publication 'Scottish Charity Accounts – A Brief Guide' provides further guidance.

Dual registered charities (i.e., registered with the Charity Commission and with OSCR) need to comply with the SORP, but the audit requirement, annual report, and trustees' responsibilities need to reflect the legal requirements of both countries.

43.1.1   General

The Charities (Accounts and Reports) Regulations 2008 set out the requirements for preparation of accounts in respect of English and Welsh charities. Whilst all charities must prepare accounts, the impact of these regulations depends on the threshold requirements as set out in the 1993 Act and on whether the charity is registered or not. These requirements can be summarised as follows:

- registered charities with gross income and total expenditure of £10,000 or less, and excepted charities which are not registered, are not required to submit annual reports or accounts to the Charity Commission, unless requested to do so. All registered charities must prepare an annual report, even if they are not requested to submit it to the Charity Commission;
- non-company charities with gross income of £100,000 or less may prepare a receipts and payments account and a statement of assets and liabilities; and
- all charitable companies and non-company charities that exceed this £100,000 threshold must prepare accounts on an accruals basis to give a true and fair view. Certain additional disclosure requirements are placed on charities whose gross income exceeds the audit exemption threshold.

The audit or examination requirements are as follows:

- gross income does not exceed £10,000 – no statutory requirement for either an audit or an independent examination;
- gross income does not exceed £500,000 in the year – an election may be made for the accounts to be independently examined. Where income exceeds £250,000 in the year the examiner must be a member of a specified body; and
- gross income exceeds £500,000 in the year, or is over £100,000 and the charity has assets over £3.26 million – a statutory audit is required.

An audit can only be undertaken by a registered auditor, unless the Charity Commission gives a dispensation.

As noted above, where the charity is a company and has not elected for exemption from the Companies Act audit requirement then the audit is conducted under the Companies Act.

43.1.2 Independent examination

An independent examination for a charity below the thresholds discussed above, does not have to be carried out by a professionally qualified individual but should be by a person suitable to the circumstances of the charity. The examiner must be 'an independent person who is reasonably believed by the trustees to have the requisite ability and practical experience to carry out a competent examination of the accounts'.

The independent examiner's report to the charity's trustees is intended to provide a moderate level of assurance (negative assurance) and should:

- specify that it is a report in respect of an examination carried out under the Charities Act and in accordance with any directions given by the Commissioners which are applicable;
- state whether or not any matter has come to the examiner's attention which gives him reasonable cause to believe that in any material respect:
  - accounting records have not been kept in accordance with the Act;
  - the accounts do not accord with the records; or
  - the accounts do not comply with the Regulations;
- state whether or not any matter has come to his attention which should be drawn to the attention of the trustees;
- disclose any material expenditure or action which appears not to be in accordance with the trusts of the charity; and
- disclose any information or explanation provided or any information in the accounts which is materially inconsistent with the trustees' report.

The duties of an examiner are set out in CC32 issued by the Charity Commission, which is available from the Commission's website.

43.1.3 *Whistle-blowing duties for auditors and examiners*

The Charities Act 2006 imposes the same duties on auditors and independent examiners of all charities, whether or not they are limited companies. Under this whistle-blowing requirement, they have to report in writing, under s44A (Duty of auditors etc to report matters to the Commission) of the 1993 Act, any matters which may be of material significance to the Charity Commission's function as a regulator, which came to light as a result of their work.

The revised Practice Note provides additional guidance in this area, and this is detailed in the section of this chapter that covers ISA (UK and Ireland) 250, Part B.

Auditors and examiners are also expected to have regard to two other pieces of guidance: the Charity Commission's Serious Incident Reporting regime, and the guidance issued in support of the Directions for Independent Examiners.

43.2 AUDIT GUIDANCE

The major source of guidance for auditors is Practice Note 11 *The Audit of Charities*, which is designed to provide guidance on the application of the various ISAs (UK and Ireland) to charities.

Table 1 sets out the ISAs which the Practice Note covers.

TABLE 1: ISAs considered by Practice Note 11
200 Objective and general principles governing the audit of financial statements
210 Terms of audit engagement
220 Quality control for audits of historical financial information
240 The auditor's responsibility to consider fraud in an audit of financial statements
250 Section A Consideration of laws and regulations in an audit of financial statements
250 Section B The auditors' right and duty to report to regulators in the financial sector
260 Communication of audit matters with those charged with governance
300 Planning an audit of financial statements
315 Obtaining an understanding of the entity and its environment and assessing the risks of material misstatement
320 Audit materiality
330 The auditor's procedures in response to assessed risks
402 Audit considerations relating to entities using service organisations
505 External confirmations
510 Opening balances
520 Analytical procedures

540	Audit of accounting estimates
545	Auditing fair value measurements and disclosures
550	Related parties
560	Subsequent events
570	The going concern basis in financial statements
580	Management representations
600	Using the work of another auditor
700	The auditors' report on financial statements
720	Section A Other information in documents containing audited financial statements
720	Section B The auditor's statutory reporting responsibility in relation to directors' reports

In July 2009, the APB issued Bulletin 2009/3, *Auditor's Reports – Supplementary Guidance for Auditors of Charities with Accounting Periods Commencing on or after 6 April 2008*. The Bulletin details changes to auditor's reports for charities following the revisions to ISA (UK and Ireland) 700 (see **Chapter 3**).

43.3 BACKGROUND

The Practice Note only covers audits of charities and considers independent examinations as a different type of engagement. It points to the problems presented by charities given:

- the complex regulatory regime involving different Regulators in different countries;
- the diversity of accounting requirements which depend on size and corporate status;
- the whistle-blowing regime;
- its governing document and the extent of its objects and powers;
- the fact that they may be responsible for public money;
- the wide public interest in them; and
- their special features, such as voluntary income, restricted funds and charitable status.

43.4 ISA (UK AND IRELAND) 200 OBJECTIVE AND GENERAL PRINCIPLES GOVERNING THE AUDIT OF THE FINANCIAL STATEMENTS

Practitioners should not undertake the audit of a charity unless they are satisfied that they have, or can obtain, the necessary level of competence. The auditors' responsibilities in this respect are not related to the level of fee charged for the audit.

Auditors also need to comply with relevant ethical requirements relating to audit engagements. Particular issues relating to charities include:

- self interest – the auditor needs to be aware of other interests in the charity which may affect the conduct or outcome of the audit. The auditor therefore ensures that none of the audit team is in any way dependent upon the charity or provide significant support to the charity.
- self review – auditors will be often asked to provide additional help and advice, often on a pro-bono basis. The provision of this service is regarded in the same way as other non-audit services in assessing whether there is a threat to objectivity.

43.5   ISA (UK AND IRELAND) 210 TERMS OF AUDIT ENGAGEMENTS

Engagement letters will normally be sent to the trustees although they may be sent to a different appointing authority. The engagement may cover reports on other funds or on the disposition of local authority grants. Auditors will need to check documentation relating to funds received by the charity for consideration requiring special reports. Where trustees are not involved in the day-to-day running of the charity, the Practice Note suggests that auditors may send an additional copy to the chief executive or person responsible for that day-to-day management.

43.6   ISA (UK AND IRELAND) 220 QUALITY CONTROL FOR AUDITS OF HISTORICAL FINANCIAL INFORMATION

As well as ensuring that the engagement team has an appropriate level of knowledge of the charity sector, the engagement partner also satisfies himself that the members of the engagement team have sufficient knowledge, commensurate with their roles in the engagement, of:

- the Charities SORP;
- the governing document of the charity;
- the legal responsibilities and duties of charity trustees; and
- the regulatory framework within which charities operate

to identify situations which may give them reasonable cause to believe that a matter should be reported to a charity regulator.

The audit also considers if an engagement quality control review is required based on the nature of the engagement, including the extent to which it involves a matter of public interest. What is a matter of public interest is difficult to define: factors that may apply to a charity include:

- the size of the charity;
- its national or local profile; and
- its source of funds, including the extent to which the charity receives public funds.

43.7 ISA (UK AND IRELAND) 240 THE AUDITOR'S RESPONSIBILITY TO CONSIDER FRAUD IN AN AUDIT OF FINANCIAL STATEMENTS

In applying ISA (UK and Ireland) 240 to charities, auditors must be aware that the trustees are responsible for the prevention or detection of fraud in relation to the charity. However, the planning process of the audit must include an assessment of the possibility of fraud being committed by any of the people involved in the operation of the charity as well as by third parties. Certain features of charities may increase the risk of fraud, namely:

- widespread branches or operations, such as those established in response to emergency appeals in countries where there is no effective system of law and order;
- the management and supervision of volunteer staff;
- transactions often undertaken in cash;
- unpredictable patterns of giving by members of the public, both in terms of timing and point of donation;
- the limited involvement of trustees in key decision making or monitoring transactions, and limited engagement with charity staff;
- informal banking or cash transfer methods used in areas remote from conventional banking systems;
- inconsistent regulation across international borders; and
- international transfer of funds.

Auditors are required by ISA (UK and Ireland) 240 to consider whether one or more fraud risk factors are present and to investigate whether unusual or unexpected relationships may indicate risks of material misstatement due to fraud. Analytical procedures may not be easily applied to the audit of charities, as the financial statements can be very difficult to predict.

The Practice Note points out that even where fraud has been reported to the trustees, the audit report must include details of any fundamental uncertainty or disagreement over disclosure of a suspected or actual instance of fraud or error.

The Practice Note lists the various authorities which regulate charities as being the proper authorities to which reports of frauds in the public interest should be made. For example, for charities established in England and Wales, except where exempt, the proper authority is the Charity Commission as well as the Serious Organised Crime Agency (SOCA).

43.8 ISA (UK AND IRELAND) 250 PART A CONSIDERATION OF LAWS AND REGULATIONS IN AN AUDIT OF FINANCIAL STATEMENTS

Because there are laws and regulations specifically made to cover charities and their activities, including laws which affect charities which undertake fundraising, auditors must have an understanding of applicable law and regulation. Auditors must be aware of the risk of money laundering given the relatively large sums of cash which many charities receive.

As in ISA (UK and Ireland) 250, the Practice Note examines this area from the point of view:

- of laws relating directly to the preparation of financial statements; and
- those which provide a legal framework within which the entity conducts its business.

43.8.1 Laws relating directly to the preparation of financial statements

Auditors here must be aware of, in particular, the 2008 Accounts and Reports Regulations and the Charities SORP. In addition, charities may also be subject to Companies Act requirements and those which relate to housing associations.

Auditors should also check whether the charity's governing document contains any special disclosure or reporting requirements.

43.8.2 Laws central to a charity's conduct of business

Guidance is given on the interpretation of 'central' in the context of charities. Laws and regulations are seen to be central by the Practice Note where:

- compliance is a pre-requisite of obtaining a licence to operate; or
- non-compliance may reasonable be expected to result in the entity ceasing operations, or call into question the entity's status as a going concern.

These laws will to a large extent be dependent on the charity's activities. They may be subject to:

- Charities Act requirements relating to fundraising, property and borrowing transaction;
- laws on raising funds through lotteries;
- laws relating to house to house or street collections;
- Trustee Investments Act;
- Children's Act requirements;
- Registered Homes Act;
- Environmental Protection Act; and
- food safety and hygiene regulations.

Auditors must be aware of the objects of the charity and the fact that the Charities Commission has powers to suspend or remove trustees, officers, agents or employees and to freeze the property and appoint a receiver and manager if they consider that the charity's property requires protection.

Auditors must also be aware of tax as, although most activities of a charity do not attract taxation, trading other than directly or indirectly in furtherance of the charity's objects may well give rise to a tax liability. In addition, the VAT position is different to that relating to corporation tax as exemptions do not generally apply.

Furthermore, charities often receive donations tax effectively, through gift aid, payroll giving, and gifts of land and shares. For most tax effective schemes, and especially for gift aid, there are detailed requirements relating to the procedures to be followed by donors and recipient charities, as well as detailed rules designed to prevent abuse.

Similar considerations to those for other companies apply where breaches of law and regulations are found.

43.9   ISA (UK AND IRELAND) 250 PART B THE AUDITOR'S RIGHT AND DUTY TO REPORT TO REGULATORS IN THE FINANCIAL SECTOR

Although the title of ISA (UK and Ireland) 250 section B refers to reports to regulators in the financial sector, the principles and essential procedures included in this ISA apply in respect of the statutory duty and the discretionary right to report to charity regulators in England and Wales and Scotland.

The Charities Act 2006 implements a more consistent whistle-blowing regime. **Table 2** sets out the Charity Commission's and OSCR's guidance on whistle-blowing.

TABLE 2: Charity Commission and OSCR guidance on whistle-blowing

The Charities Act 1993 section 44, as amended by the Charities Act 2006, places a duty on the auditors of both a non-company charity and a company charity to report matters of 'material significance' to the Commission. Section 46 of the Charities and Trustee Investment (Scotland) Act 2005 places a similar duty on auditors of Scottish charities to report matters of 'material significance' to OSCR.

Independent Examiners are subject to similar duties and should refer to CC31 for guidance on their responsibilities in this area.

The duty to report arises where the auditor, in the course of their audit, identifies a matter, which relates to the activities or affairs of the charity or of any connected institution or body, and which the auditor has reasonable cause to believe is likely to be of material significance for the purposes of the exercise by the Commission of its functions under section 8 or 18 of the Charities Act 1993 or the exercise by OSCR of its functions under sections 28, 30 or 31 of the Charities and Trustee Investment (Scotland) Act 2005.

Subject to compliance with money laundering legislation regarding 'tipping off', in the circumstances leading to a right or duty to report, the auditor is entitled to communicate to charity regulators in good faith information or opinions relating to the business or affairs of the entity or any associated body without contravening the duty of confidence owed to the entity. In addition, in England and Wales, the Charities Act 1993 provides additional statutory protection for the auditor as no duty, for example confidentiality, is regarded as contravened merely because of any information or opinion contained in the report.

The reporting of a matter of material significance is a separate report from the auditor's report on the accounts. The Charities Act 1993 and the Charities and Trustee Investment (Scotland) Act 2005 require the report to be made immediately the matter comes to the auditor's attention and in England and Wales the Charities Act 1993 requires that this is done in writing. There is no requirement under Scottish law for a report to be made in writing but it is recommended to do so.

It is not part of the reporting duty to require auditors to perform any additional scrutiny work as a result of the statutory duty nor are they required specifically to seek out reportable matters. Auditors do however include procedures within their planning processes to ensure that members of the audit team have sufficient understanding (in the context of their role) to enable them to identify situations which may give reasonable cause to believe that a matter should be reported to the regulator. Where a matter comes to light relating to a previous financial year which would give rise to a duty to report, then the auditor should still make a report.

In order to recognise whether a situation is likely to be of material significance to a regulator's function an understanding is needed of those matters which either due to their nature or potential financial impact are likely to require evaluation and, where appropriate, investigation by the regulator.

Both the Charity Commission and OSCR will always consider the following to be of material significance and hence reportable:

- matters suggesting dishonesty or fraud involving a significant loss of, or a major risk to, charitable funds or assets;
- failure(s) of internal controls, including failure(s) in charity governance, that resulted in a significant loss or misappropriation of charitable funds, or which leads to significant charitable funds being put at major risk;
- matters leading to the knowledge or suspicion that the charity or charitable funds have been used for money laundering or such funds are the proceeds of serious organised crime or that the charity is a conduit for criminal activity;

- matters leading to the belief or suspicion that the charity, its trustees, employees or assets, have been involved in or used to support terrorism or proscribed organisations in the UK or outside of the UK;
- evidence suggesting that in the way the charity carries out its work relating to the care and welfare of beneficiaries, the charity's beneficiaries have been or were put at significant risk of abuse or mistreatment;
- significant or recurring breach(es) of either a legislative requirement or of the charity's trusts;
- a deliberate or significant breach of an order or direction made by a charity regulator under statutory powers including suspending a charity trustee, prohibiting a particular transaction or activity or granting consent on particular terms involving significant charitable assets or liabilities; and
- the notification on ceasing to hold office or resigning from office, of those matters reported to the charity's trustees.

These matters are considered central to the integrity of a charity and as such will require evaluation and where appropriate investigation by the regulators. The Charity Commission and OSCR consider all such reports to have a very high intelligence value. Both state that they take a risk based and proportionate approach to inquiry work when deciding whether to open an inquiry. The duty to report applies to the auditor who must make a report whether or not the matter has already been notified to other regulators or agencies and whether or not the trustees have already advised the charity regulators, for example, by making a serious incident report to the Charity Commission.

Matters which the Charity Commission and OSCR have indicated are likely to be of material significant are set out on the charity regulators websites. Other sources of information include:

- The Charity Commission's Directions and Guidance for independent examinations;
- Annual Returns (in Scotland, Supplementary Monitoring Returns) which signpost a number of the areas that the relevant regulator considers significant; and
- In England and Wales, any serious incident report made by the trustees to the Charity Commission.

The list of 'serious incidents' is principally concerned with serious criminal or unlawful activity, or very serious incidents concerning a charity that may affect its funds, property, beneficiaries or reputation. Some of the incidents listed may not actually be criminal activity, but do flag up a risk of potential criminal activity or other risks, which if realised, would have a serious detrimental impact on the charity.

There is no serious incident reporting requirement placed on trustees in Scotland.

Where auditors make a report, they may not have all the information but should be prepared to provide as much relevant information as possible about the matter(s) they are reporting.

The auditor also has a broad discretionary right to report matters that they believe may be relevant to the work of the charity regulators but they are not under a duty to report such matters.

Auditors do not need to perform additional work as a result of the statutory duty although they will need to make members of audit teams aware of reportable matters which are likely to be encountered.

Auditors must report matters which they have reasonable cause to believe are, or are likely to be, of material significance in relation to the Commissioners power to institute enquiries or to act for the protection of charities.

Additionally, where auditors cease to hold office, for any reason, they are required to make a statement as to whether there are any matters concerning their ceasing to hold office which should be brought to the attention of the trustees. A copy of this statement should be sent to the Charity Commission.

As in the financial services sector, 'material significance' does not have the same meaning as 'material' in the context of the audit of financial statements. For example, dishonesty by a trustee may not be significant in financial terms but would have a significant effect on the commissioner's consideration of whether the person concerned should be allowed to continue to act as a charity trustee.

For dual registered charities, the auditor's duty to report is to both the Charity Commission and OSCR.

43.10 ISA (UK AND IRELAND) 260 COMMUNICATION OF AUDIT MATTERS WITH THOSE CHARGED WITH GOVERNANCE

The Practice Note suggests that the auditors' work on the charity's system of internal control may identify information on these systems which would assist the trustees in seeking to establish and maintain effective and efficient systems. Even if management letters are addressed to the executives responsible for the day-to-day running of the charity, a copy of the report should be sent to the trustees.

43.11 ISA (UK AND IRELAND) 300 PLANNING AN AUDIT OF FINANCIAL STATEMENTS

Particular issues the auditor considers at the planning stage include:

- the applicable reporting framework including:

  - the legislative requirements e.g. the CA 2006 or, in England and Wales the Charities Act 1993 or, in Scotland the 2005 Act (Scotland);
  - the Charities SORP (or sector specific SORP where one applies);
  - the governing document for the charity, which may also include specific reporting requirements;

- governance arrangements, including planning with the trustees the form and timing of communications;
- operating structures, branches and overseas operations including:

  - the extent to which the charity's activities (either of a fundraising or a charitable nature) are undertaken through branches or overseas activities and the impact this has on the auditors' required knowledge of the business (for example taxation and employment law), their risk assessments and sources of audit evidence, and
  - the structure and management of any related or connected entities, in particular the degree to which the entities are managed and controlled by the trustees and management of the charity;

- the charity's activities in the context of its stated objects and powers, including any limitations the charity's governing document, or terms and restrictions placed on material gifts or donations received;
- the likely impact on the financial statements of the charity of the activities of any related or connected entities (for example, a separate limited company set up to undertake commercial activities for the charity);
- the statutory duty to report matters to the charity regulators including whether members of the audit team have sufficient understanding (in the context of their role) to enable them to identify situations which may give reasonable cause to believe that a matter should be reported to the regulator; and
- whether other auditors' reports are required – for example special reports to funders of the charity, grant donors or EU agencies.

43.12 ISA (UK AND IRELAND) 315 UNDERSTANDING THE ENTITY AND ITS ENVIRONMENT AND ASSESSING THE RISKS OF MATERIAL MISSTATEMENT

Auditors will need knowledge of the special features of charity audits, and in planning they will need to be aware of the following:

- the existence of special regulations governing the conduct of charities;
- sources of income which may include grants from public authorities or funds held on trust. Breaches of the conditions relating to the use of such income can have serious implications to the charity;
- tax relief dependent upon a charity complying with the governing document submitted to the Inland Revenue;
- activities of the charity which bring it within the scope of other regulations, as well as those relating to charities;
- the level of involvement in the administration of the charity which can be expected of trustees; and

- the way in which the charity is managed on a day-to-day basis.

In terms of the regulatory framework the factors considered under ISA (UK and Ireland) 250 Part A above will apply.

Auditors must be aware of the way in which the charity conducts its operations, whether through:

- groups of distinct legal entities;
- associated undertakings;
- what are effectively branches; or
- by subcontracting to non-controlled organisations.

Depending on the structure, the accounting requirements will be different.

Overseas operations can also present difficulty as there is a wide range of structures which charities can adopt. Auditors must determine the legal status and decide whether their accounts need to be incorporated within the main accounts of the charity.

The source of much information about a charity will be its officers and trustees together with its governing document. For larger charities sources of information may include specialist publications and umbrella organisations which provide statistics and industry norms. ISA (UK and Ireland) 315 requires auditors to use their understanding of the entity and its environment to assess the risk of material misstatement in the financial statements and gives details of the areas that auditors of charities should consider.

ISA (UK and Ireland) 315 require auditors to obtain an understanding of the accounting and internal control systems sufficient to plan the audit and develop an effective audit approach. There is a wide variation between different charities in terms of size, activity and organisation so that there can be no standard approach to internal control and risk. Even large national charities with sophisticated control systems may have local branches that are run by voluntary staff on an informal basis.

43.12.1   Inherent risk

A previous version of the Practice Note listed the factors which may affect the auditors' assessment of inherent risk. These include:

- the significance of donations and cash receipts;
- fundraising by non-controlled bodies;
- the extent of donations by credit card or over the internet;
- the valuation of donations in kind;
- uncertainty over completeness of income;
- operational limitations imposed by governing documents;
- restricted funds;

- difficulties in identifying and quantifying liabilities arising from constructive obligations;
- sensitivity of key statistics, such as the proportion of resources used for administration purposes;
- trading activities; and
- complexities of tax rules relating to charities.

43.12.2   Control environment

Auditors must assess the adequacy of controls in relation to the circumstances of each charity. Here, the attitude rather than involvement of the trustees is likely to be fundamental.

The features of a sound control environment – for example, clearly defined authority, segregation of duties, competent staff, budgetary controls – are similar to those that apply in commercial organisations.

Auditors may also need to ensure that there is control over grants made to other bodies.

The Practice Note provides details of factors that auditors should consider when assessing the control environment of a charity. These include the:

- amount of time committed by trustees to the charity's affairs;
- skills and qualifications of individual trustees;
- trustees' understanding of the charity and its legal and regulatory environment;
- the regularity and effectiveness of trustee meetings and the level of attendance at these meetings;
- the adequacy of minutes of trustee meetings;
- independence of trustees from each other;
- the policy on dealing with trustee conflicts;
- supervision by the trustees of relatively informal working arrangements which are common when using volunteers;
- the degree of involvement, by the trustees, in key decision making or monitoring transactions and engagement with charity staff;
- the attitude of trustees to previously identified control weaknesses;
- level of delegation by trustees to senior management and the formality of this delegation; and
- the committee structure of the organisation.

In addition, auditors should review any risk register maintained by the charity to ascertain what the trustees determine to be the business risks faced by the charity and what control systems they have established to mitigate those risks. The auditors' assessment of related business processes, in line with the requirements of ISA (UK and Ireland) 315, should include ensuring that systems accurately capture details of restrictions on income.

43.12.3   *Control activities*

Tables 3 to 7 show examples of control activities which the Practice Note considers may be applicable to charities and of which auditors should gain an understanding to enable them to assess the risk of material misstatement at the assertion level and design further audit procedures responsive to those assessed risks.

TABLE 3: Controls over cash donations

Source	*Examples of Controls*
Collecting boxes and tins	<ul><li>numerical control over boxes and tins</li><li>satisfactory sealing of boxes and tins so that any opening prior to recording cash is apparent</li><li>regular collection and recording of proceeds from collecting boxes</li><li>dual control over counting and recording of proceeds</li><li>public collections are undertaken within legal requirements for public collections</li></ul>
Other cash receipts	<ul><li>clear directions to staff on how to handle cash donations</li><li>advice to donors on where to make donations securely</li></ul>
Postal receipts	<ul><li>unopened mail kept securely</li><li>dual control over the opening of mail</li><li>immediate recording of donations on opening of mail or receipt</li><li>agreement of bank paying in slips to record of receipts by an independent person</li><li>rotation of post opening staff</li></ul>
Receipts over the internet	<ul><li>sending a confirmation receipt to the donor</li><li>controls over the writing up of daybooks</li></ul>
Text giving	<ul><li>IT controls to ensure texts received are processed correctly with a full audit trail maintained</li></ul>

TABLE 4: Controls over other donations

Source	*Examples of controls*
Gift aid/Deeds of Covenant	<ul><li>establish procedures to ensure donations are initially recorded correctly with tax compliance issues being met</li><li>regular checks and follow up procedures to ensure due amounts are received</li><li>regular checks to ensure all tax repayments have been obtained</li></ul>

Source	Examples of controls
	• structured archive system in place to ensure documentation is retained for 7 years
	• procedures for the sale of goods on behalf of donors where gift aid is to be claimed on the sale proceeds
Legacies	• comprehensive correspondence file maintained in respect of each legacy and numerically controlled searches of agency reports of legacies receivable
	• regular reports and follow up procedures undertaken in respect of outstanding legacies
	• security of chattels received as legacies and procedures to establish their value and proper realisation
Donations in kind/ donated services	• in case of charity shops, separation of recording, storage and sale of stock
	• all types of activity: immediate recording of donated assets
	• procedures for recording donated services
	• logging of donated goods for distribution received which are only recognised in the accounts when distributed

TABLE 5: Controls over other income

Source	Examples of controls
Fund-raising activities	• records maintained for each fund-raising event
	• other controls maintained over receipts appropriate to the type of activity and receipt (see Tables **3** and **4**)
	• controls maintained over expenses as for administrative expenses
	• reconciliation of financial aspects of the fundraising database to the general ledger
Grants and loans, including those from government bodies	• regular checks that all sources of income or funds are fully utilised and appropriate claims made
	• ensuring income or funds are correctly applied in accordance with the terms of the grant or loan
	• comprehensive records of applications made and follow up procedures for those not discharged
	• appropriate controls procedures if stipulated by the funding agreement

---

TABLE 6: Controls over fixed assets

Source	*Examples of controls*
Existence of assets	• a register of fixed assets maintained, including donated assets
Valuation	• donated tangible fixed assets recorded at their current value at the date of the gift and then depreciated in line with other assets • donated fixed asset investments recorded at their marketable value at the time of the gift

---

TABLE 7: Controls over use of funds

Source	*Examples of controls*
Restricted funds	• records maintained to identify relevant income, expenditure and assets • appropriate allocation of income generated by restricted funds • terms controlling application of funds • oversight of application of fund monies by independent personnel or trustees
Grants to beneficiaries	• records maintained, as appropriate, of requests for material grants received not paid to beneficiaries and their treatment • appropriate checks made on applications and applicants for grants, and that amounts paid are *intra vires* • records maintained of all grant decisions, checking that proper authority exists, that adequate documentation is presented to decision making meetings, and that any conflicts of interest are recorded • controls to ensure that grants made are properly spent by the recipient for the specified purpose, for example, requirements for returns with supporting documentation or auditors' reports concerning expenditure, or monitoring visits
Related party transactions	• annual declarations of interests received from all trustees • register of interests maintained

---

Where charities have UK or overseas branches, control activities may include:

• regular reports to head office by any branch, office or individual, checks to ensure these are received and a mechanism for monitoring branch activities;
• prompt investigations of any report of the misuse of the charity's name;
• internal controls of a standard equivalent to those in the main charity for any branch where trustees have direct control;
• accounts and procedures manuals for branches;
• acknowledgements of remittances to and from branches abroad;

- clear instructions on receipt and transfer of income to identify the point at which it belongs to the main charity;
- controls over recruitment and appointment of staff to run branch operations;
- controls regarding the opening of bank accounts and the transfer of funds between bank accounts;
- periodic checks from head office or internal audit of material amounts;
- retention of documents for local inspection or for periodic transmission to head office; and
- treasury operations to ensure that overseas funds are held in a hard currency and foreign exchange exposure is minimised.

In accordance with ISA (UK and Ireland) 315 auditors are required to assess the risk of material misstatement at the financial statements level, for classes of transactions, account balances and transactions. There are many factors which may affect the risk of material misstatement in charities including the:

- complexity and extent of regulation;
- valuation of donations in kind;
- uncertainty of future income; and
- special consideration that must be made of restricted funds.

Further examples are provided in the Practice Note. Auditors must then consider whether any of these risks are significant risks for which special audit consideration must be given, including the evaluation of related controls and the planning and performance of related procedures.

43.12.4 Accounting policies

Auditors must review accounting policies and ensure these are in line with the Charities SORP and other accounting standards. Policies that may require particularly careful consideration include those for the recognition of:

- legacies receivable;
- grants receivable as voluntary income;
- grants receivable or payable on performance related conditions;
- liabilities resulting from constructive obligations;
- gifts in kind and donated services; and
- heritage assets.

43.13   ISA (UK AND IRELAND) 320 AUDIT MATERIALITY

Materiality should be considered with regard to the applicable laws and regulations and any additional reports the auditors are required to make – for example, in respect to restricted funds. The general principles underlying the consideration of materiality apply to audits of charities in a similar way to other entities.

43.14 ISA (UK AND IRELAND) 330 THE AUDITOR'S PROCEDURES IN RESPONSE TO ASSESSED RISKS

ISA (UK and Ireland) 330 requires auditors to plan and perform specific audit procedures where they have identified a significant risk of material misstatement. Common areas for the risk of material misstatement for charities are:

- ensuring completeness of incoming resources;
- overseas operations; and
- restricted funds.

Completeness of income

Typically income from charities comes from a number of different sources, such as grants and public donations, and its amount and timing is often difficult to predict. Trustees cannot be expected to have responsibility for funds until they are, or should be, within the control of the charity, but as soon as this happens, trustees should implement procedures to ensure appropriate recording and safeguarding of the funds.

The Practice Note suggests the following possible substantive procedures for completeness of incoming resources:

- to check for a loss of incoming resources through fraud, auditors can assess and test the sorts of controls described in section **43.11.3** for appeals and 'non-routine' sources, and compare donations actually received to past results for similar appeals and statistics for response rates for charities in general;
- where professional fundraisers have been used to generate funds, auditors can review terms of the agreement between the charity and the fundraiser and other relevant documentation to ensure that all funds have been accounted for;
- check the arrangements for the transferral of funds from branches, associates or subsidiaries to the main charity, to determine when funds are recognised;
- review correspondence with solicitors to determine when legacy income is reasonably certain, its value can be measured and it can therefore be recorded. These criteria will normally be met following probate and once the executor of the estate has established that there are sufficient assets, after settling liabilities, to pay the legacy. Certainty and measurability may also be affected by events such as valuations and disputes. The Auditor therefore reviews information up to when the accounts are approved for evidence relating to legacies receivable existing at the balance sheet date;
- where informal groups raise funds for a charity, without the charity's knowledge, charities have no obligation to record the income until it is

received, and so auditors should ensure that funds are not recorded prior to this time;

- examination of grant applications and correspondence to determine completeness of grant income, including direct confirmation about the amounts receivable from the grant provider; and
- auditors should consider the procedures in place for recognising and valuing non-cash donations, such as goods and services. They should also review the disclosures in the financial statements regarding the basis of valuation of non-cash donations to ensure it is reasonable.

Substantive procedures may be limited by the uncertainty affecting donations, but they may be of use to corroborate other evidence.

Overseas operations

Where overseas operations exist, auditors will be required to obtain evidence of material expenditure overseas and gain an understanding of when overseas expenditure has occurred. Where the overseas operations are part of the charity, the expenditure will not be incurred when money is transferred to the overseas branch, but when the expenditure is actually made by that branch.

The Bulletin suggests the following procedures:

- consideration of internal control procedures put in place by the charity, and how adherence to procedures is monitored;
- obtaining evidence from field officers' reports as to work undertaken;
- comparison of accounting returns of expenditure with field reports and plans for consistency and reasonableness;
- analytical review of accounting returns received from overseas branches or local agents;
- consideration of any inspection or internal control visit reports undertaken by any internal audit function;
- consideration of audit work undertaken by local auditors, and consideration of any audit reports carried out on behalf of international donors, for example government departments; and
- evidence from the audit work of another audit firm.

Where material assets are held or material funds are applied by overseas operations, the Practice Note suggests that auditors may seek observational evidence by way of site visit.

Where a charity makes a grant to an autonomous overseas charity, auditors ensure:

- receipt of the funding; and
- that the charity has exercised reasonable diligence in ensuring that the funds are used for charitable purposes.

Restricted funds

Restricted funds which are subject to specific rules about their application may give rise to a significant risk of material misstatement. Auditors should consider:

- the terms or conditions attached to the restricted funds;
- any funds in deficit;
- any income funds held in illiquid assets, preventing application of the fund; and
- capital being expended without authority.

The Practice Note suggests the following audit procedures:

- consideration of internal control procedures put in place by the charity to identify restricted funds;
- consideration of the methods used in cost allocation;
- comparison of expenditure with the terms of the restricted funds;
- consideration of the future funding to recover negative balances;
- consideration of the validity of the transfer between funds;
- consideration of the ability of the fund to meets its obligations in view of its underlying assets; and
- consideration of whether the capital of an endowed fund has been expended without express authority.

43.15   ISA (UK AND IRELAND) 402 AUDIT CONSIDERATIONS RELATING TO ENTITIES USING SERVICE ORGANIZATIONS

The requirements for auditors to review arrangements between charities and their service organisations does not vary from that which exists where a company is audited.

The use of service organisations by charities is not uncommon and includes services provided to the charity such as:

- maintenance of accounting records and payroll services;
- fundraising; and
- custodianship of assets, and investment management services.

43.16   ISA (UK AND IRELAND) 505 EXTERNAL CONFIRMATIONS

Some charities will have bank accounts in overseas locations. In this situation, the auditor considers the format of the request for information to ensure it will be fully understood by the bank.

The auditor should also assess the implications of failures of overseas banks to rely to requests for information, and whether these should be reported to those charged with governance.

43.17   ISA (UK AND IRELAND) 510 INITIAL ENGAGEMENTS – OPENING BALANCES AND CONTINUING ENGAGEMENTS – OPENING BALANCES

Because of the possibility that charities will qualify by reason of size for an audit where previously they were exempt, cases will arise where charities will not have had opening balances audited and the receipts and payments basis of accounting may have been used.

Where there has been a change in the basis of accounting, procedures may include checking bank statements, reviewing receipts and payments after the year end and physically checking any tangible fixed assets. For analytical review procedures, the auditors are likely to need to adjust the prior year management information prepared on a receipts and payments basis to enable a proper comparison.

43.18   ISA (UK AND IRELAND) 520 ANALYTICAL PROCEDURES

The Note sets out certain analytical procedures which auditors may find useful:

- comparison of actual income and expenditure to prior year figures and trends;
- comparison of actual to budgeted results;
- comparison of actual income to successful bids, legacy notifications and potential legacies reported in the minutes;
- comparison of actual expenditure to the auditors own estimate of expenditure;
- comparison of results of an individual branch to those of similar branches of the main charity;

- checking charity shop sales revenue between different periods and to other shops operating in similar locations;
- analyses of efficiency ratios such as staff or administration costs as a percentage of benefits delivered or grants made; and
- comparison of actual donations received to the amount which would be expected on the basis of available charity statistics.

43.19   ISA (UK AND IRELAND) 540 AUDIT OF ACCOUNTING ESTIMATES

Accounting estimates in the financial statements of charities should be audited using similar principles to other entities, bearing in mind the accounting requirements of the SORP. Examples of instances where estimates may be used include:

- the quantification of future charitable commitments and constructive liabilities;
- valuations of gifts in kind, particularly property;
- valuation of assets received for onwards distribution;
- valuation of fixed asset investments where no market price exists;
- valuation of heritage assets;
- valuation of intangible income derived from donated services or use of facilities;
- estimates of on-going service potential of fixed assets, in the absence of a cash flow, in an impairment review; and
- recoverability of loans made to beneficiaries in the furtherance of a charity's objects.

Auditors will ensure that techniques selected by the trustees enable the financial statements to give a true and fair view and that the financial statements disclose a description of the estimation techniques used, in order to comply with FRS 18, *Accounting Policies* and the Charities SORP.

43.20   ISA (UK AND IRELAND) 545 AUDITING FAIR VALUE MEASUREMENTS AND DISCLOSURES

While there are few references in the SORP to fair value, there are a number of areas where the application of ISA 545 may be helpful, including:

- the valuation of defined benefit pension schemes. Charities also have the specific complexities of allocating pension deficits/assets between funds and the effect of these deficits/assets on their free reserves;
- the need to recognise material grant commitments at their present value in the balance sheet;

- the need to recognise all investments (apart from programme related investments) at market value;
- the option to recognise tangible fixed assets at valuation;
- the need to recognise some heritage assets at valuation;
- the need to fair value the assets and liabilities acquired where acquisition accounting is applied (in this situation, the due diligence process may only provide limited information on the fair value of some assets such as land and buildings and heritage assets);
- the need to recognise gifts in kind (apart from second hand goods donated for resale) at a reasonable estimate of their gross value to the charity and donated services and facilities at a reasonable estimate of the value to the charity of the service or facility received.

The auditor considers the processes management have adopted for determining the fair values of these assets and liabilities and the reasonableness of these valuations. The auditor assesses the reasonableness of the valuations by comparisons with the sales value of similar assets (where these values are publicly available), gains or losses being recognised by other charities which hold similar assets, sector indices and market trends.

43.21   ISA (UK AND IRELAND) 550 RELATED PARTIES

It is a fundamental principle of trust law that a trustee should not benefit directly or indirectly from his or her trust. Neither charity trustees nor persons connected with them should transact business with the charity unless expressly permitted by the charities governing document or an appropriate authority. There are also disclosure requirements in the Charities SORP and in the regulations.

43.22   ISA (UK AND IRELAND) 560 SUBSEQUENT EVENTS

The determination after the balance sheet date of the amount of a gift aid payment to a parent charity by a subsidiary undertaking, if the subsidiary had a present legal or constructive obligation at the balance sheet date, is an adjusting post balance sheet event.

43.23   ISA (UK AND IRELAND) 570 GOING CONCERN

This can be a difficult area in the audit of charities as many charities have an apparent financial weakness which is often compounded by the uncertainty of future income. Their ability to raise revenue will often be outside their direct control, and be dependent on such matters as the voting of grants and spending of the public.

It may also be difficult for a charity to cut back on a project or grant funding in the event of a liquidity problem, and although it may have an apparently large bank balance it may be unable to meet general liabilities because the balance in question belongs to a restricted fund.

The Practice Note provides examples of conditions which may indicate that the charity is not a going concern. These include:

- inability to finance its operations from its own resources or unrestricted funds;
- decision by the trustees to curtail or cease activities;
- transfer to, or take-over by, another entity of the charity's activities;
- loss of essential resources or key staff;
- existence of tax liabilities which cannot be met from existing resources;
- deficits on unrestricted funds;
- loss of clients, for example where a public authority ends a practice or contract to refer (and pay for) clients to the charity;
- loss of operating licence;
- significant changes in strategy of major funders and significant decline in donations by the public;
- investigation by a charity regulator;
- loans made to subsidiaries which cannot be repaid;
- claw-back of grant received and gift aid refunds;
- reliance on major donors;
- failure to meet reserves policy targets; and
- persistent failure to meet the requirement for public benefit, leading to withdrawal of funding or tax liabilities.

Similar considerations apply to charities as to commercial entities. Auditors must assess whether there is sufficient disclosure of relevant circumstances to enable financial statements to give a true and fair view on this issue. The trustees' report may also contain disclosures giving indications of factors such as future expected income based on past donations or patterns of giving.

In considering going concern, the Practice Note suggests it may be helpful for the auditors to include the following points in discussions with trustees:

- the nature of management information systems covering future income and expenditure;
- shortfall of identifiable future income on forecast expenditure needing to be made up by voluntary donations of cash or other resources;
- where the charity relies on a major donor, whether it is practical to obtain comfort in relation to their future support;
- level of uncommitted reserves available;

- lists of projects supported or awards made in the year and planned for the following year;
- the reliability of the budget and cash-flow forecast for the coming year, based on past experience and the certainty of inflows and outflows;
- any reliance on support by the charity's bankers, major donors, or public authorities;
- concentration on the provision of services to a particular category of beneficiaries or objects for which future funding or demand may be limited; and
- any special operating licences or similar conditions.

The going concern concept does not apply to the preparation of financial statements on a receipts and payments basis (allowed for small non limited company charities in England and Wales which are within the income thresholds defined by legislation). In these circumstances auditors should consider whether there are matters that affect the charities' ability to continue operational existence for the foreseeable future. Auditors should not issue their report unless they are satisfied with explanations received from trustees concerning future funding arrangements. If they are not satisfied they may find it appropriate to include an explanatory paragraph in their report. They will not qualify their report on the proper presentation of the receipts and payments account.

43.24 ISA (UK AND IRELAND) 580 MANAGEMENT REPRESENTATIONS

A representation letter in respect of the financial statements of the charity is normally signed by the trustees who are responsible for the contents and presentation of the financial statements.

Where day to day management of the charity is delegated to senior management by trustees and representations are taken from those staff, auditors should ensure that the staff involved have the necessary authority and all such representations are considered and approved by the trustees.

43.25 ISA (UK AND IRELAND) 600 USING THE WORK OF ANOTHER AUDITOR

Where other auditors are used because they act for local branches, subsidiaries or other units, principal auditors must assess the degree of reliance they intend to place on the other auditors' work. Where the charity is a limited company, there is a statutory obligation on auditors of any subsidiary undertaking that is a company to communicate such information and explanations as may be reasonably required by the principal auditors. Where the charity is unincorporated, auditors have rights under s44(1)(d) of the 1993 Act of access to books, documents and records which relate to the charity. This extends beyond those actually in the ownership of the charity. Generally, the principal auditors will take steps including:

- agreeing with the client a standard mandate to be issued to the secondary auditors covering the scope of work to be undertaken and reports to be issued;
- issuing a standard questionnaire to be completed by the subsidiary auditors; and
- obtaining a report of principal findings direct from subsidiary auditors.

Similar considerations apply where auditors rely on the work of others to undertake audit work relating to overseas branches or subsidiaries of a charity.

43.26 ISA (UK AND IRELAND) 700 THE AUDITOR'S REPORT ON FINANCIAL STATEMENTS

The 2008 regulations determine that audit reports should be addressed to the trustees unless the auditor has been appointed by the Charity Commission. Companies and Friendly Societies statutes require audit reports to be addressed to the members. Scottish law requires company audit reports to be addressed to trustees and members.

The trustees' responsibilities may vary depending upon the constitution of the particular charity. The Companies Act and the Friendly and Industrial and Provident Societies Act establish duties under law. Where a charity is not subject to other regulation, the Practice Note recommends the form of words shown in **Table 8.**

TABLE 8: Example statement of trustees' responsibilities

'The law applicable to charities in England & Wales/Scotland/Northern Ireland requires the trustees to prepare financial statements for each financial year which give a true and fair view of the state of affairs of the charity and of the incoming resources and application of resources of the charity for that period. In preparing these financial statements, the trustees are required to:

- select suitable accounting policies and then apply them consistently;
- observe the methods and principles in the Charities SORP;
- make judgments and estimates that are reasonable and prudent;
- state whether applicable accounting standards have been followed, subject to any material departures disclosed and explained in the financial statements;
- prepare the financial statements on the going concern basis unless it is inappropriate to presume that the charity will continue in business.

The trustees are responsible for keeping proper accounting records that disclose with reasonable accuracy at any time the financial position of the charity and enable them to ensure that the financial statements comply with the [Charities Act

---

1993, the Charity (Accounts and Reports) Regulations 2008 and the provisions of the trust deed] [2]. They are also responsible for safeguarding the assets of the charity and hence for taking reasonable steps for the prevention and detection of fraud and other irregularities.'

Where charities are required to prepare statements which show a true and fair view then compliance with accounting standards is necessary.

The Practice Note puts forward the argument that since the Charities SORP has been developed and issued under the code of practice established by the Accounting Standards Board for the production and issue of SORPs it is authoritative guidance on the application of accounting standards to charities.

As the 1993 Act requires trustees to state whether financial statements have been prepared in accordance with SORP this provision, taken with the general status of the SORP, implies a strong presumption that the financial statements will need to follow the SORP in order to give a true and fair view.

In addition, FRS 2 and the SORP indicate that it is necessary for a reporting entity to prepare consolidated financial statements in certain circumstances.

Bulletin 2009/3 was issued by the APB to provide examples of certain opinions for accounting periods commencing on or after 6 April 2008 (for accounting periods commencing prior to this date, auditors should refer to Bulletin 2009/1). Auditors should refer to the relevant bulletin when drafting their audit report. It should be noted that revised guidance is expected to be issued by the APB in respect of accounting periods ending on or after the 15 December 2010.

43.27 ISA (UK AND IRELAND) 720 PART A OTHER INFORMATION IN DOCUMENTS CONTAINING AUDITED FINANCIAL STATEMENTS AND PART B THE AUDITORS STATUTORY REPORTING RESPONSIBILITY IN RELATION TO DIRECTORS' REPORTS

The Practice Note lists the types of other information that may be in documents containing audited financial statements.

The Charities SORP requires trustees of charities with gross income exceeding £500,000 to state in their report that the major identified risks to which the

---

[2] For Scottish charities, the references should be substituted with the Charities and Trustee Investments (Scotland) Act 2005, the Charities Accounts (Scotland) Regulations 2006 and the provisions of the charity's constitution.

charity is exposed have been reviewed and that systems have been put in place to manage such risks. Smaller charities are not required to give this information, but it is considered good practice to make a statement about risk assessment and management. Whilst auditors are not expected to verify any risk management statement made by trustees, they should consider the disclosures made in relation to their knowledge of the charity's circumstances and systems.

Auditors of charitable companies must disclose in their report if, in their opinion, the trustees' report is consistent with the financial statements. Auditors of non-company charities only need to report where, in their opinion, the trustees' report is not consistent with the financial statements

43.28   SUMMARISED FINANCIAL STATEMENTS

The Practice Note contains guidance on auditors' reports on summarised financial statements produced by charities.

Where the charity is unincorporated there is no statutory requirement for auditors to report on summarised financial statements, but the SORP states that where the summarised version has been derived from the full accounts there should be an accompanying statement of their consistency from the auditors or independent examiners. Where the charity is incorporated the requirements of s427 of the Companies Act regarding non-statutory financial statements also apply.

Inconsistency may be indicated by:

- inaccurate extraction from the full financial statements;
- summarising information in such a way that it becomes unduly selective; and
- omission of fundamental information.

Where the auditors' report on the full financial statements was qualified, the Practice Note suggests that auditors may wish to refer to the matter in their report on the summarised financial statements.

An example of an auditors' report on summarised financial statements is shown in **Table 9**.

TABLE 9: Auditors' statement on summarised financial statements

Independent auditors' statement to the trustees of XYZ charity

We have examined the summarised financial statements of XYZ charity.

Respective responsibilities of trustees and auditors

The trustees are responsible for preparing the summarised financial statements in accordance with the recommendations of the Charities SORP.

Our responsibility is to report to you our opinion on the consistency of the summary financial statements with the full financial statements and Trustees' Annual Report. We also read the other information contained in the [*summarised Annual Report*] and consider the implications for our report if we become aware of any apparent misstatements or material inconsistencies with the summary financial statement. [3]

Basis of opinion

We conducted our work in accordance with Bulletin 2008/3 issued by the Auditing Practices Board.

Opinion

In our opinion the summarised financial statements are consistent [are not consistent] with the full financial statements and Trustees' Annual Report of XYZ charity for the year ended 31 December 20. [in the following respects . . .].

Statutory auditor
Address
Date

Following the revision to ISA (UK and Ireland) 700 in March 2009, the format of the standard company audit report has changed (see **Chapter 3**). Until guidance is forthcoming on a revision to the format for Charity reports we have retained the version previously used.

43.29 AUDIT EXEMPTION REPORTS

The effect of the Charities Act 2006 s77 order is to make charitable companies which elect for exemption from audit under the Companies Act subject instead to the Charities Act requirements for audit or examination. Therefore audit exemption reports no longer apply to limited companies which are charities for accounting periods commencing on or after 6 April 2008.

---

[3] Auditors may include a 'Bannerman Statement' as part of the opening section of their report (see **3.20**).

44 PENSION SCHEMES

44.1 GUIDANCE FOR AUDITORS OF PENSION SCHEMES

Pension schemes operate in a complex legal environment and the APB has provided specific guidance to auditors of schemes in Practice Note 15 *The Audit of Occupational Pension Schemes in the United Kingdom,* most recently revised in March 2007.

This chapter is intended to guide auditors of pension schemes to the key items addressed in PN15 and to provide details of where other relevant information can be obtained.

44.2 LEGAL BACKGROUND

ISA (UK and Ireland) 250 *Consideration of Law and Regulations in an Audit of Financial Statements* sets out auditors' responsibilities to consider laws and regulations. The legislative framework for pension schemes is dominated by the Pension Schemes Act 1993, the Pensions Act 1995 ('PA 1995'), the Pensions Act 2004 ('PA 2004') and Regulations that accompany them. The subsequent Pensions Act 2007 ('PA 2007') and Pensions Act 2008 ('PA 2008') are also relevant for background knowledge but with less direct impact on pension scheme auditors.

The Pensions Schemes Act 1993 is consolidating legislation addressing the contracting out of the additional element of the state scheme (currently the State Second Pension) and the protection of members through the disclosure of information to them and by placing restrictions on employer-related investment.

The PA 2007 is primarily concerned with the provision of state pensions including the change in state pension age, increasing from 65 to 68 over the period 2024 to 2046.

The PA 2008 introduces requirements on employers to auto-enrol all employees into qualifying workplace pension schemes (including 'personal accounts') from 2012 and establishes the mechanisms for setting up the 'personal account' pension arrangements at that time.

PA 1995 and PA 2004 are both reforming legislation and primarily enabling Acts with detailed requirements set out in Regulations made under them. The principal Regulations that pension scheme auditors need to be aware of are:

- The Occupational Pension Schemes (Disclosure of Information) Regulations 1996 ('the Disclosure Regulations');
- The Occupational Pension Schemes (Scheme Administration) Regulations 1996 ('the Administration Regulations');
- The Occupational Pension Schemes (Requirement to obtain Audited Accounts and a Statement from the Auditor) Regulations 1996 ('the Audited Accounts Regulations'); and
- The Administration Regulations and the Audited Accounts Regulations have been subsequently amended by The Occupational Pension Schemes (Administration and Audited Accounts) (Amendment) Regulations 2005 ('the Amending Regulations').

PA 1995, PA 2004 and the Regulations set out the basis on which auditors are appointed, auditors' responsibilities and the form and content of pension scheme financial statements and annual reports. They also set out responsibilities for trustees such as obtaining the annual report and financial statements and the establishment and operation of internal controls.

PA 2004 also introduced The Pensions Regulator ('the Regulator'). The Regulator replaced the Occupational Pensions Regulatory Authority ('OPRA') from April 2005.

The Regulator, which is sometimes abbreviated to 'TPR' or 'tPR', has a range of powers, which include issuing:

- codes of practice, as explained further below;
- improvement notices: the ability to prevent those responsible for the scheme contravening pensions legislation;
- third party notices: the ability to take action against a third party who is preventing a person from complying with the law;
- contribution notices: to order contributions from parties attempting to avoid employer debt to a defined benefit scheme; and
- financial support directions: to secure financial support from a party associated with the principal employer if the employer is either a service organisation or insufficiently funded.

Codes of practice are primarily directed at trustees. They are not statements of law, but are an indication of what is considered to be best practice. Any departure from them should, therefore, be justifiable and not be in breach of any underlying legal requirements. All professionals involved with pension schemes should be aware of the codes of practice and should refer regularly to the Pension Regulator's website (*www.thepensionsregulator.gov.uk*). There have been 12 codes of practice issued to date. Those which are particularly relevant to the responsibilities and work of a pension scheme auditor are:

01   Reporting breaches of the law
03   Funding defined benefits
05   Reporting late payment of contributions to occupational money purchase
      schemes
07   Trustee knowledge and understanding
09   Internal controls

The codes of practice referred to above are explained in more detail in the relevant parts of this chapter.

In explaining the legal environment in which pension schemes operate, code of practice 01 refers to 'enactments or rule of law', which are broadly defined to include the Theft Act, trust law and common law. Auditors of pension schemes must, therefore, maintain an understanding of many legal requirements. In addition, there must also be familiarity with the scheme's own rules and regulations which are set out in the trust deed and rules.

44.3 ACCOUNTING GUIDANCE

The accounting guidance for pension schemes is contained in the Statement of Recommended Practice *Financial Reports of Pension Schemes* ('the SORP'). The SORP is issued by the Pensions Research Accountants Group ('PRAG') who also issue other guidance for the accounting and governance of pension schemes. Auditors of pension schemes should refer to the PRAG website (*www.prag.org.uk*) for details of the latest guidance.

The current version of the SORP was issued in May 2007 and applies to periods commencing on or after 6 April 2007.

Auditors are required by Regulation 3 of the Audited Accounts Regulations to report whether the financial statements contain the information specified in the Schedule to those Regulations. The Schedule sets out the format in which the financial information should be presented and certain disclosures that need to be made. One disclosure is whether the financial statements have been prepared in accordance with the SORP and if not, an indication of material departures.

PN15 explains that it is normally necessary to follow the guidance in the SORP in order for pension scheme accounts to show a true and fair view. Auditors must, therefore, be familiar with the requirements of the SORP and be prepared to refer to any material non-compliance with it in the audit opinion.

44.4 SCHEMES EXEMPT FROM AUDIT

A number of categories of scheme are exempt under the Administration Regulations from the requirement to appoint an auditor. The principal exemptions relate to:

- occupational schemes with fewer than two members;
- certain public sector schemes;
- occupational money purchase small schemes (prior to the Finance Act 2004 and the Amending Regulations these were known as Small Self Administered Schemes or 'SSASs') meeting specified criteria in respect of unanimous decision making and membership of the trustee board;
- occupational schemes in which the only benefits provided are death benefits and under which no member has accrued rights; and
- unfunded occupational schemes.

Any of the above schemes may be audited on a 'voluntary basis', for example where the trustees request an audit to be performed or where the scheme rules require an audit.

In addition, schemes which invest only in one or more insurance policies which specifically allocate benefits to individual members ('ear-marked' schemes) only require an auditor's statement about contributions.

44.5 CONSIDERATION OF FRAUD

Although PN15 comments that the risk of fraudulent financial reporting is low given the nature of pension schemes it also states that the potential for fraud cannot be ignored. The most likely risk is the misappropriation of assets and PN15 explains that, even if activities are delegated, the trustees retain responsibility for the prevention and detection of fraud.

Examples of the type of fraud that may occur in a pension scheme are:

- misappropriation of assets;
- non-payment of employee and/or employer contributions to the scheme;
- use of assets of the scheme either directly or as collateral for borrowing by either the employer or an associate of the employer;
- misapplication of the assets of a scheme to meet the obligations and expenses of either another scheme or of the sponsoring employer;
- dealing in scheme assets by the investment manager without the required mandate or authorisation;
- lending of scheme assets by the custodian without authorisation;
- exchange of assets without sufficient valuable consideration (for example selling assets such as property at below market value);
- assets of the scheme used for the personal preferment of the trustees or used for the personal preferment of an individual scheme member;

- benefit claims by members or their beneficiaries to which they are not entitled (for example failure to notify a scheme of the death of a true beneficiary); and
- creation of fictitious scheme records by the administrator (for example dummy beneficiary records).

PN15 states that auditors usually rebut the presumption that revenue recognition gives rise to a risk of material misstatement due to fraud. This is due to the nature of the income, the not-for-profit nature of a pension scheme and the limited scope for revenue manipulation.

There are circumstances that increase the risk of fraud and auditors need to be aware of these when planning the audit. These include:

- trustees or scheme management displaying a significant disregard for the various regulatory authorities;
- trustees or scheme management having little or no involvement in the day-to-day administration of the scheme;
- trustees or scheme management having ready access to the scheme's assets and an ability to override any internal controls;
- trustees or scheme management failing to put in place arrangements to monitor activities undertaken by third parties, including the employer;
- trustees or scheme management displaying a lack of candour in dealings with members, the actuary or the auditors on significant matters affecting scheme assets;
- the sponsoring employer operating in an industry with increasing business failures, or itself having financial difficulties; and
- significant levels, or unusual types, of related-party transactions (including employer-related investments) involving unaudited entities or entities audited by other firms.

To properly assess the above circumstances, scheme auditors should be communicating with the trustees and those responsible for the management of the scheme, conducting analytical procedures and holding a fraud brain-storming discussion. As with all other entities, an appropriate response to identified fraud risks should be determined and management representation sought on fraud.

44.6 COMMUNICATION WITH TRUSTEES

Scheme auditors must ensure that there is interaction with trustees at various stages of the audit. As well as being a requirement of ISA (UK and Ireland) 260 *Communication of audit matters with those charged with governance*, it is fundamental to the planning of the audit and compliance with ISA (UK and Ireland) 315 *Understanding the entity and its environment and assessing the risks of material misstatements*.

Auditors will communicate with the trustees on a range of matters including:

- independence;
- scope of the audit, the audit plan and any additional procedures;
- timetable;
- fees;
- access to third parties and information;
- fraud;
- procedures, controls and internal audit;
- establishing expectations for analytical procedures and discussing the results of such procedures;
- changes to the scheme;
- issues arising from a review of the minutes;
- unadjusted errors other than those that are clearly trivial; and
- communication with the Regulator.

As part of their assessment and communication of matters concerning their independence, scheme auditors should also consider services provided to the sponsoring employer of the scheme. Guidance issued in 2008 by the Regulator highlights trustees' responsibilities to assess and manage conflicts of interest, including advisor conflicts.

At the end of the audit process auditors will also communicate with trustees. Trustees should be notified of all breaches of duties relevant to the administration of the scheme discovered in the course of the audit work. These duties include those imposed by any enactment or rule of law on the trustees or managers, the employer, any professional adviser or any prescribed person acting in connection with the scheme. The notification to the trustees should be made, regardless of whether the matter gave rise to a statutory duty to report to the Regulator. If there are no matters that need to be notified, the trustees should be advised in writing accordingly.

44.7 CONTROL ACTIVITIES

ISA (UK and Ireland) 315 *Understanding the entity and its environment and assessing the risks of material misstatement* requires auditors to understand the systems and controls of entities being audited. PN15 sets out the features of an effective control environment, examples of control activities and the factors that increase the risk of material misstatement. In considering the risk of material misstatement, auditors should refer to the appendices of PN15 which explain the risks which apply to different benefit structures.

Auditors should also consider the ability of the trustees and in doing so reference should be made to code of practice 07 'Trustee Knowledge and Understanding'. The Regulator intends that trustees should, amongst other areas, be familiar with their powers and the manner in which their scheme operates. The code of practice explains how trustees might approach the task of determining the elements of knowledge and understanding which are appropriate for them and how they might acquire the knowledge and understanding needed. This is, therefore, a part of the assessment of the environment. Many pension schemes delegate activities, most commonly administration and investment management, to third parties. Of particular relevance to pension scheme auditors is, therefore, ISA (UK and Ireland) 402 *Audit considerations relating to entities using service organisations*. The responsibility for the operation of the scheme does, however, remain with the trustees when they have outsourced activities and they are responsible for ensuring that scheme has appropriate procedures and controls. Any weaknesses or gaps in the controls operated by trustees may lead to additional audit risk. In such circumstances, auditors will need to design audit procedures to address that risk.

It must be emphasised that the systems and control activities that need to be understood are those operated by the trustees and which are under their direct control. Section 249A of PA 2004 and *The Occupational Pension Schemes (Internal Control) Regulations 2005* impose on trustees a statutory obligation to operate internal controls and in considering the internal controls auditors should refer to code of practice 09 Internal Controls and the PRAG Publication, 'Outsourcing for Trustees'.

It is necessary for scheme auditors to gain an understanding of how the scheme's use of a service organisation affects the scheme's internal control. The following should, therefore, be documented and understood:

- the services provided;
- selection procedures;
- contractual terms and the relationship;
- contingency plans;
- interaction of the control systems of the scheme and the service organisation;
- the scheme's controls relevant to the service organisation and how risks are identified and controlled;
- the capability of the service organisation; and
- information available to the trustees in respect of the service organisation's operations including general and IT controls.

The directors of the service organisation may provide information to the trustees by producing an 'internal control report' in accordance with *AAF 01/06 Assurance report on internal controls of service organisations made available to third parties* ('AAF 01/06') (see **Chapter 42**).

The essential content of an internal control report under AAF 01/06 is for the service organisation to explain how control procedures achieve control objectives. Control objectives are set by the management of the service organisation, but AAF 01/06 provides mandatory objectives for pension scheme administrators, custodians and investment managers. An internal control report produced under AAF 01/06 will also contain a report from a Reporting Accountant providing an opinion on the fairness of the description and the design and operating effectiveness of control procedures.

Trustees should seek to obtain such reports from service providers and incorporate the assessment of them into their control procedures.

Having gained an understanding of the service organisation's controls, it may be concluded that these controls do not impact on the overall assessment of the audit risk in respect of the scheme. This could, for example, be because either the activities are not significant to the audit of the scheme or because the trustees have appropriate controls in place over their use of the service organisation.

If, however, the activities of the service organisation do result in audit risk, appropriate audit procedures will need to be designed. The nature of the procedures will be specific to each scheme and are dependant upon the service and the risks that have been assessed. Access to the service organisation will not always be necessary as the trustees may either hold sufficient documentation, or the service organisation provides periodic reports which contain adequate information. The internal control reports provided to trustees may also provide useful information to the scheme auditor.

44.8 CONTRIBUTIONS

Scheme auditors are required by the Audited Accounts Regulations to make a statement about contributions. This is separate to the opinion that is given on the financial statements. The statement for periods beginning on or after 22 September 2005 is whether contributions have, in all material respects, been paid at least in accordance with the payment schedule or the schedule of contributions.

Auditors need to understand the basis under which contributions are paid to the scheme by the employer. Money purchase schemes are required to have a payment schedule under s87 of PA 1995 and a defined benefit scheme is required to have a schedule of contributions under s58 of PA 1995 ('the schedule(s)').

Pension scheme auditors need to be familiar with the form and content of the schedule relevant to the scheme. Since 2005 contributions to defined benefit schemes come under the 'scheme specific funding' regime, which replaced the previous minimum funding requirements.

The schedule of contributions must be prepared in accordance with the Occupational Pension Schemes (Scheme Funding) Regulations 2005 and is required to show separately any deficit funding and 'other' contributions due from the employer. It must also be signed by the trustees and the employer.

Auditors need to ascertain when a schedule becomes effective. PN15 provides guidance on the issues that need to be considered, but it is important to be aware that a schedule of contributions cannot be effective until it is certified by the actuary and that it cannot be backdated.

Code of practice 03 'Funding defined benefits' and code of practice 05 'Reporting late payment of contributions to occupational money purchase schemes' provide guidance for trustees on the monitoring of contributions and the reporting responsibilities in the event of late or incorrect payments being made.

In order to make their statement about contributions, auditors must obtain the schedule and undertake procedures to obtain sufficient appropriate evidence to conclude whether or not contributions payable have, in all material respects, been paid at least for the amounts and within the timeframe set out in the schedule.

Auditors need to consider a range of issues, including:

- changes in rates of contributions payable and the extent to which these have been included in the schedule;
- changes in the definition of salary on which the contributions are based;
- whether the schedule is sufficiently clear;
- whether the schedule complies with legal requirements and guidance issued by the Regulator;
- whether there have been any member complaints about incorrect contributions;
- the scheme's systems for recording and monitoring contributions; and
- any reports to the Regulator of late or inaccurate contributions.

As the statement about contributions is separate to the audit opinion, PN15 indicates that it should be a separate report. PN15 also recommends that a summary of contributions paid during the scheme year under the schedule is produced by the trustees and included with the annual report ('the summary').

The summary, an example of which is included in the appendices to PN15, shows details of contributions payable during the year together with a reconciliation to the contributions shown in the fund account. The significance of the summary is that it enables the reader of the annual report and financial statements to identify which contributions the auditor's statement refers to.

As the schedule refers to both the quantum and the timing of the payment of contributions, materiality must be considered in terms of both value and time. It is normal to apply materiality to values and the pension scheme auditor should consider this in the same manner as for any other transaction stream. The application of materiality to timing is more complex.

The application of materiality is a matter of judgement for individual pension scheme auditors and the only guidance provided by PN15 is that there should be regard to the frequency of the breaches and the cumulative, as well as the individual, impact of the breaches.

In considering the application of materiality to timing there are, however, some salient factors which may be considered:

- the statement about contributions is on an aggregate basis and so materiality should not be applied based on the perception of a single member's contribution;
- late contributions are usually more significant in a money purchase arrangement; and
- the manner of the monitoring of contributions, the identification of any late contributions and the timeliness of such identification should be considered.

In the event that the auditor's statement on contributions is qualified, trustees should have already considered the need to report to the Regulator because of their responsibility to monitor the receipt of contributions. In such circumstances the auditor will need to consider the following:

- if a report has been made by the trustees, did it contain all relevant information that the Regulator would expect?
- if the trustees were aware of the issue giving rise to the qualification, have they documented why a report was not made to the Regulator and is the conclusion reasonable?
- if the trustees were not aware of the issue, are their monitoring procedures insufficient and are there wider implications?

Depending upon the results of the above, it may be necessary for a report to be made to the Regulator by either the trustees or the auditor. A qualified statement about contributions does not automatically result in a report to the Regulator. A report by the trustees to the Regulator on the timing of contributions is, however, more likely to result in a qualified statement about contributions, but the pension scheme auditor should give the matter proper consideration.

44.9   SCHEMES IN THE PROCESS OF WINDING UP

Schemes in winding up are not exempt from the requirement to produce an annual report and audited financial statements until the wind up is complete. The Administration Regulations do not require the appointment of an auditor if the membership is less than two, so potentially the statutory requirement for an audit can cease before the wind up is finalised. However, trust law and best practice indicate that financial statements should still be prepared. In these circumstances, the audit becomes non-statutory and auditors need to consider whether the existing engagement terms remain appropriate.

A schedule of contributions is no longer required once the wind up of a defined benefit pension scheme commences and auditors should only express an opinion in their statement about contributions on compliance with the schedule of contributions up to the date the wind up commences. In relation to subsequent periods, the statement concerns compliance with the scheme rules and, where appropriate, the recommendations of the actuary.

For a money purchase scheme, the payment schedule is still required during the wind up period. Trustees should revise the payment schedule to reflect the basis on which contributions are payable from the start of winding up, which is normally nil. Auditors express an opinion on the payment schedule in force up to the commencement of winding up and thereafter on the revised schedule if one has been produced.

Once winding up is formally concluded the auditor's appointment automatically lapses without the need for formal resignation. Evidence of winding up should be obtained, but, if no such evidence is available, auditors should consider formal resignation. Where no audit work has been performed for several months, it may be appropriate for auditors to include in the statement on resignation that they are not able to know of any circumstances which might affect members' interests.

44.10   OTHER REPORTING SITUATIONS

There are situations when audited financial statements are required for periods other than the usual agreed accounting reference date. These will normally coincide with the requirement for an actuarial valuation such as:

- the determination of the Pension Protections Fund Levy;
- a claim against an employer under s75 of PA 1995 due to an employer ceasing to participate in a multi-employer scheme;
- following a bulk transfer into or out of a scheme and/or a significant change in membership; and
- for the purpose of the Pension Protection Fund following the entry of the scheme into the assessment period.

The financial statements in all of these situations should be prepared in accordance with the Audited Accounts Regulations. A trustee report is not usually required and the notes to the financial statements should specify the purpose for which the financial statements have been prepared. Auditors will report on the financial statements in the usual manner, again specifying the purpose for which they have been prepared. There is not usually a requirement to give a separate statement about contributions. PN15 provides detailed guidance and examples of reports.

44.11 'WHISTLE-BLOWING' RESPONSIBILITIES

Section 70 of PA 2004 imposes on the auditor (and virtually everyone associated with the running of a scheme) a duty to report to the Regulator any breaches of the law that are likely to be of material interest to the Regulator. PN15 provides comprehensive information on the auditor's considerations leading to such a report and the manner in which this should be undertaken.

The Regulator's code of practice 01 explains the 'whistle-blowing' requirements and this, together with further guidance issued by the Regulator, should be understood by the scheme auditor. The duty to report to the Regulator arises where the trustees and others associated with the scheme have failed to comply with their legal duties. The Regulator has, however, indicated that it expects most reporting to be by trustees and, if a report has already been made, auditors should only report if there is additional information to be provided. Auditors are not required to undertake any additional work other than to fulfil their responsibilities.

45 SOLICITORS' ACCOUNTS RULES

45.1 BACKGROUND

The Rules dealing with solicitors' accounts are contained in the Solicitors' Accounts Rules 1998 (SAR98). These rules were amended on 31 March 2009 as part of a general updating process to introduce firm-based regulation and legal disciplinary practices as provided for in the Legal Services Act 2007.

SAR98 covers solicitors, registered European Lawyers and registered foreign lawyers (in partnership with solicitors or registered European Lawyers) who practice in England and Wales, who are employed by a practice or who are employed as in-house solicitors.

In addition SAR98 now cover practices with non-solicitor lawyers as managers (member, partner or director), practices with up to 25 per cent of managers who are not legally qualified (as allowed by the Legal Services Act 2007) and all employees. New definitions of 'Non Solicitors' and 'managers' have been included in Rule 2.

Solicitors who practice outside England and Wales are governed by the Solicitors' Code of Conduct 2007 Rule 15.27 (accounts), Rule 15.15 (deposit interest) and Rule 20.06 (production of documents and information). These are similar in principle to SAR98, but are less detailed and less onerous in their requirements.

All practising solicitors who handle clients' money are required to deliver a report confirming their compliance with SAR98. This must be given by an authorised reporting accountant on an annual basis to the Solicitors' Regulation Authority (SRA) (previously the Law Society) within six months of the solicitor's firm's year end. The SRA are the independent regulatory body of solicitors in England and Wales.

The amendments as of 31 March 2009 have also enabled the introduction of more-flexible, risk-based provisions for the delivery of accountants' reports. This means the SRA may request further reports if they believe it is in the public interest to do so.

45.1.1 Objective

The object of SAR98 is to ensure compliance with the Solicitors' code of conduct 2007 Rule 1 and in particular that:

- other people's money is kept separate from money belonging to the solicitor or the practice; that each client's money is used for that client's matters only;
- that money held as trustees of a trust is used for the purposes of that trust only;
- solicitors maintain adequate bookkeeping and recording systems.

Note that the amendments as of 31 March 2009 due to the Legal Services Act, have abolished the concept of a 'controlled trust', so all money held by a practice is either client money or office money. This means that the same interest provisions apply to all client money, including money previously defined as 'controlled trust money'.

All the principals in a practice must ensure compliance with the rules both by themselves and by everyone employed in the practice. This duty also extends to the directors of a recognised body which is a company, or to the members of a recognised body which is an LLP. All partners are responsible even if practical compliance with the Rules is delegated to one particular person.

Breaches of the Rules must be rectified immediately upon discovery, including the replacement of money improperly withheld or withdrawn from a client account. The duty to remedy breaches rests not only on the person causing or discovering the breach but also on all the principals. This duty extends to replacing missing client money from principals' own resources, even if the money has been misappropriated by an employee or another principal and whether or not a claim is made on the solicitors' indemnity or compensation funds.

SAR98 strongly recommends that accounting records are written up at least weekly, even in the smallest practice, and daily in the case of larger firms.

The basic principle is that any money received from a client by a solicitor must be paid into a client account unless it is received in respect of a bill rendered to the client for time costs or disbursements that have already been paid by the solicitor. Money may only be withdrawn from a client account in accordance with the client's instructions, or to settle a solicitor's fee after a fee invoice has been given to the client. The transfer to the office account to settle a fee must occur within 14 days of the receipt into the client account.

The books of account maintained by the solicitor must show the current balance on each client's ledger and balances must be reconciled with the cash books and the bank statements every five weeks. The records must be kept for a period of six years and any bank statements must be kept as issued and printed by the bank.

Where money is held in a designated client account, solicitors must account to their clients for all of the interest earned on such accounts. Where money is held in a general client account solicitors are responsible for accounting to their clients for any interest earned unless the amount of interest is £20 or less. The accounting system should have the ability to highlight this.

Rules 15(3) and (4) came into force on 14 July 2008. The rules state that:

- client money must be returned to the client promptly, as soon as there is no longer proper reason to retain it;
- payments received after the solicitor has already accounted to the client must be paid to the client promptly;
- solicitors must promptly inform a client in writing of the amount of any client money retained at the end of, or substantial conclusion of a matter and the reason for retention; and
- thereafter, the client must be informed in writing at least every 12 months of the amount of client money held and the reason for the retention.

Rules 15(3) and (4) are not designed to apply to ongoing retainers.

45.2   EXISTING GUIDANCE

The accountant's report has to be prepared by a registered auditor and strict rules for its compilation are set out in SAR98. Although it is called an accountant's report, many of the procedures involved are of an auditing nature. As the opinion confirms whether the rules have been complied with, it is a less judgemental exercise than carrying out a number of prescribed tests, similar to an audit. It is restricted to an examination of both client and office ledgers and the related bank accounts, and it does not involve the audit of a profit and loss account and balance sheet of the practice. No accounts have to be filed with the SRA.

Accountants are also required to check that the solicitor's practice holds PI insurance for the period covered by the report for the purposes of the Solicitor's Indemnity Insurance Rules 2000.

45.3   ENGAGEMENT LETTER

There is a formal requirement for engagement letters to be issued to and agreed with solicitors and both parties must keep these for three years. Rule 38 details a number of terms which need to be incorporated into the engagement letter. An example of suitable paragraphs for inclusion in the engagement letter is shown in **Table 1** below.

TABLE 1: Paragraphs to include in an engagement letter concerning whistle-blowing

In accordance with rule 38 of the Solicitors' Accounts Rules 1998, we are instructed as follows:

(i)   (a)   if we discover evidence of fraud or theft in relation to money held by a solicitor (or registered European lawyer, or registered foreign lawyer, or recognised body, or employee of a solicitor or registered European lawyer, or manager or employee of a recognised body) for a client or any other person (including money held on trust), or held in an account of a client, or an account of another person, which is operated by a solicitor (or registered European lawyer, registered foreign lawyer, recognised body, employee of a solicitor or registered European lawyer, or manager or employee of a recognised body); or

       (b)   we obtain information which we have reasonable cause to believe is likely to be of material significance in determining whether a solicitor (or registered European lawyer, or registered foreign lawyer, or recognised body, or employee of a solicitor or registered European lawyer, or manager or employee of a recognised body) is a fit and proper person to hold money for clients or other persons (including money held on trust), or to operate an account of a client or an account of another person,

we must immediately give a report of the matter to the Solicitors Regulation Authority in accordance with section 34(9) of the Solicitors Act 1974;

(ii)   we may, and are encouraged to, make that report without prior reference to you;

(iii)   we are to report directly to the Solicitors Regulation Authority should our appointment be terminated following the issue of, or indication of intention to issue, a qualified accountant's report, or following the raising of concerns prior to the preparation of an accountant's report;

(iv)   we are to deliver to you with our report the completed checklist required by rule 46 of the Solicitors' Accounts Rules 1998; to retain for at least three years from the date of signature a copy of the completed checklist; and to produce the copy to the Solicitors Regulation Authority on request;

(v)   we are to retain these terms of engagement for at least three years after the termination of the retainer and to produce them to the Solicitors Regulation Authority on request; and

(vi)   following any direct report made to the Solicitors Regulation Authority under (i) or (iii) above, we are to provide to the Solicitors Regulation Authority on request any further relevant information in our possession or in the possession of our firm.

To the extent necessary to enable us to comply with (i) to (vi) above, you waive your right of confidentiality. This waiver extends to any report made, document produced or information disclosed to the Solicitors Regulation Authority in good faith pursuant to these instructions, even though it may subsequently transpire that we were mistaken in our belief that there was cause for concern.

45.3.1 'Whistle-blowing'

Reporting accountants have a mandatory whistle-blowing duty if they discover evidence of fraud or theft in relation to money:

- held by a solicitor (or registered European lawyer, or registered foreign lawyer, or recognised body, or employee of a solicitor or registered

European lawyer, or manager or employee of a recognised body) for a client or any other person (including money held on trust), or

- held in an account of a client, or an account of another person, which is operated by a solicitor.

The mandatory whistle-blowing duty also applies if they obtain information which gives reasonable cause to believe it is likely to be of material significance in determining whether a solicitor is a fit and proper person to hold money for clients or other persons (including money held on trust), or to operate an account of a client or an account of another person.

Reporting accountants are encouraged to report directly to the SRA, without reference to the solicitors.

Matters which may indicate a requirement on the reporting accountant to report to the SRA include:

- false accounting, theft or misappropriation by any solicitor in the firm;
- evidence of theft or misappropriation by any employee, fee-earner, consultant or third party not reported to the police authorities;
- evidence leading to concerns about honesty or integrity of any solicitor;
- evidence of attempted tax evasion (either direct or indirect taxes);
- failure to properly control client money;
- failure to keep proper accounting records under the SAR98 which is so significant that the reporting accountant is unable to express an opinion in his report;
- failure to take professional advice without due consideration;
- evidence of indifference or recklessness in connection with client money or operation of a client's own account as signatory; or
- any other matters or indications of fraud or theft in connection with client money or operation of a client's own account as signatory.

45.3.2   Termination of appointment

Reporting accountants are also required to communicate with the SRA on the termination of their appointment where this has arisen from the issue of, or an indication of the intention to issue, a qualified accountant's report.

45.3.3   Independence

Reporting accountants must note in their report any possible connections with the solicitors that may influence their independence.

As part of the SAR98 report, the reporting accountant must complete a questionnaire concerning whether the reporting accountant, his principals, directors, members or employees of the accountancy practice:

- are related to the solicitor;
- normally maintain the solicitor's client accounts;
- place substantial reliance on the solicitor for referral of clients;
- are clients or former clients of the solicitor; and
- whether there are any other circumstances which may affect the reporting accountant's independence.

The SRA has indicated that the disclosure of this information is stated to relate only to that information which is within the personal knowledge of the person signing the report. They have also said that they do not expect detailed investigations to be undertaken for everyone in the firm, but they do expect reasonable enquiries to be made of those directly involved in the work. For example, if the engagement partner is aware that one of his fellow partners is related to a solicitor covered by the report, this should be noted. If he is not aware of the relationship then it need not be noted, as it could not influence the reporting accountant's independence.

45.3.4 Place of examination

SAR98 requires that the examination of the solicitor's accounting records, files and other relevant documents should be performed at the solicitor's office and not at those of the reporting accountants. They do permit an initial electronic transmission of data to the reporting accountants at their offices where this is to reduce the amount of time spent at the solicitor's premises.

45.4 PROCEDURES

SAR98 sets out the matters that should be checked. These cover:

- the adequacy of the accounting system;
- checking that any client money is properly dealt with;
- ensuring that receipts and payments of client money are properly recorded;
- the adequacy of the system of recording and transferring costs;
- examining financial transactions on client accounts to ensure they comply with SAR98;
- checking the reconciliations required at two dates, one of which should be at year end;
- ensuring that the reconciliations have been performed at the appropriate intervals throughout the period and have been retained;
- checking that any inter-client transfers have been dealt with in accordance with SAR98; and
- where acting for both purchaser and lender in a conveyancing transaction, that client funds are clearly identifiable.

Where the solicitors use a computerised accounting system, testing may be carried out on a sample basis so long as the reporting accountants are satisfied that the system is adequate and the fact is mentioned in their report.

The SRA has issued guidelines on procedures and systems for accounting for clients' money, and the reporting accountants are required to report on material departures from them which they identify during their work on SAR98. However, they are not required to undertake a detailed check on compliance with these guidelines.

Following the 31 March 2009 update SAR98 now covers practices with non-solicitor lawyers as managers and practices with managers who are not legally qualified. In the event that these managers are permitted to authorise client account withdrawals, they need to have an appropriate understanding of the requirements of the rules. Therefore, before involving these non solicitors in client account withdrawals, firms should carefully consider the level of their planned involvement, the training required and the implementation of appropriate controls over withdrawals.

45.5   PROBLEM AREAS

Reporting accountants should ensure that they are aware of the following problem areas as part of their knowledge of the business, as they are the common areas in which solicitors breach the SARs.

Additionally it should be noted that the reporting accountant has a duty of care to the SRA and is not able to cap this liability.

45.5.1   Debit balances

No client account may go into debit in the solicitor's ledger. Each client should be treated in isolation and it is not permissible to net off debits and credits on the client ledger. This would indicate a shortage of funds that should be disclosed.

The SRA does not allow debit balances to be offset against credit balances when stating the liabilities to clients as shown by the ledgers on the accountant's report form.

45.5.2   Client confidentiality

Solicitors may refuse to allow the accountant access to certain documents on the grounds of client confidentiality and where this is the case the accountant should qualify the report, setting out the circumstances.

45.5.3   Trivial breaches

During the course of the examination, clerical and bookkeeping errors may come to light. Most of these will be classified as trivial breaches and will not lead to a qualification of the accountant's report. In order for the breach to be considered trivial the following criteria must be met:

- it must have arisen due to clerical error;
- it must be rectified promptly on discovery;
- there must be no loss to the client; and
- the nature and recurrence of such a breach should not give rise to significant cause for concern.

The notes to SAR98 state that the SRA receives a number of accountant's reports which make reference to trivial breaches but also show a significant difference between liabilities to clients as shown in the ledger and client money in bank accounts. Where this is the case, the notes to SAR98 require that an explanation for the difference must be given.

45.5.4   'Without delay'

'Without delay' is defined in SAR98 as meaning the day of receipt or the next working day. This means that solicitors must have procedures to ensure that cheque receipts are banked 'without delay'. Any cheques that are not banked within this time period will constitute a breach of SAR98.

45.5.5   Other areas

Other problem areas include ensuring that the specific rules are properly applied to:

- interest on clients' money;
- legal aid receipts; and
- designated deposit accounts.

45.6   REPORTING

The accountant's report confirms that the solicitor has complied with the SAR98. Its form is set out in SAR98 and requires details of:

- the solicitor(s) covered by the report;
- the period covered by the report;
- the results of the reconciliations at the chosen dates; and
- any qualification.

The report may be qualified in respect of matters:

- on which the accountant has been unable to satisfy himself or herself, giving the reasons for that inability; or
- where it appears to the accountant that there have been breaches of SAR98.

There is some space on the standard form for details of the qualification. The details given should be sufficient to enable the SRA to understand the nature of the breach. If necessary, a separate letter may contain these details but this must be referred to in the report.

As noted in **45.3.3** any possible connections with the solicitors which might influence independence must be detailed on the report.

45.7 CHECKLIST

As well as reporting to the SRA, reporting accountants are required to complete a checklist which is kept by the solicitor and which may be reviewed by the SRA. The checklist covers the results of the test checks made by the reporting accountants on client money in the following areas:

- each office's accounting system;
- postings to ledger accounts and casts;
- receipts and payments of client money;
- the system of recording costs and making transfers;
- examination of client files for verification of transactions and entries in accounting records;
- extraction of client ledger balances for clients;
- reconciliations;
- payments of client money;
- office accounts kept separate from client money;
- client's money not held in client account;
- inter-client transfers;
- instances where the firm acts for both borrower and lender in a conveyancing transaction; and
- information and explanations requested.

Reporting accountants have to confirm whether the results of their tests are satisfactory in each of these areas and, if not, indicate that any breaches have been mentioned in the accountant's report. Where, as a result of these tests, the position has been found to be unsatisfactory, further details are to be reported at the end of the checklist.

46 INVESTMENT BUSINESSES

46.1 INTRODUCTION

This Chapter covers the audit considerations in respect of the financial statements, client assets and conduct of business rules for investment businesses. The guidance is taken from Practice Note 21 (Revised) *The Audit of Investment Businesses in the United Kingdom* which was issued in December 2007 and superseded the earlier Practice Note of the same name and APB Bulletins 2001/7 *Guidance for Auditors of Investment Business* and Bulletin 2005/2 *Audit Risk and Fraud – Supplementary Guidance for Auditors of Investment Businesses*.

This Practice Note also covers auditors' reports to the FSA, which is covered in **Chapter 8** 'Reports to the FSA on investment businesses'.

46.2 RULES AND REPORTING REQUIREMENTS

Investment businesses incorporated in Great Britain are subject to the same requirements of the Companies Act for a statutory audit of financial statements as any other company. The scope of the audit is no different, but some regulated businesses are not able to take advantage of the exemptions available for small and medium-sized entities. Investment businesses trading as sole traders and partnerships are subject to additional requirements under the FSA Handbook of Rules and Guidance (the FSA Rules) that they would not be subject to were they not regulated.

In addition to the requirements for a statutory audit, investment businesses are governed by:

- The Financial Services and Markets Act 2000 (FSMA 2000), which sets out regulatory objectives covering:

    - market confidence;
    - public awareness;
    - the protection of consumers; and
    - the reduction of financial crime;

- various European Directives including:

    - Markets in Financial Instruments Directive (MiFID) which allows cross border trading across EEA member states without obtaining separate authorisation in each country;

- Capital Requirements Directive which sets out the minimum amounts of regulatory capital which must be maintained by member firms; and
- Undertakings for Collective Investment in Transferable Securities Directive (UCITS) which allows firms to sell UCITS schemes in other EEA member states without registering in those jurisdictions.

Under Part X of FSMA 2000, the FSA has the power to make rules, the primary objective of which is investor protection. The main categories of the FSA Rules are:

- High Level Standards to ensure that firms follow the FSA's Principles for Business and meet Threshold Conditions as well as ensuring that those within the firm performing Controlled Functions meet the requirement of the Approved Persons regime;
- Business Standards consisting of:
  - Prudential Sourcebooks containing financial rules, designed to ensure that the business is financially sound, has appropriate controls and is able to meet its commitments;
  - Client Assets rules, requiring segregation of money and investments held for clients and also covering arrangements for custody;
  - Conduct of Business rules, to ensure that the business deals fairly, honestly and with due skill, care and honesty with its clients;
  - Market Conduct rules, containing the FSA code of market conduct, price stabilising rules, interprofessional conduct and endorsement of the takeover code;
  - Regulatory Process rules, containing details of the authorisation, supervision, enforcement and decision making processes; and
  - Redress rules, covering dispute resolution, compensation and complaints against the FSA.

Compliance with the FSA Rules is monitored in a number of ways, the principal ones being:

- internally, by the business itself;
- by submitting regular returns to the FSA;
- by monitoring and inspection by the FSA;
- reports to the FSA by the business's auditors.

Auditors constitute an important part of the system of supervision; as well as reporting on the financial statements which are submitted to the Regulator, they issue reports in relation to:

- whether the entity has complied with the rules concerning client assets; and
- interim profits for capital adequacy purposes.

The Practice Note splits these reports into three types:

- the audit of financial statements;
- review reports on interim profits; and
- reports to the FSA.

The audit of financial statements and the review of interim profits are discussed further in this chapter. **Chapter 8** contains details about reporting to the FSA in relation to client assets, in addition to guidance on ad hoc reporting to the FSA as set out in Section B of ISA (UK and Ireland) 250.

The introduction of the CREST system of on-line share settlement in July 1996 has meant that auditors of investment businesses which are CREST users, such as stockbrokers, fund managers or custodians, need to understand the nature of the system. Guidance for auditors comes from Audit 2/96 *Guidance for auditors of CREST users*, issued by the Audit Faculty of the Institute of Chartered Accountants in England and Wales, which gives an overview of how the system operates, its regulatory structure and some of the key audit issues. It is discussed in **46.6** below.

46.3 THE AUDIT OF FINANCIAL STATEMENTS

The Practice Note sets out guidance for the audit of financial statements on an ISA-by-ISA basis. This chapter sets out some of the major areas of which to be aware when auditing an investment business.

46.3.1 *ISA (UK and Ireland) 200 Objective and general principles governing an audit of financial statements*

In addition to the ethical guidance issued by auditors' professional bodies, there are additional independence rules laid down by the FSA. Therefore, auditors should be aware of the increased threat to their independence and review these prior to accepting any regulated audit engagement.

46.3.2 *ISA (UK and Ireland) 210 Terms of audit engagements*

The FSA Rules have various requirements in relation to accepting engagements. There is no requirement for auditors to be approved by the FSA before they can be appointed. However, investment businesses must take reasonable steps to ensure that the auditor it is planning to appoint or has appointed, has suitable skills, experience and independence with the nature, scale and complexity of the firm's business and the requirements and standards under the regulatory system to which the business is subject.

To enable the business to assess the ability of an auditor, the FSA may seek information about the auditor's relevant experience and skills. The FSA will normally seek such information by letter from an auditor who has not previously audited any FSA regulated firm. The auditor should reply fully to the letter and the regulated firm should not appoint any auditor who does not reply to the FSA.

The FSA may also seek further information on a continuing basis from auditors as it deems necessary.

Auditors should notify the FSA when they cease to hold office as auditor of an authorised firm.

The engagement letter may cover both the terms of engagement for:

- the client assets reports to the FSA; and
- the statutory audit.

If this is the case, it should be clear that the client assets report will be addressed to the FSA, not the directors to whom the engagement letter is addressed.

46.3.3   ISA (UK and Ireland) 240 The auditor's responsibility to consider fraud in an audit of financial statements

Key indicators of potential fraud and error particularly relevant to investment businesses will include:

- backlogs in key reconciliations;
- inadequate segregation of duties between back, middle and front office staff;
- inadequate management understanding of complex products;
- inadequate definition of responsibilities and supervision of staff;
- inadequate whistle-blowing arrangements;
- high management and staff turnover;
- ineffective oversight of offshore operations;
- lack of an effective audit committee;
- ineffective personnel practices and policies;
- inadequate communication of information to management;
- scope for inappropriate revenue recognition or concealment of trading losses;
- ineffective regulatory compliance monitoring; and
- elements of remuneration packages linked to revenue or profits.

46.3.4   ISA (UK and Ireland) 250 Part A Consideration of laws and regulations in an audit of financial statements

ISA (UK and Ireland) 250 Part A requires auditors to perform procedures that identify possible or actual non-compliance with regulations which are central to the entity's ability to conduct its operations. The ISA (UK and Ireland) defines laws and regulations which are central to the entity's ability to conduct its business as those where either compliance is required to obtain a licence to operate, or where non-compliance could be reasonably expected to result in the entity ceasing to operate.

The Practice Note suggests the following procedures to help identify such possible or actual breaches of non-compliance for an investment business:

- obtain a general understanding of the legal and regulatory framework applicable to the entity and industry, and of the procedures followed to ensure compliance with the framework;
- inspect correspondence with the relevant regulators;
- review the business's Scope of Part IV Permission (an FSA document which sets out the regulated activities that the firm is permitted to engage in, together with any limitations and requirements imposed on those activities);
- enquire of the directors whether they are on notice of any possible instances of non-compliance with law or regulations;
- include in the representation letter confirmation that the directors have disclosed to the auditors all those events of which they are aware which involve possible non-compliance, together with the actual or contingent consequences arising therefrom;
- hold discussions with the investment business's Compliance Officer and other personnel responsible for compliance; and
- review any work on compliance matters carried out by internal audit.

Two types of regulation are central to the investment businesses:

- prudential rules; and
- conduct of business rules.

The prudential rules' aim is to ensure the protection of clients and typical procedures auditors may carry out include:

- enquiring how management ensure that the financial resources calculations are properly prepared and submitted on time;
- enquiring how management ensure that the firm complies with the financial resources requirements;
- examining the returns to see whether they show that the firm/group has a reasonable surplus of regulatory capital. This should include the period being audited and the future period as part of work on going concern; and
- reviewing relevant correspondence with the FSA.

The auditor has no direct reporting responsibility in respect of the conduct of business rules. However, any breaches of the rules may:

- lead to material fines and/or claims by investor; and
- cause the investment business to have its authorisation restricted or withdrawn, which will threaten its existence as a going concern.

Therefore, auditors should be alert to any indications that management and staff are not monitoring compliance with these rules or that business is being conducted outside the scope of the company's authorisation.

46.3.5 ISA (UK and Ireland) 300 Planning an audit of financial statements

Auditors will usually complete their work on the annual accounts at the same time as the work required to report to the FSA, in an effort not to duplicate audit effort. Auditors must also ensure that their work is planned to meet the short timescales for reporting imposed by the FSA.

46.3.6 ISA (UK and Ireland) 315 Understanding the entity and its environment and assessing the risks of material misstatement

Auditors must seek to understand the complex business and regulatory regime within which investment businesses operate. This will include:

- obtaining a general understanding of the applicable legal and regulatory framework and the procedures followed to ensure this framework is complied with;
- reviewing the firm's Scope and Permission Notice; and
- inspecting correspondence with regulators.

The Practice Note lists example procedures that auditors may perform to assist them in understanding:

- the industry, regulatory and other external factors affecting the business, including the applicable financial reporting framework;
- the nature of the entity, e.g., the types of investment business undertaken, its risk management procedures, and the legal and operational structure of the entity;
- the selection and application of accounting policies;
- the entity's objectives and strategies and the related business risks;
- how the financial performance of the entity is measured and reviewed;
- how the entity has responded to risks arising from IT; and
- the control environment and control activities, so that they can assess the risk of material misstatement at the assertion level and design appropriate audit procedures.

Factors to be considered when assessing the control environment of an investment business are shown in **Table 1**.

TABLE 1: Factors to consider when assessing the control environment

- the nature and status of the investment business's clients and any changes in their status which may affect the application of investor protection requirements;
- a change in the market environment (e.g., an increase in competition);
- the introduction of new clients, products or marketing methods;
- claims made in promotional literature (particularly in relation to performance);
- the risk profile of the business undertaken by the entity;
- the complexity of products;

- the consistency, across geographical location, of products sold and methods used;
- the legal and operational structure of the investment business;
- financial and managerial support provided to and by any other group companies;
- the number of branches and sales offices;
- the use of appointed representatives;
- management's attitude towards control, regulation and investor protection;
- the roles and responsibilities allocated to the finance and compliance functions;
- the recruitment, training, competence and supervision of personnel; and
- the integrity, competence and experience of management.

Their understanding of the entity should then allow auditors to identify the risks of material misstatement at the financial statements and assertion levels, and to determine which risks are significant. Example risks which auditors may deem to be significant are:

- the valuation of investments, including derivatives, which could have a significant impact on the financial statements;
- breaches of the regulator's requirements;
- breaches of the terms of client mandates; and
- the calculation of performance fees to be paid by clients.

Investment businesses differ greatly in their size and the complexity of their operations, and therefore the reliance auditors place on internal control systems varies. Where client assets exist this is likely to be an area where detailed internal controls are relevant. Whilst client assets are not, in principle, part of the financial statements, any material deficiency could be indicative of poor control and may have an impact on the financial position of the business.

When the systems are designed, their dual purposes should be borne in mind. There are considerations both for the entity itself and for the protection of investors' interests. Detailed guidance on the requirements for the accounting records is included in each set of the FSA Rules.

Auditors should not accept work that they are not competent to undertake and may consider using technical specialists for more involved areas – for example, when considering trades in complex products or for a business heavily involved in e-commerce. The use of specialists is particularly important in assessing valuations of particular derivative instruments for which there is no independent fair market valuation. Guidance on the use of specialists is given in section **39.4.**

46.3.7 *ISA (UK and Ireland) 330 The auditor's procedures in response to assessed risks*

In addition to tests of controls and general substantive tests, ISA (UK and Ireland) 330 requires that, where auditors identify significant risk of material misstatement, they should plan and perform specific substantive procedures to address that risk.

For investment businesses, significant risks may include:

- valuation of investments;
- liabilities for breaches of regulations, contract or mandate; and
- calculation of performance fees.

Valuation of investments

Year end positions may be valued by marking to market or at fair value. Where securities are traded openly their value can be ascertained with little judgement, and similarly where unquoted securities may be equated to an equivalent quoted security, its valuation can be easily verified.

However, other instruments which are more complex or do not have a readily ascertainable market value, may be valued using a complex model. In such cases, auditors may require the input of an expert in such areas to determine whether the valuation is reasonable. Further details can be found in **Chapter 28**.

Liabilities for breaches

There are no substantive procedures that can identify breaches that the investment business or its advisors have not already identified. Auditors must rely on consistency of information from various sources, such as legal representatives, correspondence files etc, and obtaining representations from management about the existence of any such liabilities.

Performance fees

Auditors should obtain an understanding of the investment business's systems and controls over performance fees. Tests of detail may include:

- confirming the basis of the performance fee calculation to the underlying agreement;
- agreeing the figures used in the performance fee calculation have been correctly extracted from the underlying records;
- reviewing the reasonableness of any estimates or underlying assumptions; and
- recalculating the performance fees.

Third party information may also be available to support the performance fee calculations.

46.3.8 ISA (UK and Ireland) 402 Audit considerations relating to entities using service organizations

It is common for investment businesses to outsource some of their functions, including:

- safe custody of investments by a custodian;
- settlement or clearing of trades;

- maintenance of accounting records;
- product administration (such as unit trusts, savings schemes, PEPs or ISAs); and
- investment management.

Auditors must consider where to obtain their audit evidence where activities are outsourced. Evidence may be obtained from the investment business itself, by contacting or visiting the third party, or by relying on the assurances of the third party's auditors. Investment business should take reasonable steps to ensure that, where applicable, each of its appointed representatives and material outsourcers give auditors the same right of access to their accounting and other records as the firm itself is required to give to their auditors. See further details on ISA (UK and Ireland) 402 in **Chapter 37**.

The investment business is required to comply with the FSA Rules whether or not its activities are outsourced.

46.3.9   ISA (UK and Ireland) 520 Analytical Procedures

Analytical procedures for investment businesses may include comparison of:

- fees to funds under management and market indices; and
- commission income and expense to transaction volumes.

46.3.10   ISA (UK and Ireland) 540 Audit of Accounting Estimates

Where independent fair market valuations are not available, accounting estimates are often used for valuation purposes. Where a mathematical model has been used, auditors will review the process used to develop and test the model, as well as gaining an understanding of any assumptions used. Auditors should consider the reasonableness and consistency of the estimates, and also whether they conform with generally accepted practices.

Accounting estimates may also be used to establish liabilities for compensation payments to clients, for example where funds have been priced incorrectly.

46.3.11   ISA (UK and Ireland) 545 Auditing Fair Value Measurements and Disclosures

This ISA (UK and Ireland) deals in the most part with the valuation of financial assets, and is covered in detail in **Chapter 28**.

46.3.12 ISA (UK and Ireland) 570 Going concern

ISA (UK and Ireland) 570 sets out the areas for consideration in assessing whether an entity is a going concern. For investment businesses the attitude of the FSA towards an entity and continuing authorisation of the entity by the FSA are paramount to continuing as a going concern. Therefore, the following items should also be considered:

* FSA censures or fines;
* FSA capital shortages;
* non-routine visits from the FSA;
* reputation and other indicators; and
* general non-compliance with the FSA Rules.

Any doubts about an entity's ability to continue as a going concern may be reportable to the FSA under the guidance in ISA (UK and Ireland) 250 Section B.

46.3.13 ISA (UK and Ireland) 580 Management representations

In addition to the requirements of ISA (UK and Ireland) 580, under ISAs (UK and Ireland) 250 Section A and 550, auditors are required to obtain confirmation of the completeness of disclosure to the auditor of:

* all known actual or possible non-compliance with laws and regulations whose effects should be considered when preparing financial statements together with the actual or contingent consequences which may arise therefrom; and
* information provided regarding the identification of related parties and the adequacy of related party disclosures in the financial statements.

Possible additions to the standard management representation letter for investment businesses include:

* acknowledging management's responsibility for establishing and maintaining accounting records and systems of control in accordance with the FSA Rules;
* confirming that management has made available to the auditors all correspondence and notes of meetings with the FSA relevant to the auditors' examination;
* that all complaints have been drawn to the attention of the auditors; and
* where applicable, representation that no client money or client investments were held by the investment business.

46.3.14 ISA (UK and Ireland) 700 The auditor's report on financial statements

Details of auditors' reports to the FSA as the regulator of investment business are covered in **Chapter 8**.

46.4 HIGH LEVEL STANDARDS AND CONDUCT OF BUSINESS RULES

The prime responsibility for ensuring compliance with, and reporting breaches of, the FSA's High Level Standards and Conduct of Business rules lies with the management of the investment business. The FSA performs periodic inspections of investment businesses to review compliance with the FSA Rules.

The FSA's High Level Standards Sourcebook covers such matters as:

- Principles for Businesses;
- Senior Management Arrangements, Systems and Controls;
- Threshold Conditions;
- Statements of Principle and Code of Practice for Approved Persons; and
- The Fit and Proper Test for Approved Persons.

The FSA's Conduct of Business Sourcebook covers such matters as:

- clear, fair and not misleading communication;
- inducements and soft commission;
- reliance on others;
- Chinese walls;
- financial promotion;
- the internet and other electronic media;
- accepting customers;
- client classification;
- terms of business and client agreements with customers;
- advising and selling;
- product disclosure and the customer's right to cancel or withdraw;
- dealing and managing investments;
- reporting to customers;
- client assets;
- operators of collective investment schemes;
- trustee and depository activities.

46.4.1 Impact on the audit

Auditors have no direct reporting responsibility in respect of the FSA's High Level Standards and Conduct of Business rules, although breaches of such rules may have implications for the financial statements of the investment business, other aspects of the annual reporting requirements, or ad hoc reports. Therefore some enquiry into possible breaches is called for. Examples of such situations are:

- FSA Rule breaches, which could give rise to fines or claims by investors; or
- a restriction or withdrawal of authorisation, which could threaten the business's viability as a going concern.

46.4.2 Audit approach

Staff involved in the audit should have a general understanding of the High Level Standards and Conduct of Business rules to enable them to spot possible breaches which come to their attention. They should assess the control environment that exists, considering such areas as:

- the adequacy of procedures and training to inform staff of the requirements of the FSA and to ensure that they meet those requirements;
- the adequacy of authorities and supervision;
- the review of compliance by senior management;
- procedures to ensure possible breaches are investigated by an appropriate person and are brought to the attention of senior management; and
- the authority of, and resources available to, the compliance officer.

Possible areas, outside client assets, where compliance problems commonly occur and may have an effect on the audit include:

- conducting business outside the scope of its authority: such action could result in fines, suspension or loss of authorisation;
- customer complaints: a significant level of complaints should put auditors on guard;
- poor controls over appointed representatives: the business is liable for the acts of its representatives;
- personal dealings of its employees: the business could be liable if clients believe they are dealing with the business when in fact they are dealing with its employees;
- misclassification of customers as 'business' or 'private' investors: incorrect classification could result in claims;
- unauthorised deposit taking; and
- lack of or incomplete customer agreements.

It would normally be inappropriate to perform any direct testing for compliance with the High Level Standards and Conduct of Business rules, as it is beyond the auditors' responsibility and they may not be technically competent enough to perform the work. Ensuring compliance with such rules is part of the monitoring function of the FSA. However the general steps that may be taken to assess the impact of any breaches on the auditors' report are:

- consideration of the investment business's compliance framework, including operational manuals and the documentation of its procedures and controls;

- review of the scope and results of the internal compliance monitoring and review;
- examination of the records maintained of any breaches and notifications to the FSA;
- examination of correspondence with the FSA and the results of the most recent inspection visit;
- review of the register of complaints from customers; and
- review of monitoring returns and questionnaires submitted to the FSA.

Where auditors become aware of a possible breach of the High Level Standards or Conduct of Business rules they should identify its cause and consider whether it imposes any reporting requirements on them.

Auditors should enquire of management and staff whether any breaches have occurred and obtain appropriate representations in writing from management.

46.5 REVIEW REPORTS ON INTERIM PROFITS

All bodies subject to the Investment Services Directive are required to maintain adequate capital resources, as defined by the EC Capital Adequacy Directive. The reserves of an investment business are permitted to include interim profits as long as the interim profits have been verified. External auditors may be requested to perform this verification and report on interim profits for capital adequacy purposes.

The engagement to 'verify' interim profits is essentially a review engagement and the opinion may be given in terms of negative assurance. The report is addressed to the directors of the entity.

Auditors must state in their report that they have followed the review procedures specified by the FSA or, if they have varied the procedures used, the alternative procedures should be listed in their report. Alternatively, reference may be made to the engagement letter, where the alternative procedures may have been listed.

The FSA states in the FSA Rules the procedures they wish auditors to perform. As a minimum, auditors should:

- satisfy themselves that the figures forming the basis of the interim profits have been properly extracted from the underlying accounting records;
- review the accounting policies used in arriving at the interim profits to obtain comfort that they are consistent with those used when drawing up the annual financial statements, and adhere to the rules of the regulator involved;
- perform analytical review on the results to date, including comparisons of actuals to date with budget and prior period;

- discuss the overall performance and financial position of the business with management;
- ensure the implications of current and prospective litigation and claims, changes in business activities and provisions for bad and doubtful debts are included in the interim profit figure; and
- follow up problem areas of which they are already aware.

Additional work may be required if:

- the control environment surrounding the preparation of the interim net profits is evaluated as weak;
- the results of the procedures undertaken above are not fully consistent with the interim profits as reported; or
- there has been a significant change to the accounting system.

Auditors must also make it clear that the report is for the use of the FSA and for the purpose of the calculation of capital adequacy only.

An example review report is given in **Table 2**. This should be adapted where the entity is unincorporated, or a sole-trader, or where procedures have not been specified by the engagement letter.

TABLE 2: Example review report on interim profits for a FSA regulated investment business

Review report by the independent auditors to the board of directors of XYZ Limited ('the company')

In accordance with our engagement letter dated [date], a copy of which is attached, we have reviewed the company's statement of interim profits for the period from [date] to [date] set out on pages [x] to [x] of the attached [Note 1]. That statement is the responsibility of, and has been approved by, the directors.

Our review did not constitute an audit, and accordingly we do not express an audit opinion on the interim profits. It has been carried out having regard to [see Note 2] of the FSA Handbook and Practice Note 21: The audit of investment businesses in the United Kingdom (Revised) issued by the Auditing Practices Board.

On the basis of the results of our review, nothing has come to our attention that causes us to believe that:

- the interim profits have not been calculated on the basis of the accounting policies adopted by the company in drawing up its annual financial statements for the year ended [date of last annual financial statements];
- those accounting policies are not in accordance with the principles set out in [see Note 3]; and
- the interim profits after tax amounting to £[x] as so reported are not reasonably stated.

[Date]

Notes:

Note	Wording for BIPRU investment firms	Wording for exempt CAD firms	Wording for investment management firms	Wording for UCITS firms	Wording for personal investment firms
1	Type of firm it was prior to 1 January 2007: Investment management – financial return UCITS management – financial return Personal investment – retail media-tion activities return Securities and futures – reporting statement	Type of firm it was prior to 1 January 2007: Investment management – financial return Personal investment – retail mediation activities return Securities and futures – reporting statement	financial return	financial return	retail mediation activities return
2	2.2.102R and 2.2.103G of GENPRU	9.3.4R or 13 1A.9R of IPRU (INV)	Table 5.2.2(1) of Chapter 5 of IPRU (INV)	Table 2.2.1R of UPRU	Appendix 13(1) of Chapter 13 of IPRU (INV)
3	Type of firm it was prior to 1 January 2007: Investment management – Section 4 table 1 of Annex 5R to chapter 16 of SUP UCITS management – Section 3 table 1 of Annex 16R to chapter 16 of SUP Personal investment –	Type of firm it was prior to 1 January 2007: Investment management – Section 4 table 1 of Annex 5R to chapter 16 of SUP Personal investment – Paragraph 15 of the introduction in Annex 18BG to chapter 16 of SUP	Section 4 Table 1 of Annex 5R to Chapter 16 of the FSA's Supervision Manual	Section 3 Table 1 of Annex 5R to Chapter 16 of the FSA's Supervision Manual	Section 15 of Annex a8BG to Chapter 16 of the FSA's Supervision Manual

Note	Wording for BIPRU investment firms	Wording for exempt CAD firms	Wording for investment management firms	Wording for UCITS firms	Wording for personal investment firms
	Paragraph 15 of the introduction in Annex 18BG to chapter 16 of SUP	Securities and futures – Section 6 of Annex 10R to chapter 16 of SUP			
	Securities and futures – Section 6 of Annex 10R to chapter 16 of SUP				

46.6 CREST

Auditors of entities which use CREST need to obtain an understanding of the nature of the processing system and the controls necessary to ensure the investment assets are properly safeguarded. They also have to be reasonably satisfied as to the assets' existence and ownership and year end balances for their statutory reports and those to the FSA concerning the keeping of adequate books and records.

Audit 2/96 covers three areas where CREST may impact on the audit approach. These are:

- understanding the business;
- evaluating internal controls; and
- detailed audit procedures.

46.6.1 Understanding the business

The following matters may need to be considered in seeking to comply with ISA (UK and Ireland) 315 where CREST is used (see **16.2**):

- the extent of the interaction between the entity and CREST, including:
  - whether securities are held as principal by the entity or whether the organisation conducts investment business on behalf of other clients as agents;
  - the volume and value of transactions settled;
  - the materiality of unsettled transactions and balances relative to the entity's financial position; and
  - its relationship with other parties within CREST;
- the manner in which the entity interacts with CREST, including:

- the entity's status within CREST as a user, member or registrar;
- the structure of the member's accounts that 'contain' the entity's investments;
- details of the connection to CREST, such as gateway and network provider; and
- the systems used to interact with CREST, whether standard interface, bespoke or off-the-shelf in-house systems.

Specialists, such as computer audit staff, may need to be involved to assess the systems in the first year that CREST is used by the entity, and the effort required is likely to be greater when in-house systems are used. Once the systems have been ascertained and documented, the guidance in ISA (UK and Ireland) 315 (see **Chapter 22**) should be followed to develop an appropriate audit approach.

46.6.2 *Evaluating internal controls*

The types of internal controls which need to be considered in relation to CREST include:

- access and authorisation controls with regard to the CREST computer systems;
- adequate audit trail controls which identify CREST transactions;
- other IT controls such as security, disaster planning and authorised upgrading of the system;
- organisational and segregational controls over CREST transactions; and
- management controls such as reconciliations and follow-up of exception reports.

Auditors will need to consider controls at CREST as well as the procedures within the entity being audited in accordance with ISA (UK and Ireland) 402 *Audit considerations relating to entities using service organizations*. More reliance will need to be placed on CREST systems where the entity's records or systems are unreliable. The guidance notes that CREST Co will be commissioning its own auditors to produce an annual report on controls which will be made available to CREST members and their auditors, where it is necessary to consider CREST's own controls.

46.6.3 *Detailed audit procedures*

The extent and nature of detailed audit procedures will depend on the auditors' assessment of risk and the strength of the entity's systems and controls. The Technical Release notes several matters which the auditors may wish to take into account when planning their work on a CREST user. At present, CREST does not produce hard-copy confirmations, although they have indicated that this may change if there is sufficient demand. Auditors will therefore need to find alternative evidence. The guidance suggests that this may be obtained by:

- the auditors being authorised to use the entity's systems to obtain confirmation;
- auditors installing their own CREST link and having the entity's permission to have read-only access to their records;
- independent confirmation with the counterparty; or
- work on the entity's own systems and reconciliations.

47 REGISTERED PROVIDERS OF SOCIAL HOUSING

The term Registered Providers of Social Housing (or Registered Provider) was introduced by the Housing and Regeneration Act 2008. The previous term, 'Registered Social Landlord' (RSL) was introduced by the Housing Act 1996. Registered Providers can now come from the profit-making sector as well as the traditional non-profit making sector. They can include housing associations, local housing companies, registered housing charitable trusts and housing care and support agencies. Local Authorities managing social housing were within the regulatory framework for the first time from 1 April 2010. From 1 April 2010, a broader range of providers, such as profit-making organisations, were able to become registered providers. The entry of new forms of provider was intended to create greater competition and encourage innovation and the delivery of greater value for money by existing providers.

The Housing and Regeneration Act 2008 is a fundamental change to the way that housing and regeneration are regulated and funded. One of the most significant changes is the separation of investment from regulation. There was general consensus that a substantial degree of overlap existed between the Housing Corporation (as previous regulator and investment agency) and English Partnerships which have now been brought together. The Housing Corporation was dissolved on 1 December 2008 and two new agencies were created:

- Homes and Communities Agency (HCA); and
- Tenant Services Authority (TSA).

The HCA was formed through the transfer of the functions and assets of English Partnerships; the investment functions of the Housing Corporation; a number of delivery programmes from Communities and Local Government and the transfer of the Academy for Sustainable Communities. The statutory objects of the HCA, as listed in the Housing and Regeneration Act 2008 are to:

- improve the supply and quality of housing in England;
- secure the regeneration or development of land or infrastructure in England;
- support in other ways the creation, regeneration or development of communities in England or their continued well-being; and
- contribute to the achievement of sustainable development and good design in England, with a view to meeting the needs of people living in England.

Similar agencies exist for Wales, Scotland and Northern Ireland, with similar statutory objects to those applicable in England. The relevant bodies are:

- Communities Scotland;
- The National Assembly for Wales (Social Housing Regulation and Investment Unit of the Welsh Assembly Government); and

- The Northern Ireland Housing Executive.

The TSA is the regulator for affordable housing, having taken over the regulatory powers of the Housing Corporation. The TSA's goal is to raise the standard of services for tenants and in March 2010, they published a new regulatory framework entitled *The regulatory framework for social housing in England from April 2010*. The publication is available from the TSA's website at *www.tenantservicesauthority.org* and is effective from 1 April 2010.

This is an important document for auditors of registered providers of social housing to be familiar with.

The six standards cover:

- *Tenant involvement and empowerment* – which contains requirements relating to customer service, choice and complaints; involvement and empowerment; and understanding and responding to diverse needs of tenants;
- *Home* – which contains requirements relating to quality of accommodation; and repairs and maintenance;
- *Tenancy* – which contains requirements relating to allocations; rent and tenure;
- *Neighbourhood and community* – which contains requirements relating to neighbourhood management; local area co-operation; and anti-social behaviour;
- *Value for money*; and
- *Governance and financial viability*.

Each standard sets out the high-level outcome that landlords should achieve, followed by a series of 'specific requirements' related to that outcome.

The approach of the TSA is now one of 'co-regulation' which means an expectation of robust self-regulation by the boards and councillors of registered providers who govern the delivery of housing services, incorporating effective tenant involvement. There is still an expectation of some core regulation by the TSA.

47.1 EXISTING AUDIT GUIDANCE

47.1.1 Practice Note 14

Practice Note 14 *The Audit of Registered Social Landlords in the United Kingdom (Revised)* provides guidance on how Statements of Auditing Standards should be applied to audits of the financial statements of Registered Providers (note that the Practice Note still refers to RSLs as it has not yet been updated for the Housing and Regeneration Act 2008). The Practice Note does not have an effective date and so should be applied to any audits of Registered Providers commencing after its date of issue of March 2006.

The March 2006 Practice Note 14 (Revised) is based on legislation (including the Housing Act 2004) and regulations in effect at 31 December 2005.

Although the Housing Act 1996 introduced the term RSL in respect of England and Wales, Practice Note 14 (Revised) also uses the term RSL for housing associations in Scotland and Northern Ireland.

The Practice Note follows the framework of the ISAs and provides a commentary on the application of each ISA to the audit of RSLs. The introduction to the Practice Note stresses that it is designed to ensure the consistent application of ISAs across the social housing sector rather than provide detailed explanatory material to assist auditors on all aspects of RSL audit work. Section **47.3** below summarises the applicability of ISAs to RSL audits as interpreted by the Practice Note and should be read in conjunction with the Practice Note in order to get a full understanding of the implications for the audit of social housing providers.

47.1.2   Regulatory Circulars and Good Practice Notes

From 1 April 2010, the new regulatory framework for social housing in England resulted in the withdrawal of the majority of Circulars and Good Practice Notes that the sector had been accustomed to following.

Regulatory guidance which was applicable to the audit of Registered Providers in England included:

- Good Practice Note 7, *External audit of housing associations* – (GPN 7);
- Circular 04/07: *Requirement to submit external audit management letters and responses;*
- Circular 01/06: *Accounting requirements for Registered Social Landlords: General Determination 2006;*
- Circular 07/07, *Internal Controls Assurance* and
- Good Practice Note 15: *Demonstrating internal controls assurance in housing associations* – (GPN 15),

all of which are now withdrawn. The TSA have indicated that the above Circulars and Good Practice Notes will be subject to appropriate archiving provisions and they will continue to be available on request or through an online archive. Therefore, whilst they no longer have a place within the regulatory framework, they will continue to be useful sources of reference for good practice in the short to medium term.

Social housing providers in Wales, Scotland and Northern Ireland will have similar guidance in respect of external audit and internal controls assurance.

749

47.2   BACKGROUND

47.2.1   The nature of Registered Providers of Social Housing

Most existing Registered Providers are not-for-profit housing associations, managed under the oversight of a board or committee of management, independently from local and central government. They provide social housing accommodation (usually made available at less than market rents and allocated to applicants in greatest housing need) and other related services. With the new regulatory framework effective from 1 April 2010, councils managing social housing have also become registered providers. Profit-making organisations can also be registered providers where they are managing social housing.

Registered Providers operate under a variety of legal frameworks, including Industrial and Provident Societies, limited companies and charitable trusts. They are required, under legislation, to have an annual independent audit, although the specific auditing requirements will vary depending on the legal status. For example, some may be eligible to apply exemptions applicable to small companies, charities and industrial and provident societies. In such cases they must supply an accountant's report. The thresholds have been amended by SI 2006/265 The Friendly and Industrial and Provident Societies Act 1968 (Audit Exemption) (Amendment) Order 2006 and the Charities Act 2006. Advantage of these exemptions is only possible if permitted under the Rules under which they are incorporated.

Auditors of Registered Providers must be registered auditors, i.e. eligible under the Companies Act and registered with a supervisory body recognised under companies legislation.

Registered Providers undertake new building, refurbishment of existing property or acquisition of existing satisfactory properties, with the aim of providing affordable, low cost rented accommodation. Under certain conditions such housing may be sold to tenants (e.g., right to buy, right to acquire and shared ownership).

Registered Providers which are housing associations may be constituted in various ways, for example, as:

- industrial and provident societies (either as exempt charities or non-charitable); or
- limited companies (either as registered charities or non-charitable).

As a result, auditors must understand the statutory framework of their social housing clients as this will affect audit reporting requirements. This does differ slightly between England, Wales, Scotland and Northern Ireland. The majority of Registered Providers in the United Kingdom are registered with the TSA under the Housing and Regeneration Act 2008 and the term given to that body is the 'Regulator'. Under certain pieces of legislation, the Regulator has the power to determine the accounting requirements of Registered Providers which will be important for the auditors to understand. Practice Note 14 (Revised) contains useful guidance in its appendices covering legislation throughout the United Kingdom relevant to Registered Providers.

The constitution of Registered Providers or the legal rules under which they are incorporated usually prohibit them from distributing any surpluses or assets to the members or the board, even if they are non-charitable. Non-profit making organisations that are registered providers are required to have within their objects:

- the provision of social housing;
- not-for-profit status; and
- non-distribution of assets to members.

The majority of Registered Providers are industrial and provident societies and most reference is made to a consolidating piece of legislation, the Industrial and Provident Societies Act 1965. As industrial and provident societies, they fall under the administrative jurisdiction of the mutual societies division of the Financial Services Authority (FSA). This means that their constitution comprises 'Rules' which must be registered with the FSA. They will be governed by a voluntary board which is appointed by the members. The Industrial and Provident Societies Act 1965 contains some basic requirements for the accounts and audit. The Friendly and Industrial and Provident Societies Act 1968 sets out the main accounting and audit requirements. It requires proper financial records to be kept and that all financial statements agree with those records, that there is a satisfactory system of internal control over transactions and that the financial statements show a true and fair view of the social housing provider's financial position. Industrial and provident societies which are charitable are known as exempt charities which means they are subject to the Charities Act but are not regulated by the Charity Commission. The regulatory framework referred to above will continue to be developed during 2010/11 including work with the Charity Commission and stakeholders to gain a clear understanding of the opportunity presented by the *Charities Act* 2006 for the TSA to become the principal regulator of charitable industrial and provident societies which are also registered social housing providers ('exempt charities').

Registered Providers which are limited companies are incorporated under the Companies Act and are generally companies limited by guarantee without share capital. They will therefore need to comply with the Companies Act 2006 but also the accounting determinations issued by the relevant regulator, e.g., the TSA. Registered Providers that are charitable companies are also regulated by the Charity Commission but as Registered Providers, the Statement of Recommended Practice in the social housing sector takes precedence over the Charity SORP.

47.2.2 Responsibilities of the Board or the Committee of Management

Although day-to-day management of the Registered Provider may be delegated to subcommittees or staff, the board retains full responsibility for seeing that those functions are properly carried out.

The roles and responsibilities of the board noted in the Practice Note normally include:

- defining and monitoring compliance with the governing documents, values and objectives of the Registered Provider;
- establishing plans to achieve those objectives;
- approving each year's budget and financial statements prior to publication;
- establishing and overseeing an appropriate framework of delegation and effective systems of control;
- taking key decisions on matters that will, or might, create significant risks for the Registered Provider;
- monitoring the performance of the Registered Provider in relation to these plans, budgets and decisions;
- appointing and, if necessary, dismissing the chief executive and being represented in the appointment of key second tier managers;
- appointing and agreeing the remuneration of the auditors;
- satisfying themselves that the affairs of the Registered Provider are conducted lawfully and in accordance with performance standards set by the Regulators; and
- overseeing the Registered Provider's relationship with its regulatory body.

47.2.3 Responsibilities of audit committees

Whilst formally withdrawn on 1 April 2010 as a result of the TSA's new regulatory framework, the October 2004 Housing Corporation publication 'Improving the Effectiveness of Audit Committees: a Good Practice Guide' is still helpful. This publication addresses how audit committees can operate effectively and contribute to good governance in housing associations. It is also useful guidance for external auditors covering areas such as:

- understanding what goes into external audit management letters;
- assessing auditor performance and effectiveness;
- the independence of auditors; and
- the audit committee's role with regard to accounting policies;

The guidance covers many other areas regarding good governance and internal audit arrangements.

47.2.4   Financial reporting requirements

The financial statements of Registered Providers are prepared in accordance with the requirements of applicable law and regulations contained in accounting orders or determinations issued under the relevant statutes. The precise nature of the requirements is determined by two factors:

- how the Registered Provider is constituted (for example, as a registered charity, industrial and provident society, or non-profit making company); and
- whether the Registered Provider is registered by the relevant regulatory body.

The *Housing and Regeneration Act* 2008 sets out the requirements for accounts and audit in s127 to 143.

Generally, each Registered Provider is required to prepare financial statements which give a true and fair view and hence should comply with applicable accounting standards. The Statement of Recommended Practice *Accounting by Registered Social Landlords* (the RSL SORP) supplements these general accounting principles and provides authoritative guidance on their application. Therefore, in order to give a true and fair view, financial statements of Registered Providers are normally prepared following the provisions of the social housing sector SORP.

Although there is no specific legal requirement that Registered Providers should comply with accounting standards or with the social housing sector SORP, the various regulations require the board of a Registered Provider to state whether its financial statements have been prepared in accordance with applicable accounting standards and statements of recommended practice, which implies that the social housing sector SORP should be applied.

The latest version of this SORP is *Accounting by Registered Social Landlords 2008* which was issued in January 2008. It applies to accounting periods commencing on or after 1 April 2008.

The SORP Working Party continues to work on the next update to the SORP, and on 16 March 2010 published a SORP Exposure Draft for comment. The Exposure Draft has been prepared in accordance with the ASB's 'SORPs: Policy and Code of Practice (2000)' and comments were requested by 4 June 2010. It is proposed the updated requirements should apply to accounting periods commencing on or after 1 April 2011 but earlier adoption will be recommended. Three draft Technical Notes have been prepared as supplementary guidance to the SORP. The overall aim of the Technical Notes is to assist practitioners in the preparation of financial statements. The Technical Notes attempt to explain and illustrate what is required by the 2008 SORP. They do not form part of the SORP and are not reviewed by the ASB. They are, however, being published as part of the consultation to provide social landlords with the opportunity to comment on the proposed content of the Technical Notes. The Technical Notes cover:

- component accounting;
- impairment; and
- business combinations.

The SORP Working Party considered that the SORP would benefit from further development in the following areas:

- capitalisation of works to existing properties; and
- negative goodwill.

In addition, the SORP Working Party proposes to make a number of editorial changes to the SORP which involve updating:

- Part 3 of the SORP for new standards and Urgent Issues Task Force Abstracts that have been issued since the 2008 SORP was published; and
- references in the SORP to the Companies Act 1985 and the Housing Corporation which are to be updated where appropriate to reflect the enactment of the Companies Act 2006 and the formation of the Tenant Services Authority.

As none of the proposed editorial changes impact upon the accounting requirements in the SORP, they are not being consulted on as part of the Invitation to Comment.

The revised SORP 2008 is essential reading for auditors.

The next most likely change will be to take into consideration International Financial Reporting Standards (IFRS). There is still however some doubt as to how exactly IFRS will apply to the social housing sector. In August 2009, the ASB issued a consultation paper proposing that the process of piecemeal convergence with IFRS be replaced by a single change, the first accounting period affected being that ending on or after 31 December 2012. The main driver of the ASB's consultation was the publication by the International Accounting Standards Board in July 2009 of the IFRS for SMEs. The ASB believe that the IFRS for SMEs could realistically be applied by entities not otherwise required to apply full IFRS, resulting in the demise of existing UK GAAP on which all SORPs are predicated and that currently apply to many not-for-profits, including registered providers of social housing.

The ASB's consultation paper acknowledges that the IFRS for SMEs, like its big brother full IFRS, is written primarily with profit-making entities in mind. Therefore, the ASB proposes a separate public benefit entity standard setting out where different accounting is required by not-for-profits. If the board does take forward its proposal for a separate public benefit entity standard, questions still remain over what form that guidance should take. At one end of the spectrum it could be a standalone document distinct from the IFRS for SMEs covering all areas of accounting. At the other end it might take a minimalist approach merely requiring compliance with the IFRS for SMEs 'except for' certain specified areas. Further complications are likely to affect the social housing sector because several associations have listed debt on their balance sheets which would require their financial statements to be prepared under full IFRS. There are some fundamental areas of accounting in social housing that are different under full IFRS and the IFRS for SMEs such as the capitalisation of interest on housing property development. Matters like this will need to be resolved before the standard setters can finalise the accounting requirements.

47.2.5   *Responsibilities of auditors*

Although Registered Providers may be subject to different legislation, the statutory duties of their auditors are similar. The auditors are required to:

- express an opinion as to whether the financial statements give a true and fair view and have been properly prepared in accordance with the appropriate statutory requirements; and
- state in the auditors' report:

  - where proper books of account have not been kept;
  - where a satisfactory system of control over transactions has not been maintained; and
  - if the financial statements are not in agreement with the books and records of the Registered Provider.

There may also be a requirement imposed by the relevant regulatory body to report to them on certain returns of Registered Providers e.g. as requested by the TSA. Similarly with regard to funders, loan covenants may include the need for the auditors to report on compliance with financial covenants.

47.2.6   *Features of social housing audits*

Internal controls

Internal controls are particularly relevant because:

- Registered Providers are in receipt of substantial amounts of public funding in the form of grants; and
- legislation requires auditors to state in their report on the financial statements if the Registered Provider has failed to maintain a satisfactory system of internal control.

Other guidance

There are housing federations which represent the best interests of Registered Providers in the United Kingdom. Auditors should be aware of guidance issued by these federations, for example, codes of governance.

The long-term nature of the business

The main income source, rents, is fairly predictable, and thus analytical procedures are often a useful audit tool.

Substantial debt financing

It is common for Registered Providers to have significant amounts of borrowing. Therefore it is important for Registered Providers and their auditors to assess their medium-term financial forecasts to ensure that the going concern basis remains appropriate. Such debt financing brings with it loan covenant compliance requirements and the importance of accounting under Financial Reporting Standard 25 (FRS 25) if there are any breaches during the year.

The Auditing Practices Board (APB) Bulletin 2008/1, *Audit Issues When Financial Market Conditions are Difficult and Credit Facilities May be Restricted* and the update in APB Bulletin 2008/10, is particularly relevant to Registered Providers (see **Chapter 37**). Both were triggered by the development in the financial markets commonly known as the 'credit crunch' and the worsening economic climate and were written to apply more generally to all entities with a focus on the possible risks of misstatement to the financial statements arising from:

- the possibility of the reduced availability of finance; and
- difficulties with valuing some assets for balance sheet purposes, especially those that are required to be measured at 'fair value'.

Concerns for Registered Providers stem from the impact of significant trading difficulties in the financial markets compounded by a reduction in liquidity plus difficulties in selling social housing properties developed for sale which in turn could impact on loan covenant requirements. Registered Providers with HCA development partnering status and hence large property development commitments will be dependent on facilities from their lenders and may still have further facilities to negotiate when auditors are considering the going concern basis.

Complex direct tax, indirect tax and employee tax rules

Registered Providers are heavily involved in property transactions and this brings with it complex corporation tax and VAT requirements. As many Registered Providers are charitable housing associations they need to be aware of their primary purpose when considering property development contracts involving mixed tenure (e.g., developments where a scheme may include an element of commercial units and units for outright sale). Other examples of complexities include:

- group structures and most often the inability to be considered a group for tax purposes, i.e., group relief;
- conflicts between social housing accounting requirements under accounting

standards, and the social housing SORP and the tax treatment, e.g., first tranche shared ownership sales;

- transfer pricing, loan relationships and gift aid which can add complexity when linked to property transactions under substantial donor rules;
- partial exemption treatment for VAT purposes;
- the use of development company subsidiaries outside the VAT group to maximise the recovery of VAT on professional fees;
- potential difficulties for stock transfer associations in claiming input VAT on certain property refurbishment costs;
- the effect of employee tax for employees transferring from local authorities and tax deduction requirements on payments made to overseas landlords, e.g., under temporary leasing arrangements;
- construction industry scheme administration; and
- self employed tax rules when using consultants, especially in busy property development departments.

Auditors should be aware of joint guidance issued in May 2009 by HM Revenue and Customs, the Charity Commission and Housing Corporation titled *Affordable Home Ownership – Charitable Status and Tax.* This guidance was issued because Registered Providers increasingly venture into commercial activities which may not always fit with their 'primary purpose' or charitable status. The guidance sets out the authorities' understanding of what may or may not qualify as covered by the charitable tax exemptions and considers the question of whether particular individual families would be suitable beneficiaries. Registered Providers with home ownership activities such as shared ownership will be affected by this as will those developing residential property for outright sale. The guidance can be found on the Charity Commission's website at *www.charity-commission.gov.uk.*

Supported housing

Registered Providers involved in supported housing and providing care services have access to various sources of funding, e.g., in England, 'Supporting People'. A large amount of this funding is available through contracts with local authorities. These contracts can be complex and the available funding may not always be sufficient to deliver the service.

Housing properties

A significant number of Registered Providers including many established by means of Large Scale Voluntary Transfers, carry their housing properties at an existing use valuation. A professional valuation is obtained and, as set out in ISA (UK and Ireland) 620 *Using the work of an expert*, auditors consider the proper inclusion of the valuation in the accounts, the information on which the valuer has relied and the reasons for any changes in the valuation from the previous period.

Judgement is needed on the depreciation policy to be adopted in respect of housing properties. This covers the useful economic lives of housing properties which for most Registered Providers can cover long periods depending on property type, location and construction method. Determining the amount of cost attributable to land (which is not depreciated) and to buildings can be difficult where the properties have been in ownership for many years and records may not provide the split.

Capitalisation of works to existing properties

The principles of FRS 15 are followed and further guidance is given in the social housing SORP. The SORP recommends that works which result in an increase in the net rental income stream should be capitalised as improvements. This may arise from works carried out to existing properties, through a combination of increased rents, reduction in future maintenance costs or a significant extension to the life of the property. It is often difficult to demonstrate that any enhancement of the economic benefits of tangible fixed assets is in excess of the previously assessed standard of performance anticipated when the assets were first acquired, constructed, last replaced or revalued and should be capitalised. Registered Providers might therefore consider component accounting but this has implications for record keeping. Component accounting requirements will be clarified in the revised SORP 2008, including a Technical Note as explained above in **47.2.4**.

Impairment

FRS 11 is an important standard to consider in social housing audits. Impairments can result from a major reduction in the service potential of a property which may arise from a reduction in demand in the local area. Such impairments are recognised immediately in the income and expenditure account. Impairment reviews are also required where the estimated economic life of housing properties for depreciation purposes is 50 years or more, or no depreciation is charged because it is considered immaterial.

Auditors of Registered Providers should also be aware of a Helpsheet published by the ICAEW in February 2009 called *Impairment in the Social Housing Sector*, Reference SHSC 01/09. This helpsheet was prepared to assist practitioners and Registered Providers with identifying current thinking on impairment issues highlighted by the current economic climate. The helpsheet discusses a number of questions connected with judgements that Registered Providers and their auditors will need to make when considering the need for impairment provisions. Impairment will be clarified in the revised SORP 2008, including a Technical Note as explained above in **47.2.4**.

47.2.7   The auditors' relationship with the Regulators

The *Housing and Regeneration Act* 2008 sets out the general requirements in respect of accounts and audit. Section 127 of this Act sets out the powers of the Regulator to issue accounts directions for Registered Providers. Section 143 concerns the disclosure of information by auditors to the relevant authority.

This section applies to information that a person has received while acting as auditor or as a reporting accountant of a registered provider. Such persons may disclose the information to the regulator for a purpose connected with the regulator's functions:

- despite any duty of confidentiality; and
- whether or not the regulator requests the information.

The reference to disclosing information includes expressing an opinion on it.

47.3   ISA (UK AND IRELAND) 210: TERMS OF AUDIT ENGAGEMENTS

Engagement letters should set out additional auditor responsibilities in relation to Registered Providers, which may arise:

- under statute – such as additional returns to be reviewed;
- from recommendations issued to Registered Providers within the various codes and other recommendations from the relevant regulatory body or relevant housing federation; or
- by agreement with the Registered Provider.

Statutory requirements may also result in additional returns which a Registered Provider may require its auditors to review or sign, such as a service charge summaries under the Landlord and Tenant Act 1985. The recommendations made to Registered Providers by their regulatory bodies are not themselves binding on auditors, but Registered Providers and their auditors will generally agree to increase the scope of the auditors' work to ensure that the Registered Provider complies with best practice.

An example of an audit engagement letter is shown in **Table 1**.

TABLE 1: Example engagement letter for Registered Providers – drafted for an Industrial and Provident Society and should be amended for other types of constitution

To the Board of [name of Registered Provider]

The purpose of this letter is to set out the basis on which we are to act as auditors of the Society and the respective areas of responsibility of the Board, comprising of those charged with governance of the Society, and of ourselves.

Financial statements, accounting records and internal controls

As members of the Board ('the Board') of the Society you are responsible for maintaining proper accounting records and an appropriate system of internal control for the Society. You are also responsible for preparing the annual report and the financial statements which give a true and fair view and have been prepared in accordance with applicable accounting standards, the Industrial & Provident Societies Acts 1965 to 2002, Housing and Regeneration Act 2008 and the most recent applicable Accounting Requirements for Registered Social Landlords General Determination or Direction as issued by the Tenant Services Authority ('the Accounting Determination'). Failure to fulfil these requirements can result in your disqualification from office.

In preparing the financial statements, you are required to:

- select suitable accounting policies and then apply them consistently;
- make judgements and estimates that are reasonable and prudent; and
- prepare the financial statements on the going concern basis unless it is inappropriate to presume that the Society will continue in business.

You are responsible for keeping proper accounting records that set out with reasonable accuracy at any time the Society's financial position and for ensuring that the financial statements comply with the Industrial & Provident Societies Acts 1965 to 2002, Schedule 1 to the Housing and Regeneration Act 2008 and the Accounting Determination. You are also required to have regard to the Statement of Recommended Practice, Accounting by Registered Social Landlords, (the SORP) issued jointly by the National Housing Federation in England, the Scottish Federation of Housing Associations and the Welsh Federation of Housing Associations. As an RSL, the Society's financial statements are expected to comply fully, where appropriate, with the SORP. You are also responsible for safeguarding the assets of the Society and hence for taking reasonable steps to prevent and detect fraud and other irregularities.

It is usual for a statement of your responsibilities to be included in the Board report or elsewhere in the annual report. If no such statement is made, we are required to include one in our report.

You are responsible for filing the financial statements with the Tenant Services Authority and the Registrar within the requisite time limits. Failure to do so can result in action being taken against yourself and the Society.

You are responsible for ensuring that the Society complies with laws and regulations that apply to its activities, and for preventing non-compliance and detecting any that occurs.

For the purposes of our audit you are required by law to make available to us, as and when required, all the Society's accounting records and related financial information, including minutes of management and board meetings, that we need to do our work. We are entitled under the Act to require from the officers of the Society, such information and explanations we think necessary for the performance of our audit. We are also entitled to attend all general meetings of the Society and to receive notice of all such meetings.

Electronic Publication

We recognise that you may wish to publish your financial statements and our audit report on your website or distribute them by means such as e-mail. If you choose to do so, it is your responsibility to ensure that such publication properly presents the financial information and any auditors' report.

You agree to advise us of any intended electronic publication before it occurs, and we reserve the right to withhold consent to the electronic publication of our audit report if we assess the audited financial statements or our report to be published in an inappropriate manner.

The members of the board are responsible for the controls over, and security of, the website used for this purpose, and examination of these controls is beyond the scope of our audit of the financial statements. You are also responsible for establishing and controlling the process for electronically distributing Annual Reports and other financial information to stakeholders.

If you choose to publish our audit report electronically, the following wording must also be published:

'Financial statements are published on the Society's website in accordance with legislation in the United Kingdom governing the preparation and dissemination of financial statements, which may vary from legislation in other jurisdictions. The maintenance and integrity of the group's website is the responsibility of the members of the board. The responsibility of members of the board also extends to the ongoing integrity of the financial statements contained therein.'

OUR RESPONSIBILITIES AS AUDITORS

Audit under the Friendly and Industrial Provident Societies Act 1968

The responsibility for safeguarding the assets of the Society and for the prevention and detection of fraud, error and non-compliance with law or regulations rests with yourselves. However, we shall endeavour to plan our audit so that we have a reasonable expectation of detecting material misstatements in the financial statements or accounting records (including those resulting from fraud, error or non-compliance with law or regulations), but our examination should not be relied upon to disclose all such material misstatements or frauds, errors or instances of non-compliance as may exist.

Under the Insolvency Act 1986, you have a statutory duty of care to the creditors of the Society. You must ensure that the Society does not continue to trade if there is no reasonable prospect of avoiding insolvent liquidation. If during our audit, any factors come to our attention which indicate such a possibility we shall of course inform you. However, this will not relieve you of your statutory and other duties as members of the board.

The law requires us to report whether, in our opinion:

- the financial statements give a true and fair view, in accordance with the relevant financial reporting framework, of the state of the Society's affairs and of its surplus or deficit for the year;
- the financial statements have been properly prepared in accordance with the Industrial and Provident Societies Acts 1965 to 2002, the Housing and Regeneration Act 2008 and the Accounting Requirements for Registered Social Landlords General Determination.

The law also requires us to consider whether:

- proper accounting records have been kept by the Society;
- the balance sheet and profit and loss account are in agreement with the accounting records and returns;
- whether the Society has maintained a satisfactory system of control over its transactions;

- we have obtained all the information and explanations which we think are necessary for the purposes of our audit; and
- whether all the information in the Board's report is consistent with that in the audited financial statements.

We are only required to make a specific reference to these matters in our report if we are not satisfied.

In addition, there are certain other matters which, according to the circumstances, may need to be dealt with in our report. For example, where the financial statements do not give full details of the board's review of effectiveness of internal controls.

We are required to read the other information issued with audited financial statements and to consider whether it is consistent with the financial statements. This other information would include, where applicable, statements by the chairman, chief executive or treasurer, operating and financial review, financial highlights, corporate governance statement, the board's statement on internal controls. If we become aware of any apparent misstatements or material inconsistencies with the financial statements, we draw these to your attention. We are only required to make a specific reference to these matters in our report if we are not satisfied.

There are also certain other matters which we may have to deal with in our report. For example, the law requires us to give details of directors' remuneration, where such details are not disclosed in the financial statements. Similarly where transactions between directors (and their connected persons) and the Society have not been disclosed, we must give details in our report.

We also have a professional responsibility to refer in our report to instances of material non-compliance with applicable accounting standards. We do not need to refer in our report to those areas where, in our opinion, the non-compliance is necessary for the financial statements to show a true and fair view and is adequately disclosed.

Section 143 of the Housing and Regeneration Act 2008 applies to information that a person has received while acting as auditor or as a reporting accountant of a registered provider. Such persons may disclose the information to the regulator for a purpose connected with the regulator's functions:

- despite any duty of confidentiality; and
- whether or not the regulator requests the information.

Scope of audit

Our audit will be conducted in accordance with International Standards on Auditing (UK and Ireland) issued by the Auditing Practices Board and will have particular regard to the APB's Practice Note '*The Audit of Registered Social Landlords in the United Kingdom (Revised)*'. It will include such tests of transactions and of the existence, ownership and valuation of assets and liabilities as we consider necessary.

We shall obtain an understanding of the accounting and internal control systems in order to assess their adequacy as a basis for the preparation of the financial statements and to establish whether proper accounting records have been maintained by the Society. We shall expect to obtain such appropriate evidence as we consider sufficient to enable us to draw reasonable conclusions therefrom.

The nature and extent of our procedures will vary according to our assessment of the Society's accounting system and, where we wish to place reliance on it, the internal control system, and may cover any aspect of the business's operations that we consider appropriate.

Because of the test nature and other inherent limitations of an audit, together with the inherent limitations of any accounting and internal control system, there is an unavoidable risk that even some material misstatements may remain undiscovered.

Our audit is not designed to identify all significant weaknesses in the Society's systems but, if such weaknesses come to our notice during the course of our audit which we think should be brought to your attention, we shall report them to you.

We shall request sight of all documents or statements which are due to be issued with the financial statements.

Management representations

From time to time we may have to rely on oral representations by management which are uncorroborated by other audit evidence. Where they relate to matters which are material to the financial statements, we will request that you provide written confirmation of them. In particular, where misstatements in the financial statements that we bring to your attention are not adjusted, we are required to obtain your reasons in writing.

Use of report

Our report will be made solely to the Society's members, as a body, in accordance with Section 9 of the Friendly and Industrial Provident Societies Act 1968 and Schedule 1 paragraph 16 to the Housing and Regeneration Act 2008. Our audit work will be undertaken so that we might state to the Society's members those matters we are required to state to them in an auditors' report and for no other purpose. In those circumstances, and to the fullest extent permitted by law, we will not accept or assume responsibility to anyone other than the Society and the Society's members as a body, for our audit work, for the audit report, or for the opinions we form.

We shall not be treated as having notice, for the purposes of our audit responsibilities, of information provided to members of our firm other than those engaged on the audit (for example information provided in connection with accounting, taxation and other services).

Once we have issued our report we have no further direct responsibility in relation to the financial statements for that financial year. However, we expect that you will inform us of any material event occurring between the date of our report and that of the Annual General Meeting which may affect the financial statements.

Communication with those charged with governance

We will communicate certain information to you, including:

- Any matters relevant to the firm's independence and the integrity and objectivity of the audit engagement partner and audit staff;
- An outline of the nature and scope of the work that we propose to undertake;
- Our views about the qualitative aspects of the company's accounting practices and financial reporting;
- Uncorrected misstatements other than those that are clearly trivial;
- Material weaknesses in internal control identified during the audit;

Such communication may be oral or in writing (see management letter below). However, we will report in writing any findings from the audit that we consider to be significant or to confirm that there are no matters that we wish to report in writing. Any such report may not be disclosed to third parties without our prior written consent apart from the Tenant Services Authority. Such consent will be granted only on the basis that such reports are not prepared with the interests of anyone other than the company in mind and that we accept no duty or responsibility to any other party as concerns the reports.

Management Letter

At the conclusion of the audit, or sooner if appropriate, we shall prepare a report to the Board that will include comments on:

- any expected modification of the auditors' report,
- unadjusted misstatements,
- material weaknesses to the accounting and internal control systems identified during the audit,
- the qualitative aspects of the Society's accounting practices and financial reporting,
- matters specifically required by other Auditing Standards, and
- any other relevant matters relating to the audit.

Our audit is not designed to identify all significant weaknesses in the Society's system of internal controls. Our review of internal control systems is only performed to the extent required to express an opinion on the Society's financial statements and therefore our comments on these systems will not necessarily address all possible improvements which might be suggested as a result of a more extensive special examination.

You will forward a copy of our management letter to the Tenant Services Authority.

Summary Financial Statements

As Board members of the Society, you are responsible for any summary financial statements. Our responsibility is to report to the members whether in our opinion the summary financial statement is consistent with the full financial statements and report of the Society for the year. Our work will be conducted in accordance with Bulletin 2008/3 'The auditors' statement on the summary financial statement' issued by the Auditing Practices Board.

On recurring audits, the auditor should consider whether circumstances require the terms of the engagement to be revised and whether there is a need to remind the client of the existing terms of the engagement.

When asked to provide special reports on grants where the grant making body requires the report to be addressed to it as well as the grant recipient, auditors should refer to Technical Release 03/03, *"Public Sector Special Reporting Engagements – Grant Claims"* published by the Audit and Assurance Faculty of the ICAEW. This includes examples of tri-partite engagement letters and covers typical examples of when either high level or moderate assurance is sought or whether the approach is one of agreed upon procedures.

47.4 ISA (UK AND IRELAND) 220: QUALITY CONTROL FOR AUDITS OF HISTORICAL FINANCIAL INFORMATION

The engagement partner should be satisfied that the engagement team collectively has the appropriate capabilities, competence and time to perform the audit engagement in accordance with professional standards and regulatory and legal requirements, and to enable an auditor's report that is appropriate in the circumstances to be issued.. The Practice Note states that this will include:

- the scope and nature of the activities of the Registered Provider;
- the most significant parts of the relevant regulator's guidance; and
- the relevant general principles of the social housing SORP.

47.5 ISA (UK AND IRELAND) 240: THE AUDITOR'S RESPONSIBILITY TO CONSIDER FRAUD IN AN AUDIT OF FINANCIAL STATEMENTS

Registered Providers have been encouraged by their respective regulatory bodies to establish adequate internal controls and to report frauds over a certain limit to their regulator.

As part of their risk assessment, auditors should review any disclosures to the regulator and enquire whether the regulatory body has responded.

Various external issues could influence a Registered Provider's objectives and strategies. The Practice Note refers to the increase in consolidation within the sector, the increased focus on efficiency and cost control, and the desire to become or remain a HCA development partner. The strategies being adopted by Registered Providers to manage these issues may result in an incentive for material misstatement of the financial statements. Registered Providers often also have significant borrowings with covenants attached (generally interest cover and gearing covenants).This may create pressures on the entity that, in turn, may motivate management to take action to improve the reported business performance or to misstate the financial statements.

The Practice Note comments that where auditors suspect that there may be any matters which they believe should be included in the register they should document their findings and, subject to any requirement to report them directly to a third party, raise them with senior management or a board member as soon as possible. They should also consider reporting the matter to the board and audit committee once they are aware of all the circumstances. When considering the appropriate person to discuss these matters with auditors should bear in mind the management structure of the Registered Provider.

There is no requirement for auditors to report suspected instances of fraud to a regulatory body unless they consider it a matter of public interest or, in the case of an unincorporated, non-exempt charity they believe it would be a matter of material significance in the exercise of the Charity Commission's functions. Section **47.2.7** above on the auditor's relationship with the Regulators sets out the implications of reporting matters to the Regulator.

47.6   ISA (UK AND IRELAND) 250: CONSIDERATION OF LAWS AND REGULATIONS IN AN AUDIT OF FINANCIAL STATEMENTS

While Section A of ISA (UK and Ireland) 250 set out how auditors should plan to obtain sufficient evidence of compliance with relevant law and regulations, the Practice Note only lists those regulations with which auditors should be concerned. It does not provide any guidance on how auditors should set about obtaining evidence of compliance.

The law relating to a specific Registered Provider depends on:

- whether the Registered Provider is constituted as a registered charity, a society registered under the Industrial and Provident Societies Act 1965 or as a non-profit making company; and
- which regulatory body has granted registration to the Registered Provider.

Although, as noted above, the regulations imply that the financial statements of an Registered Provider should be prepared in accordance with the social housing SORP, consideration must also be given to any specific requirements of its governing document.

The auditor should perform further audit procedures to help identify instances of non-compliance with those laws and regulations where non-compliance should be considered when preparing financial statements, specifically:

(a) Inquiring of management as to whether the entity is in compliance with such laws and regulations;
(b) Inspecting correspondence with the relevant licensing or regulatory authorities, e.g. the TSA and HCA; and
(c) Enquiring of those charged with governance as to whether they are on notice of any such possible instances of non-compliance with law or regulations.

In the UK and Ireland, the auditor's procedures should be designed to help identify possible or actual instances of non-compliance with those laws and regulations which provide a legal framework within which the Registered Provider conducts its business and which are central to its ability to conduct its business and hence to its financial statements.

Laws and regulations which are noted by the Practice Note as likely to be central to a Registered Provider are those where a breach would have any of the following consequences:

- intervention by the regulatory body to direct the affairs of the Registered Provider – for example, non-compliance with the various laws relating to fraud and corruption under which the regulatory body possesses various powers of intervention;
- loss of necessary licences to continue a major element of the Registered Provider's work – primarily laws and regulations applicable to building and planning regulations or contaminated land, or health and safety regulations in relation to homes in multiple occupation; or
- financial effects resulting in liabilities which are likely to exceed the available resources of the Registered Provider – for example, expenditure or activities outside grant conditions imposed by the regulatory body which may lead to disallowance and repayment of grant.

Auditors of Registered Providers other than unincorporated charities have no statutory duty to report suspected or actual instances of non-compliance with the law or regulations to an appropriate authority, unless they believe it should be reported in the public interest.

In accordance with Practice Note 11, the auditors of unincorporated charities have a statutory duty to report actual or suspected significant instances of non-compliance to the Charities Commission (see **Chapter 43)**.

Given the significant cash flows involved in the purchase and development of land, all Registered Providers should be aware of the risk of money laundering occurring. Regard should be given to the Money Laundering Regulations and Practice Note 12 (revised), see **Chapter 12**.

Instances of non-compliance identified by auditors should be reported to the appropriate level of management. However, if management are involved in the breach, auditors may consider it appropriate to communicate with the Board.

47.7 ISA (UK AND IRELAND) 260: COMMUNICATION OF AUDIT MATTERS WITH THOSE CHARGED WITH GOVERNANCE

As responsibilities in Registered Providers are delegated by the Board to the management team, auditors need to consider to whom it would be most appropriate to address their reports. Whilst the management team may play a central role in the management of the Registered Provider, their powers come from the Board, and therefore it is to the Board that auditors will normally address their management letters.

ISA (UK and Ireland) 260 sets out examples of areas to consider when communicating to those charged with governance:

- expected modifications to the auditors' report;
- unadjusted misstatements;
- material weaknesses in the accounting and internal control systems;
- views about the qualitative aspects of the Registered Provider's accounting practices and financial reporting;
- matters specifically required by other ISAs (UK and Ireland) to be communicated to those charged with governance, such as fraud and error; and
- any other relevant matters relating to the audit.

All UK social housing regulators required Registered Providers to send them copies of auditors' management letters, together with management's response although this requirement no longer appears to be mandatory under the TSA's *The regulatory framework for social housing in England from April 2010*. It is recognised that the management letter addresses only those matters which have come to the attention of the auditors in the course of their audit.

47.8 ISA (UK AND IRELAND) 300: PLANNING AN AUDIT OF FINANCIAL STATEMENTS

The Practice Note comments that the auditors should obtain an understanding of the accounting principles and their impact on the audit, and that auditors should make use of internal controls, internal audit and reporting arrangements in place at the Registered Provider. At the planning stage auditors should be aware of any additional reporting requirements that they may have and plan their work accordingly.

At the planning stage, auditors should identify any additional procedures or evidence which may be necessary for work on other reports, for example, on service charges.

The auditor should develop an audit plan for the audit in order to reduce audit risk to an acceptably low level and should also document the overall audit strategy and the audit plan, including any significant changes made during the audit engagement.

47.9 ISA (UK AND IRELAND) 315: UNDERSTANDING THE ENTITY AND ITS ENVIRONMENT AND ASSESSING THE RISKS OF MATERIAL MISSTATEMENT

This section of the revised Practice Note which interprets ISA (UK and Ireland) 315 in relation to Registered Providers, has been subject to major revision and now covers how the auditor should obtain an understanding of relevant industry, regulatory, and other external factors including the applicable financial reporting framework for Registered Providers including:

- the Constitution of Registered Providers, regulation and financial reporting requirements;
- obtaining an understanding of the nature of the entity including the overall structure, activities, finances and governance of the Registered Provider;
- complex projects such as schemes developed under the Private Finance Initiative (PFI) and the accounting for such schemes in accordance with Application Note F of FRS 5;
- the development of both social housing and housing for outright sale, sometimes as part of the same overall scheme. Under such arrangements, surpluses generated on the sale of properties may be used to subsidise other social housing which may be developed without recourse to social housing grant or with lower levels of grant than would normally be the case;
- understanding a Registered Provider's selection and application of accounting policies and considering whether they are appropriate for its business and consistent with the applicable financial reporting framework and accounting policies used in the relevant industry, especially in relation to depreciation, capitalisation of works to existing properties and impairment;
- understanding a Registered Provider's objectives and strategies, and the related business risks that may result in material misstatement of the financial statements;
- measurement and review of a Registered Provider's financial performance given the considerable external benchmarking and performance review including, for example, participation in benchmarking clubs, other comparative information published by the TSA and various league tables in the housing press;
- understanding of internal control relevant to the audit including the statutory requirement to report if the Registered Provider has not maintained a satisfactory system of control; the expectation (in Wales, the requirement) that the management letter will be passed on to the regulatory body; and any additional procedures that have been agreed with the client;
- requirements of auditors in relation to control systems;
- the control environment including considering and understanding the entity's process for identifying business risks relevant to financial reporting

objectives and deciding about actions to address those risks, and the results thereof;

- control activities where the Practice Note provides many examples of those control activities which are of particular significance to Registered Providers. The list is not intended to be exhaustive as there may be other control procedures that are relevant to the activities of a particular RSL; and
- assessing the risks of material misstatement where again the Practice Note provides many helpful examples relevant to Registered Providers.

47.10   ISA (UK AND IRELAND) 320: AUDIT MATERIALITY

The Practice Note states that consideration of materiality for Registered Providers does not differ fundamentally from that for other entities. However, auditors should be aware that particular disclosures or expenditure categories may be sensitive and warrant extra attention, and the guidance suggests the Chief Executive's remuneration, restricted funds and bad debt provisions as examples.

47.11   ISA (UK AND IRELAND) 330: THE AUDITOR'S PROCEDURES IN RESPONSE TO ASSESSED RISKS

When the auditor has determined that it is not possible to reduce the risks of material misstatement at the assertion level to an acceptably low level with audit evidence obtained only from substantive procedures, the auditor should perform tests of relevant controls to obtain audit evidence about their operating effectiveness. Many social housing activities involve a large number of small transactions, e.g. rental income. Auditors seek evidence to determine the completeness and accuracy of rental income. Where auditors are satisfied, through evaluation and testing, that there are appropriate and effective controls, including, for example, the effective reconciliation of housing management and finance systems, they can use the results of this internal control testing as a source of audit evidence about the completeness and accuracy of recorded transactions.

When the auditor has determined that an assessed risk of material misstatement at the assertion level is a significant risk, the auditor should perform substantive procedures that are specifically responsive to that risk. Possible significant risks in the context of Registered Providers are listed in the Practice Note covering ISA (UK and Ireland) 315. In respect of a significant risk arising from capitalisation, the auditor considers whether the Registered Provider's policy, for example on the types of works to be capitalised, as well as the approach to the capitalisation of internal development costs and interest, is in compliance with FRS 15 and the detailed interpretation set out in the social housing SORP. The auditor will then carry out detailed checks to ensure compliance with the policy.

Auditors of Registered Providers also need to consider the risks surrounding significant and complex transactions and other factors such as:

- property development work including:
  - incorrect allocation of costs to schemes,
  - cost overruns due to poor budgeting or unauthorised expenditure leading to costs in excess of the original project appraisal,
  - fraud risks arising from purchasing frauds, such as payment for services not supplied, or
  - collusion;
- lack of experience of the Registered Provider's staff in carrying out such non-core activities;
- the complexity of the transactions, e.g. legal structures, tax, accounting and funding arrangements;
- involvement of, and reliance on, third parties;
- viability arising from cost overruns; and
- issues relating to the vires of the Registered Provider.

47.12 ISA (UK AND IRELAND) 402: AUDIT CONSIDERATIONS RELATING TO ENTITIES USING SERVICE ORGANISATIONS

Where a Registered Provider makes use of a service organisation it does not alter the ultimate responsibility of the board or the audit committee to meet their legal responsibilities, neither does it diminish auditors' responsibilities when reporting on financial statements.

Examples of activities undertaken by a service organisation may include:

- maintenance of the Registered Provider's accounting records;
- processing of the payroll;
- other financial functions which involve establishing the carrying value of items in financial statements;
- management of assets, including outsourcing of repairs, maintenance and development work;
- management of agency schemes;
- internal audit; and
- undertaking or making arrangements for transactions as agents of the user entity, e.g., property management contracts.

47.13 ISA (UK AND IRELAND) 500: AUDIT EVIDENCE

In order for the auditor to obtain reliable audit evidence, the information upon which the audit procedures are based needs to be sufficiently complete and accurate. For example, in auditing rental income and bad debt provisions, the auditor considers the accuracy of the ageing of rental debtors derived from the housing management system. Obtaining audit evidence about the completeness and accuracy of the information produced by the housing management system may be performed concurrently with the actual audit procedure applied to the information when obtaining such audit evidence is an integral part of the audit procedure itself.

In other situations, the auditor may have obtained audit evidence of the accuracy and completeness of such information by testing controls over the production and maintenance of the information. However, in some situations the auditor may determine that additional audit procedures are needed. For example, these additional procedures may include using computer-assisted audit techniques (CAATs) to recalculate the information.

Given the large number of housing properties owned and managed by Registered Providers, physical inspection is unlikely to be an appropriate means of testing existence. The auditor views or obtains confirmation of documents of title from solicitors or the Land Registry. Such tests do not establish that the valuation of properties is appropriate.

47.14 ISA (UK AND IRELAND) 505: EXTERNAL CONFIRMATIONS

Situations in which external confirmations may be used by Registered Provider auditors may include:

- Bank balances and other information from bankers;
- Loan balances and terms and conditions;
- Balances with local authorities, agencies and other partners;
- Property title deeds held by lawyers.

Confirmations are unlikely to be appropriate as a means of checking balances with tenants and leaseholders given the volume and size of individual balances.

47.15   ISA (UK AND IRELAND) 520: ANALYTICAL PROCEDURES

The income and expenditure of Registered Providers, and in particular the levels of capital and maintenance expenditure, interest payable and rental income, are predictable. This facilitates comparisons with budgets, with other organisations in the sector and proof in total tests.

In addition, as Registered Providers are required to submit a number of returns to their Regulator, many publish a comprehensive range of information and data, which may assist auditors by indicating trends and current ratios.

Examples of items to consider and features of data are detailed in **Table 2**.

TABLE 2: Analytical procedures

Capital and repairs and maintenance expenditure

- movements and unexpected or unusual relationships between current and prior year capital programme, allocations, budgeted amounts and cash planning targets for acquisitions and disposals
- comparison of the level of development department activity and professional fees with recorded additions to housing properties
- major repairs grants and repairs costs in comparison to budget and previous years' costs
- the ratio of repairs and maintenance to the cost of housing, land and buildings
- comparison against prior year and expected amounts for construction costs per property
- comparison of actual expenditure against costs in stock condition surveys
- for special need housing, comparison of the ratio of care staff to the number of bed spaces
- review of amount of grant as a percentage of development cost
- movements on any suspense or construction in progress accounts
- comparison of interest and overheads capitalised with prior years
- comparison with external benchmark indicators.

Rental income

- the relationship between the number of housing units available for occupation, the incidence of empty units and rents receivable
- movements, and any unexpected or unusual relationships, between current and prior year budgets for rent received or service charges
- movements, and unexpected or unusual relationships, between current year, prior year and budget for voids and bad debts as a percentage of rents
- rents and service charges for each month.

Other income and administrative expenses

- amounts are usually related to comparable information for prior periods
- amounts are usually directly comparable to other Registered Providers of similar size and nature

---

> • some amounts are closely related to non-financial information such as the number of units, the number of employees and the size of office buildings.

47.16 ISA (UK AND IRELAND) 540: AUDIT OF ACCOUNTING ESTIMATES

The main areas where estimates are likely to be involved in the audit of Registered Providers are:

• depreciation of housing properties, and especially the estimated useful economic life;
• the level of bad and doubtful debt provisions against tenant arrears; and
• impairment provisions, including situations where existing use valuations are below net cost but the Registered Provider assesses the net realisable value of the property, after deducting any grants that would need to be repaid or recycled, to be higher than net cost. Further judgments may be required in order to determine whether an alternative measure of service potential may be more appropriate where assets are held for social purposes.

47.17 ISA (UK AND IRELAND) 545: AUDITING FAIR VALUE MEASUREMENTS AND DISCLOSURES

Fair value measurements and disclosures are most likely to apply to those Registered Providers who hold fixed assets at valuation.

Under acquisition accounting, the identifiable assets and liabilities of the Registered Provider acquired should be included in the acquirer's balance sheet at their fair value at the date of acquisition. The auditor ensures that the valuation method and amount adopted is appropriately supported and properly reflected in the financial statements.

In principle the fair value of housing properties is the Existing Use Value Social Housing (EUV-SH) of these properties. The fair value of other assets and liabilities can be assessed in accordance with the requirements of FRS 7. The auditor considers whether the information provided is consistent with the financial records subject to audit. Fixed rate loans should be revalued in the light of interest rates at the time of acquisition.

47.18   ISA (UK AND IRELAND) 550: RELATED PARTIES

The principles and procedures set out in ISA (UK and Ireland) 550 apply to the audit of Registered Providers as for other entities. In addition, those Registered Providers that are companies need to comply with relevant sections of the Companies Acts.

Subject to certain exemptions, members of the board and those associated with them, and those associated with senior managers, are not allowed to benefit financially from their connection with the Registered Provider. If there is any evidence of the existence of such related party transactions, then both ISA (UK and Ireland) 550 and ISA (UK and Ireland) 250 *Consideration of law and regulations* applies.

In England, auditors may take account of the results of any examination of related party transactions undertaken by the TSA's review teams. However, such examinations do not remove the requirement for auditors to obtain sufficient and appropriate audit evidence that material, identified related party transactions are properly recorded and disclosed.

The auditor considers in particular whether appropriate disclosure, as required by Financial Reporting Standard (FRS) 8 – Related Party Disclosures, is made in the financial statements of transactions between the RSL and board members. The provisions of FRS 8 in the context of related parties and the Registered Provider's management, are applied to all members of 'key management' not just members of the board. Key management may be taken to include those persons having authority and responsibility for planning, directing and controlling the activities of the Registered Provider, directly or indirectly, including any director (whether executive or otherwise) or officer of that Registered Provider.

47.19   ISA (UK AND IRELAND) 560: SUBSEQUENT EVENTS

Requirements for auditors to consider subsequent events do not differ for Registered Providers compared to other entities. Auditors should be aware, however, that in most Registered Providers the non-executive board plays a crucial role in approving the financial statements. This may be a significant time after the formal audit clearance meeting has taken place.

47.20   ISA (UK AND IRELAND) 570: GOING CONCERN

Registered Providers should normally prepare accounts on a going concern basis, and where they are not the Accounting Requirements for Registered Social Landlords General Determination 2006 requires disclosure of that fact.

The Practice Note recommends that auditors consider the circumstances in which Registered Providers may cease to continue in operational existence. This takes the same form as for other entities. The board has primary responsibility to make an assessment as to whether the going concern concept is applicable.

As Registered Providers have a relatively long business cycle the board may need to consider a longer period than normal. This is likely to involve an assessment of the extent to which there may be adverse variations or uncertainties, and because of this it may be appropriate for auditors to obtain representations from the board on these. Where there are uncertainties, confirmation of particular sources of funds or revenues of the Registered Provider may need to be obtained by auditors in the same way as confirmation of facilities may be required for a company.

Factors which may indicate a potential going concern problem are listed in **Table 3** below.

TABLE 3: Factors indicating potential going concern problems

- transfers of the entire housing stock, or a significant proportion of it;
- potential action from the regulatory body;
- for a transferee Registered Provider, transfers of housing stock where the acquisition cost or carrying value is not covered by the long-term projected net rental income;
- onerous contract terms;
- inability to service interest payments;
- a significant amount of variable interest rate borrowings at a time when interest rates are rising or are predicted to rise;
- a significant short-term repair liability that the Registered Provider will have difficulty in meeting from its own resources;
- loan repayments or refinancing which cannot be met from the Registered Provider's own resources;
- housing property development commitments which cannot be met from available Social Housing Grant and available loan facilities;
- breach of loan covenants; and
- significant loans to subsidiaries involved in activities such as shared ownership or developments for sale.

In assessing going concern, the board considers the extent to which there may be adverse variations from anticipated funding or revenue, or additional unexpected costs, and any uncertainties as to whether or not the Registered Provider can continue in operational existence for the foreseeable future. Typically,

Registered Providers acquire properties with the assistance of grants or long term borrowings. This method of financing leads to predictable cash flows in that loan repayments can be predicted and, accordingly, the Registered Provider should be able to plan to meet its obligations from available resources. Registered Providers have a relatively long business cycle and, in preparing its medium term financial forecasts, the board may consider a longer period of time than for other entities.

If there are any indications that a particular source of funds or revenue may need to be renewed or renegotiated, the auditor may elect to request the Registered Provider to contact the source of such funds for confirmation that the facility, or grant, will continue to be made available to the Registered Provider. Where there continues to be uncertainty, it may be necessary for the board to disclose the circumstances in the financial statements and for the auditor to draw attention to the matter within their report.

47.21 ISA (UK AND IRELAND) 580: MANAGEMENT REPRESENTATIONS

The Practice Note guidance on the need for written confirmation of management representations does not vary greatly from that in the ISA (UK and Ireland). It does recommend, however, that auditors may include in their representation letters confirmation that all minutes and correspondence with the regulatory body have been made available to them.

47.22 ISA (UK AND IRELAND) 610: CONSIDERING THE WORK OF INTERNAL AUDIT

Auditors should make use of any internal audit function in place at the Registered Provider. Larger Registered Providers are required to determine what is an appropriate internal audit function.

The Practice Note comments that although liaison with internal audit may reduce the extent of the external auditors' procedures, this is a matter for their professional judgement, which should take account of the particular circumstances of the Registered Provider and the auditors' assessment of the internal audit function.

Auditors should also be aware of the ICAEW's Audit and Assurance Faculty guidance *'The Power of Three, Understanding the roles and relationships of internal and external auditors and audit committees'* which was published in May 2003.

47.23   ISA (UK AND IRELAND) 620: USING THE WORK OF AN EXPERT

ISA (UK and Ireland) 620, alongside ISA (UK and Ireland) 545, *Auditing Fair Value Measurements and Disclosures* are likely to be relevant where properties are shown at a valuation. The SORP requires that valuations should be on the 'existing use value social housing' basis, and any departure from this basis should be disclosed in the accounts. Normal auditing considerations apply and these are dealt with in **Chapter 28**.

The other area where auditors may rely on the work of an expert is where information is supplied by an actuary about the surpluses or deficits on defined benefit pension schemes.

47.24   ISA (UK AND IRELAND) 700: THE INDEPENDENT AUDITOR'S REPORT ON A COMPLETE SET OF GENERAL PURPOSE FINANCIAL STATEMENTS

The Practice Note contains guidance on the reports made by auditors of Registered Providers and provides example reports and responsibility statements. An example unqualified report and responsibility statement are shown in **Tables 4** and **5** respectively.

TABLE 4: Audit report for single entity registered provider of social housing that is an industrial and provident society – Not ISA 700 (Revised) UK & Ireland

Independent auditor's report to the members of Example Housing Association

We have audited the financial statements of Example Housing Association for the year ended 31 March 2010 which comprise the income and expenditure account, the balance sheet, *[the statement of total recognised surpluses and deficits, the note of historical cost surpluses and deficits, the cash flow statement,]* and the related notes. These financial statements have been prepared under the accounting policies set out therein.

Respective responsibilities of the board and auditors

The Board's responsibilities for preparing the financial statements in accordance with applicable law and United Kingdom Accounting Standards (United Kingdom Generally Accepted Accounting Practice) are set out in the statement of responsibilities of the Board.

Our responsibility is to audit the financial statements in accordance with relevant legal and regulatory requirements and International Standards on Auditing (UK and Ireland).

We report to you our opinion as to whether the financial statements give a true and fair view and have been properly prepared in accordance with the Industrial and Provident Societies Acts 1965 to 2002, the Housing Act 1996 (to 31 March 2010), the Housing and Regeneration Act (from 1 April 2010) and the Accounting Requirements for Registered Social Landlords General Determination 2006. We also report to you if, in our opinion, the Association has not kept proper accounting records, a satisfactory system of control over transactions has not been maintained, or if we have not received all the information and explanations we require for our audit.

We read the Report of the Board and consider the implications for our report if we become aware of any apparent misstatements within it. *[if there is other information in the Report of the Board, please delete this paragraph and replace with the one below]*

We read other information contained in the Report of the Board, and consider whether it is consistent with the audited financial statements. This other information comprises only the operating and financial review. We consider the implications for our report if we become aware of any apparent misstatements or material inconsistencies with the financial statements. Our responsibilities do not extend to any other information.

Our report has been prepared pursuant to the requirements of the Housing Act 1996 (to 31 March 2010), the Housing and Regeneration Act (from 1 April 2010) and Section 9 of the Friendly and Industrial and Provident Societies Act 1968 and for no other purpose. No person is entitled to rely on this report unless such a person is a person entitled to rely upon this report by virtue of and for the purpose of the above statutes or has been expressly authorised to do so by our prior written consent. Save as above, we do not accept responsibility for this report to any other person or for any other purpose and we hereby expressly disclaim any and all such liability.

Basis of audit opinion

We conducted our audit in accordance with International Standards on Auditing (UK and Ireland) issued by the Auditing Practices Board. An audit includes examination, on a test basis, of evidence relevant to the amounts and disclosures in the financial statements. It also includes an assessment of the significant estimates and judgments made by the Board in the preparation of the financial statements, and of whether the accounting policies are appropriate to the Association's circumstances, consistently applied and adequately disclosed.

We planned and performed our audit so as to obtain all the information and explanations which we considered necessary in order to provide us with sufficient evidence to give reasonable assurance that the financial statements are free from material misstatement, whether caused by fraud or other irregularity or error. In forming our opinion we also evaluated the overall adequacy of the presentation of information in the financial statements.

Opinion

In our opinion the Association's financial statements:

- give a true and fair view, in accordance with United Kingdom Generally Accepted Accounting Practice, of the state of the Association's affairs as at 31 March 2010 and of its results for the year then ended; and
- have been properly prepared in accordance with the Industrial and Provident Societies Acts 1965 to 2002, the Housing Act 1996 (to 31 March 2010), the Housing and Regeneration Act (from 1 April 2010) and the Accounting Requirements for Registered Social Landlords General Determination 2006.

XYZ LLP, statutory auditor
Town, County
United Kingdom
Date

XYZ LLP is a limited liability partnership registered in England and Wales (with registered number OC123456).

TABLE 5: Example responsibility statement for Registered Provider board

The board members are responsible for preparing the report of the board and the financial statements in accordance with applicable law and regulations.

Industrial and Provident Society law and social housing legislation require the board members to prepare financial statements for each financial year in accordance with United Kingdom Generally Accepted Accounting Practice (United Kingdom Accounting Standards and applicable law). The directors must not approve the financial statements unless they are satisfied that they give a true and fair view of the state of affairs of the association and of the surplus or deficit of the association for that period.

In preparing these financial statements, the board members are required to:

- select suitable accounting policies and then apply them consistently;
- make judgements and accounting estimates that are reasonable and prudent;
- state whether applicable UK Accounting Standards and the Statement of Recommended Practice: Accounting by registered social landlords (2008) have been followed, subject to any material departures disclosed and explained in the financial statements; and
- prepare the financial statements on the going concern basis unless it is inappropriate to presume that the association will continue in business.

The board members are responsible for keeping adequate accounting records that are sufficient to show and explain the association's transactions and disclose with reasonable accuracy at any time the financial position of the association and enable them to ensure that the financial statements comply with the Industrial and Provident Societies Acts 1965 to 2002, the Housing Act 1996 (to 31 March 2010), the Housing and Regeneration Act (from 1 April 2010) and the Accounting Requirements for Registered Social Landlords General Determination 2006. They are also responsible for safeguarding the assets of the association and hence for taking reasonable steps for the prevention and detection of fraud and other irregularities.

The board is responsible for ensuring that the report of the board is prepared in accordance with the Statement of Recommended Practice: Accounting by registered social landlords (2008).

Financial statements are published on the association's website in accordance with legislation in the United Kingdom governing the preparation and dissemination of financial statements, which may vary from legislation in other jurisdictions. The maintenance and integrity of the association's website is the responsibility of the board members. The board members' responsibility also extends to the ongoing integrity of the financial statements contained therein.

ISA (UK and Ireland) 700 also requires auditors' reports to contain any further matters required by statute or other requirements applicable to the particular engagement. For Registered Providers, these matters may be set out in a number of areas, depending on the legal form and jurisdiction of the Registered Provider:

- the Housing Act 1996, together with any Statutory Instrument or Accounting Determination or Order issued under the Act;
- the Industrial and Provident Societies Acts 1965 to 2002;
- the Companies Act 1985;
- the Charities Act 2006;
- the trust deed.

Of particular note is the requirement for Registered Providers to maintain adequate books and records and satisfactory systems of internal control which vary depending on the legislation under which they are formed. Auditors are required to report if this is not the case, and consideration should also be given to a qualification on the grounds of limitation of scope.

47.25 ISA (UK AND IRELAND) 720: OTHER INFORMATION IN DOCUMENTS CONTAINING AUDITED FINANCIAL STATEMENTS

Although there may be no statutory requirement for auditors to review other information in Registered Provider annual reports, it is noted that 'one of the fundamental principles set out in the APB's *The Auditors' Code* is that auditors allow their reports to be included in documents containing other information only if they consider that the additional information is not in conflict with the matters covered by their report and they have no cause to believe it to be misleading'.

Examples of other information that may be included are:

- statements by the patron, president, chair or chief executive;
- an operating and financial review;
- a statement concerning arrangements for corporate governance;
- the board's statement on internal control;
- a treasurer's report;
- financial summaries; and
- projections of future expenditure based on planned activity.

Where an inconsistency is identified between other information and corresponding or related amounts or disclosures in audited financial statements and conclude that the other information should be amended, they discuss the matter with management or the board of the Registered Provider with a view to appropriate amendments being made.

47.26 MISCELLANEOUS REPORTS

For many of the returns on which auditors are asked to report the guidance provided by ISA (UK and Ireland) 700 can be adapted to suit the specific circumstances.

There are many returns where auditors are asked to report which will vary from one Registered Provider to another. Due to the variety, it is impracticable to list them in this guidance. Auditors should refer to guidance contained in ISA (UK and Ireland) 700 which can be adapted to such returns and also the ICAEW's Technical Release Audit 03/03 *Public Sector Special Reporting Engagements – Grant Claims* (see **Chapter 48**).

47.27 SERVICE CHARGE AUDITS

Under the Commonhold and Leasehold Reform Act 2002 various amendments were made to the Landlord and Tenant Act 1985, notably relating to the preparation of annual service charge statements, making these mandatory rather than upon request by a tenant. As at the date of issue of the Practice Note in March 2006, the provisions relating to annual service charge statements have yet to come into force.

The Housing and Regeneration Act 2008 updates the requirements for the provision of information to leaseholders and in respect of monies held for service charges in designated accounts. It effectively replaces certain sections of the Commonhold and Leasehold Reform Act 2002 and the new requirements for the provision of service charge information are expected to be published during 2010 with implementation most likely to be from 1 April 2011.

The auditors' report is addressed to the landlord or managing agent. The Practice Note stresses that auditors must communicate clearly the basis and scope of the audit on which they are reporting. The Practice Note comments that leaseholders and tenants should understand that they are not receiving any assurance regarding whether they are being charged a reasonable amount for services or whether those services have been provided effectively.

The format of the report varies depending upon the contents of the service charge statement. The example in **Table 6** should be amended depending on whether the service charge statement is prepared in accordance with the Landlord and Tenant Act 1985, in accordance with the requirements of a lease, or voluntarily.

TABLE 6: Example service charge auditors' report

Independent auditors' report on service charge

Report of the auditors to the landlord/managing agent of [property]

In accordance with our engagement letter dated [date], we have examined the service charge statement set out on pages ... to ... in respect of [property] for the year ended [date] together with the books and records maintained by [landlord/managing agent] in so far as they relate to [property].

Under the terms of this engagement, we were not required to, and did not, form any opinion as to either the reasonableness of the costs included within the service charge statement or the standard of the services or works provided.

Respective responsibilities of the board and auditors

Under the Landlord and Tenant Act 1985/Under clause [ ] of the tenancy agreement (or lease) dated [date] between the landlord and [the tenant], the landlord is responsible for the preparation of this service charge statement in respect of the costs in respect of [property]. [The managing agent has undertaken responsibility for the preparation of the service charge statement on behalf of the landlord.].

It is our responsibility to form an independent opinion, based on our examination, on the service charge statement and to report our opinion exclusively to the landlord/managing agent. [2]

Basis of audit opinion

Our work included examination, on a test basis, of evidence relent to the amounts included in the statement and their disclosure. [It also included an assessment of the significant estimates and judgements made by the landlord/managing agent in the preparation of the service charge statement.]

We planned and performed our examination so as to obtain all the information and explanations which we considered necessary in order to provide us with sufficient evidence to give reasonable assurance that the service charge statement is a fair summary of the costs relating to [property] and is sufficiently supported by accounts, receipts and other documents which have been made available to us. In view of the purpose for which this service charge statement has been prepared, however, we did not evaluate the overall adequacy of the presentation of the information which would have been required if we were to express an audit opinion under Auditing Standards issued by the Auditing Practices Board.

Opinion

In our opinion the service charge statement presents a fair summary of the income and expenditure for the year ended [date], is sufficiently supported by accounts, receipts and other documents and has been prepared in accordance with [section 21 (5) of the Landlord and Tenants Act 1985 and] clause [ ] of the tenancy agreement (or lease) dated [ ] between the tenant (leaseholders) and XYZ Registered Social Landlord.

Registered Auditors
Address
Date

---

[2] Auditors may include a 'Bannerman Statement' as part of their report (see **3.20**).

48 PUBLIC SECTOR AUDITS

48.1 INTRODUCTION

In recent years the accountability of central government departments and other public bodies has become a topic of increasing public interest. There has been continuing debate concerning their audit arrangements with increasingly more audits being carried out by private sector auditors as opposed to the National Audit Office.

In January 2006, the APB issued a further revision to Practice Note 10, *Audit of Financial Statements of Public Sector Entities in the United Kingdom*. The revised Practice Note replaces the previous revision from April 2001, which in turn superseded the original Practice Note 10, *Audit of Central Government Financial Statements in the United Kingdom* issued in February 1996 and Practice Note 17, *The Audit of Regularity in the Central Government Sector,* issued in September 1998.

The January 2006 revision updated the guidance following the introduction of ISAs (UK and Ireland) and also included legal and regulatory developments since April 2001.

In January 2010 a Consultation Draft of a further update to Practice Note 10 was issued to revise the guidance following the publication of the Clarified ISAs (UK and Ireland) which are effective for the audit of financial statements for periods ending on or after 15 December 2010. Legal and regulatory changes to date are also included in the Consultation Draft. It is discussed in **48.30** below.

As well as providing guidance on the application of each ISA (UK and Ireland) to public sector audits, the Practice Note also considers the role of the public sector auditor.

In January 2006 the APB issued Bulletin 2006/2, *Illustrative Auditor's Reports on Public Sector Financial Statements in the United Kingdom*, which revised the example audit reports provided in earlier versions of the Practice Note. Further guidance on audit reports was published in Bulletin 2008/7 *Illustrative Auditor's Reports on Public Sector Financial Statements in the United Kingdom*. A list of reports set out in this Bulletin is provided in **48.29** below. The Consultation Draft published in January 2010 does not update these reports further.

In 2002, the APB issued Practice Note 10(1), *Audit of central government financial statements in the Republic of Ireland*. The guidance takes account of the current legislative requirements governing the financial statement audit of Irish central government bodies and is designed to promote a common approach to the application of Auditing Standards. The guidance is also consistent with the equivalent guidance for public sector auditors in the UK, set out in Practice Note 10.

In 2003, three further pieces of guidance were issued for auditors of public sector entities:

- Bulletin 2003/1 *Corporate Governance: Requirements of Public Sector Auditors (Central Government)*;
- Bulletin 2003/2 *Corporate Governance: Requirements of Public Sector Auditors (National Health Service Bodies)*;
- Technical Release Audit 03/03 *Public Sector Special Reporting Engagements – Grant Claims.*

These were joined by Bulletin 2004/2, *Corporate Governance: Requirements of Public Sectors Auditors (Local Government Bodies)* in June 2004. These documents are detailed in **48.10** and **48.11**

48.2   THE ROLE OF THE PUBLIC SECTOR AUDITOR

Those responsible for public finance and for spending public money are accountable for ensuring that public business is conducted in accordance with proper standards and the law and that public money is safeguarded and properly accounted for. External auditors are an essential part of the process of accountability and make an important contribution to the stewardship of public money.

As part of this role, external auditors may be asked to give an independent opinion on the financial statements and may also review and report on aspects of the arrangements in place to ensure that resources are used economically, efficiently and effectively.

48.2.1   Auditor responsibilities

Public sector auditors are given authority to carry out their work by mandates which are embodied in legislation or set out in codes of audit practice. These mandates will vary according to the area of central government being audited and geographical location.

Broadly, these mandates establish responsibilities in relation to:

- the financial statements;
- compliance with legislative and other authorities (also known as 'regularity');
- economy, efficiency and effectiveness ('value for money' or 'use of resources').

48.2.2   Financial statements

The legislative framework governing each public sector body sets out different requirements in relation to the preparation of financial statements. The requirements include:

- format of financial statements;
- period within which financial statements must be prepared;
- who the financial statements are reviewed by.

48.2.3   Regularity

For central government bodies in England, external auditors have to report on whether transactions included in the financial statements conform with the legislation that authorises them. The Comptroller and Auditor General then satisfies himself that expenditure and income have been applied in accordance with Parliament's wishes and reports to Parliament accordingly. Similar requirements exist or are being developed in Scotland and Northern Ireland respectively.

A similar requirement also exists in England and Wales in relation to health authorities and other specified National Health Service entities which are to be consolidated respectively into the financial statements of the Department of Health and National Assembly for Wales. In Northern Ireland this requirement exists for health and social service boards.

In other health entities and in local government there is no requirement for external auditors to report on regularity, but they should be alert to questions of legality and review the procedures in place to ensure the legality of transactions that might have a significant financial consequence. Any transactions or events of questionable legality coming to light as a result of this review should be reported to the appropriate authorities.

Auditors' responsibilities in relation to regularity are discharged at the same time as the audit of the financial statements and are covered in a separate part of the audit report.

Guidance on regularity for auditors is set out in a separate section of the Practice Note. In particular, the section considers:

- understanding the regulatory framework;
- testing for regularity, including auditing compliance with European Union authorities; and
- regularity and reporting.

48.2.4 Other assignments

External auditors may also be asked to review and report on other information prepared by public bodies on aspects of their corporate governance and on their arrangements to secure economy, efficiency and effectiveness in their use of resources. This information may include:

- *performance information* – for central government, where external auditors are invited to report on such information by the Minister responsible;
- *grant claims* – external auditors act as agents of the Audit Commission when reporting on the extent to which a grant claim has been prepared in accordance with the requirements of the government entity and that the figures presented have been properly and fairly presented;
- *corporate governance* – some public sector bodies are required to include corporate governance statements in their financial statements;
- *best value* – auditors of local government in England and Wales are required to report on whether the public bodies' Best Value Performance Plans are prepared and published in accordance with legislation and statutory guidance;
- *economy, efficiency and effectiveness* – auditors' responsibilities vary between different parts of the public sector, and so auditors should review relevant legislation for details; and
- *standards of financial conduct* – public sector auditors are required to review and report on issues relating to standards of financial conduct in public bodies and aspects of the arrangements set in place by the audited body to ensure the proper conduct of its financial affairs.

48.3 STANDARDS GOVERNING PUBLIC SECTOR AUDITS

The standards covering the conduct and reporting of the audit of financial statements in the public sector are determined by the national audit agencies. However, the objectives of the audits are no different to those in other sectors and so public sector auditors apply the basis principles set out in Auditing Standards.

The Practice Note gives auditors guidance on the application of each ISA (UK and Ireland) to the audit of public sector financial statements.

The major differences to the audit of Companies Act financial statements are set out below.

48.4 INTERNATIONAL STANDARD ON QUALITY CONTROL (UK AND IRELAND) 1

International Standard on Quality Control (UK and Ireland) 1 (ISQC 1) is relevant in its entirety to the audit of financial statements of public sector entities. Practice Note 10 (Revised) provides additional guidance in relation to withdrawing from an engagement and threats to auditor independence.

In the public sector, under statute auditors may not be able to withdraw from an engagement, and even if withdrawal is permissible, there may be other alternatives. In most cases there is a duty to publicly report matters that would have otherwise caused withdrawal from the engagement.

If a national audit agency is appointed by statute there is no option to withdraw from an engagement where threats to independence have been identified and other steps should be taken to reduce these threats. Where an audit firm has been appointed as an agent of a national audit agency, that agency will assess the firm's independence when it is appointed. The firm must comply with the requirements of ISQC 1 on independence when carrying out their work.

48.5 ISA (UK AND IRELAND) 200 OBJECTIVE AND GENERAL PRINCIPLES GOVERNING AN AUDIT OF FINANCIAL STATEMENTS

The general principles of auditing are the same in both private and public entities, but auditors of public entities often have wider duties and further responsibilities laid down in legislation, directives and codes of practice.

For public sector auditors:

- for central government, specified health entities and probation boards there is a requirement to obtain evidence on compliance with authorities; and
- in recognition of the importance of regularity to the audit of these entities, the auditors' report includes an explicit opinion on the regularity of transactions.

48.6 ISA (UK AND IRELAND) 210 TERMS OF AUDIT ENGAGEMENTS

For many central government assignments the terms of engagement are set out in legislation and no engagement letter is necessary although auditors may choose to set out their understanding in such a letter, sometimes called a letter of understanding.

Where the legislation does not prescribe the terms, these are covered in a detailed letter of appointment from the relevant national audit agency, rather than in a letter from the auditors. If the auditors choose to send a letter this will not replace the agency's letter. The agency's letter normally covers all the terms contained in a standard audit engagement letter. These terms and the nature of the engagement cannot be changed by auditors.

48.7 ISA (UK AND IRELAND) 220 QUALITY CONTROL FOR AUDITS OF HISTORICAL FINANCIAL INFORMATION

ISA (UK and Ireland) 220 requires an engagement quality control review of the audit of listed clients. In the public sector, audit teams should consider whether such a review is necessary for each client. Reviews are likely to be appropriate for larger, more complex entities or those with a high profile.

48.8 ISA (UK AND IRELAND) 230 DOCUMENTATION

In addition to the requirements of ISA (UK and Ireland) 230 (see **Chapter 19**), auditors of public sector entities may have additional responsibilities with regard to confidentiality or the retention of working papers. These may be imposed by Statute, such as the Official Secrets Act 1989 and auditors should be aware of these.

48.9 ISA (UK AND IRELAND) 240 THE AUDITOR'S RESPONSIBILITY TO CONSIDER FRAUD IN AN AUDIT OF FINANCIAL STATEMENTS

The Practice Note provides additional guidance on:

● responsibilities of the entity and the auditors;

- fraud in the context of the regularity assertion;
- consideration of fraud risk factors;
- auditors' other responsibilities relating to fraud and corruption; and
- reporting to third parties.

48.9.1   Responsibilities of the entity and auditors

For central government entities the Accounting Officer is usually the permanent head or senior full-time official of the entity and directs its management. They are personally responsible for ensuring that:

- proper financial procedures are followed;
- assets and public funds are properly managed and safeguarded; and
- funds are applied to the extent and for the purposes authorised by Parliament.

The entity's management are generally responsible for developing and maintaining effective controls to prevent fraud and detecting it when it does occur.

In local government an officer is appointed to have responsibility for the arrangements for the proper administration of financial affairs. For health entities in England and Wales, the Accounting Officer and other directors are responsible for ensuring that:

- systems are in place to produce reliable financial information and proper accounting records;
- there are controls in place over the security of financial systems and data; and
- there is a fraud and corruption policy and response plan in place.

Responsibilities in Scotland and Northern Ireland are broadly similar to England and Wales.

Under ISA (UK and Ireland) 240, auditors should plan, perform and evaluate their work so as to have a reasonable expectation of identifying the risk of material misstatement arising from fraud and error. These requirements apply to audits of public sector entities as well as private entities, but they are extended in the public sector context to ensure a reasonable expectation of detecting material breaches of regularity arising from fraud or error.

48.9.2   Fraud in the context of the regularity assertion

Fraudulent transactions cannot, by definition, be regular and where material fraud is proven a qualification on the regularity assertion is necessary. Where the auditors suspect fraud the matter should be discussed with management to discover whether the transactions are in compliance with the authorities which govern them. If management do not accept the views of the auditors it may be necessary to communicate the matter to higher authorities and to qualify the audit report.

48.9.3   Consideration of fraud risk factors

When gaining an understanding of the public entity and its environment, including its internal controls, auditors should consider whether fraud risk factors are present. The risk of external fraud may be high if the entity is making grants to the public or collecting tax revenues.

Internally, fraudulent financial reporting may occur where bodies are required to meet externally set targets, such as where financial results affect performance ratings by an inspectorate.

48.9.4   Auditors' other responsibilities

Public sector auditors are required to have a wider regard to fraud and corruption than just the potential impact on the financial statements as addressed by ISA (UK and Ireland) 240. These additional responsibilities include consideration of the financial aspects of corporate governance arrangements for local government and health entities in England and Wales, and review of Treasury and other appropriate guidance on corporate governance for central government auditors.

If auditors become aware of fraud when addressing these additional responsibilities, they should also ensure that they consider the impact of these findings on the financial statements in accordance with ISA (UK and Ireland) 240.

ISA (UK and Ireland) 240 recommends that where auditors encounter circumstances arising from fraud or a suspected fraud which bring into question their ability to continue with the audit, they should consider resigning. For public sector clients, auditors cannot decline or withdraw from an engagement if they have been appointed by statute. There is usually a statutory requirement to make a public report about any matter which would have caused withdrawal, had such action been permissible.

The ISA (UK and Ireland) requires auditors to presume that a risk of material misstatement due to fraud will exist. For some public sector entities this will not apply, and as with other entities where this presumption can be rebutted, this conclusion must be clearly documented.

48.9.5   *Reporting to third parties*

When considering whether to report a suspected or actual fraud, auditors must have regard to:

- the relevant provisions that set out management's responsibilities for reporting fraud or other irregularity;
- the duties to report to a third party set out in the auditors' terms of engagement.

When management is implicated in the fraud, or refuses to report a fraud themselves, the auditors have a duty to report to third parties depending on the type of public sector entity involved. The different entities are set out in **Table 1**.

TABLE 1: Third parties to whom fraud may be reported

Public sector type	*Fraud reportable to*
Central government departments in England and Wales	The Treasury
National Assembly for Wales and its sponsored public bodies	The Compliance Officer of the National Assembly for Wales
Central government departments in Scotland	The Auditor General for Scotland
Central government departments in Northern Ireland	The Department of Finance and Personnel
Non-departmental public bodies and executive agencies	The sponsor department
Local government entities	The relevant authority as set out in ISA (UK and Ireland) 240
Health entities	Counter Fraud and Security Management Service.

48.10   ISA (UK AND IRELAND) 250 CONSIDERATION OF LAWS AND REGULATIONS IN AN AUDIT OF FINANCIAL STATEMENTS

ISA (UK and Ireland) 250 is concerned with laws and regulations that, if not complied with, may materially affect the financial statements. These fall into two categories, those which set out the form or contents of the financial statements and those which set the provisions under which an entity is allowed to conduct its business. Auditors are required to obtain an general understanding of both categories of laws and regulations. Where auditors are required to report on compliance with certain provisions of laws or regulations, as with the regularity assertion for public entities, as well as being familiar with the law itself, they must test the entity's compliance with its provisions.

Auditors of local government and health entities have separate statutory responsibilities when matters come to their attention that indicate that unlawful expenditure has been or will be incurred or that a financial loss or deficiency will arise. This is irrespective of the potential for material impact on the financial statements. In addition, auditors must report on the elements of the local government or health entities' corporate governance arrangements that relate to the legality of transactions which might have a financial consequence.

48.11 ISA (UK AND IRELAND) 260 COMMUNICATION OF AUDIT MATTERS WITH THOSE CHARGED WITH GOVERNANCE

In addition to the requirements of ISA (UK and Ireland) 260 the Practice Note stresses the importance of reports to management as a means of reporting non-compliance with:

- regularity;
- propriety; and
- other official guidance to Accounting Officers.

Where matters relating to other duties and responsibilities are reported to management in the same letter as matters arising from the audit of the financial statements, auditors must be sure that the letter still meets the requirements of ISA (UK and Ireland) 260.

The Practice Note sets out the correct addressee of the management report for each type of public sector entity.

Public sector auditors sometimes have a responsibility to submit an annual audit letter to a third party from where it may be made public. Even where this is not the case, reports to management may come into the possession of third parties and auditors may wish to limit their liability should reliance be placed on their audit letter. This can be achieved by including a caveat in their report to management.

48.12 ISA (UK AND IRELAND) 300 PLANNING AN AUDIT OF FINANCIAL STATEMENTS

With regard to the overall audit planning the Practice Note covers the additional matters which should be considered, including:

- auditors' other responsibilities laid down in Statute or in the letter of appointment; and
- planning the audit of regularity.

48.13 ISA (UK AND IRELAND) 315 UNDERSTANDING THE ENTITY AND ITS ENVIRONMENT AND ASSESSING THE RISKS OF MATERIAL MISSTATEMENT AND ISA (UK AND IRELAND) 330 THE AUDITOR'S PROCEDURES IN RESPONSE TO ASSESSED RISKS

Auditors are required to obtain an understanding of the relevant financial reporting framework and regulatory factors and their impact on the audit. These include the financial reporting framework and other regulations set out in:

- the specific legislation that has established the audited entity and determines its activities;
- UK GAAP;
- accounts directions;
- Government Accounting and the Government Financial Reporting Manual;
- other HM Treasury guidance on the application of accounting standards, the Companies Act and the disclosure of information;
- manuals for accounts of NHS entities; and
- relevant SORPs.

An additional consideration for public sector auditors is the additional assertion of regularity. When assessing risk for reporting on the regularity assertion, auditors should consider the following specific factors:

- the complexity of the regulations;
- the introduction of major new legislation or changes in existing regulations;
- services and programmes administered under European Union authorities, where the framework of authorities may be complex;
- services and programmes delivered through third parties; and
- payments and receipts made on the basis of claims or declarations.

ISA (UK and Ireland) 315 requires auditors to obtain an understanding of an entity's business objectives and strategies and assess any resulting business risks. Public sector entities may have a number of additional business risks as a result of their closely regulated regimes, public reporting process and typically high number of transactions processed. The practice note highlights the following as possible significant risks in the public sector:

- financial transactions entered into by the entity in the period do not conform to the authorities that govern them;
- organisations issuing grants have been subject to fraudulent grant claims;
- the financial statements have been manipulated to meet externally set targets; and
- Private Finance Initiative transactions have not been accounted for in accordance with UK GAAP and guidance issued by HM Treasury.

48.14   ISA (UK AND IRELAND) 320 AUDIT MATERIALITY

When assessing the qualitative aspects of materiality auditors should consider the interest of the body to whom the audit report is addressed. Auditors should consider any higher body, into whose financial statements the results of the audited entity is being consolidated, to be the addressee of the audit report. Auditors should also be aware of any special considerations applying to the reporting of certain classes of misstatement when assessing the materiality of uncorrected misstatements.

Where public sector auditors have a responsibility to report on matters that do not affect the opinion on the financial statements, they may adopt an appropriate level of materiality for these items which differs from the materiality level applied to the audit of the financial statements.

The concept of materiality applies to the audit of regularity as to any other assertions in the financial statements. Where required to report on regularity, auditors need only to obtain sufficient evidence to give an opinion on whether expenditure and income has been applied for the intended purposes 'in all material respects'. As with other financial statements assertions, the assessment of materiality will include both qualitative and quantitative judgements.

48.15 ISA (UK AND IRELAND) 402 AUDIT CONSIDERATIONS RELATING TO ENTITIES USING SERVICE ORGANISATIONS

The requirement for public sector auditors to give an opinion on the regularity of transactions may require inspection of records maintained by service organisations beyond that in other audits. ISA (UK and Ireland) 402 does not automatically secure access rights to this information, and so it is important that the contract terms between the public sector entity and its service provider allow sufficient access by the entity's auditor. Guidance on model conditions of contract are available in the Office of Government Commerce's *Successful Delivery Toolkit*.

48.16 ISA (UK AND IRELAND) 500 AUDIT EVIDENCE

When testing the regularity assertion, auditors plan and perform procedures to confirm that the entity's expenditure and income comply with the specific authorities governing them. The principles and procedures applied are the same as those applied in the audit of any other financial statements assertion. However, there may be particular considerations in relation to the design of audit procedures as auditors may encounter difficulties obtaining reliable audit evidence in relation to some aspects of regularity, such as the eligibility for grants. For example, auditors may require access to the records of a third party who has received the grant, to ascertain whether conditions for its grant have been met.

48.17 ISA (UK AND IRELAND) 510 INITIAL ENGAGEMENTS – OPENING BALANCES AND CONTINUING ENGAGEMENTS – OPENING BALANCES

The Practice Note states that the guidance in ISA (UK and Ireland) 510 is relevant for public sector entities, and also sets out additional guidance which is reproduced in **Table 2**.

TABLE 2: Additional guidance on the audit of opening balances

Nature of opening balances	*Additional guidance*
Opening balance amounts are identifiable from the preceding period's audited financial statements for another entity.	This will require that the balances are clearly identifiable. Additional procedures may also be necessary to confirm that there are no aspects of the change in status of the new entity that result in changes to the basis on which the balances were prepared.
Opening balance amounts are not identifiable from the preceding period's audited financial statements for another entity, but have been derived from balances contained in those statements.	Subject to the arrangements for co-operation, the auditor may discuss with the outgoing auditor whether information is available that would provide substantive evidence for the opening balances. Such evidence would be considered in the context of the requirements of ISA (UK and Ireland) 600.
In the absence of evidence available through such co-operation, the auditor considers carrying out substantive testing of opening balances.	Opening balances have been calculated as part of a separate disaggregation/ merger exercise, subject to a separate specific review and report by an auditor. The auditor considers the scope of the specific review and report in the context of the requirements of ISA (UK and Ireland) 600 as if the auditor were the principal auditor. Where the work from the separate specific review cannot be used, the auditor considers carrying out substantive testing of opening balances.
Opening balances have been calculated as part of a separate disaggregation/ merger exercise, but not subject to separate specific review and report.	The audit considers carrying out substantive testing of opening balances.

ISA (UK and Ireland) 510 states that outgoing auditors have no legal or ethical obligation to provide information to incoming auditors or allow access to their work papers. In the public sector predecessor auditors are expected by the national audit agencies to adopt a co-operative approach in the interests of efficiency and reducing the audit burden.

48.18 ISA (UK AND IRELAND) 520 ANALYTICAL PROCEDURES

In addition to the relationships set out in ISA (UK and Ireland) 520, public sector auditors also consider relationships in two classes:

- programme expenditure and income; and
- management costs.

Each class has certain features that will influence the type of analytical procedures performed.

Programme expenditure and income

Programme expenditure and income relate to the actual function of the entity, for example grant payments and health care treatments. These are:

- usually closely related to non-financial information such as the number of bodies in receipt of grant or persons receiving hospital treatment;
- not always directly comparable to prior periods because of changes to eligibility rules and Government policy; and
- often comparable to expenditure plans included in published departmental or entity strategy.

Management costs

Management costs relate to the running of the entity and can be distinguished from programme expenditure as they are:

- usually related to comparable information for the prior period and are less subject to change as a result of Government policy changes;
- closely related to information such as number of employees, size of buildings, etc; and
- directly comparable to other entities with similar establishment sizes.

48.19   ISA (UK AND IRELAND) 550 RELATED PARTIES

The Practice Note provides little specific guidance on the audit of related party transactions for public sector entities. It does note, however, that related parties of these entities are subject to specific restrictions on the nature and scope of the transactions that they enter with the entity. Guidance varies for each part of the public sector and auditors should be aware of these restrictions.

48.20   ISA (UK AND IRELAND) 560 SUBSEQUENT EVENTS

For central government entities, auditors must also consider matters arising from relevant parliamentary procedures as part of their subsequent events review. Auditors should consult relevant legislation to determine the dates the financial statements are deemed to be 'issued' and 'laid before members', as this varies for each central government entity.

For auditors of local government and health entities, the concept of subsequent events is limited. The statutory audit opinion is only issued when the audit is concluded and all responsibilities have been met. Thus the auditors' duties are concluded at the date of the issue of the statutory audit certificate and their powers for that audit are at an end. Where, as is common, auditors have given an opinion in advance of concluding the audit, the final statutory opinion will contain references back to earlier opinions and any additional work performed since those opinions were given.

48.21   ISA (UK AND IRELAND) 570 GOING CONCERN

The Practice Note gives guidance on the following areas:

- auditors' other responsibilities relating to going concern;
- entities that prepare their financial statements on the going concern basis;
- circumstances affecting going concern;
- consideration of the foreseeable future;
- auditors' responsibilities in considering going concern;
- written representations on going concern.

48.21.1   Auditors' other responsibilities relating to going concern

Auditors of local government and health entities in England and Wales must review and report on aspects of the entity's corporate governance arrangements as they relate to the ongoing financial standing of the entity. Similar requirements exist for local government in Scotland. In Northern Ireland, auditors are expected to assess the financial standing of the audited entity.

These requirements are outside the intended scope of ISA (UK and Ireland) 570, but auditors should ensure that when matters come to their attention through these additional responsibilities, they consider their impact on the financial statements in line with the requirements of the ISA (UK and Ireland).

48.21.2   Entities that prepare their financial statements on the going concern basis

The legislation determining the format of the financial statements will normally indicate whether the going concern basis should be adopted.

Where central government entities prepare financial statements on a cash basis the going concern basis does not apply. However, the auditors should still report to Parliament in the rare circumstance that there are matters which may affect the entity's ability to continue as a going concern. They do not, however, qualify their opinion on the proper presentation of the financial statements.

48.21.3   Circumstances affecting going concern

It is unlikely that a central government entity will cease to operate as a result of insolvency or inability to finance operations unless they operate in a trading capacity at arm's length from Government.

Cessation is most likely to result from a decision by Government and may involve transferring the operations to another entity. In such cases the individual circumstances should be considered when assessing whether the going concern basis is appropriate.

48.21.4   Consideration of the foreseeable future

Government policy is inherently subject to political uncertainty, but political decisions are no more uncertain than the risks faced by private entities. Therefore the provisions in ISA (UK and Ireland) 570 relating to 'foreseeable future' can be applied by auditors of public sector entities.

48.21.5   Auditors' responsibilities in considering going concern

Public sector auditors should consider two factors:

* the risk associated with changes in policy direction (for example, where there is a change in Government); and
* the operational, or business, risk (for example, the entity has insufficient working capital).

Auditors need to obtain evidence concerning the government's intentions in the particular area of policy that the entity operates in. This would include whether:

* they intend to review policy, for example a manifesto commitment;
* a review has been announced;
* an efficiency review has concluded that rationalisation is necessary; or
* there is a known intention to privatise its activities.

Trading operations may also be subject to risks arising from changes in policy direction as well as operational and business risks.

48.21.6   Written representations on going concern

The Practice Note suggests that the receipt of written representations from the Accounting Officer about going concern may not be sufficient audit evidence as the officer may not be capable of making judgements about future conditions for support.

If the going concern assumption is only substantiated by written confirmation of support from the sponsoring department, auditors should consider whether there is a need to refer to these confirmations in the financial statements.

Other evidence of the intention to continue the entity's activities could come from the most recent:

- Public Expenditure Survey;
- Supply Estimates; and
- financial management and policy review.

The Practice Note contains example audit procedures in relation to going concern.

48.22 ISA (UK AND IRELAND) 580 MANAGEMENT REPRESENTATIONS

Each type of public sector entity has a person or group of people with responsibility for the preparation and signing of the financial statements. Auditors should review relevant regulations to determine to whom this responsibility falls. The responsible person signs letters of representation, including specific representations on the regularity assertion.

48.23 ISA (UK AND IRELAND) 600 USING THE WORK OF ANOTHER AUDITOR

There are five situations where auditors of public sector entities are deemed to be principal auditors:

- if the public sector entity consolidates the results of lower tier bodies into its own financial statements, the principal and other auditor relationship is identical to that within a group of companies;
- where the Comptroller and Auditor General audits the Whole of Government Accounts. This is a situation analogous to the audit of a group of companies;
- if the entity has pooled budgets or shared services audited by another auditor;
- where an entity has contracted out services to another party, a principal/other auditor relationship exists and auditors apply the guidance in ISA (UK and Ireland) 402 accordingly; and
- where there is a duty to give an opinion on regularity and the auditor of the

entity seeks to use the work of the grant recipient's auditor to reduce the extent of their own procedures.

Auditors have a duty under ISA (UK and Ireland) 600 to assess the competence of any auditor on whose work they seek to rely. Where the auditor is appointed by a national audit agency they will have had to demonstrate professional qualifications, experience and resources to the national audit agency. Whilst the principal auditor will still need to perform their own checks, this will provide a clear framework within which to make this assessment.

48.24   ISA (UK AND IRELAND) 610 CONSIDERING THE WORK OF INTERNAL AUDIT

The requirements of ISA (UK and Ireland) 610 are as relevant to the audit of public sector entities as to private companies. Internal audit is normally a mandatory element of a public sector entity's internal control framework, and auditors may have a responsibility to provide negative assurance on a Statement of Internal Control which will necessitate an assessment of the internal control function even if it is not possible to rely on its work in relation to the financial statements.

48.25   ISA (UK AND IRELAND) 700 THE AUDITOR'S REPORT ON FINANCIAL STATEMENTS

When reporting on central government financial statements the requirements of ISA (UK and Ireland) 700 should be followed, bearing in mind any specific reporting requirements of the engagement, such as to whom the audit report is addressed.

The Practice Note gives additional guidance on responsibility statements which should draw attention to the responsibilities of the Accounting Officers or other financial officer with responsibility for the financial statements, separately from those of any other officers. **Table 3** sets out the expected disclosures in a public sector entity's Statement of Responsibilities.

TABLE 3: Expected disclosures in a public sector entity's Statement of Responsibilities

Responsibility for:

- Proper accounting records that disclose with reasonable accuracy at any time the financial position of the entity and enable the entity to ensure that financial statements are prepared to comply with statutory requirements.

- Safeguarding the assets of the entity and for taking reasonable steps for the prevention and detection of fraud and other irregularities.
- Preparation of financial statements for each financial year that give a true and fair view of/present fairly the state of affairs of the entity and its performance for that period.
- In preparing financial statements:

  - Selecting suitable accounting policies and then applying them consistently;
  - Making judgements and estimates that are reasonable and prudent;
  - Stating whether applicable accounting standards have been followed, subject to any material departures disclosed and explained in the financial statements; and
  - Preparing the financial statements on the going concern basis, unless it is inappropriate to presume that the entity will continue in business.

- The regularity of the public finances for which the Accounting/Accountable Officer is answerable, where a regularity opinion is given.

The wording of the audit opinion depends on the particular auditing framework. Bulletin 2006/2, issued in January 2006 with the revision to Practice Note 10 provides examples of unmodified audit reports and reports modified for regularity issues. The opinion paragraph should clearly indicate the financial reporting framework used to prepare the financial statements and the statute which requires the financial statements to be audited. These vary from body to body and the Practice Note provides a list of alternatives.

Where auditors are reporting on regularity, a separate and explicit opinion is given on the regularity of transactions in the entity's financial statements. In addition, auditors may provide separate reports, other than through their audit opinions, on issues of regularity. Where auditors give a qualified opinion on regularity, this does not in itself lead to a qualification of the truth and fairness, fair presentation or proper presentation part of the opinion.

48.26 ISA (UK AND IRELAND) 720 OTHER INFORMATION IN DOCUMENTS CONTAINING AUDITED FINANCIAL STATEMENTS

Most public sector entities are required to include a foreword in the same document as the financial statements. The foreword usually contains the information which would be included in the directors' report in a set of Companies Act financial statements, and the auditors' opinion does not extend to the contents of the foreword.

Other information required will vary depending on the type of public sector entity.

48.27 CORPORATE GOVERNANCE

In November 2003, the APB issued two Bulletins concerning the requirements of auditors in relation to corporate governance in central government and National Health Service bodies, and in June 2004 a Bulletin covering corporate governance in local government bodies was issued. Separate Bulletins are required as public sector bodies do not operate within a common legislative framework, which means that different models of governance have evolved. The APB anticipates issuing further Bulletins to cover other areas.

48.27.1 Central government

Background

The central government sector consists of the following main types of entity:

- government departments;
- executive agencies;
- trading funds;
- bodies not administered as government departments but which are subject to Ministerial and department control, for example non-departmental public bodies; and
- the Scottish Executive, the National Assembly for Wales, the Northern Ireland Executive, their executive agencies and sponsored/related public bodies.

Whilst parts of the Combined Code and the general tenets of the Turnbull recommendations are relevant to central government, the environment is significantly different to that of listed companies. The private sector Board model that contains both non-executive and executive directors is not generally found in central government. Directors of a company have collective responsibility, but the Accounting Officer in central government has full responsibility under the Minister, for the organisation and management of the entity.

Statement on internal control

Following consideration of the Combined Code and Turnbull Report, the Treasury introduced the requirement for central government entities to:

- maintain a system of internal control, with emphasis on risk management;
- review at least annually the effectiveness of the system; and
- include a Statement on Internal Control (SIC) in the accounts.

SICs are required to including the following disclosures:

- acknowledgement of the Accounting Officer's responsibility for ensuring that a sound system of internal control is maintained;
- an explanation that the system of internal control is designed to manage rather than eliminate risk of failure to achieve policies, aims and objectives –

it can therefore only provide reasonable and not absolute assurance of effectiveness;

- reference to an ongoing process designed to identify the principle risks to achievement of the entities policies, aims and objectives, evaluate and manage them and confirmation that the process accords with Treasury guidance. A comment is also included on the staff's capacity to manage the risk process;
- confirmation that the above process was in place for the duration of the financial year and remained so up until the date of the approval of the annual report and accounts;
- acknowledgement of the Accounting Officer's responsibility for reviewing the effectiveness of the system of internal control, and describing the process for review;
- confirmation that the results of the Accounting Officer's review of the effectiveness of internal control has been discussed with the Board, the Audit Committee and, if applicable, the Risk Committee for 2003/04 and subsequently; and
- where appropriate, set out details of actions taken, or proposals to deal with significant internal control issues.

The auditors' review of the SIC is not designed to provide 'positive assurance', therefore, to avoid misunderstanding, the APB recommends that the engagement or understanding letter explains the scope of the review and that the auditors discuss the findings of their review with senior management before releasing their report. Example extracts from an engagement letter are given in **Table 4**.

TABLE 4: Example extracts from an engagement letter

Review of the Accounting Officer's Statement on Internal Control

Responsibilities

As Accounting Officer of the Authority you are responsible for ensuring that the [name of entity] complies with the guidance issued by HM Treasury entitled 'Corporate Governance: statement on internal control'. This requires you to include alongside the accounts a statement on internal control. The guidance requires the external auditors to review the statement.

Scope of review

Our review of the statement will be conducted in compliance with the relevant recommendations of Bulletins issued by the Auditing Practices Board, which, among other things, set out the scope of our review. For this purpose you will provide us with such information and explanations as we consider necessary. We may request you to provide written confirmation of oral representations which you make to us during the course of our review. We shall request sight of all documents or statements which are due to be issued with the statement on internal control and all documentation prepared in support of the statement.

Our work will be restricted to a consideration of whether your statement:

- provides the disclosures required by the Treasury guidance; and

---

- is not inconsistent with the information of which we have become aware from our audit of the financial statements.

As our work is not designed to consider whether your statement on internal control covers all risks and controls, or form an opinion on the effectiveness of [name of entity]'s risk and control procedures, our work on internal control will not be sufficient to enable us to express any assurance as to whether or not your internal controls are effective. In addition our financial statements audit should not be relied upon to draw to your attention matters that may be relevant to your consideration as to whether or not your system of internal control is effective.

Auditors' review of the SIC

The auditors' review of the SIC will be directed at:

- considering the completeness of the disclosures in meeting Treasury requirements; and
- identifying inconsistencies between the disclosures and the information that the auditor is aware of from their work on the financial statements and other work (including any 'value for money' work carried out in the year).

The auditors' assessment will, therefore, be narrower in scope than the review performed by the Accounting Officer. Auditors are not expected to assess whether all risks and controls have been addressed by the Accounting Officer, or that risks are matched by internal controls. To clarify this, the following wording should be included in the auditors' certificate on the financial statements:

'We are not required to consider, nor have we considered whether the Accounting Officer's statements on internal control cover all risks and controls. We are also not required to form an opinion on the effectiveness of the entity's corporate governance procedures or its risk and control procedures.'

Possible procedures to obtain appropriate evidence about disclosures are detailed in **Table 5**.

TABLE 5: Example procedures to test disclosure in the SIC

- Consider whether the disclosures are consistent with the auditors' review of management board and committee minutes.
- Review supporting documents prepared for the board that are relevant to disclosures made in the SIC. In doing this auditors will pay particular attention to the documentation prepared for Accounting Officers to support their statement made in connection with their effectiveness review and assess whether or not it provides sound support for that statement.
- Gain an understanding of the process defined by the Accounting Officer for his review of the effectiveness of internal control through enquiry of the senior management and comparing their understanding to the statement made by the Accounting Officer in the SIC.
- Attend Audit Committee meetings at which corporate governance, internal control and risk management matters are considered.
- Review the Head of Internal Audit's formal annual report to the Accounting Officer which includes the overall opinion of the adequacy and effectiveness of the organisation's risk management, control and governance processes.

> • Relate the statement made by the Accounting Officer to the auditors' knowledge of the entity obtained during the audit of the financial statements.

Significant internal control issues

The Accounting Officer is required to disclose in the SIC details of actions taken or proposed to deal with significant internal control issues. The term 'significant internal control issue' cannot be absolutely defined, but the following characteristics may indicate that the issue is significant enough to be reported:

• it seriously prejudices or prevents achievement of a Public Service Agreement target;

• it has resulted in the need to seek additional funding from Treasury/the sponsoring department to allow resolution, or has required funds to be diverted from another aspect of the business;

• the external auditor would regard it as having a material impact on the accounts;

• the Audit Committee advises that it should be significant;

• the Head of Internal Audit has reported on it as significant in the annual opinion on the whole risk, control and governance; or

• it, or its impact, has attracted significant public interest or has damaged the reputation of the department.

The auditors are not required to assess whether the procedures described in the SIC will remedy any underlying weakness, rather they are required to assess whether the description of the rectification process is appropriate.

Reporting on the SIC

The auditors report by exception in the opinion paragraph of their report on the financial statements, if they conclude:

• that the Accounting Officer's summary of the process applied in reviewing the effectiveness of internal control is either not supported by, or does not reflect the auditors' understanding of that process;

• that the processes disclosed to deal with significant internal control issues do not appropriately reflect the auditors' understanding of the process undertaken;

• that, when the Accounting Officer has failed to conduct a review of the effectiveness of internal control, this has not been disclosed;

• when it is disclosed that no review of the effectiveness of internal control has taken place, the disclosure is not consistent with the auditors' understanding;

• that the Accounting Officer has not disclosed that the review has not covered all the entities within the accounting boundary.

The suggested wording for the opinion paragraph is set out in **Table 6**. This form of report is not a qualified audit opinion, and should be included under the heading 'Other matter'.

TABLE 6: Model opinion paragraph when the auditor reports by exception on the SIC (Central Government)

Opinion

In our opinion:

- the financial statements give a true and fair view of the state of affairs of ... at [date] and of the net resource outturn, resources applied to objectives, recognised gains and losses and cash flows for the year then ended, and have been properly prepared in accordance with the Government Resources and Accounts Act 2000 and directions made thereunder by the Treasury; and
- in all material respects the expenditure and income have been applied to the purposes intended by Parliament and the financial transactions conform to the authorities which govern them.

Other matter

We have reviewed the Accounting Officer's description of his/her processes for reviewing the effectiveness of internal control set out on page [x] of the annual report. In our opinion the Accounting Officer's comments concerning ... do not appropriately reflect our understanding of the process undertaken by the Accounting Officer because ....

Audit committees

The purpose of an Audit Committee in the central government sector is to give advice to the Accounting Officer on the adequacy of audit arrangements, both internal and external, and on the implications of assurances provided in respect of risk and control in an organisation. Audit Committees are not mandatory in the central government section, but are strongly encouraged.

Auditors have no specific reporting responsibilities in relation to the establishment and workings of the Audit Committee.

Auditors' responsibilities

Auditors have different responsibilities for different parts of the annual report and accounts. They are required to audit the financial statements, review the SIC and read all the other information. In addition, in some instances auditors are required to report positively on their findings, in others they have to report by exception.

Therefore, it is important that there is a clear statement of the auditors' responsibilities. Examples are provided in **Table 7**.

TABLE 7: Example statement of auditors' responsibilities (Central Government)

... Our responsibilities as independent auditors [are established by statute] and we have regard to the standards and guidance issued by the Auditing Practices Board and the ethical guidance applicable to the auditing profession.

> We report our opinion as to whether the financial statements give a true and fair view and are properly prepared in accordance with the [Government Resources and Accounts Act 2000] and Treasury directions made thereunder and whether in all material respects the expenditure and income have been applied to the purposes intended by Parliament and the financial transactions conform to the authorities which govern them. We also report if in our opinion the Foreword is not consistent with the financial statements, if the [Department/Agency/entity] has not kept proper accounting records or if we have not received all the information and explanations we require for my audit.
>
> We read the other information contained in the [Accounts/Annual Report] and consider whether it is consistent with the audited financial statements. We consider the implications for our certificate if we become aware of any apparent misstatements or material inconsistencies with the financial statements.
>
> We review whether the statement on page ... reflects the [Department's/Agency's/entity's] compliance with Treasury's guidance 'Corporate Governance: Statement on Internal Control'. We report if it does not meet the requirements specified by the Treasury or if the statement is misleading or inconsistent with other information we are aware of from our audit of the financial statements. We are not required to consider, nor have we considered whether the Accounting Officer's statements on internal control cover all risks and controls. We are also not required to form an opinion on the effectiveness of the [Department's/Agency's/entity's] corporate governance procedures or its risk and control procedures.

48.27.2   National Health Service bodies

Background

Chief Executives of NHS bodies are designated by the Department of Health as Accountable Officers (rather than the Accounting Officers for central government departments). They have personal responsibility for, amongst other things, ensuring that management systems are in place which safeguard public funds, achieving value for money, ensuring that assets are safeguarded and ensuring that expenditure complies with Parliamentary requirements.

NHS bodies operate a Board model similar to that of private sector listed companies, comprising both executive and non-executive members.

Corporate governance developments in the NHS have included:

- designation of Chief Executives as Accountable Officers;
- the establishment of remuneration committees and audit committees (mandatory) and risk management committees (optional);
- adoption of measures recommended by Greenbury relating to disclosure of directors' remuneration; and
- the introduction of a statement on internal control.

The involvement of auditors

Much of the guidance in Bulletin 2003/2 relating to NHS bodies is identical to that in Bulletin 2003/1 on central government, and it is not repeated. However, some terminology differs between sectors, and for that reason a number of the example wordings and reports given in **48.10.1** are provided again below, suitably adapted for use by auditors involved in NHS reporting.

The following tables for use by auditors of NHS bodies detail:

- model opinion paragraph when the auditor reports by exception on the SIC (**Table 8**); and
- example statement of auditors' responsibilities (**Table 9**).

TABLE 8: Model opinion paragraph when the auditor reports by exception on the SIC (NHS bodies)

Opinion

In our opinion:

- the financial statements give a true and fair view of the state of affairs of [xx] NHS Trust at [date] and of its income and expenditure for the year then ended...;

Other matter

We have reviewed the Accountable Officer's description of the processes undertaken for reviewing the effectiveness of the system of internal control as set out on page [x]. In our opinion the Accountable Officer's comments concerning ... do not appropriately reflect our understanding of the processes undertaken because ....

TABLE 9: Example statement of auditors' responsibilities (NHS bodies)

... Our responsibilities as independent auditors are established by statute, and by the Code of Audit Practice issued by the Audit Commission, which requires adherence to the auditing standards issued by the Auditing Practices Board (APB) and relevant ethical standards. It also requires us to have regard to other guidance and advice issued by the APB.

We report to you our opinion as to whether the financial statements give a true and fair view of the state of affairs of the Trust and its income and expenditure for the year, in accordance with the accounting policies directed by the Secretary of State as being relevant to the National Health Service in England.

We review whether the directors' statement on internal control reflects compliance with the Department of Health's guidance 'The Statement on Internal Control 2003/04'. We report if it does not meet the requirements specified by the Department of Health or if the statement is misleading or inconsistent with other information we are aware of from our audit of the financial statements. We are not required to consider, nor have we considered whether the directors' statements on internal control cover all risks and controls. We are also not required to form an opinion on the effectiveness of the Trust's corporate governance procedures or its risk and control procedures. Our review was not performed for any purpose connected with any specific transaction and should not be relied upon for any such purpose.

We read the information contained in the Annual Report and consider the implications for our report if we become aware of any apparent misstatements or material inconsistencies with the statement of accounts.

48.27.3   Local government bodies

Background

Bulletin 2004/2 provides guidance on the corporate governance arrangements for local government bodies subject to the Local Authority SORP. In England, Wales and Scotland this is local authorities, police authorities, fire authorities, joint committees and joint boards of principal authorities, and, in England and Wales, relevant parish, town and community councils. In Northern Ireland the SORP applies to all district councils.

Local government bodies are governed by elected or appointed members who are supported by professional officers. The body itself is responsible for ensuring that a sound system of financial management and internal control are in place, but it will have three designated statutory officers each of whom has a specific role in relation to accountability and control:

- Head of Paid Service – usually the Chief Executive, responsible to the full council for the corporate and overall strategic management of the authority;
- Monitoring Officer – responsible for reporting to the authority any actual or potential breaches of the law or any maladministration, and for ensuring that procedures for recording and reporting key decisions are operating effectively; and
- Chief Financial Officer – local authorities are required to appoint an officer with responsibility for the proper administration of their financial affairs.

The involvement of auditors

As with Bulletin 2003/2, much of the guidance in Bulletin 2004/2 relating to local government bodies is identical to that in Bulletin 2003/1 on central government, and it is not repeated here. Again, some terminology differs between the sectors, and example wordings and reports given in **48.22.1** are provided again below, adapted for use by auditors involved in local government reporting.

The following tables show:

- the model opinion paragraph when the auditor reports by exception on the SIC (**Table 10**); and
- an example statement of auditors' responsibilities (**Table 11**).

TABLE 10: Model opinion paragraph when the auditor reports by exception on the SIC (Local Government)

Opinion

In our opinion the statement of accounts present fairly the financial transactions of XYZ Authority at [date] and its income and expenditure for the year then ended.

Other matter

We have reviewed the authority's description of the processes undertaken for reviewing the effectiveness of the system of internal control as set out on page [x]. In our opinion the authority's comments concerning ... do not appropriately reflect our understanding of the processes undertaken because ....

TABLE 11: Example statement of responsibilities (Local Government)

Respective Responsibilities of Chief Financial Officer and Auditors

As described on page [x], the Chief Financial Officer is responsible for the preparation of the statement of accounts in accordance with the Statement of Recommended Practice on Local Authority Accounting in the United Kingdom. Our responsibilities as independent auditors are established by statute, and by the Code of Audit Practice issued by the Audit Commission, which requires adherence to the auditing standards issued by the Auditing Practices Board (APB) and relevant ethical standards. It also requires us to have regard to other guidance and advice issued by the APB.

We report to you our opinion as to whether the statement of accounts present fairly the financial position of the Council and its income and expenditure for the year.

We review whether the statement on internal control on page [x] reflects compliance with CIPFA's guidance 'The Statement on Internal Control in Local Government: Meeting the Requirements of the Accounts and Audit Regulations 2003'. We report if it does not comply with proper practices specified by CIPFA or if the statement is misleading or inconsistent with other information we are aware of from our audit of the financial statements. We are not required to consider, nor have we considered, whether the statement on internal control covers all risks and controls. We are also not required to form an opinion on the effectiveness of the authority's corporate governance procedures or its risk and control procedures. Our review was not performed for any purpose connected with any specific transaction and should not be relied upon for any such purpose.

We read the other information published with the statement of accounts and consider the implications for our report if we become aware of any apparent misstatements or material inconsistencies with the statement of accounts.

48.28   GRANT CLAIMS

48.28.1   Background

Grants received from government departments and other funding agencies may be unconditional or may have detailed controls imposed over their expenditure. The guidance in Audit Technical Release 03/03 refers only to situations where a grant paying body has awarded a grant for specific purposes and it has requested that a special accountants' report be provided. A grant recipient may ask an accountant to provide assurance on the eligibility of amounts claimed and/or on the use of grant money and to sign special reports that have been requested by the grant paying body.

The Technical Release builds on the principles outlined in Audit 1/01 *Reporting to Third Parties* (see **Chapter 42**), and applies from September 2003.

There are three categories of people who will require consideration from the accountants when reporting on grant claims. These are detailed below:

Recipients who are entitled to rely on reports and may suffer a direct loss

A grant paying body usually requires assurance that the recipient meets the criteria for receiving the grant and that the grant monies have been spent in accordance with its terms and conditions. Even when accountants are not providing their report directly to the grant paying body, but rather to the grant recipient, the grant provider is also likely to rely on the report.

Therefore, the accountants should enter into an agreement with both the grant provider and the grant receiver, acknowledging the duty of care to both parties.

If the grant provider has a sponsoring body which is ultimately responsible for the monies paid by the grant provider, they may seek to rely on the accountants' report and should be bound into the engagement separately.

Recipients who may use them, are entitled to place reliance on them, but will not suffer a direct loss

These may include audit agencies such as the National Audit Office, Parliament and sponsoring bodies who have not entered into an engagement with the accountants.

The accountants should establish who has statutory rights of access to their report and seek to stipulate that it should not be disclosed to another person without consent from the accountants.

General access to reports where no entitlement for reliance may be placed

These reports are widely available as a result of statute, but it is not reasonable for the accountants to owe a duty of care to anyone who reads their report. Therefore, if a body writes to the accountants in an attempt to indicate reliance on their report, the accountants should issue a disclaimer in writing.

48.28.2   Terms of engagement

The accountants' understanding of the risks involved in the engagement will determine whether they accept the work. Depending on the circumstances, the accountants can either:

- accept that they owe a duty of care to the grant provider and enter into an engagement with both the grant provider and the grant receiver, limiting liability as necessary;

- engage with the grant receiver, but require the grant paying body to acknowledge in writing that no duty of care is owed by the accountants before the report is released to them;
- engage with the grant receiver, but disclaim or limit any liability or duty to the grant provider in the accountants' report; or
- refuse to accept the appointment.

Where other parties such as the sponsoring body also require access to the report, they may require input into the wording of the report. Accountants need to be clear about who is permitted access and to whom a duty of care is owed.

Where the accountants assess the report as low risk, because the grant provider could suffer little or no loss, or where the grant provider is willing to accept in writing that they are owed no duty of care, there may be no formal engagement between the accountant and the grant provider.

The possible courses of action are set out in the flow chart in **Table 12**.

An example tri-partite engagement letter is set out in **Table 13**. As there are likely to be a large number of recipients for a particular grant scheme, the provider may be unwilling to agree individual engagement letters. If this is the case, the grant paying body will issue a standardised terms of engagement, an example of which is in **Table 14**. These terms may need to be tailored in certain circumstances.

If the grant provider will agree to neither the tri-partite engagement letter nor the standardised terms of engagement the accountant may choose not to accept the engagement.

TABLE 12: Reporting accountants' process in accepting a request for a report from a grant provider

TABLE 13: Example tri-partite engagement letter

Where a sponsoring body is to be bound into the engagement process, then all references to the grant paying body should also include references to the sponsoring body.

[Grant paying body]
[Address]

[Grant recipient]
[Address]

[Date]

Dear Sirs

Government Grant reports/confirmations

We are writing to confirm the terms and conditions on which you have engaged [name of firm] to provide reports/confirmations in connection with [description or name of grant] paid by [grant paying body] to [grant recipient]. These terms and conditions will apply to the reports/confirmations to be supplied for the period [ended/ending . . .] and for subsequent periods unless otherwise agreed in writing. We will write separately to the grant recipient regarding practical matters such as the timing of our work, staffing and our charges. Our invoices will be addressed to [grant recipient], who will be solely responsible for payment in full.

Scope of our work

We will complete the relevant work specified below on the schedule (as defined in the offer letter). The schedule is to be prepared by, and is the sole responsibility of [grant recipient].

Our work will comprise the following:

[Details of planned work relevant to the nature of the claim or grant, level of assurance and form and content of report required]

[**High level assurance**] On the basis of the detailed tests carried out, we will report whether, in our opinion, we have obtained sufficient appropriate evidence that the amounts shown in the schedule are [presented fairly in all material respects in the context of reporting upon this grant claim and in accordance with the terms and conditions set by the grant paying body].

[**Moderate assurance**] We will report whether anything has come to our attention arising from the limited tests carried out (as specified in the schedule) to suggest that the amounts shown in the schedule have not been spent in accordance with the terms and conditions set by the grant paying body.

[**Agreed upon procedures**] We will complete the specified limited scope procedures set out below on the attached schedule. Upon completion of the procedures, we will provide you with a report of our findings. You have both agreed that the scope of our work, as specified below, is sufficient for your purposes.

[Preparation of any document that [grant recipient] may be required to submit to [grant paying body] in connection with our work will be the responsibility of [grant recipient]'s Directors, who will also be responsible for ensuring that [grant recipient] maintains proper accounting records and such other records as may be required by [grant paying body]. [Grant recipient]'s Directors will on request supply us with confirmation of matters affecting our work which are dependent on the Directors' judgement.]

Save as set out above, we will not seek to establish the accuracy, completeness or reliability of any of the information or documentation made available to us. Our work will not amount to an audit of financial statements and will not give the same level of assurance as an audit.

Our audit work on the financial statements of [grant recipient] is carried out in accordance with our statutory obligations and is subject to separate terms and conditions. This engagement will not be treated as having any effect on our separate duties and responsibilities as [grant recipient]'s external auditors. Our audit report on the financial statements is intended for the sole benefit of [grant recipient]'s shareholders as a body, to whom it is addressed, to enable them to exercise their rights as a body in a general meeting. Our audits of [grant recipient]'s financial statements are not planned or conducted to address or reflect matters in which anyone other than such shareholders as a body may be interested in for such purpose.

To the fullest extent permitted by law we do not and will not, by virtue of our reports/ confirmations or otherwise, assume or accept any duty of care or liability under this engagement to [grant recipient] or to [grant paying body] or to any other party, whether in contract, negligence or otherwise in relation to our audits of [grant recipient]'s financial statements.

Having set out our work we will issue reports/confirmations addressed to [grant recipient] and [grant paying body] in the form set out in the appendix to this engagement letter, if our findings support this. In determining the form of our report we will take into account, (though without being bound by it) any form of reporting that the [grant paying body] has suggested or agreed with the Institute of Chartered Accountants in England and Wales following consultation with them. We will deliver copies to [grant recipient] at the same time. This letter will be identified in our reports/ confirmations as the 'tri-partite agreement' under which our reports/confirmations have been issued. Our reports/confirmations will be released on the basis that they are not to be copied, referred to or disclosed, in whole or in part, to any other party without our prior written consent, which may be conditional. If we need to qualify our opinion, we will issue a qualified report but will continue to use the agreed form of report for all aspects that are not qualified.

Other matters

Our duties and liabilities in connection with this engagement owed to [grant recipient] and to [grant paying body] will differ.

[Detail any exclusions and limitations on the firm's liability to both the grant paying body and the grant recipient and any relevant qualifications required to satisfy statutory reasonableness criteria. See **Table 13**.]

Our duty to [grant paying body] will be limited to delivery of reports/confirmations in the agreed form to enable it to meet its statutory obligations. Delivery of such reports/ confirmations (or the supply of confirmation that we are unable to do so in the agreed form) at any time will discharge that obligation in full. We will not owe [grant paying body] any other duty, in contract, negligence or otherwise, in connection with our reports/confirmations or their preparation [(see alternative wording in **Table 13**)].

This agreement shall be subject to and governed by English law and all disputes arising from, or under it, shall be subject to the exclusive jurisdiction of the English Courts.

[Detail or append any other terms and conditions to apply to this work.]

Please confirm, by signing below your agreement to this letter. Once you have done so this letter will form a tri-partite contract between us in respect of the matters covered. If you wish to discuss any aspects of this letter, please contact [name and telephone number].

Yours faithfully
[Name of accountant]
[Grant recipient]
[Grant paying body]

TABLE 14: Example standardised terms of engagement

Where a sponsoring body is to be bound into the engagement process, then all references to the grant paying body should also include references to the sponsoring body.

The following are the terms of engagement on which the [grant paying body] agrees to engage accountants to perform [a high or medium level of assurance or agreed upon procedures] engagement and report in connection with the [name of grant claim].

An agreement between [grant recipient], its reporting accountants and the [grant paying body] on these terms is formed when [grant recipient] and the accountant signs and submits to the [grant paying body] a report as set out in Clause 3 herein. [NB: The [grant paying body] will not need to sign anything. By publishing this document the [grant paying body] makes an offer to engage on these terms. Once the offer is accepted by the [grant recipient] and the accountants then an agreement is formed. If the terms of the standardised engagement letter are to be revised, the [grant paying body] will need to confirm its acceptance of the new terms before an agreement is formed.]

In these terms of engagement:

'[grant paying body]' refers to the body that is providing the grant funding;

'the [grant recipient]' refers to the organisation that is required to submit the report to the [grant paying body];

'the accountant' refers to the [grant recipient]'s reporting accountants.

1 Introduction

The [grant recipient] is required to submit to the [grant paying body] reports as set out in Clause 3 below that are also signed by an accountant to provide independent assurance. These terms of engagement set out the basis on which the accountant will sign the report.

2 The [grant recipient]'s responsibilities

2.1 The grant recipient is responsible for producing the [information], maintaining proper records complying with the terms of any legislation or regulatory requirements and the [grant paying body]'s terms and conditions of grant ('the grant conditions') and providing relevant information to the [grant paying body] on a basis in accordance with the requirements of the grant conditions. The [grant recipient] is responsible for ensuring that the non-financial records can be reconciled to the financial records.

2.2 The management of the [grant recipient] will make available to the accountant all records, correspondence, information and explanations that the accountant considers necessary to enable the accountant to perform the accountant's work.

2.3 The [grant recipient] and the [grant paying body] accept that the ability of the accountant to perform his work effectively depends upon the grant recipient providing full and free access to the financial and other records and the [grant recipient] shall procure that any such records held by a third party are made available to the accountant.

2.4 The accountant accepts that, whether or not the [grant recipient] meets its obligations, the accountant remains under an obligation to the [grant paying body] to perform his work with reasonable care. The failure by the [grant recipient] to meet its obligations may cause the accountant to qualify his report or be unable to provide a report.

3 Scope of the accountant's work

3.1 The [grant recipient] will provide the accountant with such information, explanations and documentation that the accountant considers necessary to carry out his responsibilities. The accountant will seek written representations from management in relation to matters for which independent corroboration is not available. The accountant will also seek confirmation that any significant matters of which the accountant should be aware have been brought to the accountant's attention.

3.2 The accountant will perform the following work in relation to reports required by the [grant paying body]:

3.2.1 Grant return: The accountant will [carry out a high/medium level of assurance assignment or perform agreed tests] [as set out in the terms and conditions of the grant] and subject to any adverse findings will produce a report in the form set out in the attached Appendix.

3.2.2 Where a [high/medium] level of assurance is required by the [grant paying body], the criteria is identified as per the Appendix to this letter.

3.2.3 For an agreed upon procedures engagement, the tests are as laid out in the Appendix to this letter.

4 Form of the accountant's report

4.1 The accountant's reports are prepared on the following basis:

4.1.1 The accountant's reports are prepared solely for the confidential use of the [grant recipient] and the [grant paying body] and solely for the purpose of submission to the [grant paying body] in connection with the [grant paying body]'s requirements in connection with [name of grant]. They may not be relied upon by the [grant recipient], or the [grant paying body] for any other purpose except as provided in 4.1.2 below;

4.1.2 The [grant paying body] may only disclose the reports to others who may have statutory rights of access to the report. There may be an actual or potential liability to [other bodies] that may arise out of the eligibility and/or use of monies by the [grant recipient], and [the others] who will be entitled to rely on the report;

4.1.3 Neither the [grant recipient], nor the [grant paying body] [nor others] may rely on any oral or draft reports the accountant provides. The accountant accepts responsibility to the [grant recipient], the [grant paying body] for the accountant's final signed reports only;

4.1.4   The accountant's reports must not be recited or referred to in whole or in part in any other document (including, without limitation, any publication issued by the [grant paying body]) without the prior written approval of the accountant;

4.1.5   Except to the extent required by court order, law or regulation or to assist in the resolution of any court proceedings the accountant's reports must not be made available, copied or recited to any other person (including, without limitation, any person who may use or refer to any of the [grant paying body]'s publications);

4.1.6   Except as provided by 4.1.2 herein, the firm of accountants, its partners and staff neither owe nor accept any duty to any other person (including, without limitation, any person who may use or refer to any of the [grant paying body]'s publications) and shall not be liable for any loss, damage or expense whatsoever nature which is caused by their reliance on representations in the accountant's reports.

5 Liability provisions

5.1 The accountant will perform the engagement with reasonable skill and care and acknowledges that it will be liable to the [grant recipient] and the [grant paying body] for losses, damages, costs or expenses ('losses') caused by its breach of contract, negligence or wilful default, subject to the following provisions:

5.1.1   The accountant will not be so liable if such losses are due to the provision of false, misleading or incomplete information or documentation or due to the acts or omissions of any person other than the accountant, except where, on the basis of the enquiries normally undertaken by accountants within the scope set out in these terms of engagement, it would have been reasonable for the accountant to discover such defects;

5.1.2   The accountant accepts liability without limit for the consequences of its own fraud and for any other liability which it is not permitted by law to limit or exclude;

5.1.3   Subject to the previous paragraph (5.1.2), the total aggregate liability of the accountant whether in contact, tort (including negligence) or otherwise, to the [grant paying body] and the sponsoring body, arising from or in connection with the work which is the subject of these terms (including any addition or variation to the work), shall not exceed the amount of [to be discussed and agreed].

5.2 The [grant recipient] and the [grant paying body] agree that they will not bring any claims or proceedings against any individual partners, members, directors or employees of the accountant. This clause is intended to benefit such partners, members, directors and employees who may enforce this clause pursuant to the Contracts (Rights of Third Parties) Act 1999 ('the Act'). Notwithstanding any benefits or rights conferred by this agreement on any third party by virtue of the Act, the parties to this agreement may agree to vary or rescind this agreement without any third party's consent. Other than as expressly provided in these terms, the provisions of the Act are excluded;

5.3 Any claims, whether in contract, negligence or otherwise, must be formally commenced within [years] after the party bringing the claim becomes aware (or ought reasonably become aware) of the facts which give rise to the action and in any event no later than [years] after any alleged breach of contract, negligence or other cause of actions. This expressly overrides any statutory provision which would otherwise apply;

5.4 This engagement is separate from, and unrelated to, the accountant's audit work on the financial statements of the [grant recipient] for the purposes of the Companies Act 1985 (or its successor) or other legislation and nothing herein creates obligations or liabilities regarding the accountant's statutory audit work, which would not otherwise exist. [To be amended where the grant recipient is other than a Companies Act entity.]

6 Fees

The accountant's fees, together with VAT and out of pocket expenses, will be agreed with and billed to the [grant recipient]. The [grant paying body] is not liable to pay the accountant's fees.

7 Quality of service

The accountant will investigate all complaints. The [grant paying body] or the [grant recipient] have the right to take any complaint to the Institute of Chartered Accountants in England and Wales ('the ICAEW'). The [grant paying body] or the [grant recipient] may obtain an explanation of the mechanisms that operate in respect of a complaint to the ICAEW at *www.icaew.co.uk/complaints* or by writing to the ICAEW. To contact the ICAEW write to the Professional Standards Office, Silbury Court, 412-416 Silbury Boulevard, Central Milton Keynes, MK9 2AF.

8 Providing services to other parties

The accountant will not be prevented or restricted by virtue of the accountant's relationship with the [grant recipient] and the [grant paying body], including anything in these terms of engagement, from providing services to other clients. The accountant's standard internal procedures are designed to ensure that confidential information communicated to the accountant during the course of an assignment will be maintained confidentially.

9 Applicable law and jurisdiction

9.1 This agreement shall be governed by, and interpreted and construed in accordance with, English Law.

9.2 The [grant recipient], the [grant paying body] and the accountant irrevocably agree that the Courts of England shall have exclusive jurisdiction to settle any dispute (including claims for set-off and counterclaims) which may arise in connection with the validity, effect, interpretation or performance of, or the legal relationship established by the agreement or otherwise arising in connection with this agreement.

10 Alteration to terms

All additions and variations to these terms of engagement shall be binding only if in writing and signed by the duly authorised representatives of the parties. These terms supersede any previous agreements and representations between the parties in respect of the scope of the accountant's work and the accountant's report or the obligations of any of the parties relating thereto (whether oral or written) and represents the entire understanding between the parties.

Accountants should consider whether to include a disclaimer or liability limitation in their engagement terms. Examples are given in **Tables 15** and **16**.

TABLE 15: Example disclaimer notice for an accountant's report

Where the grant paying body signs the engagement letter

Our Report is prepared solely for the confidential use of [grant recipient] [and [grant paying body]], and solely for the purpose of [describe the purpose]. It may not be relied upon by [grant recipient] [or [grant paying body]] for any other purpose whatsoever. Our Report must not be recited or referred to in whole or in part in any other published document without the written permission of the accountant. [(Please see comments in **Table 12** item 4.1.4.)]

Our Report must not be made available, copied or recited to any other party without our express written permission in every case except for [grant paying body] may disclose the report where it has a statutory obligation to do so. Other than to [grant recipient] [and [grant paying body]], [accountant] neither owes nor accepts any duty to any other party to whom their Report may be disclosed.

Where the grant paying body does not sign the engagement letter

Our Report is prepared solely for the confidential use of [grant recipient] and solely for the purpose of [describe the purpose]. It may not be relied upon by [grant recipient] for any other purpose whatsoever. Our Report must not be recited or referred to in whole or in part in any other published document without the written permission of the accountant. Our Report must not be made available, copied or recited to any other party without our express written permission in every case to any other party, except for [grant paying body], to whom we owe no duty of care. Accountant neither owes nor accepts any duty to any other party who may receive our Report and specifically disclaims any liability for any loss, damage or expense of whatsoever nature, which is caused by their reliance on our Report.

TABLE 16: Example of a liability cap for an accountant's reporting engagement

The total aggregate liability, whether to [grant recipient] or [grant paying body] or any other party, of whatever nature, whether in contract, tort (including negligence) or otherwise, of [accountant] for any losses whatsoever and howsoever caused arising from or in any way connected with this engagement [and this transaction] shall not exceed [insert amount] (including interest). We limit liability to that proportion of the loss or damage suffered by the [grant paying body] for which the [accountant] has contributed to the overall cause for such loss or damage, as agreed between the parties, or in the absence of an agreement, as finally determined by the courts (subject to an upper limit).

Where there is more than one addressee of the engagement, the limit of the liability specified will have to be allocated between these addressees. Such allocation will be entirely a matter for the addressees, and the addressees will be under no obligation to inform [accountant] of it; if (for whatever reason) no such allocation is agreed, the addressees will not dispute the validity, enforceability or operation of the limit of liability on the grounds that no such allocation was agreed.

48.28.3   Types of engagement

There are no UK auditing standards covering this type of engagement, but international guidance does exist. This guidance sets out three types of engagement which could be performed:

- agreed upon procedures;
- assurance engagements (high level assurance); and
- assurance engagements (moderate level assurance).

The level of testing will depend on the type of engagement required, and this should be agreed at the outset of the engagement.

Agreed upon procedures

An 'agreed upon procedures' assignment involves the accountant performing certain procedures which have been specified by the grant provider, and which the provider uses to derive its assurance. Audit 1/01 *Reporting to Third Parties* suggests that this type of procedure will normally best meet the expectations of the third party and the client as the procedures are agreed in advance and set out in the engagement letter. In addition, the accountant will attach a copy of their proposed report format to the engagement letter.

Assurance engagements

For an engagement to provide a specific level assurance it needs to exhibit all of the following elements:

- a three party relationship involving a professional accountant, a responsible party and an intended user;
- a subject matter;
- suitable criteria;
- an engagement process; and
- a conclusion.

Therefore the grant provider is required to determine suitable criteria on which the accountant will conclude.

High level of assurance is usually regarded as providing a conclusion in positive terms, such as 'the grant conditions have been met'. In order to provide this opinion a significant amount of work must be performed by the accountants, up to 100 per cent testing levels.

Moderate level assurance requires the above elements of an assurance engagement to exist, but with a lesser level of testing. This will lead to a negative opinion in the style of 'nothing has come to our attention to suggest that the grant has not been spent for the intended purpose'.

48.28.4   *Reporting*

Agreeing the form of report to be given at the outset of the engagement helps to narrow any expectation gap that may arise. The grant provider should carefully consider the form of words it will require for its purpose, but good practice suggests that all parties should be involved in agreeing the wording. If possible, standard forms should be avoided, particularly those that cannot be justified by any level of work, and undefined terms such as 'review' or 'reasonable' should not be used without clarification of their meaning. Terms required by statute or legislation should be clearly defined to avoid later misunderstanding.

Typically an accountants' report will contain the following:

- addressee(s);
- identification of the applicable engagement letter and specific information on which the work has been performed and tests have been applied;
- under an agreed upon procedures engagement, a statement that the procedures/tests performed were those agreed with the grant recipient (and grant paying body);
- under a high or moderate assurance engagement, a statement of the procedures necessary to provide the agreed level of assurance;
- identification of the purpose for which the procedures/tests were performed;
- listing of the specific procedures/tests performed;
- description of the accountants' findings, including sufficient details of errors and exceptions found;
- statement that the procedures/tests performed do not constitute either an audit or a review;
- statement that the report is restricted to those parties that are bound by the terms of the engagement letter;
- statement that the engagement is separate from the audit of the annual financial statements and that the report relates only to the matters specified and that it does not extend to the grant recipient's annual financial statements taken as a whole;
- name and signature of reporting accountants; and
- date of the report.

48.28.5   *Access to accountants' working papers*

Government departments or audit agencies may require access to the accountants' working papers. Most accountants will agree to this as long as an authorisation letter is signed by the grant recipient permitting the accountants to give access to their papers and a release letter is signed by the party requiring access agreeing that no duty of care or liability exists to them. Further details can be found in **Chapter 19**.

Model authorisation and release letters are provided in **Tables 17** and **18.**

TABLE 17: Authorisation letter

We understand that the [body requesting access] believes that it would be helpful if they were to review our working papers and report on [grant claim].

Our policy does not normally allow me to disclose our working papers to any third party. In accordance with the guidance contained within Technical Release Audit 3/03 *Public Sector Special Reporting Engagements – Grant Claims* issued by the ICAEW, this firm is content to allow such access to the working papers and report providing certain conditions are met. We are now writing to confirm your agreement to the terms set out in this letter and to secure the authorisation of the grant recipient for that access.

As a condition of providing access and responding to any request for information or explanations in relation to the working papers in the course of or in connection with the review of the papers, this firm requires the [body requiring access] to agree to the terms of the letter.

Prior to making the working papers and reports on [grant claim] available, we need the consent of [grant recipient]. In addition, we will require from [body requiring access] an agreement (in the form of a release letter) that they will not acquire any rights against [name of firm] as a result of such access, and an acknowledgement from [body requiring access] that they recognise the basis on which such access is provided.

As you will appreciate, our working papers were created for the sole particular purpose of providing assurance on [grant claim] in line with [procedures/expectations] agreed with yourselves [and [body requiring access]]. They were not created for any other purpose. Furthermore, it is not this firm's function or responsibility to provide to the [body requiring access] any papers that come into existence or information that may come to the firm's attention after the date of this letter. Consequently, the working papers, report and any subsequent information and explanations provided in relation to the working papers and report are subject to the following conditions:

(1) the [grant paying body] or any other parties involved, do not misuse any confidential information obtained from their review of the working papers and reports or from any explanations provided by the firm; and

(2) the [grant paying body] accept that, to the fullest extent permitted by law, [firm] owes them no duty of care or other obligation and will incur no liability whatsoever to them in relation to or in connection with their review as a result of granting them access or providing explanations.

Please, therefore, confirm that you agree to our disclosing the working papers, reports and providing explanations in relation to the working papers and reports on [grant claim] on the terms described above by signing and dating and returning to us the enclosed copy of this letter on behalf of the [grant recipient] and returning it to us.

Yours faithfully

Name of firm

Acknowledged and agreed, for and on behalf of [grant paying body] and its directors

Director   Date

TABLE 18: Release letter

In connection with [grant claim], the [grant recipient] has requested us to allow [body requiring access] access to our working papers, reports and provision of explanations in relation to the working papers and reports as necessary.

The procedures and working papers were designed and prepared solely for the purpose of forming our opinion, in accordance with the form of report agreed in the engagement letter with the [grant recipient] and the [grant paying body]. Accordingly, we have not expressed any opinion or other form of assurance on other issues related to [grant recipient].

You should note that we have only reported on transactions related to [grant claim] in accordance with the agreed procedures/expectations for the period of [date] and to [date] and significant events may well have occurred since that date.

Neither the working papers, reports and explanations provided, can in any way serve to substitute enquiries that you may need to make for the purpose of satisfying yourself in relation to the review that you are carrying out.

Notwithstanding the purposes for which the working papers and reports were prepared, we are prepared to grant [body requiring access] access to them on the condition that the [body requiring access] acknowledges and accepts the previous paragraphs and agree to the following conditions upon which access will be granted:

[body requiring access] agrees and acknowledges that:

- to the extent that any of the working papers or reports may be construed as relating to the state of affairs of the [grant recipient] the onus will be on the [body requiring access] to verify the information directly with the [grant recipient] before relying upon it for the purpose of their review;
- to the fullest extent permitted by law, the [grant paying body] accept that the [name of firm] owes no duty of care to it whether in contract or tort or under statute or otherwise and will not bring any actions, proceedings or claims against the [name of firm] with respect to or in connection with the working papers [or report] on [grant claim]; and
- to the fullest extent permitted by law, [name of firm] has no liability to it for any loss or damage suffered or costs incurred by it, arising out of or in connection with the provision of access to the working papers [or reports], however such loss or damage is caused, including as a result of negligence.

Please confirm your agreement to the foregoing terms and conditions and your acceptance of the rest of this letter by signing, dating and returning to us a copy of this letter.

Yours faithfully

[Name of firm]

The [body requiring access] acknowledges and agrees to the provisions of this letter.

For and behalf of [body requiring access]   Date

48.29   BULLETIN 2008/7

In May 2008, the APB issued Bulletin 2008/9 *Illustrative Auditor's Reports on Public Sector Financial Statements in the United Kingdom.* The purpose of the Bulletin is to provide illustrative examples of:

- unmodified auditor's reports for auditors of financial statements of public sector bodies in the United Kingdom for auditors performed in accordance with International Standards on Auditing (UK and Ireland); and
- auditor's reports modified for regularity issues.

The reports included in the Bulletin are listed in **Table 19**.

TABLE 19: Example reports set out in Bulletin 2008/7

- Audit certificate and report for a Department preparing a Resource Account
- Audit Certificate and Report for an NDPB or Trading Fund preparing an accruals account
- Audit Report for a local government body in England that does not administer a pension fund
- Audit Report for a local government body in Wales that does not administer a pension fund
- Audit Report for a local government body in Scotland that does not administer a pension fund
- Audit Report for a local government body in Northern Ireland that does not administer a pension fund
- Audit Report for a local government body in England that administers a pension fund
- Audit Report for an NHS Trust in England
- Audit Report for a NHS Primary Care Trust/Strategic Health Authority in England
- Audit Report for a Probation Board in England and Wales
- Qualified opinion on the regularity of expenditure and unqualified opinion on the truth and fairness of accounts
- Qualified opinion for limitation of scope on regularity in England and unqualified opinion on the truth and fairness of the accounts
- Qualified opinions arising from expenditure in excess of amounts authorised
- Wording for a Primary Care Trust's/Strategic Health Authority's regularity opinion where the Revenue Resource Limit or the Capital Resource Limit has been breached.

48.30 PRACTICE NOTE 10 (REVISED) CONSULTATION DRAFT

Following the publication of the Clarified ISAs (UK and Ireland) in October 2009, the APB's industry-specific Practice Notes currently in issue required updating. The proposed revision of Practice Note 10 primarily provides guidance for auditors on their audit procedures when applying the new ISAs (UK and Ireland). It also takes account of a small number of legal and regulatory developments affecting public sector bodies in the United Kingdom since the current Practice Note 10 (Revised) was issued in January 2006. Comments were requested by 9 April 2010.

49 REGULATED ENTITIES

49.1 INTRODUCTION

In October 2003 the Audit and Assurance Faculty of the ICAEW issued Technical Release Audit 5/03 *Reporting to Regulators of Regulated Entities* to assist accountants when reporting on regulatory information.

Regulated entities, see **Table 1**, are often required to submit a large volume of financial information to their regulated body as part of the regulatory process and the exact requirements can vary significantly between industries. Regulators use this information in a number of ways, for example, in ensuring that costs and pricing are transparent, and the regulatory body often requires an independent accountant's report on elements of this information.

The guidance in Audit 5/03 is based on Audit 1/01 *Reporting to Third Parties*, see **Chapter 41**, and has been developed after discussion and consultation with a number of regulators. It does not apply to reporting to other regulatory bodies, such as the Financial Services Authority, see **Chapter 8**.

TABLE 1: Regulatory bodies

The Government appointed regulatory bodies that oversee the activities of regulated entities for the purpose of Audit 5/03 are:

- Ofgem (The Office of Gas and Electricity Markets);
- Ofwat (Office of Water Services);
- Oftel (Office of Telecommunications);
- Postcomm (Postal Services Commission);
- ORR (Office of the Rail Regulator);
- Ofreg (Office for the Regulation of Electricity and Gas in Northern Ireland);
- OfCom (Office of Communications).

49.2 DUTY OF CARE AND ENGAGEMENT CONTRACTS

As noted in **Chapter 41**, when an accountant knows that a third party obtains and relies on their report, the accountant will owe that third party a duty of care unless an effective disclaimer is in place.

Regulatory returns and regulatory accounts are required by an individual regulator, who will specify what information they will contain and who uses that information as part of its overall role. The accountant will only accept a duty of care to the regulator if either a tri-partite or bi-partite engagement contract with a written notice is in place. If the regulator will not enter into a suitable engagement contract the accountant will not accept a duty of care to the regulator and will make it clear in their report. However, the report will be addressed to the company and the regulator in order to meet the requirements of the regulatory licence.

The accountant will exclude a duty of care to any other third party by including a suitable disclaimer in their report. A third party may only rely on the report once they have become party to the engagement contract.

49.2.1   Tri-partite engagement contracts

A tri-partite engagement contract is a written engagement contract between the accountant, the regulated entity and the regulator. The contract will contain appropriate terms clarifying and limiting the scope and extent of the accountant's responsibilities and liability.

Table 2 sets out an example tri-partite engagement contract.

TABLE 2: Example tri-partite engagement contract

Private and Confidential

The Directors
[Name and address of Regulated Entity]
For the attention of [ ]

The Director General
[Name and address of Regulator]
For the attention of [ ]

[Date]

[Name of Regulated Entity] ('the Company')
Audit of the regulatory financial statements for the year ended [date]

Dear Sirs

Introduction

This letter (including the attached Appendices and the Terms and Conditions) sets out our understanding of the basis on which we act as auditors reporting on the regulatory financial statements ('the Regulatory Accounts') as specified in [licence condition or other reference] of the Instrument of Appointment of the Company as a [type of business] under the [applicable legislation] ('the Regulatory Licence') and the Regulatory Accounting Guidelines ('RAGs') [agreed with/] issued by the Director General of [identity of Regulator], [name of Regulator] ('the Regulator'). We also set out the respective areas of responsibility of the directors of the Company ('the Directors'), the Regulator and ourselves, in respect of the audit of the Regulatory Accounts (the 'Services'). This letter (with all its attachments) applies only to the audit report on the Regulatory Accounts and the scope of our work will be limited accordingly. If any additional work or report is required, separate engagement terms and conditions will need to be agreed.

This letter and the attached terms and conditions together comprise the entire contract ('the Contract') for the provision of the Services [to the exclusion of any other express

---

or implied terms, whether expressed orally or in writing including any conditions, warranties and representations unless made fraudulently] and shall supersede all previous contracts, letters of engagement, undertakings, agreements and correspondence regarding the Services.

Responsibilities of the Directors and the Auditors

The Directors are required to ensure that the Company complies with all of the terms of its Regulatory Licence [or other reference].

The Directors are required to prepare Regulatory Accounts in accordance with the Company's Regulatory Licence [or other reference] and the RAGs [agreed with/] issued by the Regulator, a copy of which are attached as Appendix [ ]. The Directors are also required to:

- [other licence conditions on which the Directors are required to give a finance-based report per the Regulatory Licence, for example];
- [confirm that, in their opinion, the Company has sufficient financial and management resources for the next twelve months];
- [confirm that, in their opinion, the Company has sufficient rights and assets which would enable a special administrator to manage the affairs, business and property of the Company];
- [Report to the Director General of [name of Regulator] changes in the Company's activities which may be material in relation to the Company's ability to finance its regulated activities];
- [Undertake the transactions entered into by the business consisting of the carrying out of the regulated activity ('the appointed business'), with or for the benefit of any group companies or related companies ('associated companies') or activities of the appointed business, at arm's length]; and
- [Keep proper accounting records which comply with [licence condition or other reference].

We refer to the above as 'the Specific Obligations'.

Other than reporting on whether or not proper accounting records have been kept by the Company as required by Condition [ ] of the Regulatory Licence [or other reference], it is not our responsibility in providing the Services to report on the Specific Obligations or on any other obligations of the Company or the Directors under the Regulatory Licence [or other reference].

The Directors are also responsible for ensuring that the Company maintains accounting records which disclose with reasonable accuracy, at any time, the financial position of the company, and for preparing Regulatory Accounts which present the results of the Company fairly in accordance with the Regulatory Licence. They are also responsible for making available to us, as and when required, all of the Company's accounting records, all other relevant records, including minutes of all directors', management and shareholders' meetings, and such information and explanations which we consider necessary for the performance of our duties as auditors.

It is our responsibility to form an independent opinion, based on our audit, on the Regulatory Accounts and to report our opinion to the Company and the Regulator.

Our report will be addressed to the Company and the Regulator and will state whether, in our opinion the Regulatory Accounts present fairly in accordance with conditions [ ], [ ] and [ ] of the Regulatory Licence [or other reference] the state of the Company's affairs at [date] and of its profit (or loss) for the year then ended, and have been properly prepared in accordance with conditions [ ], [ ] and [ ] of that Licence [or other reference].

Our report will be made in accordance with the Contract, solely to the Company and the Regulator in order to meet the requirements of the Regulatory Licence [or other reference]. Our audit work will be undertaken so that we might state to the Company and the Regulator those matters we have agreed in the Contract to state to them in our report in order to (a) assist the Company to [meet its obligations under the Regulatory Licence to procure such a report] and (b) to facilitate the carrying out by the Regulator of its regulatory functions, and for no other purpose. To the fullest extent permitted by law, we will not accept or assume responsibility to anyone other than the Company and the Regulator for our audit work, for our report, or for the opinions we will form. Our report will contain a disclaimer of liability to other parties to this effect.

The Contract does not confer benefits on any parties who are not parties to it and the application of the Contracts (Rights of Third Parties) Act 1999 is excluded.

In arriving at our opinion, and in accordance with the Regulatory Licence (condition [reference]) [or other reference], we will consider the following matters, and report on any in respect of which we are not satisfied:

- whether appropriate accounting records have been kept by the Company and proper returns adequate for our audit have been received from operating locations not visited by us;
- whether the Regulatory Accounts are in agreement with the accounting records and returns retained for the purpose of preparing the Regulatory Accounts; and
- whether we have obtained all the information and explanations which we consider necessary for the purpose of our audit.

Our responsibilities also include:

- providing in our report a description of the Directors' responsibilities for the Regulatory Accounts where the Regulatory Accounts or accompanying information do not include such a description; and
- considering whether other information in documents containing the Regulatory Accounts is consistent with those Regulatory Accounts.

The Regulator and the Company acknowledge and agree that:

- wherever the Regulatory Accounts or other Regulatory Information covered by the Independent Accountants' report are published or otherwise made available in full, our audit report will also be published or otherwise made available in full as part of that communication;
- wherever substantial extracts from the Regulatory Accounts or other Regulatory Information covered by the Independent Accountants' report are published or otherwise made available, and reference is made to the fact that they are audited or otherwise examined by an Independent Accountant, there will be explicit statements by the Regulator: (a) that the information published is only an extract; and (b) about the limitation of scope of the Independent Accountants' report and the duty of care owed by the Independent Accountants; and (c) referring to where the full set of Regulatory Accounts can be found or otherwise obtained; and
- wherever any other information is referenced from the Regulatory Accounts or other Regulatory Information covered by the Independent Accountants' report, there will be an explicit reference by the Regulator to the source of that information and the limitation of scope of the Independent Accounts' report and the duty of care owed by the Independent Accountant.

Relationship between the Regulator and the Company

For the avoidance of doubt, nothing in this Contract is intended to nor does it affect or in any way alter the relationship or the rights and obligations between the Company and the Regulator as set out in the Regulatory Licence [and all relevant legislation].

Scope of our audit

Our audit will be performed with regard to the guidance contained in Audit 05/03 *Reporting to Regulators of Regulated Entities* issued by the Institute of Chartered Accountants in England and Wales.

Our audit will be conducted in accordance with International Standards on Auditing (UK and Ireland) issued by the Auditing Practices Board except that, as the nature, form and content of Regulatory Accounts are determined by the Regulator, we will not evaluate the overall adequacy of the presentation of the information, which would have been required if we were to express an audit opinion under International Standards on Auditing (UK and Ireland). Our audit will include such tests of transactions and of the existence, ownership and valuation of assets and liabilities as we consider necessary. We shall obtain an understanding of the accounting and internal financial control systems to the extent necessary in order to assess their adequacy as a basis for the preparation of the Regulatory Accounts and to establish whether appropriate accounting records have been maintained by the Company.

We shall expect to obtain such appropriate evidence as we consider sufficient to enable us to draw reasonable conclusions therefrom. The nature and extent of our procedures will vary according to our assessment of the Company's accounting system and, where we wish to place reliance on it, the internal financial control system and may cover any aspect of the business operations.

[The Regulatory Accounts are prepared by disaggregating balances recorded in the general ledgers and other accounting records of the [name of statutory entity] maintained in accordance with the Companies Act 1985 and used, in accordance with that Act, for the preparation of [name of statutory entity]'s statutory financial statements.]

[No additional tests will be performed of the transactions and balances which are recorded in the general ledgers of [name of statutory entity] other than those carried out in performing the audit of the statutory financial statements that include the Company.]

Our audit includes assessing the significant estimates and judgements made by the Directors in the preparation of the Regulatory Accounts and whether the accounting policies are appropriate to the Company's circumstances, consistently applied and adequately disclosed.

[We will read the [specify information] ('Other Information') contained within the Regulatory Accounts, including any supplementary schedules on which we do not express an audit opinion, and consider the implications for our report if we become aware of any apparent misstatements or material inconsistencies with the Regulatory Accounts. We will not perform any audit procedures nor provide any other assurance on the Other Information.]

We will plan our work to gain reasonable assurance that the Regulatory Accounts are free from material error, whether caused by fraud or other misstatement.

The concept of materiality affects our audit planning and our consideration of matters arising from our audit. We take into account both qualitative and quantitative factors when assessing materiality. We will only express an opinion on the Regulatory Accounts as a whole and not on individual factors/components within Regulatory Accounts.

Where the Regulator requires specific factors to be reported upon by us, this should be addressed through the powers vested in the Regulator through the Regulatory Licence [or other reference]. For such reporting, we will agree a list of procedures ('Agreed Upon Procedures') that we will perform for the Regulator. These procedures will be specified in a separate engagement contract between us and the Regulator [and will be shown to the Company]. We will report the findings of the Agreed Upon Procedures separately from the Regulatory Accounts opinion, by way of a factual report to the Regulator, in which we will not express an opinion on the results of the Agreed Upon Procedures, nor the appropriateness of those procedures for the purposes of the Regulator. As with the form and content of Regulatory Accounts, the Regulator will need to make its own assessment of the appropriateness of the Agreed Upon Procedures and the reported findings.

Where Agreed Upon Procedures are required in addition to an opinion on the Regulatory Accounts, we may choose not to complete our work nor express an opinion on the Regulatory Accounts until:

- the Agreed Upon Procedures that have been specified by the Regulator have been completed and reported upon; and
- the Regulator has provided a written notice to us confirming that nothing has come to the attention of the Regulator from that report (or otherwise) that indicates that there are any matters which the Regulator believes that we should take into account in arriving at our opinion on the Regulatory Accounts. If such matters do exist we will consider, in arriving at our opinion on the Regulatory Accounts, the matters noted by the Regulator and/or agree additional Agreed Upon Procedures with the Regulator.

The Services are separate from our audit work on the statutory financial statements of the Company which is carried out in accordance with our statutory obligations under the Companies Act 1985. Our audit report on those statutory financial statements is intended for the sole benefit of the Company's shareholders as a group, to whom it is addressed, and not for any other purpose. Our audit of the Company's statutory financial statements are not planned or conducted in contemplation of the requirements of anyone other than such shareholders and, consequently, our audit work is not intended to address or reflect matters in which anyone other than such shareholders may be interested.

We do not and will not, by virtue of this report or otherwise in connection with this engagement, assume any responsibility whether in contract, negligence or otherwise in relation to our audits of the Company's statutory financial statements required by the Companies Act 1985; we and our employees shall have no liability whether in contract, tort (including negligence) or otherwise to any parties other than the Company and its members in relation to our audit of the Company's statutory financial statements.

The nature and format of the Regulatory Accounts are determined by the requirements of the Regulator. It is not appropriate for us to assess, and accordingly we will not make any assessment on, whether the nature of the information being reported upon is suitable or appropriate for the Regulator's purpose. It is a matter for the Regulator to consider whether the information being reported upon is appropriate for its own purposes and we will not give any implicit or explicit affirmation that the information being reported upon is suitable for the Regulator's purpose.

The Regulator and the Company accept that there [may be/are] differences between United Kingdom Generally Accepted Accounting Principles ('UK GAAP') and the basis of information provided in the Regulatory Accounts. Financial information, other than that prepared on the basis of UK GAAP, does not necessarily represent a true and fair view of the financial performance or financial position of a Company.

Internal audit

In developing our audit plan, we will liaise with the Company's internal auditors to ensure that our work is properly co-ordinated with theirs. It is our policy to rely upon internal audit work whenever possible, whilst ensuring that adequate audit coverage is achieved of all significant areas.

Meetings with the Regulator

We are willing to attend meetings with the Regulator to discuss the Services, if requested to do so, provided that we can agree appropriate terms on which such meetings are held. For the avoidance of doubt appropriate terms will include meeting only on a tri-partite basis in the absence of specific consent of the Company allowing us to meet with the Regulator [and its advisors].

Management representations

The information used by the Directors in preparing the Regulatory Accounts will invariably include facts or judgements which are not themselves recorded in the accounting records. As part of our normal audit procedures, we shall request appropriate Directors or senior officials/management of the company to provide written confirmation each year of such facts or judgements and any other oral representation which we have received during the course of the audit on matters having a material effect on the Regulatory Accounts. We will also ask the Directors to confirm in that letter that all important and relevant information has been brought to our attention. In connection with representations and the supply of information to us generally, we draw your attention to section 501 of the Companies Act 2006 under which it is an offence for an officer of the company to mislead the auditors.

Detection of fraud, error and non-compliance with laws and regulations

The responsibility for safeguarding the assets of the Company and for the prevention and detection of fraud, error and non-compliance with law or regulations rests with the Directors. However, we shall endeavour to plan our audit so that we have a reasonable expectation of detecting material misstatement in the Regulatory Accounts or accounting records (including any material misstatements resulting from fraud, error or non-compliance with law or regulations), but our examination should not be relied upon to disclose all such material misstatements or frauds, errors or instances of non-compliance as may exist.

Timetable

We expect to commence our work on [date] and would normally expect to issue our report by [date].

Completion of our work will depend on receiving, without undue delay, full co-operation from all relevant officials of the Company and their disclosure to us of all the accounting records of the Company and all other records and related information (including certain representations) that we may need for the purpose of our work.

Other requirements

In order to assist us with the examination of the Regulatory Accounts, we shall request early sight of all documents or statements which are due to be issued with those Regulatory Accounts.

Once we have issued our report we have no further direct responsibility in relation to the Regulatory Accounts for that financial year.

Preparation of Regulatory Accounts

Assistance with the preparation of Regulatory Accounts does not form a part of the audit function, but we shall discuss the Company's accounting principles with the management and/or the Directors and we may propose adjusting entries for their consideration.

Other services

We shall not be treated as having notice, for the purposes of our regulatory audit responsibilities, of information provided to members of our firm other than those engaged on the audit (for example information provided in connection with accounting, taxation and other services).

Fiduciary responsibilities

Because our audit work under the terms of this engagement is directed at forming an opinion on the Company's Regulatory Accounts our audit procedures will not formally extend to assets or documents of title in respect of assets that are in the Company's possession but owned by others.

Terms and Conditions

The attached Terms and Conditions set out the duties of all parties in respect of the Services. The Terms and Conditions amongst other things:

- limit our liability to a maximum aggregate amount of £[X]. This limitation shall be allocated between the Company and the Regulator. [It is agreed that such allocation will be entirely a matter for the addressees of this letter, who shall be under no obligation to inform [name of auditor] of it, provided always that if (for whatever reason) no such allocation is agreed, neither the Company nor the Regulator shall dispute the validity, enforceability or operation of the limit of liability on the grounds that no such allocation was agreed]; and
- limit the period within which a claim may be brought.

[Name of auditor] alone will be responsible for the performance of the engagement contract formed by this letter. You therefore agree that you will not bring any claim in respect of or in connection with this engagement whether in contact, tort (including negligence), breach of statutory duty or otherwise against any partner or employee of [name of auditors]. The foregoing exclusion does not apply to any liability that cannot be excluded under the laws of England and Wales.

Fees
[Details]

The fee for the work covered by this engagement letter will be agreed with, and paid by, the Company.

Safeguarding service

It is our desire to provide you at all times with a high quality service to meet your needs. If at any time you would like to discuss with us how our service to you could be improved or if you are dissatisfied with any aspect of our services, please raise the matter immediately with the partner responsible for that aspect of our services to you. If, for any reason, you would prefer to discuss these matters with someone other than that partner, please contact [ ] at [ ]. In this way we are able to ensure that your concerns are dealt with carefully and promptly. We undertake to look into any complaint carefully and promptly and to do all we can to explain the position. This will not affect your right to complain to the Institute of Chartered Accountants in England and Wales.

Acknowledgement and acceptance

Please acknowledge your acceptance of the terms of our engagement under the Contract by signing the confirmation below and returning a copy of this letter and the attached Terms and Conditions to us at the above address, whereupon the Contract will take effect from the date of the commencement by us of the Services.

Once it has been agreed, this letter will remain effective, from one audit appointment to another, until it is replaced.

If you have any questions regarding this Contract, please do not hesitate to contact us.

Yours faithfully

[Name of auditor]

I have read the above letter and accept the terms and conditions set out therein.

Signed

_____ (Name and position)   [date]

for an on behalf of [name of Company]

_____ (Name and position)   [date]

for an on behalf of [name of Regulator]

49.2.2   Bi-partite engagement contracts

A bi-partite engagement contract is a written engagement contract between the accountant and the regulated entity only. In order for the accountant to owe a duty of care to the regulator when a bi-partite engagement contract exists, there must be provision in that contract for the accountant to accept a responsibility to the regulator separately in a written notice. The contract will cap any financial liability to the regulator and regulated entity in aggregate to that which would have been paid to the regulated entity if no separate agreement had been made with the regulator.

A copy of the bi-partite engagement contract between the accountant and the regulated entity will be attached to the written notice.

Tables 3 and **4** set out an example bi-partite engagement contract and written notice respectively.

TABLE 3: Example bi-partite engagement contract

Private and Confidential

The Directors
[Name and address of Regulated Entity]
For the attention of [ ]

[Date]

[Name of Regulated Entity] ('the Company')

Audit of the regulatory financial statements for the year ended [date]

Dear Sirs

Introduction

This letter (including the attached Appendices and the Terms and Conditions) sets out our understanding of the basis on which we act as auditors reporting on the regulatory financial statements ('the Regulatory Accounts') as specified in [licence condition or other reference] of the Instrument of Appointment of the Company as a [type of business] under the [applicable legislation] ('the Regulatory Licence') and the Regulatory Accounting Guidelines ('RAGs') [agreed with/] issued by the Director General of [identity of Regulator], [name of Regulator] ('the Regulator'). We also set out the respective areas of responsibility of the directors of the Company ('the Directors') and ourselves, in respect of the audit of the Regulatory Accounts (the 'Services'). This letter (with all its attachments) applies only to the audit report on the Regulatory Accounts and the scope of our work will be limited accordingly. If any additional work or report is required, separate engagement terms and conditions will need to be agreed.

This letter and the attached terms and conditions together comprise the entire contract ('the Contract') for the provision of the Services [to the exclusion of any other express or implied terms, whether expressed orally or in writing including any conditions, warranties and representations unless made fraudulently] and shall supersede all previous contracts, letters of engagement, undertakings, agreements and correspondence regarding the Services.

The Regulator is not a party to the Contract. On condition that the Regulator accepts in writing a notice in the form appended ('the Regulator's Contract'), we will accept duties and responsibilities to the Regulator in respect of our audit work, our audit report and our audit opinion on the Regulatory Accounts. Any such agreement will be on the basis that, amongst other things, the Company and the Regulator agree that our aggregate liability to the Company and the Regulator is limited to the maximum amount which would have been payable to the Company alone in respect of any breach of our obligations to the Company. References to rights and obligations between the Regulator and the auditors in relation to the Services and the Agreed upon Procedures are included in the Contract for the purpose only of the Regulator's Contract and are not intended to create rights or obligations between the Regulator and the Company.

Responsibilities of the Directors and the Auditors

The Directors are required to ensure that the Company complies with all of the terms of its Regulatory Licence [or other reference].

The Directors are required to prepare Regulatory Accounts in accordance with the Company's Regulatory Licence [or other reference] and the RAGs [agreed with/] issued by the Regulator, a copy of which are attached as Appendix [ ]. The Directors are also required to:

- [other licence conditions on which the Directors are required to give a finance-based report per the Regulatory Licence, for example]:
- [confirm that, in their opinion, the Company has sufficient financial and management resources for the next twelve months];
- [confirm that, in their opinion, the Company has sufficient rights and assets which

would enable a special administrator to manage the affairs, business and property of the Company];

- [Report to the Director General of [name of Regulator] changes in the Company's activities which may be material in relation to the Company's ability to finance its regulated activities];
- [Undertake the transactions entered into by the business consisting of the carrying out of the regulated activity ('the appointed business'), with or for the benefit of any group companies or related companies ('associated companies') or activities of the appointed business, at arm's length]; and
- [Keep proper accounting records which comply with [licence condition or other reference].

We refer to the above as 'the Specific Obligations'.

Other than reporting on whether or not proper accounting records have been kept by the Company as required by Condition [ ] of the Regulatory Licence [or other reference], it is not our responsibility in providing the Services to report on the Specific Obligations or on any other obligations of the Company or the Directors under the Regulatory Licence [or other reference].

The Directors are also responsible for ensuring that the Company maintains accounting records which disclose with reasonable accuracy, at any time, the financial position of the company, and for preparing Regulatory Accounts which present the results of the Company fairly in accordance with the Regulatory Licence. They are also responsible for making available to us, as and when required, all of the Company's accounting records, all other relevant records, including minutes of all directors', management and shareholders' meetings, and such information and explanations which we consider necessary for the performance of our duties as auditors.

It is our responsibility to form an independent opinion, based on our audit, on the Regulatory Accounts and to report our opinion to the Company and the Regulator.

Our report will be made in accordance with the Contract, solely to the Company and the Regulator in accordance with the Regulatory Licence [or other reference]. Our audit work will be undertaken so that we might state to the Company and the Regulator those matters we have agreed in the Contract to state to them in our report in order to (a) assist the Company to [meet its obligations under the Regulatory Licence to procure such a report] and (b) to facilitate the carrying out by the Regulator of its regulatory functions, and for no other purpose. To the fullest extent permitted by law, we will not accept or assume responsibility to anyone other than the Company for our audit work, for our report, or for the opinions we will form. Our report will contain a disclaimer of liability to all other parties but we will confirm acceptance in our report of responsibility in respect of our audit work to the Regulator also if the Regulator has agreed to the Regulator's Contract by signing the written notice appended.

Our report will be addressed to the Company and the Regulator to meet the requirements of the Regulatory Licence and will state whether, in our opinion the Regulatory Accounts present fairly in accordance with conditions [ ], [ ] and [ ] of the Company's Regulatory Licence [or other reference] the state of the Company's affairs at [date] and of its profit (or loss) for the year then ended, and have been properly prepared in accordance with conditions [ ], [ ] and [ ] of that licence [or other reference].

The Contract does not confer benefits on any parties who are not parties to it and the application of the Contracts (Rights of Third Parties) Act 1999 is excluded.

In arriving at our opinion, and in accordance with the Regulatory Licence (condition [reference]) [or other reference], we will consider the following matters, and report on any in respect of which we are not satisfied:

- whether appropriate accounting records have been kept by the Company and proper returns adequate for our audit have been received from operating locations not visited by us;
- whether the Regulatory Accounts are in agreement with the accounting records and returns retained for the purpose of preparing the Regulatory Accounts; and
- whether we have obtained all the information and explanations which we consider necessary for the purpose of our audit.

Our responsibilities also include:

- providing in our report a description of the Directors' responsibilities for the Regulatory Accounts where the Regulatory Accounts or accompanying information do not include such a description; and
- considering whether other information in documents containing the Regulatory Accounts is consistent with those Regulatory Accounts.

The Company and (where the Regulator signs the written notice appended) the Regulator acknowledge and agree that:

- wherever the Regulatory Accounts or other Regulatory Information covered by the Independent Accountants' report are published or otherwise made available in full, our audit report will also be published or otherwise made available in full as part of that communication;
- wherever substantial extracts from the Regulatory Accounts or other Regulatory Information covered by the Independent Accountants' report are published or otherwise made available, and reference is made to the fact that they are audited or otherwise examined by an Independent Accountant, there will be explicit statements by the Regulator: (a) that the information published is only an extract; and (b) about the limitation of scope of the Independent Accountants' report and the duty of care owed by the Independent Accountants; and (c) referring to where the full set of Regulatory Accounts can be found or otherwise obtained; and
- wherever any other information is referenced from the Regulatory Accounts or other Regulatory Information covered by the Independent Accountants' report, there will be an explicit reference by the Regulator to the source of that information and the limitation of scope of the Independent Accounts' report and the duty of care owed by the Independent Accountant.

Where the Regulator does not sign a written notice in the form appended, the Company will procure that these events take place in the circumstances identified.

Relationship between the Regulator and the Company

For the avoidance of doubt, nothing in this Contract is intended to nor does it affect or in any way alter the relationship or the rights and obligations between the Company and the Regulator as set out in the Regulatory Licence [and all relevant legislation].

Scope of our audit

Our audit will be performed with regard to the guidance contained in Audit 05/03 *Reporting to Regulators of Regulated Entities* issued by the Institute of Chartered Accountants in England and Wales.

Our audit will be conducted in accordance with International Standards on Auditing (UK and Ireland) issued by the Auditing Practices Board except that, as the nature, form and content of Regulatory Accounts are determined by the Regulator, we will not evaluate the overall adequacy of the presentation of the information, which would have been required if we were to express an audit opinion under International Standards on Auditing (UK and Ireland). Our audit will include such tests of transactions and of the existence, ownership and valuation of assets and liabilities as we consider necessary. We shall obtain an understanding of the accounting and internal financial control systems to the extent necessary in order to assess their adequacy as a basis for the preparation of the Regulatory Accounts and to establish whether appropriate accounting records have been maintained by the Company.

We shall expect to obtain such appropriate evidence as we consider sufficient to enable us to draw reasonable conclusions therefrom. The nature and extent of our procedures will vary according to our assessment of the Company's accounting system and, where we wish to place reliance on it, the internal financial control system and may cover any aspect of the business operations.

[The Regulatory Accounts are prepared by disaggregating balances recorded in the general ledgers and other accounting records of the [name of statutory entity] maintained in accordance with the Companies Act 1985 and used, in accordance with that Act, for the preparation of [name of statutory entity]'s statutory financial statements.]

[No additional tests will be performed of the transactions and balances which are recorded in the general ledgers of [name of statutory entity] other than those carried out in performing the audit of the statutory financial statements that include the Company.]

Our audit includes assessing the significant estimates and judgements made by the Directors in the preparation of the Regulatory Accounts and whether the accounting policies are appropriate to the Company's circumstances, consistently applied and adequately disclosed.

[We will read the [specify information] ('Other Information') contained within the Regulatory Accounts, including any supplementary schedules on which we do not express an audit opinion, and consider the implications for our report if we become aware of any apparent misstatements or material inconsistencies with the Regulatory Accounts. We will not perform any audit procedures nor provide any other assurance on the Other Information.]

We will plan our work to gain reasonable assurance that the Regulatory Accounts are free from material error, whether caused by fraud or other misstatement.

The concept of materiality affects our audit planning and our consideration of matters arising from our audit. We take into account both qualitative and quantitative factors when assessing materiality. We will only express an opinion on the Regulatory Accounts as a whole and not on individual factors/components within Regulatory Accounts.

Where the Regulator requires specific factors to be reported upon by us, this should be addressed through the powers vested in the Regulator through the Regulatory Licence [or other reference]. For such reporting, we will agree a list of procedures ('Agreed Upon Procedures') that we will perform for the Regulator. These procedures will be specified in a separate engagement contract between us and the Regulator [and will be shown to the Company]. We will report the findings of the Agreed Upon Procedures separately from the Regulatory Accounts opinion, by way of a factual report to the Regulator, in which we will not express an opinion on the results of the Agreed Upon Procedures, nor the appropriateness of those procedures for the purposes of the Regulator. As with the form and content of Regulatory Accounts, the Regulator will need to make its own assessment of the appropriateness of the Agreed Upon Procedures and the reported findings.

Where Agreed Upon Procedures are required in addition to an opinion on the Regulatory Accounts, we may choose not to complete our work nor express an opinion on the Regulatory Accounts until:

- the Agreed Upon Procedures that have been specified by the Regulatory have been completed and reported upon; and
- the Regulator has provided a written notice to us confirming that nothing has come to the attention of the Regulator from that report (or otherwise) that indicates that there are any matters which the Regulator believes that we should take into account in arriving at our opinion on the Regulatory Accounts. If such matters do exist we will consider, in arriving at our opinion on the Regulatory Accounts, the matters noted by the Regulator and/or agree additional Agreed Upon Procedures with the Regulator.

The Services are separate from our audit work on the statutory financial statements of the Company which is carried out in accordance with our statutory obligations under the Companies Act 1985. Our audit report on those statutory financial statements is intended for the sole benefit of the Company's shareholders as a group, to whom it is addressed, and not for any other purpose. Our audit of the Company's statutory financial statements are not planned or conducted in contemplation of the requirements of anyone other than such shareholders and, consequently, our audit work is not intended to address or reflect matters in which anyone other than such shareholders may be interested.

We do not and will not, by virtue of this report or otherwise in connection with this engagement, assume any responsibility whether in contract, negligence or otherwise in relation to our audits of the Company's statutory financial statements required by the Companies Act 1985; we and our employees shall have no liability whether in contract, tort (including negligence) or otherwise to any parties other than the Company and its members in relation to our audit of the Company's statutory financial statements.

The nature and format of the Regulatory Accounts are determined by the requirements of the Regulator. It is not appropriate for us to assess, and accordingly we will not make any assessment on, whether the nature of the information being reported upon is suitable or appropriate for the Regulator's purpose. It is a matter for the Regulator to consider whether the information being reported upon is appropriate for its own purposes and we will not give any implicit or explicit affirmation that the information being reported upon is suitable for the Regulator's purpose.

There [may be/are] differences between United Kingdom Generally Accepted Accounting Principles ('UK GAAP') and the basis of information provided in the Regulatory Accounts. Financial information, other than that prepared on the basis of UK GAAP, does not necessarily represent a true and fair view of the financial performance or financial position of a Company.

Internal audit

In developing our audit plan, we will liaise with the Company's internal auditors to ensure that our work is properly co-ordinated with theirs. It is our policy to rely upon internal audit work whenever possible, whilst ensuring that adequate audit coverage is achieved of all significant areas.

Meetings with the Regulator

We are willing to attend meetings with the Regulator to discuss the Services, if requested to do so, provided that we can agree appropriate terms on which such meetings are held. For the avoidance of doubt appropriate terms will include meeting only on a tri-partite basis in the absence of specific consent of the Company allowing us to meet with the Regulator [and its advisors].

Management representations

The information used by the Directors in preparing the Regulatory Accounts will invariably include facts or judgements which are not themselves recorded in the accounting records. As part of our normal audit procedures, we shall request appropriate Directors or senior officials/management of the company to provide written confirmation each year of such facts or judgements and any other oral representation which we have received during the course of the audit on matters having a material effect on the Regulatory Accounts. We will also ask the Directors to confirm in that letter that all important and relevant information has been brought to our attention. In connection with representations and the supply of information to us generally, we draw your attention to section 389A of the Companies Act 1985 under which it is an offence for an officer of the company to mislead the auditors.

Detection of fraud, error and non-compliance with laws and regulations

The responsibility for safeguarding the assets of the Company and for the prevention and detection of fraud, error and non-compliance with law or regulations rests with the Directors. However, we shall endeavour to plan our audit so that we have a reasonable expectation of detecting material misstatement in the Regulatory Accounts or accounting records (including any material misstatements resulting from fraud, error or non-compliance with law or regulations), but our examination should not be relied upon to disclose all such material misstatements or frauds, errors or instances of non-compliance as may exist.

Timetable

We expect to commence our work on [date] and would normally expect to issue our report by [date].

Completion of our work will depend on receiving, without undue delay, full co-operation from all relevant officials of the Company and their disclosure to us of all the accounting records of the Company and all other records and related information (including certain representations) that we may need for the purpose of our work.

Other requirements

In order to assist us with the examination of the Regulatory Accounts, we shall request early sight of all documents or statements which are due to be issued with those Regulatory Accounts.

Once we have issued our report we have no further direct responsibility in relation to the Regulatory Accounts for that financial year.

Preparation of Regulatory Accounts

Assistance with the preparation of Regulatory Accounts does not form a part of the audit function, but we shall discuss the Company's accounting principles with the management and/or the Directors and we may propose adjusting entries for their consideration.

Other services

We shall not be treated as having notice, for the purposes of our regulatory audit responsibilities, of information provided to members of our firm other than those engaged on the audit (for example information provided in connection with accounting, taxation and other services).

Fiduciary responsibilities

Because our audit work under the terms of this engagement is directed at forming an opinion on the Company's Regulatory Accounts our audit procedures will not formally extend to assets or documents of title in respect of assets that are in the Company's possession but owned by others.

Terms and Conditions

The attached Terms and Conditions set out the duties of all parties in respect of the Services. The Terms and Conditions amongst other things:

- limit our liability to a maximum aggregate amount of £[X]. Where the Regulator accepts in writing a notice in the form appended (and on that basis we accept duties and responsibilities to the Regulator), this limitation shall be allocated between the Company and the Regulator. [It is agreed that such allocation will be entirely a matter for the addressees of this letter, who shall be under no obligation to inform [name of auditor] of it, provided always that if (for whatever reason) no such allocation is agreed, neither the Company nor the Regulator shall dispute the validity, enforceability or operation of the limit of liability on the grounds that no such allocation was agreed]; and
- limit the period within which a claim may be brought.

[Name of auditor] alone will be responsible for the performance of the engagement contract formed by this letter. You therefore agree that you will not bring any claim in respect of or in connection with this engagement whether in contact, tort (including negligence), breach of statutory duty or otherwise against any partner or employee of [name of auditors]. The foregoing exclusion does not apply to any liability that cannot be excluded under the laws of England and Wales.

Fees
[Details]

The fee for the work covered by this engagement letter will be agreed with, and paid by, the Company.

Safeguarding service

It is our desire to provide you at all times with a high quality service to meet your needs. If at any time you would like to discuss with us how our service to you could be improved or if you are dissatisfied with any aspect of our services, please raise the matter immediately with the partner responsible for that aspect of our services to you. If, for any reason, you would prefer to discuss these matters with someone other than that partner, please contact [ ] at [ ]. In this way we are able to ensure that your concerns are dealt with carefully and promptly. We undertake to look into any complaint carefully and promptly and to do all we can to explain the position. This will not affect your right to complain to the Institute of Chartered Accountants in England and Wales.

Acknowledgement and acceptance

Please acknowledge your acceptance of the terms of our engagement under the Contract by signing the confirmation below and returning a copy of this letter and the attached Terms and Conditions to us at the above address, whereupon the Contract will take effect from the date of the commencement by us of the Services.

Once it has been agreed, this letter will remain effective, from one audit appointment to another, until it is replaced.

If you have any questions regarding this Contract, please do not hesitate to contact us.

Yours faithfully

[Name of auditor]

I have read the above letter and accept the terms and conditions set out therein.

Signed

_____ (Name and position)   [date]

for an on behalf of [name of Company]

TABLE 4: Example written notice

Private and Confidential

The Director General
[Name and address of Regulator]
For the attention of [ ]

[Date]

[Name of Regulated Entity] ('the Company')

Audit of the regulatory financial statements for the year ended [date]

Dear Sirs

We refer to our engagement letter with the Company dated [date] ('the Contract') relating to our audit of the Company's regulatory financial statements for the year ended [date] ('the Regulatory Accounts'). A copy of the Contract is attached as Appendix 1 to this letter.

In the Contract we set out the basis on which we will act as auditors reporting on the Regulatory Accounts of the Company, together with the respective areas of responsibility of the directors of the Company and ourselves in respect of that audit and the scope of our audit. We also set out in the Contract the agreed extent of our liability to the Company in respect of our work. We confirm in the Contract that we will address our report on the Regulatory Accounts to the Company and, in order to meet the requirements of the Regulatory Licence, to you as well but we clarify that in our report we will deny liability in respect of our audit work and our report to any party other than the Company.

You have confirmed your interest in our audit of the Regulatory Accounts in your capacity as the Company's Regulator and your interest in the scope of our engagement agreed with the Company. You have asked us to accept responsibility for our audit work and our report to you as well as to the Company so that there is no denial of responsibility to you in our report. This letter ('the Regulator's Contract') sets out the basis on which we are willing to accept such a responsibility, in return for your agreement to the terms of this letter including the following:

- Our duties and responsibilities to you and your obligations to us will be those set out in the Contract as incorporated into this letter. This sets out, amongst other things, terms relating to the disclosure of the Regulatory Accounts and other Regulatory Information covered by the Independent Accountants' Report.
- Our aggregate liability to you will be strictly limited to £[ ] in the event of any breach of our obligations to you under the Regulator's Contract.
- You do not wish to acquire rights against us in respect of use of the audit report for any purposes other than as the Company's Regulator and accept the disclaimer of liability to any Third Party (being a person other than the Company or the Regulator) as set out in the Contract.
- You accept that the nature and format of the Regulatory Accounts are determined by your requirements and that it will be for you to consider whether the information on which we report as auditors is suitable or appropriate for your needs and purposes.
- You will not be bound by any amendment to the Contract, whether written, oral or arising from the Contract, which is not formally accepted by you in writing.

Please acknowledge your acceptance of the terms and conditions of this by signing the confirmation below and returning a copy of it and the Contract to us at the above address.

Yours faithfully

[Independent Accountants]

I have read the above letter and accept the terms and conditions on behalf of [name of Regulator].

Signed

_____ (Name and position)   [date]

[cc: The Directors, [name of Company]
Enclosure: Copy of the Contract

49.3   REPORTING

Each regulator will stipulate in its regulatory licence the information to be included in reports it receives and state that the report should be accompanied by an independent accountants' report.

The report should follow the guidelines set out in ISA (UK and Ireland) 700 *The Auditor's Report on Financial Statements* (see **Chapter 3**). An example is given in **Table 5**, which should be modified for the particular circumstances of the engagement.

Accountants should make clear in their report the regulatory information on which they are providing assurance, and that on which they are not. Where the regulatory information is part of a wider report or return, the material covered by the accountants' report should be clearly identified.

TABLE 5: Example unqualified independent accountants' report

Independent Accountants' Report to the Director General, [Regulator] ('the Regulator') and ABC Limited

We have audited the Regulatory Accounts of ABC Limited ('the Company') on pages [x to x] which comprise the profit and loss account, the statement of total recognised gains and losses, the balance sheet, [the cashflow statement] and the related notes to the Regulatory Accounts.

This report is made, on terms that have been agreed, solely to the Company and the Regulator in order to meet [the requirements of the Regulatory Licence]. Our audit work has been undertaken so that we might state to the Company and the Regulator those matters that we have agreed to state to them in our report, in order (a) to assist the Company to [meet its obligation under the Regulatory Licence to procure such a report] and (b) to facilitate the carrying out by the Regulator of its regulatory functions, and for no other purpose. To the fullest extent permitted by law, we do not accept or assume responsibility to anyone other than the Company and the Regulator, for our audit work, for this report or for the opinions we have formed.

Basis of preparation

The Regulatory Accounts have been prepared under the historical cost convention (as modified by the revaluation of certain fixed assets) and in accordance with conditions [ ], [ ] and [ ] of the Company's Regulatory Licence, Regulatory Accounting Guidelines [ ], [ ] and [ ] ('the RAGs') issued by the Regulator and the accounting policies set out in the statement of accounting policies.

The Regulatory Accounts are separate from the statutory financial statements of the Company and have not been prepared under the basis of Generally Accepted Accounting Principles in the United Kingdom ('UK GAAP'). Financial information other than that prepared on the basis of UK GAAP does not necessarily represent a true and fair view of the financial performance or financial position of a company as shown in financial statements prepared in accordance with the Companies Act 1985.

Respective responsibilities of the Regulator, the Directors and Auditors

The nature, form and content of Regulatory Accounts are determined to the Regulator. It is not appropriate for us to assess whether the nature of the information being reported upon is suitable or appropriate for the Regulator's purposes. Accordingly we make no such assessment.

The directors' responsibilities for preparing the Regulatory Accounts in accordance with conditions [ ], [ ] and [ ] of the Regulatory Licence are set out in the statement of directors' responsibilities on page [x].

Our responsibility is to audit the Regulatory Accounts in accordance with International Standards on Auditing (UK and Ireland), issued by the Auditing Practices Board, except as stated in the 'Basis of audit opinion', below and having regard to the guidance contained in Audit 05/03 *Reporting to Regulators of Regulated Entities*.

We report our opinion as to whether the Regulatory Accounts present fairly, in accordance with conditions [ ], [ ] and [ ] of the Company's Regulatory Licence, the RAGs [ ], [ ] and [ ], and the accounting policies set out on page [x], the results and financial position of the company. We also report to you if, in our opinion, the Company has not kept proper accounting records or if we have not received all the information and explanations we require for our audit.

[We read the other information contained within the Regulatory Accounts, including any supplementary schedules on which we do not express an audit opinion, and consider the implications for our report if we become aware of any apparent misstatements or material inconsistencies with the Regulatory Accounts.]

Basis of audit opinion

We conducted our audit in accordance with International Standards on Auditing (UK and Ireland) issued by the Auditing Practices Board except as noted below. An audit includes examination, on a test basis, of evidence relevant to the amounts and disclosures in the Regulatory Accounts. It also includes an assessment of the significant estimates and judgements made by the Directors in the preparation of the Regulatory Accounts, and of whether the accounting policies are consistently applied and adequately disclosed.

We planned and performed our audit so as to obtain all the information and explanations which we considered necessary in order to provide us with sufficient evidence to give reasonable assurance that the Regulatory Accounts are free from material misstatement, whether caused by fraud or other irregularity or error. However, as the nature, form and content of Regulatory Accounts are determined by the Regulator, we did not evaluate the overall adequacy of the presentation of the information, which would have been required if we were to express an audit opinion under International Standards on Auditing (UK and Ireland).

Our opinion on the Regulatory Accounts is separate from our opinion on the statutory accounts of the Company on which we reported on [date], which are prepared for a different purpose. Our audit report in relation to the statutory accounts of the Company (our 'Statutory' audit) was made solely to the Company's members, as a body, in accordance with section 475 of the Companies Act 2006. Our Statutory audit work was undertaken so that we might state to the Company's members those matters we are required to state to them in a Statutory auditor's report and for no other purpose. In these circumstances, to the fullest extent permitted by law, we do not accept or assume any responsibility to anyone other than the Company and the Company's members as a body, for our Statutory audit work, for our Statutory audit report, or for the opinions we have formed in respect of that Statutory audit.

Opinion

In our opinion the Regulatory Accounts:

- fairly present in accordance with conditions [ ], [ ] and [ ] of the Company's Regulatory Licence, Regulatory Accounting Guidelines [ ], [ ] and [ ], and the accounting policies set out on page [x], the state of the Company's affairs at [date] and of its profit (or loss) [and cashflow] for the year then ended; and
- have been properly prepared in accordance with those conditions, guidelines and accounting policies.

[Name of auditor]
[Chartered Accountants and Registered Auditors]
[Address]
[Date]

49.4 MATERIALITY

Increasingly regulators are requiring entities to include a number of different analyses of their business segments or operations and for accountants to report on them. In order to do this accountants must use their professional judgement to assess materiality in the context of the regulatory accounts as a whole and in line with the principles outlined in ISA (UK and Ireland) 320 *Audit Materiality*, see **Chapter 18**. Their opinion should be on the regulatory accounts as a whole, not on the individual analyses.

If the regulator requires specific items to be reported on in detail, this should form the basis of a separate, 'agreed upon procedures' engagement, which is reported on separately to the opinion on the accounts.

49.5 WORKING WITH INDEPENDENT EXPERTS

Accountants may need to rely on the work of independent experts when reporting on regulatory accounts and other regulatory information, such as technical or engineering experts to determine whether the cost of projects should be capitalised or expensed.

Where this is the case, the accountants would follow the guidance in ISA (UK and Ireland) 620 *Using the Work of an Expert*, and would not refer to the expert's work in their audit report. If an 'agreed upon procedures' engagement is undertaken and no opinion is given in the accountants' report, reference to the expert's work is likely. Consent should be obtained from the expert prior to issuing any report which refers to them or includes extracts of their work.

50 INVESTMENT CIRCULAR REPORTING

50.1 LEGAL BACKGROUND

Generally when shares are offered to the public for the first time, or when a company whose shares are listed on the Stock Exchange or traded on AIM enters into a major transaction, an investment circular is required which contains relevant financial information.

This information is accompanied by an accountants' report from a reporting accountant engaged specifically for the purpose. The term 'reporting accountant' may include the company's auditors where they are carrying out a role in connection with an investment circular, rather than their role as auditors reporting on the financial statements.

50.2 GUIDANCE

Until the issue of the Standards for Investment Reporting (SIRs) (previously named Statements of Investment Circular Reporting Standards) the only guidance came from Auditing Guideline *Prospectuses and the Reporting Accountant*. The current SIRs are:

- SIR 1000 – *Investment Reporting Standards Applicable to all Engagements Involving an Investment Circular*;
- SIR 2000 – *Investment Reporting Standards Applicable to Public Reporting Engagements on Historical Financial Information*;
- SIR 3000 – *Investment Reporting Standards Applicable to Public Reporting Engagements on Profit Forecasts*;
- SIR 4000 – *Investment Reporting Standards Applicable to Public Reporting Engagements on Pro Forma Financial Information;* and
- SIR 5000 – *Investment Reporting Standards Applicable to Public Reporting Engagements on Financial Information Reconciliations Under the Listing Rules.*

SIRs 1000 and 2000 are effective for reports signed after 31 August 2005, SIRs 3000 and 4000 are for reports signed after 31 March 2006 and SIR 5000 is effective for reports signed after 31 May 2008.

SIRs 1000 and 2000 were revised in 2005 following the implementation of the Prospective Directive and FSA's review of the Listing Regime. The revised FSA rules came into force on 1 July 2005 and had a significant effect on the work undertaken by reporting accountants. This is particularly so in relation to historical financial information.

Under the revised rules the issuers, rather than the reporting accountants, are responsible for preparing and presenting historical financial information and the reporting accountant's role will be to express an opinion on whether the information presents a true and fair view.

In October 2006, the APB issued the *Ethical Standard for Reporting Accountants* (ESRA). This document follows the format used for the Ethical Standards discussed in **Chapter 2**, and is applicable for all engagements where SIRs are used. It is detailed in **50.8** below. The ESRA replaces Bulletin 2005/7, *Integrity, Objectivity and Independence – guidance for Reporting Accountants undertaking engagements in connection with an investment circular* which was issued in July 2005 as an interim measure to provide limited ethical guidance so that reporting accountants could meet the requirement of SIR 1000 to consider ethical standards when deciding whether to accept or continue with an engagement. As part of the process of revising the Ethical Standards (see **Chapter 2**) in October 2007 the APB announced its intention to update the ESRA once the changes to the main ESs were finalised.

In November 1998, Bulletin 1998/8 *Reporting on Pro Forma Information Pursuant to the Listing Rules* was issued. This provides guidance on the requirement under the Listing Rules for an issuer's reporting accountant to provide an opinion on the pro forma information to be included in an investment circular and is discussed in **50.7** below.

In April 2006, the Audit and Assurance Faculty of the ICAEW issued a technical release AAF 02/06, *Identifying and managing certain risks arising from the inclusion of reports from auditors and accountants in prospectuses (and certain other investments circulars)* to provide guidance for reporting accountants. It develops the principles set out in Audit 1/03 *The audit report and auditors' duty of care to third parties*, which was issued following the Bannerman case (see **3.21**). It is detailed in **50.9** below.

50.3   STRUCTURE OF THE SIRS

The format of the SIRs is similar to that of the ISAs (UK and Ireland) with standards in bold type and further explanatory material in normal type. However, they are a separate series because the work of reporting accountants encompasses more than auditing and is not within the audit regulation regime.

Reporting accountants undertake a wide range of engagements, split into 'public reporting engagements', where a reporting accountant expresses a conclusion that is published in an investments circular and 'other reporting engagements' which typically involve reporting privately to an issue, sponsor or regulator.

Public reporting engagements are themselves of two types:

- those analogous to audits, where the reporting accountant's opinion is in terms of a 'true and fair' view on historical financial information (covered by ED SIR 2000); and
- those where the reporting accountant's conclusion is expressed as to whether financial information has been properly compiled.

50.4   SIR 1000

50.4.1   General

SIR 1000, *Investment Reporting Standards Applicable to all Engagements Involving an Investment Circular* is an overarching SIR setting out basic principles and essential procedures that apply to all engagements involving an investment circular.

50.4.2   Acceptance and continuance

SIR 1000 states that auditors can only accept or continue an engagement if nothing has come to their attention to indicate that the requirements of relevant ethical standards will not be satisfied. The *Ethical Standard for Reporting Accountants* (ESRA) was issued by the APB in October 2006. This is detailed in **50.9** below.

Reporting accountants should only accept or continue with an engagement if the scope of the engagement is sufficient to support the required report, they will be able to carry out the procedures required by the SIRs and they have personnel with the necessary professional experience and expertise to carry out that work.

50.4.3   Terms of the engagement

SIR 1000.4 states that specific terms of engagement should be agreed in writing with the instructing party. This may be either in the form of a letter of instruction from that party which is confirmed by the reporting accountants or a letter prepared by the reporting accountants and accepted by the other party.

The engagement letter should summarise:

- the obligations and responsibilities of the respective parties;
- the scope of the engagement; and
- the form of the report(s) to be given.

The engagement letter should encompass the whole of the reporting accountants' contractual responsibilities to those instructing them. The guidance to the SIR notes that it is important to clarify the requirements of the directors and the sponsors, together with the scope and content of the reports and letters at the earliest possible stage.

SIR 1000.4 states that the engagement letter should specify:

- those reports intended for publication;
- other reports that are required; and
- to whom all the reports should be addressed.

This restricts the use of the reports to those mentioned in the engagement letter.

The guidance notes that it is important that the scope of the reporting accountants' work is defined realistically. The engagement letter sets out the contractual responsibilities and reporting accountants should not accept responsibility for matters or entities in respect of which they are not specifically instructed, nor report on matters which fall into other advisers' areas of expertise.

In preparing their report, reporting accountants will need to rely on evidence supplied by, and representations from, the entity's directors, its employees or its agents. The engagement letter should limit the extent of the reporting accountants' responsibility where information which is material to their task is withheld or concealed from them or misrepresented to them. Where reporting accountants are aware of any such concealment they should inform the directors and sponsors as soon as is practicable.

Any subsequent changes to the terms of the engagement should be agreed in writing.

50.4.4 Independence and ethical standards

When conducting any engagement in connection with an investment circular, SIR 1000.5 requires reporting accountants to comply with the ethical standards issued by the APB and their professional body. These are contained in the *Ethical Standard for Reporting Accountants* (see **50.8**) and reporting accountants should be mindful of their requirements when performing their work.

50.4.5 Legal and regulatory requirements

As with an audit, the reporting accountant should be familiar with the applicable laws and regulations governing the report to be given.

50.4.6 Quality control

There are two SIRs on quality control which require:

- the reporting accountant to comply with the requirements of ISQC (UK and Ireland) 1 and ISA (UK and Ireland) 220 (see **Chapter 20**); and
- a partner with appropriate experience be involved in any work concerning an investment circular.

This would mean *inter alia* that some form of hot review would be necessary (see **20.3.7**).

50.4.7   Planning and execution

Reporting accountants should 'develop and document a plan for their work so as to perform the engagement in an effective manner' (SIR 1000.9). The objective of planning is to:

- assess whether the timescale is realistic;
- ensure that appropriate attention is directed to the various aspects of the engagement;
- ensure that potential problems are identified and procedures are designed to deal with them;
- consider the need for the involvement of specialists; and
- facilitate review.

The plan should be amended as necessary as work progresses, and these changes should be documented.

An initial plan should be prepared to document the chosen approach. At this stage a preliminary review of the information available, together with previous audit opinions may indicate issues which could lead to a qualification or modification of the report. Such issues should be reported to the entity and the sponsors immediately.

An appropriate level of materiality should be set, except in agreed-upon procedures engagements, where materiality may be determined for the reporting accountant.

Reporting accountants should obtain sufficient appropriate evidence under SIR 1000.11 on which to base their opinions, reports or letters. Evidence will be obtained from a variety of techniques including:

- inspection;
- observation;
- enquiry;
- computation; and
- analytical procedures.

The choice of procedures will depend on the circumstances of the engagement and the report being given in the context of the overall investment circular. The reporting accountant will obtain written confirmation of representations made by the entity's directors.

If evidence is withheld, concealed or otherwise misrepresented, the reporting accountant should consider whether this fact should be reported, and seek legal advice as necessary.

50.4.8 Documentation

The working papers should document:

- evidence that supports the report given and that the engagement was performed in accordance with SIRs; and
- reasoning on all significant matters that require the exercise of judgement, and the conclusions thereon.

The form of working papers will depend on:

- the nature of the engagement;
- the form of the report and the opinion, if any, to be given;
- the nature and complexity of the entity's business;
- the nature and condition of the entity's accounting and internal control system;
- the needs, in the particular circumstances, for direction, supervision and review of the work of members of the reporting accountants' team; and
- the specific methodology and technology that the reporting accountants use.

The guidance notes that working papers should be designed and organised to meet the circumstances and the reporting accountants' needs for each part of the engagement.

50.4.9 Professional scepticism

SIR 1000.16 requires the reporting accountant to plan and perform the engagement with an 'attitude of professional scepticism' to ensure that they make a critical assessment of the evidence obtained. They should remain alert to contradictory evidence and consider explanations received in the context of findings from other areas of their work.

50.4.10 Reporting

SIR 1000.17 covers the content of the reporting accountants' report, which should:

- be addressed only to those identified in the engagement letter or to the relevant regulatory body;
- identify the information to which the report relates;
- address all matters that are required by the engagement letter;
- explain the basis of the report or opinion;
- give a clear expression of opinion;

- include the reporting accountants' signature;
- include the reporting accountant's address; and
- state the date of the report or letter.

The engagement letter usually sets out the form of the report to be issued, and the report is normally signed and dated on the same date as the directors authorise the issue of the investment circular.

In all public reporting engagements the reporting accountant's report will include:

- a statement of compliance with SIRs; and
- a summary description of the work performed by the reporting accountant.

The level of assurance provided by a reporting accountant's report will vary from engagement to engagement. Therefore, the report should clarify the scope of the opinion or the level of assurance provided.

50.4.11   Modified opinions

The reporting accountant must give a modified opinion if there is a limitation on the scope of their work or where the outcome is materially misstated. In some situations, regulations will not allow the giving of a qualified opinion. Where this is the case, the reporting accountant will be unable to report, and should discuss with the party to whom the report is to be given, whether information in the investment circular can be amended to remove the obstacle to issuing an unmodified report, or whether the information itself can be omitted from the circular.

50.4.12   Pre-existing financial information

Where the issuer already has audited financial statements or audited or reviewed financial information which meets the needs of the investment circular, the audit firm is not required to consent to the inclusion of its earlier reports in the circular.

50.4.13   Consent

In certain cases, reporting accountants are required to give consent for the inclusion of their report or their name in the investment circular. SIR 1000.21 states that in these circumstances, before giving their consent, reporting accountants should consider their report in the form and context in which it appears. This involves:

- comparing their report with other information in the document to ensure that there is no inconsistency; and

- assessing whether they have any cause to believe any information in the investment circular to be misleading.

The SIR continues by requiring reporting accountants, where there is inconsistency or misleading information, to withhold their consent until the investment circular has been appropriately amended.

The reporting accountant should not give their consent for any of their reports to be included in the investment circular until all of their reports in that circular have been finalised.

The requirement for reporting accountants to give consent for the inclusion of their report comes from the relevant regulations governing the engagement. These are:

- the Prospectus Rules – which require that where a statement from an expert, including reporting accountants, is given in a document their consent is obtained and that this is stated in the document;
- the Listing Rules and the AIM rules– these have the same requirements as the Prospectus Rules for listings not subject to those Rules;
- Listing Rule 13.4.1(6) – which requires an expert to consent to the inclusion in any Class 1 circular of any report, letter or statement provided or made by that expert; and
- the City Code – which requires that where a takeover document includes an accountants' report on a profit forecast included in that document, it should be accompanied by a statement that the reporting accountants have given, and not withdrawn, their consent to publication. Any subsequent documents containing the report must include a statement that they have no objection to their report continuing to apply.

An example consent letter is given in **Table 1**.

TABLE 1: Example consent letter

The Directors
Issuer plc

Dear Sirs

We hereby give our consent to the inclusion in the Prospectus/Listing Particulars dated [. . .] issued by ABC plc of [our accountant's report]/[our letter relating to the profit estimate for the year ended 200X]/[our letter relating to the pro forma financial information for the year ended 200X] dated [. . .] [and the reference to our name] in the form and context in which [it]/[they] are included, as shown in the enclosed proof of the Prospectus/Listing Particulars which we have signed for identification.

Our consent is required by [provision requiring consent] and is given for the purpose of complying with that provision and for no other purpose.

[We also hereby authorise the contents of the [report]/[and]/[letters] referred to above included in the Prospectus for the purposes of Prospectus Rule [5.5.3R (2) (f)] [5.5.4R (2) (f)] *or* [We also hereby authorise the contents of the [report[s]] referred to above which [is/are] included in the Listing Particulars for the purposes of Regulation

---

> 6(1)(e) of the Financial Services and Markets Act 2000 (Official Listing of Securities) Regulations 2001.] *or* [We also hereby authorise the contents of the reports[s] referred to above which [is/are] included in the Admission Document for the purposes of Schedule Two to the AIM Rules]
>
> Yours faithfully
>
> Reporting Accountant

Consent is not required for documents already in the public domain unless it is with regard to an earlier report or opinion which is being repeated or referred to again. Where this is the case, the reporting accountants should ensure that there have been no events in the intervening period which mean that their report might require modification.

Although consent letters do not extend their responsibilities beyond their report, reporting accountants should be aware of the other parts of the document and consider whether there are any inconsistencies with their report.

Consent letters should be dated the same day as the relevant document.

50.4.14   Events after the reporting accountant's report

There may be situations where the reporting accountant becomes aware of events that occur after the date of their report, but before the completion date of the transaction, which may have caused them to issue a different report or withhold consent. If this occurs, the reporting accountant should discuss the matter with those responsible for the investment circular and take legal advice as necessary.

50.5   SIR 2000

50.5.1   General

SIR 2000, *Investment Reporting Standards Applicable to Public Reporting Engagements on Historical Financial Information* sets out basic principles and essential procedures that apply to all engagements involving the examination of historical financial information that is intended to give a true and fair view for the purposes of the engagement circular. The reporting accountant is required to obtain sufficient evidence to express a true and fair opinion of the financial information.

The guidance in the SIR applies only to situations where new opinions are provided by the reporting accountant, not where pre-existing audit reports are available and are used in the investment circular.

The reporting accountant's exercise will not differ greatly from that of an auditor and reporting accountants will perform or rely on work that meets the requirements of ISAs (UK and Ireland). Their work does vary in that:

- they are likely to have the evidence collected by the original auditors of the historical information available to them;
- they may have the benefit of being able to see the outcome of issues that were difficult or contentious at the time of the original audit; and
- they do not have the statutory reporting responsibilities of an auditor, for example, there is no requirement to report if proper accounting records have been kept by the entity.

In addition some of the requirements of ISAs (UK and Ireland) do not apply to the work of reporting accountants. An example would be where the ISA (UK and Ireland) requirement is based on the existence of an ongoing or continuous relationship between auditor and client, which does not exist in the same way for reporting accountants. SIR 2000 provides a list of requirements that do not apply.

50.5.2   True and fair view

SIR 2000.2 requires reporting accountants to ensure that when reporting in true and fair terms, the investment circular complies with relevant financial reporting standards to the extent that they are applicable.

For historical financial information presented in a prospectus, the relevant financial reporting standards are set out in the Prospectus Rules and the most recent years' financial information should be presented in a form consistent with that which will be adopted in the issuer's financial statements. Reporting accountants should ensure that the directors have selected appropriate accounting policies to reflect the situation of the issuer once the transaction has been completed.

For information presented in a Class 1 circular, the reporting criteria are set out in the Listing Rules and financial information should be presented in a form consistent with the accounting policies adopted in the issuer's latest annual consolidated accounts.

Directors should consider accepted conventions when establishing and disclosing the accounting principles to be used. An annexure to SIR 2000 sets out conventions that address:

- making adjustments to previously published financial statements and dealing with entities which have not previously prepared consolidated accounts;
- carve outs;
- acquisitions; and
- newly formed issuers.

The aim of presenting this information in an annexure, rather than in the body of, or as an appendix to, the SIR, is that it can be easily updated without having to re-expose the whole SIR.

50.5.3 *Professional considerations*

The applicable ethical standards and guidance relating to engagement letters is set out in SIR 1000 and the draft Ethical Standards for Reporting Accountants (see **50.9**).

Where reporting accountants rely on historical evidence obtained by auditors they should ensure that their documentation identifies the work papers used and states how the auditor addressed the risks identified by the reporting accountant's risk assessment procedures.

Reporting accountants should consider who those charged with governance are for the purpose of reporting. Where an audit committee has already been set up, the reporting accountant should report to that committee, otherwise reports should be made to the directors.

50.5.4 *Planning*

The reporting accountant is required to perform and document their risk assessment. The reporting accountant may consider the following areas as part of their planning:

- any previous modifications to the audit report on relevant financial statements;
- the nature of adjustments to previously published historical financial information and evidence to support these adjustments;
- the interaction with other roles taken by the reporting accountant, such as preparation of the long-form report;
- staffing, including relevant experience and skills;
- liaison with the auditor and terms of access to their working papers;
- the nature and timing of procedures to support their reliance on the auditor's evidence;
- whether the financial reporting framework used for the audited financial statements is the same as that applied to the financial information contained in the investment circular, e.g., UK FRS compared to IFRS;
- whether there are any special circumstances surrounding the appointment, resignation or reporting responsibilities of the auditor;
- whether there is evidence of any limitation having been placed on the work of the auditor; and
- whether corrections or adjustments to subsequent financial statements indicate possible inadequacies in the audits of earlier periods.

Where the reporting accountant intends to rely on the auditor's evidence, the reporting accountant should first consider the qualifications, independence and competence of the auditor and the quality control systems of the audit firm.

50.5.5 Understanding the entity and risk assessment

Reporting accountants are required to obtain an understanding of the entity and its environment, including internal control, sufficient to allow them to assess the risks of material misstatement of the historical financial information and to plan procedures. Many of the methods used will be identical to those employed by auditors, but reporting accountants will have regard to the fact that misstatements in earlier periods may have been detected in subsequent periods or that uncertainties may have been resolved over time. They should also have regard to any other relevant work performed in relation to the investment circular.

50.5.6 Materiality

Reporting accountants determine planning materiality for their own work and in the context of the report they will be giving. Therefore the reporting accountant's materiality may differ from that used by the auditors of the historical information.

50.5.7 Reporting accountant's procedures

Reporting accountants should perform procedures to obtain sufficient evidence that the work of the auditor can be relied upon or, where it cannot be relied upon or access is not possible, procedures to compensate for this. The procedures of the auditor and the reporting accountant together should comply with ISAs (UK and Ireland) except where a requirement of an ISA (UK and Ireland) is not relevant or where it is not possible for the reporting accountant to perform such procedures. Where the reporting accountant chooses not to meet a requirement of an ISA (UK and Ireland) they should document the reason for not meeting the requirement and why there is no impact on their opinion. This is unless the requirement is listed as not applicable Appendix A to SIR 2000.

The reporting accountant should assess whether the procedures undertaken by the auditor are sufficient to address the assessment of risk performed by the reporting accountant or are conducted to an appropriate materiality level. Where they are not, the reporting accountant would be required to perform further procedures themselves.

SIR 2000.9 requires the reporting accountant's substantive procedures to include:

- examining material adjustments made to the previously published historical financial information and considering the reasons for the adjustments;
- evaluating whether all such necessary adjustments have been made; and
- checking the extraction of the historical information in the investment circular from the previously published information.

50.5.8   Access to audit work papers

When a firm other than the company's auditor or former auditor is appointed as reporting accountant, they will require access to the audit work papers related to the historical information to be included in the investment circular. Access will usually be granted, with the auditors accepting no responsibility or liability to the reporting accountant in connection with the use of the audit work papers.

Where access is denied or is impossible, the reporting accountant has to reperform the audit procedures themselves.

Whether or not access is granted, reporting accountants should obtain from the auditors or directors a copy of any communications with those charged with governance, together with responses to those communications, for the relevant periods.

50.5.9   Post balance sheet events

Unless a post balance sheet event indicates that there has been an error in the preparation of the historical financial information in an earlier period, the reporting accountant will only consider the impact of post balance sheet events occurring up to the date of their report. After the date of their report the reporting accountant has no obligation to perform procedures or make enquiries about such events.

However, if, in the period between the date of their report and the completion date of the transaction, the reporting accountant becomes aware of matters which might have caused them to issue a different report or withhold consent if they had occurred before the date of their report, the reporting accountant should discuss these matters with those responsible for the investment circular.

If there is a significant change affecting any matter in the document or a material mistake or inaccuracy is noted once the prospectus has been approved by the FSA and before the closing date of the offering, a supplementary prospectus must be prepared.

50.5.10   Going concern

The reporting accountant will include in their report an emphasis of matter paragraph on any material uncertainty related to going concern. If the uncertainty will be resolved as a result of the offering, the reporting accountant should consider whether this is adequately disclosed in the basis of preparation note to the historical financial information.

50.5.11   Representations

Where auditors have already obtained written representations, it may not be necessary for reporting accountants to repeat the request for written confirmation. However, reporting accountants will usually require confirmation that:

- the directors or management of the entity are responsible for the preparation of the historical financial information; and
- any adjustments made to historical financial statements are necessary, have been correctly determined and that no further adjustments are required.

50.5.12   Joint reporting accountants

Where joint reporting accountants are appointed, the division of work will be agreed between the parties and may be set out in their engagement letter. The joint reporting accountants are jointly and severally liable for the report.

Each reporting accountant will participate in the planning of the engagement, will review the work of the other, and records the result of that review. A common set of working papers is normally maintained.

50.5.13   Reporting

SIR 2000 requires reporting accountants to include in their report:

- a statement that the work was conducted in accordance with SIRs; and
- reference to the basis of preparation and the applicable financial reporting framework.

The opinion is usually expressed in terms of whether the financial information gives a true and fair view of the state of affairs and profits, cash flow and statement of changes in equity.

If a limitation of scope exists, perhaps because no audit of the underlying financial information was performed and there is an absence of contemporary evidence, reporting accountants should consider whether they are able to form an opinion. Because of the reliance to be placed on the financial information by its readers, reporting accountants would not normally agree to be associated with financial information where a disclaimer of opinion needs to be given on the information for the entire period.

The reporting accountant does not refer to any audit opinions previously given on the financial statements on which the historical financial information is based. However, if the issuer has referred to details of earlier disclaimers or qualifications, the reporting accountant considers the disclosures made by the issuer and whether they may give rise to queries about the reporting accountant's opinion. If the reporting accountant is not satisfied with the disclosures they should discuss the matter with those responsible for the investment circular and ensure that further appropriate information is included either by the issuer or in their report.

An example reporting accountant's report on historical financial information is shown in **Table 2**.

TABLE 2: Example reporting accountant's report on historical financial information

The Directors
ABC plc

Dear Sirs

We report on the financial information set out [in paragraphs ... to ...]. This financial information has been prepared for inclusion in the [prospectus]/[listing particulars]/[Class 1 Circular relating to the acquisition of XYZ Limited] dated ... of ABC plc on the basis of the accounting policies set out in paragraph [...]. This report is required by [relevant regulation] and is given for the purpose of complying with that [relevant regulation] and for no other purpose.

Responsibilities

[As described in paragraph [...]] [T/t]he Directors of ABC plc are responsible for preparing the financial information [on the basis of preparation set out in [note x to the financial information]] [and in accordance with [the applicable financial reporting framework]].

It is our responsibility to form an opinion [on the financial information] [as to whether the financial information gives a true and fair view, for the purposes of the [prospectus]/[listing particulars]/[Class 1 Circular]], and to report our opinion to you.

Basis of opinion

We conducted our work in accordance with the Standards of Investment Reporting Standards issued by the Auditing Practices Board in the United Kingdom. Our work included an assessment of evidence relevant to the amounts and disclosures in the financial information. It also included an assessment of significant estimates and judgements made by those responsible for the preparation of the financial statements underlying the financial information and whether the accounting policies are appropriate to the entity's circumstances, consistently applied and adequately disclosed.

We planned and performed our work so as to obtain all the information and explanations which we considered necessary in order to provide us with sufficient evidence to give reasonable assurance that the financial information is free from material misstatement whether caused by fraud or other irregularity or error.

Opinion

In our opinion, the financial information gives, for the purposes of the [prospectus]/ [listing particulars]/[Class 1 Circular] dated ..., a true and fair view of the state of affairs of [ABC plc]/[XYZ Limited] as at the dates stated and of its profits, cash flows and recognised gains and losses for the periods then ended in accordance with the basis of preparation set out in note x and in accordance with [the applicable financial reporting framework] as described in note y] [and has been prepared in a form that is consistent when the accounting policies adopted in [ABC plc's latest annual accounts*].

Yours faithfully

Reporting Accountant

* The wording in these square brackets is appropriate for inclusion where the report relates to historical financial information include in a Class 1 circular.

50.6   SIR 3000

50.6.1   General

SIR 3000, *Investment Reporting Standards Applicable to Public Reporting Engagements on Profit Forecasts*, sets out standards to be applied when reporting accountants are engaged to report publicly on profit forecasts which are to be included in an investment circular under:

- the PD Regulation or other regulations with similar requirements;
- the City Code;
- requirements of the London Stock Exchange in respect of an AIM admission document.

Profit forecasts are inherently uncertain because they are based on assumptions and events and circumstances may not occur as expected, or may not be predicted at all. However, profit forecasts should be:

- reliable;
- understandable;
- comparable; and
- relevant.

It is the directors' responsibility to determine whether a profit forecast is relevant to, and should be included in, the investment circular. Reporting accountants are required to consider whether the profit forecast has been properly compiled, not whether it is correct to include it in the circular. In order to assess whether the forecast has been properly compiled, reporting accountants considers its reliability, understandability and comparability.

Reliability

ICAEW guidance for directors published in 2003, explains that in order for a profit forecast to be reliable it must be:

- able to be depended on by the intended user as a faithful representation of what it either purports to represent or could reasonably be expected to represent;
- neutral and free from bias;
- free from material error;
- materially complete; and
- prudent, ie a degree of caution is applied in making judgements.

If a profit forecast does not correctly predict the actual outcomes it does not mean that it was not reliable when it was made.

Forecasts will be most reliable when they are based on good quality business analysis performed by the directors.

Understandability

A profit forecast can only be understandable if it contains sufficient information to allow the reader to appreciate the degree of uncertainty it contains and the assumptions made. Reasonable disclosure will include details of the basis of preparation, the factors that will affect whether the assumptions will be borne out in practice and the likely outcomes if the assumptions do not prove to be correct.

Comparability

In order for profit forecasts to be of greatest use they must be comparable to actual results and to equivalent information for other reporting periods. This means that profit forecasts should be prepared using the same accounting policies as the historical information contained in the investment circular.

50.6.2 Compilation process

Directors are responsible for compiling the profit forecast and would typically complete the steps set out in **Table 3**. When assessing the reliability, understandability and comparability of the profit forecast, reporting accountants would consider whether these steps have been followed.

TABLE 3: Steps in the compilation of a profit forecast
The process followed by the preparer would be expected to include:
(a) an appropriate analysis of the business (what is appropriate will depend on a

number of factors including the complexity and predictability of the business and the length of the period being forecast and accordingly the content, degree of detail and presentation of such analyses may vary significantly);

(b)   identification of material uncertainties;

(c)   selection of appropriate assumptions;

(d)   where relevant, identification of, and reference to, appropriate third party information (eg market research reports);

(e)   arithmetic computation of the profit forecast;

(f)   appropriate sensitivity analysis;

(g)   appropriate disclosure to enable the intended users to understand the profit forecast; and

(h)   appropriate consideration of the profit forecast and approval of it by the directors of the entity.

50.6.3   Agreeing the terms of the engagement

Before accepting an engagement, reporting accountants should complete the procedures set out in SIR 1000 and ascertain whether the directors intend to comply with all relevant regulatory requirements. They should also consider the ethical requirements set out in SIR 1000.

Example of engagement letter clauses for profit forecast engagements are set out in **Table 4**.

TABLE 4: Example engagement letter extracts

Financial information on which the report is to be given

The [investment circular] will contain a profit forecast for the company for the period ending [date] (the 'PFI') prepared and presented in accordance with [item 13 of Annex I of the PD Regulation] [the requirements of the City Code] [other applicable regulation]. We will prepare a report on the profit forecast addressed to [. . .] expressing our opinion on the profit forecast, in the form described below to be included in the [investment circular].

We will ask the Directors to make certain representations to us regarding the PFI. If the PFI is intended only to be a hypothetical illustration, or the Directors are unable to make such representations to us, we will not wish to be associated with the PFI and accordingly, will be unable to report publicly on it.

Responsibilities

The preparation and presentation of the profit forecast will be the responsibility solely of the Directors. [This responsibility includes the identification and disclosure of the assumptions underlying the profit forecast.(omit if no assumptions)]. The Directors are also responsible for ensuring that the PFI is prepared and presented in accordance with [item 13 of Annex I of the PD Regulation] [the requirements of the City Code] [other applicable regulation].

We will require the Directors to formally adopt the PFI before we report on it. We understand that the Directors will have regard to the guidance issued by The Institute

---

of Chartered Accountants in England & Wales entitles 'Prospective Financial Information – Guidance for UK directors' in preparing the PFI.

It is our responsibility to form an opinion as to whether the profit forecast has been properly compiled on the basis stated and whether such basis is consistent with the accounting policies normally adopted by ABC plc.

If the results of our work are satisfactory, and having regard to the requirements of [item 13.2 of Annex I of the PD Regulation] [the City Code] [other applicable regulation], we shall prepare a report on the profit forecast for inclusion in the [investment circular]. An illustration of the form of our report is attached.

Scope of work

Our work will be undertaken in accordance with Standard for Investments Reporting (SIR) 3000 'Investment Reporting Standards Applicable to Public Reporting Engagements on Profit Forecasts' issued by the Auditing Practices Board and will be subject to the limitations described therein.

We draw your attention in particular to paragraph 75 of SIR 3000 which would preclude us from expressing any opinion if the Directors have not complied with the regulatory requirements set out in Appendix 2 of that SIR.

As the purpose of our engagement is restricted as described above and since the PFI and the assumptions on which it is based relate to the future and may be affected by unforeseen events, we will not provide any opinion as to how closely the actual result achieved will correspond to the profit forecast. Accordingly we neither confirm nor otherwise accept responsibility for the ultimate accuracy and achievability of the PFI.

Assumptions

We will discuss the assumptions with the persons responsible for preparing the PFI together with the evidence they have to support the assumptions, but we will not seek to independently verify or audit those assumptions. We are not responsible for identifying the assumptions.

In the event that anything comes to our attention to indicate that any of the assumptions adopted by the Directors which in our opinion, are necessary for a proper understanding of the PFI have not been disclosed or if any material assumption made by the Directors appears to us to be unrealistic we will inform the Directors so that steps can be taken to resolve the matter. However, we are required to comment in our report if an assumption is published which appears to us to be unrealistic or an assumption is omitted which appears to us to be important to an understanding of the PFI.

50.6.4 Planning and performing the engagement

SIR 1000 sets out the basic principles in respect of the planning of all reporting engagements. SIR 3000 requires the reporting accountant to obtain an understanding of the subject matter sufficient to assess the risk of the profit forecast not being properly compiled. Reporting accountants should consider:

- the background to, and nature of, the circumstances in which the profit forecast was made, including whether the forecast is being made for the first time or whether it is being updated for this purpose;

- the entity's business and the business analysis performed by the directors; and
- the procedures used to prepare the profit forecast (see **Table 3** above).

Reporting accountants discuss the plans, strategies and risk analysis of the preparer of the forecast and consider whether they are in keeping with the findings of the business analysis and review the assumptions made. It may be the case that not all the assumptions used are disclosed in the profit forecast, as only those necessary to aid understanding of the forecast are required. Reporting accountants will also consider whether there are cash flow statements and balance sheets to act as checks of omissions and inaccuracies in the forecast.

If profit forecasts are regularly prepared by the entity, reporting accountants should consider whether these regular forecasts prove close to actual outcomes and look at the directors' analysis of variances.

50.6.5   *Materiality*

For a profit forecast to be reliable it must be free from material error. In this context an error will include:

- assumptions that are not consistent with the analysis of the business;
- mathematical or clerical mistakes in the compilation of the profit forecast;
- misapplication of accounting policies;
- misapplication of stated assumptions;
- known misstatement in historical financial information embodied in the forecast without adjustment;
- failure to disclose an assumption or other explanation which is necessary for an understanding of the forecast; and
- presenting the forecast in a way that it is not capable of being compared with subsequent published results.

Materiality should be determined in relation to how users who have a reasonable knowledge of business, economic activities and accounting would be influenced by an error in making economic decisions.

50.6.6   *Historical financial information*

Where historical financial information has been included in the profit forecast, SIR 3000 requires reporting accountants to:

- consider the results of any audit or review of that information;
- evaluate the suitability of unaudited historical financial information in the forecast;
- assess whether historical financial information has been appropriately included in the forecast; and
- where any adjustments have been made to previously published historical financial information, consider whether these are appropriate.

If historical financial information has been audited, the reporting accountant would ordinarily gain access to the relevant audit work papers.

Where historical information has not been audited, the reporting accountant should perform the procedures set out in **Table 5**.

TABLE 5: Procedures in relation to unaudited historical information contained in profit forecasts

The reporting accountant should:

- understand the internal control environment of the entity relevant to the historical financial information;
- discuss with management the accounting polices applied and any differences from the method of preparing the entity's published financial statements;
- enquire of management, including internal audit, whether there have been any changes in the financial reporting systems or internal controls, or any breakdowns in systems and controls, which might affect the reliability of the financial information;
- enquire about changes in the entity's procedures for recording, classifying and summarising transactions, accumulating information for disclosure and preparing the financial statements;
- consider the accuracy of unaudited historical financial information by comparing it to audited financial statements for the same period;
- compare the historical financial information to previous budgets or forecasts prepared by the entity in respect of the period covered by the historical financial information and gain an understanding of the reason for any significant differences; and
- check the historical financial information used in the profit forecast agrees to, or reconciles with, the underlying accounting records of the entity.

50.6.7   Consistent accounting policies

Where the profit forecast relates to the expansion of the existing business the reporting accountant's primary consideration is the consistency of the accounting policies used in the forecast with those used for the most recent historical financial information in the investment circular. However, they should also consider whether these continue to be appropriate on an ongoing basis.

Where the profit forecast relates to a start up situation, reporting accountants consider only the appropriateness of the policies chosen.

50.6.8   Presentation of the profit forecast

Reporting accountants should consider whether:

- the forecast is presented in an understandable way;
- assumptions are clearly disclosed, ensuring that the significance of each assumption is apparent;
- the degree of inherent uncertainty is clearly disclosed;

- the choice of captions and subtotals are such that they allow easy comparison with subsequent historical financial information;
- additional disclosure is included with any sensitivity analysis to ensure that it is understood; and
- useful information is obscured by the inclusion of immaterial items or meaningless headings.

50.6.9   Representation letter

Many of the assumptions used in the compilation of a profit forecast will depend on the intent of directors, and so written representation of such intent is a particularly important source of evidence.

50.6.10   Reporting

SIR 3000 requires reporting accountants to include in their reports:

- a statement that the reporting accountants' responsibility is to form an opinion on the compilation of the profit forecast and to report their opinion to the addressees of the report;
- a statement that the profit forecast and the assumptions on which it is based are the responsibility of the directors; and
- in the basis of preparation section of their report, cross references to disclosures that explain the basis of preparation of the profit forecast including:

  - assumptions made;
  - accounting policies applied; and
  - where appropriate, the source of historical financial information embodied in the profit forecast.

Where the profit forecast relates to the expansion of an existing business, it is normal for the reporting accountants' report to include reference to the fact that the basis of accounting is consistent with existing accounting policies. Where this is not the case a more detailed explanation of the accounting policies used will be appropriate.

In the basis of opinion section of the report, the reporting accountant should include a statement that where the profit forecast and any assumption on which it is based relate to the future, the reporting accountant does not express any opinion as to whether the actual results achieved will correspond to those shown in the profit forecast.

Reporting accountants cannot give an unmodified opinion when the directors have not applied the criteria set out in Appendix 2 of SIR 3000, which sets out the reporting accountant's criteria as listed in relevant regulations, and the effect of this omission is material.

An example report is given in **Table 6**.

TABLE 6: Example unmodified report on profit forecasts

[Addressees]

Dear Sirs

[ABC plc]

We report on the profit forecast comprising [*insert description of items comprising the prospective financial information*] of ABC plc ('the Company') and its subsidiaries (together 'the ABC Group') for the [period] ending [date] (the 'Profit Forecast'). The Profit Forecast, and the material assumptions upon which it is based, are set out on pages [x] to [y] of the [describe document] ('the [Document]') issued by the Company dated [date]. This report is required by [relevant regulation] and is given for the purpose of complying with that [relevant regulation] and for no other purpose.

[*Substitute the following text of the last sentence of the immediately preceding paragraph, where a profit forecast is made by an Offeree in the context of a takeover.* This report is required by Rule 28.3(b) of the City Code and is given for the purpose of complying with that rule and for no other purpose. Accordingly, we assume no responsibility in respect of this report to the Offeror or any person connected to, or acting in concert with, the Offeror or to any other person who is seeking or may in future seek to acquire control of the Company (an 'Alternative Offeror') or to any other person connected to, or acting in concert with, an Alternative Offeror.]

Responsibilities

It is the responsibility of the Directors of ABC plc to prepare the Profit Forecast in accordance with the requirements of the [PD Regulation]/[Listing Rules]/[City Code]/ [guidance issued by the London Stock Exchange].

It is our responsibility to form an opinion as required by the [PD Regulation]/[Listing Rules]/[City Code]/ [guidance issued by the London Stock Exchange] as to the proper compilation of the Profit Forecast and to report that opinion to you.

Basis of preparation of the Profit Forecast

The Profit Forecast has been prepared on the basis stated on page [x] of the [Document] and is based on the [audited/unaudited] interim financial results for the [six] months ended [date], the unaudited management accounts for the [x] months ended [date] and a forecast to [date]. The Profit Forecast is required to be presented on a basis consistent with the accounting policies of the ABC Group.

Basis of opinion

We conducted our work in accordance with the Standards for Investment Reporting issued by the Auditing Practices Board in the United Kingdom. Our work included [evaluating the basis on which the historical financial information included in the Profit Forecast has been prepared and] considering whether the Profit Forecast has been accurately computed based upon the disclosed assumptions and the accounting policies of the ABC Group. Whilst the assumptions upon which the Profit Forecast are based are solely the responsibility of the Directors, we considered whether anything came to our attention to indicate that any of the assumptions adopted by the Directors, which, in our opinion, are necessary for a proper understanding of the Profit Forecast

---

have not been disclosed and whether any material assumption made by the Directors appears to us to be unrealistic.

We planned and performed our work so as to obtain the information and explanations we considered necessary in order to provide us with reasonable assurance that the Profit Forecast has been properly compiled on the basis stated.

Since the Profit Forecast and the assumptions on which it is based relate to the future and may therefore be affected by unforeseen events, we can express no opinion as to whether the actual results reported will correspond to those shown in the Profit Forecast and differences may be material.

[*This paragraph may be omitted if the document is not be distributed outside the UK –* Our work has not been carried out in accordance with auditing or other standards and practices generally accepted in the United States of America [or other jurisdictions] and accordingly should not be relied upon as if it had been carried out in accordance with those standards and practices.]

Opinion

In our opinion, the Profit Forecast has been properly compiled on the basis [stated]/[of the assumption made by the directors] and the basis of accounting used is consistent with the accounting policies used by ABC Group [*or refer to the actual policies used if different*].

Declaration [*to be given if report is included in a Prospectus*]

For the purpose of [Prospectus Rule [5.53R(2)(f)] [guidance issued by the London Stock Exchange] we are responsible for [this report as part] [the following parts(s)] of the [prospectus] [registration document] [AIM admission document] and declare that we have taken all reasonable care to ensure that the information contained [in this report] [those parts] is, to the best of our knowledge, in accordance with the facts and contains no omission likely to affect its import. This declaration is included in the [prospectus] [registration document] [AIM admission document] in compliance with [item 1.2 of Annex I of the PD Regulation] [item 1.2 of Annex III of the PD Regulation] [guidance issued by the London Stock Exchange].

Yours faithfully

Reporting Accountant

50.6.11   Consent

SIR 1000 sets out the basic requirements in respect of reporting accountants giving consent for their reports to be included in investment circulars. In addition, for profit forecasts, reporting accountants consider whether other disclosures in the circular are consistent with the assumptions and other disclosures relating to the profit forecast before giving their consent.

50.7   SIR 4000

50.7.1   General

The APB issued SIR 4000, *Investment Reporting Standards Applicable to Public Reporting Engagements on Pro Forma Financial Information* in January 2006. Pro forma financial information is defined as net assets, profit or cash flow statements that demonstrate the impact of a transaction on previously published financial information together with the explanatory notes thereto. The compilation of pro forma financial information would usually include:

- the accurate extraction of information from permitted sources;
- the making of adjustments that are arithmetically correct, appropriate and complete;
- arithmetic computation of the pro forma financial information;
- consideration of accounting policies;
- appropriate disclosure to allow the user to understand the financial information; and
- consideration and approval of the pro forma financial information by the directors of the entity.

50.7.2   Agreeing the terms of the engagement

Before accepting an engagement, reporting accountants should complete the procedures set out in SIR 1000 and ascertain whether the directors intend to comply with all relevant regulatory requirements. They should also consider the ethical requirements set out in SIR 1000.

Example of engagement letter clauses for pro forma financial information engagements are set out in **Table 7**.

TABLE 7: Example engagement letter clauses for a pro forma financial information engagement

Financial information on which the report is to be given

The [investment circular] will include a pro forma [balance sheet/profit and loss account] together with a description of the basis of preparation (including the accounting policies used) and supporting notes to illustrate how the transaction might have affected the financial information of the company had the transaction been undertaken at the beginning of the period[s] concerned or as at the date[s] stated (the 'pro forma financial information').

Responsibilities

The pro forma financial information, which will be the responsibility solely of the Directors, will be prepared for illustrative purposes only. This is required to be prepared in accordance with items 1 to 6 of Annex II of the PD Regulation.

It is our responsibility to form an opinion as to whether the pro forma financial information has been properly compiled on the basis stated and that such basis is consistent with the accounting policies of ABC plc.

If the results of our work are satisfactory, and having regard to the requirements of item 7 of Annex II of the PD Regulation, we shall prepare a report on the pro forma financial information for inclusion in the [describe document]. An illustration of the form of our report is attached.

Scope of work

Our work will be undertaken in accordance with Standard for Investments Reporting (SIR) 4000 'Investment Reporting Standards Applicable to Public Reporting Engagements on Pro Forma Financial Information' issued by the Auditing Practices Board and will be subject to the limitations described therein.

We draw your attention in particular to paragraph 62 of SIR 4000 which would preclude us from expressing any opinion if the Directors have not complied with the regulatory requirements set out in Appendix 1 of that SIR.

50.7.3 Planning and performing the engagement

In addition to the procedures set out in SIR 1000, the reporting accountant should gain an understanding of:

- the nature of the transaction being undertaken;
- the entity's business; and
- the procedures adopted, or planned to be adopted by the directors to prepare the pro forma financial information.

By understanding these areas, reporting accountants will be able to identify the risk of the pro forma financial information not being properly compiled.

Reporting accountants should obtain sufficient evidence that the unadjusted financial information has been correctly extracted from a suitable source and that the adjustments applied to it are in accordance with the criteria set out in legislation, and included in Appendix 1 to SIR 4000. The PD Regulation requires adjustments to be:

- clearly shown and explained;
- directly attributable to the transaction; and
- factually supportable.

In addition, in respect of a pro form profit and loss account or cash flow statement, those adjustments which are expected to have a continuing impact on the issuer must be clearly identified.

The requirements of the PD Regulation that adjustments must be directly attributable to the transaction and factually supported may mean that directors are not able to make all the adjustments they wish to. For any adjustment which is omitted in this way, reporting accountants should consider whether the omission renders the pro forma financial information misleading. Any concerns may be removed by providing details of the omitted adjustment in the notes to the pro forma financial information. However, where the omitted adjustment is so fundamental that disclosure is not sufficient to remove the uncertainty, the reporting accountant should discuss the matter with the directors and the issuer's advisors, and may not be able to issue their report.

Reporting accountants should also evaluate whether the adjustments made are consistent with the accounting policies adopted in the last, or to be adopted in the next, financial statements of the entity.

Reporting accountants are also required to ensure that the calculations within the pro forma financial information are mathematically correct.

50.7.4 Materiality

For pro forma financial information to be reliable it must be free from material error. In this context an error will include:

- use of an inappropriate source for the unadjusted financial information;
- incorrect extraction of the unadjusted financial information from an appropriate source;
- the misapplication, or failure to use, the accounting policies used in the last (or to be adopted in the next) financial statements;
- failure to make an adjustment required by the PD Regulation;
- making an adjustment that does not comply with the PD Regulation;
- a mathematical or clerical mistake; and
- inadequate or incorrect disclosures.

Materiality should be determined in relation to how users who have a reasonable knowledge of business, economic activities and accounting would be influenced by an error in making economic decisions.

50.7.5 Presentation of the pro forma financial information

Reporting accountants are required by SIR 4000 to consider whether they are aware of anything that would suggest that the presentation of the pro forma financial information is misleading or difficult to understand. Where there are concerns they should be discussed with the directors and the reporting accountant should consider whether to issue their report.

50.7.6 Reporting

SIR 4000 requires reporting accountants to include in their reports:

- a statement that the reporting accountants' responsibility is to form an opinion on the compilation of the pro forma financial information and to report their opinion to the addressees of the report;

- a statement that the pro forma financial information is the responsibility of the directors; and
- in the basis of preparation section of their report, cross references to disclosures that explain the basis of preparation of the pro forma financial information.

Reporting accountants cannot give an unmodified opinion when the directors have not applied the criteria set out in Appendix 1 of SIR 4000 and the effect of this omission is material. The appendix sets out the reporting criteria as listed in relevant regulations.

An example report is given in **Table 8**.

TABLE 8: Example unmodified report on pro forma financial information

[Addressees]

Dear Sirs

[ABC plc]

We report on the pro forma [financial information] (the 'Pro forma financial information') set out in Part [. . .] of the [investment circular] dated . . . , which has been prepared on the basis described [in note x], for illustrative purposes only, to provide information about how the [transaction] might have affected the financial information presented on the basis of the accounting policies [adopted/to be adopted] by ABC plc in preparing the financial statements for the period [ended/ending] [date]. This report is required by [relevant regulation] and is given for the purpose of complying with that [relevant regulation] and for no other purpose.

Responsibilities

It is the responsibility of the Directors of ABC plc to prepare the Pro forma financial information in accordance with [item 20.2 of Annex I of the PD Regulation]/ [guidance issued by the London Stock Exchange].

It is our responsibility to form an opinion as required by [item 7 of Annex II of the PD Regulation]/ [the guidance issued by the London Stock Exchange] as to the proper compilation of the Profit Forecast and to report that opinion to you.

In providing this opinion we are not updating or refreshing any reports or opinions previously made by us on any financial information used in the compilation of the Pro forma financial information, nor do we accept responsibility for such reports or opinions beyond that owed to those to whom those reports or opinions were addressed by us at the dates of their issue.

Basis of opinion

We conducted our work in accordance with the Standards for Investment Reporting issued by the Auditing Practices Board in the United Kingdom. The work that we performed for the purpose of making this report, which involved no independent examination of any of the underlying financial information, consisted primarily of comparing the unadjusted financial information with the source documents,

---

considering the evidence supporting the adjustments and discussing the Pro forma financial information with the directors of ABC plc.

We planned and performed our work so as to obtain the information and explanations we considered necessary in order to provide us with reasonable assurance that the Pro forma financial information has been properly prepared on the basis stated and that such basis is consistent with the accounting policies of ABC plc.

[*This paragraph may be omitted if the document is not be distributed outside the UK* – Our work has not been carried out in accordance with auditing or other standards and practices generally accepted in the United States of America [or other jurisdictions] and accordingly should not be relied upon as if it had been carried out in accordance with those standards and practices.]

Opinion

In our opinion:

(a) the Pro forma financial information has been properly compiled on the basis stated; and

(b) such basis is consistent with the accounting policies used by ABC plc.

Declaration [*to be given if report is included in a Prospectus*]

For the purpose of [Prospectus Rule [5.53R(2)(f)] [5.5.4R(2)(f)]] [guidance issued by the London Stock Exchange] we are responsible for [this report as part] [the following parts(s)] of the [prospectus] [registration document] [AIM admission document] and declare that we have taken all reasonable care to ensure that the information contained [in this report] [those parts] is, to the best of our knowledge, in accordance with the facts and contains no omission likely to affect its import. This declaration is included in the [prospectus] [registration document] [AIM admission document] in compliance with [item 1.2 of Annex I of the PD Regulation] [item 1.2 of Annex III of the PD Regulation] [guidance issued by the London Stock Exchange].

Yours faithfully

Reporting Accountant

50.8 SIR 5000

50.8.1 General

Whilst other SIRs, most notably SIRs 1000 and 2000, set out the majority of requirements and guidance relating to engagements involving investment circulars, SIR 5000 *Investment Reporting Standards Applicable to Public Reporting Engagements on Financial Information Reconciliations under the Listing Rules* provides further guidance when accountants are required to report on financial information reconciliations which are included within Class 1 circulars prepared for issue in connection with a securities transaction.

The Listing Rules require a target company's financial information to be included in a table within the investment circular and reconciled to the issuer's accounting policies. The need for such a reconciliation, sometimes known as a GAAP reconciliation, usually occurs when the target and issuer prepare their financial statements in accordance with different financial reporting frameworks, though they are sometimes required when different choices have been made within the same financial reporting framework.

The Listing Rules do not set out what the financial information should comprise, and accepted conventions have arisen over time. SIR 5000 sets these out in an Annexure.

There are three elements to a financial information reconciliation:

- the 'subject matter' – the target company's financial information;
- the 'suitable criteria' – the requirements of the issuer's financial reporting framework and their accounting policies; and
- the 'outcome' – the financial information of the target as adjusted and included in the Class 1 circular.

Reporting accountants are required to give an opinion on the financial information reconciliation that sets out:

- whether it has been properly compiled on the basis stated; and
- whether the adjustments are appropriate.

The accountant is not required to provide an opinion on the subject matter.

A reconciliation is not required when there are no material adjustments needed to achieve consistency between the target and the issuer's accounting policies.

50.8.2 Accepting the engagement

SIR 1000 sets out issues surrounding the acceptance of an investment circular reporting engagement. **Table 9** provides example engagement letter clauses for the review of financial information reconciliations.

TABLE 9: Example engagement letter clauses for the review of financial information reconciliations

Financial information upon which the report is to be given

The Class 1 circular will include a financial information table relating to ABC Inc prepared in accordance with the requirements of [13.5.18R] [10.5.18] [and interim financial information relating to ABC Inc reproduced in accordance with Listing Rule [13.5.30R(2)] [10.5.30(2)]].

We understand that the Class 1 circular will also include a financial information reconciliation of ABC Inc for the three years ended [date] [and the interim period ended [date]] (the 'Reconciliation'). The Reconciliation will comprise [the income statements] and [balance sheets] of ABC Inc showing the adjustments necessary to restate them to conform to XYZ plc's stated accounting policies. The Reconciliation will include supporting notes to explain the adjustments made.

Responsibilities

The preparation of the Reconciliation in accordance with the requirements of the Listing Rules will be the responsibility solely of the directors.

It is our responsibility to form an opinion as to whether the Reconciliation has been properly compiled on the basis stated and the adjustments are appropriate for the purpose of presenting the financial information (as adjusted) on a basis consistent in all material respects with the accounting policies of XYZ plc.

If the results of our work are satisfactory, and having regard to the requirements of Listing Rule [13.5.27R (2)(b)] [10.5.27(2)(b)] [and Listing Rule [13.5.30(2)] [10.5.30(2)]], we shall prepare a report on the Reconciliation for inclusion in the Class 1 circular. An illustration of the form of our report if the results of our work are satisfactory is attached.

Scope of work

Our work will be undertaken in accordance with the Standards for Investment Reporting issued by the Auditing Practices Board and will be subject to the limitations described therein.

In performing this engagement we will expect to receive, without undue delay, such:

(a) co-operation from all relevant officials of XYZ plc and ABC Inc [including its auditors];
(b) access to all the pertinent accounting records of XYZ plc and ABC Inc and any other relevant records and related information; [and]
(c) representations from XYZ plc[; and]
(d) [access to the files of the auditors of ABC Inc],

as we may need for the purposes of our examination.

50.8.3   Planning and performing the engagement

Understanding the entities

To be able to make a judgement on the proper compilation of the reconciliation and that appropriate adjustments have been made, the reporting accountant should obtain an understanding of the:

- nature of the target's and the issuer's businesses;
- accounting policies of the target and of the issuer and the application of those policies;
- requirements of the issuer's financial reporting framework;
- extent to which the issuer has employees with the requisite knowledge of the financial reporting framework used by the target, or the ability to consult with those having such knowledge; and
- the procedures and controls adopted or planned to be adopted, by the directors for the preparation of the financial information reconciliation.

The reporting accountant may obtain information about the target's business by reviewing publicly available information or by holding discussions with the management of the target or the issue, or with the auditors of the target company. In obtaining their information, the reporting accountant should consider:

- business operations, including the conduct of operations and nature of revenue sources and the products or services and markets;
- financing and investments, including group structure, the structure of finance and investment in non-consolidated entities; and
- financial reporting, including industry specific practices, revenue recognition practices and accounting for unusual or complex transactions.

Materiality

It is the responsibility of the directors of the issuer to evaluate materiality in order to determine the need for material adjustments. Materiality is determined by reference to the financial information of the target, as adjusted in the financial information reconciliation.

Reporting accountants are not required to evaluate this determination of materiality, however, if they become aware that a material adjustment is required and no reconciliation has been performed, they are required to discuss it with the directors of the issuer.

Misstatements

SIR 5000 defines misstatements in the context of the compilation of a financial information reconciliation as including:

- use of an inappropriate source for the target's financial information;
- incorrect extraction of the target's financial information from an appropriate source;
- in relation to adjustments, the misapplication of accounting policies or failure to use the issuer's accounting policies;
- failure to make an adjustment necessary for the purpose of presenting the financial information (as adjusted) on a basis consistent in all material respects with the issuer's accounting policies;
- disclosing as an adjustment the rectification of an error in the underlying financial information of the target; and
- a mathematical or clerical mistake.

Considering directors' procedures and controls

The controls put into place by the issuer will combine both high level internal controls (such as having experienced staff) and lower level accounting control activities (such as ensuring no 'one-sided' entries are made and considering whether the cash and cash equivalent position in the target both before and after reconciliation are identical). Reporting accountants should consider whether the controls in place are appropriate.

The areas where reporting accountants will concentrate their review are:

- ensuring the unadjusted financial information of the target has been properly extracted from an appropriate source. Reporting accountants are not required to perform specific procedures on the unadjusted financial information of the target;
- ensuring the completeness of the adjustments and the consistency of the accounting policies. This includes gaining evidence that the directors have understood the accounting policies of the target and assessing the directors' impact analysis of the effect of applying the issuer's accounting policies to the target's financial information;
- assessing the arithmetical accuracy of the reconciliation itself and considering whether the adjustments made are included under the appropriate financial statement captions; and
- ensuring that the presentation of the reconciliation is not misleading and that each item is adequately disclosed.

Reporting accountants should ensure that they have sufficient evidence on file to show that the issuer can support each adjustment made.

Representation letter

Example representation letter clauses for financial information reconciliations are given in **Table 10**.

TABLE 10: Example representation letter clauses for financial information reconciliations

Introduction

We refer to the financial information reconciliation set out in Part [. . .] of the [Class 1 circular] dated . . . (the 'Reconciliation'). We acknowledge that we are solely responsible for the Reconciliation and confirm on behalf of the directors of the company to the best of our knowledge and belief, having made appropriate enquiries of officials of the company [and the directors and officials of the [target]], the following representations made to you in the course of your work.

Specific representations

- We acknowledge as duly appointed officials of the company our responsibility for the Reconciliation which has been prepared in accordance with the requirements of the Listing Rules of the United Kingdom Listing Authority.
- We have considered the adjustments included in the Reconciliation. We confirm that, in our opinion, the Reconciliation includes all adjustments that are appropriate for the purpose of presenting the financial information (as adjusted) on a basis consistent in all material respects with the accounting policies of XYZ plc.
- We have made available to you all significant information relevant to the Reconciliation of which we have knowledge.
- [Any specific representations relating to information included in the Reconciliation (for example representations concerning accounting policies in greater detail than that included in the published financial statements).]

50.8.4   Reporting

The reporting accountant's report should give details of the respective responsibilities of the directors of the issuer and the reporting accountant. The reporting accountant's responsibilities are limited to the provision of the report and the opinion given.

Where the reporting accountant is not also the auditor of the target, they may state in their report that they have no responsibility for the historical financial statements of the target and express no opinion on them.

Where the reporting accountant is also the auditor of the target, they may state that they:

- are not updating or refreshing any reports made or opinions previously given; and
- accept no responsibility for such reports or opinions beyond that owed to those to whom they were originally addressed.

The reporting accountant should ensure that their report cross-refers to disclosures that explain the basis of preparation of the financial information reconciliation.

As Class 1 circulars are sometimes made available in other countries which have their own standards for reporting accountants, the reporting accountant may include a reference to the fact that their work has been conducted in accordance with the SIRs, and their report should not be relied upon as if it had been issued in accordance with the standards applicable in any other country.

An example report is given in **Table 11**.

TABLE 11: Example report on a financial information reconciliation in accordance with the Listing Rules

Dear Sirs

XYZ plc ('the Company'): proposed acquisition of ABC Inc (the 'Target')

We report on the reconciliation of [*describe items reconciled* the consolidated income statement for each of the years in the three-year period ended [date] [and the interim period ended [date]], and of [*describe items reconciled* the consolidated balance sheet as at [dates]], together the 'financial information', as previously reported in the financial statements of the Target prepared under [United States Generally Accepted Accounting Principles], showing the adjustments necessary to restate it on the basis of the Company's accounting policies [*specify the accounting policies eg* those used in preparing the company's last set of annual financial statements] (the 'Reconciliation'), set out in Part [ ] of the Class 1 circular of the company dated [date]. This report is required by Listing Rule[s] [13.5.27R(2)(b) [and 13.5.30R(2)] of the United Kingdom Listing Authority] [10.5.27(2)(b)] and is given for the purpose of complying with [that] [those] Listing Rule[s] and for no other purpose.

Responsibilities

It is the responsibility of the directors of the Company (the 'Directors') to prepare the Reconciliation in accordance with Listing Rule[s] [13.5.27R(2)(a) [and 13.5.30R(2)]].

It is our responsibility to form an opinion, as required by Listing Rule[s] [13.5.27R(2)(b)] [and 13.5.30R(2)], as to whether:

(a) the Reconciliation has been properly compiled on the basis stated; and
(b) the adjustments are appropriate for the purpose of presenting the financial information (as adjusted) on a basis consistent in all material respects with the Company's accounting policies, and to report that opinion to you.

[Insert where an audit or other opinion has been expressed on the financial statements of the Target upon which the Reconciliation is based by a firm other than the reporting accountant, or where such information is unaudited: The Reconciliation is based on the [un]audited balance sheet[s] as at [dates] and income statement[s] for [each of] the [year[s]/period[s]] then ended of [the Target] which were the responsibility of the directors of [the Target] [and were audited by another firm of accountants]. We do not accept any responsibility for any of the historical financial statements of [the Target], nor do we express any opinion on those financial statements.]

[Insert where the reporting accountant has provided an audit or other opinion on the financial statements of the Target upon which the Reconciliation is based: In providing this opinion we are not updating or refreshing any reports or opinions previously made by us on any financial information used in the compilation of the Reconciliation, nor do we accept responsibility for such reports or opinions beyond that owed to those to whom those reports or opinions were addressed at the date of their issue.]

Basis of opinion

We conducted our work in accordance with the Standards for Investment Reporting issued by the Auditing Practices Board in the United Kingdom. The work that we performed for the purpose of making this report, which involved no independent examination of any of the underlying financial information, consisted primarily of checking whether the unadjusted financial information of [the Target] has been accurately extracted from an appropriate source, assessing whether all adjustments necessary for the purpose of presenting the financial information on a basis consistent in all material respects with [the Company's] accounting policies have been made, examination of evidence supporting the adjustments in the Reconciliation and checking the arithmetical accuracy of the calculations within the Reconciliation.

We planned and performed our work so as to obtain the information and explanations we considered necessary in order to provide us with reasonable assurance that the Reconciliation has been properly compiled on the basis stated and that the adjustments are appropriate for the purpose of presenting the financial information (as adjusted) on a basis consistent in all material respects with the Company's accounting policies.

[This paragraph may be omitted if the document is not be distributed outside the UK: Our work has not been carried out in accordance with the auditing or other standards and practices generally accepted in [the United States of America] and accordingly should not be relied upon as if it had been carried out in accordance with those standards and practices.]

Opinion

In our opinion:

(a)   the Reconciliation has been properly compiled on the basis stated; and

(b)   the adjustments are appropriate for the purpose of presenting the financial information (as adjusted) on a basis consistent in all material respects with the Company's accounting policies.

Declaration

[This paragraph is only included if the investment circular is also a prospectus: For the purposes of [Prospectus Rule [5.5.3R(2)(f)][5.5.4R(2)(f)]]/[Paragraph 2(2)(f) of Schedule 1 to 'The Prospectus (Directive 2003/71/EC) Regulations 2005'] [Paragraph 3(2)(f) of Schedule 1 to 'The Prospectus (Directive 2003/71/EC) Regulations 2005'] we are responsible for this report as part of the [prospectus] [registration document] and declare that we have taken all reasonable care to ensure that the information contained [in this report] [those parts] is, to the best of our knowledge, in accordance with the facts and contains no omission likely to affect its import. This declaration is included in the [prospectus] [registration document] in compliance with [item 1.2 of Annex I of the PD Regulation] [item 1.2 of Annex III of the PD Regulation].]

Yours faithfully

Reporting accountant.

50.9   ETHICAL STANDARDS FOR REPORTING ACCOUNTANTS

Given the high level of public interested in investment circulars and the degree of similarity between the work of reporting accountants and auditors of financial statements, it is reasonable for users to expect similar ethical requirements to apply to reporting accountants as for auditors. Therefore, in October 2006, the APB issued the *Ethical Standard for Reporting Accountants* (ESRA) based on the principles contained in the *Ethical Standards for Auditors* (ESs), which are detailed in **Chapter 2**.

The ESRA replaces Bulletin 2005/7, *Integrity, Objectivity and Independence – guidance for Reporting Accountants undertaking engagements in connection with an investment circular* which was issued in July 2005. The Bulletin was issued at the same time as SIR 1000 to provide limited ethical guidance so that reporting accountants could meet the requirement of that SIR to consider ethical standards when deciding whether to accept or continue with an engagement.

The ESRA applies to all public reporting engagements to which SIRs apply, and also to private reporting engagements which are undertaken in connection with an investment circular on which the reporting accountant is intending to issue a public report.

Many of the requirements of the ESRA mirror those in the ESs, focusing on potential threats to integrity, objectivity and independence and it should be read in conjunction with the ESs. It requires reporting accountants to consider not only their relationship with the client, but also with the sponsor, other parties to the engagement letter and other entities involved in the transaction. The independence requirement will relate not only to the engagement team, but also to others who can directly influence the conduct and outcome of the engagement. As investment circulars relate to transactions that are price sensitive and therefore confidential, there is likely to be only a limited number of people within a firm who are aware of the investment circular reporting engagement. For this reason the requirements of the ESRA only apply to those within the engagement team or with a direct supervisory or management responsibility for the team and those who have actual knowledge of the engagement, unless certain requirements of the ESRA specifically state that they apply to the whole firm.

The ESRA does not prohibit audit engagement partner and senior audit staff from being members of an investment circular reporting engagement team. Rather than lose the accumulated knowledge held by the audit team, the ESRA prefers to require such involvement of audit team members to be disclosed to those charged with governance and any other persons from whom the engagement letter states the reporting accountant should take instructions.

Contingent fees for investment circular reporting are prohibited by the ESRA, as are contingent fees in respect of other work performed by the firm during the relevant period where the:

- contingent fees are material to the firm; or
- the outcome of the service is dependent on a judgment made by the reporting accountant in relation to the investment circular.

The ESRA is effective for investment circular reporting engagements commencing on or after 1 April 2007. There are transitional arrangements for business relationships, loan staff arrangements and the supply of other services which were in place at 31 October 2006 but which are now prohibited by the ESRA.

In October 2007, the APB announced its intention to update the ESRA once the revisions to the Ethical Standards and ES – PASE were complete (see **Chapter 2**).

50.10 LIMITING RISKS FOR REPORTING ACCOUNTANTS

50.10.1 *Background*

Technical Release AAF 02/06, Identifying and managing certain risks arising from the inclusion of reports from auditors and accountants in prospectuses (and certain other investments circulars) was issued in April 2006 to expand the guidance in Audit 1/03 issued following the Bannerman case, for reporting accountants.

Audit 1/03 *The audit report and auditors' duty of care to third parties*, suggested that auditors might be able to manage the risk of taking on duties to their parties by inserting appropriate paragraphs in their audit reports. Audit 01/03 and the relevant paragraphs to be inserted are detailed in section **3.17**.

The risk that a third party may seek to prove that reporting accountants had a duty of care to them is not limited to reports made on financial statements under section 235 of the Companies Act 1985 and many other types of report now contain similar paragraphs to that outlined in Audit 01/03.

There has been no court ruling on the extent of an reporting accountant's liability to third parties when their audit report or a separate reporting accountant's report is included or referred to in a prospectus or certain other investment circular. The Prospectus Rules set out the parts of a prospectus for which a reporting accountant is responsible. The reporting accountant should take care that these responsibilities are stated in the prospectus and not left open to third parties.

50.10.2   Inclusion of a statutory audit report in an investment circular

It could be argued that by giving consent for their audit report to be included in an investment circular, reporting accountant's are accepting responsibility for their report beyond that intended when the report was first issued. AAF 2/6 states that there will be no widening of responsibility as long as auditors:

- consent to the inclusion of the audit report only;
- clarity when consenting the specific purpose for which the consent is given; and
- consider and follow SIR 1000 in connection with the form and context in which the audit report appears in the investment circular.

There is no need to insert additional clarification over and above that in the section 235 audit report itself, and auditors should not consent to the inclusion of anything other than their original section 235 report. An example consent letter is given in **Table 1** above.

In some situations, for example where an audit report has previously been issued) auditors are not required to given consent for the republication of their report. In such a situation, auditors should not send a consent letter where it is not needed, as this may be construed as providing additional assurance about their audit report.

50.10.3   Special purpose reports

Even when reports are prepared specifically for inclusion in a investment circular, the entity responsible for the circular must obtain the reporting accountant's consent for the inclusion of their report. Their report should include a Bannerman type statement, see **Table 12**. Care should be taken that the wording of their consent letter does is consistent with this statement and does not undermine its meaning.

TABLE 12: Example wording for inclusion in a reporting accountant's special purpose report

This report is required by [applicable rule or regulation] and is given for the purpose of complying with that regulation and for no other purpose.

Save for any responsibility arising under [applicable rule or regulation] to any person as and to the extent there provided [, and save for any responsibility we have expressly agreed in writing to assume], to the fullest extent permitted by law we do not assume any responsibility and will not accept any liability to any other person for any loss suffered by any such other person as a result of, arising out of, or in connection with this report [or our statements, required by and given solely for the purposes of complying with [applicable rule or regulation], consenting to its inclusion in [document].

50.10.4   Other financial information

In some situations there may be a requirement for certain historical financial information other than audited financial statements to be included in an investment circular. In such situations, the acceptance of responsibility or the granting of consent by the auditor is not an issue as it not permissible for the audit report which relates to any statutory accounts from which the non-statutory financial information was extracted to accompany the non-statutory information.

50.10.5   Addressing the report

Any person who is to be an addressee of the reporting accountant's report should be party to the engagement letter. Where a reporting accountant is asked to include a party as an addressee to their report, they should consider:

- why the person has asked to be included as an addressee;
- the role the person will undertake in relation to the transaction or investment circular; and
- whether, how and to what extent the person has assumed responsibility in relation to the transaction or investment circular.

APPENDIX

EXISTING GUIDANCE AT 30 APRIL 2010

Table A sets out the Ethical Standards. Table B lists the ISAs (UK and Ireland) and Clarified ISAs (UK and Ireland) issued for comment by the APB. Table C sets out Standards for Investment Reporting (SIRS), Practice Notes and Bulletins. These are all issued by the APB and are extant as at 30 April 2010.

Table D lists the ICAEW Statements extant on 30 April 2010.

TABLE A

APB Guidance	Status
The scope and authority of APB pronouncements (revised)	ISSUED
ES1 (Revised) Integrity, objectivity and independence	ISSUED
ES2 (Revised) Financial, business, employment and personal relationships	ISSUED
ES3 (Revised) Long association with the audit engagement	ISSUED
ES4 (Revised) Fees, remuneration and evaluation policies, litigation, gifts and hospitality	ISSUED
ES5 (Revised) Non-audit services provided to audit clients	ISSUED
ES (Revised) Provisions available for smaller entities	ISSUED
Ethical Standard for Reporting Accountants	ISSUED

TABLE B

ISA (UK and Ireland)	Status	Clarified ISA (UK and Ireland)	Status
Summary of changes in the new ISAs (UK and Ireland)			ISSUED
Glossary of Terms	ISSUED	Glossary of Terms	ISSUED
200 Objective and General Principles Governing an Audit of Financial Statements	ISSUED	200 Overall Objectives of the Independent Auditor and the Conduct of an Audit in Accordance with International Standards on Auditing (UK and Ireland)	ISSUED

TABLE B (continued)

ISA (UK and Ireland)	Status	Clarified ISA (UK and Ireland)	Status
210 Terms of Audit Engagements	ISSUED	210 Agreeing the Terms of Audit Engagements	ISSUED
220 Quality Control for Audits of Historical Financial Information	ISSUED	220 Quality control for an audit of financial statements	ISSUED
230 (Revised) Audit Documentation	ISSUED	230 Audit Documentation	ISSUED
240 The Auditor's Responsibility to Consider Fraud in an Audit of Financial Statements	ISSUED	240 The Auditor's Responsibilities Relating to Fraud in an Audit of Financial Statements	ISSUED
250 Part A Consideration of Laws and Regulations in an Audit of Financial Statements	ISSUED	250 Part A Consideration of Laws and Regulations in an Audit of Financial Statements	ISSUED
250 Part B The Auditor's Right and Duty to Report to Regulators in the Financial Sector	ISSUED	250 Part B The Auditors' Right and Duty to Report to Regulators in the Financial Sector	ISSUED
260 Communication of Audit Matters with those Charged with Governance	ISSUED	260 Communication with Those Charged with Governance	ISSUED
		265 Communicating Deficiencies in Internal Control to Those Charged With Governance and Management	ISSUED

TABLE B (continued)

ISA (UK and Ireland)	Status	Clarified ISA (UK and Ireland)	Status
300 Planning an Audit of Financial Statements	ISSUED	300 Planning an Audit of Financial Statements	ISSUED
315 Understanding the Entity and its Environment and Assessing the Risks of Material Misstatement	ISSUED	315 Identifying and Assessing the Risks of Material Misstatement Through Understanding the Entity and its Environment	ISSUED
320 Audit Materiality	ISSUED	320 Materiality in Planning and Performing an Audit	ISSUED
330 The Auditor's Procedures in Response to Assessed Risks	ISSUED	330 The Auditor's Responses to Assessed Risks	ISSUED
402 Audit Considerations Relating to Entities Using Service Organisations	ISSUED	402 Audit Considerations Relating to an Entity Using a Service Organisation	ISSUED
		450 Evaluation of Misstatements Identified During the Audit	ISSUED
500 Audit Evidence	ISSUED	500 Audit Evidence	ISSUED
501 Audit Evidence – Additional Considerations for Specific Items	ISSUED	501 Audit Evidence – Specific Considerations for Selected Items	ISSUED

TABLE B (continued)

ISA (UK and Ireland)	Status	Clarified ISA (UK and Ireland)	Status
505 External Confirmations	ISSUED	505 External Confirmations	ISSUED
510 Initial Engagements – Opening Balances and Continuing Engagements – Opening Balances	ISSUED	510 Initial Audit Engagements – Opening Balances	ISSUED
520 Analytical Procedures	ISSUED	520 Analytical Procedures	ISSUED
530 Audit Sampling and other Means of Testing	ISSUED	530 Audit Sampling	ISSUED
540 Audit of Accounting Estimates	ISSUED	540 Auditing Accounting Estimates, Including Fair Value Accounting Estimates and Related Disclosures	ISSUED
545 Auditing Fair Value Measurements and Disclosures	ISSUED		
550 Related Parties	ISSUED	550 Related Parties	ISSUED
560 Subsequent Events	ISSUED	560 Subsequent Events	ISSUED
570 Going Concern	ISSUED	570 Going Concern	ISSUED
580 Management Representations	ISSUED	580 Written Representations	ISSUED
600 (Revised) Using the Work of Another Auditor	ISSUED	600 Special Considerations – Audits of Group Financial Statements (Including the Work of Component Auditors)	ISSUED
610 Considering the Work of Internal Audit	ISSUED	610 Using the Work of Internal Auditors	ISSUED

TABLE B (continued)

ISA (UK and Ireland)	Status	Clarified ISA (UK and Ireland)	Status
620 Using the Work of an Expert	ISSUED	620 Using the Work of an Auditor's Expert	ISSUED
700 (Revised) The Auditor's Report on Financial Statements	ISSUED		
701 The Independent Auditor's Report on other Historical Financial Information	DRAFT		
		705 Modifications to Opinions in the Independent Auditor's Report	ISSUED
		706 Emphasis of Matter Paragraphs and Other Matter Paragraphs in the Independent Auditor's Report	ISSUED
		710 Comparative Information – Corresponding Figures and Comparative Financial Statements	ISSUED
		720 A The Auditor's Responsibilities Relating to Other Information in Document Containing Audited Financial Statements	ISSUED
		720 B The Auditor's Statutory Reporting Responsibility in Relation to Directors' Report	ISSUED

TABLE B (continued)

ISA (UK and Ireland)	Status	Clarified ISA (UK and Ireland)	Status
		ISRE (UK and Ireland) 2410: Review of Interim Financial Information Performed by the Independent Auditor of the Entity	ISSUED
		ISQC 1 (UK and Ireland) 1	ISSUED

TABLE C

	Status
SIR 1000 Investment reporting standards applicable to all engagements involving an investment circular	ISSUED
SIR 2000 Investment reporting standards applicable to public reporting engagements on historical financial information	ISSUED
SIR 3000 Investment reporting standards applicable to public reporting engagements on profit forecasts	ISSUED
SIR 4000 Investment reporting standards applicable to public reporting engagements on pro forma financial information	ISSUED
SIR 5000 Investment reporting standards applicable to public reporting engagements on financial information reconciliations under the Listing Rules	ISSUED
PN10 Audit of financial statements of public sector entities in the United Kingdom (Revised)	ISSUED
PN10 Audit of financial statements of public sector bodies in the United Kingdom (Revised)	DRAFT
PN10(I) (Revised) Audit of central government financial statements in the Republic of Ireland	ISSUED
PN11 The audit of charities in the United Kingdom (Revised)	ISSUED
PN12 (Revised) Money laundering – Interim guidance for auditors in the United Kingdom	ISSUED
PN12 Money Laundering – Guidance for auditors on UK legislation	DRAFT

TABLE C (continued)

	Status
PN14 The audit of registered social landlords in the United Kingdom (revised)	ISSUED
PN15 The audit of occupational pension schemes in the United Kingdom (revised)	ISSUED
PN15(I) Interim guidance for the auditors of occupational pension schemes in the Republic of Ireland	ISSUED
PN16 Bank reports for audit purposes in the United Kingdom (Revised)	ISSUED
PN19 The Audit of Banks and Building Societies in the United Kingdom	ISSUED
PN19(I) The Audit of Banks in the Republic of Ireland	ISSUED
PN20 The audits of insurers in the United Kingdom (Revised)	ISSUED
PN21 The audit of investment business in the United Kingdom (Revised)	ISSUED
PN22 The auditors' consideration of FRS17 'Retirement Benefits' – defined benefit schemes	ISSUED
PN23 Auditing Complex Financial Instrument (Revised)	ISSUED
PN24 The audit of friendly societies in the United Kingdom (Revised)	ISSUED
PN25 Attendance at stocktaking	ISSUED
PN26 Guidance on smaller entity audit documentation (Revised)	ISSUED
PN27 The audit of credit unions in the United Kingdom	ISSUED
PN27(I) The audit of credit unions in the Republic of Ireland	ISSUED
Bulletin 1997/3 The FRSSE: Guidance for auditors	ISSUED
Bulletin 2000/3 Departure from Statements of Recommended Practice for the Preparation of Financial Statements: Guidance for Auditors	ISSUED
Bulletin 2001/1 The Electronic Publication of Auditors' Reports	ISSUED
Bulletin 2001/3 E-Business: identifying financial statement risks	ISSUED
Bulletin 2002/2 The United Kingdom Directors' Remuneration Report Regulations 2002	ISSUED

TABLE C (continued)

	Status
Bulletin 2002/3 Guidance for reporting accountants of stakeholder pension schemes in the United Kingdom	ISSUED
Bulletin 2003/1 Corporate Governance: Requirements of public sector auditors (central government)	ISSUED
Bulletin 2003/2 Corporate Governance: Requirements of public sector auditors (NHS bodies)	ISSUED
Bulletin 2004/2 Corporate Governance: Requirements of public sector auditors (local government bodies)	ISSUED
Bulletin 2005/3 Guidance for auditors on first time application of IFRSs in the United Kingdom and the Republic of Ireland	ISSUED
Bulletin 2006/1 Auditor's reports on financial statements in the Republic of Ireland	ISSUED
Bulletin 2006/4 Regulatory and legislative background to the application of Standards for Investment Reporting in the Republic of Ireland	ISSUED
Bulletin 2006/5 The Combined Code on Corporate Governance: Requirements of auditors under the Listing Rules of the Financial Services Authority and the Irish Stock Exchange	ISSUED
Bulletin 2006/6 Auditor's reports on financial statements in the United Kingdom	ISSUED
Bulletin 2007/2 The duty of auditors in the Republic of Ireland to report to the Director of Corporate Enforcement	ISSUED
Bulletin 2008/1 Audit issues when financial market conditions are difficult and credit facilities may be restricted	ISSUED
Bulletin 2008/2 The auditor's association with preliminary announcements made in accordance with the requirements of the UK and Irish Listing Rules	ISSUED
Bulletin 2008/3 The auditor's statement on the summary financial statement in the United Kingdom	ISSUED
Bulletin 2008/4 The special auditor's report in abbreviated accounts in the United Kingdom	ISSUED
Bulletin 2008/5 Auditor's reports on revised accounts and reports, in the United Kingdom	ISSUED
Bulletin 2008/6 The 'Senior Statutory Auditor' under the United Kingdom Companies Act 2006	ISSUED

TABLE C (continued)

	Status
Bulletin 2008/7 Illustrative Auditor's Reports on Public Sector Financial Statements in the United Kingdom	ISSUED
Bulletin 2008/8 Auditor's Reports for Short Accounting Periods in Compliance with the United Kingdom Companies Act 2006	ISSUED
Bulletin 2008/9 Miscellaneous Reports by Auditors Required by the United Kingdom Companies Act 2006	ISSUED
Bulletin 2008/10 Going Concern Issued During the Current Economic Conditions	ISSUED
Bulletin 2009/1 The Auditor's Reports – Supplementary Guidance for Auditors of Charities with 31 March 2009 year ends	ISSUED
Bulletin 2009/2 Auditor's Reports on Financial Statements in the United Kingdom	ISSUED
Bulletin 2009/3 Auditor's Reports – Supplementary Guidance for Auditors of Charities with Accounting Periods Commencing on, or after, 6 April 2008	ISSUED
Bulletin 2009/4 Developments in Corporate Governance Affecting the Responsibilities of Auditors of UK Companies	ISSUED
Bulletin 2010/1 XBRL Tagging of Information in Audited Financial Statements – Guidance for Auditors	ISSUED
Directors' compliance statements: Reports by auditors under company law in the Republic of Ireland	ISSUED
Guidance for auditors on first-time application of IFRSs in the United Kingdom	ISSUED
Effective communication between audit committees and external auditors	
Briefing Paper: Providing assurance on internal control	
Consultation Paper: Aggressive earnings management	
Communication between auditors and audit committees	
Improving the auditing of entities subject to common control	
Fraud and audit: Choices for society	
Consultation Paper: Auditing Standards relevant to group audits	
Consultation Paper: Audit firms providing non-audit services to listed companies that they audit	

TABLE D

ICAEW Statements on Auditing

FRAG 27/93: Paid cheques

FRAG 1/94: Reading of auditors' reports at annual general meetings

AUDIT 1/97 Derivatives in a corporate environment: a guide for auditors

AUDIT 2/99: The receipt of information in confidence by auditors

AUDIT 1/00: Guidance for reporting in accordance with Global Investment Performance Standards

AUDIT 4/00: Firm's reports and duties to lenders in connection with loans and other facilities to clients and related covenants

AUDIT 1/01: Reporting to third parties

AUDIT 2/01: Requests for references on clients' financial status and their ability to service loans

AUDIT 1/02: Practical points for auditors in connection with the implementation of FRS 17 'Retirement Benefits' – defined benefit schemes

AUDIT 2/02: New arrangements for reporting to the ABTA

AUDIT 3/02: Bank reports for audit purposes – explanatory note

AUDIT 4/02: Management representation letters

AUDIT 1/03: The audit report and auditors' duty of care to third parties

AUDIT 2/03: New arrangements for reporting to the Civil Aviation Authority (CAA) in connection with the Civil Aviation (Air Travel Organisers' Licensing) Regulations 1995

AUDIT 3/03: Public sector special reporting engagements – grant claims

AUDIT 4/03: Access to working papers by investigating accountants

AUDIT 5/03: Reporting to regulators of regulated entities

AUDIT 1/04: Reporting to the Audit Bureau of Circulations Limited (ABC)

AUDIT 2/04: Chartered accountants' reports on the compilation of financial statements of incorporated entities

AUDIT 3/04: Audit implications of IFRS transition

AUDIT 1/05: Chartered accountants' reports on the compilation of historical financial information of unincorporated entities

AUDIT 2/05: Guidance on the implications of the Freedom of Information Act 2000

AAF 1/06 Assurance Reports on internal controls of service organizations made available to third parties

TABLE D (continued)

ICAEW Statements on Auditing

AAF 2/06 Identifying and managing certain risks arising from the inclusion of reports from auditors and accountants in prospectuses (and certain other investment circulars)

AAF 3/06 The ICAEW Assurance Service on Unaudited financial statements

AAF 4/06 Assurance engagements: management of risk and liability

AAF 1/07 Independent accountants report on packaging waste

AAF 2/07 A framework for assurance reports on third party operations

AAF 1/08 Access to information by successor auditors

AAF 1/09 Paid cheques

AAF 2/09 New arrangements for accountants reporting to the Civil Aviation Authority

AAF 1/10 Framework document for accountants' reports on grant claims

Exposure Draft: The audit of related parties in practice

Auditing in a group practice context: practical consideration for auditors

Index

All indexing is to paragraph number

competence and objectivity, 26.5.6
and insurance provisions, 39.4.7
results assessment, 26.5.9
retirement benefit schemes,
26.5.6–26.5.9
work of, as audit evidence, 26.5.7
see also EXPERTS, USE OF
ad hoc reports, to FSA
auditor's right to report directly to
regulators, 8.6.5
closely linked entities, 8.6.4
communication by FSA, 8.6.7
compliance with management
requirements, 8.6.3
cumulative minor breaches, 8.6.4
fit and proper person requirement,
8.6.3
form of report, 8.6.6
going concern, doubt as to entity's
status as, 8.6.3
guidance, 8.6.1, 8.6.3
identification of matters requiring
report, 8.6.4
items reportable on ad hoc basis, 8.6.4
material significance considerations,
8.6.3
other auditors, reliance on, 8.6.4
planning, 8.6.4
procedures, 8.6.4
relationship with other reporting
responsibilities, 8.6.8
reporting, 8.6.5
right and duty to report, 8.6.2
risk of loss, 8.6.3
statutory provisions, 8.6
supervision and control, 8.6.4
'adverse' opinion
going concern, doubt as to entity's
status as, 13.6.1
modified reports, 4.2.2, 4.2.4, 4.2.5
affiliates
Ethical Standards for Auditors, review
of, 2.7.6
Affordable Home Ownership –
Charitable Status and Tax, 47.2.6
aggressive earnings management
Consultation Draft, 22.1, 22.5.1
AICPA (American Institute of
Certified Public Accountants)
auditing in economic downturn, 22.5.1,
22.5.3

on risk factors, 22.1
AIM (Alternative Investment Market)
and Directors' Remuneration Report
Regulations, 3.17.2
AIU (Audit Inspections Unit), 2.1, 2.14
American Institute of Certified Public
Accountants (AICPA) *see* AICPA
(AMERICAN INSTITUTE OF
CERTIFIED PUBLIC
ACCOUNTANTS)
analytical procedures
audit evidence, evaluating, 10.6
audit procedures, 24.2.4
auditing standards, 25.1
see also ISA (UK AND IRELAND)
520 (*ANALYTICAL*
PROCEDURES); SAS 410
(*ANALYTICAL PROCEDURES*)
charities, 43.18
defined, 25.2
e-commerce, 41.7.3
investment businesses, 46.3.9
in overall review at end of audit, 25.6
practical problems, 25.3
public sector audits, 48.18
recording, 25.8
Registered Providers of Social
Housing, 47.15
risk assessment, 22.3.3, 25.4
as substantive procedure, 25.5
acceptable differences, 25.5.4
data reliability, 25.5.2
precision of expected results, 25.5.3
suitability of using analytical
procedures, 25.5.1
substantive procedures as, 22.4.2
suitability of using, 25.5.1
unusual items, investigating, 10.5.3,
25.7
Analytical Review **(APC Guideline)**,
25.8
announcements, preliminary *see*
PRELIMINARY
ANNOUNCEMENTS
annual report
non-financial information, assurance
on, 42.10.3
significant problems, 15.6.3
anti-money laundering measures *see*
MONEY LAUNDERING
PREVENTION

ACCOUNTANTS IN ENGLAND
AND WALES)
**Institute of Chartered Accountants of
Ireland** *see* ICAI (INSTITUTE OF
CHARTERED ACCOUNTANTS
OF IRELAND)
**Institute of Chartered Secretaries and
Administrators (ICSA)** *see* ICSA
(INSTITUTE OF CHARTERED
SECRETARIES AND
ADMINISTRATORS)
Intangible Assets **(SSAP 29)**
fair values, 37.8.4
integrity
defined, 2.5.1
of financial statements, monitoring,
15.13.5
ICAEW *Code of Ethics*, 2.9.2
and reports to management, 9.8.3
security measures, e-commerce, 41.6.4
*Integrity, Objectivity and Independence
– Guidance for Reporting
Accountants in Connection with an
Investment Circular* **(APB Bulletin
2005/7)**, 50.9
interim financial information
complete set, 16.7
interim profits
investment businesses, 46.5
interim reports, review of
assurance provided, 16.4
communication, 16.15
comparative periods, 16.11
date of review report, 16.16.3
departure from applicable financial
reporting framework, 16.16.1
documentation, 16.8
engagement letters, 16.5
evidence, 16.7
general principles, 16.3
going concern, 16.10, 16.16.1
guidance for auditors, 16.2
limitation of audit scope, 16.16.1
Listing Rules requirements, 16.1
management representations, 16.11,
16.12
modification of review report, 16.16.1
other information, 16.13
planning, 16.6
procedures, 16.7
reporting

date of review report, 16.14.6
modification of review report,
16.16.1
prior period modifications, 16.16.2
requirement for, 16.16
review engagement, requests to
discontinue, 16.18
significant uncertainties, 16.16.1
subsequent events, 16.9
internal audit
auditing standards, 39.2.1
corporate governance, auditor
procedures in relation to, 15.6.3
defined, 39.2.2
effect on external audit procedures,
39.2.2
evaluating specific work, 39.2.4
ICAEW guidance booklets, 15.13.6
public sector audits, 48.24
Registered Providers of Social
Housing, 47.22
understanding and assessment of,
39.2.3
internal auditors
Ethical Standards, review of, 2.7.5
internal control
activities, 22.3.5
assurance on, 15.8.1
components, 22.3.5
control activities, 22.3.5
control environment, 22.3.5
corporate governance, auditor
procedures in relation to, 15.6.3
CREST, 46.6.2
deficiencies in
identifying and reporting, 9.13.4
significant, 9.13.4
failure to conduct review of, 15.6.3
information system, 22.3.5
limitations of, 22.3.5
management override of controls,
10.5.5
manual and automated elements, 22.3.5
material weaknesses in systems,
15.11.4
monitoring of controls, 22.3.5
providing assurance on
background, 15.10.1
framework, 15.10.2
knowledge of entity's business, need
for, 15.10.3

937